The War of the Austrian Succession

The War of the Austrian Succession

BY REED BROWNING

ST. MARTIN'S PRESS
NEW YORK

First published in the United States of America 1993

Printed in the United States of America

ISBN 0-312-09483-3

Library of Congress Cataloging-in-Publication Data

Browning, Reed.
  The War of the Austrian Succession / Reed Browning.
    p. cm.
  Includes bibliographical references and index.
  ISBN 0-312-09483-3
  1. Austrian Succession, War of, 1740-1748. I. Title.
D292.B76 1993
940.2′532—dc20   93-12439
                                    CIP

To Susan, with love

■Contents■

■ PREFACE ■

I want to take a moment before beginning my narrative to offer three points of advice about how this book should be dealt with. First, I urge the reader to be attentive to names. There will be a plethora of them before the tale is told, and unfortunately many of the individuals whose careers we will be examining were named Charles. The reader must be prepared to keep Charles Albert and Charles Emmanuel separate, to realize that one Charles VII ruled as Holy Roman Emperor while another reigned as King of the Two Sicilies, and to distinguish Prince Charles (of the House of Lorraine) from Bonnie Prince Charlie (of the House of Stuart). Second, I urge an attentiveness to place. Twentieth-century readers cannot be expected to have maps of eighteenth-century Europe impressed upon their brains, and so to avoid the fog of directionlessness the reader will probably need to consult the charts at the back of this book whenever geographical references become obscure. Third, I urge the reader to keep in mind the fact that this war, more than most we are accustomed to speaking of, was marked by frequent shifts in fortune. National prospects waxed and waned, belligerent armies advanced and retreated, and no ruler or minister was spared the agony of seeing hopes dissolve into dread. It was a war in which overextension was invariably punished, in which hubris regularly suffered its appointed fate. The reader should therefore expect that the tale will be burdened by the irritation of apparent inconclusiveness.

A few other cautions are necessary. Throughout the work I shall use the Gregorian calendar. It had not yet been adopted in Britain and Russia in the 1740s, and so some of the dates I give may seem oddly errant to those conversant with the internal histories of those lands. The reader also may be struck by the suspiciously rounded character of the numbers used in the citing of battle statistics. During the eighteenth century there was no reliable means of counting either combatants or casualties—even commanders were usually quite uncertain of the numbers they commanded—and so the relative sizes of fighting forces and the balances of carnage that ensued from combat are very uncertain. Finally, the reader may be puzzled by some of the European place-names. The general principle I have followed is to employ the names used by the governments that exercised sovereignty over the sites at the beginning of 1992. This principle has implications for all border regions, and most dramatically it means that I will use Czech and Polish names when mentioning towns in Bohemia, Moravia, and Silesia, even though these towns were typically designated by German names in the documents of the eighteenth century. Only in cases where history has fixed the names of events or the conventions of the English language control the consciousness of readers will I violate the rule: Hohenfriedberg will thus remain Hohenfriedberg, Prague will remain Prague, and Aix-la-Chapelle will not yield to Aachen.

As a final caution I should note that the name conventionally given to the war that wracked Europe and its dependencies between 1740 and 1748 — and consequently the name of this book — is not much more than a century and a half old. In fact, for many years the belligerence lacked a generally accepted title. It was not one single war but several that happened to coincide: the war of Bohemia, the two wars of Silesia, the war of the Alps, the war of Italy, the Forty-Five. And even if contemporaries realized that the various military actions occurring in scattered theaters around the world were parts of an organic whole, they were likelier to denominate the struggle the War of the Pragmatic Sanction or even the War of 1741 than to call it a succession struggle. There were, of course, those who from the very beginning seized upon the analogy to earlier wars over dynastic claims. Prussian ministers, for example, and even Frederick II himself, were ascribing the war to the "Austrian succession" as early as 1741. But it was not until the nineteenth century that the usage of our day became current, and even in our own century it has not won universal assent. We may draw an important conclusion from this nomenclatural uncertainty: the conflict we are about to trace is neither well understood nor well charted.

Finally, I wish to thank some friends and colleagues. Will Scott, a colleague on the Kenyon College Department of History, provided seminal advice early on. Jeremy Black, Grete Klingenstein, Karl Roider, and Don Smith — distinguished historians all — provided timely encouragement. Two members of the fine staff of the Olin and Chalmers Libraries at Kenyon were especially helpful: Nadine George assisted in researching place-names, and Carol Marshall supplied me with an abundance of interlibrary loans. The manuscript was prepared chiefly by Roberta McPhail and Mary Hopper. The charts were drafted in part by Kimberley Highfield. Support from the National Endowment for the Humanities and from Kenyon College enabled me to visit major libraries in Europe. I am grateful to all these people and institutions for their faith and help. Finally I am grateful to my wife, Susan. She has been living with the War of the Austrian Succession for more years than the war itself lasted. She has been wonderful.

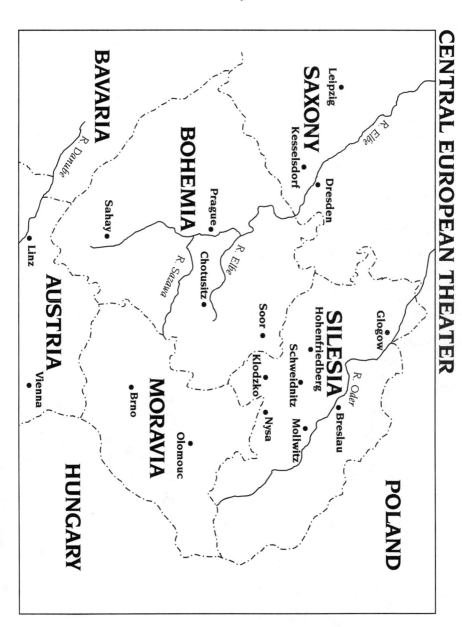

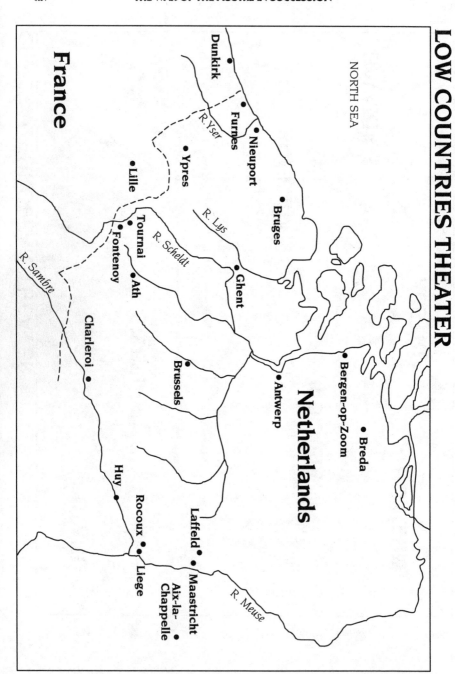

LOW COUNTRIES THEATER

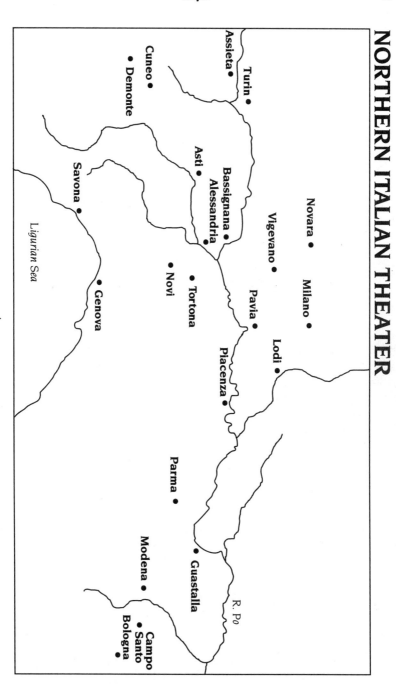

NORTHERN ITALIAN THEATER

P·R·O·L·O·G·U·E

The Designs of Europe

1

The Framework of War

THE ORDER OF ARMS

To understand the War of the Austrian Succession we need to understand the military thinking of the age. The chief constituent of any eighteenth-century army was the infantry. At the time of the War of the Austrian Succession, it provided three-fourths of the troops in an ordinary army. Life for the infantryman was hard. His feet were his chief mode of transportation. Though actual engagements were rare—on the average in the mid-eighteenth century, significant battles among belligerent states occurred less than once a month—the soldier spent his days in camping, marching, and perhaps training. When encamped, he subsisted on meager rations; when on the move, on scantier ones still. On his back he bore over sixty pounds of equipment. As he trudged along, his thighs lashed against each other, often drawing blood. He was not without diversions. An encamped army was joined by wives and whores, and improvised recreations, especially dancing, were commonplace. But the rigors of military life were never far off. There was, for example, the weather. Steamy summers exhausted armies on campaign. And when the cold season appeared and campaigning ended, armies conventionally settled into winter quarters to begin their hibernal struggle to keep warm and safe amid campfires, tents, and generally hostile civilian populations. Disease was another rigor. In an age of primitive medicine and hygienic ignorance, infections of the digestive tract and lungs were frequent. Veterans built up immunities to the more ravaging diseases, but young recruits were invariably vulnerable. About one-fourth of all deaths due to disease were among soldiers in their first year in uniform. Illness, in fact, exacted a higher toll of soldiers than combat.

By far the greatest part of the remaining portion of an eighteenth-century army was the cavalry. These were the soldiers who, in the tradition of medieval knights, went into battle on horseback. The generic term cavalry embraced several different modes of combat. In western Europe there were usually two types of cavalry, called horse and dragoons respectively. The horse fought only on horseback and therefore rode large animals capable of delivering a forceful charge. The dragoons might engage either in the saddle or on foot, and so they rode smaller steeds. They also received training with firearms. In the east—and most prominently in the Habsburg realm, where the rulers could draw upon warriors accustomed to the military ways of Hungary and the Balkans—there were regularly three kinds of cavalry. The cuirassiers, or heavy cavalry, corresponded to the horse in the west, and the dragoons, or medium cavalry, corresponded to their namesakes in the west. The hussars, or light cavalry, were one of the sensations of the war, so successful at harassing enemy flanks that several countries that entered the war without such troops tried to create them as the hostilities continued. A frightened French soldier dubbed them "vermin."[1] As a nondisciplined, irregular element in an otherwise ordered army, they provided commanders a wider degree of flexibility in their operations.

The artillery constituted a third section of the army, minuscule in size but important in many situations. Several figures suggest the exiguity of artillery forces. In 1740 Prussia had only one battalion—perhaps 600 men—of field artillery. For the purposes of the war, it was found sufficient to do no more than double that number. Britain in 1741 had 593 men in service. Its wartime expansion was virtually identical to Prussia's, for at the end of the struggle artillery personnel totaled 1,025. Considering the importance of their function, it is almost certain that these men who were charged with tending and deploying cannon were the most productive in uniform. Their work was hard and dangerous. The cannons themselves were heavy, impediments to swift troop movements. Transporting them as part of an army on campaign required patience and sweat and, when in the vicinity of hostile forces, exposed the men to enemy fire. During combat all artillerymen faced the threat of the unexpected explosions caused when powder encountered residual sparks in the barrel. Since the artillery was a service of recent origin, it lacked the prestige associated with the far older and more conventional infantry and cavalry. Its appeal was different from theirs, and rarer too. Men of mathematical or mechanical curiosity might prefer it. Most, however, thought its rewards dubious. By yoking enhanced danger to low dignity, the artillery kept itself a service of comparative eccentrics.[2]

The warfare of the mid-eighteenth century was dominated by two smoothbore weapons—the flintlock musket and the cannon. The flintlock, a muzzle-loading firearm, was the weapon of the infantry and most of the cavalry. By modern standards this musket was primitive, requiring a four-step reloading procedure after each discharge. Though capable of killing at 300 yards, its accuracy disappeared at half that distance. But if rudimentary in our view, the flintlock was nevertheless an improvement on its seventeenth-century predecessor, the matchlock, since in the hands of a skilled infantryman it could be discharged as often as three times a minute, a rate that allowed a trained fighting force to increase its firings by 50 percent. Cannon at midcentury came in a variety of calibers, ranging (in the terminology of the day) from the mobile three-pounders to the cumbersome twenty-four-pounders. (The figures refer not to the weapons themselves but the weight of the iron balls propelled by the cannon.) The lighter pieces were assigned to infantry battalions, for which they provided close fire support in combat. Because for short periods they could be fired as often as four times a minute, shredding an enemy with clusters of iron bits, their usage has been likened to the employment of machine guns in more recent times. Larger pieces were employed as massed batteries. When directed against the heart of the enemy formation, they could quickly disrupt the developing scheme of the opposing commander. The largest cannon were siege weapons, designed to pummel walls and fortifications with crushing blows and incendiary threats. Though in principle cannon project their missiles farthest when raised 45 degrees from the horizontal, eighteenth-century mountings limited the angle of inclination to 15 degrees. The point of this limitation was to encourage gunners to send their cannonballs *bouncing* through the enemy lines. The three-pounders had a range of perhaps 2,500 yards; the twenty-four pounder increased that range to little more than 3,300 yards. In general, in the War of the Austrian Succession the flintlock musket was the controlling weapon in central Europe and Italy while cannon played a similar role in the Low Countries.

The outcome of wars is in large measure a consequence of the outcome of battles. Thus it is important to recall that in the eighteenth century, except in instances of surprise, battles were fought only when both commanders wanted them. This important truth is a consequence of the fact that positioning an army for battle took more time than withdrawing an army from a proposed field of combat. Thus a force that chose to avoid combat could always impose its will on the moment, though usually at the cost of ground. It therefore follows that battles occurred only when each commander saw nothing to be gained by delay or withdrawal. This was not often the case, for if the two rival armies differed significantly in size, the smaller would have little inducement to hazard a battle; even if they were approximately the same size, both commanders would have to conclude independently that the promise of victory was great enough to warrant running the risk of defeat. And risk it was, for one almost certain consequence of a battle was to widen the margin of superiority that one army enjoyed over the other. Thus, in the aftermath of most major battles, the winners took over the artillery and baggage of their enemy, while the losers, nursing their wounds, yielded the area and withdrew to recover, regroup, and reconsider. Of the major commanders of the War of the Austrian Succession, only Frederick II of Prussia actively sought battle. More characteristic of the age was the view of Maurice of Saxony, who, commanding the often inexpert French army, preferred to triumph by maneuver rather than battle. As he told Louis XV, "the issue [of a battle] is always doubtful when one cannot rely on the discipline of one's troops."[3]

Although armies marched to battlefields in columns, they engaged from line formations. This term means that, when confronting the enemy prior to battle, the infantry presented itself as a long line of soldiers facing the enemy and standing shoulder to shoulder. This formation was preferred to all alternatives because it allowed an army to deliver the greatest volume of fire. The line might extend for several miles and was composed of three or four ranks, separated from each other by a distance of several yards. The precise procedures for firing varied from army to army, but the general principle was everywhere identical: the rank in front would fire a volley and then step back behind the other ranks, reload, and move back to the front as the other ranks followed in sequence. By firing in this manner it was possible for a line of infantrymen to maintain a rate of four to six volleys a minute. Commanders rarely committed all their infantry to the front line. They preferred, even at the initial sacrifice of firing power, to withhold some troops at a distance of 150 to 450 yards behind the front line, ready to advance and reinforce that line if it showed signs of cracking at any point. Flanking the infantry in a regular battle formation was the cavalry. Their task was to deal with the cavalry of the enemy, to protect the flanks of their own infantry line, to capture hostile artillery emplacements, and, if possible, to harass the infantry of the foe. It is important to understand what cavalry could and could not do. They were ineffective when charging unaided against the front of a hostile line of infantry, for as they drew near they were exposed to enemy fire that they could not hope to match in force or accuracy. But they were far more effective when assaulting the flank of an enemy line of infantry, for their enemy was not positioned to fend them off and their horses' speed allowed them to move in quickly and devastatingly. A good cavalry could not compensate for a poor infantry, but a commander who could rely on his cavalry had at hand a flexible tool that widened his options both offensively and defensively.

A good commander also paid attention to topography, weather, and the time of day, for all might aid him in implementing schemes of deception. The covers of disguise were numerous. Once the sun had set, a commander had the hours of darkness to move his troops about. But even when the sun illuminated the battlefield, an able commander had several tricks he could resort to. Hills and woods provided screens behind which troops could be moved. Even gently rolling terrain offered depressions through which battalions could be filtered unseen. For want of any natural feature, a commander could create an artificial screen by sending his cavalry into a position between the enemy and the troops he was shifting. The point of this effort at deception was to secure a local advantage that could be exploited before the enemy could either reinforce its outnumbered sector or discover where the attacker had weakened himself in order to create the local advantage. Speed was thus important, and an army bedeviled with difficult terrain that retarded troop movements was at a clear disadvantage. Because a company ensconced in the buildings of a village enjoyed a high measure of protection, such settlements often became the fulcrums of battles. It was not uncommon for a commander to infuse men into a village secretly, in the hope that the incautious enemy would either send an outmatched detachment to take it or, believing it innocuous, choose to ignore it entirely.

In addition to the battle, there was one other type of major engagement to which eighteenth-century troops might be committed: the siege. The besieging of fortified towns had become the most formalized part of warfare by the middle of the eighteenth century. Among its practitioners were not only commanders schooled by experience but engineers trained in principles of construction and demolition. Eighteenth-century Europe was studded with walled fortifications, some small, some mammoth. Because an attacker rarely dared simply to bypass such a fortification (since he would thereby expose his rear to the foe), he had no choice but to try to oust the enemy. The effort to oust was called siege warfare, and it was the most toilsome and dangerous part of soldiering. In fact, if the besieging commander did not have an advantage of at least five to one in troops—and ten to one was preferred—he would often decline the operation. Each fortress was architecturally and positionally unique, but they all had several common features. The most prominent was the wall, which formed a continuous ring around the precinct that it protected. Because it was backed with piled and packed earth, it could resist pummelings by the enemy artillery. Because a ditch lay just outside its circumference, creating a height of perhaps ten yards for potential attackers to scale, it could resist assaults by the enemy infantry. Behind earthen ramparts on the wall sat artillery emplacements, able to reply blow for blow to the attacker. And through the cunning placement of bastions, which were triangular structures projecting outward from the wall, it was possible for protected marksmen to bring any spot along its base under fire. If a garrison was amply endowed with supplies and ammunition, it might be able to hold out against a besieging army for several months.

The men who served in eighteenth-century armies were usually drawn from the poorer sectors of society. In Prussia and Austria the peasantry constituted the backbone of the national fighting force. In France and Britain it was city folk who preponderated. The pay these men were offered is usually called miserable, but in most instances, though low, it sufficed to keep voluntary enlistments coming and peacetime armies at adequate levels of manning. Troop levels also were maintained by the incorporation of foreigners, who constituted an important element in all the major continental armies. When war broke out, however, the manning methods of peacetime failed and all European countries resorted to some variation of conscription. Prussia's method, which involved obliging geographical areas called cantons to keep the regiments assigned to them at full strength, was easily the most effective. All wartime armies suffered from high rates of desertion, especially among the young. In fact, for fear of offering opportunities for desertion, commanders tended to avoid such exercises as night marches, encampments near wooded areas, and the sending out of small detachments to gather supplies. The other sources of wartime attrition in manpower were illness and injury. About the former little could be done; its toll, as noted, was invariably higher than that attributable to combat. But wounds offered a different prospect to eighteenth-century physicians, and it is a notable commentary on the uneven diffusion of medical knowledge at the time that in Prussian camps the mortality rate among wounded might rise to 80 percent while in British camps the duke of Cumberland operated by the rule of thumb that two-thirds of those wounded would fight again.[4]

Keeping an army supplied with food was a staggering task. Commanders tended to agree that the best way to avoid being constrained by a shortage of victuals was to live off the land. As long as an eighteenth-century army kept on the move and did not retrace its steps, it could hope to secure adequate food and fodder from the countryside, and the pressing need for grass for grazing animals—"the most important restraint of all," in the words of a French officer—was quite expeditiously met in this manner.[5] It was only during siege operations that armies preferred the sedentary to the mobile life, and in such circumstances they quickly discovered that they needed magazines, ovens, and cumbersome supply trains.[6] These considerations correctly imply that eighteenth-century warfare, despite its reputation for relative benignity, in fact bore exceedingly heavily on the civilian populations of Europe. Armies cut swaths through the agricultural countryside, leaving desolation in their train. Understandably, therefore, rulers preferred their armies to campaign, even to winter, in foreign lands.

THE WORLD OF THE FLEET

The conflict of the 1740s spread to the seas. Its maritime aspect will not detain us for long, because engagements on the vastness of the deep were rare. But a paucity of combat does not imply an irrelevance of theater. Control of the seas conferred enormous advantages on the country that could secure it: safety for one's own trade, a stifling of enemy trade, the ability to move troops by sea, and the opportunity to threaten the coastal cities of the enemy. Precisely because naval supremacy imparted such leverage, the states that bordered the Atlantic had recently been pushing their naval programs. But despite improvements in the navies of Spain and France, Britain remained the dominant maritime power. Its traditions infused its commanders with boldness. Its financial resources gave it the capacity to sustain combat for long periods of time. Its pool of experienced seamen assured it of trained crews. It is true that they were not always contented crews: in time of war Britain supplemented voluntary enlistments with the activities of the press-gang. But despite the problems posed by manning ships through coercion—despite too the surprising but acknowledged fact that French ships and French naval technology were superior—Britain was the recognized mistress of the sea. France's navy was not inconsequential: though shackled to the jejune notions of a *guerre de course*, it still played an important role in the struggle. But the fleet that His Britannic Majesty could put to sea could overawe the naval power of any other nation. For that reason the opponents of Britain usually sought maritime allies. Alone, they had little chance.

The ships of eighteenth-century navies came in many sizes, but even though corvettes and frigates had their uses, the strength of a fleet was measured basically by the number of ships of the line it contained. This term designated all three-masted ships with sixty or more guns; the largest such ship boasted over one hundred. These cannons were eighteen- to thirty-two-pounders, placed within the confines of the hull on one of the two or three decks of a ship. Smaller vessels posed no challenge to these behemoths, for in an engagement between mismatched ships the larger could simply sit outside the range of the smaller and, though pitching atop the restless ocean, hurl enough cannon fire at it to assure its eventual destruction. Remarkably self-sufficient, a ship of the line, if it avoided combat and heavy storms, could shelter 700 men at sea for as long as five months before fouled hulls, the thirst·for fresh water, and disrepair aloft necessitated a visit to port. Advances in the skills of rigging and handling sails permitted eighteenth-century ships to keep their sails full even when plowing to within 70 degrees of the wind. But sailing with the wind at one's back was far easier and swifter. And the worst fate of all, in an era in which wind supplied the power of motion, was to become becalmed.

When war came, the navy was expected to perform two duties—to protect commerce and to render the enemy fleet ineffectual. Since the commercial vessels of a belligerent state were the lawful prey of their foe, a nation that valued its trade would act to defend its merchant marine against the warships and privateers of the enemy. Thus merchant ships were encouraged to sail in convoys, to which warships would be attached as protectors. This device saved ships and goods, but the men of commerce disliked having to adjust their sailings to the schedule of the convoys. And since any merchant who broke from a convoy in mid-passage to race ahead—and who managed to evade the enemy—stood to gain large profits by beating his rivals to the transoceanic market, it was difficult to keep convoys intact for the duration of a journey. The still more important function of the navy in time of war was to keep the enemy at bay. In many instances this goal could be accomplished by establishing a blockade—more accurately, a "close watch"—off an enemy port, stationing a squadron within view of the port and thereby preventing the enemy from bringing its fleet out. But if the enemy fleet was already at sea, then battle was the best expedient for rendering an enemy ineffectual. The loose tactical principles that explain battle at sea in the eighteenth century were quite independent of the tactical principles applicable to battle on land.[7] Since the sea afforded no screens, commanders had no opportunity to engage in the hidden maneuvering that characterized land engagements. Since the number of ships on one side rarely exceeded twenty-five and since victory usually went to the side with the numerical advantage, however small, there was no incentive for holding part of a force back in reserve. Since there was no maritime equivalent to the distinction between infantry and cavalry, there was no imperative to establish two sets of rules for deployment. Since communications within the fleet were usually limited to flag signals, only the simplest of maneuvers were practicable. Finally, since the slowest vessels of a retreating force would invariably be overtaken by the swiftest vessels of the pursuing force, flight in the face of an approaching enemy left stragglers to the certain threat of capture or destruction and was therefore inadvisable. In fact, the logic of engagement at sea was precisely the reverse of the logic of engagement on land. When armies met, they fought only if both commanders sought to do so; when navies met, they withdrew only if both chose to do so.

Fleets (and their subdivisions, squadrons and detachments) generally prepared for engagements by falling into lines behind their lead vessels. This formation was called line of battle ahead. When moving into position to engage each other, the fleets maneuvered until they had aligned themselves in a roughly parallel formation (though the lines might still be several miles apart), whereupon individual ships began to fire broadsides on the vessels holding analogous spots in the enemy's line. Because the largest ships, including the flag ship, sailed near the center of the line, this procedure assured that size would be pitted against size. But a commander had the option of beginning an action before the two forces were completely aligned. If he saw that he could secure a temporary local advantage by doing so, he might start the affray even when some of his ships were without obvious targets. If one force had a greater number of ships, it would be able at some point along the line of engagement to commit two ships against one of the enemy. The exchanges of cannon fire that marked the opening stage of a battle might occasionally shatter the hull of a ship unlucky enough to be hit in a vulnerable spot, but they were likelier to damage the upperworks and rigging. A dismasting could quickly immobilize a vessel and make it a choice candidate for capture as a prize. As a battle continued, its linear structure became increasingly disordered and coordination gave way to melees.

In light of the logic of engagement, the reader might well wonder why naval battles were rare events. In fact, enemy sightings were exceedingly uncommon. In an age innocent of high-speed communications, fleets at sea wandered in a void, directed by instructions months out of date and following up on information that had been stale weeks earlier. Commanders might yearn for action, but unless fortune flung an enemy before them, they could expect months, even years, of watchful but fruitless sweeps across seemingly limitless seas. A British commander expressed his frustration to the first lord of the admiralty: "'Tis all chance to which we must submit, and content ourselves with the merit of deserving success by our diligence whether we meet with it or not."[8] Still, it is true that the British were likelier to meet with it than the French, not merely because they had ampler resources but also because their strategic thinking placed a far greater emphasis on finding and destroying the enemy. The French held to a conservative strategic theory that posited the priority of defending trade. It was a strategy of folly: it kept the battle fleet below full strength, and when that enfeebled fleet finally met its predictable defeat, it left the convoys exposed to attack as well. Bolder by experience as well as instructions, the British commanders probed and hunted with ever mounting diligence as the war proceeded, and when negotiators finally sat down to try to end the carnage of the War of the Austrian Succession, command of the seas gave Britain its best card.

2

The Constellation of States

THE MAP OF WAR

To understand the War of the Austrian Succession, we must understand the topography of Europe. When nations went to war in the early modern period, they regularly found themselves operating in the same few regions. We may therefore speak of a military geography of Europe. Certain topographical features—mountain ranges, for example, and wide stretches of water—divided the arena into theaters, each of which was relatively cut off from the other theater. Other features—river valleys and mountain passes—funneled military activity into narrow areas. It is true that national ambitions, as embodied in strategic planning, might tempt a commander to test the constraints that geography imposed on his army. And sometimes he even succeeded in vaulting these constraints. But the more general practice was to treat the constraints with respect. In an age of cumbersome and slow armies, of forbidding support problems and imperfect discipline, of communications no faster than the fleetest horse, it would have been foolhardy for leaders to ignore the implacable commands of nature.

The War of the Austrian Succession fell into three theaters. To the west the Low Countries hosted, as they so often had, a set of avaricious armies that sat heavy on the land, occasionally engaging in battles, more often undertaking sieges, but most frequently simply lurking, waiting, and preying. To the east, in the region centered on Bohemia and including Saxony, Silesia, Moravia, Upper Austria, and Bavaria, a war of greater movement occurred, as armies ebbed and flowed across the land while Prague, situated at the heart of the theater, endured three sieges and two occupations. To the south the expanse of northern Italy provided campaign grounds for the armies of no fewer than six nations and even an occasional opportunity for demonstrations of the impact a vigorous navy could have upon military operations. This distribution of military activity into three cockpits was no accident. Rather, it followed very neatly from the existence of the two dominating geo-

graphical divides of the era: the awkward block posed by the Rhine River
and the still more forbidding partition created by the Alps.

The first cockpit, the region called the Low Countries, was the stretch of
land in northwestern Europe through which the Scheldt, much of the
Meuse, and the lowest reaches of the Rhine coursed their ways to the sea. A
reticulation of virtually innumerable tributaries across generally flat countryside made transportation easy and cultivation profitable. Villages abounded—
over 7,000 in the Austrian Netherlands alone—and Flanders was so thick
with people that the Spanish described the entire county as "but one city."[1]
Yet the region also boasted the most productive agricultural sector in
Europe. In extent the Low Countries included the seven provinces of the
Dutch republic, the various districts of the Austrian Netherlands (with the
embedded but independent bishopric of Liege), and parts of northern
France. Traditionally, therefore, Europe's largest battles occurred within its
precincts. But the region also offered ample opportunity for siege operations.
The Low Countries had often served as a route for French attacks on the
Dutch. Consequently there stretched across the middle of the region, from
Furnes by the English Channel to Maastricht on the Meuse, a chain of fortifications that had been built within the previous half century to serve as a
Barrier—and that is what they were collectively called—against future
French probes. When these probes came in the 1740s, the French were faced
with the need of taking each of the fortresses one by one. Finally, these fortifications lay within territory that was, by virtue of the Treaty of Utrecht of
1713, under Austrian control. But by the terms of the Barrier Treaty of 1715,
many of the fortifications were manned by Dutch, not Austrian, troops. This
unusual arrangement was by itself sufficient to assure that the Austrian
Netherlands would have a peculiar international status.

Four hundred miles to the west lay Bohemia, the center of the second
cockpit. Unlike many political entities in this part of Europe, the old kingdom possessed geographically intelligible frontiers. Rimmed by hills and
mountains, Bohemia had the topography of a bowl. These rugged border-
lands impeded a military entrance into the central plain, but they by no
means prohibited one. Because most of the troops that saw action in
Bohemia in the 1740s came from beyond its borders, the lands adjacent to
the kingdom also must be seen as part of the cockpit, each playing a distinctive role in the military activities of the decade. In two instances that role was
secondary. Since Moravia was mountainous and possessed of two fine
fortresses, it posed tactical problems that potential invaders preferred to
avoid. Since Saxony was so flat that an army could sweep across it in a matter of days, it was not the scene of lengthy campaigning. The roles of Bavaria

and Silesia, however, were primary. The electorate of Bavaria was divided into three geographical bands. In the north and the south it was mountainous. But across its middle, like a great belt, stretched the Danube valley, fed by the Isar and the Inn—a route of easy access for armies moving either westward or eastward. Where the Rhine was a barrier, the Danube was a highway. As for the duchy of Silesia, though it was a dependency of the crown of Bohemia, it lay beyond the Sudetes and is better viewed as a part of the southern tier of the north German plain than as a land placed amid the central German mountains. The Oder River flowed northward right down its middle, draining its lands into the Baltic Sea. It is of the greatest moment to the present story that this Habsburg land of Silesia, rich and prosperous, buffered by Moravia and Bohemia from its distant overlord in Vienna, thrust itself almost like a pointing finger into the regions dominated by the Hohenzollerns of Brandenburg.

Almost 500 miles to the south from both the Low Countries and Bohemia lay the third cockpit—the valley of the Po River. Stretching across northern Italy from its source in the mountains west of Turin until it flowed into the Adriatic south of Venice, the Po and its many tributaries provided a fertile band of land that lay cut off from Gallic and Teutonic Europe by a sleeve of mountains. All along its northern stretch it faced the Alps. At its narrow western end it still met the Alps. And along its southern limit, though now not far from the waters of the Mediterranean, it still fronted onto mountains—the Maritime Alps and the Apennines. These mountains provided remarkable protection for northern Italy, and especially for Piedmont, the principality that occupied the westernmost recess of the valley. In 1713 Piedmont had secured the western Alps from France and thus, although the principality lay adjacent to France, its rulers felt no compelling need to be unduly submissive to the monarchs at Versailles. Only a few passes wound their tortuous ways over and through the lofty and inhospitable mountains, and these passes the Piedmontese zealously guarded. Thus moving troops from France into Italy was no small task. The mountain passes might be stormed, but even when such assaults achieved success they often entailed the incapacitation of an entire army. The narrow coastal path might be hazarded, but it exposed a strung-out army to withering fire from ships offshore. A seaborne invasion might be chanced, carrying troops from Toulon to Spezia or Orbetello, but unless the attacker was assured of command of the Mediterranean—and only Britain (and its allies) could be reasonably confident of such command—such a plan threatened to abort in a maritime disaster. Because nature had so munificently shielded the Po valley, this cockpit was easily the most independent and isolated of the three.

THE CATALOG OF ASPIRATIONS

The paramount power in Europe as 1740 opened was France. The Bourbon kingdom had been guided to preeminence in the seventeenth century by the decisions of two shrewd ecclesiastics, cardinals Richelieu and Mazarin, and by the determination of the renowned Sun King, Louis XIV. This preeminence rested on several considerations: a centralization of sovereign authority that, though loose by modern standards, was second only to Britain's among European states; a population of 23 million that exceeded by a factor of three that of its island enemy; an economy that, by the standards of the Old Regime, was diversified; a geographical compactness that left it without exposed territorial salients; and a large and successful army. France was the only European nation whose geographical situation allowed it to contemplate acquiring dominion either on land or on sea. We must not be surprised to learn, therefore, that France was the only nation in which the notion of preserving a European balance of power was challenged: a cant prescription almost everywhere else because it promised the maintenance of European peace through the creation of countervailing forces, the idea of an international equilibrium aroused little enthusiasm among those French policymakers who preferred to ground their hopes for European peace in the establishment of a France capable of overawing all other states. These men nourished, in short, the old dream of a universal monarchy. They were not the only section of foreign policy thinkers in France; they were not even, in 1740, the section in command. But only in France was such a view conceivable.

The French goal in 1740 may be succinctly expressed: to maintain French dominance in Europe. In general, and especially after the acquisition of the expectation to Lorraine, dominance did not imply territorial expansion. France sought not to bludgeon its neighbors but rather—by a judicious combination of coaxing, prodding, and bullying—to persuade the states of Europe to pursue policies acceptable to Versailles. Equipped with the most skillful corps of diplomats in Europe, the French government had a pool of capable agents through whom it could explain and try to effect its purpose of dominance. These agents could then employ the various instrumentalities that legitimized the exercise of French influence. Subsidy treaties with a number of second-level states, especially Sweden and Bavaria, gave it opportunities to affect decisions in the heart of Scandinavia and Germany. The Bourbon family tie, which extended to the kingdom of Naples, meant that the wishes of France could not be ignored in southern Italy. Centrally important—and therefore resolutely defended—was France's role as guarantor of the treaties of Westphalia of 1648. This role allowed France to act as defender of the rights of the numerous body of German princes in the

empire. It was a marvelously serviceable policy for France, for while assuring the friendship of at least some of Germany's rulers, it simultaneously
inhibited Austria's efforts to tighten imperial control for Vienna's benefit. The
goal of dominance required the deliberate pursuit of divisions among potential rivals. Operating from its base of power, France had of late known nothing but success.

The man who had directed French affairs during the triumphant decade of
the 1730s was Cardinal Fleury. Though in his eighties and beginning to make
concessions to age, he stood as the preeminent figure in European politics.
Even more remarkably, he managed to combine a reputation as a cunning
wartime minister with celebrity as a lover of peace. His gifts were those of
the manager: repressed ambition, unbounded patience, a keen sense of the
limits of the possible. He had recently decided, as the War of the Polish
Succession wound down, that rather than smiting Austria, France would be
better served by protecting the coherence of its old rival. In 1738, therefore,
through the long-sought peace treaty, Fleury finally secured an alliance with
the Habsburg state. Then in 1739, at the pinnacle of his influence, Fleury
directed French policy to three dramatic triumphs: French mediation of a
Swedish-Turkish defense alliance, French service as honest broker in the
treaties of Belgrade that ended Austria's humiliating war with Turkey, and
the conclusion of a treaty with Prussia that, while reaffirming French influence in Germany, also initiated a decade of Franco-Prussian cooperation.
With Britain isolated and Austria subdued, "the Nestor of politics" had
earned, he believed, the right to rest. He expected to end his days as the
faithful servant of Louis XV, guiding the affairs of France and, through
France, of Europe along the fabled paths of peace.

The state most manifestly in need of peace as 1740 began was Austria.
Geography and recent history had conspired to illuminate the weaknesses of
the Habsburg realm. In fact, only by the loosest of usages could these
domains even be considered a state. Flung out across the political map of
Europe from the English Channel to the Carpathians and from north of the
Oder to south of the Po, the European power that we conventionally call
Austria was actually an archipelago of historically diverse regions that over
centuries had been combined, through matrimony and conquest, into the
Habsburg realm. But this combination was not a fusion. Indeed, in its governmental, cultural, linguistic, and economic diversity this realm of more
than 16 million people was an administrative nightmare. The task of integrat-
ing this vast patrimony had been beyond the capacity of even the ablest of
recent Habsburg ministers. The dislocations of war only complicated the
task, and thus to the extent that the directors of Austrian policy believed

Austria's salvation to lie in constitutional and economic centralization, they would be proponents of peace.

They had another reason as well for wishing to forgo war: Austrian arms had of late been distinguished only by their feebleness. It had not always been so. In the protracted struggle against Louis XIV and the Turkish empire that had opened the century, Austrian forces had triumphed magnificently. But in these wars Austria had overextended itself. Money, bureaucratic discipline, and, finally, vision were all deficient for the perpetuation of the ramshackle state created by war. Prince Eugene himself, the hero of the era of expansion, faltered, his grip relaxing as his mind dimmed. Bloated and vulnerable, Austria stumbled from humiliation to humiliation in the 1720s and 1730s. Unsuccessful in defending commercial interests in the Netherlands and recently acquired territory in Italy and the Balkans, Austria within a generation receded from its position as the continent's most impressive state to the status of victim. It is no wonder that Austrian leaders sought protection in a tie with Bourbon France. Immediate war held scant prospect of gain.

Throughout the previous two decades of embarrassment, one thread of consistency had marked Austrian foreign policy. Whatever else was changing, Austrian diplomats had worked steadily and, by Vienna's lights, successfully to secure European guarantees of a document called the Pragmatic Sanction. Latter-day observers have been inclined to adjudge this campaign a monumental misallocation of energy. Its purpose was to assure that on the death of Emperor Charles VI the Habsburg inheritance would pass intact to his daughter, Maria Theresa. In issuing the Pragmatic Sanction, Charles VI violated his own sworn promise to support the terms of a family compact promulgated by his older brother, Joseph I. But Charles VI was not concerned with such matters: he had fixed his mind upon assuring that his daughter would succeed him. The Pragmatic Sanction thus became the talisman of his reign, the putative salvation of Habsburg hopes, and the obsession of Austrian diplomats. By purchasing promises of support from Spain, Russia, Prussia, Britain, the United Provinces, and France, Charles VI thought that he was purchasing his daughter's unchallenged succession. Rarely has the foreign policy of a major power been more persistently fatuous.

There was a separate yet related problem. For centuries—in fact, since 1438—the elective office of Emperor of the Holy Roman Empire of the German Nation had been held by Habsburgs. But imperial law forbade a woman from becoming emperor, and so the failure of Charles to sire a male heir meant that, with his demise, the most distinguished secular title in Europe would pass to a non-Habsburg. The imperial office was not inherently a powerful one. The peace of Westphalia had set the radical decentralization of the empire in stone: since each member state had the right to maintain an army and follow its own foreign policy, an emperor was almost powerless to compel demurring princes to obey his direction. What Charles VI worried about, therefore, was not the loss of power that his death would bring to the family but the loss of dignity. There was no shortage of German rulers who might seek the office for themselves. The best solution to Charles VI's awkward dilemma would have been to get Maria Theresa's husband, Francis Stephen, Duke of Lorraine, chosen as King of the Romans—the official title of an elected heir presumptive in the empire. But even though Charles VI courted the idea of securing Francis's election, the fact that the duke was hostile to France (which had, after all, forced him to give up Lorraine for Tuscany) and his own undistinguished military record against the Turks induced the emperor to lay that plan aside until a more propitious hour. So those who presided over affairs in Vienna as 1740 began could expect that the death of the emperor, whenever it came, would create challenges against both the integrity of the Habsburg realm and Austrian prestige in Germany.

In 1740 the direction of Austrian foreign policy lay chiefly in the unlikely hands of Johann Christoph Bartenstein. His had been a triumph of intellect and industry over birth. The group that made foreign policy decisions for Austria was called the Conference, and technically Bartenstein was not even a member of that august body. But as its registrar he was in a position to give verbal expression to its deliberations. And as the passing years gave him experience, his opinions were more and more heeded by the distrustful but superannuated members of that body. Bartenstein was notorious abroad for stubbornness and for the acerbic tone he could give to his lengthy and detailed papers. But most foreign observers saw only part of the man. Though proud, he was not inflexible. A British diplomat well acquainted with him noted that it was "the nature of the fellow to stick out as long as he can, but that nobody runs faster into a thing when once it is necessary and ripe."[2] Unlike his imperial master, Bartenstein did not turn a blind eye on the complexities and uncertainties of international affairs. He thought that Austria would be ill advised to entrust its fate simply to one powerful friend, and so, though he was determined to be faithful to the French tie as long as it was beneficial, he secured a treaty with St. Petersburg in 1739. Bartenstein's fault lay not in an absence of vision. It lay rather in his tendency to become immersed in detail and thereby to get his priorities wrong.

It is perhaps needless to add that the international situation of Austria in 1740 was thoroughly unhappy. The state's coffers were empty after decades of mismanagement, the state's leading military commanders languished in prison as punishment for their ignominious collapse before the Turks, the state's army was but half its authorized size and so widely scattered as to make it a sieve. A French diplomat lamented "the disorder which reigns in the finances of the Emperor." A Dutch envoy despaired of the "dissensions, confusions, disagreements, protractions, indecisiveness, mistrust, jealousies, intrigues, cabals" that tore the court of Vienna apart. A British agent dismissed the Habsburg domains as "a mere state of anarchy." And a leading Austrian nobleman, Frederick, Count Harrach, could only hope that he might predecease the dying realm.[3] In retreat on its frontiers and in disarray at its center, Austria seemed to owe its continued existence to nothing more substantial than inertia.

It is a common error of historians to undervalue the importance of Spain in the affairs of eighteenth-century Europe. Scholars have too readily seen Bourbon Spain merely as a satellite of Bourbon France. But in the late 1730s and for much of the 1740s, Madrid was almost as influential as Versailles in the Bourbon alliance. This influence resulted not from any margin of Spanish superiority in power—Spain's population was only 8.5 million, and it lacked France's administrative coordination—but from an odd combination of familial, psychological, and strategic factors that in the years around 1740 provided the leaders of the Spanish kingdom with impressive leverage at Versailles. Louis XV's eagerness to be helpful to his uncle Philip V, the complementary intransigence of the Spanish queen, and the temporary centrality of Italian concerns within a larger European context combined to assure that Spain's clear voice was heard within the Bourbon alliance.

Spain's first preoccupation was Italy. For decades Philip V and his Italian wife, Elizabeth Farnese, had devoted their full efforts to securing the establishment of their sons, Don Charles and Don Philip, as important Italian rulers. The War of the Polish Succession had been the vehicle for getting Don Charles planted in southern Italy, as Charles VII of the kingdom of the Two Sicilies. But the price had been embarrassing, for Spain had been required to relinquish to Austria the duchy of Parma and Piacenza, a territory rich with Farnesan associations. Having succeeded with the elder son, the royal couple was now working to establish Don Philip in the peninsula, and the duchy so recently handed over to Vienna gleamed as an appropriate core for the younger son's presumptive principality. Elizabeth Farnese was a driving force behind the campaign. Her ambitions for her sons were a staple of the diplomatic banter of the day. She was the personification of maternal blindness, so formidable, the Prussian king once declared, because she blended Spartan pride, English obstinacy, Italian finesse, and French vanity.[4] But Elizabeth Farnese's resolve to see her offspring placed in the land of her ancestors is not an adequate, still less a complete, explanation for Spain's interest in Italy. The Spanish had ruled in parts of Italy for much of the preceding two centuries. Strong pro-Spanish factions prospered in Sardinia, Corsica, Tuscany, Genoa, and even Milan. Many Spanish nobles owned land in Naples and Sicily, while many Italians resided in Spain. All these considerations bore in upon the king's consciousness, persuading him that Spain should reassert itself where once it had ruled. The envoy from the court of Turin understood the king's commitment: "the intention of this sovereign has always been to restore to his crown, or at least to place in his sons' hands, all those states that were subject to his throne when he ascended it."[5]

Spain's other preoccupation was America, and though Italy loomed potentially larger in the old-fashioned minds of the royal couple, it was in the New World that affairs had become urgent as 1740 opened. The basic cause of the problem was not complex. Spain wished to control its American empire with the same absolutist and xenophobic spirit that it exercised at home. But in 1713 the Iberian kingdom had reluctantly yielded to British demands that British traders be given at least minimal access to Spanish markets in the Caribbean basin. The appetite of Spanish America for slaves, when conjoined to Spain's reluctance to engage directly in the transatlantic traffic in human beings, provided the foundation for such access, and the British were awarded the Asiento, the contract to supply 5,000 slaves annually for thirty years to New Spain. An additional Spanish concession allowed the British to send a single commercial vessel each year—the so-called Annual Ship—to Porto Bello. To the Spanish authorities in Madrid such a concession to British commercialism, extorted under duress, seemed already excessive; to the British it was risibly meager. And so British merchants began to resort to smuggling. The blocking of such illicit trade posed immense problems for Spain. The protection afforded smugglers by nighttime darkness, the high-handedness of Spanish commanders charged with distinguishing legitimate from illegitimate British voyages in the international arena of the West Indies, and the Spanish settlers' own eagerness to purchase goods that only Britain could supply conspired to subvert Spain's efforts to guard its empire without provoking the British. Several ancillary quarrels—Britain's refusal to give Gibraltar back, disagreements over the location of the boundary between Florida and Georgia, the dispute over logwood, and the counterclaims advanced by the Spanish government and Britain's South Sea Company about losses incurred during recent wars—also poisoned Anglo-Spanish relations.

For most of the decade of the 1730s, patient diplomacy had served as a firebreak against inflammatory proposals, but in the fall of 1739 the will to peace succumbed to the intransigence of grasping British merchants and proud Spanish bureaucrats. The British government declared war on Spain and began to fit out its fleet for attacks on Spanish holdings in the West Indies. The directors of Spanish policy in Madrid realized that in a maritime struggle the advantage lay with Britain: London's treasury was ampler, its fleet three times as large. To neutralize these British advantages, the Spanish decided to take steps designed to make Britain wary of shifting the preponderance of its naval might westward across the Atlantic. The Spanish assembled an army opposite Gibraltar, poised for an assault on the strategic rock so recently lost. They gathered troops in Catalonia, from where they might strike at Minorca, the former Spanish island the British had secured in 1713. And they created a minatory force in Galicia, hinting that they were considering the still bolder plan of invading Scotland or Ireland. Behind these troop dispositions Spain nourished a more basic hope: that France might come to its aid. For the truth of Spain's situation—a truth that Spanish leaders ruefully but correctly discerned—was that Spain needed the help of its Bourbon ally if its hopes, presently for America and in the future for Italy, were to be realized.

To observers in London the international situation in 1740 was no occasion for joy: with its 7.5 million people, Britain stood awkwardly isolated. The isolation had two sources. In part it was self-inflicted, for in 1733 Britain had declined to honor a treaty obligation to come to the aid of Austria, thereby saving British lives but also poisoning its relationship with the court of Vienna, traditionally its most important continental ally. In significant measure, however, Britain's isolation was a consequence of Cardinal Fleury's brilliant diplomatic initiatives during the 1730s. Because they controlled the world's largest fleet and could tap financial resources unparalleled in any other land, isolation did not terrify the British. They had over 120 ships of the line in their fleet, while France had but 50 and Spain, 40. But if not panic-struck, they were uneasy. Virtually friendless in the face of Bourbon restlessness, the British were often reduced to imagining a world subject to Bourbon hegemony. Should events come to such a pass, Britain would have to acknowledge that it had been thwarted in its effort to realize its two primary diplomatic goals: the maintenance of an equilibrium of power on the continent and the establishment of a world receptive to British traders.

The desire to keep a balance of power operative on the European continent constituted the oldest and most persistent theme in British foreign policy. In the 1720s and 1730s Britain had pursued this goal by adopting policies that paralleled France's, whether in opposition to Madrid's scheme to overturn the Utrecht settlement or to Vienna's hope to plant a commercial empire in the Austrian Netherlands. The British inclination to remain friendly with France culminated in Britain's neutrality in 1733. This policy of entente was the product of the cautious mind of Whig leader Sir Robert Walpole, who had become first lord of the treasury in 1721. Thereafter, as chief minister, he had steadily widened his authority in the British government. Walpole believed that peace promoted prosperity. He was determined therefore to keep Britain out of war, and he thought that cooperation with France was the policy likeliest to achieve that end. He failed to realize that by elevating peace to the rank of first priority in diplomacy, he might be compromising Britain's self-defined role as equilibrator of Europe by depriving the nation of its weapon of last resort. When historians call Walpole "the Fleury of England," they have in mind his love of peace.[6] The comparison is apt. But it should not be pressed beyond its core meaning. Walpole was not Fleury's peer as a diplomatic strategist, and as the 1730s progressed, international advantages accrued disproportionately to France. This uneven allocation of rewards could not pass unnoticed, and by late in the decade British critics of Walpole's policy were becoming increasingly vocal. Moreover, the initial French reason for supporting Anglo-French cooperation—the fear of violent disputes over the French succession should Louis XV die without heir—had disappeared with the birth of the dauphin. Whether Britain would continue to equate the pursuit of an equilibrium with amity toward France was thus open to question by the end of the 1730s.

The other chief goal of British policy was the promotion of commerce. And in the eighteenth century trade was booming. Exports exceeded imports by a healthy margin, both mounted throughout the century, and with the striking exception of France, almost all areas of Europe accessible by sea experienced buoyant trade with Britain. Because most Britons who gave thought to the matter believed that British prosperity was inextricably linked to British trading success, the government paid the closest attention to commercial voices when elaborating the kingdom's foreign policy. But these voices did not speak in unison. Traders represented diverse and often conflicting interests. They fell into quarreling parties on almost every discrete issue of the day. The war with Spain that Britain initiated in 1739 is a case in point. When the British government declared war on Madrid, it was bowing to the demands of those merchants who believed a fortune was to be made by trading with Spain's American empire and rejecting the advice of that separate, more prosperous group of merchants who already traded with Old Spain and who foresaw that the outbreak of war would steal their markets from them. What the verdict of time has rather oddly called the War of Jenkins' Ear—oddly, because Captain Jenkins had been separated from his ear back in 1731—was essentially a commercial conflict, but not all men of commerce endorsed it. Indeed, Sir Robert Walpole resisted the calls for belligerence to the end. His defeat on the issue signaled not only a decline in his political power but also the acceptance by a significant proportion of Britons of the rightness of using war to realize commercial goals.

A final complication must enter our analysis of Britain: the kingdom's close ties with the United Provinces and Hanover left the trajectory of its policy ever vulnerable to deflection. The alliance with the Dutch republic had been forged in the wars against Louis XIV. So close had the cooperation between the two commercial and liberal states become that Europeans spoke of them jointly as the Maritime Powers, even after they ceased to share princes. Britain had always been the stronger of the two, and in the years after 1713 British power had waxed while Dutch had waned. But the memory of cooperation endured, and since both shared a keen determination to prevent France from gaining control of more of the Low Countries, leaders in both states worked consciously to keep their policies generally coordinate.

The tie with Hanover had arisen in 1714, when the Elector of Hanover succeeded to the throne of Britain. In 1740 George II, like his father before him, was prince in both lands. Hanover was geographically vulnerable. "It would only be a breakfast," a Prussian warned the British envoy to Berlin in 1738.[7] Most Britons would therefore gladly have ended the tie: they believed that Hanover held Britain in thrall. But George II loved what he called "his country-seat."[8] Since it could not be cast off, it had to be included in diplomatic calculations.

The distinctive fact about Prussia was the size of its army. Like all nations, Prussia had objectives it hoped to realize in the world. But with a standing army numbering 80,000—constituting almost 4 percent of the entire realm of only 2.2 million—it had access to a club of disproportionate magnitude wherewith it might pummel all but the largest of the states that stood in its way. In Prussia the army was the chief business of the nation. Fortunately for Europe the king of Prussia, Frederick William I, valued his army too much to risk it in war. Political geography defined his objectives. Like the Habsburg domains, the lands of the Hohenzollerns were discontinuous. Far to the east, beyond the Holy Roman Empire, lay the kingdom of Prussia, or East Prussia, as contemporaries often called it. Far to the west, on the Rhine and the Weser rivers, were several outlying clumps of territory. Between these flanking outposts to east and west, but contiguous with neither, were the homeland of the Hohenzollerns, the Mark Brandenburg, and other adjacent territories. To the north lay the Baltic Sea; to the south, Saxony. And for a short stretch of about forty miles, where the Oder divided Brandenburg from Silesia, the Hohenzollern domains fronted onto the holdings of the Habsburgs.

A long-term goal of Prussia was to acquire the intervening territories in Germany. Pomerania, which separated the core holdings from East Prussia, was a part of Poland and therefore relatively immune from Hohenzollern grasping, for any effort to seize it would trigger Russian and Austrian assaults upon Prussian territory. Hanover separated the core holdings from the smaller territories lying farther west. Any effort to wrest this electorate from its ruler would certainly bring British and Austrian forces into the field. Consequently Prussian leaders in the 1730s were contemplating less controversial possibilities. The immediate issue as the decade drew to a close was the reversion to Jülich and Berg, two Rhenish territories that, if joined to existing possessions, would make Prussia a significant force on the middle Rhine. But the Prussian claim was not uncontested, and so the foreign policy of Frederick William I had been directed toward securing international support for Prussia's reversionary right to Berg, even at the cost of renouncing Jülich. In diplomatic as in military affairs, Frederick William was a cautious man.

To the south, in the northwest corner of Italy, sat the strategically important state of Piedmont-Sardinia. The three chief components of this state of 2.3 million inhabitants were the island of Sardinia, economically unimportant but the source of Charles Emmanuel III's royal title; the duchy of Savoy, the mountainous province from which Charles Emmanuel's family had earlier sprung; and the principality of Piedmont (with contiguous territories), the core of the realm and seat of its capital at Turin. Following the course laid out by his father, Victor Amadeus II, Charles Emmanuel bent his own energies to securing more land for his realm. His hopes lay in the east, for to have envisioned plucking territory from France would have been insane and to have chosen an Alpine struggle against Switzerland would have been stupid. The region to be looted—peeled like an artichoke, leaf by leaf, as the expression ran—was therefore Lombardy. Spain had held it until the War of the Spanish Succession; Austria had ruled it thereafter. Neither of these major states was prepared to yield its ambitions for the regions, and thus both were regarded as the enemies of Turin. The key tactical problem facing the diplomats of Piedmont-Sardinia was to discover how, in a world of powerful enemies, a smaller state could expand.

Since coming to the throne in 1730, Charles Emmanuel had played his enemies against each other dexterously. He dangled hopes of his support or at least of his neutrality before one and all. He was determined to keep Britain as an ally and thereby, whatever else might happen, to maintain a route (through Nice) to the outside world. He so maneuvered his state that he never faced the combined armed might of Austria and Spain. He called bluffs opportunely, he made threats credibly. He was—though the world did not fully acknowledge the fact in 1740—the master diplomat among the princes of his day. Since it was Austria that held the land that Charles Emmanuel desired, it was Austria that would be required to yield it up. But to the king, it was a matter of indifference whether Austria transferred the land as an indemnity to a victorious enemy or as a reward to a useful friend. Piedmont-Sardinia was prepared to serve in either capacity in order "to play," as the Austrian envoy had said in 1727, its "two-sided role."[9]

Finally there was Russia. Peter the Great had made western Europe aware of the citadel of Orthodoxy. Then the penetration of 12,000 Russian troops to the Rhine in 1735 had forced western Europe to stop relegating the land of the czars to the periphery of its consciousness. If nothing else, Russia boasted an army that was composed, in the words of a French observer, "of very fine troops, perfectly disciplined, accustomed to hard work and deprivation."[10] But western understanding of this vast and alien empire of 14 million souls was a jumble of hope, fear, and misinformation. Though the empress Anna, who had reigned since 1730, was German by background and in her interests, she was also indolent, and thus the main lines of Russian foreign policy remained unaltered from the direction given it by Peter the Great. By this definition Russia had two goals: moving southward at the expense of Turkey and moving northwestward at the expense of Sweden. Because France supported both these nations, Russian leaders were not notably tender-hearted toward Versailles. Because Austria followed an anti-Turkish policy parallel to Russia's, there were opportunities for cooperation between Vienna and St. Petersburg, and treaties concluded in 1726 and 1739 identified the character of that cooperation. But essentially, Russia was an international loner, protected by distance. It was free to choose to ignore Europe. If complications in the notoriously vicious politics of St. Petersburg should further distract the attention of Russian leaders from the affairs of the west, it would become a monumental task to dislodge Russia from its inactivity.

THE NETWORK OF CONFLICTS

National leaders in the eighteenth century were confident that the fundamental conditions of the international order were enduring. Above all, they believed that antipathies between states were more determinative than friendships—in fact, that persisting international rivalries provided the fixed points upon which any sound understanding of the world of international relations had to be based. They were right, and the earlier discussion of national aspirations directs our gaze immediately to the four contentions that seemed paramount to the statesmen of 1740. The first pitted France against Austria in a struggle for influence in Germany. The second found Austria and Spain as rivals in a conflict over territory in Italy. The third involved Britain and Spain in the competition for trade in America. The fourth cast Britain and France as adversaries in a contest for nothing less than dominance in Europe. None of these contentions was of recent origin; all, in fact, may be traced at least to the seventeenth century. They thus satisfied the eighteenth-century presumption that the foundations of the international order should be persistent. And foundations they were, for in the mind of almost every person who gave thought to the reality of international relations these four great conflicts constituted the starting point of policy formulation.

It is easy, but also misleading, to see the contention between France and Austria as a contest between rival ruling houses. Whatever it may once have been, the struggle had by the middle of the eighteenth century become one in which national motives transcended dynastic motives. France sought to make Germany responsive to its wishes so that Paris need feel no threat from beyond the Rhine. Austria sought to make Germany compliant to its will so that the integrity of the Austrian state would not be challenged. Thus, though nominally allies in the odd twilight years of the late 1730s, France and Austria were in fact wary antagonists for power in Germany. And even though recent trends—the gaining of the reversion to Lorraine and the tightening of the alliance with Bavaria—had worked to the advantage of France, two further considerations posed severe constraints to the potential further widening of French influence. First, the Germans did not much care for the French. Whether because they remembered the brutalities of Louis XIV's troops or because they had been exposed to the prevailing French contempt for things Teutonic, the inhabitants of the Holy Roman Empire nursed a keen distrust of their Gallic neighbors. Second, Austria had a friend in Russia. To policymakers in Paris this ominous connection might be translated into military support that would allow Austria to send its armies sweeping across Germany with impunity. Fleury was therefore quite sincere when he assured Charles VI that Louis XV would "observe with the most exact and inviolable fidelity the obligations he has taken."[11] Both from personal inclination and from his reading of the international situation, Fleury had concluded that France's chances for success in the struggle for influence in Germany were best if the contest remained diplomatic in nature.

A second great conflict focused on Italy. Here Austria and Spain were the contenders, and their duel revolved less on influence than upon the sheer acquisition of territory. Unlike the contests between Austria and France for influence in Germany, the struggle between Austria and Spain for land in

Italy was essentially dynastic. Spain had long been the dominant foreign power in Italy, ruling in the sixteenth and seventeenth centuries in both Naples and Milan. But this had been the Spain of the Habsburgs. Thus, when the Bourbons replaced the Habsburgs in Madrid—and especially after the War of the Spanish Succession was fought precisely over this issue—it became possible for both the new Bourbons, now ensconced in Spain, and the dispossessed Habsburgs, driven back to their Austrian redout, to advance pretensions to the old Spanish Habsburg holdings in Italy and thereby to claim valuable real estate at both ends of the peninsula. Charles VI styled the council that ran Italian affairs from Vienna the Consejo de España, and he hoped to use his son-in-law's new duchy of Tuscany as a *point d'appui* for an Austrian recovery of southern Italy. But the Spanish rulers were equally determined. Having won Naples for Don Carlos, they now eyed Milan for Don Philip. There were those in Vienna and Madrid who could justify the struggle for Italian territory by reference to presumptive economic or strategic advantage. But at root the struggle was familial, fueled by dynastic pride and fought for dynastic pretensions.

The third great conflict, however, was anything but dynastic. When Britain challenged Spain's command of the Caribbean by declaring war in October of 1739, the government was responding to the demands of a frustrated British public and an ambitious commercial sector. It was to be a war for trade, and Britain believed it would prevail by interdicting the lines of trade that bound the Caribbean to Spain and thereby isolating the scattered New World settlements of the Iberian kingdom. The organization of Spanish Caribbean trade suggested that the plan would not be difficult to effect. On the mainland that rimmed the sea Spain had three secondary ports—Vera Cruz, Porto Bello, and Cartagena—each of which fed its trade into Havana, on the island of Cuba. From Havana the cargoes crossed the Atlantic, most of them going to Cadiz. In theory, therefore, Spain presented several vulnerable Caribbean targets. In practice, however, there were several problems for the British. They had only eight ships of the line and eleven smaller vessels in the region. Even though that number could be augmented by squadrons from Europe, such a transfer would mean the weakening of either the Mediterranean or the Channel defenses of Britain and perhaps invite a Spanish attack in European waters. Moreover, their Caribbean ships could not remain at sea indefinitely, and Britain lacked the Caribbean dockyard facilities for building new vessels that Spain possessed at Havana. And so, despite boasting a fleet that numbered over one hundred seaworthy ships when the war began, the British were uneasy. No one knew better than they that naval warfare was riddled with vagaries.

Britain won an early victory when, in December of 1739, Admiral Vernon captured Porto Bello with six ships. At home the British people were jubilant: Vernon was memorialized in dozens of medals for beginning the war so auspiciously. But in truth the achievement was nugatory. The defenders had offered no resistance, and after the British left, the Spanish resumed their use of the port. British ministers soon began to realize that maritime activities alone would be insufficient to make Spain yield to British demands. What was needed, they came to believe, was the capture of an important Spanish port in the Caribbean. Havana and Cartagena were the two choicest targets, but a divided ministry could not choose between them. So in December of 1739 it decided to dispatch a joint military-naval expedition to Jamaica with the orders that a Council of War, convoked in Jamaica, should make the final determination of target. But while Britain pondered strategies and tactics, Spain acted with alacrity to relieve its distressed forces in the Caribbean. Philip V sent a squadron under Admiral Torres to the West Indies. Meanwhile, with a series of feints on land and sea, Spanish commanders in Europe kept Britain's naval directors thoroughly confused about Spanish plans for the eastern rim of the Atlantic. Above all, Spain sought and received pledges of French assistance. By October of 1740 Vernon was digesting the thoroughly unpalatable news that two French squadrons, one under the Marquis d'Antin and the other led by Admiral Laroche-Alart, had escaped British detection in European waters and were cruising near Martinique.

The mention of French commanders indicates that this third great conflict of the era was impinged upon by the fourth. And the fourth was the greatest of all. For if Britain and Spain were contenders for trading advantages in America, Britain and France were contenders for dominance in Europe and the world beyond. By one criterion that the eighteenth century respected, Britain and France stood apart from all other states as the only two great powers: France had the military might to command the land of western Europe, but Britain had the naval might to control the sea and the financial resilience to purchase allies almost indefinitely. What these two powers sought was not so much territory as influence. They deployed their foreign policies with an eye to assuring the continuance of a world order suitably malleable to their wills. The problem lay in the unhappy fact that their wills did not coincide. The rivalry touched North America and the West Indies, India and West Africa, but it focused on Europe, where both France and Britain purchased friends and influence. Sweden lay in France's orbit, Denmark and the United Provinces in Britain's. Britain enjoyed better relations with Russia than France did, and in 1740, prompted by Hanoverian misgivings and its own fear that war in the Caribbean might leap the

Atlantic, Britain campaigned to secure closer ties with Prussia. France in turn had its Bourbon nexus to rely on, its important German friends, and its capacity to stir the Turks to action. As if in fear of contamination, the two rivals eschewed trade with each other. But elsewhere their merchants struggled incessantly for the upper hand. The Baltic was Britain's sea, the Mediterranean (though more narrowly) France's. The war in the Caribbean now threatened to ignite this tinder-box of cross-purposes, for even a generation of superficial Anglo-French amity had not reduced, still less expunged, these multiple tensions. Cardinal Fleury viewed the dispatch of d'Antin's squadron as decisive; in August he declared that "one can not reasonably doubt that the English will declare war in due form."[12]

A consideration of these four great conflicts suggests that Europe fell into two rival camps. In one sat France and Spain, each with its particular quarrels against both Britain and Austria. In the other sat Britain and Austria, each with a particular quarrel with the respective Bourbon kingdoms. France's recent policy of pampering Britain and patronizing Austria had confused the picture somewhat, but no one believed that if general war came to Europe either London or Vienna would side with Versailles. It is true that relations between Britain and Austria had soured since the halcyon days of the Duke of Marlborough and Prince Eugene. In 1725 the two states had joined rival alliances, and in 1733, two years after the earlier rupture had been repaired, Britain had refused to honor commitments to come to Austria's aid in the War of the Polish Succession. But if the two states had not in recent years been notably friendly, they continued to find in their common suspicion of France a basis for cooperation. And since the Austrian decision to abandon its Ostend dreams had eliminated the last serious point of contention between London and Vienna—and since London was seeking allies in the face of its West Indian problems—all the elements were in place that would conduce to more amicable ties between Britain and Austria and perhaps to joint international actions. Bourbon relations also had known their rocky moments. In 1719 France had joined an international effort to compel Spain to accede to a revised territorial settlement; in 1724 France had broken off the engagement of the Spanish infanta to the French dauphin; in 1727 France had forced Spain to abandon its military effort against Gibraltar. But unlike the London-Vienna axis, the Paris-Madrid tie was grounded in commercial relations that both sides valued. So a political rapprochement was central to Fleury's thinking. In 1731 the two states had agreed to an alliance, the first sign of the Family Compact that would promote the coordination of Bourbon policies off and on for three decades. And in the war that followed over the Polish succession, the two had cooperated with stunning success.

That war was now the great object lesson for Europe. For if Lorraine and Naples constituted proof of the value of Bourbon solidarity, they were equally proof of the fatuity of Austro-British bickering.

Of the unengaged states of Europe, Russia was the least involved with any of the foregoing disputes. It had growing trade ties with Britain and France, though the relations with the latter were complicated by France's support of the three countries—Sweden, Poland, and Turkey—that comprised the so-called eastern barrier against Russia. It had virtually no relations with Spain, for these two seats of empire—guardians of pieties as dissimilar as the nativistic Orthodoxy of the czarist state and the baroque Catholicism of the Iberian peninsula—viewed each other with suspicious incomprehension. Only with Austria, its nearest neighbor among states already considered, did Russia have considerable intercourse. The two were, as noted, allies. But their friendship was strained. A half century of lukewarm cooperation against the Turks had led each to realize that the other coveted land and allies in the Christian regions taken from Islamic control. The issue was not sharp in 1740. But it cast a shadow on Austro-Russian ties. And one recent event also bedeviled those ties. In the just concluded war with Turkey, Austria had been so desperate for peace that it had, with considerable French prompting, accepted a separate treaty of peace, leaving its ally Russia isolated. All these considerations united to reinforce the impression that geography gave: Russia had no adequate reason to become immersed in the disputes of western and central Europe.

A second unengaged state was Piedmont-Sardinia. Unlike Russia, it had powerful reasons for choosing to enter a European war, should one break out. Alone, the armies of Charles Emmanuel III could not hope to wrest Lombardy from Austrian control. But in a time of general war, when Austria would need troops to defend Brussels and Prague as well as Milan, the possibilities for success would multiply. Nevertheless, Charles Emmanuel faced a vexing dilemma: how could Piedmont-Sardinia acquire land from the Habsburgs without simultaneously weakening the Habsburg capacity to check Bourbon ambitions in Italy? There were several alternative approaches from which the king, always inventive in stratagems, might choose. But one thing he needed to take into account, whatever course he chose, was the feebleness of support for Piedmont in the lands he coveted. The inhabitants of Lombardy had no desire to become part of Turin's growing northern Italian empire. Nourished in the municipal traditions of ancient Lombardy, many of the middle-class inhabitants of the Milanese viewed Piedmont-Sardinia as a land of pernicious centralization, unrelieved monarchism, and stultifying agrarianism. The sum of these considerations was clear to observers across

Europe: Charles Emmanuel could be expected to take advantage of any emerging opportunity to secure unwilling subjects, but the means he would choose could not be predicted. Waiting upon events had become the hallmark of Piedmont-Sardinian foreign policy.

There were parallels between the conditions of Piedmont-Sardinia and of Prussia, the last of the important unengaged states. Rulers in both had embarked upon deliberate programs of centralization, encountering in the process resistance from their nobilities. Rulers in both had formulated reasonably clear plans for territorial expansion at the expense of adjacent states and were looking for opportunities to implement these plans. Two important dissimilarities, however, defined their essentially divergent situations. First, Piedmont-Sardinia had natural and defensible frontiers; Prussia did not. In one sense this dissimilarity gave an important advantage to the leaders in Turin. But the second dissimilarity flowed in part from the first and more than compensated for it. Prussia had the army of a major power; Piedmont-Sardinia did not. The difference is most graphically suggested by figures. Piedmont-Sardinia, no laggard in this matter, had the equivalent of one out of every 77 subjects in the army; France, for comparison, had one out of every 157. But Prussia, through draconian discipline and an unyielding commitment to military might, had managed to put the equivalent of one out of every 28 Prussians in arms. It is no wonder, then, that European courts eyed the Hohenzollern succession uneasily. Prussia yoked the appetite of Piedmont-Sardinia to the military potential of France. Frederick William was a prudent man, a practitioner of peace. But it has always been the chanciest of foreign policies to hazard all on the life of a single individual.

In May of 1740 the King of Prussia died. Of his successor, Frederick II, much has been written. Twenty-eight when he ascended the throne, he later became known as "the Great," a sobriquet he would earn in the war he was soon to unleash. Frederick was an unpleasant person. He bullied his associates, saddled them with blame for his own failures, and lied with abandon. His conception of himself was exalted, and as early as 1731, when not quite twenty, he likened himself to Alexander, seeking new worlds to conquer. To some degree these unattractive traits can be imputed to the loveless childhood and frightened adolescence that the new king had endured. But to some degree they reflect deliberate choice—the calculated behavior of a ruler who, despite a publicized critique of Machiavellianism, operated on the assumption that private virtue was inconsistent with princely function. Frederick was also a man of high intellect and wide reading, unafraid to make bold decisions. He valued accurate information and browbeat his representatives abroad to learn all they could about the courts and countries to which they were posted. He lived, by royal standards, austerely; he worked, by royal standards, arduously. Throughout his long life he knew only rarely the joy of friendship. He meant to be feared, not liked.

Nine years before acceding to the throne, Frederick had set forth his ideas on Prussia's foreign policy. The government, he had declared, should seek to enlarge the territory under its control and thereby link up the separated territorial blocks that comprised the state. He identified three targets for incorporation — Polish Prussia (West Prussia), Swedish Pomerania, and Jülich and Berg — and he inaugurated his reign by declaring his unwillingness to accept his father's renunciation of Jülich. But even as he was bending his energies to realizing the old Hohenzollern dreams for more Rhenish territory, he also had his eye upon Vienna. In 1737 he had written: "The present situation of the House of Austria is very critical. If the emperor should die today or tomorrow, what kind of upheaval would the world then not experience. Everyone would want to share in his inheritance, and we would see as many factions arise as there are rulers." In the year of his accession he was blunter: "The emperor is the old spectre of an idol who formerly had power. . . . but who at present is nothing."[13] Some commentators have seen in these remarks only the ruminations of the intellectual in politics, somewhat dramatically couched but essentially analytic rather than programmatic. Perhaps the commentators are right. But in light of what followed we should not lightly dismiss the possibility that the new king began his rule with aspirations that far transcended the acquisition of a Rhenish principality. Frederick was himself later to say of the opening of his reign: "Ambition, the opportunity for gain, the desire to establish my reputation — these were decisive, and thus war became certain."[14] In any event, as his words suggested and his actions showed, the young man who had come to the throne of Prussia, unlike his fellow sovereign in Turin, was one of those rare rulers who would not be content to wait upon events but would choose instead to shape them.

P·A·R·T I

The Lure of Depredation
(October 1740 – July 1742)

3

The Temptation of War
[October 1740 — April 1741]

EUROPE EYES THE INHERITANCE

Our story begins with a death. On 20 October 1740, after a brief illness, Emperor Charles VI, the elected head of the Holy Roman Empire of the German Nation, commended his soul to God. The demise could scarcely have come at a worse time for the Habsburg domains. He left behind a divided body of councillors and a loose collection of member states, each determined to sustain its prerogatives. His heir was his daughter, Maria Theresa. Had her father invested half the energy into educating her about statecraft that he expended in securing pledges of support for the Pragmatic Sanction, her sense of command might sooner have asserted itself and her earliest decisions been wiser. Instead, however, her virtues were domestic, and her skills were those of the accomplished young woman—reading, dancing, and music. She knew little of matters of state, less of the weaknesses of her father's ministers. Thrown suddenly into a world of responsibility vastly more extensive than any she had hitherto encountered, she fell back for guidance on two principles: she would accept her father's advice to retain his councillors, and she would defer in most other matters to her presumably more experienced husband, Francis Stephen, Duke of Lorraine. The decision to adopt these principles, though natural, was deeply unfortunate. A decade later Maria Theresa bitterly recalled that at the opening of her reign, "I found myself, without money, without credit, without army, without experience and knowledge of my own and finally, also without any counsel."[1] It was thus a deceptively simple task for the new ruler to choose her policy in October 1740. Dismissing the possibility that foreign rulers might try to seize her territorial inheritance, she turned her attention instead to her deepest and most fervent hope: securing the office of Holy Roman Emperor for Francis Stephen. Her thinking reflected both her marital and her princely obligations: if her gender precluded her from gaining the imperial dignity for herself, she would fall back on the next best outcome by gaining it and its glory for her husband.

In surveying the German scene, Maria Theresa and her advisors concluded that the chief challenger to Francis Stephen was likely to be Charles Albert, Elector of Bavaria. Of the possible contenders for the elective office, only Charles Albert met all the conditions that should define a candidate: he was German, he was Roman Catholic, he ruled Catholic subjects, and he held an extensive principality within the empire. Charles Albert possessed some practical advantages as well. Two members of the electoral college — the Elector Palatine and the Elector of Cologne — were close blood relatives of his, and France, a guarantor of the settlement of Westphalia, had long offered him its protection. Some people harbored reservations about Charles Albert's ability, finding him to be lazy, undisciplined, and peculiarly vulnerable to the self-deceptions that flow from an improper articulation of means and ends. But to these flaws Charles Albert was of course blind. In contrast to Francis Stephen's ancestry, which was more French than German, Charles Albert held up the example of his own family: "an old, old German rock, even one of the first founders, from which in part the creation of the empire issued forth."[2] Confident of the justice of his candidacy, Charles Albert moved as early as November 1740 to mobilize the means of pressing his campaign. Indeed, catching Vienna off guard, he extended his claim not simply to the imperial dignity but also to significant portions of Maria Theresa's territorial inheritance.

The Elector of Bavaria was not the only ruler interested in Maria Theresa's lands. Piedmont-Sardinia had never accepted the Pragmatic Sanction, and Charles Emmanuel III's chief minister had several times been heard to dismiss the document as "the same thing as nothing."[3] The kingdom had a well-trained army of 30,000 men. But uncertain of Spanish intentions and alert to the need of maintaining an Austrian counterweight to the Bourbon presence in Italy, the leaders in Piedmont-Sardinia soon decided to stick with their usual policy of caution, even dispatching Piedmontese recognition of Maria Theresa's title in November. In Madrid, on the other hand, there was unconcealed jubilation at news of the death: Elizabeth Farnese even suggested that the occasion called for dancing. The Spanish court commanded an army of 130,000, and so after a brief search of the archives the Spanish ministry cobbled together a paper that explained Philip V's rights to vast portions of the inheritance. Behind the extravagance of these claims lay a far more precise goal: the grabbing of some of Austria's Italian territory, to serve as a principality for Don Philip. When Elizabeth Farnese proposed joint military action to France, she identified her true priorities: "Let the Spanish enter Italy without delay, and let the French seize the Low Countries."[4]

It was in Prussia, however, that the gravest threat to Maria Theresa's peaceful succession lay. Though in bed at Rheinsberg with fever when he learned on 26 October of the emperor's death, Frederick II promptly summoned his two key aides, Heinrich von Podewils, his minister for foreign affairs, and Kurt Christoph von Schwerin, his most trusted military commander. Citing the recent promise by the Austrians to support the Elector Palatine's claims to Berg—a promise that contravened Austria's pledge to support a Prussian claim to the duchy—Frederick II declared himself free of all commitments to the court of Vienna and announced his intention to secure Silesia. He would offer Maria Theresa the chance to cede it to him. If she refused, he would join her foes. But in any case the province was to be his. And to assure that outcome, he revealed to his two advisors his intention of seizing Silesia by armed force as a preliminary to any other actions. With a keen sense of the implications of his decision, he wrote to Voltaire on 28 October: "It is the moment for the total transformation of the old political order."[5]

It did not trouble Frederick that an attack on Silesia was likely to trigger a general war in Europe. Indeed, he was counting on the spread of belligerence. With Britain already at war with Spain and close to war with France, he calculated that either Britain or the Bourbon states would make his cause theirs. Either way, Prussia would have a powerful friend. Lesser allies were also at hand. Frederick knew of Charles Albert's hopes for grandeur and assumed that Bavaria would pursue an anti-Austrian course in Germany that parallelled Prussia's. He presumed that Spain would snatch its opportunity and launch an assault in Italy. Once all these fires had been ignited, the Austrians would be surrounded by flames. Any troops sent to extinguish conflagrations in Lombardy or the Danube valley would be soldiers unavailable for service in Silesia. Only Russia worried the Prussian monarch. But Frederick took heart from reports that the Empress Anna lay near death. It was, in sum, time to gamble.

Sitting on the flanks of Europe, both Russia and Britain were cognizant of how the lure of plunder was imperiling the peace of the continent. But neither state was free to intervene. In Russia the empress's death, which came on 28 October, monopolized attention. Her grandnephew Ivan, an infant of five months, succeeded her on the throne, and various high officials struggled for influence and power. Under these circumstances Russia had little interest in foreign affairs. In Britain all eyes were on the Caribbean. The French squadrons wending their way across the ocean were far more fearsome to political leaders at Westminster than the rumors of war drifting in from Germany. In fact, Charles VI's death might even be regarded as a godsend. After all, with affairs in Germany catching the interest of policymakers at Versailles, French attention would now be diverted from America.

The death of the emperor revealed the centrality of France. As the most formidable state in Europe, the kingdom of Louis XV was now courted by friend and foe alike. Charles Albert sought French financial aid. The Spanish royal family bombarded Fleury with letters beseeching French aid. From Vienna came Maria Theresa's assurances of friendship and pointed reminders of France's commitment to the Pragmatic Sanction. Reacting to these importunities, Cardinal Fleury saw the emperor's death as an occasion for securing French advantage. He had realized almost immediately that there was a distinction between the Bavarian Elector's imperial aims and his territorial aims. The former were congruent with long-standing French policy: as early as 1715 the French government had issued instructions declaring that if the emperor died, "the intention of the king will be to use all the means in his power to elevate the Elector of Bavaria to the imperial dignity."[6] But Fleury had no interest in endorsing Charles Albert's territorial ambitions and thereby in setting free the hounds of war. By smiling benignly, counseling restraint, and probing for weaknesses, the crafty old ecclesiastic hoped to extend French influence into the heart of the empire.

The first step in any political campaign on behalf of Charles Albert was to mobilize the electors of the empire. Only a man of high ability and credit could be entrusted with the delicate assignment. After casting about for a suitable diplomat to serve as ambassador to the imperial Diet, Fleury chose the Count Belle-Isle, then fifty-six years of age and governor of Metz. The reasons for the choice remain puzzling, for although there could be no doubts of Belle-Isle's energy and imagination, there were grounds for worrying about his judgment. What Fleury needed for this exacting mission was a man who appreciated the cardinal's concern for caution and shared his aversion to armed conflict. What he got was an envoy whose ambitions for acquiring a marshal's baton were notorious and whose distaste for temporizing was legendary—a man who had once described himself as the "great foe of the defensive."[7] It is therefore appropriate to regard the appointment of a figure so clearly at odds with the policy he was to implement as an early sign of the aged cardinal's slide into lethargy, confusion, and indecision.

No such difficulties beset King Frederick as he prepared his state for war and yet kept his neighbors guessing about his aims. It was, of course, impossible to conceal the fact that regiments were being gathered. But at least it was possible to disguise the target. Frederick fostered the belief that the

Prussians were readying themselves to snatch Jülich and Berg. The entire exercise was a diplomatic feint. His orders to Podewils were explicit: "You will try to amuse the foreign ministers in Berlin and to set them on a false scent."[8] The king studied maps of Silesia, met daily with Schwerin and Podewils, and authorized the printing of manifestoes justifying the imminent despoliation. Podewils's rationale for the assault he commended as "the work of an excellent charlatan."[9] As November passed into December Prussia's pretenses dropped away. Frederick's envoy in Vienna, Major General Borcke, began advancing the king's contention that Prussian support for Maria Theresa's succession could be bought only with a territorial concession. The archduchess had independent grounds for worry. To get firsthand information on the situation in Prussia, she had sent the Marquis Botta d'Adorno to Berlin. He was now warning the young ruler to expect an attack on Silesia by mid-December. These portents of trouble were fulfilled on 9 December, when Frederick announced to Botta d'Adorno that Prussia would save Silesia for the beleaguered Maria Theresa by sending in troops to protect her rights. The marquis replied that if Frederick wished to help his mistress, he could deploy his troops to fend off any Bavarian or Saxon probe, but that if he invaded Silesia, he would be violating the Pragmatic Sanction and face certain Austrian resistance. The king of course was unbowed. Four days later, after a nocturnal masquerade ball, he slipped out of Berlin, and on 16 December 1740 he led his troops from Crossen across the border into Silesia. The War of the Austrian Succession had begun.

But would it be a European war? The Prussian action virtually assured a war in Germany; only if Austria chose not to resist could an armed struggle be avoided. But if hostilities were almost certain, their scope was far more problematic. Cardinal Fleury had committed France to a policy that aimed at the maintenance of peace: the Bourbon kingdom would help the Elector of Bavaria secure the imperial throne, but it would not aid in the dismemberment of the state inherited by Maria Theresa. Did this distinction make sense? Belle-Isle was quick to argue that Charles Albert's imperial hopes in fact depended on his territorial claims. After all, the electoral college was quite evenly divided. The Bohemian vote might therefore be the crucial one. And yet it was precisely over Bohemia—and hence over the disposition of its vote—that Charles Albert and Maria Theresa were contending. And so Belle-Isle was able to argue that if the French wanted Charles Albert elected, they would find it necessary to lend him aid in his coming military effort to acquire the kingdom of Bohemia. It was a dilemma that Fleury would agonize over while, as the winter swept across Europe, Frederick II crisply compelled Silesia to submit to his will.

PRUSSIA SEIZES SILESIA

On the map of eighteenth-century Europe, Silesia lay like a distorted ellipse against the mountainous northeastern frontiers of Bohemia and Moravia. About 220 miles in length along its northwest-southeast axis and approximately 80 miles broad at its widest, the province was drained by the Oder River, which, rising in Moravia to the south, flowed up the middle of the territory toward Brandenburg and the northwest. The province enjoyed an economic vitality unusual for central Europe. Because its woolen-cloth industry had been expanding rapidly for two decades, and because it was a major crossroads for both east-west and north-south trade, its wealth had become a central element in Habsburg finance: fully one-quarter of all the direct tax revenues derived from the hereditary lands came in to Vienna from Silesia. Bartenstein did not mislead when he later called Silesia "the true jewel of the house of Austria."[10]

Frederick II knew that his decision to invade Silesia was momentous. On the evening of the day he led his troops across the frontier, he invoked the most powerful of historical parallels: "I have crossed the Rubicon."[11] He was counting on speed to bring success to his 27,000 men. The defending commander in Silesia was Maximilian Browne. One of those many Irishmen who, denied military opportunity in Protestant Britain, pursued careers as soldiers of fortune for the Catholic princes of Europe, Browne had displayed his formidable intelligence both in his elegance as a tactician and in his reasonableness as a negotiator. Now summoned from Italy, he was deemed the man to put Frederick's army to the test. But his resources were sadly deficient. Even the virtual quadrupling of Austrian troops in Silesia between October and December—from less than 2,000 to perhaps 7,500—left the defenders badly undermanned. Most of the major Silesian fortifications— Glogow in the north, Brzeg to the southeast of Breslau, Klodzko close to the Bohemian-Moravian frontier—lay in scandalous disrepair.[12] Only Nysa, commanding the river of the same name, was both strong and ample. Surveying this reality, Browne was realist enough to know that necessity enjoined initial recourse to the ploy of the outmanned: trading space for time.

The Prussian king did not delay in his campaign of occupation. Despite heavy rains he pushed his army southward up the Oder valley at a pace of close to four miles a day. He bypassed the Austrian outpost at Glogow and instead set in motion a pincers movement designed to bring most of Silesia under his control within a month. One contingent was entrusted to Field Marshal Schwerin. At fifty-five years of age, Schwerin had known service at Ramillies and Malplaquet. His task was to march southward to the mountains, then move in a southeasterly direction along their foothills, capture

Klodzko, and prevent any Austrian relief force from penetrating from Moravia. The other contingent, which Frederick himself commanded, took responsibility for seizing Breslau and the fortifications along the upper reaches of the Oder. Schwerin's troops, meeting virtually no opposition, were in control of Opava on the Moravian frontier within five weeks. Frederick's troops were only marginally less successful. By the second week in January they had either seized or neutralized every important Austrian post along the Oder to Nysa. Only when Frederick tried to occupy Nysa itself did he begin to meet difficulties. Ingeniously defended, the town refused to yield, and Frederick, needing to return to Berlin to attend to diplomatic affairs, finally called off the siege. It was an anticlimactic end to his triumphal march up the Oder-Nysa valley, but it mattered little. "Silesia," Frederick declared on 14 January, "is as good as conquered."[13] By the time he returned to Berlin, reality conformed to prediction.

The swift conquest was accompanied by an intense Prussian diplomatic offensive in Vienna. By forcing talks on the Austrians, Frederick hoped to blunt their military response to his aggression. He may have hoped as well to find them, beset as they were by a host of foes, somewhat tractable. Frederick's public proposal was ostensibly designed to meet the needs of both Austria and Prussia: if Austria would only acknowledge Prussian sovereignty over Silesia, Prussia would then undertake to guarantee the remainder of Maria Theresa's inheritance and to join Austria in allying with Russia and the Maritime Powers. Privately the king even expressed a willingness to settle for less than the entire province of Silesia. Within the Austrian camp there were those who inclined toward some type of compromise. Francis Stephen, for example, told the Prussians that although yielding would be difficult, "I do not say that all hope is lost."[14] But most of the Austrian advisors were opposed to concessions, arguing that an Austrian acquiescence in the violation of any part of the Pragmatic Sanction would nullify the entire document. Maria Theresa's sentiments lay with those who counseled resistance, and so she moved quickly to stiffen her husband's vacillating resolve. She even stationed herself right behind the closed doors of the conference room whenever he talked with the Prussians. Fortified by her firmness, Francis Stephen talked tough. On the day after the Prussian entrance into Silesia, he exclaimed to Borcke: "Better the Turks before Vienna, better the surrender of the Netherlands to France, better every concession to Bavaria and Saxony, than the renunciation of Silesia!"[15] Inclined to regard Austria's position as desperate, Frederick was reduced to venting astonishment at Austrian adamance. He had in fact received his first taste of Maria Theresa's fabled stubbornness.

It was not out of any confidence in prompt vindication that Maria Theresa and her advisors were acting when they chose to fight rather than submit. They knew how Browne was pleading for reinforcements, they knew what Botta d'Adorno had said of Prussia's military preparations, they knew of Schwerin's high reputation. But the conviction was firm in Vienna that in the long run, victory would nevertheless be Austria's. Prussian troops might look more stylish, but Austria's were more experienced. Once Austria had assembled a force equivalent in size to Prussia's, the Austrian advantages would allow their troops to undo the Prussian conquest. From the very beginning, however, financial stringency hindered these preparations. Because funds were scarce, the army could not enter into contracts for troops and horses, could not acquire wagons for bearing provisions, and could not transport artillery to Silesia. The shortage of money even affected the choice of commander, for Count Neipperg, the successful candidate, argued that the liberation of Silesia could be effected with fewer troops and less money than Count Khevenhüller, his rival, proposed to use. The choice of Neipperg had its piquancy: after all, he had been one of the commanders imprisoned for incompetence after the recent Turkish war. But he was an experienced commander, eager to rehabilitate his reputation, and sanguine of success. "Confidence in defeating the enemy and recovering Silesia," the Venetian ambassador wrote, "is universal."[16] In a scene too familiar to need depicting, a people embarking on war were systematically repressing what both experience and common sense taught about belligerence, suspending all reasonable calculation of probabilities, and mistaking hope for reality.

The Prussian army used February and early March to tighten and protect its hold on Silesia. Faithful to the principle that fear is the great tranquilizer, the Prussian authorities acted to make Silesians respectful of Prussian power. Silesians were conscripted into the Prussian army, new financial exactions were imposed, strategic towns were laid waste. The yoke became so burdensome that even many Protestants, initially delighted at the arrival of their co-religionist from Berlin, came to resist Frederick; and Catholics, for whom the situation had never been ambiguous, often fled to Poland or, staying put, cooperated with the small bands of Austrian troops that Browne sent out to harry the enemy. The hostility of the south was particularly intense, leading Schwerin to advise Frederick in March that "all the people between the Nysa and the Oder are sworn enemies of your majesty."[17] Frederick probably needed no convincing. Late in February he himself had almost been seized or killed at the outpost of Baumgarten by an Austrian detachment that had relied on the sympathy and silence of the peasants to allow it to approach undetected. There was even a story circulating that various Silesians had taken an oath to assassinate him. He ruled a restive province.

But the most pressing danger to Frederick's control of Silesia lay just over the border in Moravia, where Austria was assembling its relief army. Frederick was uncertain of the size of this Austrian force, though he knew that earlier Austrian hopes of gathering 40,000 men had proved extravagant. What most worried him, however, was his ignorance of Austria's choice for an invasion route. He assumed the town of Nysa was the initial goal of the Austrian advance, for the stubborn garrison there would be a useful addition to Neipperg's army. But there were two possible routes out of Moravia, and Frederick and Schwerin disagreed over which was the likelier choice. The king therefore tried to cover both, dividing his forces between Schwerin and himself. Neipperg meanwhile was giving the lie to all those, then and after, who have condemned him for irresolution: though commanding a force of only 15,000, he decided to delay no longer. The element of surprise, he calculated, would more than compensate for a deficiency in troops. And so, on 29 March 1741, along that more westerly route that Frederick had espied and Schwerin had ridiculed, Neipperg led the Austrian relief army across the frontier into Silesia.

FRANCE AT THE CROSSROADS

The Prussian invasion of Silesia posed a dilemma of massive proportions for French policymakers. By the treaty of 1738 France had pledged itself to uphold the Pragmatic Sanction. But France had also pledged to support Charles Albert's just claims, and obedience to this obligation—assuming the claims to be just—would draw France into the circle of powers hostile to Austria. In theory the two obligations were not contradictory. But in practice it could not be otherwise, since it was inconceivable that France would support Bavarian efforts to despoil Vienna while opposing Prussian efforts to do precisely the same thing. Fleury's love of peace, his distrust of Frederick II, and his suspicion that Charles Albert's ends were disproportionate to his means all disposed the cardinal to hope to minimize French cooperation with anti-Austrian hotheads. But there were countervailing considerations, powerful because grounded in history and emotion. France had long sought the humbling of Austria: a choicer opportunity for effecting this goal could scarcely be envisioned. Moreover, popular opinion among the educated and politically attuned supported a vigorous French response to events in central Europe. Finally there was Count Belle-Isle. The darling of the young—the man who, it was said, could start his own religion—Belle-Isle was calling upon the cardinal and other royal advisors to seize the moment. It was a great tug-of-war for the soul of France, with the immediate destiny of Europe waiting upon its resolution.

Belle-Isle was an energetic and thorough advocate of war. In the fourth week of January 1741, he outlined a scheme that called for France to send 35,000 troops to Germany, to become an auxiliary of Prussia, to give financial and military support to Bavaria, to unleash Spain upon Austrian holdings in Italy, and to prod Turkey into hostilities against Vienna in the east. Moreover, to prevent Russia from aiding the enemy, France should instigate a northern war between Stockholm and St. Petersburg; to keep Britain at bay, France should send troops to the Hanoverian frontier to overawe the electorate. In the ensuing continental belligerence, Austria would stand bereft of allies. Prussia would seize Silesia, Bavaria would take Bohemia, Piedmont-Sardinia and the Spanish royal family would partition northern Italy. And France, the engineer of the despoliation, would emerge as the unchallengeable dominator of Europe. The scope of Belle-Isle's vision invites comparison with the breadth of the dreams of Louis XIV before him and Napoleon I after him. "Kingdoms are not conquered," he admonished, "and an empire is not obtained without fighting battles, and to think and to act on other principles is to wish to risk all and even to lose all."[18]

It is impossible to mark the exact moment in early 1741 at which Fleury finally embraced Belle-Isle's idea that France should wage war. In a sense, he never embraced it at all, but instead drifted along, hesitantly and with reservations, until events contrived to have the idea embrace him. He valued his reputation as a lover of peace. But the very senescence that he sought to protect left him helpless when confronted with the energy of the more youthful Belle-Isle. Moreover, it was far from clear to Fleury that adhering to a policy of peace would enhance his fame. It was argued that since Frederick's attack on Silesia had ended the possibility of keeping Europe at peace, the only question now before the French government was whether France would act to make gains from a war that was inevitable. In a sense, Frederick was playing a cunning diplomatic game, threatening to come to terms with Britain if France failed to give him fuller support. But in his prime the cardinal had been a master game-player himself. What is significant here is that by 1741 Fleury was well past his prime, weary and failing. And so he ended up accepting, even endorsing, a military effort against Austria that addressed no definable French need. The judgment of historians has properly been severe: Cardinal Fleury lived too long for his good name.

Relations with Prussia lay at the heart of French calculations about Germany in early 1741. In the War of the Spanish Succession, Austria had been able to array all of the important members of the Holy Roman Empire, with the exception of Bavaria, against France. But in the circumstances of early 1741 it appeared possible for France to secure Prussia as an ally, thus shattering the virtual unity that the empire had earlier shown. As early as December Frederick II had proposed a defensive treaty to France, whereby the two kingdoms would ally with each other to bring a candidate unrelated to the house of Austria to the imperial throne. After two months of soul-searching the French foreign ministry notified Berlin late in February that France was prepared to come to terms with Prussia. Specifically, if Frederick would renounce his claim to Jülich and Berg, Louis XV would guarantee Prussia's right to Lower Silesia and provide Bavaria with financial support. By this time, however, Frederick was stiffening his terms, waiting for talks with the British and Austrians to ripen before deciding how to commit his kingdom. And so no Franco-Prussian alliance was forged in the early months of 1741. But by acquiescing to Prussian demands that Frederick's claim to at least part of Silesia be recognized, France had already hopelessly compromised itself with Austria.

In early March Belle-Isle finally set out on his diplomatic mission to the empire. His assignment in Germany was multiform: to win over the ecclesiastical electors, to confer with Charles Albert, to draw Frederick II into the circle of those supporting the election of the Bavarian, and finally to attend the imperial Diet. Recently awarded the marshal's baton, he traveled as the very embodiment of power—the man who had outflanked Fleury and, in effect, seized control of French policy. His initial stops were at the courts of the archiepiscopal electors of Trier, Cologne, and Mainz. Collectively these three archbishops constituted fully one-third of the electoral college. Belle-Isle charmed, cajoled, and menaced them by turns. The burden of his argument was simple: the interests of Germany would best be served if Austrian influence was reduced and if Francis Stephen, a non-German, was denied the imperial throne. Bribing and bullying worked, and when Belle-Isle proceeded on to Frankfurt to overawe still other Germans with the trappings of his power, he felt reasonably confident that he had secured the support of the three ecclesiastical electors.

There remained one awkward element in France's grand design: French policymakers could not decide how to deal with Spain. Belle-Isle urged a Spanish assault on Milan, but for Fleury and most of his ministerial colleagues, the situation was far more ambiguous. A Spanish strike into northern Italy would surely force Piedmont-Sardinia to cast its lot with Austria. It might suck Britain into the struggle, at least in the Mediterranean. Neither prospect was happy, and the latter was fearful. But Spain could not be blithely ordered around. The kingdom had an empire, a navy, a reasonably efficient bureaucratic apparatus, and a history of international glory. What it lacked was a route for moving its army to Italy. The Mediterranean would ordinarily have been the avenue of first resort, but the British fleet made it dangerous. So Spain looked to France for help, because French territory was the land-bridge between Spain and Italy. The first Spanish sounding for aid came as early as November 1740. "Just wait four months," Fleury counseled the Spanish ambassador, the Prince of Campo-Florido, "the situation will be clearer."[19] But even as the situation took on definition, Fleury remained an opponent of Spanish military initiatives. It is true that his thinking shifted. In November he reminded Campo-Florido that Spain had renounced its claims to Italian territory; by February he was conceding Parma, Piacenza, and Mantua to Don Philip as part of a putative settlement of the war. But on the key point— Spain's wish to march 40,000 troops into Italy—he was unbending. He even argued, in a contention that struck the Spanish as a gross misunderstanding of priorities, that Spain's chief goal should be the election of Charles Albert to the dignity of Holy Roman Emperor. "What a misfortune," Campo-Florido wrote, "that the death of the emperor should occur during the life of the cardinal."[20]

Spain, however, was only a sideshow at this point. By March 1741 the various elements of the French design were falling visibly into place. All that was missing from the design was the capstone to which everything else had been preparatory—a promise of French military assistance to Charles Albert. On 15 March that promise finally came: within three months, Fleury pledged, France would send at least 30,000 troops as auxiliaries to the Bavarian elector. A tangle of technical problems remained to be worked out, but the key commitment had finally been made. Belle-Isle had prevailed, and a halting Fleury had submitted to the combined force of logic, reality, public opinion, and youth. Secure in this promise, Charles Albert could now inaugurate preparations for a Danubian campaign. By choosing as they did, the leaders of France had decreed that a bilateral conflict was to be widened into an international war.

DIPLOMATIC PROBES

Aside from Maria Theresa, the European ruler most enraged by Frederick's attack on Silesia was George II of Britain. Like his father before him, he was of Germanic stock, at ease with the language and versed in the exotic details of Teutonic genealogy. He also—a matter of no small moment—was fascinated with the military and saw himself as a man of martial ability. The uncle of the Prussian king, George regarded his nephew as an upstart, at once callow, arrogant, and insensitive to the interests of Germany. At the opening of Parliament in 1740 George had spoken of

Britain's obligation to support Austria as a counterweight to France. After the invasion George translated this general principle into an explicitly anti-Prussian formula. Dismissing Frederick as "a faithless prince," he declared that the Prussian king "must have his wings clipped."[21] In George's view the invasion constituted a *casus belli* under the terms of the Treaty of Vienna of 1731. But eager as George was for combat on behalf of an affronted Austrian archduchess, Britain needed to be cautious, lest it get out of step with Hanover and the United Provinces. The Hanoverians spoke first, advising Britain in mid-January 1741 that the Prussian attack required a military response from the electorate. In adopting this view, the Hanoverian ministers were accepting the reluctant conclusion of Gerlach Adolf von Münchhausen, George II's chief electoral advisor. Prussia's planning and Frederick's behavior proved, in the words of Hanover's advice, that "neither faith nor confidence are to be expected of him; consequently each neighbor must guard against the worst."[22] The Dutch gave their response soon afterward. As might be expected from a nation that earned its livelihood from trade, the United Provinces did not profess any enthusiasm for war. But the States General acknowledged that the republic was obliged by the Treaty of 1731 to provide 5,000 troops to aid Maria Theresa. Britain was now free to declare itself.

And so in February 1741 London urged the government in Vienna to reject Prussia's offer of a compromise settlement: help was on the way. George envisioned a coalition of anti-Prussian powers uniting to teach Frederick his seasonable lesson and even to make him disgorge territory. The Austrians, the Hanoverians, and the Saxons would take up arms against Prussia; Hessian and Danish troops, purchased by the ample coffers of Britain, would join the allies; the Dutch would dispatch a contingent; and meanwhile the Russians would march into East Prussia. Surrounded and outmanned, Frederick would then be compelled not only to relinquish Silesia but also to yield up some of the Brandenburg patrimony—with Hildesheim being George's apportioned share. Dreaming of leading troops into battle against the forces of his nephew, George called upon the Austrian government to waste not a moment in dispatching a general to London to concert military plans.

Meanwhile, at the king's prompting, delegates from several interested states gathered in Dresden, the spacious capital of Saxony, to lay schemes for the presumptive operations against Frederick. The choice of site was itself significant, for Saxony had hitherto been reluctant to support Maria Theresa. Not only was Augustus III fearful of what the Prussians might do to his ill-trained army of 31,000, he also was not without hopes of winning the imperial crown for himself. And his chief minister, Count Brühl, hoped to use the outbreak of war in Silesia to seize a strip of land through Bohemia and Moravia and thereby to realize Augustus's greatest goal by binding his Saxon electorate to his Polish kingdom. Nevertheless, these anti-Austrian views did not prevail in Augustus's court in the opening months of 1741. The elector preferred to heed instead his Habsburg wife, Maria Josepha, and to see the occasion of war as a way to try to crush the forbidding northern neighbor. Dresden was thus an appropriate locale for an anti-Prussian conclave, and Augustus's representatives gladly joined with envoys from Britain, Russia, Austria, Hanover, and the United Provinces to affirm a collective intention of upholding the Pragmatic Sanction. George II seemed well on his way to forming his anti-Prussian army.

That was precisely what Frederick II feared. As long ago as the secret sessions at Rheinsberg, the Prussian king had spoken as if he did not care whether it was Britain or France that finally sided with him. But in fact he was not indifferent on the matter. He much preferred the prospect of the British tie. Fleury seemed unreliable and devious, and Britain, while it could make its weight powerfully felt in European affairs, lacked the capacity to inundate Germany with troops. The distinction between the sizes of the British and French armies was central. Frederick had not staked his future on military activities in Silesia just to allow Louis XV's writ to run in Frankfurt, Prague, and Berlin. By this reckoning Britain seemed the less threatening potential ally and France only a "last resort."[23] Frederick was therefore campaigning for George's favor when in March he received firm evidence of the coalition adumbrated at Dresden. Podewils despaired at the news. "Pandora's box is opened," he wrote, mindful of his October warnings of international reprisals; "we are entering the most fearful crisis that has ever faced the house of Brandenburg."[24]

The intelligence about the decisions at Dresden compelled Frederick to adjust his diplomatic strategy toward France. An approach that had been detached and cautious became both fervent and urgent. Frederick sought to make France's friends his own friends. Thus, abandoning all earlier pretenses of impartiality in the coming election, he urged the Elector of Bavaria to bind himself to Versailles, snatch the territories that he claimed, and thereby seize the irrecoverable moment. Frederick even contemplated Prussian military cooperation with Bavaria, despite his well-founded belief that the Bavarian army was untrained, ill equipped, and disorganized. But if one road to Paris ran through Munich, another was more direct. On 18 March 1741, just days after receiving confirmation of the anti-Prussian gathering, Frederick ordered Podewils to conclude a quick and secret alliance with France. He hoped to disguise his intentions from the British as long as possible, but as Podewils wrote: "the camp of the King of England and that of France and Bavaria are incompatible, like fire and water."[25] Forced by Britain's enmity to make a choice, Frederick fell back on the Bourbon kingdom.

By one of those ironies of history, especially common when belligerence disposes all to be impatient with patience and distrustful of trust, Britain's ardent enmity was at this precise moment turning to cold ash. The British leaders had been assuming that France would not act to extricate Frederick from the problem he had brought upon himself. But the news, received in March, that the Bourbons planned to assist Bavaria gave the lie to this assumption. Aiding Bavaria would bring France into phase with Prussia, at least operatively; and de facto cooperation would probably allow the fitful Franco-Prussian talks to conclude at last in success. Suddenly Britain faced the likelihood of driving Prussia into France's embrace. Immediately the British government abandoned its language of justice and took up the cry instead that Austria needed to come to compromise terms with Prussia. Britain even proposed to mediate an accommodation between Berlin and Vienna and sent the Earl of Hyndford as a special envoy to Prussia, entrusted with the task of enlisting Frederick II and Maria Theresa in an anti-French alliance. His appointment startled the ministers in Vienna, who could see no compelling reason to bury their hostility to a northern neighbor that had just inaugurated a campaign of plunder in order to ward off what was still but a presumptive threat from Gallic lands to the west of the Rhine. A military engagement was thus necessary. Britain might hope to promote peace by transforming enmities, but Austria preferred to promote it by crushing enemies.

MOLLWITZ

When Neipperg led 15,000 Austrian reinforcements into Upper Silesia at the end of March 1741, he caught the Prussians off guard. They had expected him to wait until the spring had melted the heavy winter snows. Neipperg, however, counted on surprise. Though Prussia had 60,000 troops in Silesia, they were scattered in various winter quarters throughout the restive province. With 28,000 troops Austria could at least regain some of the province and perhaps, if the enemy remained dispersed, inflict a major defeat on Prussia. The two chief Prussian armies were separated by twenty-five miles. Neipperg hoped to keep them apart and to deal with each in turn. He shared the common Austrian belief that the experienced Austrian troops would prevail in any engagement with the uninitiated Prussians. Indeed, Austrian hussars held their Prussian counterparts in such contempt that they took to bleating "Baa! Baa!" at them.[26] Heavy mountain snow slowed the pace of the Austrian advance, but on 5 April the Austrians reached Nysa and were greeted by the Catholic inhabitants as liberators. Rather than giving his exhausted troops a chance to rest at Nysa, however, Neipperg immediately led some of them into Brzeg. Only here did he rest, just outside the town of Mollwitz. The decision was an unhappy one. Now that Neipperg was north of the Neisse River, he was in Protestant territory, and while the inhabitants were scarcely fond of their newly installed Prussian master, they were not as ready to keep the Austrians informed about Prussian troop movements as the Catholics of Upper Silesia had been. Neipperg was thus ignorant of the position of the Prussian armies.

And the Prussians had contrived to bring Schwerin's and Frederick's armies together. They lay, moreover, to the south of Neipperg's force—that is, between the Austrian army and its Moravian base. Though the Prussian detachments stationed along the frontier had refused to engage the Austrians and had withdrawn at their approach, they had been giving their main-force colleagues time to establish communications. Once the two Prussian armies had been brought together, Frederick knew that he had a larger force than Neipperg. He knew also that he commanded far more artillery than the Austrian. Therefore Frederick had only to wait for the opportune moment, confident after his juncture with Schwerin that victory in the imminent battle would be Prussia's. Nevertheless, he prepared his ministers for disaster, instructing Podewils that if Austria should seize him, the Prussian government was to give no heed to any orders he issued from captivity. "I am king," he ringingly declared, "only when I am free."[27] On the morning of 10 April 1741 he began marching his troops north through the snow toward Mollwitz, hoping to force a battle that very day.

The surprised Austrians, learning of the Prussian threat, drew themselves as quickly as possible into a disorderly line formation. Numbering only 16,000, they knew that their prospects against 23,400 Prussians were grim. And yet events initially broke propitiously for Neipperg's forces when the battle began at 2:00 in the afternoon. The cavalry on Austria's left wing swept wide and then wheeled back on the Prussian cavalry. Though a fierce exchange of charge and countercharge followed, the Prussians soon yielded the ground. By then moving behind the Prussian line, the Austrians threatened to turn a local victory into a total rout. Fearing that Austria was on the verge of a victory, Field Marshal Schwerin advised Frederick to leave the battlefield, lest he be taken prisoner. The king acceded, escaping on horseback to the southeast. But then the fortunes of battle dramatically reversed their course. After defeating the cavalry on Prussia's right, many Austrian horsemen, averse to discipline, abandoned blood for booty, preferring the easy rewards of sacking the Prussian camp to the risks of continuing their assaults on Prussian troops. The Austrian cavalry's outstanding commander, Lieutenant-General Römer, fell before enemy fire. Meanwhile, the Prussians rushed into action three grenadier divisions that had been held in reserve. Above all else, the Prussian infantry showed its mettle. All the drill field exercises now paid off: the infantrymen did not break ranks, they fended off cavalry assaults, they awaited instructions, and, having received them, they followed them. The Prussian artillery smashed the Austrian front, driving the panicked Austrian infantry into flight. "It was a pity," an Austrian observer noted, "to see these poor recruits hiding one behind the other."[28] Then the Prussian infantry surged forward like "moving walls," firing with fearsome rapidity, apparently unfazed by the carnage in their own ranks.[29] By 7:00 in the evening, finding that he could no longer regroup his troops, Neipperg ordered a withdrawal. It was smoothly effected under the protective cover of the cavalry. But the field of Mollwitz was Prussia's.[30]

Casualties in this first major battle of the war had been virtually equal on both sides, Austria's numbering about 4,500, Prussia's about 4,600.[31] The Austrian cavalry had performed well, justifying Neipperg's confidence in them. But it was the Prussian infantry that everyone talked of. Their ability to maintain order and to fire swiftly astonished the Austrians—Neipperg spoke of their "hellish platoon fire" while another Austrian observer called the Prussian fire "a continuous role of thunder"—and justified the long hours spent at training.[32] Thus, the real hero of Mollwitz was Frederick William I. Many commentators thought that Neipperg had not handled his infantry well, criticizing especially his failure to support early cavalry successes. The nearness of the miss invites speculation that had the abler Khevenhüller and his larger army been chosen to carry out the relief of Silesia, the crucial initial battle might have had a different outcome. Certainly there were ironies aplenty to contemplate on the morrow of the engagement. Frederick had emerged victorious, even though he had fled the fight and spent the night, unaware of its outcome, cursing God and hiding in a mill. The Austrians had planned to win with a frontal assault; they had almost won with a flank attack. The Prussians had planned to win with a flank attack; they did prevail with a frontal assault. Already war was showing itself to be an unpredictable genie.

The consequences of the battle for Austria were seen to be devastating. It is true that Austrian troops remained in Upper Silesia and the Prussians avoided a new test of arms. But the military lesson was clear: a powerful cavalry could not compensate for deficiencies in infantry and firearms. And the diplomatic results were nothing less than calamitous. Some wavering states, now convinced that Prussia could make good its claim to Silesia, became far readier to join the looting party; others, though still reluctant or unable to prey upon Maria Theresa's inheritance, retreated from commitments to help her in the now-desperate task of defending it. As Austrians sought to assess responsibility for the debacle, attention focused naturally on Neipperg; he, after all, had aroused the expectation of victory. Observers noted that he had stupidly misjudged his enemy. He had even—the last failing one would have expected from a general whose name was a byword for caution—allowed himself to be taken by surprise. And then he had tried to blame the dead Römer for the loss! "What else can one expect," one commentator asked, "from a man who had been released from prison to be placed at the head of the army?"[33] Eventually Maria Theresa would agree.

For Prussia the consequences of the battle were exhilarating. Victory vastly strengthened Frederick's hand as he turned his cajoleries and threats upon such states as France, Saxony, and Hanover. He had, it is true, learned that Austrian power was not to be despised; he had seen weaknesses in his own army, especially the cavalry, that he moved quickly to repair. But in general he felt that Prussian practice had vindicated Prussian methods. About his own conduct he was, quite simply, embarrassed. He blamed Schwerin for urging him to leave the battlefield, and he even begrudged him his wound. But Frederick also recognized that Schwerin had saved the day and perhaps the monarchy. He was resolved never again to flee a battle, and without casting Schwerin aside, he moved to distance himself from the prickly field marshal. Meanwhile, he turned his attention to diplomacy. Both France and Britain were pursuing him, Belle-Isle and Hyndford were seeking audiences, and in the emerging diplomatic auction he might be able to win still more territory for the Hohenzollern state.

4

France's Diplomatic Noose
[April 1741 — September 1741]

THE NOOSE BEGUN

Cheered by the outcome at Mollwitz, France moved to press its advantages by isolating Austria, knowing that the starting point of any diplomatic campaign in Germany was of necessity Bavaria. Belle-Isle dispatched his chief aide, Count Mortaigne, to Munich with instructions to assess Bavarian readiness and to thrash out a plan for the coming military campaign. There was quick agreement on the first step in any march against Austria: the bishopric of Passau, commanding the Danube valley, had to be taken. But thereafter two choices beckoned. The Bavarians might march eastward down the Danube valley, seize Linz and besiege Vienna, and by thus penetrating to the very core of the Habsburg realm compel Maria Theresa to yield up vast chunks of territory. Or they might march northward into Bohemia, seize Prague, and by commanding the Bohemian vote in the electoral college assure the victory to Charles Albert in the imminent election. Ultimately it was the lateness of the approaching campaign that settled the issue. Mortaigne shrank from the prospect of setting out on a campaign that might wind up after six months with the Bavarian army stalled and benumbed beneath the frigid walls of Vienna, and in mid-April he persuaded Charles Albert to assail the far more vulnerable capital of Bohemia. It was — though the truth was not immediately apparent — the most important military decision to which Charles Albert ever acquiesced.

French efforts to win over Saxony in the spring of 1741 were less successful. Belle-Isle hoped to wean Augustus III from his visceral Prussophobia and thereby secure the use of the Saxon army. But when he arrived on 15 April he found the Saxon court in disarray, traumatized by two reports that left its policy in shambles. The first described how Britain, rather than fighting Prussia, would seek to mediate the Silesian dispute. The second, telling of the battle of Mollwitz, dramatically underlined the potency of Prussian arms. Realizing that a court that was habitually sluggish in its deliberations was unlikely to abandon the shelter of lentitude in a time of crisis and confusion, Belle-Isle wasted less than a week in Dresden.

The French also sought allies outside of the empire, but their campaign to win over Piedmont-Sardinia was even less successful than their efforts with Saxony, for in the early months of 1741 the Piedmontese were negotiating with both sides. When Count Kaunitz returned from Turin to Vienna to report of Charles Emmanuel's abiding fear of the Bourbons, the Austrians concluded that Charles Emmanuel would eventually cast his lot with Vienna. But the wily king and his tough-minded foreign minister, Marquis d'Ormea, were not going to be stampeded into committing themselves. Ormea was a man of strength, vision, and ability. Frederick II called him a student of Machiavelli; Kaunitz praised his acting ability. Both traits stamp his career—a clear-minded servant to a supple king. Together, the two men offered their support to Austria for a price—the immediate cession of Italian territory, guarantees and money from Britain, a promise that Austria would not abandon its truncated Lombardy—and the Austrians found the price too high. Thus Versailles's feelers to Turin were not rebuffed. As long as France refused transit to Spanish troops, the Italian peninsula would remain largely untouched by hostilities beyond the Alps. In such circumstances Charles Emmanuel could enjoy the luxury of being courted by both camps.

France's chief diplomatic effort during the spring came at the court and camps of Frederick II. Whereas Saxon support and Piedmontese assistance were nonessential and Bavarian adherence categorical, the accession of Prussia to France's plan was neither a frippery nor a certainty. By mid-April, in fact, Belle-Isle's situation had become somewhat anomalous. He had successfully won Fleury and France over to a policy of war by arguing that Frederick's attack on Silesia gave Versailles an unexampled historical opportunity. Now he was confronted with the embarrassing prospect of Frederick's withdrawal from the conflict and France's consequent isolation. To Belle-Isle it was a matter of both pride and strategy that Prussia's formal adherence to his plans be promptly obtained. And so, when he quitted Dresden, he sped directly to Breslau, arriving on 22 April.

He encountered Europe's man of the hour. By triumphing at Mollwitz, Frederick had made himself indispensable. Foreign diplomats swarmed so thickly at Breslau that Neipperg likened the gathering to the Congress of Soissons. In this crowd Belle-Isle could only wait his turn. But when serious talks began on 27 April, the marshal made clear France's disappointment that Frederick would pay heed to British blandishments, and he called for

Frederick to accept the treaty that negotiators had been working on for months. Frederick countered with biting reflections on the tractability of Fleury and observed that with Prussia so exposed to Russian and British hostility, it would be folly for Berlin to commit itself to war until it knew that France had formally entered the struggle. Had Belle-Isle been absolutely in command of French affairs, the problem would have been resolved easily. But Fleury was still a force to be reckoned with back in Paris, and he was insisting on some assurance that Prussia would not leave France in the lurch. In short, Frederick wanted an irreversible French commitment before he would sign a treaty, while Fleury wanted a binding pledge before he would launch the troops. Since neither side would yield, Belle-Isle left Breslau angry and empty-handed on 2 May.

Frederick was playing his favorite diplomatic game. Poised between France and Britain, he was keeping both off balance while maximizing his own free-dom of action. But the situation was, in fact, inherently unstable. The king had stymied Belle-Isle's campaign to win an alliance not because he thought a treaty with France inappropriate—on the contrary, as he told Podewils as early as 12 April, unless Britain could truly mediate, "it will be necessary to close with France"[1]—but because he dared not pass up the faint chance that Hyndford could stitch together a settlement between Berlin and Vienna. The British envoy arrived as Belle-Isle left and found Frederick quite cheerless. The recent decision by the British Parliament to approve a subsidy of £300,000 for Austria seemed prima facie evidence of Britain's lack of impar-tiality. Still, Frederick made an offer: if Vienna recognized Prussia's right to Lower Silesia, Prussia would pay Vienna 3 million thalers (£1 million). Hyndford sent the proposed terms to his colleague in Vienna, Sir Thomas Robinson. Then monarch and emissary sat back to wait. The fate of Europe now seemed to depend on the diplomatic skills of two British agents in Germany, authorized to mediate between two powerful combatants who would not even talk to each other directly.

At the Bavarian capital, meanwhile, the French diplomatic campaign con-tinued to enjoy success. Bavaria's most pressing need was money, and France had been working to funnel funds to Charles Albert by urging Spain to pay him subsidies. On 28 May Belle-Isle presided over the conclusion of an agreement between Madrid and Munich. Spain promised Bavaria an imme-diate payment of 800,000 livres (£32,000) and monthly subsidies of 80,000 Dutch florins (£7,250), while Bavaria reciprocated with a pledge to use the money to put 6,000 additional troops in the field and to exercise its influ-ence—potentially considerable, if Charles Albert became emperor—to secure Italian lands for Don Philip. This agreement was the Treaty of

Nymphenburg, the first formal pact concluded among the allies of Austria. Charles Albert pledged his loyalty in unmistakable terms: "I will never separate myself from my friends and never conclude peace without their knowledge and approval."[2] The significance of the treaty lay not in its obligations, which were quickly evaded or rendered irrelevant, but in its symbolism: foes of Austria in two different regions of Europe were prepared to join forces to despoil Maria Theresa.

Scarcely had Belle-Isle effected his Spanish-Bavarian coup when he received even more heartening news: Frederick II was announcing his readiness to accept the Franco-Prussian treaty. As the Prussian king had anticipated, the Austrian court, though divided, had rejected his proposal for financial compensation for Silesia. The Prussian king wasted no time in reacting. On 30 May he retreated into the only choice that was left and authorized Podewils to accept the treaty with France and to accede to the Treaty of Nymphenburg. Five days later, on 4 June 1741, Valory and Podewils signed the Treaty of Breslau. Its terms favored Prussia. France promised to give Bavaria as much aid as was necessary to guarantee Prussia's peaceful possession of Lower Silesia, and, in an effort to protect Prussia's eastern flank, to prod Sweden into hostilities against Russia. Prussia in turn ceded its claims to Jülich and Berg to France's most loyal Rhenish ally, the Elector Palatine, and gave Louis XV the privilege of determining how Prussia should vote in the upcoming election. Each side promised to send 6,000 troops in assistance if the other were attacked. The term of the treaty was fifteen years, its operative contents a secret.[3] The reactions of the various parties took predictable forms. Fleury remained unpersuaded of Frederick's loyalty—"he is false in everything, even in his caresses"[4]—but all the cardinal could do now was marginally impede mobilization. Belle-Isle luxuriated in the fawning adoration of the court at Munich. Podewils maintained the deception, prolonging his talks with Hyndford and expressing hopefulness for Austro-Prussian amity even as Prussia prepared for new military exertions. And Frederick II, denied the peace he wanted, moved with customary thoroughness to ready his army for the wider war that his treaty with France invited.

CARTAGENA

Because news traveled no faster than steeds and ships in the eighteenth century, events that had occurred months earlier in America came to bear on European affairs only as word of them reached the capitals of the major states there. Thus it was that even as France and Prussia were coming to terms in June 1741, information about a startling reversal of fortune in the Caribbean in April had not yet reached London, Paris, or Madrid. The outbreak of war in central Europe had already compelled Britain and the Bourbon states to reexamine their military priorities, and without exception they had concluded that they should bring most of their vessels back to European waters. But 1741 was a transitional year, and before these ships could be brought home, they had opportunity—and their commanders still had orders—to make war on their enemies. The British squadron under Vernon numbered ten ships of the line; it had been reinforced by a fleet of twenty-six (and 10,000 troops) under Sir Chaloner Ogle. Britain thus had thirty-six ships in the Caribbean basin. The Spanish squadron under Torres had fourteen ships, and six other Spanish ships raised the number of vessels in the Caribbean owing obedience to Madrid to twenty. D'Antin's French squadron consisted of fourteen ships, and Laroche-Alart's squadron numbered eight. The French thus commanded twenty-two ships of the line in the same region. Never before had Britain and its Bourbon rivals committed so large a proportion of their navies to American waters.

But why then did no naval engagements occur? With respect to Vernon, the question is readily answered. Because his squadron was for several months dangerously outnumbered, he deliberately forswore combat. It is, however, rather more difficult to account for the failures of the French and Spanish to seize the initiative, and it seems fair to conclude that Bourbon maritime leadership was exhibiting its characteristic excess of caution. To be sure, France faced difficulties in the Caribbean. D'Antin arrived in Hispaniola to find food in short supply, and the land forces of Martinique, which he needed for an assault on any British holding, were unprepared for action. Moreover, disease was beginning its insidious march through the French forces. A bit of conventional wisdom that the British admiral, Sir Charles Wager, entrusted to Vernon in 1740 applied with equal force to all Europeans in these inhospitable regions: "soldiers, no more than other people, cannot do anything when they are dead, and that will be their fate if they stay too long in Jamaica."[5] The swath cut by malaria and yellow fever—2,000 deaths ensued—reduced the capability of the French so dramatically that d'Antin finally decided to abandon plans for combat. As for the Spanish, they were even more quiescent. Torres waited at Cartagena for d'Antin to act, and when he learned of the Frenchman's recall, he moved to Havana. Timidity controlled both Bourbon commanders.

But not—once Ogle reached American waters—the British. They cast their eye on Cartagena, the most formidable fortress on the Spanish Main. They knew the Dutch saying: "He who is master of Cartagena is master of

America."[6] By taking it, the British would totally disrupt the pattern of Spanish trade in the area, give themselves a base from which to prey on the great Spanish bullion fleets, and make the whole western Caribbean unsafe for Spanish vessels. Because the operation would employ both land and sea forces, it was subject to joint direction, with Admiral Vernon directing naval operations and Brigadier General Thomas Wentworth directing land operations. The two commanders faced a daunting task. The fortification was built on a spit of land that, thrusting southward, separated the turbulent Atlantic to the west from the large anchorage of the secluded Bay of Cartagena to the southeast. An oceanic assault was deemed too risky, and so the British decided to disembark troops in the quieter waters of the bay and to take the fortress by land operations. Against such schemes Cartagena was well protected. A permanent garrison, disease-hardened and capable, manned the extended and winding defenses. The opening to the bay was guarded by several fortifications, including Boca Chica castle. Because Spanish batteries covered much of the anchorage, the British would be compelled to offload their troops under fire, and those troops that survived would then find their route to the fortress laced with swamps, waterways, and several strategically placed outworks. With good reason the Spanish believed they could not be dislodged.

The British arrived before Cartagena near the middle of March 1741 with a force that may have numbered as many as 30,000 men and thirty ships of the line. Command of the defenders lay with the viceroy of New Grenada, Don Sebastian de Eslava, and the general of the galleons, Don Blas de Lezo. The Spanish garrison protecting the fortification and the harbor numbered 3,000. The opening stages of the assault focused on the beleaguered castle of Boca Chica and the secondary forts positioned nearby. From the sea the British subjected all the fortifications to crushing fire; by land they pressed on Boca Chica with a slow and steady advance. But already Vernon and Wentworth were at odds. Wentworth tarried while his engineers labored; the troops then took their time making their camps; days passed into weeks. Vernon raged because all the while Spanish cannon fire nibbled at the British squadron. Only on 6 April did British ships sail into the bay, and a jubilant Vernon finally predicted victory: "It is the Lord's doing, and seems marvellous in our eyes."[7]

He celebrated too soon, for disease was making devastating inroads into the British force as troops moved ashore. And then an ill-conceived assault on an outlying fortress cost Britain fully half of its attacking force of 7,000 while Spanish casualties numbered twenty.[8] Wentworth thereupon withdrew, ostensibly to make plans for another attempt. But since combat was now threatening those whom disease did not disable, the British decided to cut their losses and called off the campaign. The British troops embarked onto ships where "our meat is salt as brine, our bread as it lays on the table swarms with maggots, and the water here fluxes us all."[9] But ashore the situation was grimmer still, for the beaches and roadways that the British abandoned were—in a Spanish report—"littered with corpses and with traces of recently dug graves."[10] Thus, an enterprise begun in confidence and under apparently favorable conditions had ended in a debacle. The British, by sustaining damage to seventeen of their ships, had stumbled from a position of dominance back into a position of vulnerability. The proportion of casualties to combatants was appallingly high.[11] The quality of military leadership was astonishingly low. But the chief explanation for Britain's failure was, quite simply, the fever. Tropical disease had destroyed Britain's Caribbean army.[12]

THE RESUMPTION OF CAMPAIGNING

By June 1741 the Austrians were proceeding in an ignorance that in retrospect can only be called blissful. The grant of £300,000 voted by the British Parliament in April, coupled with assurances that Britain would secure 6,000 troops each from Denmark and Hesse-Cassel, heartened their mobilization. Reports from London of Maria Theresa's popularity among the common people there constituted further evidence of Britain's determination to aid the beleaguered Austrian realm. Meanwhile, although the battle of Mollwitz could not be undone, Austria was sending bands of Hussars out from Nysa into Prussian-controlled Lower Silesia to maraud and harry, and the Prussians, licking their wounds after the close call near Brzeg, were proving reluctant to engage these mounted warriors in direct combat. Finally, Austrian diplomats and generals in Dresden, St. Petersburg, and The Hague were laying plans for military operations against Prussia. When Maria Theresa traveled to Bratislava to receive, on 25 June, the "Holy Crown" of Hungary, she was convinced that her foes would soon be compelled to choose between yielding to the threat or submitting to the application of force.[13]

In fact, Maria Theresa misread the situation in Britain. Her staunchest supporter in the kingdom was George II himself, but elsewhere the disposition to seek an accommodation with Prussia that had taken root even before Mollwitz continued to flourish. It received important reinforcement from Hanover and the United Provinces. Münchhausen advised the king at the end of May that Hanover ought to avoid getting sucked into Austria's hopeless quarrels. The Dutch cast their vote on the same side, advising Maria

Theresa that "it is often requisite and necessary to sacrifice a small portion in order to keep and protect the whole or larger portion."[14] Lord Harrington, Britain's northern secretary, expressed the cabinet's point of view when he told Robinson in Vienna that Britain would provide no further aid and instructed the envoy to work for a peaceful settlement of Austro-Prussian differences. As long as France remained the greatest threat to Europe, a war against Frederick, though perhaps unavoidable, would certainly be misdirected and might be counterproductive.

Neither divided counsel nor fundamental ignorance lamed Frederick II's preparations. Right after the battle of Mollwitz, he besieged and took Brzeg. Thereafter he encamped at Strzelin and held aloof from further combat, using the time thereby gained to drill his disappointing cavalry, to increase the mobility of his heavy artillery, and to weed out those officers whose dedication was less than wholehearted. Though allowing the charade of talks with Britain to continue—"is it my fault if they are so stupid?"[15]—he watched attentively for the French and Bavarian advances to begin in the west, confident that Maria Theresa would be compelled to dispatch Neipperg's troops to deal with them. Upper Silesia would then be his, secured in a bloodless operation. Since this strategy waited upon the initiative of his new allies, Frederick peppered France and Bavaria with letters of expostulation and admonition. It was important, he reminded them, to begin hostilities early enough in the year to allow time for the anti-Austrian alliance to prevail within one campaign. As he told Valory, in a judgment that lay at the core of his strategic thinking, "a long war cannot be borne."[16]

Frederick's worry about French lethargy was well founded. By any calculation, France was the cornerstone of the anti-Austrian alliance, and yet French preparations for war were both sluggish and confused. The source of the difficulty was Cardinal Fleury. France may have adopted Belle-Isle's plan, but with the marshal away in Germany lining up support for the Elector of Bavaria, the administration of the plan lay chiefly with Fleury. His feebleness and his preference for the subtle over the direct combined to make flaccidity the mark of his direction of affairs. He delayed making financial arrangements with Bavaria, even though Charles Albert's poverty was notorious.[17] He declared that France's contribution to the Franco-Bavarian force in the Danube valley would not exceed 25,000 men, disregarding Belle-Isle's argument that a force of fewer than 40,000 would be dangerously insufficient. He sent a letter to Belle-Isle to explain that because the season was so advanced, it would be impossible to implement the plan of operations worked out at Munich in the spring. Fleury even had the audacity to lay the fault at Frederick's feet: it was Prussian delay, the letter asserted, that was forcing the change in plans. Belle-Isle was so outraged by this self-serving epistle that he immediately set out for Paris for a showdown with the cardinal.

Into this environment of dithering in France, discipline in Prussia, division in Britain, and delusion in Austria, two startling reports burst at the very end of June. The first, escaping after four weeks of confinement, revealed the existence of the Franco-Prussian treaty and shattered Austrian swagger and British presumption. The other, finally traversing the Atlantic, told of the startling result at Cartagena. It was the latter that most affected thinking in the chancelleries of Europe. The Treaty of Breslau, though unpleasant for the Austrians and the British, was not exactly a surprise. But the account of the unexpected British defeat in the Caribbean sharply altered the political scene. Philip V was so delighted by the happy news that his knees buckled upon hearing it. Britain's Lord Hardwicke addressed the same theme, more somberly, when he stated that "now America must be fought for in Europe."[18] If Britain could not prevail where it could muster all its maritime advantages, what fatality might await it when it engaged—as now it must—under severe disadvantages?

Marshal Belle-Isle received word of the events at Cartagena as he sped toward Versailles. The reports only increased his rage at the bumbling direction that Fleury had given to military preparations in his absence. Belle-Isle feared that through a combination of Fleury's incompetence and envy France might lose the opportunity of the century. To deal with this danger—and to humble Fleury—he insisted upon full and lengthy meetings of the council. When the series of sessions ended on 13 July, the ministry and the king had submitted to the force of his personality and argumentation and had rededicated themselves to a swift and crushing campaign. The councillors committed themselves to pushing 15,000 troops into Germany by mid-August and another 25,000 in September—the full 40,000 that Belle-Isle had pronounced necessary. They agreed to send a separate army, also of 40,000, into Westphalia, where it would do triple duty as defender of Prussia's Rhenish territories, intimidator of vacillating Dutch politicians, and menace to Hanover, should George II misbehave. It was, in every respect, a dazzling performance by the virtuoso of French politics, and it did not go unappreciated. Ignoring Fleury, Louis XV spoke only to Belle-Isle when the two waited upon the monarch. Meanwhile, notable French observers celebrated Belle-Isle as an authentic hero who, after years of the cardinal's deviousness and caution, was restoring energy and purposefulness to French policy. These were heady days for the marshal.

In summoning Europe to war, Belle-Isle was deliberately leaving one area of the continent to Fleury. This was Italy, entrusted to the cardinal as much because the marshal was unfamiliar with it as because it was the arena for the perhaps insoluble clash between the Spanish monarchs and the King of Sardinia. Fleury made an effort, proposing terms for Piedmontese-Spanish cooperation in Italy. In effect, Charles Emmanuel III would shift his eastern frontier farther to the east, across part of Austrian Lombardy to the Adda River; Don Philip would get Parma and Piacenza, Mantua, and the remainder of Austrian Lombardy that lay between the Adda and the Venetian republic; and France would receive Savoy from Piedmont-Sardinia. Neither Charles Emmanuel nor the Spanish royal couple found the proposal acceptable. The King of Sardinia, after often threatening to turn to Vienna, was actually beginning secret talks with the Austrians, and he had no interest in jeopardizing them by coming to terms with Spain. "If one means to negotiate by fragments," Marquis d'Ormea explained, contemptuously dismissing France's jigsaw proposal, "the treaty will not be concluded for ten years."[19] Philip V, for his part, was astonished that a Bourbon ruler in France would not give Don Philip, a blood relative, more regard than he showed to such strangers as Charles Albert, Frederick II, and Charles Emmanuel. "I will not make war for the King of Sardinia," he bluntly declared.[20] As a consequence, Austria would remain unchallenged for a while in one of its most exposed salients.

If French pressure was ineffective in Italy, it was exceedingly effective elsewhere. No one felt it more acutely than George II, shocked by the double blow of the Franco-Prussian treaty and Cartagena. His advisors had finally clustered around the idea that Britain's interest was the preservation of a suitable continental equilibrium. As long ago as November 1740 the Duke of Newcastle had told the House of Lords that "the preservation of the balance of power and liberties of Europe, does not . . . depend upon preserving entire the dominions of the House of Austria."[21] By mid-July Münchhausen was counseling George II that "it is never allowed to be a healthy policy to begin a war for which one lacks the strength requisite for an advantageous conclusion."[22] By then the king-elector needed no persuading. The sight of Prince Leopold's Prussian army menacing to the east and the prospect of a French army approaching from the west, both presumably intending to perch on the Hanoverian frontier, so debilitated George that he took to his bed. Worried about Prussia, he contemplated seeking a neutrality treaty with Frederick. Even more frightened of France, he offered Versailles both Hanoverian neutrality and French control of the Hanoverian vote in the coming imperial election. Meanwhile, he repudiated all recent commitments he had made on behalf of the electorate to Austria. Elector George was scurrying for shelter, and he did not care what effects his precipitous disavowal of international promises would have on either his kingdom or the Austrian state that he had pledged to aid.

For the Austrians, the prospect by late July was genuinely grim. Whereas June had produced nothing but good news, each week in July brought reports of some new disappointment. The shocks of the Treaty of Breslau and the disaster at Cartagena were still being absorbed when Sir Thomas Robinson returned from Silesia with Prussian demands for further Austrian concessions. Reports from Austrian authorities in Bohemia told of a populace that might well prefer Charles Albert to Maria Theresa as sovereign. An envoy in Bavaria wrote that despite three separate Austrian-authorized overtures, Charles Albert would spurn any offer of compromise. Then came word of George II's decision to withdraw his support. The Conference had little choice but to summon troops from the east. But all knew that the drawing down of forces in Hungary might invite a Turkish attack. A desperate Queen of Hungary, burdened now with pregnancy as she faced a disintegrating international scene, wrote plaintively to her sister: "I do not know if a town will remain to me for my delivery."[23]

It was Bavaria that struck first. Though pressed for money and consequently short of supplies, Charles Albert had managed to gather an army of 21,000 men at Schärding. The target, as planned, was Passau, the strategically located bishopric that commanded the Danube and lay nestled at the near junction of Bavaria, Bohemia, and Upper Austria. Cardinal Lamberg protected his ecclesiastical territory with a garrison of only seventy, and when a Bavarian detachment rushed through the gates behind a nocturnal traveler in the predawn hours of 31 July 1741, the town yielded without a struggle. Though only a small and bloodless action, the seizure of Passau thrust the war in central Europe into a new phase. Hostilities had thus far been confined to Silesia; only one international frontier had been violated. Now belligerence found a new arena, a second border had been infringed, and Vienna, already outgunned to the north, faced a threat along the Danube as well.

Help was not at hand. Britain's defection meant that salvation from the west was improbable. And now a putative eastern ally disappeared too. Throughout the spring and summer of 1741, Austrian leaders had believed that if war came, Vienna would be able to rely on the support of Russia. But French policy was to distract Russia, and the policy succeeded brilliantly. While the French envoy to St. Petersburg worked to undermine pro-Austrian sentiment in Russia, French agents in Stockholm prodded the irredentist Swedes into a war of recovery against the czarist state. Their timing could not have been better. As the summer proceeded, Swedish preparations held Russia's attention. And on 4 August 1741, immediately after the seizure of Passau, the Swedes declared war on Russia. Thus, at exactly the moment when Vienna needed St. Petersburg, a resumption of the great northern conflict gave Russia a set of priorities that excluded Austria. There would be no salvation from the east for Maria Theresa.

With Bavaria on the march and Russia diverted, there remained but one final action to be taken for Belle-Isle's plan of conflict to be realized. That action occurred on 15 August 1741, when the French army destined for the Danube crossed the Rhine, precisely on schedule. Their hats decked out in the blue and white ribbons of Bavaria, a sign that they were auxiliaries rather than principals, the troops began an orderly march across Germany. Belle-Isle was not yet in command, for he had agreed that he should retain his diplomatic role until Charles Albert was elected emperor. But all knew that the army was, in effect, his; and even before the march got under way, Frederick II was speculating on which of the two leaders might be Marlborough and which Eugene. Belle-Isle delighted in the flattery. He expected, moreover, to be able to answer the speculation promptly, for the goal of making Charles Albert emperor seemed near at hand. With French armies afoot in Germany, even the most Austrophile of princes and ministers would find it advisable to heed French suggestions. The constricting noose was drawing tighter around the Austrian neck.

THE HUNGARIAN MOMENT

In this darkening summer of Maria Theresa's discontent there was one shaft of sunlight. Against all expectations, the kingdom of Hungary emerged as the most visible defender of the young ruler. Recent history suggested that the proud aristocrats of the Magyar kingdom might use a crisis in Austria's relations with France to pry themselves loose from Vienna's grasp. That, after all, is exactly what had happened in 1711. But from the opening of her reign, Maria Theresa had shown greater solicitude than her father had for the Latinate magnates who held power east of Bratislava. As the dispute with Prussia intensified, she listened with respect to advice that the old distrust of Hungary might safely be set aside. She noted with pleasure that Count Palffy, the Judex Curiae of Hungary, upon learning of Frederick's attack, had ordered a local mobilization in the Danubian districts of Hungary and had come to Vienna to discuss the defense of his homeland. Palffy was a Hungarian through and through: though offering to supply troops, he insisted that Hungarians command them. But he was also a loyal subject, and that somewhat surprising fact was not lost on the new ruler. She therefore chose to make him her chief Hungarian ally as she looked ahead to the convocation of the Hungarian Diet that her accession triggered. She knew that the session would be difficult. But as the Venetian ambassador reported, "the queen allows herself to hope that she can persuade the Diet with her presence."[24]

The formalities of a Hungarian coronation were intricate. Only after the Diet signified its approval could a coronation occur, and that approval would be preceded by an exchange of demands between the monarch and her subjects. Maria Theresa came to Bratislava[25] determined to win over the Magyars. She spent the spring honing her equestrian skills because the coronation required that she ride a galloping steed. When she drifted down the Danube to her appointed reception on 20 June, she traveled on a ship bedecked in Hungarian colors. Garbed in Hungarian attire, she used the occasion of her arrival at Bratislava to honor the nobles and churchmen who greeted her. Maria Theresa was later to acquire celebrity as a monarch who understood the importance of a ruler's public persona. At Bratislava she revealed for the first time how skillfully she could project dignity and simplicity, evoking simultaneously esteem and affection from her subjects. A desperate Austrian ruler was quite willing to let a feudal ethos serve where a more calculating political philosophy could only fail, and on 25 June 1741 Maria Theresa received the crown of St. Stephen.

She had, however, enjoyed her new title but a few days when the revelations of late June showed that the fundamental assumptions of Austrian policy in the west were insupportable. By August she needed help wherever she could find it, and Bartenstein supported her private view that one source of assistance might be Hungary. It was, in the context of recent history, a bold idea. If Hungary was to help, it would have to be armed. But Vienna's situation was desperate, and thus cautious talks were begun with leading Hungarians to try to arrange for Hungarian participation in the widening war without sacrificing Austria's remaining powers in the kingdom. It was, of course, impossible that there should be no quid pro quo: Maria Theresa acknowledged certain laws and privileges to be "fundamental," granted tax exemptions to the nobility, and accepted the obligation to keep the Hungarian administration separate. But she did not have to concede at every point, for she was shrewd enough to realize that a flattering coquetry could sometimes do duty for donative ingratiations. The Hungarians gladly accepted both kinds of attention. And thus the Hungarian leaders had already been won over when, in September 1741, Maria Theresa made her second great visit to Bratislava.

Once again the queen showed her gift for theater. She came to Hungary with two goals in mind. First, she wanted the Diet to call out a *generalis insurrectio*—the Hungarian version of the *levée en masse*. Second, she hoped to have Francis Stephen chosen as coregent. What occurred during two lavish September weeks was a unification of purpose and will between queen and Diet. On 7 September Maria Theresa told the Upper House of her harried situation; her invocation of Hungary as the last defense of her crown moved the body to promise to provide 40,000 soldiers, mostly cavalry. On 11 September, now addressing the full Diet, she apostrophized Hungarian bravery and received the fervent and memorable adjuration: "*vitam et sanguinem consecramus.*" On 13 September the Diet added more troops to its commitment—30,000 infantry and another 35,000 cavalry. On 19 September, after legislating a set of limitations, it agreed to make Francis Stephen coregent. Then on 21 September, with both her goals secured, Maria Theresa climaxed this extraordinary visit by appearing for a final time before the Diet and (according to some accounts) triumphantly holding aloft her infant son Joseph, born the previous March.[26] She had earlier told the Hungarians that she wanted to be their "mother"; she now capped her visit to Bratislava with rituals designed to underline her fecundity and love.

In assessing the significance of Maria Theresa's two visits to Hungary, it is important to separate fact from fancy—but also to realize that fancy can have an impact. As the coming chapters will make clear, Hungary's promise of over 100,000 insurrection troops was risibly disregarded by the Magyar magnates. Count Palffy was later to mock the *insurrectio* "that cost so much and produced so little."[27] But even though the euphoria of Bratislava was ultimately betrayed by the failure of Hungarian nobles to honor their commitments, the immediate effect of the Diet's action was to quicken Austrian resolve to resist Franco-Bavarian aggression and to give Maria Theresa's foes pause. It came at the most propitious moment possible. It demonstrated that the French were not the only camp in the widening European struggle that could enlist allies. It worried Frederick. Above all, it raised Austrian hopes. In the grim opening days of the autumn of 1741, it was the only development that did.

THE NOOSE COMPLETED

The desperation that beset the Austrians as the French noose tightened is starkly revealed in their fumbling after allies. Gone now was all realistic hope of maintaining the territorial integrity of the inheritance. The Austrians sought Charles Emmanuel III's support by offering him the Vigevano district of Lombardy and some rather vague promises of help in securing the Mediterranean port of Finale. They sought Charles Albert's forbearance by offering him his choice of the Austrian Netherlands or Lombardy. They sought Louis XV's assistance by proposing territorial settlements for Bavaria and Spain and the transfer of Luxembourg from Austrian to French control. But the proposed beneficiaries of this sudden burst of Viennese largesse were not taking the bait. Charles Emmanuel and Marquis d'Ormea were not yet persuaded that the reward for aiding Austria was worth the risk of inviting Bourbon attacks. Charles Albert and his military commander, Count Törring, saw no reason to settle for only a small portion of Maria Theresa's inheritance when, with but a little effort, they might wrest the major part of it from her. Belle-Isle and Fleury shared Charles Albert's conviction and wanted besides to avoid giving Frederick II any cause for alarm. In sum, Austria afforded observers a classic case of offering too little too late.

Simultaneously with all these negotiations, Austria was continuing its talks with Prussia. It did so because, although Frederick had been an ally of Louis XV since 4 June, his own guns in Silesia had remained strangely silent, even after Bavaria had seized Passau and the French army had begun its transit of Germany. In fact, on 21 August Frederick's and Neipperg's armies were but two miles from each other, and yet the king abstained from attacking. The Austrians therefore had no doubt that peace with Frederick could still be bought; the only problem was contriving to find the right price. The bartering that ensued in August and September found Frederick blustering—"let those who want peace give me what I want, or let them fight me again, and be again beaten"—and Maria Theresa, by her own description, "very depressed."[28] The king rebuffed two Austrian offers of territory before finally expressing interest in a set of Viennese concessions that a dispirited Maria Theresa had authorized with the mournful notation: "*Placet,* because there is no other source of help; but with the greatest sickness of heart."[29] Her mood notwithstanding, when the king's reply arrived, the queen received it excitedly and immediately authorized direct Austro-Prussian talks.

The reason for the sudden haste was the news that the Franco-Bavarian army had finally broken camp and was advancing down the Danube on Linz. This advance struck at the heart of the Habsburg domain. Even before the attack began, reports were circulating in Europe suggesting that a deep disenchantment had set in among Maria Theresa's subjects. Once the enemy began its approach, Austrians, already disaffected, began to seek refuge in nonresistance or flight. And in Vienna a panic set in. If Maria Theresa thought the situation so dangerous that she ordered her infant son to be removed from the court and brought to her at Bratislava, who could blame the good citizens of the city for adopting *sauve qui peut* as their slogan? The wealthy left for Bratislava and Graz, bearing books and furniture with them.

Those residents who could not flee turned their energies to fortifying the weakened city walls. Regiments of the elderly were called out; preparations for a siege were begun; morale crumbled. Not since the Year of the Turks had the grand Habsburg capital been so threatened.

On 15 September Linz received Charles Albert, who proclaimed himself "friend, lord, and sovereign" of Upper Austria.[30] The city had offered no resistance to the 18,000 invaders, and Austria's small defensive force had withdrawn so precipitously before their advance that it had even neglected to destroy the bridge that crossed the Danube at the city. The invading Franco-Bavarian force arrived with some fissures emerging: neither nation's army trusted the military leadership of the other. But these quarrels between allies, though boding ill for the future, were forgotten in the heady opening days of the elector's occupation of the capital of Upper Austria. Charles Albert declared himself Archduke of Austria. He held sumptuous court, entertaining and accepting the good wishes of the leading figures of the province. Later, on 2 October, he exacted from many of them an oath of allegiance. All his convictions about the inclination of the Austrian people toward the House of Wittelsbach and about the ease of the developing campaign were confirmed. One French commander confidently wrote that "before the end of the month we will be at Vienna."[31]

At almost the same moment, Saxony finally disappointed Austrian hopes. In midsummer a French observer reported from Dresden that "the more I enter into this court, the greater the mystery I discover; it is filled with faithlessness and fear."[32] As evidence accumulated in July to suggest that Austria could not win the coming conflict, the Saxon ministry decided to explore the possibility of cooperation with the French-sponsored opposition so that Saxony might secure the coveted land-bridge between Augustus's German electorate and his Polish kingdom. But neither Prussia nor Bavaria was interested in handing over part of its putative winnings to Saxony, and without the help of one of these states, the land-bridge could not be created. The Saxon initiative thus failed, and yet Augustus did not repent of it. Instead, in a decision that suggested nothing so much as a failure of will, he announced in early September that he would give Belle-Isle carte blanche to make terms for him. The strain of persisting isolation and the stress of carrying out simultaneous but incompatible negotiations—tensions that Frederick and Ormea found exhilarating—were unbearable for the Elector of Saxony and his fainthearted ministry.

Belle-Isle took full advantage of the opportunity that Augustus's complaisance afforded him. On 19 September 1741, at Nymphenburg, Bavarian and Saxon diplomats signed a treaty that promised Moravia and Upper Silesia (without Nysa) to Saxony, and Bohemia (including Klodzko), the bulk of Upper Austria, the Tyrol, and Further Austria to Bavaria. A separate Spanish-Saxon treaty and Prussian accession to the new Treaty of Nymphenburg promptly followed. This arrangement omitted the land-bridge, and so to placate Augustus Belle-Isle threw in a few sops. Moravia would become a kingdom (and Augustus thereby a king of the nonelective variety) and a toll-free road would cut across Bohemia, joining the two portions of Augustus's disjunct realm. But Augustus would undertake an obligation too. The treaty pledged him to supply 18,000 troops and artillery when his allies launched their assault on Prague. The treaty was received jubilantly in Munich and coolly in Dresden. After all, as any observer could see, its fruits were a large, agglutinated Wittelsbach state and a territorially divided Wettin realm. But both governments ratified it, and Saxony thereby joined the anti-Austrian coalition.

Throughout the long summer, the abiding fear of both French and Prussian policymakers had been that, if general war broke out, Britain would lend its aid to Austria. The pressure on Hanover that France's Westphalian army under Count Maillebois and Prussia's Brandenburg army under Prince Leopold exerted was designed to make British leaders think seriously about the implications of helping Maria Theresa. George II was clearly nervous. He huddled with his frightened German ministers, hearing from Münchhausen his fear that "a single battle [would] draw in its train the entire loss of royal land, because we have neither resources nor fortresses."[33] The king-elector ignored a call from Parliament to return to Britain and directed the Hanoverian envoy to France to affirm his own determination to assure that "no foreign troops enter and [be] stationed in our vicinity."[34] The events of September were then decisive, and on 25 September, in an exchange of declarations between French and Hanoverian representatives, George II as elector pledged not only to cast his vote in the electoral college for Charles Albert rather than Francis Stephen, but also to refrain from using his troops against France or its allies. By 12 October the exchange of declarations was converted into the Protocol of Neustadt: Hanover had formally declared its neutrality. In Britain the reaction was shock, disbelief, and incomprehension. George had acted against the advice of his British ministers and in the face of their promises to defend Hanover if Britain's support of Maria Theresa provoked assaults on the electorate. At no time in his entire reign was the double role of George as king of the United Kingdom of Great Britain and elector of Hanover less understood or, if understood, more condemned.

With the emasculating of Hanover and the stymieing of Britain, France had completed its noose.[35] Excepting only the kingdom of Hungary, Austria was now isolated. Belle-Isle wrote to Louis XV to compliment him (and himself of course) on his enormous success. The king, he said, had achieved what had been the goal of French policy ever since the days of Francis I: the giving of an emperor to Germany. "Your Majesty," he added, "will assure forever the peace of his subjects, the splendor of his crown, and the immortality of his glory."[36] Nine months earlier French policymakers had been asked to choose between two strategies for assuring peace. Fleury had framed his proposals in the categories of eighteenth-century thought about the fitness of a balance of power: he had urged that Austria not be humbled, lest France appear too threatening to one and all. Belle-Isle had framed his proposals with the assumptions of the seventeenth century: he had held out the vision of a mighty France giving the law to a set of middling German states. By the end of September 1741 it was Belle-Isle's doctrine that had decisively prevailed. The noose was his handiwork, wrought by his unshakable resolution, his keen eye for detail, his inexhaustible drive, and his robust presence. The only relevant question was: would the noose be sufficient to choke off the capacity and spirit of the Austrians?

5

The Abasement of Austria
(September 1741 – January 1742)

THE INTERLUDE OF KLEINSCHNELLENDORF

In October 1741 Frederick II launched his first great surprise of the war. Having spent the late summer spurning several proposals from Vienna— and having at one point ordered Podewils to "fuck the Austrians"[1]— Frederick suddenly decided that his intransigence had rendered Maria Theresa sufficiently tractable to warrant the renewal of serious talks. His policy had been based on the assumption that Silesia could be secured only as an aspect of a wider anti-Austrian war, but even if this assumption were true, he reasoned, it did not follow that as Europe lurched into armed conflict, Prussia was obliged to participate. And so Austro-Prussian discussions began near the Austrian redoubt of Nysa. Maria Theresa authorized Neipperg to negotiate for Austria and acknowledged the impossibility of retaining possession of Prussian-occupied Lower Silesia; her situation, she bluntly explained, was "everywhere desperate."[2] Frederick deputed Colonel Goltz to represent the Prussian side. In light of Neipperg's manifest inadequacy as a negotiator in the recent Turkish war, he was not a happy choice. But the queen felt that the alternative—continued reliance on British intermediaries—was unhappier still, and so she reposed her trust in a man who, if muddled, nevertheless held her interests at heart.

The talks became snagged on two difficult issues. Goltz spoke at one point of a "general pacification," but that was precisely what Maria Theresa least wanted.[3] To her way of thinking, the sole virtue of freeing Austria from the need to defend Upper Silesia was to be able to unleash her troops against the Bavarian poachers in Upper Austria. A peace that ended hostilities altogether would cost her not only Silesia but also important areas of the Danube valley. Similarly contentious was Frederick's desire to add the strategically important county of Klodzko to his Lower Silesian prize. Klodzko was a dependency of the Bohemian crown and not historically a part of Silesia; the queen was determined to resist a cession that would not only be militarily disadvantageous but would also reopen the question of the integrity of the inheritance. Frederick understood. Wanting relief for his army, he bowed to the queen's obdurance. Thus, on 9 October 1741, at the Starhemberg castle of Kleinschnellendorf that lay just east of Nysa, with torches illumining the nocturnal setting, Lord Hyndford served as witness to an exchange of promises between Neipperg and Frederick and then drafted a paper that particularized these oral agreements. This odd document was the Convention of Kleinschnellendorf.

By its terms, a cease-fire fell across Silesia. Prussia would get Lower Silesia and Nysa but not Klodzko. To maintain the mask of secrecy, Austrian troops would briefly pretend to hold out at Nysa before yielding the town to their foes. In return for the certainty of this triumph, the Prussians would allow the Austrians to leave the area and to travel wherever they wished. Frederick pledged himself to forgo hostilities against either Austria or Hanover and to limit his territorial demands to Lower Silesia and Nysa. Meanwhile, Prussia would be allowed to establish winter quarters in Upper Silesia (but not in Moravia or Bohemia) and to stay there until April 1742. The procedure that generated the convention was extraordinary—Hyndford alone signed the paper—but it assured that there would be no documentary evidence to embarrass the Prussians at a later time. And embarrassing its revelation would predictably be, for Frederick, the "undying" ally of Charles Albert and Louis XV, was unequivocally abandoning both of these pledged friends.

Events were soon to overtake the Convention of Kleinschnellendorf, and a document that might have transformed the structure of the war became within two months but an archival curiosity. From a military and strategic perspective it was an error for Frederick to have accepted it. He secured one short-term gain: the opportunity to rest his exhausted troops. But the price he paid was high and is best understood by considering the three likeliest scenarios for the post-Kleinschnellendorf future. Either Austria would now repel France and its German allies, or France and those allies would continue the despoliation of Austria, or the two sides would get bogged down in a war of attrition along the Danube valley and across Bohemia. If the first scenario ensued, Austria could be expected to use its demographic preponderance, its now mobilized might, and its awakened élan to reopen the battle for Silesia. If the second scenario ensued, Prussia would find itself cheek to jowl with an expanded Bavaria and Saxony, both backed by a cocky France, and all nursing grudges against the perfidious Prussian king. Only if the third scenario ensued was Prussia reasonably safe. And even then the safety would be of the qualified sort, for protracted warfare, ceaselessly lapping at the frontiers of the Hohenzollern state, would be the hallmark of Germany, and it is notoriously hard to be an island of tranquility in an ocean of turbulence. Not surprisingly, therefore, Frederick's ministers counseled against accepting the convention. It is true that Frederick made his reputation by defying conventional wisdom. But in this instance conventional wisdom was right.

THE FALL OF PRAGUE

After lingering three weeks in conquered Linz, Charles Albert confounded plans and expectations alike by directing the Franco-Bavarian army to march down the Danube valley directly on Vienna. In the Austrian capital, the pause in the Franco-Bavarian advance had not been squandered. Under the energetic direction of Count Khevenhüller, the situation in the city had been stabilized. Conscription had created a labor force to repair the walls; requisitioning had provided the horses needed to move materials; troops posted at Plzen in Bohemia had been recalled to strengthen the garrison; the military authorities had even taken the precautions of ridding the city of unnecessary combustibles and storing water for extinguishing fires. The Franco-Bavarian advance triggered new pressures — an influx of refugees displaced by the enemy and a renewed efflux of the fearful — but the order and spirit that Khevenhüller had created were proof against even these dislocations. On 21 October the Franco-Bavarian army encamped at St. Pölten, only thirty miles from the city.

At that point prudence finally prevailed over boldness in the Franco-Bavarian camp. Despite his wish to make Prince Eugene's glorious residence at Belvedere his home, Charles Albert saw ominous signs. He was short of siege artillery. His lines of communication with Bavaria were stretched thin, and his army was vulnerable to isolation if an Austrian attack should fall toward the west. Fredrick II, though nominally an ally, was being peculiarly unhelpful, reinforcing the suspicions triggered by recent rumors of an Austro-Prussian reconciliation at Kleinschnellendorf.[4] And if these considerations were not adequate, there was a final and clinching one. Charles Albert foresaw the unpleasant possibility that while he was besieging Vienna, the Saxons might snatch the opportunity he was providing them to do with Bohemia what the Prussians had done with Silesia — and with two added benefits: the control of the Bohemian electoral vote and the claiming of the Bohemian crown. And so, after his brief essay in boldness, Charles Albert reverted to the original decision and directed his army to march on Prague. The news cheered Belle-Isle. But the marshal's analysis retained force: "For two months the Elector has done nothing but float from one opinion to the other. . . . He has sinned against all true principles, and has adopted false ones."[5] He had also lost irredeemable time.

The elector's decision sealed the fate of the kingdom of Bohemia. For the next four years it would be the heart of warfare in central Europe. Immediately three hostile armies penetrated its mountainous rim. Out of Upper Austria came 12,000 Franco-Bavarian troops, marching by way of Budejovice. Out of the Upper Palatinate a smaller Franco-Bavarian force struck to take Plzen. Finally, 20,000 Saxons invaded along the Elbe valley. To defend the kingdom, Maria Theresa vowed to spare nothing and no one. In what is probably the most chilling letter she ever penned, she explained her resolution to Count Kinsky: "My mind is made up. We must put everything at stake in order to save Bohemia . . ., and to this end I shall have all my armies, all my Hungarians killed off before I cede so much as an inch of ground."[6] To command the defending army that Austria was assembling, she turned to her husband, Francis Stephen. Though now disillusioned about his political capacity, she believed that he might still show himself a military man. But since caution tempered conviction, she dispatched his younger and more experienced brother, Prince Charles of Lorraine, to assist and watch over him. With the invading Franco-Bavarian force numbering about 13,000, the invading Saxons mustering another 20,000, and the defending Austrians totaling 40,000, the incipient Bohemian conflict promised to be significantly larger than the struggle for Silesia.

Early in October Cardinal Fleury had described the French situation in central Europe as "very brilliant." Then he added a characteristic qualification: "even as it has the luster of glass, it has its fragility."[7] It was the latter that impressed the leaders of the French, Bavarian, and Saxon allies who gathered outside of Prague as the fourth week of November began. The Bavarian army had been well received by the Bohemians. The Bohemian peasantry had turned out to gawk at the brash elector from Munich who proposed to end the Viennese stranglehold on the imperial crown. But there had been no rush to transfer formal loyalty from Habsburg to Wittelsbach, for the majority of the people of Bohemia were waiting to see how military affairs broke before committing themselves to one side or the other. And the prospects for an allied military success at Prague did not seem good. Frederick was offering no help, and Charles Albert lacked both the charisma to establish an ascendancy over the French commanders and the experience to plan an effective siege. The three armies were therefore on the verge of acting independently. Meanwhile, two enemies approached: the sluggish but large Austrian army under Francis Stephen and the inevitable bitterness of winter. In their frustration the allied commanders in Prague appealed for the arrival of Marshal Belle-Isle, but in yet another stroke of allied misfortune the marshal at that very moment lay abed at Dresden, too ill to mount a horse. Outnumbered and isolated, the allies felt their vulnerability.

Prague meanwhile prepared for their attack, its Austrian commander, Count Ogilvy, dubious of his own prospects. The fortifications of the city were daunting, but within them lived 40,000 people of uncertain loyalty. The commercial middle class was hostile to the new wartime taxes, the Jewish sector was eager for an end to persecution. The Austrians therefore dared not arm the citizenry. Earlier calls from Maria Theresa for assistance had depleted the Austrian garrison stationed in the city to a meager 2,500 men. Even the geography of Prague made the defensive task difficult. The Vltava flowed northward through the city, separating the Old Town on the east bank from the Lesser Town on the west bank. The Charles Bridge was the only span linking the two parts of the city. If it became necessary to speed detachments of the thin and scattered garrison across the river, only the circuitous and delaying route of the bridge was available. For all these reasons many inhabitants expected the imminent assault to be successful.

On the afternoon of 25 November 1741 the Saxon commander, Count Rutowski, declared his intention of breaking the impasse to which allied operations had seemed to come. Since a traditional siege offered no hope of a quick triumph, Rutowski proposed an escalade. The walls of the city were forbiddingly high, but with a diversion to pull defenders away from the point of attack and with the protection of darkness, an assault by ladder might succeed. All that was needed, he argued, was for a few men to prevail long enough within the city to get a gate open and a drawbridge lowered. Then the allied troops waiting on the outside could swarm in. To the French generals the proposal seemed ill judged, but if Rutowski was willing to sacrifice his own men in a harebrained scheme, they agreed to mount the far less risky diversion. To command one of these feints, they chose Maurice of Saxony (who, despite his name, commanded in the French, not the Saxon, army).

Maurice of Saxony was forty-five on that chilly November day. His life had already been tempestuous. One of the many illegitimate progeny of Augustus the Strong, he was the half brother of the present elector of Saxony, Augustus III (and interestingly, of Count Rutowski, the chevalier de Saxe, and Count Cosel, all present in the Saxon army at Prague). At the age of twelve he had entered the imperial army; later he had joined the service of the French crown. He was as famous for his debauched life as for his extraordinary strength. But even while living as a wanton Hercules, he had applied his mind to mathematics and military science, and during an illness in

1732 he had written his *Reveries*, a two-volume discussion of the art of war that revealed its author to be at once an analyst and a mystic. Maurice was a man of complex loyalties and interests. He sought to help the house of Wettin from which he had sprung. He sought to help Louis XV, to whose support he had pledged his service. And he sought to help himself—perhaps by recovering the duchy of Courland (from which, though the elected duke, he had been driven by the Russians) and certainly by winning glory for himself through military exploits. When war had broken out in the autumn of 1740, Maurice had written: "here is the general muddle, and I have a part to play in it."[8] Now, a year later, the part could begin.

As a man who had been chastised by Prince Eugene for foolhardiness, Maurice was scarcely to be satisfied with commanding a mere diversion. In choosing those who would accompany him to the east side of the river, he culled the ablest troops. In making his semicircuit of the city he gathered ladders, ropes, and axes. At 3:00 in the morning on November 26, Maurice and his troops reached a position adjacent to the New Gate, the point of entry he had selected. The rattle of gunfire and the thunder of the defensive artillery in the west allowed the French to approach undetected. Maurice positioned his cavalry so that they might charge into the city as soon as the bridge was lowered. He directed his chief aide, Lieutenant-Colonel François de Chevert, to begin a furtive escalade. Only two of the ladders were tall enough to reach the battlements, but they were adequate to get ten men onto the top of the wall before the Austrians discovered them. A brief engagement ensued, in which the French, trusting to silent bayonets rather than noisy fire, defeated the confused defenders. With resistance nullified, a new wave of scalers swept over the wall. The invaders then made their way to the New Gate, overcame the guard there, and lowered the bridge. Like a bolt, Maurice and the French cavalry came crashing across, shouting *"Vive le roi!"* By the time Maurice reached the Charles Bridge, intending to move into the Lesser Town and open the Charles Gate to Rutowski, Ogilvy was ready to accept an invitation to surrender. Prague had fallen.[9]

The capture of the capital of Bohemia was a strategic coup for the allies and a stunning triumph for Maurice. Charles Albert embraced him; his half brothers congratulated him. Allied failure at Prague had been averted by only the narrowest of margins—the Austrian relief army began to arrive on the very day the city fell—and no objective observer could doubt, despite Rutowski's courage and Chevert's spirit, that the victory was essentially Maurice's. At a cost of only fourteen lives and twenty-two other casualties, the allies had wrested the jewel on the Vltava from Maria Theresa's grasp. If the loss of Silesia had been wounding to Austria, the loss of Bohemia—for that is what the capture of Prague portended—would be fatal. The queen, still in Hungary, wept on learning of the catastrophe. Her inheritance was evaporating, her pride crumbling. The resolve, to be sure, remained: despite the desperation of her fainthearted councillors, she would not abandon the struggle. But the odds had shifted dramatically, for Frederick II and Maurice of Saxony— the two names may at last be linked—had dealt a double blow to Maria Theresa that threatened to place her and her staggered regime beyond hopes of recovery.

SPAIN WIDENS THE WAR

In the fall of 1741 Philip V and Elizabeth Farnese finally found the will to defy France's disinclination to support Spanish goals. Early in the year, with Fleury unwilling to allow a Spanish army to march into Italy by way of Provence and with Britain's Admiral Haddock patrolling the western Mediterranean, ready to pounce upon an armada of troop carriers, they had felt compelled to keep Spanish troops safe at home. But as the year proceeded, the situation in Italy and the Mediterranean changed. First, the Austrian holdings from which Don Philip's realm was to be carved became exposed. Faced with military dangers nearer to home, Maria Theresa had redeployed large portions of her Italian army to the northern side of the Alps. Second, though Piedmont-Sardinia was not yielding to French efforts to make it more tractable, neither was it securing allies. By sitting unattached it was also remaining vulnerable—if not to attack, then at least to manipulation. Third, the British squadron was acting as if its commander dared not risk his vessels in battle. Admiral Haddock had begun the year with a Mediterranean squadron of five ships. He had access to another five sailing off Cadiz. This small force, though it grew marginally as the year progressed, was not adequate even for the checking of Spanish privateering against British merchantmen. And while it might have been sufficient for an engagement against Spain's Mediterranean squadron alone, Haddock feared that in the event of an imminent battle, the French squadron at Toulon would join the Spanish, creating a "Gallispan" force that Britain could not hope to defeat. Therefore Haddock was behaving circumspectly.

Spain's response to this expanding opportunity was devised by two able men. José del Campillo had been installed as secretary of finance in March 1741. A man of energy and vision, Campillo had expanded his authority until, by autumn, he was secretary for war, the navy, and the Indies as well. Campillo was urging that Spain shake off the French leash and seize some Italian acreage. Fully supporting this recommendation was Spain's most celebrated military man, the Duke of Montemar, who in the War of the Polish Succession had led the army that had expelled the Austrians from Naples and permitted Don Charles—Charles VII in Neapolitan history—to be established there. It seemed clear to both men that Spain had no reason to fear Haddock's timid squadron. Therefore they recommended that Philip V authorize a fleet of Spanish ships to convey the 40,000 troops assembled at Barcelona to Italy. Campillo wanted the chief landing to be effected at Orbetello; Montemar preferred the Genoese port of Spezia for the disembarkation. This dispute loomed large at the time, but it did not disguise the major areas of agreement between the two men. The Austrian holdings in Lombardy, they insisted, and above all the city of Milan should be targets of the Spanish attack. The royal couple accepted the general proposal with delight, and in October Philip V chose Orbetello as the landing site in Italy. The French ambassador soon reported on a conversation with the king and queen in which they announced "that they are going to take possession of what belongs to them in Italy and that if the King of Sardinia makes opposition he will be declaring himself their enemy and be treated as such."[10] It was a declaration of Spanish independence.

It was no easy matter to launch an army across the expanse of water that linked Catalonia to Tuscany. When Montemar arrived at Barcelona to assume command of the army, he found its morale and readiness low. But he was successful at putting affairs in better order, and meanwhile a fleet of troop transports finally numbering 220 was assembled in the harbor. From Versailles Cardinal Fleury authorized Vice Admiral Claude-Elisée de Court la Bruyère (conventionally called Court), commander of France's Toulon squadron, to supply a qualified protection for the Spanish troop carriers on their voyage to Italy. Court even provided a further service. By feigning a dash toward Gibraltar, he forced Haddock to move the British squadron westward so as to prevent the threatened junction between the Toulon and the Cadiz squadrons. Then the weather broke in Spain's favor, and the British, now numbering twelve ships, were dispersed in a storm. By early in November almost 14,000 men were under sail. Haddock dared not challenge the superior force, and so the Spanish troops were carried unimpeded to the Italian target, where they began disembarking in the fourth week of November. Spain had brought the war to Italy.

Leaders across Europe reacted with predictable concern, for the hope of containing the struggle between Maria Theresa and her enemies dissolved in November of 1741. In the north Bohemia became an arena; in the south, Italy. The court at Vienna was the government most distressed by the Spanish initiative. The queen immediately ordered the regiments marching northward from Lombardy back into Italy and supplemented them with troops from north of the Alps. Her goal was to restore her Italian army to its prewar size of 24,000. The court at Turin could only suppose that Spain's intrusion meant that Madrid had decided to seize first and talk later. Ormea sounded out various Italian sovereigns on the possibility of resisting the Spanish but met only hostility, indifference, or resignation. In Britain the Walpole administration was deeply embarrassed by the Spanish action. A parliamentary opposition that had been growing stronger ever since the outbreak of the war took the Spanish coup as another sign of the prime minister's inability to guide a military effort. Throughout Europe rulers and ministers were compelled to accept the unwelcome fact that Philip V and Elizabeth Farnese were as ready as Frederick II to sacrifice lives in pursuit of territory.

Although Madrid was delighted at the success of the voyage to Orbetello, it needed a larger army in Italy before it could begin to undertake offensive actions. Once Haddock had indicated he would not pick a fight when outnumbered, the Spanish concluded that they could complete their plans for a second sailing. It left Barcelona for Spezia in mid-December, comprised of fifty-two transports carrying almost 12,800 men. The protective convoy that guarded this second voyage was even more formidable than the convoy that had protected the first, and Haddock again chose not to sacrifice the men and ships entrusted to him. The success of this second Spanish sailing, which reached Spezia in January 1742, heightened Europe's mystification about the whole affair. Some observers attributed Britain's inaction to Machiavellian cunning in the British government. Such speculations presupposed, however, a far finer hand behind London's inactivity than in fact existed. If Britain had been able to give Haddock the ships he needed, the voyages would have been repulsed. Haddock's orders, after all, were to destroy troops sent out from Spain. The task had simply been too great for him. And by late in January 1742 Spain had placed over 25,000 soldiers in Italy.

Though the Spanish troops were aimed against Austria's interests in Italy, they impinged on Piedmont-Sardinia's as well. During the previous summer the Marquis d'Ormea had warned France against trying to corner his master. "He has," the marquis had remarked, "a natural aversion to cloisters, they are a kind of architecture he cannot endure."[11] Now suddenly feeling himself dangerously hemmed in, Charles Emmanuel accepted the conclusion that Piedmont-Sardinia should align itself with Britain: only London among the major powers saw the preservation of balances of power as vital to its own interest. The political algebra was therefore ineluctable: Charles Emmanuel had no choice but to make common cause with Maria Theresa, both because she was Spain's foe and because she was Britain's friend. Eager to be compensated for cooperation, Charles Emmanuel and Ormea demanded cessions from Vienna: the tiny Vigevano triangle (with its control of the junction of the Po and the Ticino), the Angera region northward to the Swiss mountains, the region called Oltrepo (that is, the part of Pavia that lay south of the Po), and Finale on the Mediterranean coast. The first demand was designed to make the Ticino River the basic eastern boundary of Charles Emmanuel's realm north of the Po, the second was aimed at giving Turin a modest base beyond the Ticino, the third was intended to thrust that realm down toward Tuscany and central Italy, and the last was proposed so that the kingdom might have fuller access to the Mediterranean. Through all the vicissitudes of the next six years, these four goals would remain the touchstones of Turin's policy.

THE NADIR OF AUSTRIAN FORTUNES

The Franco-Bavarian capture of Prague was a tonic for the anti-Austrian camp. With Prague in Bavarian hands, Charles Albert was in a position to insist that the crown of Bohemia be recognized as his. Using the city as a *point d'appui,* the French army could begin to nibble away at those areas of Bohemia still under Austrian control. The victory, moreover, sent a message to all of Europe: French might was formidable, French policy vindicated. The king of Prussia was quick to take notice. The capture of Prague meant that he had misread the military situation in central Europe and in concluding the Convention of Kleinschnellendorf had sided with a loser. It was not too late to undo his error. On the very day he learned of the events in Prague he ordered Prussian troops to join with French and Saxon troops in a march to the Moravian frontier. Soon afterward he dispatched additional troops into Upper Silesia and Bohemia. The sudden offers of aid amused Belle-Isle. "I understand," the marshal noted, "he comes to our aid when we no longer need him."[12] But Frederick's goal in fact was not limited to aiding his rediscovered allies; he wanted nothing less than to bend French success to Prussian purposes by imposing a political settlement that would compel Bavaria and Saxony to look to Berlin, not to Versailles, for guidance and protection.

At the time, however, the elector of Bavaria did not feel much need for guidance and protection from anyone. He controlled Prague and half of Bohemia. From his position as liberator, he played upon the political ambivalence of an aristocracy that, though appreciative of the value of links with Vienna, nevertheless suspected that their own city, already freer and more relaxed than the capital of the Habsburgs, might gain added luster if it could escape the shadow of Austrian authority. He won friends among all classes by insisting that his own troops abstain from pillage, brutality, and all the other savageries that conquering armies often indulge in. And he moved quickly to legitimize his authority, by having himself proclaimed king of Bohemia. Nevertheless, despite his dominance in Prague, an anomaly was obtruding: a Bavarian might reign in Bohemia, but it was French bureaucrats who administered. Never attentive to bureaucratic concerns, Charles Albert delegated to a Frenchman, Jean-Moreau de Séchelles, the task of handling quotidian affairs. Thus, in the very hour of his Bohemian glory, Charles Albert was countenancing administrative actions that threatened to dissipate the groundswell of genuine support he was generating.

There was moreover still a war to be won. Charles Albert and his French advisors knew that the final triumph would not be his until he had used the city as a staging area for the conquest of southern Bohemia. And so the Franco-Bavarians, in a set of related maneuvers undertaken by small forces, fanned out from Prague to assail Cheb, Pisek, Chrudim, and Havlickuv Brod. During these actions French troops marched farther east than any had gone since the near-mythic times of Charlemagne. The attack on Cheb failed to dislodge the Austrians, and the French troops were forced to begin an investment of the town. But in their other efforts the Franco-Bavarians were successful. These various victories, scattered and small though they were, gave the invaders control over virtually three-quarters of the kingdom of Bohemia and by mid-January 1742 confined the Austrians to the southern crescent. If Charles Albert had not delayed for a full week after taking Prague, the invaders might have proceeded even further, for Austrian resistance still lacked teeth. Even so, as both camps dug in for a winter that was soon to become legendary for its ferocity, Charles Albert could consider himself master of Bohemia.

The Prussians were also on the move. One army, led by the Hereditary Prince of Anhalt-Dessau (the son of Prince Leopold), entered eastern Bohemia.[13] The other, commanded by Count Schwerin, drove south into Upper Silesia. Frederick was determined not merely to add to his booty but also to effect a distribution of other territories among his allies that was conducive to Prussian security. The Hereditary Prince's target was Klodzko, and although an Austrian garrison held out in the castle until spring, the county itself submitted to Prussian control in the second week of January. Meanwhile, Schwerin's troops overran Upper Silesia. On 22 December the Prussians crossed over into Moravia, and on the day after Christmas Olomouc surrendered, delivering the northern portion of the province into Prussian hands. Prussia might have struck farther had not Saxony been seized by one of its characteristic spasms of hesitation. All of Frederick's unwonted winter activity had a purpose. In his geopolitical vision, Bohemia (stripped of Klodzko) was to be Bavaria's and Moravia was to be Saxony's. Such an allocation, Frederick believed, would create a buffer between Austria and Prussian Silesia and compel the suspicious rulers in Munich and Dresden to treat him as an ally against future Austrian irredentists.

Only one development confused the situation in Europe. At the very time that the French army was stirring forth out of Prague to press the Austrians southward, an extraordinary decision issued forth out of Paris to confound France's allies and foes alike: Marshal Belle-Isle was relieved of his military command. The marshal had, of late, acknowledged that he had been too ambitious in insisting on doing double duty as both soldier and diplomat. Cardinal Fleury seized upon this admission to win Louis XV's approval for a division of those duties. Belle-Isle would remain France's ambassador to the imperial Diet. But in his stead as commander of the French army in Bohemia, the Duke of Broglie would be installed. The new commander seemed singularly ill-suited to his task. Approaching seventy when he arrived in Prague on 19 December 1741, he was still recovering from a stroke and bore such marks of his years as poor hearing, poor vision, poor memory, and poor temper. Consequently, some observers believed that Versailles was reconsidering its commitment to the war. Even though the cardinal assured Belle-Isle that he would remain "the soul of our counsels,"[14] that assurance lost much credibility when seen in the light of Belle-Isle's separation from military authority. And yet subsequent events gave the lie to those who suspected a French volte-face. Broglie's tenacious and successful defense of Pisek against Austrian counterattacks during the winter of 1741-42 indicated as clearly as one could hope that France was honoring its commitment to Charles Albert. Broglie's proposal for a winter assault on Jihlava, a Bohemian town nestled close to the Moravian frontier, indicated that France was not abandoning boldness. Rather, France was shifting its vision somewhat. Within the French government Count Maurepas had been arguing for an intensification of naval warfare against Britain. Maurice of Saxony wanted a campaign to win territory in the Netherlands. Belle-Isle had achieved most of the goals he had set for himself in central Europe; now it was time to shift the focus of the struggle westward. The French decision was less a repudiation of Belle-Isle than a reminder to him that not everyone defined French interests as he did, and not everyone found his monopolization of power wise.

With Saxon troops hesitant and the French command in flux, Frederick decided in mid-January that some dramatic stroke was needed to reinvigorate the anti-Austrian coalition. Giving only scant warning, he arrived personally in Dresden, ready to make his case for a Moravian campaign in the most forceful terms possible. Augustus III was easily overmatched in this royal confrontation. A votary of the sybaritic life, he was resourceless when faced with Frederick's iron character. With quick argument, incisive reasoning about Saxon interests, and some well-chosen warnings about the consequences of a Prussian departure from the war, Frederick won Augustus over to an assault on Moravia. Meanwhile, he also overbore French demands for a Prussian attack on Upper Austria by insisting that a thrust into Moravia, with its implicit threat to Vienna itself, would compel the Austrians to ease up at Linz and defend their capital. Only Maurice of Saxony refused to bow before the will and dash of the Prussian king, pointedly reminding him of the difficulties of campaigning in winter in a hostile and ravaged land without extensive preparations. The first two months of 1742 were the occasions for the only meetings during the war between these two giants, and their exchange neatly typified their strengths. Frederick's great military virtue was boldness; Maurice's was thoroughness. By the time the snows began to melt, the world would know whether a winter campaign in Moravia was an example of considered audacity or of reckless folly.

Meanwhile, Maria Theresa's troubles were compounding. While Frederick's Saxon diplomacy removed all ground for hoping that the change in the French command might portend relief for Austria, an almost simultaneous change in the government at St. Petersburg crushed nascent hopes that Russia might at last give aid to Austria. It is true that the swiftness of Russia's victory over Sweden in September had seemed to explode France's scheme to keep St. Petersburg preoccupied. Thereafter, with the Swedish threat contained, the czarist government had moved, though haltingly and obliquely, toward fuller support for Austria, capping an autumn of diplomacy on 28 November 1741 by concluding a defensive treaty with Britain that made St. Petersburg an ally of Vienna's ally. But abruptly Austria's hopes were dashed, when on the night of 5-6 December 1741 Elizabeth Petrovna seized power from her rival, the regent Anne. The French minister to Russia, the Marquis de La Chétardie, claimed credit for managing the startling coup, and his claims received wide credence throughout Europe, for the coincidence of a military victory in Bohemia and a diplomatic victory in Russia suggested the final irresistibility of French power and skill. The situation was, however, more complex, for Elizabeth had acted without La Chétardie's knowledge and nursed no desire to make Russia a French puppet. Still, Russia's approach to Austria was unquestionably at an end—Elizabeth scorned the territorially bereft Maria Theresa as "the naked queen"[15]—and in the early months of 1742 the French emerged as the dominant foreign presence in Russian governmental circles. For a second time within six months Vienna was denied salvation from the east.

The testiness of Vienna's negotiations with Piedmont-Sardinia, conducted during December in the shadow of the Spanish military incursion into Italy, was a sign that salvation from the south was not imminent. Austrian mistrust of Charles Emmanuel III ran deep. Already the Viennese were likening the king of Sardinia to the king of Prussia. The Piedmontese proffer of military aid was contingent upon a guarantee of territorial compensation, whatever the outcome of the war. The Austrians were especially galled that London supported Turin's demands. After all, if Austria kept buying support by ceding land, it would soon become a state not worth supporting. When Sir Thomas Robinson appeared before the Conference on the final day of 1741, he came with some sweeteners. If Vienna accepted Turin's proposals, he declared, Britain would place a squadron off Italy to intercept Spanish convoys, supply a subsidy to Piedmont-Sardinia to allow it to honor its defense obligations, and add some Swiss troops to its payroll. But he also came with a threat. If the queen spurned Charles Emmanuel's proposal, Britain would withhold the assistance. In terse phrases Robinson defined Britain's position: "no treaty, no squadron; no treaty, no subsidy; no treaty, no Swiss."[16] Reluctantly the Conference decided that just as it had agreed to the loss of Lower Silesia to protect Bohemia at Kleinschnellendorf, so it must now agree to the loss of the Vigevano région to protect Milan. But the ministers needed no reminding that Frederick II had repudiated the Convention of Kleinschnellendorf at his convenience.

Not everything was going wrong for the Austrians as winter set in. The British subsidy of £300,000 had, in the reported judgment of the ministers, "saved the House of Austria from total ruin."[17] With the easing of Bavarian pressure on Vienna, life in the city returned to more normal rhythms. Maria Theresa reentered the capital on 11 December 1741, jubilantly received by a citizenry that had missed her and was coming to appreciate the virtues of Habsburg rule. She was now a far wiser person than the ingenuous young woman who had assumed the throne only a year earlier, and she was beginning the overdue task of weeding out the incompetent military commanders. Neipperg, of course, was dismissed. So was Francis Stephen, whose lethargy in marching to save Prague had angered the queen. Meanwhile, the queen set the military priorities for the coming year. Although she installed her brother-in-law, Prince Charles of Lorraine, as her commander in Bohemia, she defined as the first task—ahead even of a counterattack on Bohemia or Silesia—the recovery of Upper Austria. And to effect this goal she chose

Count Khevenhüller, the man who had mobilized Vienna. Entrusted with 16,000 men, Khevenhüller left the capital on 20 December with shouting throngs attending his carriage and prayers for success echoing in his ears. These various signs of an Austrian revival were not much. But a desperate and afflicted people finds its joys in little things.

EMPEROR CHARLES VII

While the soldiers were contending for control of German real estate, the diplomats were deliberating about the future of the German crown. Though the decision was to be a German one—all nine electors represented states deemed to be German[18]—France had declared its interest in the outcome very early on, and no less a figure than Marshal Belle-Isle had been sent as Louis XV's emissary to the imperial Diet at Frankfurt. Resident at Frankfurt, he was an observer—and, whenever possible, a mover—of the complicated procedures by which the empire chose its leaders. The electoral representatives at Frankfurt spent much of the autumn debating minor matters until the outcome of engagements should reveal who actually held power. In this context the Franco-Bavarian capture of Prague was decisive. If the loss of Silesia had damaged Maria Theresa's capacity to impose her husband on the empire, the loss of Bohemia destroyed it. Charles Albert, elector of Bavaria and disposer of Bohemia, had validated his candidacy by arms; the slow debilitation of the house of Austria had finally cost it its German preeminence.

The march toward a final decision began on 4 November 1741, when the representatives of the electors, apprised of the outcome at Prague, voted to exclude Maria Theresa's Bohemian representative, reducing the number of electoral votes to eight. They then spent over a month debating the conditions they would impose on a new emperor and, that matter disposed of, set 24 January 1742 for proceeding with the election itself. With the opening of the new year, princes and nobles from throughout Germany and from lands beyond began to arrive in Frankfurt, gathering in this historic home of imperial elections and coronations to attend the two most splendid ceremonies the old empire could stage. Balls, illuminations, and a variety of enchanting spectacles gave the dignitaries ample opportunity to display the most sumptuous finery of the age. Splendid dinners gave master chefs an arena for displaying their culinary arts. The election itself was but a formality: with only Austria opposing (for Bohemia had been banished and Hanover cowed), Charles Albert was chosen to succeed Charles VI as Holy Roman Emperor. The victor arrived a week later, and briefly bore the redolent title of king of the Romans. Then on 12 February, amid ceremonial splendor, he received the sword of Charlemagne, the scepter and globe, the great mantle, and finally, from the hands of his archiepiscopal brother of Cologne, the crown of Charlemagne. Charles Albert became Charles VII. For the first time in more than three centuries a non-Habsburg wore the German imperial crown.

The coronation marked the height of French influence in Germany during the war. At enormous cost France had finally wrought what for a century it had sought to effect: depriving the house of Austria of the imperial dignity. Belle-Isle, the man who had mobilized French resources to accomplish this goal, believed that by establishing the foundation of a French hegemony he had secured immortality for himself. We can now see that the marshal was grievously mistaken. He had failed to recognize what Frederick II readily saw: that the imperial dignity was hollow, a grand vestige of hoary presuppositions that amid the sovereignties of eighteenth-century Europe was awkwardly puny. French celebrations about the events at Frankfurt were thus inappropriate. Rather than weakening German freedom, France had served as an unwitting accomplice in the amalgamation of the state that would eventually become the fulcrum of German power and independence. The French leaders were not, of course, clairvoyant; they cannot be indicted for failing to see Bismarck. But some were already sensing a disproportionality between French exertions and French gains in the war. As one wrote immediately after the election, "it is now necessary to work for peace and to endeavour that France, after so many difficulties, risks and expenses, should draw some advantage from them."[19]

For Maria Theresa the election was a catastrophe. By the end the outcome was not a surprise. But its predictability did not make it less galling. The first task she had set herself after succeeding her father was getting her husband elected emperor. She had failed. And actuarial expectations being what they were, it was unlikely that the imperial throne would soon be vacant again. The queen undertook a campaign of harassment against the empire that had spurned her candidate. She refused to recognize the election, holding that Bohemia's exclusion, a disregard of the Golden Bull, and the fact that the election was held though the empire was not at peace were grounds for regarding it as invalid. But she ran the danger of being nothing more than the sponsor of petty impediments unless she could demonstrate to the world that the choice of Charles Albert over Francis Stephen had violated the fundamental truth that only those who ruled vast territories had the independent strength needed for effective service as emperor. Thus it became her mission to cut the new emperor down to size and then to use his exposure to secure commitments from him and his supporters that the imperial dignity would return to Vienna after its Wittelsbach interlude.

What of the new emperor himself? Hardly had he been crowned when he took sick. To his diary he confided an extraordinary admission about his coronation: "in the moment of greatness I felt more than ever that I was only a frail man."[20] His was not the only uneasiness. An observer of the election discerned "not the least cry of joy in the whole town, which had, on the contrary, a very serious air."[21] There was about Charles VII a fundamental likeableness—in his casual indolence, in his affability, in his kindness, even in the carelessness of his ambitions. But his all-too-human qualities made him unsuited for the lofty office he had been given. There was, by way of contrast, a supreme self-confidence in Frederick II. And while Maria Theresa, unlike her Prussian rival, could at least feel the terror of holding power, she was determined to rise above what she regarded as the weakness of her human spirit. Charles VII lacked Frederick's vanity; he lacked Maria Theresa's determination to transcend human debility. And if his character was his enemy, so too was his situation. He was denied the political means—trained officials, a capable army, financial resources—to make Europe pay heed to him. He was even denied a reign in peacetime, though only in time of peace could a person of Charles VII's stamp have hoped to rule with a modicum of success. A reign of virtually unrelieved disappointment was commencing, and the new emperor, by reading his own character and plight, had received premonitions of what was to come.

6

The Turn of the Tide
[January 1742 – June 1742]

AUSTRIA'S WINTER COUNTERATTACK

On the night that inaugurated 1742, Count Khevenhüller led his army of recovery across the Enns River into Upper Austria. The unexpected winter strike caught Maria Theresa's enemies unprepared. Within days the French who held Upper Austria had either withdrawn westward across the frontier into Bavaria or had clustered into Linz, seeking the protection of Count Ségur's large garrison there. Ségur himself had advised against holding the provincial capital, but Charles Albert had directed him to remain in the city, looking forward, as emperor, to proposing "a reasonable compromise" to Maria Theresa.[1] Events, however, broke against him. On 17 January an Austrian force of 4,000 under Baron Bernklau drove 7,000 Bavarians under Count Törring into a disordered retreat from Schärding, thereby carrying the war back into Bavaria. Khevenhüller was not afraid to leave an unconquered Linz to his rear. Maria Theresa, however, was of a different mind. Though in a now-famous letter she had addressed a spirited injunction to the count—"Act, o hero and true vassal, as if you will have to justify yourself before God and the world. . . . do what you think is right!"[2]— she in fact instructed him to recover the symbolically vital city. Linz had no wall. And since Ségur lacked artillery, he had no hope of keeping the Austrian light troops at bay. So he resorted to wide ditches, palisades, and mines to make the Austrian advance costly. Then, having exacted a toll from Austrian attackers, he exercised his one remaining point of leverage by threatening to destroy the city in a conflagration if Khevenhüller did not show some readiness to compromise. On 24 January the Austrian commander yielded to this threat, exchanging the freedom of the 10,000-man French garrison for the return of an intact Linz. Only later could Maria Theresa savor the irony: on the very day that Charles Albert was being chosen emperor in Frankfurt, he was losing his chief prize in Austria.[3]

At this point the campaign of recovery became, in part at least, a campaign of punishment. It is true that Austria needed negotiating leverage for any postwar settlement and that Bavarian territory was ideal for the purpose. But the savagery of the Austrian sweep through the electorate bespoke the existence of more visceral motives. The new emperor's resources were insufficient for the task that Maria Theresa was forcing on him, and the imminence of his imperial responsibilities only complicated the situation, for at a time when he needed to be looking after the defense of his homeland, he was in western Germany and his ministers were scrambling for imperial sinecures. The parlous position of Charles VII was neatly captured by the story of the coin struck in Florence, bearing Francis Stephen's head and the words *Aut Caesar aut nihil* on the obverse and the new emperor's head with the words *Et Caesar et nihil* on the reverse.[4] The chief carriers of Austria's campaign of punishment were Croats and Borderers—men who could not, in Khevenhüller's words, "be confined like monks in their cloisters."[5] Instead, they ravaged the south of Bavaria, burning houses, looting farms, and planting terror in the hearts of the inhabitants of the electorate. The Bavarian peasantry responded with their own clandestine war against the invaders, exacting a price in lives. Meanwhile, Munich became a football between the two sides, as the Austrians occupied it on 12 February, withdrew under pressure on 28 April, and snatched it back again on 6 May. By that time much of the new emperor's patrimonial territory was submitting to foreign rule, and the Bavarian army had fallen back on Ingolstadt. Confident advisors in Vienna were mulling the possibility of continuing westward, conquering Alsace and Lorraine, and replanting Charles VII in that far-off land.

There can be no doubt that Austria's military recovery in the winter and spring of 1742 was remarkable. It was not, however, inexplicable. Vienna was the beneficiary of the great countervailing factor of most wars—the tendency of allies to fall out with each other. Mutual suspicions between France and Bavaria increasingly lamed their capacity to deal with Austria's counteroffensive. Vienna also benefited from the realization of most nobles in the Habsburg realm that their claims to their scattered estates would become suspect and difficult to enforce if the realm itself was shattered. Several deliberate choices made by the Austrians enhanced their military effectiveness. By insisting on a winter campaign, Maria Theresa caught her enemies off guard. By reorganizing the administration of foreign affairs, while yet retaining Bartenstein as her key advisor, Maria Theresa took the first steps toward the improvement of administrative efficiency that was to be a hallmark of her reign. Meanwhile, Austria continued to have access to money, in part because the British subsidies kept coming in and in part because new exactions were successfully imposed. Finally, it is important to realize that from one perspective the Austrian army by late 1741 had not so much been crushed as unlucky: at Mollwitz the cavalry had proved itself strong, and in Bohemia the grievous fault had been Francis Stephen's, not the troops'. Once given sound leadership and any foe less drilled than the Prussians, the Austrians revealed themselves to be strong and dangerous warriors.

THE CAMPAIGN IN MORAVIA

The fertile mind of Frederick II continued to generate plans during the season of Austria's Bavarian success. His chief hope in January 1742, as it had been for at least a month, was to secure Moravia for Saxony and thereby to complete the formation of the buffer between his lands and the queen's. Prussian troops already slept in the town of Olomouc. If Jihlava could be secured, Frederick believed, virtually all of Moravia (except for the area around Brno) would be his to dispose of. Moreover, if Jihlava were in Prussian hands, either Khevenhüller or Prince Charles would be compelled to retreat from the areas he held, lest a sizable Prussian army be allowed to roam unmolested nearer to the city of Vienna than any prospective defending force. And so early in February Frederick ordered an advance on Jihlava. Outnumbered and unwilling to engage in a futile battle, Prince Lobkowitz abandoned the town and its magazines before the anti-Austrian allies arrived on 15 February. Frederick was exultant, explaining in a letter to Belle-Isle that Prussian valor and skill were now allowing the French to recover Linz, to conquer Budejovice, and to breathe freely in Prague. Frederick was fulfilling a recently confided aspiration: "I see myself the arbiter of the war."[6]

But at this point affairs began to go awry for the Prussian monarch. His allies awakened to the fact that he had commandeered and deployed an international force so that it covered the direct routes from Austria to Upper Silesia, and in thus protecting his own winnings he had pulled Saxon and French troops away from the Bohemian area where they would soon be needed. Fearing that Frederick would lead the French contingent farther eastward, Marshal Broglie ordered the French troops to leave Moravia and return to the upper reaches of the Sazava River in Bohemia. Initially the Saxon government reached the same conclusion, commanding Rutowski to proceed no farther into Moravia. Frederick exploded in rage at these defections. But whereas a French decision was not susceptible to overturning, a Saxon decision, given Augustus's weakness of character, was more vulnerable. By appealing to Augustus's lust for Moravia, the Prussian monarch was able to prod him into reversing his decision. Maurice of Saxony's comment to

Brühl upon this reversal was terse: "You no longer have an army."[7] In fact, however, by March, with the Prussian campaign in Moravia mired in the slough of late-winter flirtations with the freezing point, it was really Frederick himself who was in danger of losing an army.

Frederick's greatest problems were neither French withdrawal nor Saxon inconstancy. Rather, they were Moravian resistance and Austrian elusiveness. The Prussians encountered no large forces to prevent their moving about in Moravia. Thus on 19 February 1742 they easily seized Znojmo, adjacent to Austria, and sent striking parties into Lower Austria. The Austrian military leadership, deprived of any army large enough to challenge the Prussians in Moravia, relied instead on their special weapon—the legendary Hussars. These Hungarian light troops picked off small Prussian detachments, slaughtered foraging parties, and killed Prussian stragglers. Moreover, because the Prussians and Saxons had embarked on their winter campaign without adequate preparations, it was incumbent on them to find ways of extracting food, fodder, wood, clothing, and other goods from the civilian population of Moravia. Frederick urged his commanders to be harsh: just as resistance in Silesia had snapped beneath the crushing weight of occupation, so too would resistance in Moravia. The result was a savagery that exceeded even the brutality of the Austrian occupation of Bavaria. Not surprisingly, the peasants who suffered beneath the yoke resented it. They quickly began to prey on the invaders, visiting their notion of condign justice upon individuals or groups of Prussians whom they could isolate. Maria Theresa encouraged this resistance, sending military officers to Moravia to organize a peasant militia. This force finally numbered about 4,000 and, acting in loose cooperation with the hussars, emerged as the second component in Austria's defense of the province.

Frederick's chief strategic failure in Moravia was his inability to take Brno. He quickly regretted his decision of early January not to continue the advance out of Silesia past Olomouc. Austria had taken advantage of the delay to send 6,000 troops into Brno, transforming a weak outpost into a formidable fortification. The Prussians dared not bypass it on the road to either Vienna or Bratislava, and as long as it held out they could not reap the full benefits of their occupation of Moravia. The Austrians in Brno enjoyed several advantages as the brief investment proceeded. Since the Prussians lacked artillery—another consequence of the hastiness of Frederick's plans—they could not sit off at a distance and pummel the city. Their proximity then made them vulnerable targets for sorties. Since the populace, within and without the city, loathed the Prussians and supported the Austrians, Maria Theresa's forces benefited from the intelligence work, the protection, the provisioning, and all the other aids that a friendly sea of civilians can devise for their defenders. Finally, since Hungary lay nearby, it was possible for the Austrians to threaten their enemies with an influx of Hungarian troops. "We are going to be flooded with Hungarians," Frederick wrote to Fleury, "and with the most cursed brood that God has created."[8] At that point the Saxons, under renewed orders to return home, raised the siege. And an Austrian army commanded by Prince Charles arrived in the province to liberate it.

By the beginning of April Frederick's Moravian dream had become a nightmare. Both of his allies had left him, each fearing menaces farther west. His provisions were running out, and though he blamed Schwerin for the difficulties, he knew that in truth the problem was a consequence of inadequate preparations. He had now exhausted his financial reserves, and even though some money could be extracted from the sullen Moravians, such taxes only increased their inclination to obstruct Prussian rule in the land. Brno had not fallen, remaining not only a symbol of Austrian resolve but also the center of the apparatus of peasant and hussar resistance that made life miserable for the Prussians in Moravia. The region was awash with elusive mounted foes. In the distance he heard the drums of the approaching Hungarians. Though sometimes foolish, Frederick was not a fool. On 2 April 1742 he called the adventure off, and before April was out the invaders had withdrawn back into Bohemia. Prince Charles entered Olomouc to feverish acclaim. As for Maria Theresa herself, the saving of Moravia gave her new grounds to trust her own judgment: she had overridden Bartenstein's advice in choosing to send Prince Charles into the province. When conjoined to Khevenhüller's success along the Danube, the recovery gave her grounds to believe that Austria could actually win the war.

Why had Prussia failed so egregiously? We can begin to answer that question by noting that Maurice of Saxony had been proven right. A campaign undertaken in winter into hostile territory without extensive preparations was a stupidity. Frederick acknowledged as much when he wrote Fleury a few months later that "in a word, the heart played a greater role in my Moravian expedition than prudence."[9] Frederick had run afoul of a basic law of warfare: coalitions become unstable as belligerence proceeds. Specifically, France came to doubt the wisdom of military adventurism so far from home; Saxony began to wonder if the Prussian force in Brandenburg was entirely innocuous; Bavaria found itself with an appetite far exceeding its capacity; Prussia discovered it could no longer manipulate its friends. When the stresses in the coalition began to play upon a campaign that had been poorly conceived, Frederick concluded that by trying to transform Bohemia and

Moravia into buffers, he had temporarily lost sight of the reasons for which he had begun the war. The plan now stood revealed as a reckless expenditure of Prussian resources for the gains of others. Frederick had no use for altruism. He left Moravia, bloodied for the first time and wiser from the experience.

WAR COMES TO ITALY

The importance of foreign rulers in Italy and the absence of any sense of Italian corporateness analogous to the feeling of German commonality fostered by the Holy Roman Empire meant that a peninsular quarrel between Spanish Bourbons and Austrian Habsburgs seemed to many Italians only a monumental nuisance. Some major states took refuge in nonparticipation. Venice, for example, though fearful of a wider Bourbon presence in Italian affairs, sought safety in neutrality. The pope, though preferring the Bourbons to the Habsburgs as defenders of Catholicism, declared that "the sword is not appropriate in the hands of him who, however unworthy, is the vicar of Jesus Christ."[10] Francis Stephen's own duchy, strategically sensitive Tuscany, also remained neutral—and with well-founded confidence that its neutrality would be honored, since a Bourbon attack on it would immediately bring the French claim to Lorraine into question. Aside from Piedmont-Sardinia, the only major Italian power to find the grand duel for the peninsula of sufficient interest to warrant participation was the sprawling kingdom of Naples. But even here the participation was less than wholehearted, for King Charles VII sought prosperity through peace for his kingdom and agreed to enter the war only after a browbeating from his parents, Philip V and Elizabeth Farnese.

Spain's advance into Italy forced Maria Theresa and Charles Emmanuel to begin conversations early in 1742 to explore the possibility of making common cause. The talks took place at Turin, where the Austrian envoy, Count Schulenburg, negotiated with Ormea. Although the Conference had decided in December that Vienna would accede to Charles Emmanuel's demand for the Vigevanesco, this entire discussion was now overtaken by reports of the mounting Spanish troop presence. Thus Ormea wanted an agreement that would be swift and, if circumstances changed, easy to extricate Piedmont-Sardinia from. To achieve this end he laid aside the four earlier demands. Thereupon the two sides found it easy to come to terms. They agreed to supply troops to defend Lombardy against Spanish attack. They agreed that troops from Piedmont-Sardinia should occupy the duchy of Modena, the small independent state just south of Lombardy whose central location and Bourbon inclinations made it an inviting choice for emplacing the outer defenses of Austria's Italian realm. They agreed that for the duration of the convention, Piedmont-Sardinia would not push its claims to portions of Lombardy but that such restraint would not imply abandonment of the claims. And finally they agreed that Charles Emmanuel, if he chose, could renounce the convention by giving one month's notice, though he would then be obliged to withdraw his troops from any Austrian fortifications they might have occupied. On 1 February 1742 Ormea and Schulenburg signed the Convention of Turin.

Both countries promptly threw themselves into their joint enterprise. Charles Emmanuel led 18,000 Sardinian troops into the Austrian principality of Parma, just west of Modena, and prepared to meet the Spanish advance. Command of the Austrian force of 12,000 fell to Count Traun, field marshal in Maria Theresa's army and governor of Austrian Lombardy. Traun, though sixty-four years old, was the only Austrian commander to have won credit during the War of the Polish Succession, when he directed the defense of Capua. He moved his forces into the area around Bologna, just to the east of Modena, where he awaited the actions of the Spanish. The final element in the multilateral defense of Italy against Spanish ambitions was the British navy. The undermanned Haddock had twice been compelled to stand aside and allow troop carriers to move soldiers from Spain to Italy. But with the arrival in early February 1742 of additional ships from Britain, the British naval presence in the Mediterranean increased in size to twenty-one ships of the line and was enabled to become bolder. The Bourbon squadrons, jointly comprising twenty-four ships of the line, still outnumbered the British, but by a far smaller margin than before, and their commanders were left to regret their earlier decision not to attack Haddock's squadron when it was most vulnerable. By the time that a weary Haddock transferred command of the British squadron to Commodore Lestock in April 1742, it was clear that Britain had recovered a significant measure of authority in the waters around Italy.

It was against this loose but effective coalition that the Spanish labored to create a domain for Don Philip. Initially the Spanish had planned to have the army that had landed at Orbetello march north to join the army that landed had Spezia, and then to have both continue north through the mountains into nearby Parma. But one of the earliest chroniclers of the war made an observation about maps of northern Italy that bears repeating: "it is difficult to compass the Alps and all the mountains on a map, for one gets false ideas of the distances that are reduced to scale."[11] So the Spanish decided not to throw their men against the formidable wall that guarded Parma from the west. Rather, they would send their troops eastward across the mountains at a safer place farther south and, having gathered them beyond the Apennines, march them northward across the plains from the southeast toward Parma. As a consequence of this plan, the Marquis of Castelar and his 12,000 men made their way from Spezia across Italy through Tuscany, and the Duke of Montemar and his 13,500 troops marched from Orbetello across the peninsula through the Papal States. At Spoleto the army from Orbetello was joined by 12,000 Neapolitan troops under the Duke of Castropignano—the first fruit of the pressure the Spanish royal couple was putting on King Charles. But this augmentation was virtually canceled out by the staggering rate of desertion and disabling sickness that beset the transiting Spanish troops, and when the entire Bourbon force gathered at Rimini, it numbered just 30,000.[12]

Meanwhile, early in February, after receiving reports of the signing of the Convention of Turin and of the approach of a new British naval squadron, Spain renewed its request to France for permission to march troops through Provence into Italy. Madrid wanted to convey Don Philip into the territories he was claiming. Shaken by news of the Convention of Turin, Fleury agreed to permit the transit, and on 22 February 1742 Don Philip set out to enter his prospective principality.[13] Yet this decision was only half a solution, for once the Spanish had crossed Provence and reached the border town of Antibes, they were still blocked from entrance into Italy by Charles Emmanuel's coastal town of Nice and by the Genoese republic. Throughout April the Spanish army at Antibes swelled while diplomats and strategists considered various possibilities for moving it to where it was needed. A naval passage, though shorter by far than the earlier trip from Barcelona, was out of the question, for Lestock and the British fleet hovered out at sea off Antibes. A march through Nice and Genoa was deemed unwise on multiple grounds: the Piedmontese army blocked the key passes, the British navy could bombard a coastal advance, and the possibility of winning Charles Emmanuel over remained alive. And so Don Philip's army sat stranded in Antibes, disobliging its French hosts, fretting at its confinement, and serving no useful purpose in Spain's Italian campaign.

It was in Emilia that the fate of that campaign was being decided. The Duke of Montemar found his situation very difficult. Desertion had so ravaged his Napolispan army that by May it numbered but 25,000 and was shrinking daily.[14] The combined forces of Austria and Piedmont-Sardinia outnumbered his own and stood ready to defend Parma. Montemar received a bit of assistance on 30 April 1742 when, in the Treaty of Aranjuez, the Duke of Modena pledged 5,000 troops to the Spanish side in return for being given Guastalla. But the duke quickly paid the price for his decision: on 10 May the Austrians and Piedmontese began a siege of his citadel, and on 29 May Modena capitulated. In June Montemar marched his troops forward to the Modena frontier on the Panaro River. But there he stopped, understanding how difficult it would be to move an army across a defended river. When orders arrived from Campillo in Madrid demanding an attack and a victory, the Spanish officers noted wryly that while it was possible to order an offensive, it was beyond human power to ordain a triumph, and Montemar finally ordered a withdrawal from the frontier. The ensuing retreat resulted in the loss of a few stragglers to enemy fire, but by the end of June the two opposing armies were again separated, though their movement was now southward, as the Austrians and Sardinians followed and harassed the dispirited remnants of Spain's Italian force. Without a battle, the Bourbon threat to Austria's Italian holdings and to Piedmont-Sardinia's Italian preeminence had been thwarted. The salvation of Lombardy took its place beside the recoveries of Upper Austria and Moravia and the occupation of Bavaria as a token of the vast shift in Maria Theresa's fortunes that occurred during the first half of 1742. We do not need to search far to discover the immediate reasons for the Italian outcome during these months. The Austrians found an effective ally in Piedmont-Sardinia—an ally who, whatever its distant hopes, viewed the prospect of an increase in Bourbon power in Italy as obnoxious. Together Vienna and Turin were able to put a well-trained, well-led, well-motivated army in the field. They held the important defensive sites; they were adequately supplied. The Spanish on the other hand suffered under multiple disabilities. The army was long on infantry and short on cavalry. It was without artillery. Its ranks were riddled by desertion and disease. By the time it got close enough to the enemy to consider combat, it was outnumbered. Montemar, therefore, acted prudently at the critical moment: though he could not achieve victory, he kept the core of a Bourbon army in existence and thus provided the nucleus for a later Bourbon military expansion. As for the more distant reasons for the turn of events in Italy, it suffices to note that France's refusal to allow Spain to move into Italy when Vienna had been most vulnerable was continuing to haunt Versailles. The basic reason that Spain did not conquer large portions of Lombardy in the War of the Austrian Succession is that for the first year of the war France, though a foe of Austria in Germany, was a de facto ally south of the Alps.

THE VITALIZATION OF BRITISH POLICY

Throughout 1741 Sir Robert Walpole's grasp on power in Britain had manifestly been slipping. He was weary of office, and two decades of ministerial dominance had won him many enemies. Unlike any of the other countries involved in the war, Britain possessed constitutional mechanisms that had the effect of allowing public opinion significantly to influence policy. Leaders on the continent knew as much, and in the general election of 1741 both Maria Theresa and Frederick II had directed funds to the anti-Walpole cause—the queen because she found him insufficiently supportive, the king because he disliked Britain's policy of subsidizing Austria. (It was, of course, a measure of how poorly continental rulers and ministers understood British affairs that both the king of Prussia and the queen of Hungary should seek to oust Sir Robert.) The general election itself had been a disaster for Walpole. His effective majority in the House of Commons shrank to less than twenty, a figure that meant that he could not depend on winning the key votes. Thus, when the new Parliament began its session in November 1741 by berating the government for the failure at Cartagena and for the Hanoverian neutrality, Walpole decided not to fight on. A genuine proponent of peace, Sir Robert had never been a happy warrior. He would give way to a man more in tune with belligerent aspirations.

That man was Lord Carteret. His role as a leader within the anti-Walpole group made him an obvious candidate for office. His diplomatic experience—he had been southern secretary in the 1720s—suggested where his talents could most advantageously be used. His facility with the German language provided a powerful inducement to George II to endorse his promotion. And so for a confluence of reasons Carteret became secretary of state for the southern department. He was a vain, educated, amiable man who, because he took all of Europe for his domain, had no interest in the staples of internal British politics. He was shortly to make a celebrated remark: "What is it to me who is a Judge and who is a Bishop? It is my business to make Kings and Emperors, and to maintain the balance of Europe."[15] The statement explains why he was the most internationally informed of all the kingdom's politicians of his day, but it also explains, though only in part, his final failure. Lord Carteret's career followed the trajectory of tragedy and provides one of the most dramatic demonstrations of the painful truth that the war was too blindly propulsive for even the most gifted of men to guide.

When Carteret came to office in February 1742, determined to give coherence and force to British policy, he deemed it essential to military success to define the objective of the war more clearly. His first aim was to focus British attention upon the threat of a Bourbon ascendancy and to coordinate an appropriate British response. Specifically, he set out to compel the Bourbons to give up the gains they had made in the War of the Polish Succession. In Carteret's view these gains had undone the balance of power in Europe and given France and Spain a launching pad from which to campaign for

Bourbon dominance in Europe. To the end of confining the Bourbons, Carteret proposed to create a league of allies. The chief constituents of this league would be Britain and Austria, but Carteret believed that three other important rulers could be won over: Charles Emmanuel III, Frederick II, and the Emperor Charles VII. His initial policies fell into two categories: those designed to strengthen Britain's military presence on the continent, and those aimed at inducing the emperor and the kings of Prussia and Sardinia to lend their aid. But both categories had the more distant goal of creating a military force strong enough to chasten Versailles and Madrid. Carteret recognized that sacrifices from Austria might be the price necessary to secure these allies. Therefore, he affirmed Maria Theresa's right to compensation elsewhere, presumably at Bourbon expense, if she was compelled to cede territories to her coalition partners. Carteret was a tribune of the European balance of power.

Since Carteret's vision governed British actions for almost three years, it is useful to pause to assess it. A crucial point can quickly be established: Carteret had no interest in upholding the Pragmatic Sanction. Britain may have justified its involvement in European affairs in late 1740 by citing the need to support Maria Theresa's claims to her father's bequest, but even then the underlying reason for Britain's decision was a fear that a diminution of Austrian power would create a vacuum into which French influence would flow. Carteret now made that thinking clear: though Maria Theresa should not emerge a loser from the shuffle in territories that was likely to ensue, there was nothing inviolable about the integrity of her scattered inheritance. This consideration is but an aspect of a broader point: Britain's goals were not identical to Austria's. Carteret made Austria a means to an end. Maria Theresa, naturally enough, made Austria the end itself. An aspect of this disjunction would quickly emerge as Britain identified France as the key enemy while Austria cast Prussia in that role. And this formulation leads to a final point. Despite his determination to impose coherence on British policy, Carteret remained trapped within one crucial ambiguity: whereas the Bourbons were the enemy within his conceptualized view of foreign policy, in practice France alone played that part—and yet Spain, not France, had been the chief gainer from the War of the Polish Succession.

Carteret began his career as de facto war minister by assuring one and all of his desire for good relations. His actions, however, comforted chiefly the Austrians. First, he trimmed back hostilities in America so that the European theater could be emphasized. Second, he pressured George II into rejecting a renewal of the Hanoverian neutrality. The Duke of Newcastle later called this action "the best thing he ever did,"[16] and its consequences for the war were powerful. The end of neutrality meant that northwestern Germany was no longer a nonbelligerent zone and that France, already strained in central Europe, needed to worry about defending itself in Flanders. Third, he prodded Parliament into responding to a Dutch request for assistance by approving the dispatch of 16,000 British troops to the United Provinces. They were to join a force of 20,000 Dutch troops that the States General had recently called into being. Hitherto in the struggle Britain had refrained from committing troops to the European theaters; now, with Carteret in command, that restraint was abandoned. Finally, he induced Parliament to approve an additional £300,000 for Maria Theresa. Early in May Horace Walpole, an uninvolved observer of all this activity, wrote that "We are now all military!"[17] So fervent were some gentlemen in their lust for military glory that they contemplated forming private British regiments to help the queen of Hungary.

Carteret also began his efforts to mobilize a coalition. At the time he came to office, Piedmont-Sardinia had just concluded the Convention of Turin with Austria, and so Charles Emmanuel was already cooperating with Count Traun. Parliament signaled its approval of this cooperation by voting a subsidy of £200,000 for the king of Sardinia. As for Charles VII, his relationship with Maria Theresa was patently so bad that Carteret wasted no effort seeking his support at this time. It was therefore to Prussia that Carteret directed his attention. When he let it be known that Britain was ready to try again to mediate an Austro-Prussian settlement, Frederick was delighted. "I look upon the English ministry," he told Podewils, "as the master-spring of the Austrian machine."[18] The Anglo-Prussian talks, however, showed that while Frederick could be modestly flexible on territorial matters, he had no intention of making Prussia an ally of Austria. His aim, Podewils explained to Hyndford, was to end Prussian participation in the costly bloodletting. He was asking, in effect, for a return to the terms of Kleinschnellendorf. But what the queen of Hungary had been willing to accept in October, when Austria's very survival seemed in doubt, was no longer satisfactory. When Maria Theresa declined Frederick's terms in early May 1742, the king ended the talks with Hyndford. His patience exhausted, he decided to invoke the sword instead of the pen. His plan was stark and simple: "to reduce the court of Vienna to the point of humiliation where it must be."[19]

CHOTUSITZ

Frederick was encamped at Chrudim, a Bohemian town seventy miles east of Prague and situated about equidistant from the Sazava River to the south and the Elbe River to the north. He felt safe, for Klodzko had finally surrendered, and he expected the Austrians, having cleared Moravia of the Prussians, to put pressure on the French army still holding on at Pisek. The failure of the negotiations with the queen disappointed Frederick, but if belligerence was what she wanted, he was ready to march on the Austrians at Havlickuv Brod and Jihlava. Toward the French he could scarcely be civil. Even the reappointment of Belle-Isle to the command of the French army in Bohemia and the shift of Broglie from that army to France's Bavarian force did not encourage Frederick to expect aid. Frederick made his plans and dreamed his dreams without reference to the feckless French. A showdown with Austria was needed. He wanted a battle and he hoped they did too.

The Austrians seemed bent on obliging. After Prince Charles had chased the Prussians from Olomouc in late April 1742, he turned westward to Bohemia. He knew he was a man with a difficult task. Scarcely older than the Prussian king, he had been charged with defeating the man who was already fostering the legend that continues to envelop him. His own military abilities were untested, but it counted for something that he did not seem to be as lethargic as Francis Stephen or as vain as Neipperg. He was, in fact, noted for a wide-ranging curiosity, and Maria Theresa liked him very much, despite a relatively ill-disciplined life that consorted very uneasily with her far stricter notions of propriety. Prince Charles entered Bohemia determined to liberate Prague. He planned a methodical approach to the occupied capital, but poor intelligence had led him to believe that Frederick II had sent the bulk of his army to cover Upper Silesia and that the small force the king had allotted to Bohemia would have no choice but to withdraw north of the Elbe and allow the Austrians to move ahead unimpeded. Thus, the Austrians moved into eastern Bohemia ignorant of the fact that the main Prussian force lay directly ahead of them. In Moravia the peasantry had been the eyes and ears of the Austrian army; in Bohemia it kept its silence and waited for the Austrians to stumble into trouble.

When at the end of the second week of May 1742 Frederick learned that the Austrians were almost upon him, he conducted about 10,000 men—a full third of his army—toward Kutna Hora to block the road to the capital. Crown Prince Leopold was under orders to follow the next day. Thus for one crucial day the Prussian army was divided. Prince Charles, meanwhile, was slowly becoming aware that the region he was penetrating contained far more Prussians than he had counted on. The realization made him cautious, and for this reason the prince, although finding himself in the unexpected and enviable position of sitting between two outnumbered Prussian forces, failed to call for an attack on one of them. Instead he sought confirmation about the size of Frederick's force. While the Austrians hesitated, Crown

Prince Leopold hurried his force of almost 20,000 men in a long northern arc around the Austrian force in a frantic effort to link up with Frederick before a battle began. Almost simultaneously the king hastily beat a path back toward the larger portion of the Prussian army. The two Prussian forces succeeded in reuniting, and on that success hung the tale of the battle. Charles, after hesitating for a day, decided on an attack against Frederick's force and began his approach toward the king on the evening of 16 May. But Crown Prince Leopold, by marching all that night, was able to bring his tired and hungry troops into the little town of Chotusitz and into contact with Frederick's force at about 2:00 the following morning, a few hours before the Austrians drew near. Thus, the delay of a day had cost Charles his first great opportunity against Frederick.

The two armies were virtually equal in size, each numbering about 28,000.[20] The Austrians had about 2,000 fewer infantry and 2,000 more cavalry than their foes. The Prussians faced east, into the rising sun; the Austrians faced west. Despite the haste with which they had assembled, the Prussians deployed themselves advantageously. Their left touched the walls of the castle at Sehuschitz; their right bordered on a string of ponds. Clearly one lesson of Mollwitz had been learned: the flanks were to be covered. Some of the Prussian center hid in the abandoned houses of the village of Chotusitz. The Austrians, meanwhile, advanced steadily in four columns through the night of 16-17 May and drew up in order of battle just east of the village. As at Mollwitz, the Austrians had cut the Prussians off from their Silesian bases. Both armies adopted the conventional eighteenth-century formation, stationing cavalry on the wings and infantry in the middle. Oddly, each army had chosen the morning of 17 May 1742 to attack the other— Leopold, in fact, was appalled on reaching Chotusitz to learn that the king expected his exhausted men to move immediately into battle—but it was the Austrians who took the initiative.

At about 8:00 A.M. Charles ordered the attack—the first and only time in the war the Austrians started a major battle—and the assault triggered the most even and symmetrical engagement of the conflict. On the southern wing the Prussians gained a quick advantage. Their cavalry, led by Marshal Buddenbrock, exploded against the Austrians, scattering the cavalry of Austria "like a house of cards."[21] But their excitement soon became their undoing, for they failed to regather properly and fell instead into disorder. The Austrians used the opportunity to regroup and thereupon to drive the Prussians back. The battle on the southern wing soon disintegrated into a melee. On the northern wing, where Count Königsegg commanded the Austrian right, it was the Austrian cavalry that grabbed the initiative. Their opening charge disconcerted the Prussian cavalry and cost them many steeds. A countercharge by the Prussians finally halted the Austrians, but it was so forceful that the Prussians soon found themselves isolated and compelled to seek safety by circling behind the entire Austrian army to rejoin their own force on its right wing. This unexpected departure of cavalry on the Prussian left allowed the Austrian right to drive the Prussians from Chotusitz and set fire to the town. The burning was an error, for the Austrians thereby deprived themselves of the protection the settlement could afford them. But they quickly fell into a greater error. Rather than maintain their formation, the Austrian right, sensing a victory, disintegrated into looting parties and totally squandered its positional advantage and momentum. This diversion of Austrian energies allowed the Prussians to force a slow but steady recovery of the smoldering town. The battle entered its penultimate stage when the cavalry on the Austrian left, again successful in a charge, set out in a pointless pursuit of those who had fled, leaving the left flank of their own infantry equally exposed. Frederick II saw the opportunity that Austrian ill-discipline gave him, and he directed heavy fire and reserve battalions against that flank. At last the Prussian advantage in infantry—both in skill and in numbers—paid off, and at about noon the Austrians began their withdrawal.

Whereas Mollwitz had created 9,100 casualties, Chotusitz generated 11,100. Among the dead, wounded, or missing were 4,800 Prussians and 6,300 Austrians. Many officers on both sides lost their lives. Over all, fatalities came to 3,000, with the Prussians bearing two-thirds of that total.[22] The battle had been brief—less than four hours—and it had been uncommonly bloody.[23]. The Austrians had missed no fewer than three opportunities to triumph. First, for want of experienced leadership, they failed to capitalize on the division in the Prussian army on 16 May. Second, for want of discipline, they squandered the considerable advantages their right wing had won in securing the town of Chotusitz. Third, again for want of discipline, they lost the considerable advantage that their final routing of the cavalry on the Prussian right afforded them. The Prussians were consequently grim in their success. For a second time the Austrians had shown themselves to be formidable. Despite all their disadvantages, including an ineptitude of leadership that continued to amaze Frederick, they had almost fought the Prussians to a standoff. The casualties—especially the fatalities—had underlined Prussia's long-term manning problem in a war with a state that had a far larger population. If Frederick had resolved upon battle in order to force Maria Theresa to see the virtues of peace with Prussia, the battle itself, in both its evenness and its toll, had pointed up the risks for Prussia of continuing at war with Austria.

THE TREATY OF BERLIN

Podewils used a picturesque image to describe Austria after the battle: "it is true that lovely feathers have been torn from its wings, nevertheless that will not stop it from flying quite high."[24] Frederick concurred. All he wanted to do, therefore, was to persuade the Austrians that a continuing struggle with Prussia was the least profitable way to snatch up compensation for the loss of Silesia. Indeed, his task was narrower still, for the queen had already appreciated the difficulty of challenging Prussia. The only reason that peace talks had failed before Chotusitz was the royal disagreement over whether Prussia should be obliged to help Austria in its coming campaign for indemnification. Maria Theresa would not end hostilities without such a promise; Frederick would not end them if so bound. Had the queen now given up her hope for positive Prussian support? That was the key question. And so in the aftermath of Chotusitz, Frederick again turned to Lord Hyndford to explore the possibilities of peace on terms satisfactory to Berlin.

In Vienna, chastened by the second major defeat of her troops at Prussian hands in as many years, Maria Theresa was leaning toward accepting Frederick's offer. The sanctity of the Pragmatic Sanction no longer troubled her; her calculations by now were of a different order. She was determined not to emerge from the conflict a loser, and if she could not have Silesia, she would find an equivalent elsewhere. Recent successes of her armies against the French and Bavarians and the British closure of the Mediterranean pointed to a field farther west for the evolving war. As early as February 1742 Count Khevenhüller had warned that Frederick "is the only one who can make trouble."[25] Chotusitz underscored the lesson. If it was true, why not then end the struggle with this troublemaker, let him keep his ill-gotten gains, and free her army for service elsewhere in a war of compensation? Bartenstein objected to the remedy. He told the queen that Bavaria's army was in tatters, France's in trouble, Saxony's disappearing, and even Prussia's licking its wounds. He declared that what was needed was abler commanders, not surrender. "It is true the country will suffer longer," he acknowledged, "but that is less evil than losing provinces."[26] These were the kinds of arguments the queen ordinarily had found congenial, but this time she rejected them. If the Bohemian war was to be won, the Silesian war required settlement.

The situation in Bohemia shifted startlingly in the spring of 1742. On 19 April the Austrian-held town of Cheb, the western gateway to Bohemia, had finally yielded to a masterly French encirclement directed by Maurice of Saxony. On 25 May, scarcely a week after Chotusitz, the French won another engagement, when for the first and only time Belle-Isle and Broglie combined their talents to drive an Austrian force from Sahay. But even as the battle at Sahay was occurring, the larger configuration of forces in southern Bohemia was shifting dramatically against the French. Prince Charles was marching his troops from eastern Bohemia into the southern part of the kingdom where, by joining them to Lobkowitz's, he created an army of 65,000 men, far larger than Broglie's discouraged force of 40,000. The French commander ordered an immediate retreat toward Prague. It turned quickly into a rout. The frightened French abandoned many of their provisions. The Croats and Hussars dealt pitilessly with stragglers from the French ranks. The hitherto indifferent Bohemian peasants, finally sensing that a decision was at hand and that France and Bavaria had lost their gamble, joined in on the assault on those who dawdled. On 13 June Broglie and the harried French army finally staggered into the safety of Prague, and three days later an appalled Belle-Isle arrived to deliver a dolorous judgment. France ought, he said, to have stood and fought. "Our destruction would not be greater; we should at least have made the enemy buy it dearly."[27]

The tales of the French collapse, though they seemed to vindicate Frederick's judgment, also worried him. The military situation in central Europe was now shifting too rapidly, and Prussia might become a casualty if Frederick could not quickly conclude a peace. On 9 June he ordered Podewils to come to terms with Hyndford, two days later the provisional treaty of peace was completed at Breslau, and on 13 June it lay before the king for his consideration. The provisional treaty represented Hyndford's and Podewils's appraisal of the balance of forces in the central European cockpit.[28] Whereas the Convention of Kleinschnellendorf had given only Lower Silesia to Prussia, the provisional treaty recognized Prussia's stronger position in the spring of 1742 by conferring Lower Silesia, Klodzko, and all of Upper Silesia except the area around Cesky Tesin (henceforth Austrian Silesia) on Prussia. The document also dealt with nonterritorial issues. Frederick promised to withdraw his troops from Austrian lands within sixteen days of the signing of the preliminaries and to protect the faith and property of Roman Catholics in Silesia. He accepted a small portion of the financial obligation involved in the so-called Silesian Loan, a territorial debt owed to creditors in several countries, especially Britain and the United Provinces. When the draft arrived in Vienna Maria Theresa raised several minor objections, but Frederick yielded on them, and on 28 July 1742, in Berlin and not in Breslau, the treaty ending the first Silesian war was signed. Coincidentally, on the same day the Saxons acceded to the preliminary treaty, and though they waited until September before concluding their state of war with Austria in the Treaty of Dresden, they too, like the Prussians, had ended their hostilities with Vienna long before that date.

The Treaty of Berlin—and I shall use that term, preferring accuracy to custom on this matter—marked the end of the first phase of the War of the Austrian Succession. This phase resolved one fundamental issue: it demonstrated that Austria would not be shattered and that a power vacuum in central Europe would not appear. It is true that Austria was the loser in the struggle that ended with the exchange of signatures at Berlin. The cession of virtually all of Silesia deprived the Austrian treasury of an income that had reached 3.5 million florins (£410,000) in the final year of peace. It was this truncation that Bartenstein had in mind when he called the treaty "the second volume of the peace of Belgrade."[29] But when we compare the situation of Austria in July 1742 with the initial hopes of the predators—or when we compare it with Austria's own situation only six months earlier—the impression received is of Austrian resiliency, resolution, and latent power. All of Austrian Lombardy was intact, despite the covetous strategies of both Spain and Piedmont-Sardinia. All of Moravia and Upper Austria were intact and their foreign occupiers driven off. The bulk of Bohemia was back in Austrian hands, and if Prague remained unliberated, Austria enjoyed the satisfaction of knowing that Austrian troops were in control of most of the homeland of the puppet whom France had foisted on the empire as its leader. Austrian armies had established creditable records north and south of the Alps, cooperation with Piedmont-Sardinia raised the prospect of recovering some of the Italian territories lost in the 1730s, and cooperation with Britain, besides providing funds for the waging of war, compelled France to divert troops to its Flemish frontiers. The Treaty of Berlin was thus a sign of Austria's phoenician recovery: by ridding itself of its nettlesome Prussian enemy, resurgent Austria was poised to find compensation elsewhere.

Frederick II was, naturally enough, pleased with the outcome of the campaign. The acquisition of Silesia raised the population of the kingdom by almost 50 percent—from 2.2 million to 3.2 million—and provided access to much-needed funds. But it left two legacies that deeply worried the king. First, it had not excised the core of Austrian strength. If Vienna was now able to drive the French and Bavarians from Bohemia and thereby recover control of that vital kingdom—an altogether likely prospect, he feared—then Maria Theresa would turn her attention back to the lost province of Silesia and "we will have a new war to endure in four or five years."[30] Second, the war had cost the king every vestige of personal credibility. The betrayals at Kleinschnellendorf and Berlin did not inhibit the king from claiming that the course of the war had been "a skein of marks of good will that I have shown to my allies" or from denouncing a Saxon effort to alter the terms of an agreement with the remark—risible in any Frederician context—that countenancing Saxon treaty violations would mean that there was "nothing sacred, nothing inviolable in the world."[31] But the king knew that such moral posturing was seen as the huffing and puffing of a man without principles. The revelation of the terms of the Treaty of Berlin shocked European leaders. Frederick had not simply left the war; he had abandoned his allies. His position on the morrow of the peace may thus be easily summed up: his kingdom was stronger and more feared than before, but any gains in security were problematic, and he was the most distrusted man in Europe.

The French were devastated by news of the treaty, the British exultant. At Versailles Cardinal Fleury broke down in tears. What he feared most was that Austria, now free from defending itself against Prussia, would launch a major offensive in the west. He could take no comfort from Maurice of Saxony's explanation for the disastrous results of the Bohemian campaign, for to fault "the indiscipline of the soldiers" and "the negligence of the officers" was to blame the two aspects of campaigning least susceptible to swift remedies.[32] As a consequence of all of these considerations, the cardinal ordered Belle-Isle to make peace proposals to Austria immediately. At London there was a deep sense of satisfaction. Carteret had come to office determined to end the Austro-Prussian conflict, and he had succeeded. He now hoped to humble France. It is true that Frederick would not join the anti-Bourbon alliance, but at least Maria Theresa's armies were available for service in the west.

Two final questions obtrude. Why was Prussia the only one of the predatory powers that succeeded? And why, since Prussia had begun the war, did hostilities not end when Prussia withdrew? The answer to the first is quite clear, though it is useful to explore it briefly. For success a combatant needed three advantages: the will to win, the power to prevail, and access to the victim. Saxony lacked the will. Augustus III hesitated through much of the summer of 1741 and then again in the spring of 1742. His desire for acquisition paled beside his love of comfort. Bavaria lacked the power. Charles VII's army was puny and ill led,'his financial support system almost worthless. Spain lacked access. Philip V was unable to get troops into Italy at the right moment and unable to reinforce those whom he later smuggled through. Only Frederick II had the determination, the strength, and the propinquity to snatch land from Austria. The answer to the second question is rather more interesting. In effect, the war did not end because the purposes of the belligerents had changed and because several of the combatants thought they had more to gain from a continuation of combat than from peace. Preeminent in this group was Austria, for Maria Theresa was bent upon getting compensation for Silesia. "It is thus to be seen," she wrote to Khevenhüller of Silesia, "that this loss is made up for elsewhere."[33] Spain was also a belligerent notably averse to making peace. With the royal couple demanding heroics from Montemar, the war in Italy remained alive. And finally there was Britain, where Carteret wanted to turn the struggle into an anti-Bourbon crusade. For all these reasons, the Treaty of Berlin was an aspect of the redirection of the war, not the start of its resolution.

P·A·R·T II

The Redefinition of Goals
(July 1742 – August 1744)

7

All Eyes on Bohemia
(July 1742 – December 1742)

EXPLORING OPPORTUNITIES

Prussia's departure from the war opened up a wide range of possibilities for those who remained combatants. It was Britain, however, that nourished the boldest hopes and most expansive dreams. The recent string of Austrian successes in central Europe had led the British to believe that Vienna boasted an army superior to Versailles's. This conviction only intensified the already grand scope of Carteret's ambition. On 12 July Ignaz von Wasner, Austria's minister in Britain, reported to Count Königsegg that Carteret's "plan is nothing less than to chase the house of Bourbon from Italy, to return Lorraine to the house of Lorraine, and to round off a bit the states of her majesty the queen in Germany, to compensate in that way for the sacrifices she has just made to the King of Prussia."[1] Two familiar constraints, however, held the British at least somewhat in check. One was the Hanoverian tie. Although George II had accepted Carteret's advice late in the winter and had refused to extend the neutrality agreement between Hanover and France, he balked at paying the costs of keeping his electoral army at its increased size, which obliged a disgruntled British ministry to assume the burden of maintaining the Hanoverian force. The other constraint was the reluctance of the Dutch government to make irrevocable commitments to war. Though the republic enlarged its army by another 20,000 troops in March 1742, pressure from Versailles made the Dutch uneasy about assigning a part of that army to any force that might invade France. In the long run the French efforts to discourage the Dutch failed; the grand army— the Pragmatic Army, as it would be called—was to be born. But in the short run the efforts enjoyed modest success, laming Britain's hope to mount a serious threat to northern France in 1742.

Ambition also ran high in the Austrian capital. The successful campaigns of the first half of 1742 had ended a decade of military disappointment, and if, for reasons of both prudence and honor, Maria Theresa had committed herself to observing the terms of the Treaty of Berlin, she found neither of those considerations counseling forbearance with France. Moreover, she had learned that Fleury had recently been so incautious as to say that "the house of Austria no longer exists."[2] For this impertinence France deserved condign punishment. Underlying all her punitive impulses was her determination to gain compensation for the lost province of Silesia. And in her way the queen of Hungary was almost as global in her thinking as Carteret, for she mused of having the chance "to humble the faithless crown of France and to fix such limits that in the future the common peace and freedom will not have to contend so much with its presumption."[3] Maria Theresa's first goal was the recovery of Bohemia: all else was in principle to be subordinated to the campaign to cleanse this kingdom of French and Bavarian invaders. But the queen was so sure of her strength that she was determined to seize the initiative elsewhere too, and her eye alighted on Italy. She viewed Neapolitan participation in Montemar's army as a violation of King Charles VII's treaty obligations to Vienna; she was privy to reports that a strong Austrophile party continued to hope for a Habsburg restoration in Naples. She knew that Charles Emmanuel's aid would be required for an Italian campaign, but that prospect did not daunt her. After all, she calculated, if the Kingdom of the Two Sicilies was overthrown, Austria could recover the peninsular component for itself and, by allowing Charles Emmanuel to have the large island of Sicily, satisfy the King of Sardinia's territorial ambitions without sacrificing portions of the duchy of Milan. And so the queen of Hungary was driven to deal more closely with the wiliest monarch, save Frederick, in Europe.

Since May 1742 talks had been proceeding in London designed to convert the loose alliance between Austria and Piedmont-Sardinia into something more substantial and enduring. The venue bespoke Carteret's influence. British mediation on the model of Hyndford's diplomacy in central Europe was deemed essential by all parties. Carteret posed as the honest broker in the negotiations, but in fact he tilted his mediation in favor of Piedmont-Sardinia. He justified his solicitude for Charles Emmanuel by calling him "the prince who holds the balance in Italy. If you lose him," he told Maria Theresa (through Robinson), "you lose Italy: if you keep him you may gain an ample equivalent."[4] Austria, however, was unsympathetic to Piedmontese proposals that would cede portions of Lombardy to Turin even if an Austro-Piedmontese campaign in the south was unsuccessful. Instead, Maria Theresa asserted that all cessions should depend upon an Austro-Sardinian conquest of the Neapolitan kingdom. Neither Carteret nor Maria Theresa understood the situation well. Carteret presumed that the queen valued

Italian winnings as highly as German trophies; Maria Theresa presumed that Charles Emmanuel coveted Sicily. It is not surprising then, with both Britain and Austria building their plans on fancies, that their schemes were not realized during the summer of 1742.

If Piedmont-Sardinia worked with its wonted finesse to sort out its options in the post-Berlin world, Spain lurched ahead with that insensitivity to situation that was the hallmark of Elizabeth Farnese's era of influence. To a ruler who had once expressed the hope that Austria might come to terms with Prussia on the grounds that any agreement that sanctioned a transfer of territory would nullify the Pragmatic Sanction, the peace between Vienna and Berlin, though strategically unsettling, had one striking advantage: the entire Habsburg inheritance was now fair game for partition. In early August Philip V sketched out a plan whereby France and Spain would respond to the British challenge to Bourbon might by forming their own league. As prospective members he cited the emperor and the kings of Sardinia, Poland, Sweden, Denmark, and Portugal. Such an aggregation would frighten Maria Theresa into negotiations, and if the Bourbons would promise her aid in a new war to regain Silesia, she would cede Italian territory to Don Philip in appreciation. The blithe disregard of political contexts that permeates this Spanish proposal makes it even less congruent with reality than Maria Theresa's hopes or Lord Carteret's dreams.

Another ruler who hoped to manipulate the French was the emperor Charles VII. But whereas the Spanish royal couple looked to French aid to widen their influence, the Holy Roman Emperor needed it if he was to realize even the most elementary of his political goals—recovering his Bavarian homeland. Charles VII shared Spain's fear that France would now depart the war. If it chose to withdraw behind its frontiers, it would leave Wittelsbach ambitions and the political situation in central Europe in shambles. Britain was bidding for the emperor's support, but since London proposed that he be willing to swap Bavaria for lands along the Rhine, the British soundings could not be taken seriously. The emperor remained what he had been for months—the prisoner of French policy, beholden to French administrators and officers for the activities of his government and army, and dependent on French funds for those few comforts he could still enjoy. In fact, he lived in a dream world, declaring that he would accept peace with Austria only if he received the Tyrol, Further Austria, Bohemia (or the western part of it), and either Upper Austria or the Austrian Netherlands. One would scarcely have guessed that the man who advanced these demands was living in Frankfurt as an imperial indigent.

From the point of view of Versailles, the dominant fact at the outset of the summer of 1742 was the encirclement of the French army in Prague. Once numbering 40,000, it counted but 25,000 men as summer passed. Disease, desertion, and campaigning had taken a severe toll. Still, the first priority of the French government could only be to rescue it. The most obvious option available to France was to send a relief force into Bohemia, but the Danubian army, now under the timid Duke d'Harcourt, was too small for the task, and the Westphalian force, still led by the Duke de Maillebois, was guarding northern France against possible menaces from the increasingly bellicose British. The former was not adequate; the latter could not be spared. Adding confusion to this difficult situation was Cardinal Fleury's deteriorating health. In such an exigency the worst fears of the emperor were realized. France steadily distanced itself from the man it had raised above his station, clearly willing to offer up his lands if Austria insisted on claiming booty. Fleury was desperate for peace — "whatever the cost," said the papal nuncio, ". . . and to succeed he will negotiate on all sides."[5] In June Fleury countenanced secret talks between himself and Francis Stephen's Tuscan envoy in France. From these talks he learned of Maria Theresa's belief that she, as a Habsburg, continued to represent the true interests of the German princes, despite the investiture of the Elector of Bavaria with imperial office. In July he authorized Belle-Isle to abandon the demand for an Austrian withdrawal from Bavaria if that demand was the sole obstacle to extricating the French army from Prague. "I am just," the cardinal declared "and I appreciate that the Queen of Hungary must be fully compensated for what she has suffered."[6] A creature of the French, Charles VII would be their victim too, if that served their interests.

In addition to the intermittent discussions that Fleury conducted at Versailles in June and July, France established two other lines of contact with Austria. The first involved Belle-Isle, who on several occasions came out from Prague to talk with Austria's Count Königsegg. These conversations ended on 20 July 1742, when Königsegg informed Belle-Isle that Maria Theresa rejected even the marshal's final and extraordinary proposal that Austria keep Bavaria and simply allow the French to leave Bohemia unmolested. Feeling that the trapped French had no option but surrender, Maria Theresa wanted nothing less than a total French capitulation. The second line of contact involved a correspondence between Fleury and Königsegg. As part of this exchange the ecclesiastic, representing himself as a known and ancient friend of amity between Versailles and Vienna, sought to place the blame for French belligerence on Belle-Isle. "Your Excellency," he wrote, "is too well informed of what occurs not to easily guess who it was who placed all in motion in order to determine the king to enter upon a line which was so contrary to my tastes and to my principles."[7] A bitter queen exacted her revenge, arranging to have the groveling letter appear in the public press. Fleury's embarrassment was considerable: he was caught disavowing failed policies he had endorsed and trying to shift responsibility to others. With Vienna not even willing to observe the diplomatic niceties that ordinarily quarantined discussions among the leaders of states from curious public opinion, France realized it was left with only one course of action.

So the council set about planning a rescue of the king's trapped army. Obviously some of the assumptions of the late spring, when rescue seemed impossible, required adjusting. In the spring, when Carteret was beginning to funnel British troops into the Austrian Netherlands, the presence of Maillebois's army in Westphalia had seemed indispensable. By midsummer, with the Dutch visibly seeking to dampen British enthusiasm, it did not. Orders therefore went out to Maillebois to lead his 40,000 troops across Germany and to bring the surrounded army of Bohemia home from Prague. Lest Britain take advantage of this redeployment, a smaller defense force, commanded by the Duke de Noailles, was created to harry any who dared to intrude into Flanders. To enhance the threat that Maillebois's "army of redemption" was designed to pose to Austrian interests, Maurice of Saxony was given command of the 20,000-man army of Bavaria and ordered to lead them to a juncture with the Westphalian force in the Upper Palatinate. Both Maillebois and Maurice had reputations as aggressive commanders; their united armies would number 60,000. The French government hoped that this force would be able to penetrate Bohemia and compel the Austrians to lift the siege of Prague.

ITALIAN SPARRING

When the Treaty of Berlin was concluded, Spain had two armies dedicated to Italy. Both were in difficulty. Montemar's force that had been so laboriously gathered on the Adriatic coast was still in retreat into the Papal States, hounded by the Austro-Sardinian army and shriveling beneath the hot Italian sun. Meanwhile, Don Philip's force, blocked at the Var and unable even to enter Italy, continued to clog the French town of Antibes. The end of the Silesian war promised further problems for Spain, for Austria now had the opportunity to redeploy some of the troops it had assigned to central Europe. With Fleury desperately seeking a peace in the summer of 1742, Spain could expect no assistance from France. And yet, if a Spanish debacle was to be avoided, Spain would need to find a way to relieve the pressure on Montemar and provide opportunities for Don Philip. So, with the purpose of shifting Spain back onto the offensive, the ministers in Madrid directed Don

Philip's army to march northward and occupy Piedmont or Savoy. In this fashion Spain would acquire a territorial pawn and, by forcing Charles Emmanuel to break away from Traun, relieve the pressure on Montemar. In his northward march Don Philip had the assistance of Count Glimes, who though serving as his nominal second-in-command, was in fact in charge of military activities. When it became apparent that the passes into Piedmont were well defended, the Spanish army invaded Savoy, and with the duchy's quick capitulation in September, Spanish arms had finally won some territory.

The effect that this démarche had on military affairs in north-central Italy was precisely the one that the Spanish had hoped for. When Charles Emmanuel learned that Don Philip's army had begun to move to the north from Antibes, he immediately halted his own campaign. Traun believed that Montemar's army was close to disintegration. But to deliver the coup de grâce he needed Charles Emmanuel's help, and so he urged the king to ignore the promptings that argued for a return to Turin. The king, however, was not listening. Instead, he divided his troops, personally leading one section back into Piedmont to defend his patrimony and sending the other section into fixed encampments near Parma and Piacenza. Maria Theresa was stunned: the campaign to recover Naples had in a stroke been undone, and the notion of Piedmontese troops establishing "winter quarters in August in Italy" was so baldly absurd as to invite fears that a total betrayal was at hand.[8] Now it was Traun, not Montemar, who was vulnerable, and so he too staged a withdrawal northward, expecting Montemar to move to the attack. But at this point British sea power interceded spectacularly.

When Haddock had transferred control of the Mediterranean fleet to Lestock in April, the command was temporary. Upon the arrival of Admiral Mathews, Lestock resumed his position of second-in-command. Mathews's charge was to aid the military campaigns of Britain's allies. To this end he dispatched Commodore Martin with thirteen vessels (including five ships of the line) to the handsome harbor at Naples to deliver an ultimatum: either Charles VII must recall the 10,000 men he had supplied to Montemar, or the city would be subjected to naval bombardment. Martin arrived on 19 August 1742, the day after a major earthquake had already damaged Naples. The vast city, Italy's largest with well over 300,000 people, sat helpless before the British threat, its flat-roofed houses inviting destruction from shelling and its rubble providing prolific kindling for conflagrations. The king, called from church services offered as a response to the first emergency, quickly convoked his council to deliberate about the second. The council voted its fears. "This prince," the French ambassador reported, "was surrounded only with people too caught up in terror to be able to give good advice."[9] Yielding to *force majeur,* Charles VII recalled his troops. This success at Naples encouraged Martin to work similar wonders at Genoa, where another ultimatum quickly induced the republic to cease allowing Don Philip's army to store goods within its territory. With the Mediterranean cleansed of enemies, the British navy could now transport Austria's much-needed bullion subsidy for 1742 into the harbor at Genoa.

And yet, if Britain's action at Naples deprived Montemar of his Neapolitan troops, it did not deprive him of his opportunity. The departure of the Sardinians had left Traun with insufficient force to resist a Spanish advance, and late in August the Spanish resumed their march on Lombardy. Almost simultaneously they changed generals, as the Spanish royal couple, despairing at Montemar's hesitations, replaced the hero with Count Gages, a transplanted Walloon noted for his courage and common sense. Gages's orders, of course, were to advance, and in October he occupied Bologna with a force that exceeded 13,000. At that point, however, the advance halted, for the Panaro was no less formidable for Gages than it had been for Montemar. It was widely suspected that Gages, blocked to the north, would turn to the west and occupy Francis Stephen's duchy of Tuscany. But when France vigorously opposed any action that might have the consequence of calling its own claim to Lorraine into doubt, the campaign in north-central Italy stalled in all directions. The year 1742 ended with the two armies, almost equal in size and separated by scarcely more than a river, eyeing each other guardedly.

Farther west, Spain's other army was prospering as the year ended. The seizure of Savoy gave Spain a powerful point of leverage against Piedmont-Sardinia. The duchy was part of Charles Emmanuel's realm. To regain it, he would either have to launch a difficult transalpine campaign of recovery or win territory elsewhere that could provide the basis for a subsequent territorial exchange. And regaining it was essential, for Savoy was, in the king's later words, "a barrier between us and France . . . , it keeps her at a distance, so that she cannot fall suddenly on Piedmont."[10] Ignoring Ormea's reminder that the duchy was always a casualty of belligerence and that, especially with winter approaching, it lay beyond the possibility of successful recovery, he launched a counterattack at the end of September 1742 that, by mid-October, had apparently restored Savoy to Piedmontese control. An enraged Elizabeth Farnese thereupon denounced Don Philip as "the second edition of Montemar" and lent her blessing to the chilling notion that it would be better for her son to be dead than dishonored.[11] More usefully, Philip V replaced Glimes with the Marquis de La Mina, a commander who had once said that, if so ordered, he would hurl his army into the ocean. Charles Emmanuel, meanwhile, came to appreciate the deeper wisdom of Ormea's forebodings. The Spanish sent raids into Savoy from the sanctuary of France, November brought on the cold season and the attendant problems of hunger and disease, and the wall of mountains at his rear interdicted the king's supply lines with Piedmont. Thus outnumbered, and threatened by La Mina with isolation, Charles Emmanuel decided late in December to cut his losses. He withdrew his men back over the treacherous mountains, and by the opening days of January 1743 Savoy was again Spain's. Though it would be strictly incorrect to say that there had been no military engagements in Italy thus far, clearly there had been no major battles. Instead, in both north-central Italy and Savoy there had been an ebb and flow of armies, with the Spanish holding the advantage as 1742 ended. The government at Madrid had replaced two hesitant commanders with men of a more aggressive stripe, and the changes had been rewarded with success. Spanish occupation in Italy, like Austrian occupation in Bavaria and Prussian occupation in Moravia, was unpleasant for those subjected to it. Gages's army sucked provisions out of Bologna until the city and its environs were exhausted. And in Savoy, where the Spanish expected to stay at least until the end of the war, an administration was established that tolerated acts of aimless vandalism and committed deeds of calculated terror. Everywhere in Savoy a hatred for Spain surged forth, and a local versifier denounced the occupiers as "pitiless people! detestable thieves, criminals."[12] But in Madrid there was grim satisfaction as the year ended. If Don Philip's principality remained unsecured, at least he had a bargaining chip.

MANEUVERING IN CENTRAL EUROPE

"All Europe," Voltaire wrote of the summer of 1742, "had its eyes on Prague."[13] After all, France stood in danger of a defeat of proportions unparalleled in living memory. Before the end of June the Austrians gathered almost 70,000 troops into an army of investment adjacent to the city. The encircled French numbered barely 25,000, and while that number was far more formidable than a mere garrison, it also meant that they would face problems of supply that should finally prove insoluble in a city cut off from the outside. Life in besieged Prague was harsh for everyone. The French imposed a curfew on the entire civilian populace, forbade gatherings of more than three people, required that windows be lit at night, and punished violators with peremptory shootings. But as the weeks passed even the privileged occupiers fell subject to ever severer shortages, and with the disappearance of fodder, cavalry steeds were transformed into horse steaks. Disease exacted its toll, Austrian bombardments left everyone exposed to the chance of random death, and messages that were smuggled out bespoke a trenchant pessimism. "There is no appearance," one missive from a French officer said, "of being able to mount a protracted resistance."[14] French sorties were sometimes locally successful, but because they were invariably costly in French lives, Broglie finally forbade them. The decision led Belle-Isle to rage that "the Marshal de Broglie, who understands nothing about the defense of a town, has hampered me here as much as the enemy."[15]

Meanwhile, Maillebois's relief force moved rapidly across Germany. When Charles VII learned of its dispatch, he wrote to Fleury that with the news "I change over from the most severe pain to the most complete joy."[16] The French in Prague knew of its coming before August was out, and the report stiffened their resolve. By mid-September, when the force of 40,000 met Maurice's 20,000 men in the Upper Palatinate, the army of redemption had become a formidable threat to the Austrians surrounding Prague. Maurice proposed that the relief force probe in the direction of Litomerice, north of Prague; simultaneously, Broglie's army should break out of Prague and approach the army of redemption. Maurice calculated that the Austrians would be reluctant to try to impede Broglie's escape because to do so they would need to insert their army between the two French forces. After consultations, Maillebois approved the scheme. The Austrians responded to the challenge by choosing to break off the siege of Prague so that the bulk of the Austrian army might be transferred westward to block and, if necessary, engage the French. On 13 September, leaving only General Festetics and 9,000 troops to maintain a loose investment, the Austrian commanders — Francis Stephen, Prince Charles, and Count Königsegg — advanced with 60,000 men toward Plzen in western Bohemia, where on 27 September they were joined by Khevenhüller's force from Bavaria. This redeployment had one quick and unhappy consequence for Austria. By shifting Khevenhüller's army into Bohemia, Austria left its Bavarian conquest guarded by only 5,000 men. This was an opportunity that the Bavarian army, now under the command of Count Seckendorff, quickly seized, and by the end of October 1742 Seckendorff's troops had recovered all of Bavaria except Schärding.

Maria Theresa briefly feared that she would lose everything — that by too hastily spurning the French summertime offer of Bavaria she had committed Austria to a policy that would now cost it Bohemia too. But her own army there turned out to be considerably more enterprising than she had suspected. It defended the routes of entry into Bohemia, using internal lines of communication to respond quickly to French moves and its control of the heights to secure advantageous emplacements. The French were short of supplies and saw no way of transporting artillery over the mountains. At various times the two main armies were quite close to each other. But Maillebois's orders were to avoid battle if the outcome was doubtful, and the Austrian commanders, though ready to fight, calculated that battle was silly if its goal could be effected without combat. Therefore neither side initiated hostilities. Maillebois eventually despaired of success. "I have . . . knocked at all the doors," he wrote in mid-October, "or rather at all the gorges, which lead into Bohemia; everywhere I have found the Grand Duke well placed before me."[17] Sobered by this impasse, a French council of war met on 17 October 1742 to advise discontinuance of the mission, and over the next ten days the French withdrew to the Upper Palatinate. France was embarrassed by Maillebois's decision. The almost simultaneous withdrawals of a French army from the perimeter of Bohemia and a Spanish army from Savoy suggested that the Bourbons had again overextended themselves. In fact, even before Maillebois acknowledged his failure, the council, deciding to replace him with someone better acquainted with the situation in Bohemia, appointed Marshal Broglie to succeed him. It was, under the circumstances, a most peculiar choice: Broglie's recent actions suggested that bleak despair had reduced him to a spiteful lethargy. But the appointment had one happy corollary for France: full command of the army in Prague was simultaneously transferred to Belle-Isle.

The instructions that accompanied the commission gave Broglie more latitude than Belle-Isle. Broglie was even permitted to conclude that no assistance for beleaguered Prague was practicable. Belle-Isle, however, was given an unequivocal order: whatever Broglie might choose to do, he was to lead the besieged army out of Prague. Broglie received his new assignment late in October and immediately escaped from the city under cover of disguise. He promptly chose the easiest course of action: rather than moving to help those he had just left, he marched the army into Bavaria and set up winter quarters. The French army he left behind at Prague had enjoyed its two months of respite from siege. But confident of the success of Maillebois's army, it had not used the opportunity to flee the city, presuming instead that its own task was to hold the prize. When the Austrians, having repulsed the army of redemption, returned to the outskirts of the city, they began systematically to push the French back behind the walls of Prague, and by the end of November a French army was once again shoehorned into the capital of Bohemia. The Austrians no longer held their great summertime advantage in numbers—the two armies were, in fact, about equal in size at 20,000 each—but they retained a powerful cavalry advantage. In such circumstances the Austrian strategy was obvious: they would wait implacably until the rigors of winter and want drove Belle-Isle to seek terms.

ESCAPE FROM PRAGUE

"In war," Belle-Isle wrote, seeking to distinguish his own attitude from Broglie's, "it is precisely the things which are thought impossible which most often succeed, when they are well conducted."[18] In considering the French alternatives in blockaded Prague, Belle-Isle turned three options over in his mind. The first and most straightforward was to persevere in the city as long as possible, sustained by the provisions gathered during the two-month hiatus in the blockade. The French believed that they might hold out for at least four months. Perhaps events elsewhere in the interval would save the French in Prague. The second option was to let the 3,000 cavalry troops escape. Unburdened by small artillery pieces, supply wagons, and slow-footed infantry, the mounted troops would stand a good chance of evading Austria's porous net. The third option was to break out of Prague with all able-bodied troops and march westward until reaching the French-held Upper Palatinate. The risks of this course were great: the Austrian cavalry could easily assail an army slowed to the pace of its foot soldiers, and the Austrians were healthier and better fed. But if detailed planning and the element of surprise could be conjoined, such an escape might succeed. Temperament invariably directed Belle-Isle to prefer the audacious to the tame; calculation on this occasion pronounced the same lesson. And since the French authorities at Versailles were eager at all costs to avoid the calamitous surrender of a French army in foreign lands, they concurred. Amelot exhorted Belle-Isle to boldness: "Nobody can replace you in a task as difficult and as demanding of wisdom as well as of detail."[19] The third option was thus the chosen one.

In the growing chill of late autumnal Prague, Belle-Isle set about devising and implementing a scheme that, for detail and perspicacity, was unparalleled in the war. There was a multiplicity of problems to be worked out. A route was needed that was both practicable and yet unexpected. Since the Topler Mountains lay between Prague and the safety of the French-held town of Cheb, Belle-Isle's options after crossing the plains immediately west of Prague seemed limited to one of two roads: that which ran to the south via Plzen and that which lay to the north via Karlovy Vary. A second problem was one of supply. The march to Cheb would require about ten days; in winter there was no hope of living off the land, especially since enemy troops would be everywhere, and so the French had no alternative to carrying their supplies with them. The weather constituted a third problem. What was feasible in the heat of a verdant summer was not necessarily possible when snow and ice buried mountain roads. And even if the roads were open, there was the matter of the cold. It was a measure of the boldness of Belle-Isle's hope that he proposed to defy the elements for ten days.

The undermanned Austrians inadvertently aided Belle-Isle's planning by choosing not to challenge the small foraging parties sent out daily from behind the walls. The regular appearance of these groups accustomed the Austrians to seeing activity outside the city. Meanwhile, through subterfuge, Belle-Isle managed to keep his plan a secret even within the city. The food and fodder were ostensibly intended for the army in Prague; only at night did a small number of men tie the supplies up into compact bundles suitable for an army on the march. Belle-Isle also contrived to have some bogus orders from Versailles fall into Austrian hands; in this fashion he led the Austrians to believe that he was hunkering down for the winter, not readying himself for a dangerous dash. Secrecy was, he later wrote, "not the least difficult part since I had to work to two contraries at once so that my true object should be hidden in seeking to persuade people of the other."[20]

In choosing the day for escape Belle-Isle balanced the advantages and disadvantages of the passage of time. Each additional day provided a greater store of supplies, but each day also brought the onset of deep winter nearer and, with the steady arrival of Austrian reinforcements from Moravia, increased the numerical advantage of the enemy. Prague was, moreover, the focal point for a dysenteric illness. The sooner the troops got out of the afflicted city, the likelier they were to avoid the disease. On 16 December, with the temperature falling and the ground hardening, the marshal decided that the time had come to make the break. He sealed off the city so that the unmistakable evidence of an imminent departure could not be passed on to the Austrians. He sent the cavalry out on their presumably innocuous daily foraging expedition, and if it was a larger group than usual, the Austrians did not notice. He took his leave of the 5,000 troops who, by reason of wounds or disease, would perforce remain behind under the command of Chevert. Once the sun had set, the mobilized infantry began to exit the city through Charles Gate and then to group at preestablished assembly points, while the baggage trains wound out through St. Margaret Gate. An hour before midnight Belle-Isle himself, slumped with exhaustion and illness, left the city in a carriage. "Never has an operation," he wrote on that day, "been so perilous."[21]

The French army that fell into order outside the walls of Prague numbered 14,000. It was comprised of 11,000 infantry and 3,000 cavalry, who were marching westward with 30 small artillery pieces, 6,000 pack animals, and 14 important hostages—lawyers, educators, clergy, and community leaders. Belle-Isle envisioned the march to Cheb as an operation of two phases, the swift escape across the plain and then the slower surmounting of the Toplers. During the first phase the greatest enemy would be the Austrian army itself, and Belle-Isle had given much thought to aligning his troops for the maximal interplay of protection and speed. He had sought and secured the advice of the Chevalier de Folard, who sent Xenophonic suggestions that the marshal adapted to the Bohemian context. The French column was thus organized into five autonomous divisions, each with infantry, cavalry, and artillery. The vehicles bearing supplies were buried deep in the core of each division. The artillery was horse-drawn and uncommonly mobile. If the French survived the first phase, Belle-Isle planned in the second phase to send his cavalry and infantry along different routes to Cheb, thereby increasing the likelihood that at least one would get through. He even had some surprises in mind as he set out on what was, all things considered, the greatest gamble of the war.

The immediate task was obvious: to put as much distance as possible between the French army and Prague before the Austrians discovered that the entrapped had escaped. Belle-Isle's hopes to befuddle the Austrians were fulfilled. Though General Festetics, lodging to the south of Prague, grew alarmed on 17 December and began to mobilize for action, Prince Lobkowitz, encamped to the east of the city (in contravention, incidentally, of orders from Vienna), did not learn of the breakout until 18 December. Effectively, therefore, the French won a day's advantage, traveling twenty miles from Prague without meeting serious resistance. The end of the plain—and of the terrain that left the French vulnerable to Austrian cavalry attacks—was only two days away. At this point Belle-Isle sprang his first surprise. Knowing that the Austrians were in pursuit and that their mounted troops could quickly catch up with the slower French, he ordered nocturnal marches. Thus it was not until 19 December that the Austrian light cavalry caught up with the French. As planned, the French divisions swung around to meet their attackers, and on three occasions major exchanges of fire occurred. But the French were not diverted from their path, and by the evening of 20 December they had reached the foothills of the Topler Mountains.

Hitherto the French had moved almost directly west. Now, however, they were at a point of decision. Lobkowitz, understanding the French to be thoroughly hemmed in by the mountains, believed that they would march south to join the road to Plzen; he deployed the bulk of his troops to prevent such an advance. On the off chance that the French selected the less traversable northerly path that would bring them to the road to Karlovy Vary, Lobkowitz placed the Austrian garrison stationed there on the alert, with orders, if necessary, to destroy the vital bridges that alone made a winter crossing of the Eger River possible. In the Austrian view, therefore, the French were confined. Belle-Isle, however, had foreseen this dilemma and now unveiled his second surprise. On 21 December he led the infantry and artillery off the road entirely and marched them directly west into the mountains. Rather than circumventing the heights, the main portion of the French army would try to surmount them. Only the cavalry continued along the more northerly route toward Cheb, and even these mounted troops had no intention of directly challenging the Austrians at Karlovy Vary. On 22 December, when the infantry dragged itself into Zlutice and found the village unprotected, Belle-Isle was confident that the French had seen the last of their human foe in their dash from Prague.

But an implacable inhuman foe—the season of the year—had still to be faced. With his customary self-assurance Belle-Isle wrote on 21 December that "I will force nature in order to arrive with the corps safe."[22] Nature, however, unlike the Austrians, could not be evaded; indeed, in the very dodging of the Austrians the French were choosing to combat nature on its own fiercer ground. The winter solstice was at hand, and the French were compelled to cope with the absolute minimum of daylight hours. Snow blanketed everything, hiding unsuspected clefts and crags, and the forest grew so thick that the van could press ahead only with axes flailing at stubborn conifers. By daylight the troops struggled against the disorienting glare of sunlight on a stark snowscape; by night they plunged forward into a darkness that masked mortal dangers for those who stumbled. And at all times there was the cold—penetrating, enervating, inescapable. To keep spirits hopeful Belle-Isle made himself a visible and active figure during these days of trial. The general trajectory of the weary army was upward until, on Christmas morning, it reached the highest point of its route. Thereafter the course was swiftly downward, out of the forest and into gentler weather. On 26 December 1742 the French infantry, still hauling its cannon, staggered into Cheb. The cavalry had already arrived. The escape had succeeded.

"It is certain," Belle-Isle instructed his brother to write, "that this march does honor to the arms of the king."[23] No one, of course, could disguise the fact that the French had been dislodged from Bohemia. But Belle-Isle's bold stroke had saved 14,000 troops from captivity. And Chevert's cool daring— he threatened to burn down Prague if Lobkowitz did not give him and his ambulatory troops free passage—spared another 4,000 from a similar fate.[24] Estimates about the number of French soldiers who died during Belle-Isle's harrowing retreat from Prague are very uncertain; men who got lost and were presumed dead kept straggling into Cheb in early 1743, while others who held onto life during the arduous march lost it when gangrene attacked their frostbitten extremities or an effort at amputation failed. The figure of 1,500 fatalities is a good medial guess—perhaps 1,100 infantry and 400 cavalry. Grim tales of men lashed to death by the wind while marching or frozen to death while standing guard duty made their way across Europe, and when the spring thaws came the bodies of many who had sunk from sight during the march reappeared. Their luckless tales were, however, only footnotes to a broader story. When the war finally wound down and arms had been put away across Europe, the two great military figures of the struggle would be Frederick II and Maurice of Saxony. But the greatest single exploit of the war was the well-engineered retreat from Prague.

The wonder of it, however, was lost on Maria Theresa. She had counted on capturing a whole French army and using it for political leverage. All she managed to secure from the campaign was Prague. Even more galling was the reflection that she could have secured Prague four months earlier, and not have lost Bavaria, had she been more flexible. Nevertheless, she immediately set about restoring Austrian authority in the recovered kingdom. As she had in Upper Austria, she established a tribunal to identify those who, in violation of oaths, had cooperated with the French occupation forces. It was important to her that the lesson be unambiguous: enemy occupation was not a sufficient excuse for disloyal behavior. The departing French tried to protect their friends by extorting a promise from Lobkowitz that there would be no reprisals. Maria Theresa simply ignored the promise. She had many Jews banished from the kingdom. She specified that any people who had so much as accepted an honor from the French or Bavarians would never be allowed to enter her service again. Severer provocations summoned severer sentences: high fines, loss of property, life imprisonment, maiming, even death. The queen occasionally tempered rigor with mercy, and the capital sentences were later commuted. But in general she was determined to make the Bohemians pay for their disloyalty. When she finally received the crown of the kingdom in 1743, she called it a "fool's cap."[25] The departure of the French did not end the misery of Prague.

8

Britain Seizes the Initiative
(January 1743 – September 1743)

FRENCH DISARRAY

For almost seventeen years Cardinal Fleury had directed French foreign policy. At the height of his power in the 1730s, he had bestrode the world like a wizened wizard, but in the 1740s his command began to unravel. A man with a stronger sense of self-esteem might have stepped aside, using his disagreement over policy to enter into a retirement that age and accomplishment had earned. But Fleury was greedy for office—or greedy, at least, for the opportunity to restore France to peace. So the wraith of Issy stayed in the council during his recessional, laming a war effort that needed vigor if it was to succeed and hence serving the cause of neither victory nor peace. By the summer of 1742 his sight and hearing were failing, his stool was perpetually loose, and his once serene mood was increasingly subject to depression. By November the likelihood of his imminent demise dominated political talk in Paris. The situation passed understanding: incapable of directing affairs himself, Fleury could nevertheless still block others from doing so. Yet not until 29 January 1743 did the era of the cardinal finally end. The immediate issue for France then became who should succeed him. The broader question, however, was whether his death would free the kingdom from its paralysis.

Most observers could agree that French policy stood in need of a firm hand. Rather than squandering its might in scattered activities, France needed to identify clear war aims and focus its resources upon their realization. But it was unclear who might supply that sense of direction. Cardinal Tencin, a minister without portfolio who had joined the council as a disciple of Fleury's in August 1742, shared his mentor's distrust of Belle-Isle but not his aversion to war per se. Described as "hard, spiteful, and vindictive by temperament, serious and prudent in his station,"[1] he saw Britain as France's true enemy and was wont to repeat Pontus's apposite remark that the Romans could be defeated only in Rome. Count Maurepas, who with Fleury's death was now the minister with the longest tenure in office, shared Tencin's belief that Britain was the true enemy but not (at least early in 1743) his faith that a grand upwelling of anti-Hanoverian sentiment lay just below the surface in British politics. His preference, understandable for the minister of marine, was for a naval and colonial war; he was coming to believe that the future prosperity and strength of France would rest upon the kingdom's continuing ability to work its will in the Indies and America. The soberer side of the argument was best represented by the Duke of Noailles, yet another marshal of France. A close advisor to Louis XV, Noailles nursed rather larger fears of British power than Tencin and Maurepas. But his great hero was Louis XIV, and he held that a formal war with Britain was just a matter of time. Therefore, he argued, France should seek to channel confrontations into a region where French power could be maximized. The Low Countries caught his attention—valuable in themselves, easily entered, adjacent to the kingdom, populated by French-speaking inhabitants, and posing more formidable logistic problems to Britain than to France.

The role that the king assumed in this struggle to control French policy was peculiar. He was as much puppet as puppet-master, and in the ambiguity of that role lay many difficulties for France. Hitherto he had scarcely concerned himself with the war at all. His preference for peace had not aided Fleury; his secret hankering for glory had not served Belle-Isle. In light of the flaccidity of French policy in Fleury's final months, it is not surprising that many people came to believe that what France needed was fuller royal engagement in affairs. Marshal Noailles, for example, was urging the king to emulate Frederick II: "a king is never so great as when he is at the head of his armies."[2] The suggestion that Louis play his great grandfather to Fleury's Mazarin was another element in this campaign. The king was flattered by the attention, but his contributions to the debate about policy constituted a peculiarly jumbled mix: a belief that Bourbon solidarity obliged France to lend fuller support to Spain conjoined with a belief that the war was a burden; a belief that monarchs won glory through feats of arms complemented by a belief that France should seek an honorable peace. Louis XV was, quite simply, muddleheaded: to expect coherence from him was to expect poetry from a pig. And as a consequence, as the spring of 1743 approached, the continent's dominant power continued to treat war as a matter for autonomous and squabbling departments of state.

CAMPO SANTO

With the future of French policy so uncertain at the opening of 1743, Madrid needed to find a way to solidify the Bourbon alliance. Nothing seemed likelier to accomplish that goal than a military victory, and so attention focused on the army that had spent the past ten months marching and countermarching across the Italian countryside between the Panaro and the heart of the Papal States. Its new commander, Count Gages, was both frustrated and perplexed. He could not get at the enemy without crossing the Panaro into Modena; he dared not risk the exposure of a river crossing until he knew that the enemy had been tricked into deploying its forces elsewhere. And yet Gages, no tyro at tactical maneuvering, had been unable to hoodwink his foe. Either through superb intelligence or inspired guessing, the Austrians and Piedmontese had met all his feints with appropriate responses. At this point there arrived from Madrid an ultimatum: Gages was to move onto the offensive within three days or tender his resignation. Faced with that brusque alternative, the Spanish commander, under the cover of a grand ball held to lull the enemy, snuck out of Bologna and led his troops northward across the flat countryside. On 3 February 1743 he and his army, finally fooling the enemy, forded the Panaro and entered Modena. If it was possible to force a battle, he would contrive to find a way.

It turned out not to be a difficult feat. Hitherto battle had not occurred because the Austro-Sardinians preferred not to engage. But by the opening days of February, that preference had shifted. Count Aspremont, leader of the Piedmontese troops, had for some time been willing to oblige Gages by offering battle, for he burned to use his opportunity to win a great triumph. But Count Traun, the supreme commander in this theater, had restrained him. Traun was in his element maneuvering defensively. Battle for Traun was a last tactical resort, not a preferred tactical means. But Traun was becoming aware that his enemies at the court in Vienna were campaigning to have him ousted. Bartenstein complained that he was too compliant toward the Piedmontese, too careless with money, and too cautious: "if Traun is not summoned back, Italy is not to be saved."[3] Eager to justify his behavior and protect his reputation, Traun resolved to engage the Spanish. He was also moved by strategic considerations. The Austrians were uneasy about Charles Emmanuel's decision to abandon Savoy to the Spanish; they feared it portended covert negotiations between Madrid and Turin. To undercut such talk and to lock Piedmont-Sardinia more closely into its ill-defined relationship with Austria, Traun proposed to commit the Austro-Piedmontese forces to battle. The shedding of some blood in anger might dissolve any secret Piedmontese longing for a volte-face.

When Traun learned that Gages was penetrating beyond the river, he quickly gathered an army to block any Spanish advance farther into Modena. The crossing occurred at the little village of Campo Santo, and by the time the Spanish drew themselves up in battle formation on the outskirts of the settlement on 8 February the town was in ruins. Spain's army faced northwest and numbered 13,000. Traun had only 11,000 troops and consequently felt impelled to gamble with the unorthodox. He followed convention in placing his infantry in the middle of his formation with his cavalry on the wings, but rather than aligning his troops directly opposite Gages's, he shifted them to the northeast. The effect of this shift was to place the center of the Austro-Piedmontese infantry approximately opposite the gap between the infantry and the cavalry on the Spanish right wing. The benefit of this formation for the allies lay in the numerical advantage it would thereby secure for them in the fighting on their left wing, where the Piedmontese cavalry under Aspremont was positioned; the complementary liability lay in the way in which this formation left the Austrian right open to a flanking attack by the unopposed Spanish left. Traun recognized the danger and was relying on cavalry elements on his right to delay and confuse the Spanish left. But his greatest need was for a battle that was brief. The longer the fighting continued, the more time Gages would have to grasp and neutralize the Austrian plan. It was thus a fortunate stroke for Traun that Gages, having drawn his troops up into formation, chose to launch the attack at 4:00 in the afternoon on 8 February 1743 rather than wait until the following day. In early February there were but two hours of daylight left.

Initially the battle went well for Spain. Neither the Austrian cavalry, whose exploits at Mollwitz and Chotusitz had won acclaim, nor the Piedmontese cavalry, now being tested for the first time in the war, was able to withstand the charge of Spain's mounted warriors. On both wings the allied army was threatened. But then the same madness that had beset the Austrian cavalry at Mollwitz infiltrated the Spanish cavalry on the right. Having scattered the enemy horse, they chose to pursue them ineffectually across the plain rather than turn their attack against the exposed left flank of the Austrian infantry. Traun, meanwhile, dispatched assistance to his left to stabilize it and then led his infantry troops into a fierce, swarming struggle with the Spanish enemy. The pressure on the Spanish army intensified when Count Schulenburg regrouped the Austrian cavalry on the right and led it in a counterattack, while General Leutrum, replacing the fatally wounded Aspremont as commander on the left, managed a similar feat on his wing. With all sectors of the allied army finally advancing, Gages chose to retreat while it still seemed possible to avoid a massive loss of life in the currents of the Panaro. In the thickening twilight the Spanish began to withdraw across the river they had passed less than a week earlier, and the first major battle of the Italian phase of the war was over.

Though the armies had been small by central European standards and artillery had been notable for its absence, the battle was by one yardstick the most savage of the war thus far.[4] Spain suffered 4,000 casualties, including soldiers lost to imprisonment, the Austrians and Piedmontese another 2,000. Thus, fully one-quarter of all those engaged in the battle became casualties, a proportion marginally higher than the figure for Mollwitz and decidedly higher than the figure for Chotusitz.[5] Over 30 percent of Spain's army was counted among the casualties, a figure that exceeded even the 27 percent casualty rate that Austria experienced at Mollwitz. Because initial reports made the battle still more sanguinary, the impression that it had been a bloodletting was indelible. Gages spent the entire battle in the center, never fathomed Traun's plan, and so never mobilized his own left for a massive attack on the allies' great vulnerability. Traun on the other hand was the embodiment of attentive activity. Twice horses were shot from under him; twice he mounted new steeds. At every important point—from his imaginative off-center formation at the beginning to his final infantry thrust—he outthought and outmaneuvered Gages. With the modesty that comes from self-respect, Traun attributed the allies' success to the fortitude of the Austrian and Piedmontese troops. Many observers, however, gave the laurel to Traun himself.

Gages tried at first to represent the battle as a Spanish victory. To justify that claim he could point to the successes of Spain's cavalry and to the fact that the allies withdrew from the field of battle to lick their wounds at a greater distance from the Spanish force. But the general's special pleading fooled no one: as Elizabeth Farnese tartly noted, Gages's report about the engagement was penned in Bologna, not Parma. Beset by further desertions and riddled with disease, the Spanish army could not hold even Bologna. On 26 March 1743, as the Austrians arrived at one end of town, the Spanish, reduced to 6,000, left from the other to seek cover at Rimini. There the lines stabilized. The only gain that Spain received from the embarrassing failure of its campaign north of Bologna was a French promise to widen their assistance. This turn lent an ironic touch to the engagement at Campo Santo: the Spanish had sought out the battle on the presumption that victory could solidify the Bourbon alliance; as the event showed, defeat could accomplish the same purpose. For Austria, the victory at Campo Santo meant that Maria Theresa's Italian holdings were secure. Moreover, by demonstrating that Austro-Piedmontese cooperation could hold Bourbon expansionism in Italy in check, it also meant that, for a while at least, Austria remained the dominant force in the peninsula.

THE PRAGMATIC ALLIANCE PROSPERS

Lord Carteret's war aim was to enlist virtually all the non-Bourbon states of Europe into an anti-Bourbon league. By the Treaty of Berlin he had broken Prussia's tie with France. On 29 November 1742 he advanced his cause again, securing in the Treaty of Westminster a defensive alliance with Prussia that, while excluding the current hostilities, nevertheless pulled Berlin further away from Versailles. On 22 December Britain concluded a defensive treaty with Russia in which each power promised aid to the other if it was attacked in Europe. Then in the spring of 1743 the Dutch finally yielded to Carteret's coaxing. The French had devoted much time to telling the Dutch that the British were like "the bites of the tarantula, which force those who are attacked to dance without pause or rest until their powers are exhausted —the true dance of the dead."[6] But since French arms seemed more dangerous than British bullying, the preponderance of Dutch opinion swung slowly to the anti-Bourbon side. Moreover, if the republic ignored treaty obligations to Austria, it might jeopardize the margin of protection that the Austrian Netherlands offered. When the Dutch became persuaded by the British Parliament's financial support for the upkeep of the Hanoverian troops that Britain was wholeheartedly committed to widening the war, the States General finally took the steps Carteret had been asking for. Though with only dilute support from the discreet grand pensionary, Anthonie Van der Heim, it acknowledged the justness of Vienna's claims upon its assistance and voted both money and 20,000 additional troops to meet that obligation. With this vote the Dutch had 65,000 men under arms.

Throughout the months in which Carteret worked to stitch his league together, he was also successful at defusing Prussian interference. Frederick's chief concern was to halt hostilities in Germany, even if that involved nothing more than shifting them to Flanders or Lorraine. When he realized during December 1742 that Britain proposed to send the Pragmatic Army into Germany, he threatened to respond with military measures of his own. Carteret judged the king to be bluffing, however, and Hyndford told Podewils that if war erupted between George and Frederick, the outcome would turn on "which of the two had the longer sword and the longer purse."[7] That was a contest Frederick could not relish, and he quickly backed down. Instead, he advanced two new proposals, either of which might forestall a German war. By the first, France would be induced to leave

Germany because Charles VII would be given adequate satisfaction; France's departure would dissolve Britain's grounds for entrance. Specifically, Charles VII would be granted new holdings not at Austria's expense but rather through the secularizing of bishoprics adjacent to the electorate (for example, Passau and Salzburg) and the mediatizing of adjacent or embedded princely states (for example, Ulm and Augsburg). By the second proposal, the empire would establish an army of observation to protect Germany against both France and Britain. The former proposal had few supporters. The church and the Catholic emperor opposed secularizations; the imperial princes opposed mediatizations. The latter proposal foundered on the awkward fact that any German army would be largely a Prussian army. The princes of the empire had no desire to entrust the protection of their liberties to the king of Prussia. And so Frederick was frustrated in his efforts to mount a resistance to Britain's entry into Germany.

That entry came in April of 1743, when the Pragmatic Army—so named because its purpose was the defense of the Pragmatic Sanction—began to cross the Rhine under the command of Lord Stair. The Duke of Aremberg, commander of the sizable Austrian contingent, was Stair's chief aide. The army itself numbered almost 60,000. Austria supplied 20,000 troops (mostly Flemings), Britain 16,000, Hanover another 16,000, and Hesse 6,000. Multinational forces often suffer from ethnic tensions, but this one—well fed and well cared for—enjoyed high spirits. "[The British and Hanoverians] get drunk very comfortably together, and talk and sing a vast deal without understanding one syllable of what they say to one another."[8] The advance into Germany meant that at the very time that French strategic thinking was embracing the notion of withdrawing from the empire, the Pragmatic Allies were pouring a large new army into the theater.

Understandably, the French felt imperiled. But the council remained divided and gave no leadership to French commanders. The cautious Broglie felt he had no choice but to remain on the defensive with his 48,000 troops, and Charles VII's return to Munich in April 1743 did not prompt the marshal to alter his resolution. The 15,000 troops under Seckendorff's command were an even sorrier lot than the French. "No money, no bread, no forage, no food, no arms, and also scant powder and lead, and nevertheless wanting to conduct war," the commander wrote—"it is impossible."[9] He was right, and Broglie knew it. French troops might harass the advancing Austrian units, but Broglie had no intention of committing them to large battles they were unlikely to win.

What therefore ensued in Bavaria in the spring of 1743 was, from Austria's perspective, a model campaign. Prince Lobkowitz moved out of

Bohemia into the Upper Palatinate to tie down the French troops there. Meanwhile, various Austrian forces accomplished their respective tasks in the electorate. On 9 May Prince Charles's detachment defeated Count Minuzzi's imperial (that is, Bavarian) army at the town of Simbach and thereby swept past the imperial garrison at Braunau. On 16 May Count Leopold Daun led the first noteworthy engagement against the French in Bavaria, taking the town of Dingolfing on the lower Isar. Two days later, joined by Prince Charles's force, he marched into Landau, still farther down the Isar. By now the French pattern of withdrawal was becoming clear. To cover their retreat they were burning villages to the ground, and to deprive the Austrians of provisions they were spoiling or destroying all supplies they could not carry away with them. Croats in the Austrian army were also wreaking havoc on civilians: at Dingolfing they slaughtered 500. On 27 May Count Browne's more disciplined force took Deggendorf, on the Danube just above its junction with the Isar. On 9 June, after the hapless emperor had fled, Bernklau enjoyed the pleasure of retaking the Munich he had been driven from the previous autumn. When Friedberg, located on the Lech River, fell just five days later, Bavaria was effectually in Austrian hands. By picking off riparian garrison towns, Austria had conducted a textbook operation.

And where were the French? Although some had held out in the various defensive posts that Broglie had planted in Bavaria, most withdrew with the marshal. They had in fact fallen back to Donauwirth, on the western edge of Wittelsbach territory, before orders arrived from France allowing the army to return home if it could not be of service in Bavaria. Broglie embraced the opportunity, explaining that a shortage of food and Noailles's need for him mandated his withdrawal. The emperor's envoy was aghast. "It is an action," he told Broglie, "which I did not think you capable of."[10] Before fleeing Munich Charles VII had invoked Franco-Bavarian treaty obligations to try to replace Broglie as commander of the timorous French army. Now the marshal presumed to order Seckendorff to withdraw his battered imperial army over the Lech, abandoning all of Bavaria to the Austrians. This command exhausted Charles VII's patience. He had endured what he called "the weakness, the incompetence, and the wicked intentions" of Broglie for long enough.[11] On 25 June 1743 the emperor declared Bavaria separated from its faithless ally. France's German policy now lay in ruins, its German friends virtually gone.

To prevent further destruction of his electorate, Charles VII needed to secure an armistice with Austria. He deputed Seckendorff to negotiate with Khevenhüller, and the two men reached an agreement quickly. In effect, Seckendorff saved his army from destruction by giving up the electorate to

Austrian administration. The 12,000-man imperial force was neutralized, and the Austrians were given explicit permission to march through Bavaria to carry the war to France. The two men signed the document on 27 June 1743 at the monastery from which the convention took its name: Niederschönfeld. The convention never officially took force because neither Maria Theresa, who disapproved of recognition for the emperor, nor Charles VII, who balked at the concessions that the overwrought Seckendorff had made, ratified it. But in most important respects it was observed. When we link Niederschönfeld with Campo Santo, with the recovery of Bohemia, with Broglie's ignominious retreat, with Prussian isolation, with Dutch troop commitments, and with the launching of the multinational army from the Low Countries, we must conclude that the fortunes of the Pragmatic Allies were now stunningly happy. Indeed, on the very day that Khevenhüller accepted Bavaria's submission, the Pragmatic Army was elevating prospects for Pragmatic prosperity to unparalleled heights.

DETTINGEN

Once encamped near Mainz, the Pragmatic Army waited for the arrival of George II, who, against the advice of his British ministers, had decided to lead it personally in the coming engagements. Inactivity is an insidious foe of military organizations, and the discipline that had characterized the early days of the Pragmatic Army broke down. Pillaging bands began to scour the countryside for food, and the local peasantry, in anger and frustration at the military depredations, often drove their cattle away to prevent the troops from seizing them. By mid-June, when the Pragmatic Army crept into Aschaffenburg, its condition was desperate. The French, who were in general better off, watched the difficulties with glee and pondered how to take advantage of the situation. Noailles contributed to the allies' misery by interdicting supplies from higher up the Main. Meanwhile he moved his main force close to the river itself. Not until 19 June 1743 did the British king finally arrive in the Pragmatic camp, the battle still unjoined and misery in the allied camp mounting.

The British monarch quickly realized that the condition of the army he had envisioned as his vehicle to fame was wretched. Attributing the difficulties to the testy Stair, he virtually ignored the earl, huddling instead with the Hanoverian generals encamped at Aschaffenburg. These commanders decided that safety lay in retreating back down the Main River through the villages of Klein Ostheim and Dettingen to the town of Hanau, where they expected to find supplies and reinforcements. The plan involved some problems.

The lie of the land on the right bank—the proximity of the Spessart Hills to the bed of the river—would funnel the retreating troops toward the riverside, where they would become targets for the artillery that Noailles had planted along the left bank. Moreover, just in front of Dettingen lay a shallow ravine harboring a bog, with only a single bridge permitting easy transit. This natural obstacle would retard the retreat in the best of circumstances and, if guarded by the enemy, might even block it. But an army without food cannot remain immobile, and it seemed more prudent to march in the direction of friends than to plunge even farther into an uninviting Germany.

Because the Pragmatic plan was conservative, it was predictable, and therefore Marshal Noailles guessed that the multinational troops would seek to resolve their difficulties by withdrawing westward back down the Main. He conceived a response that Frederick II later praised as "worthy of a great captain."[12] Noailles placed elements of his army on the north side of the Main, downstream from the allies. As soon as he received evidence that the enemy was retreating, he would send additional units across the Main to block the withdrawal at the ravine just outside of Dettingen. Simultaneously he would send other troops across the river into the town of Aschaffenburg that the allies were abandoning. With these two deployments the French would bottle the Pragmatic Army up and could expect to destroy it almost at leisure. The ravine would allow the French to block any further Pragmatic retreat downriver. The protection of Aschaffenburg would allow the French to prevent any Pragmatic effort to escape upstream. The river itself and the Spessart Hills, confining a plain scarcely more than a mile wide, completed the confinement. And meanwhile, French artillery from the left bank, though too distant to be devastating, could add yet another complication for the cribbed enemy.

Just after midnight on 27 June 1743 the Pragmatic Army began its retreat. Awakened at 1:00 in the morning, Noailles directed that the planned disposition be effected immediately. One section of infantry began to file across the river behind the withdrawing allies and into Aschaffenburg. Simultaneously, another section moved to the north bank ahead of the allies. This blocking force, which mounted in size to 26,000, turned toward the allies and posted itself just short of Dettingen. All of these maneuvers took time, and it was not until 8:00 A.M. that a startled George II was notified that the French had blocked his army's route of exit. But then the French commander on the north bank, the Duke of Grammont, made the monumental error upon which the whole battle turned. Rather than keeping the soggy ravine ahead of his troops at Dettingen, a natural obstacle to the enemy, he began to move the French across the bridge at Dettingen and to deploy them with the swamp at their rear. In one stroke this advance radically altered the tactical situation: the topographical feature that had promised to mire the withdrawing allies was transformed into a potential sinkhole for the out-manned French. Grammont later explained his error by claiming that he feared that the slowness of his own movements had let the bulk of the Pragmatic Army slip past him. However one accounts for the mistake, its consequences were profound. Since the French could no longer wait at their leisure for the troops crossing at Aschaffenburg to become involved, the advantage in manpower suddenly shifted to the multinational force. Numbering 35,000 against Grammont's 26,000 French, the Pragmatic Army could expect the momentum of its movement to drive the French back into the quagmire or into disabled retreat across the river or through the hills.

But the ensuing battle was not an easy one for the Pragmatic Army. Three times the French charged the advancing allies, displaying (in the words of a British observer) "more courage than conduct," and only after the third charge did the French lines begin to break.[13] The allies then surged forward, pushing the French through the bog and taking Dettingen. British infantry fire, untested in European warfare since the days of Marlborough, again proved formidable. Hanoverian artillery fire from the right was deadly, by one account doing "incredible execution, and contribut[ing] not a little to the general confusion and retreat of the enemy."[14] When Noailles realized the gravity of Grammont's miscalculation, he rode to the right bank to assume command. But his chief task very quickly became the saving of as much of Grammont's force as he could, and in this task he was, considering the diffi-culty of the French position, remarkably successful. Still, when the battle ended at 4:00 in the afternoon, it was unquestionably an allied triumph. French casualties (including prisoners) numbered 4,000, allied casualties but half that figure.[15] George II basked in his long-sought (and unmerited) glory.

Thus, while Austria steadily chewed away at France in the Danube valley, advancing along several lines toward an inexorable victory, the Pragmatic Army made its contribution to the alliance with one galvanizing stroke. Europe measured strength by victories. First, Broglie's army had been bro-ken; now Noailles's was whipped. The Duke of Montijo, Spain's ambassador to the emperor, spoke tartly to some French officers afterward: "All Europe was saying that the French do not want to fight. . . . Now one must say: they fight like fools."[16] But the saddest and grimmest assessment came from Noailles himself. The French troops suffered from indiscipline, he reported to Louis XV, and "if we do not labor with the most serious and regular atten-tion to remedy this, the troops of Y[our] M[ajesty] will fall into the utmost decadence."[17] In Britain there was rejoicing, tempered only by confusion over the king's behavior. Of his raw courage there could be no doubt. Mindful perhaps of Frederick's maiden engagement, he declined suggestions that he leave the battlefield with the stinging rebuke: "What do you think I came here for, to be a poltroon?"[18] But his partiality for his electorate—he wore Hanoverian rather than British insignia into battle—was galling, and his decision to leave the wounded behind, though an indication of how shattered the military administration of the Pragmatic Army had become, was taken as a sign of a fundamental indifference to British interests.

The importance of Dettingen has sometimes been exaggerated. In terms of proportions of casualties it was not as sanguinary as Mollwitz, Chotusitz, or Campo Santo. It was not (as some who seek to rescue French glory claim) the event that prevented the Pragmatic Army from linking up with Prince Charles's army in Bavaria, for the Pragmatic Army had not been destined for Bavaria in the first place. Nor did it lead to the destruction of Noailles's benumbed force, for George II, despite Stair's pleading, made no effort to pursue the enemy, and the Pragmatic Army spent the rest of the summer mending its lesions. An interesting aspect of the battle is the fact that Britain and France, as auxiliaries, were not at war with each other when the battle occurred and did not go to war as a consequence of it. The most telling point about Dettingen is that, although Grammont's tactical error undid an excellent plan, Noailles had already in fact committed a graver strategic error. He knew that Broglie's army was falling back toward him from the east. Had he waited for it, even if waiting involved allowing the Pragmatic Army to retreat to Hanau, he would have had a force of close to 90,000 troops at his disposal. Such an army would have compelled the allies to withdraw from the Rhineland or, if they were unwise enough to give battle, to have defeated them. But the dismal tenor of the reports from Bavaria prompted Noailles to seek a quick and exhilarating triumph for French arms. He threw away a massive advantage for a marginal one, and then the fates of war undid even that residual advantage.

THE RUSSIAN WILD CARD

The empress Elizabeth had come to power in Russia in the coup of December 1741 that unseated Ivan. As daughter of Peter the Great, she was determined to brook no opposition to her claim to the succession. Yet her training for rule had been meager and patchy. She handled foreign languages well, preferring the French tongue to the German that had dominated at the court during the 1730s. But she was ignorant of foreign lands and, in surprising ways, ignorant of her own. Observers noted that she was quick-witted, pious, commonsensical, self-indulgent, and amiable, but the two traits that stood out above all others were her sensuality and her inconsistency. In June 1743 the dominant ministers at the Russian court were the Bestuzhev brothers —Michael and Alexis. Michael Bestuzhev was grand marshal of the imperial household; Alexis was vice-chancellor. Both brothers had been educated at Copenhagen and Berlin; both evinced a taste for western European ways; both had mastered the art of dissimulation. Of the two, Alexis was the abler, the more ruthless, and the more ambitious; but in the middle of 1743 it was Michael who held the more important post. On most central issues the Bestuzhevs thought alike. They wanted to make cooperation with Austria the axiom of Russian policy, since progress against the Ottomans seemed possible only with Vienna's blessing. They viewed cooperation with Britain as a vital corollary to this axiom, both because Britain's navy could transform the Baltic Sea into a British lake and because British money was central to Austrian success. They looked upon France as the chief foe of Russia because Versailles was the friend of traditional enemies such as Sweden, Poland, and Turkey. For all these reasons they were inclined to believe that Russia should aid the Pragmatic Allies.

Because the rewards of securing Russian help promised to be so ample, the states of Europe campaigned assiduously and expensively to win the favor of the empress and her ministers. A powerful pro-French party was led by the Armand Lestocq. A Huguenot by background, a Hanoverian by birth, and a physician by training, Lestocq wielded wide and mysterious influence with the empress. Austrian interests were represented through most of 1742 by Marquis Botta d'Adorno, who suspected that Elizabeth's Gallophilia made any hopes of engaging Russia in the war against France extravagant. But even in his hope to make Elizabeth suspicious of Frederick he was largely unsuccessful, and before 1742 was over he had left St. Petersburg to represent Maria Theresa in Berlin. Through Sir Cyril Wich, who represented George II in Russia after April 1742, Britain too worked to stoke Elizabeth's amity. Wich negotiated the Anglo-Russian defensive treaty of December 1742, but his struggle to find grounds for making George II an acceptable mediator for the Russo-Swedish war ended in failure.

The European capital most interested in Russia's doings was Berlin. From the opening of his reign, Frederick II lived in dread of what Russia's army might do if unleashed against East Prussia. And so Frederick was the fixed foe of the Bestuzevs' policy and the unambiguous friend of the pro-French party. As he told his envoy at St. Petersburg, Axel von Mardefeld: "there is nothing in the world I would not do in order to always live on good terms with that empire [Russia]."[19] Mardefeld lent support and gave money to

Lestocq, he kept his royal master fully informed on the intricacies and surprises of Russian politics, and he flattered the empress in as many ways as he could devise. After the conclusion of the Treaty of Berlin, Russia loomed even larger in Frederick's mind. He was separated from France but not aligned with Britain. In such a situation Russia's friendship would relieve many problems. But the defensive treaty concluded between Berlin and St. Petersburg in March 1743 failed to cheer Frederick, for Russia—pointedly and ominously—refused to comprehend Prussian Silesia within the lands to be guaranteed.

On 1 August 1743 a sequence of events began in St. Petersburg that would totally overturn this structure of Pragmatic hopes and Prussian fears. On that day Lestocq produced a set of documents that spoke of a long-standing plot to restore Ivan to the throne. A cunning combination of forgeries and excerpts from authentic documents, the evidence aroused the ire and vindictiveness of the empress. Among those implicated was Botta d'Adorno. A series of trials, tortures, and punishments followed. By the middle of September the internal ruckus had subsided, with Elizabeth still firmly in control. Michael Bestuzhev had fallen from his high position, but not from grace, since Elizabeth sent him as ambassador to Berlin. Alexis Bestuzhev and, of course, Lestocq remained a close advisor of the empress. But if the domestic scene quickly returned to its former shape, the foreign scene did not. Elizabeth regarded Botta d'Adorno as a dabbler in conspiracy. She could not punish him herself, for he had left the country, but she made clear her belief that Maria Theresa should do so. The queen of Hungary, however, after investigating the charges, found no basis for the Russian imputation and refused to take her emissary to task. The disagreement quickly became a test of wills. All hope of Russo-Austrian cooperation vanished. And Frederick II suddenly stood as the beneficiary of a marvelous stroke of luck: "the revolution in Russia . . . is one of the most fortunate conjunctures that can happen for Prussia at the present moment."[20]

THE TREATY OF WORMS

While abrupt events like the battle of Dettingen and the disclosure of the Russian plot punctuated the summer of 1743 and caught a disproportionate share of the attention of political discussants, the activities that ultimately bore most heavily upon the course of the war were negotiations that were proceeding slowly and usually quietly in three separate locations around Europe. At Worms the British were mediating discussions between the envoys of Austria and Piedmont-Sardinia that envisioned transforming the provisional relationship established by the Convention of Turin into something durable and hence reliable. Meanwhile, at Hanau the British were exploring with a representative of the emperor the possibility of resolving the outstanding differences between Charles VII and Maria Theresa. Finally, at Versailles the French were superintending exchanges between Spain and Piedmont-Sardinia that had as their goal the weaning of Turin from its ties with Vienna. It was impossible that all three talks should succeed: the aims of talks at Worms and Versailles were absolutely contradictory, and the means for realizing the aims of the talks at Worms and Hanau were incompatible.

The effort to bring Austria and Piedmont-Sardinia into a more orthodox relationship had been under way in London since the spring of 1742. Though the two states had cooperated in blunting Spanish thrusts into northern Italy, their ties remained informal. Lord Carteret had made the forging of a firmer alliance a key part of his grand design. It was not difficult for him to win acknowledgments in Vienna and Turin that the creation of an alliance would be useful. More important, the two sides were not very far apart on the terms of an agreement. Turin had set a price for cooperation: the cessions of Angera, Vigevano, Oltrepo, Piacenza, and Finale. As early as the summer of 1742, Vienna had accepted the need to yield on the first three territories, and the British were confident that the Austrians could be induced to concede a bit more. The chief obstacles to a treaty arose rather from competing expectations about the fulfillment of these terms. The Piedmontese demand postulated that Turin's gains be immediate and irrevocable while any Austrian gains — Naples and Sicily perhaps — be contingent upon military success. The Austrian demand insisted that Turin remain loyal to Vienna until Austria had secured compensation for both the Italian cessions and Silesia. Neither court thought the other's requirement acceptable. And so, in May 1743, in an effort to curtail the time lost in communicating with home courts, Carteret moved the talks to Worms.

The talks at Hanau were of much more recent origin. Carteret had long made clear his hope to win the emperor over to the anti-Bourbon league; the British secretary viewed Charles VII and the empire as "an essential spring in this great work."[21] But Austria had shown little interest in talking with Charles VII as long as it was handily defeating his troops and overrunning his lands. And Charles himself had been reluctant to enter into talks with representatives of Maria Theresa lest he thereby sacrifice French support. But in May 1743, with the French army in Bavaria disintegrating, Charles VII shifted his thinking, appointing Prince William of Hesse to negotiate with Carteret at Hanau on his behalf. The first discussions were not encouraging: William proposed a simple cease-fire, while Carteret wanted immediate commitments that Charles VII would abandon his claims against Maria Theresa, not seek lands from Austria, and detach himself from France. The prospects for an agreement were not enhanced when William countered in early July with Charles's offer to dismiss French troops only if the Austrians withdrew from Wittelsbach lands, the Pragmatic Army left Germany, and Charles VII was assured an adequate revenue. But whatever his short-term problems, at least Carteret had begun a process that might bring queen and emperor together.

Even as these explorations were carrying Carteret back and forth between the two German cities, the third set of talks was under way at Versailles and designed to upset Carteret's grand strategy by winning Piedmont-Sardinia over to the Bourbon camp. On 11 April 1743 Spain's chief minister, José del Campillo, suddenly died. Philip V replaced him with the Marquis Ensenada, the man who had been administering occupied Savoy. Ensenada shared, naturally enough, the royal interest in creating a state for Don Philip; having helped Don Charles to a kingdom, he could hope to provide the younger brother with at least a principality. But he saw in Campo Santo clear evidence that Spain needed the support of Piedmont-Sardinia if it was to realize its goals. His assumption of power allowed French leaders to believe that Madrid would be more forthcoming in negotiations with Turin. Thus, in May 1743 the French ministers at Versailles began discussions with the Piedmontese envoy to France, designed to explore the possibility of effecting a shift of Piedmont-Sardinia from Austria's side to Spain's. Amelot told Campo-Florido brusquely that "it is necessary to satisfy the King of Sardinia, whatever the price might be."[22] At first, Elizabeth Farnese was uninterested. But by July the Spanish government had proposed that Charles Emmanuel's reward for helping Spain be the long-coveted state of Milan, sweetened further by the title of king of Lombardy, while the island of Sardinia be transferred from the house of Savoy to Don Philip, thereby raising Don Philip to the eminence of royalty. Charles Emmanuel pondered the proposal, basking in the happy knowledge that he was being courted by the Austrians at Worms and the Spanish at Versailles.

The key point to keep in mind amid the details of diplomatic maneuvering that follow is that there were two crucial decisions to be made. The first lay with Lord Carteret. It was a central assumption of Carteret's grand design that both Charles Emmanuel and Charles VII be enlisted in his anti-Bourbon league. In both cases the rulers were demanding territorial concessions as their price; in each case Austria was to be the source of territory. If, however, it was not possible to get Austrian support for cessions to both of the two potential allies, who would be the more valuable to secure, Charles

Emmanuel or Charles VII? The second decision lay with Charles Emmanuel. He had to choose between Spain and Austria. Spain was offering him a very attractive package, for the addition of Milan to Piedmont would make the king the dominant force in Italy; but its acquisition depended on military success and Spanish fidelity to commitments. Austria, though holding out on a few of Piedmont-Sardinia's demands, could probably be induced to relent and cede territory outright. But that territory would not include Milan. Thus the decision that lay before Charles Emmanuel reduced itself to this question: was the small, delimited but virtually certain gain consequent upon cooperation with Austria or the large but problematic gain implicit in alliance with Spain the more advantageous?

The hour of decision struck first at Hanau. In mid-July 1743 Carteret presented two rough documents to Prince William that in combination defined the terms of a possible peace between Maria Theresa and Charles VII.[23] The emperor would dismiss his French troops, renounce his claims to Austrian lands, and add his and the empire's weight to the campaign to compel France to accept a general and just peace. The queen would respond by returning Bavaria and the Upper Palatinate to the emperor. The documents also promised the emperor a monthly revenue from Britain. There were difficulties with the proposal, but Prince William was overcome by "an indescribable joy on learning that the affair had taken so happy a turn."[24] Celebration was soon undone. The government in London found much to fault in the documents, especially the British commitment to pay money to the emperor. Newcastle denounced Carteret for negotiating about Austrian interests without notifying the authorities in Vienna. When in early August the ministers notified Carteret that the British government could not accept the proposals, the secretary realized that by seeking to bridge the gap between the emperor and the queen at a time when the emperor had only his title to distinguish him from the paltriest German prince, he had offended the Austrians and raised doubts in both Vienna and London about his commitment to Maria Theresa. And so, though allowing the talks at Hanau to continue, from early August 1743 Carteret was looking to Worms for his success.

Whether Carteret could in fact bring Austria and Piedmont-Sardinia into alliance depended as much on what happened at Versailles as on deliberations at Worms. Charles Emmanuel nursed a long-standing belief that a tie with Vienna was preferable to one with Madrid. He found Spain's insistence that he violate agreements he had reached with Vienna unsettling: "the King of Sardinia," he wrote of himself, "can deduce from the betrayals and treacheries proposed to him what Spain has in store when it believes the occasion propitious."[25] But two considerations gave him pause. The first was the fact that France was investing much energy and high hopes in the mediation effort. Before Piedmont-Sardinia could risk disappointing French hopes, Charles Emmanuel needed to be sure that he had suitable protection against the wrath of Versailles. The second consideration was that while Spain was offering generous terms, Austria was withholding even modest ones. For these reasons Charles Emmanuel continued to encourage the French to try to mediate the differences between Turin and Madrid. At the very least the protracting of the talks would give Austria time and inducement to alter its strict aversion to new concessions; and if Austria proved intractably hostile, such talks might yet pave the way for an understanding among Charles Emmanuel, Louis XV, and Philip V.

The ploy devised by Ormea to prolong the talks was to seek exorbitant concessions of Spain through France, and then wait while the two Bourbon states haggled over a response. Thus in August 1743 Turin put forward four new demands that were to supplement, not replace, the points already conceded by Madrid and that in their extravagance seemed certain to raise alarm signals in Versailles. There was numb disbelief in Turin when France signaled its prompt acceptance of these terms and pledged itself to win Spain over to them. The backfiring of the ploy suddenly threatened to snare Piedmont-Sardinia in an alliance with Spain. On 23 August Louis XV wrote Philip V of the presumptively good news. "The cause of France and Spain is today the same," he declared. Madrid's response was more shaded, but Campo-Florido stated that on balance the agreement seemed advantageous, since it would give Spain a foothold in northern Italy. At Turin, however, a kind of desperation overtook the government, and it fell back on its last hope to win adequate terms from Vienna: an ultimatum. As delivered to Wasner at Worms (and as explained to the French), its terms were very clear: either Austria agreed to all of Piedmont-Sardinia's territorial demands or Piedmont-Sardinia would ally itself promptly with the Bourbon states.

There was an element of bluff in the ultimatum. Charles Emmanuel did not yet have Spain's acquiescence. In fact, what he had was deeply disturbing—a copy of a letter from Amelot to Campo-Florido in which the Frenchman recommended Spanish assent to the terms on the grounds that "a treaty is only a piece of paper easily torn to shreds."[26] It therefore seems likely that, had Austria remained obdurate, the king would still have evaded Bourbon clutches. Wasner, however, was not privy to Charles Emmanuel's thoughts. All he knew was that an ultimatum had been tendered and that he himself had already been authorized, if necessary, to concede Piacenza to Turin. He could not hesitate—the ultimatum did not allow time for consultations with Vienna—and so he consented to conclude the treaty. The requisite signing of the defining documents occurred on 13 September 1743. Charles Emmanuel renounced his claim to Milan and guaranteed the Pragmatic Sanction, while Maria Theresa handed over the portion of Angera that lay west of the Ticino and Lake Maggiore, the Vigevanesco west of the Ticino, the Oltrepo region, Piacenza, and Vienna's rights to Finale. The two monarchs also agreed to form a joint Italian army, with Austria supplying 30,000 troops and Piedmont-Sardinia providing 40,000. Britain pledged to keep a "strong squadron" in the Mediterranean, to help secure all the compensation that was possible for Austria, and to continue paying subsidies to both Vienna and Turin "for as long as the war continues"—later an important turn of phrase. A secret article envisioned the expulsion of the Bourbons from Italy, with Naples going to Austria and Sicily to Piedmont-Sardinia. This agreement was the Treaty of Worms.

Piedmontese diplomacy had never known a greater success. With cool daring Charles Emmanuel and Ormea had held Bourbon military probes at bay for an entire summer and had then induced the Austrians to pay them for not doing something they almost surely would not have done anyway. With the expulsion of Austria from all lands west of the Ticino River, that stream (and Lake Maggiore) became the clearly demarcated and readily defensible eastern frontier of the Piedmontese realm. The new areas south of the Po River, fronting on weaker neighbors, promised enhanced revenues and made access to Tuscany and the Ligurian coast far easier. Even though the total area of the five cessions together was considerably smaller than the area of ceded Silesia alone, these transfers were of a strategic significance equal to Silesia's. Carteret was quoted by an Italian diplomat as saying that "the cessions will sooner or later make the Sardinian king master of Italy."[27] And there was another gain for Charles Emmanuel. By putting Turin's subsidy from London on an equal footing with Vienna's, the kingdom had clarified its financial situation. The only visible flaw in the pact was the transfer to Turin of Vienna's claim to the marquisate of Finale. Not only was the claim probably worthless, it also was certain to alarm the rulers of the hitherto-neutral Genoese republic. One Piedmontese noble remarked that "the Genoese, on learning of it, will find this article strange, and I admit that it appears so to me, good Piedmontese though I am."[28]

Austria's response to the treaty was more subdued. The commitment to joint military endeavors made possible the contemplation of a Habsburg restoration in Naples. That prospect was not unpleasant. But Sir Thomas Robinson had long since warned Carteret that Vienna would turn to Italy only *faute de mieux*. The treaty also prevented Piedmont-Sardinia from joining the enemy—a matter of much importance, since in August Botta's dispatches from Berlin began warning of the possibility of a preemptive Prussian attack on Austria. It made Turin an ally of Austrian authorities in Milan in the effort to defend Lombardy against the Spanish. And it pleased the British. The last was a particularly important point, for British support—whether in the Pragmatic Army, on the Mediterranean, or through the Treasury—was vital to hopes for Austrian success. And so, despite the cessions, the government at Vienna agreed to Wasner's action. Suspicious of its new ally and suspicious too of the state that had mediated the treaty, it nevertheless felt it had no choice.

Among disinterested observers the Treaty of Worms reinforced a sense that Carteret was a diplomatic genius. If the Treaty of Berlin had been the first great achievement of his ministry, the Treaty of Worms was the second. To induce the Austrians to agree to these treaties, Carteret had deliberately alternated browbeating with flattery. During the summer of 1743, for example, he warned that if Vienna was not more forthcoming he would advise Charles Emmanuel to cast his lot with Spain; but then he entertained Prince Charles with a toast more intoxicating than the beverage—"Dunkirk, Lorraine, Alsace."[29] There were risks in gathering together a league of anti-Bourbon powers. Some states that watched from the sidelines—Genoa, perhaps, or the ever-unpredictable Prussia—might decide that the balance in Europe had been dangerously skewed. But these were risks for the future. In September 1743 Carteret enjoyed the satisfaction of achievement. Against long odds and in the notoriously slippery field of foreign affairs, he had seen his grand design virtually realized and Bourbon Europe virtually isolated. It was Carteret's greatest hour.

9

Bourbon Solidarity
(September 1743 – April 1744)

FRANCE REDEFINES ITS GOALS

Piedmont-Sardinia's decision to come to terms with Austria rather than Spain swept away the flimsy foundation that for over two years had justified France's policy toward Madrid. It confirmed what Spain had long been warning about Piedmontese deviousness. A stunned and embarrassed Louis XV wrote Philip V to assure his uncle of his resolution "to unite my forces with those of Y[our] M[ajesty] to wreak vengeance for so black a betrayal."[1] This union assumed institutional shape on 25 October 1743 when the two kingdoms concluded the Treaty of Fontainebleau, committing themselves to use military force to establish Don Philip in Milan, Parma, and Piacenza. France promptly declared war on Piedmont-Sardinia; Spain had done so at the end of September. The treaty took cognizance of the festering belligerence between Spain and Britain, envisioning Spain's recovery of Gibraltar and Minorca from Britain and the annulment of the Asiento contract and the Annual Ship; and to make this goal feasible, Versailles pledged to declare war on London at some appropriate (but unspecified) point in the future. France sought little for itself: the treaty spoke only of the return to Versailles of two small but strategic fortresses that the Treaty of Utrecht had assigned to the house of Savoy in 1713. Finally, Versailles and Madrid offered reciprocal guarantees of their territories and engaged themselves to eschew all negotiations with the enemy unless their ally consented to the action. The Treaty of Worms thus created not one, but two, groupings: while consecrating the marriage of convenience between Vienna and Turin, it triggered the reaffirmation of blood affection between Madrid and Versailles.

Even the most cursory reading of the terms of the Treaty of Fontainebleau shows it to be a victory for Spain. At virtually no cost to itself Madrid had won pledges of French support for Spanish goals. The problem in explaining the origin of the treaty lies then not with Spain's participation but with France's. Why would Versailles, after the embarrassments of a German campaign predicated on an asymmetrical sharing of obligations with Bavaria, enter into a similarly asymmetrical agreement with Spain? Part of the answer lies in Louis XV's sense of guilt. "I have unfortunately been the channel that has been made use of to deceive you," he confessed to Philip V.[2] But behind Louis XV's peculiar vulnerability lay another explanation for France's acquiescence to a treaty so apparently at odds with its interests. Count Maurepas had for many months been a critic of French aimlessness. The shock of the Treaty of Worms, following so closely on the heels of the humiliation at Dettingen, created a crisis in the council that called for leadership. Maurepas now stirred himself from his habit of departmental parochialism to try to confer an element of coherence on French policy. It was he who negotiated the Treaty of Fontainebleau, crafting the terms with his old friend, the Prince of Campo-Florido. The treaty thus met his specifications, and some of its mysteries evaporate when seen in the light of his hopes.

In Maurepas's judgment, France's key enemy was not Austria but Britain. Money from London kept Vienna and Turin afloat; Carteret's diplomacy threatened to array Europe against the Bourbons; British troops were clustering dangerously close to France's northern frontier; the British navy prevented the Bourbons from exploiting their maritime proximity to Italy. The count concluded from this mournful litany of British actions that France had no choice but to turn its full force against the island kingdom. As minister of marine, Maurepas had brought the French navy up to fifty-eight ships of the line. It was now a force that might, if complemented by Spain's, deprive Britain of its command of the seas. If that goal could be accomplished, then Bourbon military strength could prevail in the appropriate European theaters. Where the flamboyant Belle-Isle had intoxicated France with the dream of a compliant empire, the bureaucratic Maurepas now tempted the ministry with visions of a bridled Britain. He proposed, in fact, mounting a double challenge to British sea power. The first, predictably, was to be in the Mediterranean, across which he wanted to send 30,000 troops. To clear the seas for this vast enterprise, he proposed to unite the Mediterranean fleets of France and Spain and to send them out against Mathews's British fleet. The second challenge that Maurepas proposed was a more surprising one: he wanted to confront Britain in the English Channel, thereby to gain control of Britain's famous moat, and then to dispatch troops to invade the British Isles. Each of these challenges involved combining a naval campaign with a military thrust. But in each instance the maritime aspect had a chronological and situational priority.

By the middle of November 1743 the ministry had accepted Maurepas's plans. But the ministry remained a body divided, and Maurepas, though temporarily preeminent, was not absolutely dominant. Thus, other ministers were able to influence France's emerging new strategy, and Maurepas's rivals on the council, especially Noailles and Richelieu, insisted on broadening the plans that their colleague had proposed. They won endorsement for carrying the war into Flanders and for mounting diplomatic efforts to assert French influence in Germany. Flanders was doubly attractive. First, since Louis XV had consented to lead a French army, the most suitable theater for playing the soldier was the Low Countries, where sieges rather than field engagements were customary and where the chance of capture by the enemy was minimal. Moreover, the United Provinces needed to be chastened: "only the success of the armies of the king," the French envoy at The Hague advised, "can solidly attach the republic to the maxims of wisdom and moderation."[3] The decision to renew efforts—even diplomatic ones—in Germay may seem odd, for France had only recently succeeded in extricating its army from the lands beyond the Rhine. But France feared that its former friends would gravitate toward Austria unless offered encouragement. Moreover, there was still the emperor, "an idol [said Noailles] to be presented to the empire to prevent it from surrendering blindly to the views of the English and the Austrians."[4] Neither of these reasons was precisely compelling, but together they suggested that France dared not ignore Germany. Consequently, Anne-Théodore Chavignard de Chavigny was sent into the empire to try to organize well-disposed princes, especially the Protestants, into a pro-Bourbon league.

In effect, in recognition of Britain's pervasive hostility, France was redefining the war. Its center of gravity was shifting westward; the relative weights of Austria and Britain were being reversed. Nevertheless, if we may conclude that the French ministry had now gained a somewhat clearer understanding of the belligerence it was caught up in, we must continue to assess its strategic decisions as both muddled and unwarrantedly ambitious. France now proposed placing four irons in the fire. To effect its various goals it needed to be able to send large armies into Italy and the Low Countries, a smaller force into Britain, and, potentially, another large one into Germany. It also needed to be able to defeat Britain twice at sea. Such projects entailed vast expenses, and while France was scarcely impoverished, its financial capabilities were more rigid and less extensive than Britain's. Moreover, by simultaneously working to place a Catholic on the throne of Britain while seeking to mobilize support among the Protestant princes of Germany, France was entering the minefield of confessional politics. For France's array of bold initiatives to succeed, many of the accidents of war would have to break its way. A grand plan that includes good fortune among its requirements for success is a plan ill conceived.

TOULON

The Mediterranean component of France's redefined purpose was its most predictable element. The Duke of Newcastle advised Admiral Mathews late in 1743 that "the war in all probability will now be carried on with great vigor in Italy."[5] France, in fact, chose to underline its commitment to vigor by raising fully 30,000 troops for its Italian expeditionary force and entrusting them to the Prince of Conti. To deal with this threat representatives from Britain, Austria, and Piedmont-Sardinia met at Turin late in December to assess the situation. They were right in predicting a Bourbon assault on the peninsula. What they did not guess, however, was that the proposed attack in northern Italy was intended to come not by way of the coast but from a southerly direction. The French plan involved transporting Conti's army and part of Don Philip's to the central Italian coast, from where the troops could link up with Gages's Spanish army in the Papal States. The key stage in this plan was the transporting of the Bourbon forces across the waters from southwestern France to west-central Italy. It would require—as Maurepas had foreseen—the neutralizing of Mathews's Mediterranean fleet.

The French decision to challenge Britain's command of the western Mediterranean meant that, for the first time in the war, a major naval engagement loomed. Late in 1743 observers began to note that the Bay of Toulon, which harbored approximately twenty French ships and about fifteen Spanish, was awash with activity. Two high seamen were on hand to superintend these activities—France's ancient vice-admiral Court, a participant at Malaga in 1704, and Spain's Don Juan José Navarro, also a veteran of the War of the Spanish Succession, now commander of the entire Spanish fleet, and as famed for his erudition as for his knowledge of ships and the sea. Admiral Mathews received reliable intelligence about all that happened in the great harbor. Increasingly, therefore, he focused his attention on Toulon, shifting his personal base from Villefranche to Hyeres in early January 1744 so that he might be closer to the heart of Bourbon Mediterranean operations. A cocky seaman, Mathews was fully confident that his fleet, numbering over thirty and growing, could defeat the conjoined French and Spanish fleets if they dared to sail out and accept battle.

Both sides were nagged by problems. Britain's fleet was still inadequately supplied, short of the cruising vessels so vital to intelligence gathering and communications among squadrons, and desperately in need of dry-dock servicing. Moreover, Mathews knew that at Brest Versailles was preparing an additional twenty-one ships for imminent sea duty. He was uncertain of France's intention for this fleet, but a lively possibility was that it might put to sea and link up with the Toulon fleet in the Mediterranean. The final British problem was the reciprocal detestation of Mathews and his second-in-command, Lestock. In sea battles, where cooperation and a kind of intuitive understanding of common purposes among commanders are important to success, this animosity boded ill. Bourbon problems were also considerable. Admiral Court was an astonishing seventy-eight years old. Whether he had the stamina, vigor, and flexibility for the task at hand was a matter for legitimate concern. His task was, moreover, complicated by the international nature of his fleet. It is always difficult to meld contingents from different nations into a coordinated unit, and the difficulty in this instance was enhanced by Spanish suspicions of French faithlessness and Spanish resentment at French presumption. Finally, they were bound by some peculiar instructions. Since France was not at war with Britain, Court was under orders to avoid initiating the engagement he was expected to win. If Britain did not oblige by attacking the Bourbons, then the Spanish were to inaugurate the battle, with the French joining the fray, as auxiliaries, only after the British had returned fire on Navarro's ships.

On 19 February 1744 the Toulon fleet, numbering thirty-two ships of the line, sailed forth. It headed due south, arrayed for battle in an extended line, with the French in the van and the Spanish in the rear. Court commanded from his flagship, the *Terrible*, located somewhat ahead of the center of the line. Once the fleet was fully at sea on the following day, a distance of over six miles separated the leading French ship from the final Spanish ship. The British learned of the egress immediately, and by 21 February their thirty-eight ships were also at sea, located to the east of the enemy and standing to the southwest to draw closer. Unlike the Bourbon fleet, which was not divided into subsections, the British fleet fell out into three divisions: Rear Admiral William Rowley commanded the van, Lestock commanded the rear, and Mathews, aboard the flagship *Namur,* commanded the center. By the morning of 22 February, Lestock's division of thirteen vessels had fallen at least seven miles behind the rest of the British fleet. Nevertheless, with the wind gently blowing from the east and the enemy in view, Mathews placed his fleet under full sail, standing to the south, line of battle ahead. Since the Bourbons maintained a similar direction and formation, the two fleets moved like two long serpents, coursing southward through the Mediterranean along roughly parallel trajectories, the Bourbons lying to the west and the British to the east. The Bourbon line was also somewhat ahead of the British. If custom had been followed, the Bourbon commander would have directed his fleet to heave to and await combat. Instead, Court kept his fleet on its southward course, displaying little immediate interest in engaging the enemy. This action posed a dilemma for Mathews, who was under orders to commence an attack only when the vans were adjacent. Since the Bourbon hulls were less fouled than the British, however, Mathews knew he could not overtake his foe. He therefore chose to close and engage with the enemy, even though the alignment of the fleets did not meet the Admiralty's requirements.

The battle brought credit to neither side. If Mathews was correct in deciding to hazard combat despite a disordered line, he was unquestionably wrong or careless in his implementation of his decision. Incredibly, he left aloft the flag signal for maintaining a line of battle, and thus he was visibly taking one course of action while visibly ordering another. The commanders of the various British ships were, naturally enough, perplexed; and while Rowley correctly intuited what Mathews intended, many did not. Thus, instead of a whole series of engagements along the overlapping sections of the two lines, there occurred only patches of fighting. Equally incredibly, the Bourbon fleet did not take advantage of its numerical superiority. Although Lestock's division remained miles distant, Court never brought the Bourbon van back northward to sweep past Rowley's division from the east.

Where combat did occur, it was intense. The *Namur*, for example, in league with the ship immediately behind it, the *Marlborough*, engaged with Admiral Navarro's *Real Felipe*, the flagship of the Spanish portion of the Bourbon fleet and, with 114 guns, the largest ship then afloat. The crushing exchange of broadsides almost destroyed the *Marlborough* and severely damaged the *Real Felipe*; the captain of the *Marlborough* lost his legs and then his life, while Navarro was wounded and 500 of his men killed or disabled. The greatest British success of the day was enjoyed by Edward Hawke, who commanded the *Berwick* in its successful battering of the *Poder*. Through the afternoon hours Lestock's division slowly approached the battle, and by 4:00 P.M. it was close enough to begin long-range firing. But then, while still at a distance, it hove to for the night. Meanwhile, Court finally decided that Navarro needed assistance and directed his squadron to tack to the northwest. This maneuver allowed the *Real Felipe* to escape under protection of friendly fire. As night fell, the two sides disengaged, and when they reformed for their nocturnal anchorings, they stood approximately six miles apart.

At dawn on 23 February 1744 the Bourbon fleet, reduced to twenty-two effective ships, set sail to the west. Court had no further taste for fighting. In fact, the Bourbon fleet broke up into its national components on this day. Mathews, in accordance with the Articles of War, ordered a pursuit. Now it was Lestock's division that assumed the van, and the unenterprising admiral of the previous day became a commander champing for the chase. But when evening came the British had still not closed with the enemy, and on the next day, after several hours of further pursuit, Mathews called off the chase. He feared that the British were being drawn too far from the north Italian coast they were expected to protect, and he doubted that his ships could overtake the fresher Bourbon ships. With this decision the battle effectively ended.[6] In fact, neither of his judgments was sound. The Articles of War clearly subordinated other assignments to the hunting down of a disabled enemy after a battle, and while the Spanish fleet was trimmer, it was also slowed by the need to tow the disabled *Real Felipe*. By suspending the pursuit, Mathews lost his opportunity to transform a marginal British victory into a crushing one.

The great sea battle of February 1744, the largest of the war, is usually called the Battle of Toulon. As one might expect after such a peculiarly disjointed and haphazard affair, the views of leaders in the various national capitals were inconsistent. Though Britain had by most acceptable measurements won the battle, the mood at London was angry. In the succeeding months Mathews and Lestock engaged in an unedifying exchanges of vilification and recriminations; eventually, in an effort to establish responsibility for the failure of the larger British fleet to destroy its ill-led and outnumbered enemy, a long series of naval trials ensued. Mathews accused Lestock of hanging back; Lestock accused Mathews of lack of courage. The verdict of the panel of sea officers remains controversial: Lestock was acquitted—unfairly, it is usually felt—of all charges of noncooperation, while Mathews was found guilty of failing to continue the pursuit and cashiered.

In Madrid the mood was peculiarly exultant. A Spanish squadron that had been confined to a French harbor for two years had finally broken free and returned home; a Spanish admiral, showing great courage, had fought the British to a virtual standoff; Spanish sailors, tested at last, had proved resilient, if somewhat ill disciplined. At Versailles there was the sense of resignation that the leadership was becoming inured to. Court was banished, and Louis XV, afflicted with "the most keen grief," agreed with his Spanish uncle that the Spanish force had been superior to the French.[7] The most important consequence of the Bourbon inability to defeat the British was the scuttling of plans to transport Bourbon troops to Italy by sea. Since the only alternative route of access to Italy was along the Ligurian coast, the failure meant that northern rather than central Italy would be the chief peninsular theater in the coming campaign. Thirty-eight ships had changed the shape of the war.

THE DESCENT ON ENGLAND

In Maurepas's encompassing vision the design of descending upon Britain—and "descent" is the name that the operation acquired—complemented the simultaneous Mediterranean initiative. Three considerations gave the French grounds for hope that the audacious enterprise might succeed. The first was the enfeebled status of Britain's military establishment at home. According to a memorandum that the French examined in October 1743, Britain had only 16,000 troops in England, Wales, and Scotland, and these men were scattered in garrisons throughout the country. The second consideration was Britain's naval vulnerability. With obligations in the Mediterranean and the Caribbean, Britain had been compelled to stretch its resources very thin. If France could secure control of the Channel for only a few days—scarcely an impossible feat—it would have the opportunity to transport an army across the straits. The third consideration was Jacobitism, the movement that sought the restoration of the house of Stuart. Insofar as Jacobites were numerous in Britain—and some reports lent credence to estimates of millions—they constituted a force of potential allies for an invading army. As long as France had hoped to avoid formal hostilities with Britain, it had forsworn use of this Jacobite weapon. But after Worms the situation was changed. In November 1743 Amelot notified the Jacobites in France that Versailles had decided to work for the restoration of James Edward Stuart, and in December Louis XV wrote Philip V of "a project I have formed in the greatest secrecy for destroying at one blow at its foundations the league of the enemies of the House of Bourbon."[8] In the Europe of the old regime there was no military action more radical than seeking to unseat a dynasty: France's decision implied a commitment to total war with Britain.

Secrecy was essential to the preparations for the descent. Since neither an army nor a fleet could be assembled without catching attention, the French were forced to resort to misdirection rather than concealment. The government chartered merchant vessels, but ostensibly for trade with America and the United Provinces. It gathered troops at Dunkirk, but inasmuch as France was aggregating a major army in the Low Countries to protect the kingdom against an attack from the Austrian Netherlands, the detachment on the coast could readily pass as a portion of this defensive force. At Brest the Atlantic fleet, assigned to the aged Count Roquefeuil, was fitted out, and while all the world could infer from the bustle in the harbor that France was contemplating some initiative, only those privy to French plans could know the intended target. On the appointed day—initially set for 20 January 1744—all these elements would move into action. According to the plan, the Brest fleet would engage Britain's Channel fleet, perhaps defeating it and certainly distracting it. The squadron of transports would meanwhile convey 12,000 French troops, commanded by Maurice of Saxony, from Dunkirk to Maldon. Only then would the British people realize what was at hand. Maurice possessed written authorization from James Edward to operate in Britain on his behalf. Lord Sempill, a Jacobite agent in France, was ecstatic: "the success is infallible."[9]

The British felt vulnerable to maritime assault, for Carteret had neglected the navy. Like many British leaders, before and since, he assumed that the navy somehow took care of itself, rising to the occasion when war began. The consequence of this folly was that Britain, although acting on the continent in a manner very likely to trigger a war with France, was leaving its fleet dispersed, its ships in disrepair, and (in the Mediterranean) its commanders at each other's throat. Fortunately for Britain, the Channel fleet was under the command of Sir John Norris. Although a seadog in his eighties, Norris was a man of prudence and common sense. The chief task of the fleet, as always, was to assert British control of the narrow straits separating Britain from the continent. As intelligence trickled in during January and February of 1744, Norris and the British government slowly fathomed the scope of French plans. When all was clear, so was his task: he was at all costs to prevent a crossing of the Channel.

Had the Brest fleet put to sea on 20 January 1744, the day fixed by the plans, it would have taken the British very much by surprise. But delays bedeviled French preparations, and the fleet did not sail out of the harbor until 8 February. Four days later Norris learned that Roquefeuil was at sea. Though he was reluctant to leave Dunkirk unattended, Norris finally concluded that he had no choice but to sail westward to engage the enemy. By the afternoon of 6 March the British and French fleets lay close to the British coast, eight miles apart and hence in view of each other. Roquefeuil had fifteen ships under his command (four others had recently slipped through into Dunkirk), and Norris had nineteen. On the coastal hilltops of Kent a crowd was gathering to watch the coming battle. But at that point an implacable force of nature intervened to seize control of events. For several days the weather had been unsettled. Now the sky began to darken, the winds to rise, and the seas to swell. By dawn on 7 March a violent gale was tearing at the fragile artifacts of human ingenuity that bobbed, scattered and impotent, on the turbulent waters. The great gale raged throughout the day. All but one of Britain's ships were damaged; five of them were placed out of action and one sank. The French fleet suffered several dismastings, but the storm was most devastating to the French in its assault on the Dunkirk harbor, where transport vessels were swept aground and the provisions and tents that the

French had so arduously been collecting for several months destroyed. Few lives had been lost (though Roquefeuil himself died at sea on 8 March—like Court, he was almost eighty), but the damage in the harbor was so great that if France wanted to pursue its plans for a descent, it would be forced to start again virtually at the beginning. For such a renewal no one at Versailles had the stomach, and so plans for a descent were allowed to lapse. Maurice of Saxony pronounced a terse and accurate judgment: "the wind is not Jacobite."[10]

The battle for the Channel was the great nonevent of the war. But it is important to realize that, had the battle been fought, Britain, with its numerical superiority and sharper élan, would probably have prevailed. Indeed, by causing greater damage to the British fleet, the storm had marginally served French ends. Nevertheless, Maurepas's grand scheme had failed, and Britain had maintained its dominance (though not a command) of the sea. The minister of marine relinquished his pretensions to overall command of the council and withdrew to the safety of naval matters. Amelot became a starker casualty of the failure, losing in April the office he had so unimpressively filled since the outbreak of the war. But even failures will have consequences. As a result of the two-pronged maritime challenge that France threw against Britain in the late winter of 1744, these two kingdoms now regarded themselves at war with each other. Formalities would follow; in the meantime, belligerence had revealed yet again its tendency to expand and consume.

THE MOMENTUM TOWARD BELLIGERENCE

By the spring of 1744 Maria Theresa was deploying the skills of her servants well. Count Kaunitz was moved from diplomacy in Turin to administration in Brussels, where he would now serve as lord high steward and direct the government of the vulnerable Austrian Netherlands. To underline still further the importance of this detached province, Maria Theresa appointed the princely newlyweds, Charles of Lorraine and her own sister Maria Anna, to be joint governors of the region. She also shifted military commands, bringing Count Traun to Bohemia (on the untimely death of Khevenhüller), Prince Liechtenstein to Moravia, and Count Batthyany to Bavaria. Only in her somewhat earlier decision to replace Traun with Lobkowitz in northern Italy did she stumble, giving new opportunities for mischief to the pompous blunderer who had allowed Belle-Isle to escape from Prague. She also won a triumph on the diplomatic front when, on 20 December 1743, Austria and Saxony formed a defensive alliance. The key clause gave a Saxon guarantee to the Austrian succession (without Silesia).

In return, Saxony received a promise that, if Maria Theresa's heirs should die, the succession to Austria and its appurtenances would pass to her aunt, Maria Josepha, the wife of Augustus III and thereby titular queen of Poland. Saxony promised to supply 6,000 troops if requested—no such request was made at the time—and Austria promised (deviously, in light of its Italian policy) not to seize Naples, where a Wettin queen sat at the side of King Charles VII.

Maria Theresa knew exactly how she wanted Austria's mounting power to be employed. After listening to Prince Charles's brief on behalf of a military campaign in Flanders in 1744 and rejecting it, she authorized instead an attack on Alsace. Her decision was chiefly a consequence of her resolution to avoid any intermingling of her troops with Britain's beyond what necessity obliged her to accept. The queen had read Charles's earlier description of a British headquarters—"it is like a republic, for each speaks and seems to have a different sentiment"[11]—and she contemned British informality as fully as she distrusted British sensitivity to Austrian interests. Alsace was a region with old Habsburg ties and was less firmly defended than French Flanders. Though it might prove advantageous to stage a diversion in the Low Countries, the major Austrian push in the west would come along the Rhine. The queen displayed similar resolution toward the imminent Italian campaign. "The conquest [of Naples]," Francis Stephen told Lobkowitz, "has become essential to the queen, if she really wishes to keep a foot in Italy."[12] With 18,000 troops, Gages had no desire to challenge Vienna's force of 25,000, and so the Spanish retreated. Despite Lobkowitz's fears that priests in central Italy would serve as spiritual guerrillas arrayed against the Austrians, his subsequent transit of the Papal States was almost leisurely, and before the month of April was at hand, the Austrians were encamped on the north bank of the Tronto, with the Neapolitan kingdom gleaming on the hither shore.

France was also laying plans for 1744, for even while the scheme to best the British on the seas faltered, the collateral scheme to engage and humble the Pragmatic Allies in the Low Countries proceeded apace. The suspension of the plan for the descent, though devastating to Maurepas's hope, simply meant that Maurice of Saxony could remain on the continent. Louis XV still relished the prospect of leading a campaign; the enemy was fortifying its strongholds in the Low Countries and reassigning troops in an ominous manner. Consequently the French laid careful plans for an attack on the fortress town of Menin, which sat just beyond the French border, and for proceeding thence northwest toward the sea, whereby they would bring maritime Flanders under control. Meanwhile, a smaller army would guard

Alsace against Austrian probes. The key to the plan was the appointment of Maurice as chief assistant to Louis XV in the Flemish campaign, and on 26 March 1744 Maurice was made Marshal of France. At forty-seven he was the youngest marshal in the kingdom—most of the other eleven were in retirement—and certainly the ablest. With Louis XV observing convention by addressing him as "my cousin," it may finally be said that the Saxon bastard had arrived.

On the diplomatic front France was similarly bellicose. To induce the United Provinces to realize the consequences of excessive Anglophilism, Versailles withdrew its ambassador late in 1743. When he returned in April 1744, he limited his activity to repeating a warning that Britain was seeking to subvert the Dutch constitution. Then, after ominously declaring that France would defend itself, he dramatically departed again to assume an officer's position in the French army. Meanwhile, in November 1743 Chavigny began his mission to Germany to lobby for the formation of an association of German princes. During a visit to Frankfurt in November 1743, he found enough interest in the association scheme to justify further efforts to promote it. His chief concern, as he explained during a return to France in February 1744, was the paralyzing effect that French efforts to unseat a Protestant ruler in Britain were having on simultaneous French efforts to mobilize German Protestants. One of them, Prince William of Hesse, asked pointedly: "Does France therefore want the universal monarchy for its favorite religion?"[13] It is understandable then that Chavigny was among those delighted when, with the abandonment of the idea of the descent, the ambiguity in France's confessional diplomacy also disappeared.

The movement toward war in Prussia was of necessity more circumspect than in France, but predictably enough it was also more coherent. Frederick II had foreseen that the Treaty of Berlin might merely mark a truce; the Treaty of Worms confirmed him in that judgment. He feared that Carteret's handiwork had conferred strategic dominance on the anti-Bourbon allies and that they would use it to impose a peace on Europe that Prussia would have no voice in. Even worse, at some point Austria would be free to renew its campaign to recover Silesia. Frederick was particularly alarmed to note that the Treaty of Berlin was not cited at Worms among the pacts to be upheld. And so he redoubled his efforts to find appropriate defenses for Prussia, reviving a proposal to create an association of princes who, in return for French subsidies, would create an army of 60,000 to serve imperial interests in Germany. His central decision, however, was far more portentous: it was time, he concluded, for Prussia to return to the war. From one point of view that was a grim conclusion. "One should never," he noted, "hazard the certain for the uncertain. Silesia is held." But finally distinguishing between a "momentary security" and a "real security," and believing himself in danger of being lulled by the former, Frederick concluded early in 1744 that only the use of armed force could secure the latter.[14]

The king calculated that his army would not be fully prepared to assume the offensive until the summer of 1744. In the meantime he needed to restore an effective working relationship with Versailles. His envoy for this purpose, Count Rothenburg, arrived in France in March, at the very moment that the maritime schemes against Britain were being reduced to shambles. He was charged to keep all discussion topics secret. The similarities between Chavigny's association plan and Frederick's provided a starting point for discussions, and concurrence on the outlines of strategic cooperation came easily. France agreed to the Prussian demand to declare war on Britain and on Austria. (Frederick insisted on these actions because they would lock France into hostilities and decrease the likelihood that it would do what Prussia had recently done: desert its ally.) On other points—a military strategy for defeating Britain and Austria, the winnings each partner could expect—the discussants were slower in finding agreement. But the delay in reaching final terms did not discourage Frederick: "this war," he wrote, "is far from being finished."[15]

The directors of Spanish policy eyed France's renewed fixation on the empire with a combination of worry and satisfaction. If too intense, the fascination might lead Louis XV to neglect his familial duties to Don Philip. But if moderate, it portended the resumption of campaigning in central Europe and the consequent attenuation of Habsburg military power in Italy. The Treaty of Fontainebleau had shown that Spain understood the connection between the German and the Italian theaters: it pledged Bourbon support to the emperor's campaign to recover and, if possible, increase his territories. Moreover, Louis XV remained personally determined to help his Spanish relatives. On 15 March 1744 France took the expected but momentous step of declaring war on Britain: no longer merely auxiliaries, the two ancient foes would now formally resume their struggle for the capacity to superintend the destiny of Europe. Somewhat over a month later, on 27 April, France completed its season of belligerence by declaring war on Austria. Meanwhile, on the first day of April the Bourbon allies plunged eastward across the Var River to begin their campaigning in northern Italy. There was springtime satisfaction at Madrid: France had unreservedly engaged itself against Spain's enemies, and a Gallispan army had taken the field in the region where Spain sought trophies. Bourbon military solidarity, forged at Fontainebleau, was finally unleashed at the Var.

10

The Engulfing Maelstrom
(April 1744 — August 1744)

THE STRUGGLE FOR NAPLES

Since the Bourbons were challenging Austria's claims to territory in northern Italy, the Austrian government had no reluctance to reciprocate by contesting Bourbon claims to territory farther south. Not surprisingly, the king of the Two Sicilies regarded this challenge as sufficient grounds for repudiating the promise extorted by Commodore Martin. Declaring that "the neutrality promised to England offends the interests of my house," the king acted in the early months of 1744 to attach his army of 13,000 to Gages's Spanish army of 12,000 in order to confront the Austrians before they penetrated his kingdom.[1] Lobkowitz was a thoroughly unaggressive foe. Fearful of contact with the enemy, he was deliberately hesitating, hoping to receive orders from Vienna to retreat. While waiting, he directed his 25,000 men to encamp in the environs of Rome, which then became the center of Austrian recreations. Soldiers visited the city and heard the crowds cheering for Maria Theresa, and Pope Benedict XIV, despite his partiality for the Bourbon cause, received both Lobkowitz and Browne at the Vatican. Bartenstein's terse remark captured the Conference's astonished despair: "time lost, everything lost."[2] Only when alerted to the approach of the Napolispan army did Lobkowitz try to rouse his troops from their Roman revels and, denied the authorization for retreat he had sought, shift them southward to face their foes.

From June through August of 1744 the ancient town of Velletri, birthplace of Caesar Augustus, was the focal point of military maneuvering. The Napolispans held the town itself, transforming it into a formidable fortification; the Austrians controlled the hills to the north. But they also remained ensnared in the sweet temptations of the Roman countryside, filling their camps with prostitutes and strawberries. Gages took advantage of Austrian carelessness. On the night of 16-17 June, guided by several Spanish-born soldiers who had defected from Austrian service, he led 5,000 troops in a surprise attack on Austrian positions. The result was a debacle for Austria. The men guarding the advance posts were caught asleep; their commander was visiting a winery. A besotted and confounded unit of 1,000 Austrians was virtually wiped out, and three important hills passed from Austrian to Spanish hands. This engagement, sometimes called the battle of Nemi and otherwise (as here) called the first battle of Velletri, conferred upon the Napolispan forces both military credibility and strategic advantage. But rather than capitalize on their success, the Spanish then lapsed back into the warfare of immobility and wasted their opportunity. At the time the reasons for prudence seemed powerful. The great enemy of all armies in Italy—the unstaunchable flow of deserters —worried the Spanish commander. But the fruit of prudence was a month and a half of wasteful inactivity.

Lobkowitz and Browne, meanwhile, set about imposing discipline on their slack army. They dispatched a battalion to Abruzzi to proclaim Maria Theresa queen of Naples; it won a measure of support but was finally expelled. They also authorized the circulation of a proclamation setting forth Maria Theresa's plans for the kingdom if her family should be restored to power. Some of her promises were attractive—a rolling back of taxation, an end to conscription, the abolition of a notorious tribunal— but she lamed their effect by pledging to expel Jews from the kingdom, forgetting that her personal brand of intense anti-Semitism was uncongenial to many people in this most cosmopolitan of Italian cities. Finally, Lobkowitz and Browne elaborated a scheme to embark about 2,500 Austrian troops on British vessels and to land them near the city of Naples. Steps to implement this extraordinary plan were well under way when in early August electrifying news reached Lobkowitz. King Charles VII had arrived at Velletri, a scant few miles from Austrian outposts. Instantly all had changed. Rather than capture a kingdom, Lobkowitz proposed to kidnap a king.

The abrupt shift in objectives produced changes in the nature of planning; speed and secrecy were now of the essence. Velletri sat on a ridge between two coursing streams, and its gates were guarded against intruders. But intelligence suggested that the same incaution that had cost the Austrians so dearly in June was making inroads among the Neapolitan occupiers of the town. And so in the predawn hours of 11 August 1744 Lobkowitz launched a daring abduction scheme. Led by Browne, 6,000 Austrian troops moved quietly to the southern gate of the city, through which they swept into the streets of Velletri. They had so successfully caught the Napolispans unaware that Gages was away from the city inspecting hilltop outposts, and the Austrians' major immediate danger was posed not by enemy troops but by irate citizens, who fired on them from their windows. But at this point the plan began to unravel. Rather than moving quickly on the Ginetti Palace, where Charles VII was lodged, the Austrians took to looting and drinking. In behavior reminiscent, *mutatis mutandi*, of behavior at Chotusitz, the Austrian force squandered its great initial advantage. Guards at the palace, which was located at the northern edge of the city, had ample warning of what was ensuing. The monarch quickly escaped the palace by a window and fled, half dressed, on horseback. He then began to regroup his forces outside the city for a counterattack. Once alerted to what was happening in Velletri, Gages did likewise. When Browne realized that his quarry had eluded capture, that expected reinforcements were delayed, and that his own force was in danger of encirclement, he ordered a retreat. It was disorganized, for many of the Austrians were now drunk and most were trying to carry their plunder with them. A number perished in the nearby streams, and many of those who tarried too long in the city met even crueler deaths beneath Bourbon axes. But by 9:00 A.M. most of the attackers had succeeded in returning to the Austrian camp.[3] For the third time in the war—Frederick II at Baumgarten and George II at Dettingen being the earlier occasions—a king had narrowly escaped capture.

The second battle of Velletri saved the Bourbon regime in Naples. Had King Charles VII been captured, Austria would have controlled a hostage of monumental significance. Had Velletri fallen—not Lobkowitz's purpose but still a possibility—the road to Naples would have lain open and the discontented in the kingdom encouraged to revolt. But neither happened. At the cost of 3,500 casualties (including 2,100 prisoners), the Napolispan army had foiled the Austrian plot. Moreover, the king had behaved bravely and his Neapolitan troops magnificently. Charles VII used the victory to consolidate his rule. It effaced the memory of his submission to Commodore Martin's demands. On 8 September 1744 he celebrated the triumph with a festival, and in later years this annual celebration became the kingdom's national holiday. The choice was apt: the second battle of Velletri had preserved the realm and—though no one could then have known it—repulsed the last Austrian threat to southern Italy until the nineteenth century.

Oddly, however, though King Charles VII viewed the battle as a victory, Lobkowitz did not initially construe it as a defeat. Austrian losses, numbering 1,500, had been far fewer than Napolispan.[4] Lobkowitz reported the raid to be a success, and even such a cautious analyst as Charles Emmanuel at first credited the report. But in the next three months the deeper meaning of the ambiguous battle revealed itself: the Austrian march on Naples was stalled. And in the last reckoning the chief blame for the stalling rested with the willful torpor of Lobkowitz. In November 1743 he had argued that he needed 25,000 troops if he was to conquer Naples. Maria Theresa had contrived to give him the number he requested. Even so, he had not used them. In the last analysis Lobkowitz was an ineffective leader, yet another example of Maria Theresa's flawed judgment in assessing her generals. The orders he received shortly after the assault on Velletri—they had been drafted in Vienna three days prior to the battle—underlined Austria's acknowledgment of this fact: Lobkowitz was instructed to transfer an infantry regiment northward to the beleaguered Charles Emmanuel. Manpower was not to be wasted where it could not be usefully employed.

PIEDMONT EXPOSED

When the Gallispan army surged across the Var on 1 April 1744, a facade of unity cloaked fundamental differences between the two Bourbon allies. Some of the disagreements were personal. The Prince of Conti, for example, despaired of reasoning with the Marquis de La Mina. The Spanish commander, in Conti's view, "defers blindly to all the orders that come from Spain."[5] Other differences were rooted in competing national prides. Bourbon solidarity might yoke Versailles and Madrid, but it did not dispose Jacques and Juan to cooperate. The central difference between the French and Spanish armies, however, was strategic: although the 30,000-man Bourbon force had been launched so that the world might have no doubts about the effectiveness of the Family Compact, in fact the purpose of the campaign once Nice and Villefranche had been conquered still remained undetermined. Two choices were available. Either, as Spain insisted, the Bourbons could continue marching eastward along the coast, slicing through the Genoese republic (while perhaps enlisting its support) and striking finally into the Parmesan region that Don Philip sought as his own; or, as France replied, they could wheel to the north and attack the fortress principality of Piedmont, hoping to force Charles Emmanuel to abandon Austria and withdraw from the war. The strategic quarrel pitted the unlettered adamance of Elizabeth Farnese against the sober reasonings of French military advisors. When the French warned that an advance along the narrow paths of the Ligurian coast exposed a defenseless army to a pummeling from the sea, Elizabeth Farnese ignored the point completely. "We have no need that any one should propose plans to us," she said with the blithe peremptoriness born of the habit of being obeyed; "we make the plans and order their execution."[6] When asked to justify her obstinacy, she explained that she knew the coastal route well because she had been carried along it in a sedan chair on her wedding trip to Spain!

But Conti was not to be stampeded into a campaign he thought unsound by reasonings he thought bizarre. From the perspective of Versailles, the key purpose of Gallispan campaigning was to defeat Piedmont-Sardinia, not to occupy Don Philip's future realm. "The King of Sardinia has failed us," Louis XV explained to Philip V, "we must make him repent of it."[7] The standoff ended, as Bourbon family quarrels usually did, with a compromise. On 11 June 1744, having wrung commitments from France that an attack on Lombardy would swiftly follow the humbling of Piedmont-Sardinia, the Spanish king assented to France's priorities. Indeed, a thorough humbling was not required: all that France sought was the taking of the strategically vital fortress at Cuneo. The season was still young. With 33,000 invading troops against 26,000 defenders, the Bourbons could anticipate a reasonably prompt success at Cuneo and ample time for proceeding thereafter against the Italian lands of Maria Theresa. From Spain's perspective the entry into the promised land was thus deferred but not discarded.

The basic problem for anyone who proposed to attack Piedmont from the west was gaining entry through the Alps, still snow-capped in June. The scheme for accomplishing this goal was devised by Lieutenant-General Pierre-Joseph de Bourcet, France's foremost authority on Alpine warfare. Bourcet believed that the Gallispans could most effectively use their numerical advantage by putting simultaneous pressure on several outlying defense works and by rushing troops into Piedmont wherever the Piedmontese army finally crumpled. He saw no value in head-on, suicidal assaults against entrenched fortifications. He preferred indirect approaches, for they could permit invaders to envelop a fortification and mount attacks from unexpected directions. From all these general considerations a plan coalesced. The Bourbons should regroup in Dauphiné. They should then march eastward into the mountains along nine different routes, seizing Piedmontese outposts as they advanced and filtering down into the valleys of the Varaita, the Maira, and the Stura rivers. These advancing units should remain in communication with each other. When the extended Piedmontese defense perimeter finally cracked, the probing units should promptly reunite to push through the hole. Bourcet's calculation was that although the dividing of forces was an unsound procedure in flat country, it could be advantageous in the mountains if communications and a capable staff permitted well-articulated coordination.[8] The Alps would test his belief.

The regrouping began in June. Leaving infantry units at Nice and Antibes and artillery units south of the Tenda pass, Conti moved the bulk of his army into Dauphiné. There they gathered adjacent to the Piedmontese frontier, extending from the vicinity of Briançion southward through Barcelonnette to St. Étienne. On 5 July 1744 the advance from these encampments into Piedmont began, and by the middle of the month all nine divisions were in motion. Experience in earlier wars had taught the French that they could expect to force no more than 4,800 troops through an undefended mountain pass a day. So the advance on all fronts was slow as the troops pushed first to the fall line and then descended cautiously down the eastern flank of the range. La Mina's carelessness about security—drafts of the Spanish plan of campaign circulated freely—drove Conti to distraction and prompted him to inform Versailles that "it is impossible to carry on war with an ally whose incapacity, ill will, and bad faith upset every arrangement."[9] But despite these problems, the scheme unfolded successfully. Outlying garrisons submitted or withdrew. The Bourbon army crept toward the heart of Piedmont-Sardinia.

The first electrifying triumph occurred along the Stura. Having filed through the Argentière pass to enter Piedmont, several Bourbon divisions then fanned out as they proceeded down the high valley of the churning Stura River. The chief obstacle before them was the aptly named Barricades, a spot where the Stura valley narrowed to a defile less than twenty feet wide between precipices and where the path leapt from one shore to the other across an insubstantial bridge. Heeding Bourcet's advice, the Gallispans turned the position by filtering troops through to the north and the south until finally the strong point was in danger of being surrounded. Rather than fall victim to a well-laid pincers movement, the Piedmontese withdrew, and in mid-July the Barricades passed bloodlessly to Gallispan control. The feat—one of the great achievement of arms of eighteenth-century mountain warfare—vindicated Bourcet and astonished Europe. It constituted, moreover, the breakthrough Conti had reckoned on, and orders immediately went out along the communications network for the Gallispan divisions to suspend probing operations elsewhere and converge toward the Stura.

As these orders were wending their way through the Alps, the Gallispans enjoyed a second victory. Casteldefino stood near the headwaters of the Varaita. Commanding a height, it dominated the surrounding area. Charles Emmanuel himself directed its 2,000 defenders. Initially the French commander, Lieutenant-General Givry, was inclined to be cautious, but François de Chevert, a hero at Prague in November 1741, persuaded Givry to authorize an attack. On 19 July, in the face of unremitting artillery fire, 4,500 French troops scrambled up the rock, climbing on the shoulders of living comrades and the bodies of the dead to scale the wall and fling themselves on the defenders. Whereas the Barricades had fallen without a shot being fired,

Casteldefino fell only after a horrendous bloodletting that cost the Gallispans 1,600 casualties and the Piedmontese 900.[10] Givry himself was among the victims. Although Spanish troops participated in the engagement, it was the French who distinguished themselves. "There will be occasions when we will do as well as the French," the Spanish commander wrote to La Mina, "for it is not possible to do better."[11] And in France itself the political nation, at last given grounds for celebration after two years of embarrassment, toasted the triumphs of Conti and his troops.

The Stura valley remained the preferred avenue, its path to Cuneo protected now only by the fortress at Demonte. Though slowed by the need to bring up artillery and harried by a peasantry that greeted the invaders by destroying livestock, Conti moved his forces into the vicinity of Demonte early in August, and on the night of 8-9 August 1744 (a scant thirty-six hours before the second battle of Velletri was to begin several hundred miles to the south), he initiated the siege of the town. Its course was swift and devastating. By raining artillery bombs into the precincts of Demonte, the Gallispans ignited much that was flammable. Food supplies perished in the fires, houses were lost, and, most fearsome of all, the powder magazine was in peril. On 17 August 1744 the municipal authorities surrendered the shattered stronghold to the Gallispans, who then pillaged the town, sending a message of intimidation across the entire principality. From Demonte they could look down on the plain of Monferrat and the great stronghold of Cuneo. Savoring his triumph and exulting in the havoc wrought by his weapons and men, La Mina relished the prospect of an imminent end to the campaign in Piedmont. "We are going straight to Cuneo," he boasted, "which will naturally have the same fate as Demonte."[12]

THE BERLIN-VERSAILLES AXIS RESTORED

One of the lessons Frederick II had learned from his Moravian embarrassment of early 1742 was that success in military campaigning depended on adequate preparations. And so he fixed two prerequisites for a resumption of Prussian military action in 1744: a pact of cooperation among the important German rulers and an alliance with Louis XV. The German arrangement came first. As early as January 1744 Joachim Wilhelm von Klinggräffen had begun negotiations at Frankfurt with the emperor's chief advisor, Count Seckendorff. On 22 May they signed the Recess of Frankfurt, a limited but useful document. Its chief accomplishment was the calling into existence of a confederation of four German princes—the emperor and the rulers of Prussia, Hesse-Cassel, and the Electoral Palatine—who pledged themselves to defend the imperial constitution. This confederation was styled the Union of Frankfurt. The four called for a truce in the war so that the imperial judiciary could pronounce on the controverted issue of the Habsburg succession in German lands. But since they thought a truce unlikely, they also pledged to support one another and offered guarantees of one another's possessions. The document went further still. It invoked the peace of Westphalia by calling upon France to protect Germany in accordance with the terms of that settlement; thus, whereas eight months earlier Frederick had sponsored a proposal designed to keep France out of the empire, he was now accepting a document that invited France in. The terms of the Recess were to be kept secret for the present. But rumors about the pact slowly spread among the chancelleries of Europe, and a continent already uneasy about Prussian intentions became more disquieted still.

When Frederick agreed to the terms of the Recess of Frankfurt, he already knew that Versailles was mobilizing itself for a military initiative in Germany. Count Rothenburg's talks with Noailles and Tencin, though far from smooth, were progressing toward an agreement on that point. Owing to the Botta affair, Frederick felt confident that Russia would not attack him. But he still worried that once Prussia had returned to the war, France might withdraw, exposing him as a friendless treaty-violator to Maria Theresa's savage wrath. To render a French withdrawal unlikely, he proposed a timetable for action that would put French troops into Germany prior to a Prussian reentry into the war. On this point the French were chary. The Low Countries were, after all, their chief priority. But they did not want to appear unreceptive to Prussian proposals, since the Union of Frankfurt constituted, in Chavigny's words, a "barrier which will be forever useful to us."[13] Therefore, Noailles and Tencin assured Rothenburg that a vigorous French push in the Low Countries coupled with the stationing of an army in Alsace would prevent Austria from rushing troops back into Bohemia when Prussia invaded it. When Louis XV left Versailles on 3 May 1744 to join the French army destined for Flanders, thereby signaling France's determination to seize the initiative in this Austrian-controlled region, that action sufficed for Frederick. On 5 June 1744, almost exactly three years after the signing of the earlier Franco-Prussian treaty, Tencin and Rothenburg signed the Treaty of Paris, and the two kingdoms became partners once again.

As with the Recess of Frankfurt, the existence of the Treaty of Paris was to be concealed. Secrecy might prevent, and would certainly retard, Austrian preparations to counteract Prussia's reentry. That reentry, as envisioned by the treaty, was to be an explosive one. Frederick pledged to unleash 80,000 troops on Bohemia in August—an army over three times the size of the one he fired into Silesia in 1740. The declared purpose of the invasion was to secure Bohemia for Charles VII and, more generally, to restore the emperor's authority in the empire. But Prussia, as we have seen, expected to be rewarded for its service, and if Charles VII would not sanction the reward, Frederick would settle for the approval of Charles's paymaster. The treaty identified not only Bohemian lands north of the Elbe as Frederick's dessert but also the Kolin and Pardubice regions south of the Elbe and the small chunk of Silesia left to Austria in 1742. France in turn pledged itself to march into the Austrian Netherlands, with the avowed purpose of seizing and annexing the barrier fortresses of Ypres, Tournai, and Furnes; and simultaneously to place an army along the Moselle, whence it could protect Frederick's Rhenish holdings and intimidate the Hanoverians. Frederick had wanted a French invasion of Germany; he settled for a French promise to pursue Austria's Rhenish army if it withdrew from the Rhine to assist in the defense of Bohemia. Each power compromised to please the other, Prussia retreating from its initial demand that France declare war on the Dutch, and France dropping its insistence for direct Prussian aid for Spain. With France now having agreed to the dismemberment of Bohemia, Emperor Charles VII could not hope to hold out. And on 24 July 1744 the three relevant entities — Prussia, France, and the emperor—agreed to confirm Prussia's claims to important portions of conquered Bohemia. The diplomatic structure for a renewed campaign against Austria was now totally in place.

If we reflect for a moment on the renewed coalescence of the anti-Habsburg alliance in 1744, we are struck by two puzzling points. French officials had begun the year resolved to minimize the German war. Why were they now reentering it? Prussia had deliberately left the war in 1742 to enjoy the benefits of peace. Why was Frederick now putting aside those benefits? For France the answer is clear. Versailles accepted Frederick's tender because renewed Prussian pressure against Austria would force Vienna to pull troops back from Italy, and because the terms of the alliance allowed France to continue to treat the Low Countries as the primary theater. For its part Prussia reentered the war both because it feared the type of peace a victorious Austria might impose on Europe, and because Frederick had decided that a renewal of military involvement could allow Prussia to secure valuable central European real estate. But the whole matter is susceptible to an even simpler explanation. As Frederick proleptically assured Fleury in the summer of 1742, Maria Theresa would never forget either Lorraine or Silesia, and "consequently our interests will always be the same."[14]

BELLIGERENCE ALONG THE FRENCH PERIMETER

France placed four armies in the field in 1744. Two of these were comparatively small: in Italy, as we have already noted, the Prince of Conti commanded a force that numbered somewhat more than 30,000; and between the Meuse and Moselle rivers a 17,000-man force led by the Duke d'Harcourt kept Luxembourg tranquil. A far more sizable army, led by the Duke of Coigny and totaling approximately 57,000 soldiers, patrolled the left bank of the Rhine with the task of shielding Alsace from Prince Charles. Meanwhile, the largest French army gathered along France's northern frontier, preparing to advance into the Austrian Netherlands. The army of Flanders, numbering 87,000 troops, was in turn divided into two corps. The larger, consisting of about 50,000 men, was assigned to the king, who would be advised in his military decision making by the Duke of Noailles. To this corps was assigned the chief offensive task of conquering various barrier fortresses in the Austrian Netherlands. The smaller corps, embracing 37,000 men, was entrusted to Maurice of Saxony, whose task was to guard the king's force from any threats that the allied army in the province might offer. On 17 May the army of Flanders, which had gathered in the vicinity of Lille, invaded the Austrian Netherlands. The French outnumbered the allies in the Low Countries by a ratio of about four to three. Even if Austria should respond to the attack by sending Prince Charles's Rhenish army of about 80,000 men into Alsace, the armies of Harcourt and Coigny stood ready to meet them. When all the various forces are summed up, the French had the preponderance of manpower in the region from the middle reaches of the Rhine to the lower reaches of the Meuse and the Scheldt.[15] And they knew that in August Prussia would hurl a large army against the Austrians in Bohemia, further tipping the scale their way.

The allies proposed to meet this challenge with a force that by June numbered about 65,000, including the 15,000 troops then manning the barrier fortresses. This allied army, clustering chiefly near Ghent, was bedeviled with leadership problems. The Dutch contingent—a force of 20,000 ill-prepared troops—was present because the Barrier Treaty required Dutch participation when the Austrian Netherlands were threatened, but the Dutch commander, Prince Maurice of Nassau, had little taste for fighting. In fact, the United Provinces, unlike Britain and Austria, were still at peace with France and supplying the Bourbon kingdom with, among other items, naval stores.[16] The Austrian contingent, scarcely 7,000 strong, was commanded by Leopold, Duke of Aremberg. He held lands in Hainault and sometimes showed an unprofessional preference for protecting that region rather than others.· The bulk of the defending army was comprised of British and

Hanoverian troops. They numbered 38,000 and were led by the septuagenarian field marshal, George Wade, whose minor reputation rested upon nothing more spirited than his superintendence of road-building activities in the wilds of Scotland. In theory the three commanders shared equality of status. In practice, Wade exercised dominant influence by virtue of commanding the largest component in the allied army. He was ill disposed toward offensive action, even rejecting Prince Charles's proposal for an attack on the French in April. "Never have I seen people more indecisive than they," the prince spit out with disgust after his talks with the bickering commanders.[17]

The fortress at Menin was one of the creations of that master craftsman among Louis XIV's military engineers, Marshal Vauban. It sat just within the territory of the Austrian Netherlands, the first obstacle facing any army advancing north from Lille. Fifteen hundred Dutch troops manned its crumbling defenses. The French began digging the trenches for their siege on the night of 28-29 May 1744. The Dutch resistance was feeble and marked by amiable chatting between defenders and besiegers. On 5 June the garrison surrendered. Swift as this siege was, Maurice asserted that it might have been still swifter had it not been, in effect, Louis XV's nursery in warfare. "The king takes a great liking to this profession," Maurice added, "and it seems to me that he has never recognized his power so well."[18] The king's next target was Ypres. It was one of the three fortresses—Knocke and Furnes were the other two—which Vauban had regarded as a collective and virtually impassable wall to invaders from the south. The French were accordingly wary. But the operation at Ypres mocked all caution. The siege began on 15 June, and just nine days later the Dutch garrison surrendered. Knocke was next on the French agenda, and here the resistance was risible. Within hours of the opening of the Duke of Boufflers's siege on 29 June the fortress surrendered. Less than two weeks later the capering campaign succeeded again, as Furnes surrendered. The vaunted fastnesses of Vauban were perishing like pricked bubbles, and the whole southern sector of maritime Flanders was in French hands.

Of all the allies, the Dutch were the most confused by the ease of the French advance. "There is anarchy in Holland," Carteret wrote in June,[19] and the remark was apt. On one side there were those, led by William Bentinck, who suffered under the knowledge that their once proud nation had become a European laughingstock. They prescribed the elevation of William, Prince of Orange, to the vacant stadholderships of several of the provinces; Bentinck was even willing to ask the British to aid in toppling the feckless republican government and in installing the prince. On the other side there were those who felt that peace on almost any terms was now essential for the republic. They contrived to have the Dutch government dispatch Count Wassenaer-Twickel to Louis XV to plead for a general settlement. Wassenaer (as he was usually called)[20] reached the king in Lille, even before the campaign began, but the French, confident in May and triumphant thereafter, were not inclined to listen to entreaties from their enfeebled neighbor. It was not until 22 July that the Duke of Noailles and the Count d'Argenson informed the Dutch envoy that they found his proposals unacceptable. Feebleness at home and feebleness abroad were proving to be mutually reinforcing.

The strategic situation had abruptly changed, however, on 30 June 1744 when Prince Charles of Lorraine began to direct his 70,000-man Austrian army across the Rhine into Alsace, toward the land that gave his family its title. Although the Austrian attack did not surprise the French, they had hoped it would not fall. And in truth there were many in Austria who doubted the wisdom of an invasion of Alsace in the summer of 1744. Maria Theresa had chosen that target the previous winter, when she had decided to rip from France or from French protection some Rhenish lands that had once been part of the empire. The fact that Lorraine, her husband's ancestral home, was among the lands only quickened her determination. But as rumors about the Recess of Frankfurt spread, the queen's councillors grew cautious. Some argued that if Prussia was actually planning to return to the war, it was inadvisable to send Prince Charles's force beyond the Rhine. Others suggested that a campaign in the west might still be appropriate, but that it ought to use the Austrian Netherlands as its base and thereby protect that outlying province. The queen was unmoved by these reasonings. "Do not let yourself be troubled by the King of Prussia," she wrote one commander; "do not think of him."[21]

Alsace had belonged to France for less than a century. Most of its inhabitants spoke German. Though still farther west, bilingual Lorraine was not yet France's: according to the terms of the settlement of 1738, this region, wrested from Prince Charles's brother and given as a sop to the would-be king of Poland, Stanislas Leczinski, would pass on Stanislas's death to the house of Bourbon. The French government was deeply worried about the Austrian invasion into this region of dubious loyalty. And so by 20 July Louis XV and an army of about 32,000 were marching toward Alsace. Marshal Noailles had already sped ahead to Metz to confer with Marshal Belle-Isle. The rest of the army of Flanders, numbering 55,000, was left with Maurice of Saxony, who was under orders to forgo offensive action. The king's advisors did not disguise their worries: Louis XV, still a novice at siege warfare, was preparing to engage the enemy in battle formations he had no experience with. It seemed to some an invitation to catastrophe.

It also—in light of the obvious option of entrusting the army to Noailles—seemed unnecessary. By crossing the Rhine, Prince Charles had made himself a captive of geography. It is true that Coigny had withdrawn toward Strasbourg, leaving various Alsatian towns to the Austrians. On one occasion, memorialized as the "affair of the wigs," the invaders so frightened the valets of a French detachment that in the ensuing scramble the French officers were knocked into the ditch by their own servants and their valises (and wigs) were carried off on stampeding horses. The advance heartened Prince Charles, and he wrote his wife that he might soon be addressing her from Paris. But in fact the fragility of the Austrian position grew daily clearer. With Coigny stiffening his troops, the army of Flanders approaching from the west, Harcourt approaching from the Moselle, Belle-Isle mobilizing his garrison, and Seckendorff regathering imperial troops, the Austrians stood in danger of soon being outnumbered and trapped with their backs to one of Europe's great rivers. Prince Charles had scarcely set foot in France before he began repenting of the enterprise.

Nevertheless, for several weeks the outcome was unclear. Fighting flared up at Wissemburg, as the French first recovered and then again relinquished the town. Neither side was placatory. The Austrian Pandours surged into battle calling out "Allah! Allah!" The French retorted with a chilling "Kill! Kill!"[22] Together the two armies sustained almost 3,000 casualties in the largely meaningless engagement. And meanwhile, in the Austrian Netherlands, the allies finally bestirred themselves. By marching on Tournai and then Lille, Wade hoped to lure Maurice away from Courtrai and into battle. But Maurice did not budge. From his stronghold at Courtrai he protected maritime Flanders, and he knew that the enemy, lacking the equipment to besiege Lille, would soon be forced to withdraw from French territory. Thus in the opening weeks of August a tactical and cautious struggle of moves and countermoves marked both Alsace and the Low Countries. But then at a stroke all changed: on 15 August 1744 Frederick II declared war on Maria Theresa. With that act Europe's most celebrated soldier and most efficient army were once again belligerents.

PRUSSIA REJOINS THE FRAY

It was not until 12 July 1744, when Frederick II received confirmation that Prince Charles had taken his army beyond the Rhine and into France, that the king sent his final commitment to Louis XV. He set forth a bold vision. The success of the anti-Austrian alliance would depend, he declared, on conquering three territories—Bohemia, Hanover, and Bavaria. The first target was entrusted to Prussia, and Frederick planned a swift victory. The second target was assigned to France, and it was to encourage French vigor in an assault on Hanover that Frederick peppered Louis XV with both advice and flattery—including the oleaginous assurance that "I would not dare to tell Your Majesty that his initial efforts are masterstrokes; but no one will prevent me from thinking it."[23] The third target was a joint responsibility, with France asked to fund the emperor's liberation of his electorate while Prussia supplied auxiliary troops. Frederick had spent two years increasing his army to 140,000 men and imposing stern discipline on them; he had taxed his subjects onerously so that he might stuff his coffers with close to 6 million thalers (£1.5 million), twice the sum expended on the first Silesian war. He was therefore confident that Prussia could accomplish its allotted task, and his only worries concerned Hanover and Bavaria.

Yet even as he prepared his exhortations for the French king, Frederick knew that at least one aspect of his carefully crafted scheme was falling apart. Gallingly, the failure was not even his own fault, but France's. Late in 1743 Versailles had sent the vain Marquis de La Chétardie back to Russia. He began his second posting to St. Petersburg inauspiciously, when he received a ridiculous wound after picking a fight with the man who had recently represented French interests. Worse soon followed. He tried to overbear the empress, reminding her of her many obligations to him. Elizabeth had a genuine affection for this man who had once been her champion, but as a ruler of a vast realm she was not accustomed to being lectured to by presumptuous foreigners. In irritation at her intractability, La Chétardie began to confide his judgments of her to coded dispatches: she was, he noted, "frivolous and dissipated," immersed in "voluptuous lethargy."[24] That was his great mistake. Alexis Bestuzhev had the dispatches intercepted, and he showed their contents to the astonished empress. Her response was swift and decisive. On 28 June 1744 La Chétardie was expelled from Russia—"I never saw a pickpocket drummed out of a garrison with more infamy than La Chétardie was *culbuté* out of this Empire," the British envoy wrote[25]—and on 6 August the empress rewarded the loyal Bestuzhev by naming him grand chancellor. Meanwhile, French-instigated negotiations among the Russians, Prussians, and Swedes were broken off.

When Frederick notified Louis XV that the attack on Bohemia was scheduled for mid-August, he did not yet know the full extent of the damage wrought by La Chétardie's stupidity. But he knew enough to warrant adding to his letter the assertion that his decision to engage was a mark of his goodwill, since the stipulated conditions with respect to Russia had not been fulfilled. As the day of the attack drew near, Frederick slowly dropped all subterfuge. On 5 August he asked Saxony's permission to march troops through the electorate into Bohemia; the request was an empty formality, for when the Prussians moved nine days later permission had not been secured. On 8 August Frederick's envoy in Vienna informed the Austrians of the existence of the Union of Frankfurt and issued minatory statements about Prussian support for the emperor and empire. The Austrians were already reading the signs aright. On 5 August Count Batthyany, commanding the queen's troops in Bavaria, received notification from Vienna that Prussia would soon attack. On 8 August the same notification reached Prince Charles, who was directed to send the bulk of his forces back across the Rhine to contend with the king of Prussia. The lingering suspense finally ended less than a week later when, on 14 August 1744 (the day before the final declaration of hostilities), a force of 80,000 Prussian troops began storming across the frontier into Bohemia. War had returned to central Europe.

Frederick explained his action in different ways to different audiences. He accused Maria Theresa of cultivating plans to recover Silesia. The attack was thus preemptive in nature. He condemned Carteret for neglecting Prussian interests in Britain's vast diplomatic schemes. The attack was, by this light, protective. He fretted that his ally France was enduring an invasion. This perspective transformed the attack into an act of loyalty. In his formal public explanation he said simply that he was acting so that he might "render liberty to the Empire, dignity to the Emperor, and repose to Europe."[26] In fact, of course, all of these rationales missed the key points. Frederick acted because he feared that Austria was restructuring Germany in a manner that would be inimical to his interests, and because he suspected that the Austrians had now so extensively committed themselves throughout Europe that their central European lands again offered trophies for the plucking. He was not a protonationalist of German dimensions. He was not a defender of the ancient usages of a still more ancient empire. He was a calculating European politician, still the richest embodiment among all his ruling contemporaries of the ethic of raison d'état.

The British were mortified. Carteret's grand design had signally failed, both by underestimating Bourbon tenacity and by exaggerating Prussian malleability. It is now conventional to denounce the Treaty of Worms as a disaster. But it is important to realize that Britain's fundamental error was not the treaty itself but the underlying belief that the Bourbon states were conquerable. In fact, under the configuration of forces then existing, there was nothing Britain could have done to create a situation that might have allowed London to impose terms on Versailles. The third phase of the war, now opening, would give the clearest evidence possible that while Carteret's technical skills as a diplomat may have been considerable, his strategic vision was flawed. And if London was embarrassed, Vienna was frightened. Not only was the war wider than it had ever been, it was also shifting in an anti-Austrian direction. The southwestern portion of the Austrian Netherlands was in French hands. Bourbon troops controlled the Stura valley and were advancing on Cuneo. Other Bourbon troops blocked an Austrian incursion into the Neapolitan kingdom. And now the Prussians had challenged the Austrians far closer to home, at a time when Austria's major army was over 400 miles away and isolated by a great river. For over two years Vienna had enjoyed more successes than failures. But overextension now threatened to exact a savage price. Bartenstein's compact prose captures the mood of the hour: "the situation of Her Majesty is dangerous in the highest degree; on one side wicked enemies, and on the other false friends."[27]

P·A·R·T III

A Cacophony of Purposes
(August 1744 – December 1745)

11

The Worms Alliance Flourishes
(August 1744 – January 1745)

PRUSSIA'S BOHEMIAN FOLLY

In German historiography, the conflagration ignited by Prussia in August of 1744 is called the Second Silesian War. The name, though disguising a Bohemian provenance, is apt. Frederick had deliberately reopened territorial issues presumably resolved in the summer of 1742. Maria Theresa thus felt herself absolved from all obligations to honor the terms she had agreed to at Berlin. But before the Austrians could hope to dislodge the Prussians from Silesia, they had to find a way to defend Bohemia against the triple thrust of Prussia's assault. Frederick's own column, numbering 40,000 troops, swept past Dresden to enter Bohemia from the north. The Young Dessauer commanded 16,000 troops·who attacked the kingdom from the northeast. Count Schwerin led yet another 16,000 out of Silesia in the east. All three made haste for Prague, which was defended by an Austrian garrison of only 17,000. Batthyany stood in the Upper Palatinate with an additional 21,000 regular troops, but against the converging Prussian columns he dared not risk his precious and outmanned force. Vienna, it appeared, would be unable to defend its Bohemian kingdom unless it could manage to extricate Prince Charles's army from beyond the Rhine and bring it swiftly into the central European theater.

At this point Austria enjoyed a stroke of beneficent fortune. In the second week of August, while moving through Lorraine to bring his French army into a position to engage the Austrians, Louis XV fell ill of smallpox. Clogged by fears that the king might die, the French military effort ground to a halt. The enfeebled king urged Noailles to continue the offensive, but when the Austrians began to recross the Rhine on August 23, they encountered virtually as little resistance as they had met upon entering France. Frederick II, who recognized immediately the strategic implications of the eastward escape of 50,000 Austrian troops, was reduced to expressions of astonishment and rage. He concluded that the best way to deal with the new situation was to place a firm clamp on Bohemia before Prince Charles could unite his force with Batthyany's. The operation had its brutal moments—on 12 September Frederick saw a cousin's head blown away by an artillery shell—but on the whole it was not a bloody siege, and on 16 September Prague surrendered. In predictable fashion the Prussians began to impress inhabitants of the city into the Prussian army and to lay financial exactions on the entire populace. These actions led the Viennese ministry to hope that Frederick had finally overreached himself. "It will be much to crush this devil. . . ," Francis Stephen wrote, "and to end his capacity to frighten us. And that is what I hope for from divine providence."[1]

As August passed into September, four developments coincided to strengthen Vienna's hand in its forthcoming struggle with Berlin. First, precisely at this moment Austria became the beneficiary of a new British grant. The Convention of London, signed on 11 August 1744, pledged the British to pay £150,000 to Vienna so that the Austrians might put 20,000 more men into the field. Second, the Saxons agreed to supply 20,000 troops to the campaign against Frederick II. Stung by the disappointments associated with the cooperation with Prussia in 1741 and 1742, Count Brühl used the summer of 1744 to catalyze anti-Hohenzollern sentiment and return Saxony to its more customary course of opposition to Prussia. Third, Maria Theresa dashed to Bratislava and won a promise from the Hungarian nobility of 25,000 additional Insurrection troops. Fourth, Bohemia itself proved loyal. Upon entering the kingdom, Frederick had issued a patent on behalf of the emperor. But mindful of how in 1742 Maria Theresa had exacted retribution for disloyalty, the Bohemian nobility removed themselves from Prussian-controlled areas, either to journey to Vienna to display their fealty or to rally partisans to assail the invaders. Meanwhile, the Bohemian peasantry greeted the Prussians with the same belligerent free-spiritedness that the Moravians had displayed in 1742.

These developments presented Frederick with a dilemma. The prudent line of thought advised the fortification and reinforcement of Prague. From that redoubt the Austro-Saxon forces could be repulsed and the northeastern quadrant of Bohemia secured. The presence of 33,000 fresh troops in Prussia would inhibit any Austrian effort to besiege the city, and a standoff therefore seemed likely. The Prussian monarch, however, prompted by past successes and by confidence in his troops, chose a bolder course. Rather than confining himself to the northeastern quadrant, he grabbed the eastern half of Bohemia, defying his enemies to wrest it from him. Frederick's mood was apparently caught by a French diplomat who, after conversations with the king, reported that "he proposed nothing less than to crush the phantom of the House of Austria; these are his favorite expressions."[2] Prince Charles, however, viewed all these matters in a different light. Astonished at Frederick's blithe disregard of the dangers of overextension, Charles believed that the Prussian king had arrogantly invited the miseries of deprivation and even starvation to attend his own army. "In truth," he wrote, "I believe that God has blinded him, for his movements are those of a fool."[3]

In fact, Frederick was not as sanguine as his bravado suggested. On 2 October 1744, the very day the Prussians captured Hluboka nad Vltavou, Prince Charles joined his army with Batthyany's in the Upper Palatinate. This Austrian force of 55,000 then plunged into Bohemia. On 22 October the 20,000 Saxons linked themselves in turn to this army, swelling its size further to 75,000. The two junctions radically transformed the balance of forces in Bohemia. The Austro-Saxon army now outnumbered its Prussian foe and enjoyed the additional advantage of operating in a friendly environment. Frederick knew that he had to decamp as quickly as possible, and as early as 8 October he had withdrawn behind the Vlatava River. His only remaining hope, if anything was to be salvaged from the reopening of the central European war, was to hold Bohemia beyond the Elbe. Astonishingly, however, the retreat rapidly deteriorated into a rout. Prussian garrisons that had been left behind to defend Bohemian towns yielded swiftly to the Austro-Saxon forces. Frederick's intelligence network collapsed. The peasantry of Bohemia rose to repay his harshness with their own cunning exactions. Dysentery and hunger carved vast gaps in the once-proud Prussian army. And, in the most damaging and frightening development of all, the vaunted discipline of the Prussian soldier and the fabled efficiency of the Prussian support system dissolved before the king's eyes. In desperation he authorized Podewils to explore the possibility of negotiating a peace "in which each belligerent party would concede some of its pretensions."[4] But Maria Theresa was uninterested in talk of compromise. By early in November the choice facing Prussia was starkly clear: if Frederick wanted to maintain his grip on Silesia, he would have to give up Bohemia entirely.

The Austro-Saxon advance against the Prussians—the remorseless pressure that it exerted against the troops of Frederick—was brilliantly conceived. And the tactician who devised it was a figure we have met before: Count Traun. After his recall from Italy, Traun had borne several secondary commands before joining his troops with Prince Charles's in April of 1744. Maria Theresa and Bartenstein continued to question his ability, even though Campo Santo still stood as Austria's finest moment in the Italian theater, but Prince Charles quickly learned to draw on Traun's talents. Once the junction with Batthyany had been effected, it was Traun who determined how the Prussians were to be expelled. The theater and season invited recourse to Traun's favorite tactic of Fabian pressure. The Austro-Saxons, he advised, should employ marches and countermarches to confine and confuse the enemy while relying on the deepening cold and the vulnerability of the Prussian support system to a hostile populace to compel Frederick to withdraw his troops. Many years later Frederick acknowledged the aptness of the plan when he called the Bohemian campaign of 1744 "his school in the art of war and M. de Traun . . . his preceptor."[5]

Forced to choose between Bohemia and Silesia, Frederick decided to defend his earlier trophy rather than his more recent plunder. This decision meant that he would guide his troops eastward, even at the cost of abandoning the large but indefensible Prussian garrison at Prague. On 8 November 1744 the Prussians began to retreat to the northern side of the Elbe. After several feints, superintended by Traun, the Austrian army swept across the river on 19 November. This maneuver completely isolated the Prussian garrison stranded in Prague, and so on 26 November the Prussians began to withdraw from the city, drummed out by a delighted, stone-flinging populace. This retreat resembled Belle-Isle's celebrated escape from Prague solely in the rigors of the season. In the midst of these horrors Frederick handed command over to the Old Dessauer and withdrew to Silesia. This action, though necessitated by the need to secure his loot from the first Silesian War, was soon reckoned a deed of shame, and in later days observers held it to be akin to his lapse at Mollwitz. Early in December the remnants of the Prussian forces began staggering into Silesia. The Austrians promptly followed them, and by 21 December 1744 Prince Charles was settled at Prudnik, and both Klodzko and Upper Silesia were back in the hands of troops obedient to Maria Theresa. The figures told an astonishing story: of the 70,000 Prussian troops sent into Bohemia, 30,000 were lost.

Three considerations explain this debacle, and Frederick, though sometimes imperfectly, recognized them all. First, his calculation about the activities of other countries was seriously flawed. France's failure to apply pressure from the west, because it was a consequence of Louis XV's sudden illness, was of course unpredictable, but Saxony's decision to oppose Prussia was, if not certain, at least likely enough to have warranted more prudent behavior than Frederick showed. Second, his logistical preparations were inadequate. He had done much since mid-1742 to hone the fighting skills of his soldiers; he had also fattened his treasury. But he had neglected the prosaic requirements for food, fodder, clothing, and medicine. The results of this neglect were captured in the accounts of the survivors: "the number of the sick increased each day, while at the same time half-starved horses died in front of the wagons, blocking gorges and mountain roads with their heavy, still bodies."[6] Third, Frederick overextended his army. A prudent calculation suggested that, with France hapless and Saxony hostile, Prussia should fortify itself in that quadrant of Bohemia defined by the Elbe and then confine itself to repelling assaults by its enemies. Instead, the Prussians tried to defend half the kingdom. Now Frederick faced a bleak future, for his failure had not simply embarrassed but truly endangered him: as violator of treaties and two-time aggressor, he had forfeited Austria's acceptance of the cession of Silesia and given Maria Theresa ample grounds—legal, moral, prudential, and emotional—for seeking to recover the province. He had also given the queen the opportunity to lodge her troops in the land. All things considered, the Bohemian campaign of 1744 was the greatest miscalculation of Frederick's reign.

The government in Vienna was overjoyed at the good fortune of Prince Charles's army. In December Maria Theresa authorized her brother-in-law to commence with the retaking of Silesia. In a gesture that neatly mocked Frederick's Bohemian patent of August, she issued an appeal for Silesians to rise up against the usurping Hohenzollern. Prince Charles and Count Traun were the heroes of the hour. Although Prince Charles was now resentful of the attention Traun received, the queen and Bartenstein realized that credit should be shared by the royal brother-in-law and his self-effacing aide. In Silesia itself the Austrians stubbornly resisted Prussian counterattacks, and although they were forced finally to yield Klodzko and Upper Silesia to the Old Dessauer, they retained their capacity to send forays of light troops far afield. Only after mid-January 1745 did the various armies begin to move into winter quarters. Meanwhile the Austrian government rebuilt its Bohemian administration. Again, as in 1743, the disloyal were punished. But since the nobility, burned by the earlier experience, had remained largely faithful, the numbers involved were small. For the queen and the Conference, however, these Bohemian perturbations were only a sideshow as 1744 came to an end. Their chief goal now was to transform Frederick's war for Bohemia into Maria Theresa's war for Silesia.

PIEDMONT SAVED

The pentagonal fortification of Cuneo sat on a bluff on the wedge of land defined by the junction of the Stura and Gesso Rivers. Surrounded by mountains on three sides and protected by the two swift streams that coursed past it, the formidable fortress was a keystone to the defense of Piedmont. So severe was the Gallispan threat in August 1744 that Maria Theresa, despite her own problems in Bohemia, had dispatched 3,000 Croats from Lombardy and a detachment of cavalry from central Italy to aid Charles Emmanuel. But if Cuneo was to be held, the burden of defense had to be borne by the forces of the king of Sardinia. In Cuneo itself he had installed Major-General Frederick de Leutrum, whose heroics had helped save the day at Campo Santo. Leutrum's advanced age had been reckoned a disadvantage, but the clear-sighted Marquis d'Ormea had urged his appointment. The king had also summoned his militia, counting on their stealth, their knowledge of the mountains, and their devotion to their plots of land to make them superb guerrillas in the region around Cuneo. Still, the king's chief weapon could only be the standing army of 25,000. Charles Emmanuel kept it near Saluzzo, ready for whatever steps might be necessary to protect Cuneo from the invaders.

The Prince of Conti had devised a detailed plan for taking Cuneo. It proposed that the wedge of land between the confluent rivers be the fulcrum of the siege. Conti believed that three armies would be required: the first to keep Charles Emmanuel's own army at bay, the second to dig and defend the trenches for the siege, and the third to patrol the lands east of the Gesso River and prevent this region from becoming the staging area for guerrilla attacks. Since the Bourbon army totaled only 50,000 while Charles Emmanuel's counted fully 25,000 and Leutrum commanded another 3,200 troops inside Cuneo, the numbers did not confer on the attackers the preponderance of power that besiegers preferred to operate with. For this reason La Mina opposed Conti's scheme. He offered no plausible alternative, however, and so on the night of 12/13 September 1744 the Bourbons began to dig the trenches that would permit an enfiladed approach to Cuneo from the south. The advance was arduous. Leutrum found ways of illumining the nighttime sky so that the zappers faced hostile fire around the clock, and Piedmontese sorties kept the attackers off balance. But the advance was also measurable, and on the night of 27/28 September the Bourbons, moving eastward, began to lay trenches beyond the Gesso.

It was at this point that Charles Emmanuel decided to implement a complex scheme he had long been coaxing into shape. The scheme was comprised of five separate elements, and its success depended on being able to initiate all five at approximately the same time. The centerpiece was to be a full-scale battle. Though Charles Emmanuel hoped, naturally enough, to win the battle, the success of the scheme—and here we see its true brilliance—did not depend on a battlefield victory. For the battle, though potentially decisive, was designed chiefly to divert the attention of Conti and La Mina from the four other actions. First, he would send supplies into Cuneo and bring out the sick and injured. Second, the king would send detachments to attack various Bourbon outposts near Cuneo, especially a hospital facility and an arms depot. Third, he would direct Leutrum to dispatch a sortie from Cuneo to destroy the siege works that the Bourbons had begun on his side of the Gesso. Fourth, he would unleash his peasant militias to assail Bourbon lines of communication along the Stura valley. Charles Emmanuel was playing for time. When the snows began to fall, the Bourbons would be faced with some difficult choices. If Cuneo was not theirs, the king reasoned, they would despair of capturing it and withdraw.

To implement this multifaceted scheme, Charles Emmanuel needed to bring his army closer to the Bourbons. The advance from Saluzzo had already begun by the final week of September, and the Prince of Conti responded by moving his main force forward to meet the Piedmontese. By the evening of 29 September 1744 the Gallispans manned and controlled the road running from Caraglio eastward to Madonna dell'Olmo, and the next morning the Piedmontese began to array themselves in a line opposite their foes. The two armies were virtually equal in size, but Conti enjoyed a distinct advantage in the number of mounted troops. The battle began about midday on the thirtieth when Croats in the king's army pushed prematurely against Madonna dell'Olmo and found themselves exposed. Charles Emmanuel, still on the Piedmontese right when the engagement opened, was compelled to make haste back toward the center. In the west, where the Gallispans pressed their attack, the French cavalry stumbled into ditches and tore itself against the barricades. But in the east, where the Piedmontese hoped for success, the Spanish defenders of Madonna dell'Olmo repelled the charging Croats and grenadiers. Thus it was in the center and not on the wings that the outcome of the battle was decided. And the decisive element was the French artillery. It ravaged the Piedmontese line and gave cover for a French infantry charge. The ensuing collision of hostile foot soldiers initiated an ebb-and-flow struggle that was both brutal and sanguinary. Late in the afternoon the King of Sardinia, realizing that he would not be able to capture Madonna dell'Olmo, directed an exemplary retreat.[7] "Your army, Sire," Conti quickly wrote to Louis XV, "has done prodigies of constancy and vigour." Even the normally caustic La Mina had a kind word for the French: they "helped us like good partners."[8]

On the night after the battle a sleepless Charles Emmanuel walked among his men, muttering "my poor soldiers, my poor soldiers."[9] His losses were indeed painful: of the 25,000 men he had led into battle 4,400 were killed or

wounded. Bourbon losses in the engagement were considerably lower —
2,700 out of 26,000 — and seemed to leave Conti with a formidable fighting
force.[10] But as the night proceeded, the prince discovered that while the main
event had brought rewards for the Bourbons northwest of Cuneo, a set of
Piedmontese sideshows had gone far toward neutralizing the advantage
Conti had putatively gained. The Piedmontese had successfully infiltrated
reinforcements into, and withdrawn invalids out of, the beleaguered fortress
of Cuneo. They had swept out against the siege works to the east, reducing the
Bourbon area to ruins. They had run wild across the mountain folds and passes
behind the Gallispan army, falling upon small Bourbon outposts and demol-
ishing bridges that had allowed Conti to maintain communications with
Demonte and beyond. Only the attack on a Bourbon hospital town had failed.
By daybreak on the first of October 1744 the Prince of Conti knew that,
though victorious on the battlefield, he was further than ever from his goal.

Then a new and still more devastating mishap befell the Bourbons. On the
same first of October the rains began to fall, and they did not relent for six
awful days. Fed by torrential mountain streams, the Stura River rose twelve
feet. Bridges cast by the besiegers across both the Stura and the Gesso were
swept away in the flood. The ground became soft and unstable, and there
was no sanctuary from the damp. When the weather finally lifted, the
Piedmontese snuck 1,200 fresh men into Cuneo, and damage to Bourbon
hopes was placed beyond remedy. It was not just that time, already precious,
had been lost. It was rather that the waters, by weakening trenches and wip-
ing out roads, had measurably set the siege back. "You will grant me, Sir,"
the prince wrote to the minister of war, "that it is indeed terrible after so fortunate a campaign . . . to be fought and perhaps beaten by the weather and
the torrents."[11] Like many commanders before him, Conti now found himself
with no recourse but to bow to the might of Cuneo.

On 11 October 1744 the callow Don Philip, an ineffectual spectator of the
fevered efforts in his behalf, convoked a council of war to plan for the retreat.
Peasant pressure, reinforced by Piedmontese regulars, was making any section of Piedmont unsafe for the invader. The ugly war between Bourbon soldiers and peasant partisans had reached new levels of savagery in early
October, when angry French troops began repaying guerrilla brutalities with
a ruthlessness that brought the terror of eastern European warfare to western
Europe. The Bourbons withdrew first to Demonte and then began filtering
back through the Barricades on 15 November. Within four days they were
over the divide, and with their departure Leutrum's fame spread swiftly
through Europe. As it turned out, the Gallispans escaped Piedmont not a
moment too soon, for on November 20 the snows, already impeding their

retreat, swept in to bury the pass. The Gallispan departure brought to a disappointing end a campaign that had begun with dash, triumphs, and hope. Once again nature and art had contrived to protect Piedmont.

The French government accepted the failure with the same resignation that it had shown on the occasion of so many earlier misfirings. Versailles blamed La Mina for much that had gone wrong, and so Conti emerged with his reputation largely intact. The rulers in Spain, as was their wont, were less forgiving. Like the French, they focused attention on La Mina. They could not believe that the successes of the summer had proved so fugitive. His recall, disgrace, and exile followed inexorably. The Gallispan retreat from Piedmont was, proportionally considered, almost as disastrous as the virtually simultaneous Prussian retreat from Bohemia. Total losses from the Cuneo campaign and its epilogue numbered 15,000. During the forty days of the siege, the Bourbon armies had rained 1,000 cannonballs a day on the fortification. But nothing availed. Those who were beginning to liken the king of Sardinia to the king of Prussia had sound instincts.

It had been a good autumn for the Worms allies. At exactly the same time that Austria was clearing its central European realm of Prussians, Piedmont-Sardinia was expelling the Bourbons from its own lands in northern Italy. The two campaigns bore some revealing similarities. In both Bohemia and Piedmont the aggressors overextended themselves, their supply lines proved startlingly vulnerable, and their retreats before a lowering winter were painful and costly. The campaigns thus confirmed some timeless truths of warfare. The farther from home one plunges, the more difficult the logistical requirements become; the side that can make the weather its ally has a powerful friend; the army that is fighting for its own land fights with fiercer commitment. But several contextual truths were also becoming visible, and the most important was the clear indication that the rural populations of Europe were neither indifferent nor inured to the misery of foreign occupations. War tends, as it procedes, to abrade the habits of quiescence that are a central component of social order. These early indications of social stress redounded to the advantage of the legitimate rulers of the regions involved, but the time was not far off when the pressures of protracted belligerence would begin to rot the cake of political custom.

THE NEW ORDER IN FRANCE

Ever since early in 1744, when the failures of Maurepas's scheme for assailing Britain had sent him scurrying back to the relative seclusion of naval affairs, no single figure had set his stamp on French foreign policy.

Then Amelot's dismissal in April left France literally without a foreign minister. Ostensibly the king assumed the responsibilities himself; in practice an informal committee composed of the Duke of Noailles, the Count d'Argenson, and Jean-Gabriel de la Porte du Theil deliberated and acted on foreign affairs. But the period between the spring and the autumn of 1744 saw the direction of external affairs slide into unrelieved confusion. Sadly for France, if the sublimely self-centered king was to be persuaded that blundering did not constitute policy, it would require a stimulus more personal and immediate than rational argumentation. The monarch's grave illness was precisely such a prod. It brought out that sense of moral obligation that usually shriveled before the king's pious but venal conscience; it also gave his advisors a splendid opportunity to make the credible argument that his recuperation required a curtailing of responsibilities. The clinching consideration was an ironic reversal of the moral one. As his health returned, he repented of his fever-induced decision of August to rid himself of his mistress, Madame de Châteauroux. Instead, reflecting on his own disposition and true interests, he decided that the pleasures of wantonness exceeded those of command. He was therefore ready, when he was welcomed by a jubilant Paris in November, to make an appointment to the vacant office of foreign minister. His first nominee declined. Then, almost as an afterthought, the post was offered to a person who seemed to have nothing but a well-placed brother to commend him. Thus on 18 November 1744 did René-Louis de Voyer de Paulmy, Marquis d'Argenson, become secretary of state for foreign affairs.

From almost any perspective the choice was a surprising and puzzling one. It is true that the marquis was the elder brother of the secretary of war. But many things seemed to nullify that advantage. In society he was sober and unmannered—ill at ease in the polite world of Paris. In politics he was inexperienced, and his political naïveté soon became legendary. His thinking was heterodox, and his candor made him a poor candidate for a successful life at court. What was oddest of all, however, was his innocence of contact with foreign affairs. All his experience—and he had had little—was with domestic matters. He had developed some shrewd ideas about the situation of the peasantry and the dysfunctionality of France's sprawling and knavish bureaucracy. He had even concluded that France needed—if proof is required of his eccentricity, here it is—a large measure of democracy and centralization! But his knowledge of the world beyond France was derived from books. In fact, it had even been distilled into one: his *Treatise on Statecraft*, written in 1737 and published in 1764. It would not be long before people would be saying that he dropped into foreign affairs out of Plato's republic.

With the Marquis d'Argenson we meet a kind of figure who has not previously entered our story: a visionary utopian. The marquis came to office determined to act on the basis of certain principles. After almost four years of confusion, he wanted to bring coherence to French foreign policy. According to the marquis, France was a satiated power. It did not covet territory. It was therefore ideally positioned to craft a disinterested peace settlement and supply armed arbitration. In trying to conceive of a European world fixed into an enduring peace, the marquis tended to conflate his abstract (and sometimes novel) notions of fairness with prevailing older notions of French interests. The resultant amalgam was uneasy.

He construed—Richelieu would have agreed—Austria as the chief enemy of peace. Therefore, Austria should be weakened. In this regard at least, Belle-Isle's campaign to make the Holy Roman Empire independent of Vienna was sound. Britain too he saw in traditional terms—an overly ambitious state that threatened France's overseas empire and trade. Richelieu had not worried about Russia, but d'Argenson's views about Elizabeth Petrovna's empire corresponded with those of his immediate predecessors: Russia needed placating, and a policy of cultural and political contacts would win the empire of the czars over to friendship. But in two areas his thoughts had abruptly discontinuous implications. First, he cast Spain among the troublers of peace—a country that sought more than its due. Second, he saw Italy as the primary victim of the greed of the great, and so he proposed to expel all foreign rule, whether Habsburg or Bourbon, from the peninsula. The marquis wrote that France had helped Germany "to shatter a colossus of greatness that had enchained their liberty. Well, let us do as much in Italy."[12] To realize this array of international goals it was necessary that France be the strongest military power in Europe. If, as earlier suggested, Belle-Isle embodied the seventeenth century in his foreign policy goals and Fleury the eighteenth century, the Marquis d'Argenson represented, at least in part, the future—the nineteenth century in his ardent prefiguring of Italian nationhood and the twentieth century in his Wilsonian faith in the attainability of armed impartiality. What was missing was a sense of the relative intractibility of the real world of international affairs.

D'Argenson's career in office, which lasted for over two years, was lived out in a middle world somewhere between dizzy dreams and fettering facts. The results (to anticipate what is to come) were calamitous for France. As a consequence of his faith in reasonableness, he was easily duped—most famously (as we shall see) by Charles Emmanuel but also by Frederick II and Lord Sandwich. Because he was comfortable with theorizing but inexperienced at devising concrete policies, he saw nothing anomalous in embracing mutually incompatible means to secure a desired end and was perplexed that others, judging only from the means, should regard him as inconsistent. He never realized that his contempt for Spain—he openly called Elizabeth Farnese a "bitch" and a "fucker"[13]—was untranslatable into policy as long as Louis XV honored family ties. He never understood that Ormea and Charles Emmanuel were Piedmontese patriots, not Italian irre-dentists. And he was blind to other matters too. He thought that because Louis XV kept him in office, the king also supported his policies. (The assumption was not, of course, an unreasonable one; d'Argenson's fault was failing to read the many signs that Louis was the silliest of kings.) We may well ask how the Marquis d'Argenson managed to stay in power for two weeks, much less two years. The fuller explanation lies ahead, but two points may be made here. First, in an era of half-time administration and casual office-holding, he stood out as a man ready to apply himself vigorously and at length to his task. Second, he was the indirect beneficiary of the turn in France's military fortunes. These considerations extended a political career far beyond the term that accomplishment warranted.

But the career began well. By a remarkable coincidence the arrival of the apostle of peace on the scene in November 1744 was immediately followed by the departure, whether temporary or permanent, of two apostles of war. The reinstallation of Madame Châteauroux as the king's mistress had brought a spirited defender of military vigor back into close association with the monarch. But scarcely had she returned to his bed than she took ill—again the smallpox—and on 8 December she died. Belligerent pillow talk no longer posed a threat to d'Argenson. Meanwhile, Marshal Belle-Isle had been chosen for a military embassy to Frederick II. The road he followed passed through the Hanoverian town of Elbingerode, where he was detained by the postmaster on the grounds that he had no passport. A comedy of errors was then played out, in which Belle-Isle carelessly compromised his position by claiming prisoner-of-war status rather than diplomatic immunity and Baron Münchhausen neglected to search his papers, leaving the marshal ample time to destroy valuable ones. No one in Hanover and then in London seemed quite to know what to do with the man who had brought France into the war, but everyone agreed that he was too valuable to give back freely. And so Belle-Isle was removed to Britain and placed under loose confine-ment at Windsor Castle. The war offered no incident more ironical than this—the scourge of Vienna stumbling into British captivity.

THE NEW ORDER IN BRITAIN

At virtually the same time that the Marquis d'Argenson entered upon his responsibilities in France, Lord Carteret resigned his office in Britain. It was an event susceptible to misinterpretation by observers on the continent, for whom the nuanced world of British politics was totally alien. Carteret fell, secondarily, because his policies were faltering and, primarily, because his politics were fatuous. It might at first seem surprising that his policies were regarded as deficient, for during the autumn of 1744 Austria was flushing Prussia out of Bohemia and Piedmont-Sardinia was dislodging France from Cuneo. These triumphs were neither unnoticed nor unapplauded in Britain, but in the larger view two failings eclipsed them in the view of British political nation, and both cast discredit on Carteret. The first was the miserable campaign that the allied army had waged in the Austrian Netherlands. Much had been expected of the Pragmatic Army in 1744. Instead, General Wade, the Duke of Aremberg, and the Prince of Nassau had quarreled, bickered, and stickled. Part of the blame for the inaction of the army inevitably attached to Carteret, who, because he directed foreign affairs, ought to have given direction to the leaders of the army. The second failing was still more severe. Carteret's first great triumph in office had been the Treaty of Berlin, which ushered Prussia out of the war. Now, however, in an action that hit London "like a bomb," Prussia had returned to the struggle.[14] And the chief reasons behind Frederick's attack on Bohemia were his concern over the implications of the Treaty of Worms—a pact that Carteret had proudly superintended—and Britain's continuing inability to get Austria to restore Bavaria to the emperor. Carteret had successfully insisted that he be given preeminent power to determine war policy; he thus had left himself no sanctuary when the policy began to unravel.

But to discuss policy is to miss the larger point. Carteret fell from office because he had so disobliged his fellow ministers that they could no longer endure serving with him. He was arrogant, bold, unconventional; he ignored the sensibilities of Parliament. His great source of strength, as he bullied his way through affairs, was the support of the king. He forgot that the king in Britain was not free to choose whomsoever he wished to be his minister. In September 1744 the "Old Corps" Whigs—led by Henry Pelham, Lord Hardwicke, and the Duke of Newcastle—began a campaign to oust Carteret. They seized on the minister's inability to wrest a firm engagement from the Dutch to help in the war against France, and in a memorial denouncing his conduct of the war they threatened the resignation of the Old Corps ministers if Carteret was not dismissed. To a Parliament smarting from the mounting cost of war, the assertion that the Dutch could be made to contribute more to the effort was very attractive. George II received the memorial in November, made several futile efforts to parry its threat, and finally (and sullenly) acquiesced. On 5 December, after consulting with the king, Carteret resigned the seals of office. An Old Corps Whig passed a fair judgment on his meteoric career: "Had he studied Parliament more and Demosthenes less, he would have been a more successful minister."[15] He fell victim to political cecity.

For almost three years Lord Carteret had been the dominant figure in the shaping of British war policy and the only European leader with an encompassing view of European affairs. He had come to office with a mandate from the king and the political nation to vitalize Britain's war effort. By the Treaty of Berlin he detached Prussia from the anti-Austrian coalition. By a set of treaties he put together the structure of an anti-Bourbon league.[16] But he failed to see that these two achievements were incompatible. It was impossible to assure security to Prussia while at the same time enhancing the strength of Prussia's enemy Austria, curtailing the might of Prussia's partial ally France, and prodding the Russian empire into action along the eastern reaches of the Hohenzollern realm. Newcastle hinted at the flaw in the grand design when he wrote late in 1743 that he hoped "our active Secretary, will at last find out, that dexterity with Princes, to seem to promise all, and intend nothing, will as little do, as with private persons."[17] European observers saw the problem too. This was why many of them expected Carteret's fall to presage a change in policy. The heart of the matter, however, was missed by all. Carteret's policies, howsoever confused, were *not* the chief reason for his resignation. Almost all leading Britons believed in the necessity of hammering France into moderation; and thus these policies survived the dismissal of their shaper.

The Duke of Newcastle succeeded Carteret as the dominant force in the shaping of British foreign policy. In one respect Newcastle was superbly qualified for the tasks he was assuming, since he had served as southern secretary for fully twenty years. But during those two decades he had always been subordinate to other men, and he had in fact never even set foot on the European continent. He conceived of European relationships through the alembic of what he called the "Old System," seeing France as Britain's chief foe, Austria as Britain's chief friend, Spain as a nuisance, and Prussia as a German rather than a European power. His model of wartime alliances was defined by the age of Marlborough, and his hope was to bind the United Provinces more firmly to the war, to use that bond to beat back the challenge in the Low Countries, and thereby to complete the defeat of France that Carteret had compassed. Other changes in personnel attended the rise of

Newcastle. Lord Chesterfield, recently of the opposition and a diplomat with experience in The Hague, was appointed to undertake a mission to the Dutch republic. General Wade was replaced as commander of the British army in the Netherlands by Lieutenant-General Sir John Ligonier, whose reputation as a man of parts was growing. The new administration inaugurated its tenure auspiciously when, on 8 January 1745, through the Treaty of Warsaw, the Quadruple Alliance was formed, committing Saxony to supply Austria with 30,000 troops in return for subsidies of 1 million gulden (£100,000) from the British and 500,000 gulden (£50,000) from the Dutch. But since the negotiations that led to the treaty had been begun under Carteret, their success should have alerted the world to the truth that, in changing men, Britain had not changed measures.

And yet there is more to the story, for change came where no one looked for it. Britain's performance at sea during the war had ranged from the acerbically mediocre at Toulon to the stupidly disastrous at Cartagena. "We have already lost seven millions of money and thirty thousand men in the Spanish war," Horace Walpole complained in 1744, "and all the fruit of all this blood and treasure is the glory of having Admiral Vernon's head on alehouse signs."[18] The blame had in significant measure been Carteret's. Inattentive to naval interests, he had allowed lethargy and aimlessness to clog the admiralty. When Carteret departed, so did his naval administration. The most important of the newcomers to the admiralty was Lord Anson, who had just returned from an extraordinary three-year circumnavigation of the globe. The invigorated admiralty soon found mechanisms to begin easing the superannuated out of commands they could no longer handle, to open up promotions to men of merit, and to tighten discipline throughout the force. Though their outcomes were not immediately visible, few developments of 1744-45 equaled these in significance.

THE WITTELSBACH TRAGEDY

In many ways Emperor Charles VII, hidden away at Frankfurt, was the forgotten man of Europe—not literally, of course, for his high office was too august to allow its incumbent to slip from mind, but effectually, since Charles was so bereft of resources. Though both Versailles and Berlin proclaimed their support for him, neither displayed more than a marginal interest in translating these words into a campaign to restore him to his Bavarian homeland. A rebuke from no less a figure than Louis XV bore testimony to the emperor's secondary status: "you must know how I dislike the ceaseless complaints you send me."[19] Still, the initiatives of the autumn—Prussia's attack on Bohemia and a siege of Freibourg by French arms—created a context for an imperial offensive. Count Seckendorff led 32,000 imperial troops, some of whom were French, on a slow march into Bavaria. The Austrians could not reinforce their occupying army in the electorate, and so Bernklau chose to retreat, withdrawing on 17 October back across the Inn and yielding the bulk of Bavaria up to its lawful ruler. On 23 October, after two years of exile, the emperor entered Munich. Yet all who spoke with him at this time were struck by his bitter gloom. Brooding about his health, he fell victim to a paralysis of will that prevented him from authorizing even the simplest of actions that would make Munich more defensible. Charles VII had long suffered from gout; by the autumn of 1744 its pains were scourging him. Novel afflictions were adding further miseries. A kidney stone wrenched his innards; a strange malaise disordered his digestion; he was short of breath. Though only forty-seven, the emperor was breaking down as if his body were seventy.

And then his world caved in. In November the Austrian surge that he had feared materialized. Austrian troops swept into the Upper Palatinate. The ongoing strife between the savage Croats serving in Maria Theresa's army and the embattled peasants living in the Wittelsbach realm crested again, with the Austrians—"they are raging animals, and not men," Batthyany had recently written of his own troops in Bavaria[20]—bringing rapine and despair to the town they favored with visits. The beleaguered emperor appealed desperately to France. But the government at Versailles had more pressing concerns and finally replied that even the help Belle-Isle had promised would not be forthcoming. Meanwhile, Count Ségur, the French officer charged with the defense of Amberg in the Upper Palatinate, handed the town over to Austrians arriving from Bohemia. The litany of Charles VII's miseries concluded in the third week of January 1745. On the eighteenth the emperor's hobbled body finally gave out, driving the titular ruler of Germany to bed with a high fever, an elevated pulse, and troubled respiration. A scant two days later, after entrusting Chavigny with superintendence of his son, the Holy Roman Emperor died. An autopsy revealed lesions in his lungs, his stomach, his liver, and his heart. "Misfortune will not leave me," he had recently declared, "before I leave it."[21]

To understand the significance of this death we must forget the man and remember the office. The throne of the Holy Roman Empire was again, and unexpectedly, empty. Such a vacancy in 1740 had triggered the current war, and the new vacancy offered all sorts of possibilities for redirecting or resolving that war. In Austria, where a loathing for Wittelsbach presumption burned intensely, there was fervent rejoicing. An anonymous court document declared that "divine providence, which watches over Your Majesty the Queen, is again to be observed in it."[22] In Prussia there was consternation. Frederick could no longer use the emperor's putative interests as a pretext for his own actions. "It seems," he wrote to Louis XV, "that there is a strange fatality which . . . is pleased to thwart and overthrow all that we are building."[23] In France the reaction was mixed. To the uncertainties of d'Argenson's new priorities were now added the uncertainties of a new diplomatic landscape. Some dreamed of peace: with the death of its imperial puppet, France no longer had German obligations that brought it into conflict with Austria. Others, however, cheered by the disappearance of the German distraction, saw an opportunity to emphasize the Italian or Flemish wars. All that could be certain was that the death of Charles VII had shattered Europe's matrix of expectations.

Maximilian III Joseph succeeded his father as ruler of Bavaria. He was a friend of peace, but he was also, at seventeen years of age, a novice at accepting responsibility. The territories he inherited were in chaos, and his council of advisors was fundamentally divided. Some of these men, chiefly Count Seckendorff, urged the new elector to seek an immediate peace with Austria on the grounds that events since 1741 had shown the fatuity of a Wittelsbach challenge to Vienna. But others, led by Count Törring, held that the war could still be won. Behind Törring stood the French and Prussian envoys, Chavigny and Klinggräffen, with their promises of financial aid. With his first actions the young man seemed to choose the path of continuity; assuming the titles of king of Bohemia and archduke of Austria, he asserted that "we . . . make no concessions at all of our inherited rights nor do we renounce them to our prejudice."[24] But since it would have been folly to concede immediately and without demurral what might later be sold at some profit, Europe awaited clearer signs before assuming that it knew the new elector's course.

12

Maurice and Frederick
(January 1745 – June 1745)

THE GREAT DIVIDE

Frederick II was a chastened man in the opening months of 1745: the Bohemian campaign had tempered his arrogance and softened his causticity. What he needed above all else was peace. But because Prussia had no leverage in Austria, Frederick hoped that the diplomatic road to peace might run through London, "England being," as he said, "the prime mover of this whole alliance."[1] In this hope Frederick was disappointed, for conversations with the British, authorized only one day after he learned of Charles VII's demise, ran aground on London's inability to soften Vienna's obdurance. In March Frederick traveled from Berlin to his army in Silesia. Trusting more to the fist than the tongue, he put his troops through their arduous paces to prepare them for the consequences of diplomatic failure. His sole aim was the holding of Silesia, where he hunkered down, in effect daring the Austrians to dislodge him from their old province. He calculated that the advantage swung to Prussia in such an engagement, since the support of the civilian populace, the readiness of the army, and the relative ease of communications made Silesia a vastly different land from Bohemia. But Frederick was also a realist. The difficult truth was that Prussia could expect no substantial aid from its nominal allies. "Never has a crisis been greater than mine," he declared, ". . . the game I am playing is so considerable that it is impossible to view its outcome with composure. . . . Pray for help from my lucky star."[2]

Peace was also proving elusive at Versailles. To be sure, the French saw their goals as restrained. A document approved by the king sounded a note of moderation: "we want only a temperate peace, which prevents war in the future and delivers the world from tyrants."[3] Clearly the boldest dreams of Belle-Isle had been dismissed. But d'Argenson needed greater specificity, and shortly after coming to office he asked the king to identify the kingdom's war aims. Louis's reply posited five aims for any general settlement. First, Don Philip was to receive a domain (Nice and Savoy were the king's suggestion). Second, the Genoese republic was to keep Finale. Third, Charles Emmanuel, as compensation for the loss of Savoy, Nice, and (presumptively) Finale, was to receive lands now under Austrian rule in the Milanese. Fourth, France was to give back its conquests in Flanders but in return to be relieved of all restrictions governing its use of Dunkirk. Fifth, Britain was to recover both the Annual Ship and the Asiento. Somewhat reluctantly d'Argenson accepted these items as a reasonable framework for peace. His subsequent efforts to effect them revealed his diplomatic fatuity.

The idea that Don Philip should be established in the peninsula ran against d'Argenson's sense of justice and contravened his dream for Italy. He derived a measure of cheer from the fact that Savoy and Nice would make Don Philip only an Italian princeling, nothing more. Still, the creation of even a small principality raised practical dilemmas. D'Argenson recognized that Charles Emmanuel would find the establishment of Don Philip as a neighbor thoroughly alarming. It was only fair that Charles Emmanuel should be compensated for his losses. The marquis proposed therefore a remarkable ratio as a guideline: "I hold it as a principle that we are not able to give, so to speak, *one* to Don Philip without giving *three* to the King of Sardinia."[4] What d'Argenson was suggesting, therefore, paradoxical as it might appear, was that the major goal of the next Gallispan campaign in Italy was the winning of land not so much for Spain as for Piedmont-Sardinia. With a foreign minister who preferred an enemy to an ally, France was stumbling into Italian policies that would soon have much of Europe perplexed.

The first Italian misstep occurred late in March of 1745 when France finally and reluctantly accepted the Spanish plan of campaign for the coming year. This plan was striking for its boldness and breadth. The army of Don Philip—really the same Franco-Spanish army whose failure at Cuneo had cost La Mina his command—would use the coastal route to return to Italy. The army of Gages would march north from the region near Naples to unite with Don Philip's force in the Genoese republic. In this fashion the junction of Spain's two Italian armies, long intended but invariably delayed by circumstances, would finally be effected. This vast army would then be able to overrun the Milanese, divide the Austrians from the Piedmontese, and, if necessary, defeat each enemy army in turn. D'Argeson recognized that if successful, the plan would subvert his Italian schemes—both his visionary private hopes and his more considered policy proposals. He never-

theless agreed to it, because the alternative was to have no Spanish cooperation at all, and that too would defeat the marquis's goals. D'Argenson had, in
fact, defined Italian ends that defied French means.

Louis XV's hopes for a settlement in Germany were undermined by a similar maladroitness. France was unwilling to countenance a settlement that
would restore to Vienna any of its losses or permit it any compensatory
gains. This fixed principle had, after the death of Charles VII, two corollaries: Max Joseph must be restored to authority in all his hereditary lands, and
Francis Stephen must be prevented from winning the imperial throne. To
install the new Elector of Bavaria in all the patrimony of his father,
d'Argenson argued that the firmest expressions of French support were
needed. He turned aside the suggestion, plausible in any case and fatal if
true, that Bavaria might seek its own settlement with Austria. Meanwhile, to
block Viennese access to the newly vacant imperial crown, d'Argenson proposed full French support for a rival candidate: Augustus III of
Saxony. Despite the exceedingly awkward fact that King Augustus received
the proposal coolly, France launched an extensive diplomatic campaign to
secure his election—a campaign that included the warning to Austria that
France, rather than accept Francis Stephen's election, would "make war for
forty years."[5] Taken together, these two corollaries defined a major French
stake in German affairs. In February 1745, in recognition of that fact,
d'Argenson proposed that Versailles defend the stake by relegating warfare
in Italy and the Low Countries to secondary status and emphasizing the
German theater.[6] With respect to Germany, d'Argensonian reasoning was
coming perilously close to issuing in Belle-Islian conclusions.

With respect to the British, Louis XV's statement of December spoke
clearly: they could not be expected to accept a peace if they were consigned
to the category of losers. Reasoning in this manner, the French king had
adumbrated a settlement that saw Spain yielding to British interests in
America while France forbore from threatening British interests on the continent. It followed from these principles that French restraint in the Low
Countries was called for. Such circumspection would assure Britain that it
need not fear for the balance of power in the region and might allow France
to wean the Dutch republic from its close British ties. The argument for forbearance, however, flew directly in the face of France's budding military
plans. In December 1744, after his successful defense of the French conquests of the previous summer, Maurice of Saxony returned to Paris to discuss with the new foreign minister and other officials the plans for a
springtime offensive. Maurice was doubly pleased. An offensive strategy
seemed to him far likelier than a defensive one to persuade Britain that peace

was appropriate. Moreover, he liked the choice of the Low Countries as a theater. Victories elsewhere posed problems for the occupying French army and at best secured only bargaining chips, but "on the side of Flanders it is not the same: we can make conquests there."[7] By adopting an offensive strategy, France embarked on a policy of muddle. In a decision remarkably like the one it made for Piedmont-Sardinia, France was hoping simultaneously to soften the enemy with sweets and clobber him with a club. Such inconsistencies cannot be glossed as the complementary components of a complex design. They are rather the mark, pure and simple, of political incompetence.

If d'Argenson's implementation of royal policies toward Italy, Germany, and the Low Countries testifies to his confusion, a final consideration underlines his extraordinary eccentricity. A glance at the foregoing aims reveals a startling and deliberate omission: France was seeking nothing for itself! D'Argenson's administration was raising and extending already onerous taxes, seizing private funds, conscripting men into the army and the navy, disrupting communal and agricultural life, countenancing a military occupation of part of the Austrian Netherlands, and planning an invasion of the Ligurian coast. And it was doing all these things so that a bedizened Spanish prince might set himself up as an Italian potentate, a Prussian plunderer might retain his pelf, a German youth might be restored to lands his father had thrown away, and a British nation might be spared the shame of defeat. The earnestness of d'Argenson's longing for peace can scarcely be denied. "I feel," he wrote, "that I am turning into Fleury."[8] But if his sincerity lies beyond cavil, then his sense must be judged deficient. If war was deemed necessary, then its aims should be French. If peace was deemed essential, then warmaking should be abandoned. The Marquis d'Argenson may well have been the most fatuous foreign minister of a great power that modern Europe has seen.

The enemies of France and Prussia were not idle in the early months of 1745. The new British administration quickly placed its mark of approval on Austro-Saxon plans to attack Prussia and granted £200,000 to Austria so that Vienna might have a contingent of Hanoverian troops. The new admiralty board made its first important decision, establishing in rudimentary form what would shortly become the fearsome Western Squadron. Meanwhile, from Vienna the queen sent out the ablest clutch of commanders she had thus far mustered—Prince Charles (Silesia), Count Traun (the Rhineland), Count Königsegg (the Austrian Netherlands), and later, Count Schulenburg (Italy). She even flashed a mordant sense of humor when, in remarking on the Quadruple Alliance's hope to partition Prussia, she noted that "before dividing up the bear's skin [they] needed to worry about killing it."[9]

The role of Saxony loomed large in Austrian and British thinking. Through the Treaty of Warsaw Saxony had unambiguously steered itself into the Austrian camp. Augustus III's reluctance to be France's candidate for emperor was in large measure a consequence of the prudential judgment that Maria Theresa might be unwilling to lend military cooperation to a man who was trying to deny her husband the imperial crown.

In April 1745 Austria celebrated a glorious triumph. Vienna had responded to the accession of Max Joseph in Munich by offering both peace and a restoration of territory to the young elector. Count Seckendorff urged Max Joseph to accept; Count Törring urged him to resist. The elector hesitated between the two camps, immobile and hence at war. Maria Theresa finally lost patience and authorized the application of pressure: "it is not to be doubted that . . . [Bavaria] will be brought to peaceloving thoughts all the more quickly."[10] On 21 March 1745 Batthyany launched a blitzkrieg, assisted by Bernklau and Browne. All the Bavarian garrisons in the east fled, Törring's army sat divided and paralyzed, and the French army under Count Ségur engaged Batthyany at Pfaffenhofen only to lose. Max Joseph abandoned Munich for the imperial city of Augsburg, and Batthyany marched his army to the edge of the capital. For the third time in four years Bavaria was overrun by the enemy. And so on 18 April 1745 Max Joseph announced that "if no one wants to have peace, yet I want to have it" and authorized the Prince of Fürstenberg to conclude.[11] Just four days later, on 22 April 1745, the Treaty of Füssen was signed. By its terms Max Joseph renounced all claims to Austrian lands and the imperial crown, approved the Pragmatic Sanction and Maria Theresa's right to control the Bohemian vote in the electoral college, and promised to support the candidacy of Francis Stephen in the coming election. Maria Theresa in return acknowledged the legitimacy of the late emperor's reign and abandoned all Austrian claims to Bavarian territory as defined by the boundaries of 1741. She withdrew most of her troops immediately, keeping only three towns as occupied hostages to be evacuated after Francis Stephen had become emperor; and she exacted no indemnity.

The Treaty of Füssen is the first of the pacts that over the course of the next three-and-a-half years defined the end of the War of the Austrian Succession. It is remarkable for its lenity and endurance. After a half century of enmity and a rivalry that was older still, Austria and Bavaria settled into a relationship that, if not amiable, was at least smooth, grounded in Bavarian acknowledgment of Austrian superiority in power. Widely celebrated as the cradle of Austro-Prussian dualism, the War of the Austrian Succession was also the deathbed of Austro-Bavarian dualism. "Everything that is harmful originates in the division of our two houses," Maria Theresa promptly wrote to the young elector, "and only through their unity can it again be set right."[12] Austria's forbearance in victory was deliberate. As policy, Maria Theresa was resolved upon ending the Bavarian war so that she could focus her forces against Prussia. Besides, she hoped that the vanquished state might gravitate—if not immediately, then, like Saxony, after a reflective interval—into the anti-Prussian camp. Confident that Silesia would soon be regained, she was in principle willing to purchase Max Joseph's surrender by abandoning her insistence on a Bavarian equivalent.

The reaction in Paris to word of the Treaty of Füssen was astonishment enlivened by anger. Only five days prior to the signing of the treaty, the Marquis d'Argenson boasted of assuring Louis XV of Max Joseph's "fidelity in any event."[13] The marquis read three implications into the unexpected treaty. First, with her Bavarian worries dissolved, Maria Theresa would have less reason than ever to seek an amicable settlement with Frederick II. Second, Munich's commitment to support Francis Stephen's candidacy made the likelihood of blocking his election far bleaker. Third, Bavaria's repudiation of its French ties meant that France could be free of German involvement. In light of the February resolution to give priority to the German war, the volte-face of April was astonishing. But d'Argenson, though wanting in consistency, never lacked commitment. Part of the Rhenish army was sent to Flanders, France itself renounced any plans of meddling in the coming election, and a request from Frederick for French financial help was turned down. The view that crystallized at Versailles in the weeks after Füssen was that the treaty offered France a grand opportunity to concentrate its energies on Italy and the Low Countries.

While German affairs were extruding the French, Italian affairs were sucking them in. A French army led by Count Maillebois—Conti and Maillebois in effect exchanged commands for the 1745 campaigns—and a Spanish army under Don Philip set out late in May on a slow march along the Ligurian coast to penetrate the Genoese republic and eventually to position themselves for a plunge into Parma, Piacenza, and the Milanese. A month earlier Gages had caught Lobkowitz unawares and, having followed the Austrians as far as Modena, bolted suddenly to the west through Lucca to seek the junction with Don Philip's force that Bourbon strategy called for. This crossing of the Apennines, effected when snows still covered the passes, aroused the admiration of Europe. On the western side of the range the Spanish troops forded the churning and ice-filled Magra in the teeth of Austrian resistance and finally reached the safety of the Genoese republic. Thereupon they took up positions north of the capital city in the Bocchetta Pass—the Thermopylae of Genoa—and before May was out stood ready either to defend the republic or to strike out toward Piedmont or Piacenza. The operation had effected the long-sought union of Spain's two Italian armies.

And diplomacy had meanwhile broadened the base of Bourbon power. Within weeks of the conclusion of the Treaty of Worms, the government of Genoa had learned that the treaty called for the transfer of Finale to Piedmont-Sardinia. The leaders of the republic were astonished. Finale was a Genoese possession—not Austria's to hand over cavalierly. The effect of Worms therefore was to force neutral Genoa to prefer a Bourbon victory, and during 1744 this inclination widened into the gambling resolve to aid the Bourbons and, in the process, pluck off portions of Piedmont. The Spanish, hating Charles Emmanuel, had no compunctions about Genoese territorial expansion at Piedmontese expense; the French, however, ever hopeful of winning over the king of Sardinia, tried to temper Genoa's appetite. And so the ensuing negotiations were protracted. Finally, however, on 1 May 1745, as Bourbon armies converged on the republic from west and east, the Genoese signed the Treaty of Aranjuez. By its terms the republic promised weapons, facilities, and a force of 10,000 men to the Bourbons, and Spain pledged in return a monthly subsidy of 30,000 piastres (£5,375), assistance in capturing vital Apennine approaches, and protection from Charles Emmanuel's army. On 26 June Genoa declared war on Piedmont-Sardinia. If want of time and want of might had undone the Bourbon campaign of 1744, then the Bourbons and their new ally—the "galligurinapolispani" in the word of one wag[14]—could expect success in 1745. By beginning their campaign in May and mobilizing fully 100,000 men for the Italian theater, they looked forward to a grand reunion in Milan before the year had ended.

During the first five months of 1745, therefore, the political shape of belligerent Europe had been transformed. The entrance of Genoa put an end to the forward momentum of the Worms allies; the numbing incompetence of d'Argenson—"he is without capacity, he doesn't know how to govern," the incredulous Campo-Florido wrote[15]—condemned France to incoherence; the withdrawal of Bavaria meant that Maria Theresa had vanquished the last pretender to the Habsburg inheritance. But above all else a chasm had opened in the anti-Austrian camp. On the one side stood Prussia, isolated against Austria and Saxony, in imminent danger of reaping the whirlwind. On the other side stood France, committed to warfare in Italy and the Low Countries while hastening to rid itself of Teutonic engagements. Berlin and Versailles were not enemies: they still had Vienna as their common foe. But they were no longer allies either. Though the decoupling had been long in coming—France's failure to block the Austrian retreat across the

Rhine and Prussia's duplicitous negotiations with Britain were aggrava-tions—it was the Treaty of Füssen that had signaled its arrival. Both Prussia and France had regarded support for Bavaria to be in their own interest. With the departure of Bavaria, there would be two simultaneous but sepa-rate wars in Europe, one along the arc defined by Bohemia's border with Silesia and Saxony and the other rolling back and forth across Italy or squeezing inexorably toward the United Provinces. The participation of Austria in both wars lent them a common denominator. But Austria's foes had now abandoned almost all pretense of providing mutual aid or devising common strategy. It was at this point that, in the course of a mere four weeks, the two most important battles of the entire war were fought.

FONTENOY

On the final day of March 1745, Maurice of Saxony set out from Versailles to join his army at the frontier. During the previous autumn at Courtrai he had drilled his troops as no French troops had been drilled in decades, snapping them through maneuvers, insisting on target practice, instructing them in foraging, and beginning the transformation of the inept army that had muddled at Dettingen into the disciplined army that would prove invincible in the Low Countries. Ever since late in December, when he had persuaded the council that Tournai was the appropriate target for France's springtime offensive, he had been mastering maps and charts. He had assured himself of the services of Count Löwendahl, a Dane whose bold-ness and experience in the Great Northern War gave him a background that French commanders lacked. He had even won the services of Marshal Noailles. Detached from the confusions surrounding the Marquis d'Argenson's conduct of foreign policy, he fixed his mind on one goal: gaining control of the upper Scheldt basin and hence of the heart of the Austrian Netherlands. Maurice had requested a vast army, for he needed a large force to besiege Tournai, a second force to serve as an army of observation, and additional units to employ in feints and to hold as reserves. He had not received all he had sought, but with 95,000 men entrusted to him he still had command of the largest national army thus far seen in the war.[16] He also boasted a rich array of artillery and France's superb engineering corps. The marshal anticipated a difficult campaign, but he expected to succeed.

The coming campaign was also the object of allied thinking. For a variety of reasons the allied army, like the French, was also smaller than its comman-ders had hoped, numbering 43,000 in April, but growing. The Hanoverian force was led by General von Wendt; it was under orders to fight in close coordination with the British. The Dutch contingent was led by the Prince of Waldeck. The Austrians were not numerous, recruited chiefly from the Austrian Netherlands. But their commander, Count Königsegg, the seventy-five-year-old veteran who liked to soothe his scarred body in baths of milk, was expected to supply the ballast of experience sorely wanting elsewhere in Pragmatic leadership circles. His chief pupil was to be George II's second son, the Duke of Cumberland, who had been appointed captain-general of the British forces and commander-in-chief of the united allied force. Cumberland had served in the navy in 1739 and later at Dettingen, but he was only a stripling, and the task before him was forbidding. For a brief time the buoyant Cumberland hoped to launch a campaign that would culminate in Paris, but Ligonier, prompted by a cooler vision, warned that France's numerical advantage meant that "they must, by their situation, be masters of besieging wherever they please."[17] And so the allies fell back on a defensive strategy, while awaiting clear evidence of France's intentions.

The two rival commanders, Maurice of Saxony and the Duke of Cumberland, made their headquarters at Maubeuge and Brussels respectively. By the third week in April 1745 a game of cat-and-mouse had begun. By selecting Maubeuge rather than St. Amand, Maurice surprised the allied command. They had calculated that the French would direct their attack at Tournai. But the choice of Maubeuge raised doubts. Tournai was still a possible target, especially since the bulk of the French army extended westward from Maubeuge in a semicircle ending just beyond the French frontier at Warneton. Still, Mons sat so close to Maubeuge that Cumberland dared not neglect it. This was precisely the state of perplexity the marshal hoped to induce. To keep his opponents guessing, he dispatched two smaller columns toward Mons. The allied council, when it learned of these movements, decided on 23 April to send troops to aid the threatened town. Meanwhile, however, Maurice slipped his main force into motion down the Scheldt River, one column on the left bank to carry out the investment of Tournai and two columns on the right bank to cover the siege and engage the enemy in battle. The whole operation proceeded so smoothly and swiftly that the governor of Tournai, in Brussels for consultations with Cumberland, did not have time to return to his post before the siege operation began on 30 April.

Tournai was defended by a Dutch garrison of 7,000 troops. Its valetudinarian commanders were as dispirited as the Dutch commanders at Menin and Ypres had been in 1744, and besides, they had expected the French attack to fall at Mons. They were thus exceedingly unready when the French suddenly appeared beneath the walls. Their fortress, however, was unquestionably formidable: it was a creation of Vauban's and employed the waters of the Scheldt to keep invaders out. But time and moisture had weakened the mortar, the artillery was rusty and flimsy, the muskets had rotted stocks. Maurice entrusted the siege to Löwendahl, who exploited every advantage, even bribing the Dutch engineers in the fortress to neglect various defensive measures. Meanwhile, Maurice turned his mind to the allied army gathering nearby. Months earlier he had concluded that a siege of Tournai, useful in itself because it would secure the guardian of western Flanders, would also serve to lure the enemy into a battle, and his intelligence reports now confirmed this judgment, for the Pragmatic troops were slowly making their way from Brussels toward the French. When it became clear that an engagement would soon develop, Maurice sent word to Louis XV to hasten from Versailles if he wished to observe. The king responded immediately, reaching the French encampment on 8 May.

Knowing the road the allies were taking, Maurice had the advantage of choosing the battlefield. He selected a plain lying before the French on the eastern side of the Scheldt, about two miles southeast from Tournai. From the ridge near the river that he proposed to use for the French position, the ground sloped gently downhill toward the south and east. The main road by which the allies were approaching ran toward the French from the southeast through the plain, while smaller roads on both sides spliced the newly green fields together. Two natural obstacles created a funnel to direct any advancing army onto this plain. On the left as the French looked out over the plain were the Woods of Barry, scarcely impenetrable but certainly impeding. On the right was the town of Antoing, with its back on the river. The allied commanders would have no choice but to channel their troops into the sector defined by these two barriers. Almost immediately ahead of the French sat the white houses and ocher roofs of the town of Fontenoy. It was ideally situated to impede the allied advance, and so Maurice ordered it leveled and sent troops in to construct fortifications on its eastern and southern flanks. Protected by rubble and their own defenses, they could neither be ignored nor easily dislodged by an enemy. Finally, Maurice resurrected an old device to assure that the enemy chose to funnel its troops only through the gap to the north of Fontenoy. He placed three firm wooden stockades, each with its own cannon, between that town and Antoing. These redoubts threatened to splinter an enemy advance. That left only the Fontenoy-Barry gap. Maurice placed a fourth stockade, called the redoubt of Eu, at the tip of the Woods of Barry that lay closest to Fontenoy. Insofar as it was practicable, Maurice had bent his cunning to creating a battlefield appropriate to his goals.

The Pragmatic Allies drew near to the French on 10 May 1745. Scouts informed Cumberland of the deployment of his enemy, and the allied commander resolved upon an attack the following day. Cumberland read the prospective battlefield as Maurice had foreseen. To the Dutch he assigned the duty of capturing Fontenoy from the French; to the Austrians—chiefly mounted troops deployed on the left—was allocated a feint toward Antoing, staged to confuse the French; to the British and Hanoverian infantry, deploying in a ravine behind the cover of the British cavalry, fell the chief task—the storming of the Fontenoy-Barry gap and the dislodging of the main French army. Though warned that the French had stationed troops in the Woods of Barry and that the allies ought to flush them out before initiating their attack, Cumberland rejected the suggestion. A few sylvan snipers, he held, posed no substantial danger. In general, he was sanguine. His experience at Dettingen had given him great confidence in the valor and shooting skills of the British soldiers.

But Maurice was also confident. He shared Cumberland's view that the British infantryman was an abler soldier than his French counterpart. His whole design had therefore been to find adequate compensation for this deficiency. If the battle unfolded as he planned, the allies would advance up the gap between Fontenoy and the Woods of Barry. Since they would be able to carry neither the woods (with the redoubt of Eu) nor the town, their advance would increasingly expose them to devastating flanking fire. Moreover, they would be advancing not into the French infantry—for this was no ordinary eighteenth-century deployment—but into the face of the French field artillery. Off to his left, under the command of the reliable Löwendahl, Maurice stationed his reserves, hidden from the allied right by the woods and by hills. He left the besieging French army of 21,000 in place at Tournai, thereby keeping the Dutch garrison bottled in and sparing himself the embarrassment of a possible attack from the rear. In effect, Maurice proposed to have the French stand their ground and allow the Pragmatic Allies to march into a meat grinder of artillery fire from the front and rifle fire from the flanks.

The day of decision, 11 May 1745, began with a surcease of the rains. Even before dawn the Pragmatic Allies were astir, completing their disposition under cover first of the fading night and then of the fog that huddled in cupping declivities and extended tentacles along each line of trees. As soon as the French were aware that the allies were grouping—by 5:00 A.M.—they began firing their artillery at the shadowy movements along the allied front. But the allies worried less about the cannon ahead of them than the sharpshooters they suddenly discovered on their right in the Woods of

Barry. The Grassins, the regiment holding the redoubt, were a unit of specially trained cavalry and infantry troops, and Cumberland quickly realized how vulnerable his troops were to flanking fire from the woods. He made efforts to purge the woods of the French, but they were unsuccessful, and when the mass of the British infantry was ready to march, he decided simply to ignore the danger on the flank. To compound his problem, the commander charged with leading the cavalry maneuver that was to disguise the infantry deployment lost a leg to enemy fire from the redoubt of Eu and died before 6:00 A.M., without having revealed his orders to any other officer. Thus, very early on, the British army found itself with an infantry exposed to lacerating fire from the right flank and with twelve of its cavalry squadrons uninstructed and confused.

The task of taking the town of Fontenoy had been given to the Dutch, and they were unequal to it. The French, sheltered behind walls and piles of brick and straw, allowed the Dutch to draw very near before releasing a hail of fire upon their foe. Some of the Dutch fell and the rest fled. Waldeck, who had bragged about what his troops would do when they faced the French, regathered his frightened men and led them in a second assault, aided now by some Austrian cavalry units. But again the French, ensconced amid the litter of a leveled town, drove them off with punishing fire. The Dutch never tried again. The allies did not use their artillery at all in the assault on Fontenoy, an omission that speaks to Cumberland's inexperience. The French were astonished that their Dutch opponents were so feeble, but Maurice, though delighted that Fontenoy remained his to control, knew that the battle was not over yet. When he was congratulated on having routed the Dutch on the French right, he replied simply that "all is not said; let us go to the English, they will be harder to digest."[18]

It was now close to 10:00 in the morning. The British infantry, accompanied by several thousand Hanoverians, stood fully ready to march forward. But neither the Woods of Barry nor the town of Fontenoy had been subdued. The choice lay with Cumberland whether to sound the advance even though the flanks were fearfully vulnerable to raking fire, or to order a retreat and thereupon await a more propitious opportunity. Cumberland chose the forward course. He chose, moreover, to guide it in person. And so, despite Ligonier's and Königsegg's frantic monitions, he abandoned his position of oversight to lead what would become celebrated as one of the great infantry advances of the eighteenth century. He set the deliberate cadence, not even a thousand yards per hour. In effect, he defied the French to gun him down. As the allied column advanced, a startling transformation occurred. Initially the infantry was arrayed in two extended lines. But the narrowness of the gap between Fontenoy and the Woods of Barry—half a mile at most—and the felt need of firing back upon the French secreted in the woods and lodged in the town compelled the wings of the British lines to fall behind and face outward. The linear formation thus became a hollow square—or, more accurately, an oblong—with six battalions (still in two lines) facing the front and three on each wing facing outward.[19] Until they approached to within thirty paces of the French line they withheld their fire. But then they began delivering volleys that demonstrated that, howsoever much the French infantry had improved under Maurice's stern tutelage, it was still not a match for the best that Britain could put in the field. By noon the British column had taken the ground on which the French officers had stood when the sun rose. Ligonier believed the Pragmatic Allies had won.

Maurice was seriously ill on the day of the battle. He hoped that his deployments would require him to be nothing more than a sharp-eyed spectator of a bloody allied retreat, and as late as 9:00 in the morning, when he passed along the French line to inspect his forces, he remained slumped within his wicker carriage. But when word of the allied advance arrived, Maurice shifted immediately to horseback and, despite pain so great that he spent much of the battle biting bullets, he began to direct the French actions personally. Initially he did not fear that the French were in danger, for by his calculation the objective situation still translated into a French victory. Fairly quickly, however, the gravity of the allied challenge imposed itself on him. Thereupon, he defined two immediate goals for his soldiers. First, the French needed to prevent the column from dividing in two, since in its present compacted shape it was a plug that denied British cavalry units transit through the Fontenoy-Woods gap and thus kept these units away from the battle. Second, the French needed to keep the town of Fontenoy out of allied hands—a task now complicated by an advance that had given the allies the opportunity to attack the town from the unbarricaded north. To achieve these ends Maurice hurled French cavalry squadrons against the column. The cost in lives was high—the missions were almost suicidal—but under the pressure the British column slowly lost its momentum. Nevertheless, there were those among Maurice's aides who thought the French had lost. Marshal Noailles actually urged Louis XV to withdraw to the safety of the farther side of the Scheldt. But Maurice appealed both to the king's courage and to his trust by declaring that the situation was not desperate, that the French would prevail, and—not entirely consistently—that "it was necessary to conquer or die."[20] The king stayed.

The swift climax to the battle came at about an hour after noon. The British had tried to get their cavalry into action, but without success: the great column blocked off direct access and fleeing Dutch and Austrian units impeded an effort to circle around to the left. Meanwhile, Maurice had summoned all his available forces—the reserves on the left, the artillery beyond the river, even the troops in the Fontenoy-Antoing gap—flinging them all against the British column in a dramatic pitting of force against force. The column ground to a halt. All along its front and flanks, in the bright and shadowless heat of a lofty sun, white-jacketed French troops and red-jacketed British troops intermingled with green foliage and brown mud in a kaleidoscope of carnage. The critical moment came when Maurice, drawing on his final reserves, sent the cavalry of the *Maison du Roy* against the foe. Cumberland, already halted and increasingly on the defensive in a desperately exposed situation, decided he had no choice but to yield. Almost simultaneously the forbidding British discipline began to dissolve and the British troops to seek cover in retreat. In the course of ten short minutes the outcome had taken on visible form: in a gigantic clash of wills and force, the French had won.[21]

When Louis XV rode forward after the battle to congratulate Maurice of Saxony for avenging Poitiers and establishing French dominance in the west, he found the marshal prostrate in the dirt, tortured by his disorder, his lips awash with yellow sputum. Maurice was later criticized for failing to pursue the vanquished enemy. His physical condition provides ample grounds for understanding his decision. The allies withdrew precipitously but not in total disorder. When they finally reached the safety of Ath, Cumberland "lost all command over his passions, and burst into a violent fit of crying"—in regret over the lives lost, it was said, but also surely in disappointment. Maurice too was struck by the enormity of the battle: "Sire," he reminded Louis XV, "now you see what war really means."[22] The figures for casualties reached absolute levels Europe had not seen in over thirty-five years. The two forces had been approximately equal in size when the battle began, each numbering about 50,000. And the two sides suffered approximately the same number of casualties, between 7,000 and 7,500. Even the tallies of deaths were startlingly similar—about 2,500 for each army.[23] France was adjudged the winner not because it had imposed a clear majority of the casualties on its foe—it had not—but because it held the field when the battle ended and because its army was thereafter free to move largely as it wished in Flanders and Hainault. The margin of victory had been narrow; the fruits thereof were nevertheless abundant. "It is," Maurice wrote to his brother, "very sweet to win battles."[24]

The battle of Fontenoy seized Europe's attention for many reasons. By dealing defeat to the allies, it overturned the mystique of British military superiority. It pointed up the importance of artillery. It raised Maurice of Saxony to heroic status, crowning a career that had seen him step from triumph to triumph through a landscape littered with the broken reputations of other French commanders. Louis XV lavished gifts, including the royal chateau of Chambord, on this Teutonic savior of French glory. On the allied side criticism fell on two targets: the Dutch army and the leadership of the Duke of Cumberland. It was bad enough that the Dutch could had not taken Fontenoy; it was even worse that, at the height of the battle, they had made no effort to distract the French riflemen in the town from firing on the advancing allies. Cumberland was faulted for neglecting to clear the Woods of Barry, to establish an adequate intelligence system, to make his orders clear, and to use his cavalry effectively. In a very real sense, the allied army had the abler soldiers, but the French army had the abler commanders.

HOHENFRIEDBERG

Frederick II was thinking apocalyptically in the spring of 1745: "Either I want to maintain my power or I want everything to perish and even the name 'Prussia' to be enshrouded with me."[25] Though nursing well into May a lingering hope that Austria might accept a return to the settlement of 1742, the king directed his attention to stiffening the defensive capability of his army in Silesia. He did not know where an Austro-Saxon attack would fall, and so he scattered 85,000 men in units throughout the province. At the same time he ordered Prince Leopold to have a special corps placed at Magdeburg, poised to strike at Saxony if Augustus III abetted the Austrian invasion. It was a sign that many of his advisors were far from sanguine that he was obliged to hold Maria Theresa up as an example of courage: are you, he asked, less sturdy than the woman who did not blanch even when Vienna itself was in peril?

Iron-willed as ever, Maria Theresa looked forward with grim pleasure to the coming clash. The honor of leading Austria to its triumph she reserved for Prince Charles of Lorraine. The choice was understandable. He had recently directed the expulsion of the Prussians from Bohemia. It is true that those who best understood such things knew that Count Traun had been the true engineer of Frederick's embarrassment, but Traun had received an appropriate reward in being given command over the important western German army. What was needed in Silesia was not cunning or brilliance, but rather the conventional skills of a seasoned commander. These Prince Charles could muster — and he could bring too all the prestige that attaches to relationship to royalty. And so the queen held to the pattern she had intermittently manifested—a tendency to choose her military commanders on the basis of title or seniority rather than merit—and waited for reports from the north with the ever-present regret that her gender disqualified her from emulating the military career of her hated Prussian rival.

Prince Charles's plan of campaign envisioned an attack on Silesia out of Bohemia. With Breslau as its ultimate target, the main Austro-Saxon army would gather near Hradec Kralove and, having entered Silesia, sweep the beleaguered Prussians before them. To keep Frederick guessing about his foe's intentions, the plan prescribed a second concentration of troops at Olomouc in Moravia: if the king felt obliged to protect the upper reaches of the Oder, he would have fewer troops to deploy to the northwest. As a final element the plan appointed light troops to swarm through Upper Silesia, with the purpose of keeping Prussian lines of communication insecure. Though both the Bohemian and the Moravian gatherings formed slowly, Prince Charles and the Saxon commander, the Duke of Sachsen Weissenfels, were unconcerned. With 75,000 troops at their disposal—20,000 Saxons and 55,000 Austrians—they believed themselves superior in numbers as well as in spirit. Their espionage network had apparently penetrated the Prussian officer corps, sending them information about Prussian deployments, and they chose to base their predictions about Prussia's capacity to fight not on Chotusitz but on the more recent Bohemian campaign. Prince Charles's confidence thus bordered on cockiness. Sieges were possible, he admitted, "but I believe it is better to seek and defeat the enemy army first, . . . then we will have no trouble."[26]

But trouble, of course, was precisely what Frederick had in mind for his enemies. The Prussian intelligence system was working splendidly, and so even before March had passed the king knew that the major attack would fall along the Bohemian frontier. Accordingly, he made Zabkowice Slaskie his headquarters and began drawing in the units he had earlier scattered loosely throughout the province. Frederick in fact knew much more about what the Austro-Saxons were doing than Prince Charles knew of what the Prussians were doing, and the king's plan depended on this asymmetry. In a paradigmatic example of disinformation, he used a double agent to feed the Austrians the story that the Prussians were withdrawing from the frontier back on Breslau. Properly reinforced, such a story was not merely plausible, but so much in accord with Prince Charles's expectations that he did not closely scrutinize it. "One cannot catch mice without setting the trap," Frederick said.[27] News of the French victory at Fontenoy seemed a good sign. But still, all depended on the accuracy of Frederick's assumptions about Austrian gullibility, and the citizenry of Berlin, privy to neither special information nor omens, began in May to seek safety in flight.

An Austro-Saxon army of 59,000 lumbered into Silesia at the opening of June 1745. When Prussia offered no resistance to their entry across the mountains, Prince Charles abandoned all lingering reservations and accorded full credit to reports of a Prussian withdrawal. During the day of 3 June the invading army completed its dusty descent to the Silesian plain, and because reports placed the wary Prussians at Swidnica, Prince Charles allowed his troops, exhausted by their passage of the mountains, to settle in for the night without completing the dispositions that might, in more danger-ous times, be appropriate for an army camping in enemy territory. The town of Strzegom was their target for the next day, and their strung-out line of encampments stretched in an uneven and sprawling semicircle from Hohenfreidberg (now Dobromierz), which lay southwest of Strzegom, to Pilgramshain, which lay northwest. The Saxon van, bivouacked on the Breite Berg near Pilgramshain, was less than a mile from Strzegom. The Austrians, encamped by Hohenfriedberg, were five miles away from the town. The Striegauer Brook flowed out of the mountains through Hohenfriedberg and toward Strzegom and thus formed what was potentially the southern bound-ary of the proposed assault on the latter town. All seemed well as night fell, and with the mountains behind them the commanders' vespertine thoughts were on their coming triumphs. "God must no longer be in heaven," Charles mused, "if we do not win this battle."[28]

While to Austrian eyes all appeared placid to the east, Frederick had set his army of 59,000 on the march. He had spent the previous days closely observing the arrival of his foe. "Now," he said on the evening of 3 June, "the enemy is where we wanted him."[29] With a silence and orderliness that dumb-founded a French observer, the Prussian army spent the night moving into a position that would allow them, they hoped, to catch the Austro-Saxons unawares, unprepared, and disoriented. Moving northwest from the vicinity of Swidnica, the Prussians waded through streams and arrived at the Striegauer Brook about midnight. There they halted for two hours to rest, and then at 2:00 A.M. they resumed their course to the northwest and north, crossing the brook in two columns. The Prussian left deliberately marched into the sinus formed by the Anglo-Saxon arc. The move was risky, but only in this manner could the Prussians gain the positional advantage Frederick sought. The Prussian right—farther from the enemy—marched toward Pilgramshain, where, once deployed, it was to initiate the combat. The Prussian left was meanwhile to move into a position fronting the Austrians and wait for the success of the Prussian right; then they were to join with the right in assailing the enemy before them.

Crepuscular dimness gave the Prussians their first success. At about 4:00 A.M. they startled five Saxon grenadier companies lodged on the Breite

Berg and drove them off almost effortlessly, securing a valuable height for their artillery in the process. Thereupon the Prussian cavalry—led by Buddenbrock, Rothenburg, and Stille—charged upon the still-dazed Saxon cavalry by Pilgramshain, and in two assaults smashed through the defenders' lines. Stunned into action, the Duke of Sachsen-Weissenfels used the time consumed by these cavalry engagements to organize the Saxon infantry, which deployed itself desperately on the sodden ground near Pilgramshain. Some of the most brutal fighting of the war promptly followed, for Frederick had encouraged his troops to regard the Saxons as particularly perfidious foes, whose abandonment of the Prussian alliance constituted heinous betrayal. "No pardon to a Saxon" was understood to be the command of the day—an order thoroughly congenial to troops now possessed by what one of them called a "demonic bloodlust."[30] By 6:00 A.M. the Prussians had prevailed on this front.

When Prince Charles first heard the sounds of gunfire to his left, he assumed they were echoes of the Saxon attack on Strzegom. It took an hour for him to realize that the Prussians—in far greater numbers than the Austrians had supposed—were threatening to overwhelm his army. He turned immediately to his mounted troops as he sought to improvise a defense, and a ferocious cavalry battle ensued, as General Berlichingen, commanding the Austrian right, drew down his reserves to keep repulsing the Prussians, while Prince Ferdinand of Brunswick, Hans Joachim von Zieten, and the Duke of Wurtemberg, commanding the Prussian left, flung their mounted men against the defenders in an effort to erode Austrian resistance. For an hour the battle was in doubt, but then slowly the Prussians asserted a dominance, and at the end the Austrian cavalry broke apart in disorder. By 7:00 A.M. the Prussian situation was truly enviable: they had shattered the allied cavalry on both wings and had put the Saxon infantry to flight. Only the Austrian infantry still contested the field, stripped of its ally and exposed as never before in the war.

And yet the Austrian infantry, whose inferiority to Prussia's had helped shape the outcomes at Mollwitz and Chotusitz, mounted an unexpectedly stiff resistance, at one point driving Prussian infantry back from ground it had seized. Still, it was finally too exposed, too confined, and too deficient in numbers to be able to prevail. The final stroke was delivered when General Gessler, with his Bayreuth Dragoon regiment, chose to intervene decisively and bring the engagement to a swift and clear-cut conclusion. Directing the Prussian infantry to divide and thereby form an avenue to the front, he led two mounted columns in a charge that became one of the legends of Prussian military history. The exhausted Austrians could not cope with this new challenge—ten mounted squadrons sweeping upon and through them—and the final flickers of Austrian resistance died out. By 8:00 A.M. the shock tactics of the Bayreuth Dragoons had closed the battle.[31] They also made the Prussian victory at Hohenfriedberg a peculiar complement to the Prussian victory at Mollwitz: whereas in 1741 the infantry had rescued the cavalry, now it was the mounted soldiers who brought decisive aid to the hard-pressed foot soldiers.

Frederick II had followed the vast sweep of the engagement from his position on the Fuchsberg, a dome situated a mile south of Strzegom. He had dispatched instructions to his commanders as the fighting progressed. Insofar as it is possible during the turbulent course of something as chaotic as a battle, he had orchestrated the victory. The usual variations in figures appear in the accounts of the toll of the battle.[32] The two armies that met at Hohenfriedberg were virtually equal in size, each numbering about 59,000. The engagement was, therefore, larger than Fontenoy by almost 20,000 combatants. As at Fontenoy, about 15 percent of the participants were finally counted among the dead, the wounded, the captured, or the missing, but unlike Fontenoy these casualties were not equally distributed between the two camps. Prussian losses totaled 4,750; only the Pragmatic Army at Dettingen suffered a lower proportion of casualties in a major battle of the war. The losses for the Austro-Saxon army, on the other hand, were substantial—13,700 men, constituting 23 percent of the combatants. The proportion was not out of line with the figures for earlier Austrian battles against Prussia; 23 percent had been counted as casualties at Chotusitz and 27 percent at Mollwitz.[121] But in these previous engagements Prussian losses also had been heavy. At Hohenfriedberg the slaughter was distinctly one-sided.

As European military thinkers contemplated the events of 4 June 1745, they were unanimous in their judgment: Frederick II was the hero of the hour. Prussia's success at Mollwitz may have been Schwerin's doing; the success at Chotusitz might be credited to Crown Prince Leopold. But at Hohenfriedberg the glory was the king's. It was he who had laid a strategic trap, and he who had closed the trap with a difficult tactical maneuver—the flank march—that only a well-trained army could have effected. Surprise and shock tactics had then carried the day. Prince Charles was so embarrassed by the battle that he asked Francis Stephen to convey the news to the queen. There were sound grounds for the prince's embarrassment. During his tenure as commander the Austrian cavalry, the strongest branch of Vienna's fighting force when the war began, deteriorated in both skills and spirit. Hohenfriedberg was dramatic evidence that Prussia now boasted a superiority in horse comparable to its superiority in foot. And on the eve of the battle Charles had committed his most egregious error. Rather than waiting for the next morning, he had brought his troops out of the mountains as the day faded, allowing them no opportunity to array themselves for battle if they should be challenged. General Stille summed up his account with an old and accurate aphorism: "in war mistakes are never made with impunity."[33] Prince Charles made many. King Frederick made few. Since at Hohenfriedberg—and at this point the contrast with Fontenoy becomes clear—the ablest generals and the ablest troops were engaged on the same side, the outcome of the battle was dramatically one-sided.

13

The Worms Alliance Withers
(June 1745 – September 1745)

FRANCE CHALLENGES THE MARITIME POWERS

Maurice of Saxony held a dominant military position in the Austrian Netherlands after the battle of Fontenoy. Once he had secured Tournai, which surrendered on 20 June 1745, he began to besiege Ath, the powerful barrier fortress on the Dender. At the same time he sent Löwendahl with 5,000 men along the Lys to lay siege to Ghent. Löwendahl's operation succeeded almost effortlessly. On 15 July French soldiers swam the moat and gained control of the drawbridge, and the Dutch commander of the large garrison, caught totally unawares, capitulated within hours. Extensive stores of supplies passed to the French, and the allied commander, his army reduced to less than 35,000 men, had no choice but to fall back from Lessines to the vicinity of Brussels. Oudenarde and Bruges soon capitulated, and by the end of July the French stood on the threshold of Zeeland, the southwestern tongue of the Dutch republic. At that point d'Argenson stayed their hand. Believing that there existed a powerful peace party among the leaders of the republic—men who "burned with a keen and sincere desire for pacification"[1]—d'Argenson did not want to drive them into British arms and therefore ordered the army to give its attention to mopping up enclaves of resistance in the western sector of the Austrian Netherlands and positioning itself for an attack on either Antwerp or Brussels in the following year. One French force seized Termonde, positioning itself to swoop downriver on Antwerp whenever it chose. Another force marched back toward the Atlantic shore and quickly picked off Nieuport. Only at Ostend did the French meet a short-lived resistance, but on 24 August Ostend too passed to French control, and Britain thereby lost its final non-Dutch landing site for troops.

The whole series of allied surrenders was stuffing French detention facilities with prisoners of war. So disproportionate in France's favor was the balance of captives that Versailles was enabled to enforce a triumph of a different sort. In return for allowing Britain to implement a prisoner exchange, France insisted on the liberation of Marshal Belle-Isle, and on 13 August 1745 the celebrated commander sailed out of Dover on a royal yacht. He had, in general, been pleased with his treatment in Britain, but he left with scant respect for British military power, declaring (according to one account) "that he would engage with five thousand scullions of the French army to conquer England."[2] Events in the Low Countries lent plausibility to the boast. When Ath finally surrendered early in October, France controlled almost half of Austria's Atlantic province, and Brussels was as vulnerable to French attack as Antwerp.

There were those in France in the heady summer of 1745 who wanted to control Britain too. But, despite Belle-Isle's puffing, more than 5,000 men — and well-trained men, not scullions — would be needed for that task. Noailles declared that 30,000 would not be too few "if Your Majesty truly wishes the Mass to be said in London,"[3] a figure that approximates Maurice of Saxony's estimate of 1744. Because this was a very substantial number of troops, the Marquis d'Argenson had spurned Jacobite proposals that France support a Stuart restoration. But d'Argenson did not exercise exclusive control over French foreign policy, and no one was better positioned to conduct an independent policy course toward the island kingdom than the promoter of the ill-fated "descent" plan of early 1744, Count Maurepas, minister of marine. He and Cardinal Tencin still harbored hopes of restoring the house of Stuart to a throne in Britain. The military successes in the Low Countries in 1745 created an environment propitious to a new effort, and although Maurepas could not supply French troops — the brothers d'Argenson controlled troop allocations — he could offer various kinds of naval assistance. And so, in this backhanded fashion, even while it was squeezing the British in the Low Countries, France began to challenge Britain on its home soil as well.

The bearer of the challenge was Charles Edward Stuart, more commonly styled "the Young Pretender" and, at twenty-four, one of the youngest figures of significance in our story. His father, James Stuart, was the pretender to the thrones of England and Scotland, and Charles Edward was determined to win back the Stuarts' patrimony. Staggeringly ignorant of military matters and surprisingly uninformed about history, Charles Edward gave full credit to stories he heard from Irish supporters about England's hatred for the Hanoverians. He seemed oblivious too to the shabby treatment he received from the French government. It is not surprising, therefore, that the Marquis d'Argenson saw little utility in supporting such a blinkered and quixotic adventurer. But Charles Edward read the signs differently. The

British defeat at Fontenoy compelled the British government to send more troops to the continent and reduce their home force to 8,000. Never had the island been more vulnerable. Charles Edward proposed therefore to sail to Britain, raise an army from among the legions of his supporters, march on London, and drive "the Elector of Hanover"—for so the Jacobites styled George II—back to his German satrapy.

Though Louis XV knew little or nothing of the scheme, and the Marquis d'Argenson not much more, nevertheless France (through Maurepas) underwrote the venture. Charles Edward sailed on 15 July 1745 on the *Du Teillay*, a small ship owned by a prominent French privateer, Antoine Walsh. The escort that covered it, *l'Élisabeth*, was a regular ship of the line, temporarily chartered by Walsh. The arms the ships carried were supplied by the Ministry of Marine. On 20 July the British ship of the line *Lion* sighted the two French ships and drew between them. A fierce engagement ensued, in which the *Lion* suffered over 150 casualties and *l'Élisabeth* over 200. But the tiny *Du Teillay*, too insignificant to attract any concentrated British attention, slipped away during the battle with only minor damage and made for the western isles off Scotland. There, on the island of Barra, on 3 August, Charles Edward stepped onto Scottish soil for the first time in his life. Less than a month later, at Glenfinnan on 30 August, the Young Pretender raised the royal standard in his father's behalf and proclaimed James Stuart king of Scotland. Just as imperial Germany would later send Lenin into Russia in the hopes that his cause would undo the enemy's war effort, so too did France in 1745 send Charles Edward into Britain to foment civil strife.

THE NETTLE OF LOUISBOURG

The only setback endured by the French in their struggle with the British in 1745 occurred in North America. In this transatlantic world amid (and at the expense of) indigenous peoples who were struggling to discover strategies of survival, settlers from both nations cultivated their empires. New France was a realm sustained and defined by two great rivers, the St. Lawrence and the Mississippi. British North America sprawled up and down the eastern coast of the continent, divided into fourteen autonomous colonies ranging from Georgia in the south to Nova Scotia in the north. The peoples of the two empires contemned each other. New France was Catholic and authoritarian; British North America was Protestant and populist. The economy of New France rested largely on the fur trade; the economy of British North America embraced commercial farming, mercantile enterprises, slave-trading, and primitive manufacturing. There was a severe demographic imbalance between the two realms: settlers in British areas outnumbered settlers in French areas by a ratio of twenty to one. But because the Appalachian Mountains separated the Atlantic coast from the Mississippi basin while the Abenaki Indians separated New York from Canada, the only region where French and British interests actually impinged was where Nova Scotia abutted on Cape Breton Island.

The key to the defense of New France was the great fortress of Louisbourg, designed by no less a figure than Vauban. Famed as "the Gibraltar of the West," it sat on the eastern coast of Cape Breton Island, facing out to the Atlantic. French privateers took sanctuary within its precincts, French fishers profited from its protection, and in this sparsely settled region it was a desirable landing site for ships that had completed the exhausting crossing of the ocean. With stone walls rising to thirty feet, covering almost one hundred cannon, it was deemed impregnable against assault. Such was not, however, the conclusion of the men who directed the affairs of Massachusetts, the most populous and important of Britain's New England colonies. Reports that French cannon at Louisbourg were in disrepair, that French militiamen were untrained and disgruntled, and that the fortress was vulnerable to attack from the land side circulated in Massachusetts and whetted Anglo-American appetites. Governor William Shirley accepted the reports and early in 1745 secured by a narrow margin the support of the colonial legislature for an attack on the fortress. The legislature then chose the popular president of the council, William Pepperell, to lead the expedition.

Massachusetts besought the aid of other interested parties, and several neighboring colonies chose to lend assistance. Connecticut sent 500 troops, New Hampshire sent 450; Rhode Island sent a ship, New York ten cannon, Pennsylvania and New Jersey funds. To Britain a request for naval support was addressed, and the government in London also agreed to help, directing Commodore Peter Warren to leave his station in the West Indies and lead his squadron to the enterprise. Meanwhile, recruiting parties spread out across Massachusetts, enticing young men to volunteer for the venture with such diverse lures as drink, music, sermons, and appeals to patriotism. All these various pieces then fell into place in the spring of 1745, and early in May the expedition gathered near Canso—4,200 troops, 34 cannon, approximately 100 transport vessels, about a dozen small armed boats, and a British naval squadron of four ships, including one boasting 60 guns. Though by the standards then obtaining in Europe, or by contrast with Cartagena, this was not an extensive project, by North American standards it was large.

The crossing from Nova Scotia to Cape Breton Island was begun on 10 May 1745, and within forty-eight hours the invasion force was securely ashore at Gabarus Bay, a scant three miles west of Louisbourg. A detachment of seventy-five French troops sent out to oppose the landing was abysmally inadequate, and the governor of Cape Breton, Louis Dupont Du Chambon, was left with no recourse but to summon the 4,000 loyal inhabitants of the region to accept the protection of the walled fortification and to wait for the attackers to spend all their energies and resources in trying to breach the ramparts. Thereupon, each side stumbled into stupid mistakes. At the very opening of the operation, Pepperell dispatched 400 men to march around to the north side of the harbor and reconnoiter the centrally important Grand Battery. Its defenders simply abandoned this dominating enclosure with its twenty-four cannon, neglecting even to blow it up. Thus, without firing a shot, within days of landing, the attackers had occupied a key element in the defense perimeter of Louisbourg. But where the French were too timid, the Anglo-Americans were incautious. On one occasion a besotted militiaman betrayed an entire operation by raising a cheer to success within earshot of previously unsuspecting French troops. Sixty besiegers were promptly gunned down. In general, the conflict may be said to have pitted the feckless against the feeble.

In the long run, however, the siege was successful. The Anglo-Americans were able to subject Louisbourg to crushing artillery fire. They had brought their own cannon with them, and with the capture of the Grand Battery they had taken possession of still larger pieces. By late June, in Cambon's words, "all the houses in the town were demolished, riddled with holes, and not fit for habitation."[4] Even the French hope for provisions proved doomed. A French supply ship was intercepted by Commodore Warren's squadron, and its foodstocks, originally intended for the besieged, passed to the commissary of the besiegers. On 26 June Pepperell and Warren concluded plans for a joint assault. But by then the defenders had seen the hopelessness of their situation: "they did not," a French observer in the town remarked, "want to be put to the sword and were not strong enough to resist a general assault."[5] After only a day given over to negotiation, on 28 June 1745 Chambon surrendered. The Gibraltar of the west, like its namesake across the Atlantic, was in British hands.

Word of this achievement took two months to vault the ocean. But when it reached Britain late in August, it thrilled a people starved for good tidings. The ministers, recalling Cartagena, were delighted that a venture which combined land and sea operations and united British and colonial forces could prosper.[6] They were pleased that at a cost of less than 450 casualties Britain had seized a celebrated enemy stronghold. They immediately understood that the acquisition gave Britain a useful pawn in any negotiations to end the war. The enthusiasm of the British people unnerved politicians who were inclined to take the longer view. Henry Pelham, to cite one example, feared that just as a refusal to hand over Gibraltar had protracted the war with Spain in the first decade of the century, so too would Louisbourg "do the same with France."[7] His concerns were, however, a minority view. Across the Channel in France, where reports of military successes in the Low Countries seized attention, the events at Louisbourg figured less prominently than in Britain. But no French minister could safely contemplate the loss of so important a fortress, and Count Maurepas quickly resolved to use the next year to recover the citadel.

THE CONVENTION OF HANOVER

Frederick II was confident after Hohenfriedberg that Austria's situation had become desperate. Pressed in Italy and pummeled in the Low Countries, its Russian friends aloof and its Dutch allies abased, Austria stood isolated. In such a situation Frederick saw ample room for patient probing. To keep the pressure on Austria, he marched his army out of Silesia into western Bohemia, occupying Hradec Kralove before the first of July and seizing the gorged magazine there. But then he stopped, waiting for leaders in Vienna, Dresden, Versailles, Munich, and London to reflect upon the implications of his military advantages. "I wage war only to attain peace," he assured Podewils.[8] But events did not unfold in quite the manner Frederick expected. A major grounds for his optimism in June 1745 was the presence near Frankfurt of a large French army. Commanded by the Prince of Conti, whose recent Italian exploits had earned him much applause, this army of 40,000 men was positioned to influence the imperial election. No one appreciated this truth more keenly than Maria Theresa, who launched Count Traun out of occupied Bavaria to join his forces with Batthyany's on the Rhine. Had Conti been in receipt of vigorous orders, he might have responded to this challenge by seeking out and humbling Batthyany's army before Traun's reinforcements could arrive. But the prince was hobbled by confining instructions that reflected France's post-Füssen disengagement from Germany and stood by as a mere spectator while Traun marched his army into the Rhineland. Then faced with an enemy that numbered 45,000, Conti ordered a withdrawal behind the Rhine. Most Europeans who attended to such matters were appalled at France's timidity. Frederick II spoke for many when he said that Conti, "having played the baron in Italy, has just played the ninny on the banks of the Rhine."[9]

The British ministers had read Fontenoy and Hohenfriedberg as signs that again in 1745, as before in 1742, the Pragmatic Allies needed to cut their losses. Silesia, they stated, could not be recovered, Britain could not afford to keep funneling money to fuel Austria's megalomania, and therefore both Britain and Austria stood to gain if Prussia could again be extruded from the war. When British diplomats agreed to meet their Prussian counterparts at Hanover in June 1745, Frederick received confirmation of his intuition that London would seek terms with Berlin. And so, on 5 August, the king gave formal approval for a diplomatic initiative with London. The negotiations took place at Hanover, whither George II had sped at the opening of the summer to free himself from the vexations of British politics. Lord Harrington accompanied the monarch, and his intense pourparlers with the Prussian envoy Andrié constituted his reintroduction to the world of diplomatic give-and-take. On 26 August Andrié and Harrington concluded the Convention of Hanover. In it the Prussian state agreed to accept a peace that brought it neither territorial nor financial gain, and Frederick even promised to cast his vote for Francis Stephen. The problem, of course, was that Britain was not Prussia's chief foe. True peace was available only in Vienna. But once again, as in 1742, Britain was now pledged to try to end the Austro-Prussian war and given a space of six weeks in which to effect that goal.

The Convention of Hanover marked an important phase in Prussia's historic relationship with Britain. One turn to London, as in 1742, might be dismissed as an expedient seized upon by a nation casting about for help; a second such turn, however, defied such construction and suggested instead that something of enduring significance was occurring. From Berlin's perspective it had long been a matter of dispute whether Versailles or London was the more useful ally. But by 1745 the answer seemed clearer: despite its unwillingness to send troops into Germany, Britain offered the prospectively more fruitful alliance. London had influence in Vienna, firmer control over its own policy, a sound understanding of the importance of international equipoise, and above all money. Correlatively, from London's perspective the war had raised serious doubts about the value of the traditional Anglo-Austrian tie. An accommodation based in any case more on the absence of disputes than on shared interests, the bond between London and Vienna had been made still more tenuous by the inability of the two allies to agree after 1741 on which of their enemies was the more threatening and on whether compromise was wiser than firmness. What was wrought in secrecy at Hanover in August of 1745 did not yet shatter the old configuration of Europe. But new articulations were struggling to be born.

Events occurring at Dresden even as Harrington and Andrié haggled in Hanover afforded clear evidence that Britain's judgment about a policy dissonance between itself and Vienna was sound. The battle of Hohenfriedberg had left Maria Theresa unshaken in her resolve to wrest Silesia from Prussia. If Britain was reluctant to help Austria in this campaign for justice, there remained Saxony. In July the queen sent Count Joseph Khevenhüller to the Saxon capital to explore the possibility of more extensive Austro-Saxon cooperation. She had feared that the unhappy outcome at Hohenfriedberg might drive Augustus III to seek security in neutrality, but Khevenhüller reported that the lure of land held Augustus in thrall. With Augustus's greed and Maria Theresa's wrath thus making common cause, on 29 August 1745 the two allies declared their alliance indissoluble, pledged themselves to send still larger armies against their foe, and resolved to press the struggle even into the chill of winter. Thus, a scant three days after Britain had pledged itself to lead Vienna to peace, Austria and Saxony rededicated themselves to war.

FRANCIS I

Despite all its misfortunes, Austria stood on the brink of one major success as the summer of 1745 passed—the securing of the imperial crown. No sooner had her father died in 1740 than Maria Theresa had resolved that her husband should be emperor. When the Elector of Bavaria was chosen instead, she had responded with procedural obstructionism and a covert campaign to have her young son Joseph chosen king of the Romans and hence heir presumptive to the title. But then in early 1745, against actuarial probability, the new emperor had himself died. The strategy that favored Joseph for heir was immediately abandoned for one that proposed Francis Stephen as title-holder. Neither he nor his wife was in a concessive mood. Though vowing that he would not, even for an empire, yield up a "hand's breadth" of Austrian territory, he also vowed to succeed.[10] And an emerging imperial consensus strengthened his candidacy: the German princes, having lived through the consequences of their choice of a middling prince as their nominal leader, were inclined to agree that only the greatest of princes could maintain the office of emperor. Francis Stephen was merely a princeling in his own right, it is true, but he was husband of the woman who ruled the vastest realm west of Muscovy. By the summer of 1745 the Austrian leadership anticipated Francis Stephen's election.

What Austria expected, France feared. In a letter to Maurice of Saxony, who was spending August mopping up resistance in the Austrian Netherlands, the Marquis d'Argenson explained that if France failed to block Francis Stephen's election, Versailles "would not be able to refrain from continuing the war and engaging . . . down to the last cent and the last man."[11] On the other hand, however, d'Argenson also refused to give the Prince of Conti the support he needed. His army's departure from the vicinity of Frankfurt left France with only an ineffectual diplomatic presence there. D'Argenson's problem was that the man he supported as a rival candidate, Augustus III, though flattered by French attention, doubted that he could muster a majority in the electoral college and saw little to be gained even if he could. A successful campaign, after all, would only be an invitation to the type of misery Bavaria had so recently borne. Augustus therefore followed a characteristic course: not wanting to disoblige anyone, he let it be known that he would not seek the imperial office but neither would he spurn it. Oddly, this was enough to keep d'Argenson active in his behalf. And the marquis had alternative ideas as well, including the remarkable suggestion, paralleling in some ways his hopes for Italy, that the German princes might dispense with an emperor entirely and transform the empire into a federal republic!

Against France's feeble opposition Austria mounted a vigorous campaign. The military aspect of it was complete when Traun and Francis Stephen encamped near Heidelberg to make their presence felt at Frankfurt. Building on this military advantage, Austrophile flacks proceeded to control public discussion of the electoral issue by spreading broadsheets throughout Germany and beyond that proclaimed the Habsburg case. The title of a famous one—*Germania triumphans sub aquila Austriae*—suggests the tone of the briefs. Simultaneously, Austria's agents sought out representatives of the electoral states to try to persuade them of the need to choose Francis Stephen. A useful line of argument was elaborated by Johann Jakob Moser, the celebrated legal writer who at Hanover's behest drafted two memoranda on the issue. What the empire needed, he asserted, was "neither an all-too-powerful nor an all-too-powerless emperor."[12] It was an argument that many German leaders were eager to hear.

As the day of the election drew near, the various foreign diplomats whose presence had turned Frankfurt into a congress by day and a fete by night withdrew from the city in respect for the old convention that called upon those who could inhibit electoral freedom to absent themselves from the vicinity. An exception was made for the French diplomat Saint-Séverin, who lay abed with illness and could not comfortably depart. Even the envoys of Prussia and the Electoral Palatine, unhappy at the triumph of the Austrian party, chose to depart. The representatives of the seven remaining electors then set about to consummate their solemn business, and on 13 September 1745 Francis Stephen was unanimously chosen king of the Romans. Cannon blasts quickly signaled that the conclusion was at hand, and the citizenry of

Frankfurt, in sharp contrast to their sullen behavior in 1742, hailed the choice of the Duke of Tuscany with parties and parades. Word meanwhile spread to Vienna, where Maria Theresa had been waiting, pregnant and eager, for her day of vindication. She had already decided that she would leave her hereditary lands for the first time in her reign to see her husband crowned emperor. Despite Francis Stephen's pleading, however, she refused to participate in the ceremony. Her reasoning was characteristically shrewd: though some thought that she stayed in the shadows so as not to diminish her husband's luster, she actually played the incognita so as not to diminish her own. On 4 October 1745 (not coincidentally the feast day of St. Francis), Maria Theresa watched as Francis Stephen, astride a black charger and adorned with the jeweled crown of Jerusalem (symbolic of his nominal status as Duke of Lorraine), rode forth to receive his new dignity. When the imperial diadem replaced the crown of Jerusalem on his head he became the emperor Francis, and Maria Theresa became, in the style of the day, the empress-queen.

THE CORSICAN REVOLUTION

The island of Corsica sits in the ample fold formed by the sweep of the north Italian coastline from Nice to Orbetello. Today a part of the French republic, in the first half of the eighteenth century it moved within the orbit of Italian civilization, and its political order was imposed by Genoese overlordship. And yet Corsica was sui generis, for its mountainous terrain provided a defense against foreign penetration. Habits of local self-government, through which rural communities chose their own leaders, had long been nourished. Meanwhile, the primacy of clan and the concomitant politics of family warfare had long provided a tradition of violent feuding that much of continental Europe found repugnantly backwards. Corsican tradition generated two types of notables—the so-called fathers of the communes and the clan chiefs. Three hundred years of Genoese rule had not crushed Corsican customs, and although nominally in command of the entire island, the republic was generally pleased if it could control the woebegone coastal towns. The impoverished island was important because, the Mediterranean Sea being the great highway for southern Europe, Corsica was a centrally located waystation on the trade routes of the West.

In the opening decades of the eighteenth century, the pattern of mutual forbearance that had allowed Corsica to accept Genoese control finally began to unravel. The governors sent out by Genoa were all too often insensitive. As misgovernment became intrusive, the bulk of the Corsican leaders

decided that the Corsican people needed Corsican direction. In 1729, provoked by a tax increase and an attack on Corsican soldiers in Finale, the
notables decided to take up arms in an effort to alter the political arrangement
with Genoa. The republic in turn sought help in suppressing the rebellion,
and a force of imperial troops temporarily arrived on the island. But the
revolt continued, and to lend it coherence the notables chose a luckless
German adventurer, Baron Theodore von Neuhoff, to be their king. They
also won a measure of British support. So Genoa again sought aid, and in
1738 it was France's turn to dispatch troops to the island. Versailles was no
more successful than Vienna had been at getting Genoa to temper its policy
toward its dependency. But under French rule the island came at least to
know the benefits of efficient administration. King Theodore meanwhile fled.
The uneasy peace that prevailed on the island after the French left in 1741
was grounded in prostration, not compromise. It allowed Genoese authority
to recover some of its influence. But its chief product was a new generation
of Corsican leaders.

As this account makes clear, the major powers of Europe were prepared to
intervene in Corsican affairs. Charles VI had boasted, among his many titles,
that of king of Corsica. His readiness to send aid to Genoa in 1731 bespoke
his hope to win Austrian access to the port of Saint Florent. Britain, with
deeper commercial interests, pursued a contrary strategy. Rather than court-
ing Genoese favor, Britain hoped to sever Genoa's tie with Corsica and transform the island into a British satellite. But of all the major states of Europe,
France was the one most interested in Corsica. It coveted Corsican timber,
and as possessor of the naval base at Toulon it wanted to keep Corsica out of
hostile hands. Briefly in 1735 Versailles flirted with the heretical idea of supporting the insurgents. But the implications of having a king of France sanction a revolution were so patently fearful that by 1737 the foreign ministry
had committed France to upholding Genoa's claim. It was this pro-Genoese
policy that prevailed throughout the War of the Austrian Succession, whether
Cardinal Fleury or Count Maurepas or Marquis d'Argenson directed
French actions in the Mediterranean.

The pressure of international events finally forced the Genoese government to reconsider its adamance toward the island. Though fearful of losing
face if too concessive, the Genoese were increasingly fearful of losing Corsica
if they were too stubborn, and in early 1743 they sent Pietro Maria
Giustiniani, a man of moderate views who was known and respected by
Corsicans, as commissioner general to Corsica. His promises of reform came
too late. By the time he publicly proclaimed them in June of that year, the
Corsican insurgents had organized themselves into a regency (on the fiction

that they were ruling on behalf of King Theodore), besought Turkish protection, and created for the first time in their fourteen-year revolt an alternative structure of government. An assembly convoked to reply to the Genoese concessions agreed to allow the republic to continue appointing governors and lieutenant governors. But the assembly also proclaimed that Corsicans alone could determine the arrangements under which Corsica would live. Not unnaturally, the Genoese government feared that the assembly's claim would incite thoughts of independence among Corsicans and viewed the existence of the Corsican regency as an invitation for hostile intervention by a foreign power.

The Genoese fears were well founded. As the regency extended its de facto authority across almost the entire island in the second half of 1743, nearby states saw an opportunity for grasping advantage from the republic's colonial dilemma. As long as Genoa remained impartial in the spreading European war, those who hoped to profit from Corsica's contumacy were given pause by the reflection that aid to the rebels would incur opposition from the republic. But once the Treaty of Worms was concluded, Genoa's neutrality was known to be spurious. Approaches from France soon followed, and Genoa gravitated quickly into the Bourbon camp. That shift removed all grounds for Pragmatic hesitation, and in July of 1744 the king of Sardinia authorized Domenico Rivarola, a latter-day condottiere, to raise a regiment in Corsica to fight for Piedmont-Sardinia. The regency made no effort to impede Rivarola's pursuit of soldiers; Theodore had even encouraged it. The republic, however, was enraged and in August responded by declaring that it would seek military assistance from the Bourbons. The following spring it accepted the Treaty of Aranjuez.

Meanwhile, Genoese authority in the island virtually dissolved. The few Genoese troops and officials who remained dared not venture forth from their isolated bastions. Thus there was no resistance when a general assembly met at Orezza in August 1745 to make explicit what had for years been implicit in the Corsican insurgency. Abandoning both the fiction that they were serving an absent king and the notion that nominal ties between Genoa and Corsica should be maintained, the clan chiefs and the local magistrates established a consulate and laid claim to Corsican independence from the republic. Power was assigned to two protectors, Alessio Matra and Gian Pietro Gaffori. The former had served in the French army until mounting debts had prompted him to flee. The latter, a physician who had attended Theodore, was an admirer of French efficiency. Together they set about to try to create a Corsican state from Corsican society. Meanwhile, by one of those exquisite coincidences that history occasionally conjures up, on the very day that the assembly finally completed its work, Charles Edward Stuart raised his standard in the Highlands. With the benefit of hindsight we can see that in August 1745 the ligaments of political obedience in Europe were beginning to snap.

BASSIGNANA

Bourbon strategy for the campaign in Italy in 1745 involved two important changes from the thinking of the previous year. First, rather than divide their forces, the Bourbons would aggregate and coordinate them. Then, rather than approach Piedmont-Sardinia from the southwest, they would attack from the southeast, thus leaving their enemies in doubt about whether the ultimate target of the advance was Piedmont or Lombardy. Bourbon strategists calculated that the pressure they would apply would induce their foes to split apart, with the Austrians regrouping around Milan and the Piedmontese falling back on Turin. Once this division was effected, the Bourbons would have precisely reversed the situation of the previous year, when it had been the Worms allies who had coordinated their operations and the Bourbons who had deliberately separated their Italian forces. The Gallispans used two converging routes of entry into Charles Emmanuel's realm in June 1745. One lay along the courses of the Bormida and Tanaro rivers, and it was assigned to Maillebois, a connoisseur of Italian warfare. Bourcet stood at his side. The other avenue into Piedmont, the Scrivia River, was allotted to Gages, whose Italian exploits were beginning to win the attention of European observers. Like most good military schemes, the Bourbon plan was simple. The two armies would advance simultaneously. Piedmont-Sardinia would be unable to defend itself along both avenues of attack. Wherever the defense finally crumbled, the Gallispans, coordinating their movements, would rush through, securing access to the plains that ran northward from the Tanaro and the Po to Turin and Milan. The key to success would lie in the numerical advantage enjoyed by the Gallispans, in their superior generalship, and in their ability to exploit their proximity to keep in communication.

The Worms allies knew of the Bourbon convergence on Genoa. Maria Theresa was so appalled at Lobkowitz's failure to impede Gages's passage of the Apennines that she finally recalled her faltering commander, sending him to Silesia and replacing him in Italy with Count Schulenburg. The count acted quickly to repair some of the damage caused by Lobkowitz's paralysis, leading 18,000 Austrian troops west from Modena toward the Piedmontese fortifications on the Scrivia. Meanwhile, Charles Emmanuel prepared to

parry the expected Bourbon thrust against his kingdom by sending reinforcements to Acqui on the Bormida and to Novi and Tortona on the
Scrivia. Since the Bourbons (with their Genoese allies) were pouring 87,000
troops into the small triangle defined by the valleys of the Bormida, the
Scrivia, and the Po, and since the Worms allies were replying by stationing
40,000 defenders in the area, the scope of Italian belligerence in the war rose
in the summer of 1745 to levels equivalent to those found in the German theater. On 26 June Novi fell to Gages; on 11 July Acqui submitted to
Maillebois. Soon thereafter the two commanders met at Acqui. The juncture
of Bourbon forces, dreamed of in Madrid and dreaded in Turin, had finally
been effected.

But all was not harmonious in the Gallispan camp. Maillebois and Gages
contended with each other for theater command. The issue was referred to
Madrid and Versailles, and Louis XV, yielding to his Spanish uncle, ordered
Maillebois to defer to his Spanish counterpart. Only two limitations were
placed on French subordination: Maillebois should protect his communications with France, and he should stay out of the Milanese unless its defenses
crumbled at the Bourbon approach. Behind this dispute over command lay a
deeper yet more diffuse quarrel between the French and Spanish governments about Bourbon war aims. In May Maurepas had assured Campo-
Florido that France would not abandon Spain. He went so far as to assert
that Maurice was conquering territory in Flanders precisely for the purpose
of trading it to secure a holding for Don Philip. To the Marquis d'Argenson
this assertion seemed indefensible: in the same month that Maurepas offered
his promise, d'Argenson suggested that if Spain could be appeased with trophies elsewhere, France would be free to retain Maurice's winnings in the
Low Countries. Fortunately for the Gallispan commanders in Italy, this
division over the future of Flanders did not lame the military advance. On
8 August 1745 Gages began his siege of Tortona. The town surrendered less
than a week later, and while the fabled citadel held out until early in
September, Gages knew much earlier that it would be forced to yield.

The victory at Tortona enabled Gages to take advantage of his numerical
superiority. For years the Spanish royal couple had longed to plant Spanish
banners in the ancient Farnesan lands they intended for Don Philip. It was
now possible to do so. Schulenburg's march toward Piedmont had left Parma
and Piacenza uncovered. Gages sent out a tentacle of 8,000 men, under the
command of the Duke of Vieuville, to seize these prizes in the east. Piacenza
yielded to an escalade attack on the night of 15 September, Parma surrendered a day later, and Bobbio was soon occupied. The Bourbon force then
retraced some of its route, crossed the Po near Stradella, and, while marching

back westward, seized Pavia, a gateway to Milan, on 22 September. Elizabeth Farnese was overjoyed at the news: her patience, her obstinacy, her tirades had finally been rewarded. As far as she was concerned, the immediate question was no longer whether Don Philip would secure his own Italian establishment; it was rather whether Charles Emmanuel and Maria Theresa could retain theirs. And Bourbon successes did not end with the conquest of the Parmesan and Oltrepo. When Pavia surrendered, Schulenburg felt he could no longer leave all of Lombardy vulnerable. And so, despite the pleas of Charles Emmanuel, he began on 22 September to withdraw his troops across to the northern bank of the Po and direct them toward Vigevano. The disjunction of the Worms allies had been effected. If the Bourbons could now seize the great fortress at Bassignana, the north Italian plain could be theirs for the taking.

Like Cuneo, the Piedmontese fortification at Bassignana sat on a triangular wedge of land defined by two rivers. But whereas mountains and crags cupped Cuneo, Bassignana basked in the milder environs of the lower Tanaro and middle Po, where riverbanks rose gently rather than abruptly. Gages and Maillebois realized that the prerequisite to the conquest of Bassignana was the placing of an army west of the village. To achieve this goal they needed to be able to ford the Tanaro and thereby move troops into the triangular wedge. This task proved easy, for a dry summer had left the Tanaro only knee deep in places, and by inviting the Piedmontese defenders to chase probing detachments out of the wedge Bourcet cunningly discovered the sites of the fords. As soon as Gages learned that Schulenburg was retreating, he drew his forces in from scattered encampments. During the night of 26-27 September he set up batteries on the southeasterly shore of the Tanaro so that he could cover the troops that the Gallispans began sending across onto the wedge. The Piedmontese learned on 26 September that an assault was imminent. Charles Emmanuel sent a plea for Schulenburg's return. But the defenders were outmanned, and by crossing the Tanaro the Gallispans were already tipping the scales mightily in their favor.

The Bourbon army totaled 50,000, with Gages commanding the right and Maillebois leading the left.[13] Against this powerful force Charles Emmanuel pitted 30,000 defenders. Barring only the battle of Parma in 1734, this clash was the largest to occur on Italian soil in almost forty years. The numbers foretold the outcome. The Piedmontese line was stretched too thin to be able to fend off the Gallispan advance. With communications intact, the divided Bourbon units maintained an exemplary coordination. The heaviest attack fell on the center of the Piedmontese line. Charles Emmanuel's hardened soldiers held their ground for a while, and his cavalry succeeded in harassing the Bourbon army. But the sheer weight of the Gallispan attack finally wore down Piedmontese resistance and split the center of the defense. This rupture exposed the Piedmontese left to an internal flank attack from the Spanish, and the king soon ordered a tactical withdrawal, leaving the town of Bassignana to Gages. The Spanish commander then used his control of the tip of the wedge to destroy the bridge that might have let Schulenburg's returning forces join the fray. When he learned that the Austrians could not return, Charles Emmanuel ordered a full retreat, and the Piedmontese effected it with their wonted discipline, regathering at Casale.[14] But Bassignana now sat in enemy hands.

Of all the large battles of the war, Bassignana was the least sanguinary. The Gallispans suffered only 1,000 casualties, the Worms allies only 2,500 (most of whom were prisoners of war).[15] But its comparative bloodlessness does not bespeak an insignificance. It culminated a campaign that had been as crisply executed as any in the war. Some commentators have credited Gages with the success; others have given the trophy to Maillebois. Each commanded with flair, and as a team they were superb. They exerted pressure relentlessly. Though mountains separated their armies from their bases in Genoa, they kept their troops adequately supplied with food and ordnance. And thus the Gallispans stood at the end of September with Milan but forty-five miles away in one direction and Turin not much farther in another. What the Convention of Hanover had done to Austro-British cooperation, the battle of Bassignana did to Austro-Piedmontese cooperation. As a consequence, the Worms alliance had splintered into its beleaguered constituent elements.

14

Infelix Austria
(September 1745 – December 1745)

SOOR

The successful conclusion of the Austro-Saxon negotiations at the end of August 1745 allowed Prince Charles to resume stalking his Prussian foes. His immediate aim was to drive them from Bohemia and carry the war back into Silesia. But since the Saxons would now launch an independent assault on Brandenburg itself, moving north from Leipzig toward Berlin, Frederick would be compelled (his enemies serenely believed) to divide his forces, thereby exposing each of his armies to the rigors of undermanned battle. The plan was sound. The combined Austro-Saxon army would outnumber the Prussian army, and the allies were maneuvering to secure a significant numerical superiority at each of the two points of prospective combat. Frederick, deprived of accurate intelligence in the hostile environs of Bohemia, responded by choosing to withdraw back toward Silesia. The king, however, was also banking on one of the persisting traits of the Austrian army during the war: the habitual sluggishness of its commanders. In this expectation Prince Charles accommodated him splendidly, first hesitating for over a week before setting his army in motion and then choosing to guide his troops on a ten-day flanking march rather than engage his foe. There were occasions when the two armies were in sight of each other, and so the Austrians were accurately informed of the size of their enemy. But nothing could stir them to swift action. More graphically than any other campaign of the war, the September march of 1745 reveals how Austria was, in many ways, its own worst enemy.

When the moment for battle finally came, however, the Austrians could not have chosen a more propitious situation. The Prussian force, numbering 22,500, was encamped just west of the small Bohemian village of Burkersdorf.[1] The site was surrounded by ridges, and in the fourth week of September the

Austrians (with some Saxon reinforcements), numbering almost 40,000, infiltrated these hills. From the heights Charles and his aides had a view of the entire Prussian camp, and on the basis of what they saw they elected to try to surround their enemy and then to initiate constrictive combat. On the night of 29-30 September a group of irregulars used mountain roads to loop around to the Prussian right. Concurrently, the Austrian main force drew itself up west of Burkersdorf in readiness for an order to march and fire. By any reckoning the Austrians controlled the situation. They held the hills and the routes of egress; they enjoyed a dramatic numerical advantage and were well provisioned; they moved amid trees, which hid their actions from their enemy. Even the weather seemed to cooperate, for in the early dawn of 30 September a light fog swirled through the woods, giving further protection to the already masked deployments of Prince Charles's troops. "We hold them," one of Charles's aides remarked, "as though in the middle of a handkerchief."[2]

King Frederick had already decided to move his army on the thirtieth and he was meeting with his generals at 5:00 in the morning to discuss implementation of the march when he received reports of enemy cavalry activity on the right and a dust cloud directly ahead. The king rode to scout the scene for himself and immediately realized that the situation of his army was far more parlous than he had believed. The enemy was lining up for battle and had already covered his lines of retreat. So Frederick decided to count once again on Austrian torpor and to lash out at his enemy even as they lumbered into formation. He would lead his forces in an uphill charge on the enemy position before him. If the heights could be gained, then his troops might yet prevail against the larger but scattered enemy force. In any event, seizing the initiative was preferable to sitting in an exposed camp and waiting for the sky to fall. And so the apostle of the unexpected chose the course that temperament and tactics alike commanded.

The Prussian commanders set about whipping their troops from their sleep, pulling them forward from their camp, wheeling them about to the right, and lining them up into a fighting formation. Astonishingly, Prince Charles made no reactive adjustments in his own plans. The Austro-Saxons still had not attacked when, at about 8:00 A.M., the Prussians began two simultaneous assaults. On the right the Prussian cavalry, led by the intrepid Buddenbrock, charged against their Austrian counterparts and in an hour of fierce mounted encounters destroyed an important portion of what had hitherto been Austria's most successful fighting force. In the center, where infantry opposed infantry, the Prussians swarmed up the hill into the face of unremitting enemy fire. Twice their line cracked before the defenders, but on the third charge it was the Austrians who broke. After a fierce melee at the top of the hill, the beaten Austrian infantry sought cover in the forest behind them. Thereupon, the Prussians wheeled upon the Austrian right. The Habsburg troops quickly sought safety in the woods. The Prussians followed them to the edge of the forest but then swung back to the right to repulse a regathering Austrian force. By noon the Prussians had cleared the field and won the day. Against astonishing odds Frederick II had fashioned yet another triumph.[3]

The battle of Soor was the first major engagement of the war in which a decidedly outmanned army won.[4] Fewer than 23,000 Prussians had savaged a force of almost 40,000 Austrians and Saxons. Casualty statistics tell the story most dramatically. Whereas the victors sustained 3,900 casualties, the losers counted more than 7,400 among their dead, wounded, missing, and captured.[5] These numbers represent 18 percent of the combatants, but that figure misleads about the ferocity of the battle, since many on the Austrian side in fact were scarcely involved before fleeing. At its heart the engagement was, in the words of one participant, a "bloodbath."[6] Only one consideration kept the day from being viewed as a total success for the Prussians. During the course of the battle Nadasdy's light troops approached the Prussian rear and, instead of entering the fray, used the occasion of the engagement to attack the Prussian camp. After brutalizing the civilians, they captured the royal war chest, containing 85,000 thalers (£20,000); seized much of Frederick's baggage, including his clothes, books, snuff boxes, and favorite hound; and carried off several hundred prisoners, including two cabinet councillors and the king's personal physician. They even discovered the king's correspondence, but, hungry for objects of more obvious worth, simply threw much of this epistolary treasure away, unthinkingly denying Prince Charles access to a fund of potentially useful information. The Prussians labeled these irregulars "thieves and robbers";[7] certainly they were inept spies.

No battle of the war more tellingly demonstrates the advantages of having well-trained and well-equipped fighting men. The Austrians, to be sure, had committed their usual complement of errors. Their right stood inexcusably immobile while the struggle for the center raged. Nadasdy's Hussars wasted themselves in a silly foraging excursion. Lobkowitz had made himself so detested that his men refused to follow his example of personal bravery. Above all, Prince Charles failed to attack the Prussians when they were virtually unaware of his presence and certainly in no formation to fight. "God," the queen said, on learning the facts, "is against us."[8] But the obverse of the matter is Frederick's skill as a commander. He understood the importance of speed and momentum. He read topography well. He knew the capabilities of his men and the thought processes of his enemy. He even found ways to overcome, at least for a crucial hour or so, much of the manpower superiority of his foe. After the battle the king heaped praise on his troops, and they merited it. But taken in tandem with Hohenfriedberg, the engagement at Soor was sufficient to persuade most Europeans that Frederick II was a military genius. The king himself thought he had finally won. "I am of the opinion," he wrote Podewils, "that this is the last venom the court of Vienna vomits on us, and that henceforth it will be unable to resist the pressing entreaties of the English."[9]

THE FALL OF LOMBARDY

With the victory at Bassignana the Bourbons had completed that part of their Italian campaign in which both geography and strategy counseled cooperation. From France's perspective enough had been done. "The war in Italy," d'Argenson had written early in the summer, "deprives us of more resources and troops than it costs Vienna," and consequently France wanted to find a way to reduce its Italian commitments.[10] If France was unwilling to proceed further, then Spain would perforce be obliged to act alone. The Spanish had two options: marching on Turin or marching on Milan. Each possibility had points to recommend it, but France, though unwilling to participate, was nevertheless prepared to exercise its veto, declaring Piedmont-Sardinia to be off limits. That prohibition left Lombardy as Spain's only choice. Gages was reluctant to invade a province that he suspected might be well defended, and so he hesitated along the Po, clearing out points of minor resistance. But Elizabeth Farnese, covetous for Lombardy, could not understand his hesitations and bombarded him with orders to break off from mopping-up exercises and to march promptly to Milan. The Spanish commander defied the orders as long as he dared, but by the end of November all plausible grounds for nonobservance had been overcome, and on 28 November, against French remonstrances, Gages crossed the river. Then, while the French settled uneasily into winter quarters, the Spanish began their advance on the capital of Lombardy.

This separation of the Bourbons immediately caused the correlative separation of their foes. Schulenburg had shown in September that if Milan was threatened, the Austrians would defend it, even if such action entailed a rupture with Piedmont-Sardinia. His successor, Prince Liechtenstein, operated with the same priority, for the city was peculiarly vulnerable. Indeed, Milan maintained a tradition of yielding peacefully to attackers who successfully traversed the Ticino or the Adda, preferring the physical preservation of the city to any struggle for abstract notions of lawful sovereignty. Therefore, if Milan was to be defended, it would require an external Austrian army. The signs, however, were ominous. The Austrian governor, Count Pallavicini, fled the city in October. A strong Spanish party existed in Milan, ready to cooperate in a Spanish restoration. Aware of these considerations, Maria Theresa had no illusions about the prospects for her Italian holdings. "In those parts," she declared in late November, "I regard everything as lost."[11] When the Spanish army began its invasion, Liechtenstein responded by falling back toward Milan. For the foreseeable future Turin and Vienna would fight apart.

In Lombardy, however, there was not much fighting at all. Liechtenstein saw no reasonable chance for success if he committed his outmanned force against Gages's troops, and so he forbore. The civilians of Milan scurried to show their pleasure at the approach of their Iberian conquerors. Many of the landholders of the region, their estates divided by the cessions of Worms, had found their ingrained dislike of Piedmont so thoroughly reinforced by a comparison of their simultaneous experiences under Savoyan and Habsburg rule that they were fixedly resolved, should Vienna fail them, to prefer Madrid to Turin. Accordingly, Gages met little opposition, and on 16 December Milan surrendered. That capitulation set the stage for Don Philip's triumphal entry into the city of 250,000 three days later. The foppish prince proclaimed himself king of Lombardy and set himself up in splendor. Dining and entertaining, dancing and receiving, he assumed the mantle of patron and benefactor. Meanwhile, Milan having yielded, cities like Lodi and Como ended their hesitations and accepted their new ruler. By the end of 1745 across the whole expanse of Lombardy only the fortress at Mantua and the castle within Milan honored a sovereign in Vienna.

The discerning eye could discover potential problems in the Bourbon situation. The French and Spanish armies were separated by two rivers, and the enemy armies, though steadily retreating, had not been defeated. Milan, unwalled and by custom unresisting, was vulnerable to the predictable counterattack. Enclaves of fortified resistance—the citadels at Alessandria and Asti in Charles Emmanuel's lands and the fortresses at Milan and Mantua in Maria Theresa's—stubbornly held out. The Genoese were withdrawing their troops (though not their amity) in order to deal with their mounting Corsican troubles. Count Maillebois interpreted these problems as parts of a portentous pattern. Reminded of how French stubbornness had undone Belle-Isle's Bohemian dreams in 1742, he indicted Spanish intransigence in 1745. "I foresee," he explained, "total destruction, if they insist on remaining in the Milanese."[12] But in the fevered exaltation of triumph Madrid was not heeding doomsayers. Don Philip now controlled virtually all of Lombardy and perhaps a fifth of Charles Emmanuel's continental realm. By Spanish reckoning, it required but a peace settlement to have Don Philip honored as one of the rightful sovereigns of Europe.

THE SCOTTISH REVOLUTION

At the end of August 1745, when Charles Edward Stuart declared his intention to restore his father to the Scottish throne, he had already gathered an army of 1,300 men. Each day he issued appeals for Scots to link their fates to his; each day the ranks of his supporters slowly increased in number. Who were these men whose sympathies might lie with rebellion? Some few were ideological Jacobites—individuals who could not brook the violation of the proper succession countenanced by the Glorious Revolution. Others, more numerous, were dynastic Jacobites, whose devotion was given to a ruling house that had sprung from Scottish soil. A tiny portion were Roman Catholics, far less numerous than legend relates but almost unanimously adhering to the cause of a Catholic pretender. Many were people disgusted with English corruption, and some were genuine Scottish nationalists, hoping to use England's troubles to dislodge London from its paramountcy north of the Tweed. At all levels of society there were those who thrilled to the prince's promise "to make you a free and happy people."[13] This following came out hesitantly, however, for they recalled the Fifteen, when (in 1715) an earlier Jacobite uprising had been beaten down and its supporters punished. Therefore, much depended on what happened in the first weeks in Britain. If the loyalist forces could rout the Young Pretender's followers, the silent would prudently hold their peace. But if the Jacobites gave indications that they could prevail in battle, the uncertain might abandon caution to sign on, and the brook would become a torrent.

The defense of Hanoverian rule in Scotland was assigned to Lieutenant-General Sir John Cope. A veteran of Dettingen, Cope was initially inclined to adopt the strategy that had succeeded in 1715—to wait in the south of Scotland and defeat the Jacobites in territory known to be inhospitable to them. But advisors declared that a show of force was necessary to persuade the many waverers to stick with George II, and so on 31 August 1745 Cope set out into the north with 2,000 troops. His intelligence was so poor that he knew no more of Charles Edward's movements than Frederick II knew of Prince Charles's. Meanwhile, he suffered desertions, and when he reached Inverness on 10 September he resolved to return to Edinburgh immediately by way of the safety of the sea. All the while Charles Edward was parading southward. When he reached Perth on 18 September, he attended a Scottish Episcopal service, probably the first Protestant service he had ever witnessed, and he gained two signal adherents—the titular Duke of Perth and Lord George Murray. When he reached Edinburgh on 27 September, the city capitulated without a struggle, and the loyalist garrison of 600 was reduced to hunkering down in the castle and praying for relief from the south. Charles Edward then issued a proclamation that claimed Scotland for his father. But he knew that his first real test was at hand, for on that same day Cope was disembarking his troops at Dunbar.

The test proved shockingly easy. Cope chose the battleground, a stubble field near Prestonpans that allowed ample space for his cavalry to maneuver in. He was relying heavily on this mounted force, for he knew that the Jacobites were deficient in cavalry. He was delighted that Murray chose to attack from the east, for he knew that the 2,400 Jacobites were maneuvering themselves into a position behind a formidable bog, and he believed that any charge from that direction would be mired in the slough. What he did not know was that the Jacobites had a guide who, in the post-midnight darkness, could lead them across a defile and give them access to the field Cope's troops were camped on. Thus, at sunrise on 2 October 1745 the Jacobites mounted a swift and absolutely unexpected assault on the loyalists. Both Murray on the left and Perth on the right swung wide to engulf Cope's men in a double flanking attack. But even before that plan had time to develop, the front line of the loyalists, after firing but one volley, broke ranks and ran before the war cries of the charging Jacobites. It was all over in a bloody ten minutes—a fact that makes the engagement at Prestonpans the shortest of the entire European war. Using the celebrated "Highland charge," a century-old tactic that involved inducing enemy troops to fire a volley and then using the interval after it to slice them down with broadswords, the Jacobites turned the battlefield into "a spectacle of horror, being covered with heads, legs, and arms, and mutilated bodies."[14] At a cost of 30 dead and about 75 wounded, the Jacobites killed 300 loyalists, wounded another 450, and captured 1,400.[15] Scotland now belonged to Charles Edward Stuart.

The battle of Prestonpans shocked the British government as few other events of the Hanoverian era. When news of Charles Edward's landing in the west had first reached British leaders, the government had been more bemused than alarmed. As they surveyed the condition of their army in Scotland, however, these leaders grew more concerned. Only 4,000 troops, scattered in various garrisons, defended the entire realm. By disarming the Highlands after the Fifteen, the British government had created a situation in which only its foes were likely to have firearms. And so by early in September the government had prevailed upon George II to curtail his Hanoverian holiday and upon the Dutch government to agree to send 6,000 troops, who landed in Britain the day before word of Prestonpans reached London.[16] Had they not come so opportunely, the Duke of Newcastle surmised, "the confusion in the City of London would not have been to be described, and the King's crown, I will venture to say, in the utmost danger."[17] Cope's astonishing defeat ended all pretense that events north of the border might be a sideshow, and the British military leadership in the Netherlands, including the Duke of Cumberland, was now recalled to deal with "these infamous Rabells."[18] Just as the Corsican revolt was forcing Genoa to withdraw from campaigns for Piedmont, so too was the Scottish revolt compelling Britain to withdraw from campaigns for Flanders.

While England shuddered, Jacobite leaders in Edinburgh struggled to impose Stuart authority on their confused realm. Many clans, especially the northernmost ones, spurned Charles Edward's appeal for support, and although Edinburgh endured his rule, the professional classes of this partly anglicized city did not hide their preference for the union. Nevertheless, Charles Edward was, for many, the embodiment of an inchoate Scottish nationalism, and that role sufficed to earn him deference. Since he commanded the only effective fighting force in the realm, the prudent emulated the deferential. The French sent a representative, the Marquis d'Éguilles, who promptly assured Tencin that "Scotland is ours."[19] France thereupon added a few officers, a bit of money, a small supply of ammunition, and six cannon. By early November 1745 Charles Edward commanded a force of 5,000 infantry and 300 cavalry. But were they an offensive or a defensive force? That was the question that most exercised the minds of observers on both sides of the border.

From the beginning of his adventure, Charles Edward had claimed that he was entering Britain not simply to reestablish the old Stuart kingdom of Scotland but to recover the entire British realm. His early successes had served to mask his more sweeping hopes. By using Scotland as his staging area, by appealing to many kinds of Scottish symbols, and by repudiating the Act of Union, he had drawn on the reserves of pro-Scottish, anti-English sentiment in the northern kingdom. In Scotland Jacobitism and Scottish nationalism were mutually reinforcing. But if Charles Edward should now choose to pursue his broader goal by invading England with his Jacobite army, he would shatter that concordance. Yet did he have a choice? Whether he invaded England or not, he could be confident that the British government would attack him: George's ministers would not tolerate a usurper. So the issue presented itself as a practical one: Was it wiser to fight England north or south of the Tweed? The ongoing deliberations on this matter climaxed on 10 November 1745. Against the advice of Lord George Murray, Charles Edward persuaded a bare majority of his advisory council to approve an invasion of England. Ever the optimist, Charles Edward professed to believe that a grand upwelling of support would greet him in England. With this decision he transformed a challenge to the periphery of Britain's domestic concerns into a threat to the core of British political life.

The first decision to be made was whether to move southward on the eastern or the western side of the Pennines. Following Murray's advice, the prince chose the westerly route, thereby evading the force that Wade was gathering near Newcastle and moving into the region of England presumed to be most friendly to Jacobite hopes. The 5,000-man Jacobite army moved out of Edinburgh on 12 November and a week later crossed the border. Its first major target was Carlisle, defended by an aged garrison of eighty. The siege was brief, and on 29 November the city surrendered. The county militias that might have posed resistance dissolved at the swift approach of the Highlanders. When the Jacobites reached Manchester bonfires and illuminations celebrated their passage, and several hundred men signed on. Meanwhile, the two army groups charged with defending England kept their distance. Wade was fooled by the ambiguity of Murray's march through Scotland; he stayed at Newcastle and soon found himself with no choice but to track the invaders south, separated from them by the Pennines. Cumberland too was fooled and withdrew to defend Wales and Jacobitical Bristol, leaving the road to London uncovered. On 15 December the Jacobite army stepped handsomely into Derby, a week's march from the capital. London was seized by panic, and Charles Edward could hope that just as a splendid parade from Glenfinnan to Edinburgh had won Scotland, so too would a procession from Carlisle to London win England.

Although the Jacobite insurrection occurred on British soil, the expedition had the effect of influencing events in other theaters of the war. By engaging against Britain and by compelling London to look to its own defense, Charles Edward gave aid to France and Spain and damaged the hopes of Austria and Piedmont-Sardinia. The government that most clearly saw the interconnectedness of all these activities was France's. Count Maurepas had authorized support for the Jacobites in the summer, and the Marquis d'Argenson took up the cause in the autumn. Prestonpans then won over the wavering. On 24 October 1745, at Fontainebleau, France concluded a treaty with representatives of the pretender. Already at war with Great Britain, France now withdrew its recognition of the elector of

Hanover as king of Great Britain, recognized instead James (VIII) as king of Scotland, promised to acknowledge him as James III of England if the nation and a free Parliament summoned him, and pledged in the meantime to send aid. Immediately France began assembling a fleet and an army, and fixed Christmas day as the target date for the attack. By the middle of December the mood in London was understandably somber. Jacobites were approaching by land, French were menacing by sea, and George II was preparing a getaway ship. What had begun as a revolution in Scotland was transforming itself into a struggle for Britain.

THE THREADS OF DIPLOMACY

When the Marquis d'Argenson assumed primary responsibility for directing French foreign policy at the end of 1744, he had made no effort to disguise his hope to end the war. But once in office, he had been unable to discover a policy that might produce peace. A peculiar feature of his administration had been his reluctance to end the connection with Frederick II. "I am Prussian from my head to my toes," he once declared, "because" — a puzzling explanation—"I am a good Frenchman."[20] Not surprisingly then, the Convention of Hanover shocked him. Recoiling from this rebuff, d'Argenson decided in September 1745 to authorize separate peace negotiations with three adversaries: the Piedmontese, the Dutch, and the Austrians. Only the British, against whom he was pressing a Scottish insurrection, lay beyond the diplomatic pale. The marquis was dealing from strength in adopting these initiatives: Fontenoy and Charles Edward had revealed Britain's vulnerability, Bassignana had frightened Charles Emmanuel, and the retreat of Austrian forces in Lombardy and Bohemia had reawakened visions of a beleaguered Maria Theresa.

The most hermetic and concrete of the negotiations were the talks with representatives of the Sardinian monarch. D'Argenson hoped to persuade Charles Emmanuel to break with Austria and Britain and align himself with France. (It is useful to note that once again d'Argenson's means were inappropriate to his end: though it was Bourbon pressure he was relying on to make Charles Emmanuel more tractable, that same pressure portended precisely the expansion of Spain's role in Italy that Charles Emmanuel dreaded and that d'Argenson himself found so repugnant to his dreams for Italy.) It was mid-September when the marquis sent word of his interest in negotiations to Turin. Charles Emmanuel had a new foreign minister, Marquis Gorzegno, who, though lacking the late Ormea's flair for the imaginative, was a skilled technician and a shrewd councillor. He and the king pondered the proposal for a short time and then accepted it. The negotiations began in Paris in October, with Gérard-Claude Lévesque de Champeaux representing France. The sweep of France's plan for a reordering of Italy soon unsettled the Piedmontese, however, and to assure that the message was properly understood, d'Argenson decided to dispatch Champeaux to Turin in early December to carry the scheme directly to the king and his minister. Posing as Abbé Rousset, Champeaux crossed the frigid St. Bernard Pass and reached Turin on 20 December, at a time when, in light of Gages's triumph in adjoining Lombardy, Piedmont-Sardinia was feeling a wintry draft of isolation.

The Dutch, like the Sardinians, sat adjacent to France, and in both instances the barriers upon which the small nation relied—mountains in the southeast and a buffer state in the north—had by the fall of 1745 failed. Beset by approaching foes, both governments were receptive to proposals that negotiations might be in order. But there were also important dissimilarities between France's two neighbors. Piedmont-Sardinia possessed a toughened fighting force; the United Provinces possessed a risible one. Piedmont-Sardinia was beholden to no foreign powers; the United Provinces were closely involved with Britain. Most important from France's point of view was the fact that there existed in the Dutch Republic a French faction. Its members felt that the United Provinces had become supine before Britain; though they had no intention of making the republic a French satellite, they believed that by distancing itself from Britain, the Dutch state might induce France to be less menacing. Therefore France suggested in September that the United Provinces, technically neutral, become the site of a congress of belligerents. The Grand Pensionary, Anthonie Van der Heim, grasped eagerly at the proposal. A timorous soul, ill suited for the rough-and-tumble of international politics, he feared that the Francophile party might force the republic into a separate peace, and he saw in the proposal for a congress a means of thwarting the hopes of those who favored unilateral action. The British, to whom Van der Heim perforce turned for advice, insisted that Cape Breton be excluded from the agenda—a veto that assured the aborting of the idea. So an immediate congress was not in the cards. But the Grand Pensionary did not want to reject French soundings entirely. He therefore persuaded the States General to nominate his friend, Colonel Larrey, for a covert mission to France in November. The colonel was directed to propose that, since both France and the United Provinces were on record as renouncing any intention of gaining territory from the war, they were already in agreement on a major point: from this agreement the basis for a future congress might yet be forged. Louis XV was among the many who understood the true import of this feeble contention: "this mysterious envoy," the king said, "proves their fear."[21]

France's third concurrent set of negotiations was with the Austrians. The court of Vienna could be neither browbeaten like to Dutch nor patronized like the Piedmontese. Austria was an equal, and if French ministers hoped to succeed with the prickly men who advised Maria Theresa, they would have to acknowledge that status. It was not easy even to bring the two powers into contact. But Maria Theresa remembered well the various oblique soundings that had emanated from Versailles over the past three years, and when she learned that Britain had concluded the Convention of Hanover with Prussia, she lost all reservations about dealing with France, authorizing her representatives in Dresden and Munich to sound out their French counterparts. She thrilled to learn that Count Chavigny offered assurances that if Prussia broke with France, Louis XV was prepared to let Frederick II meet his deserved fate; and she found tolerable the suggestion that if Vienna helped establish Don Philip in Italy, France would then relinquish the Austrian Netherlands. With these initial contacts proving satisfactory, Maria Theresa decided to pause in Munich on her September progress to Frankfurt to discuss with her advisors the possibility of an Austro-French agreement.

The Saxons were especially solicitous for the success of Austro-French conversations. Count Brühl believed that if France could be persuaded to abandon Prussia, Saxony and Austria could crush the Hohenzollern kingdom and then disassemble it. Brühl thus proposed for himself the role of mediator. But he found himself hemmed in by d'Argenson, who remained, oddly and even perversely, a friend of the Prussian tie. D'Argenson's ensuing proposals seemed designed to chill Austrian enthusiasm. They threw a few sops to Vienna, but they specified that, contrary to Chavigny's hints, France was to retain Furnes, Ypres, Nieuport, and—with conditions—Tournai. They insisted that Don Philip was still to receive an establishment in Italy. Above all, they cautioned that "whatever subject of discontent the king [Louis XV] may have with the King of Prussia . . . , His Majesty wants it absolutely understood that there be no questions of stipulations tending toward depriving him [Frederick II] of Silesia."[22] Lamed as they were by this declaration, the negotiations nevertheless lurched uneasily ahead. One Saxon observer professed to believe that "France and Spain show a decided wish to treat with the Queen of Hungary to the exclusion of the King of Prussia."[23] No one could be confident of the future, and so the governments at Versailles and Vienna preferred to keep options open.

The twists and turns of Russian policymaking added to the complexity of these autumnal diplomatic explorations. At first the announcement came forth that Russia was finally ready to cast its lot with Saxony and therefore with Austria. The decision had not been easy. But Elizabeth had yielded to the force of Alexis Bestuzhev's insistent question: "in light of the enhanced power of the King of Prussia, and especially in light of his sly, discreet, and land-hungry nature, who can give assurances that he does not hatch plans against Russia?"[24] Reports of this decision led leaders in Vienna and Dresden to assume that they could allow their hopes for the future to be conditioned by an expectation that 80,000 Russian troops would open up a new front in 1746. They had already agreed that Brandenburg rather than Silesia was their appropriate target, on the principle that if the limb proved stubborn, perhaps the trunk would be frailer. Russia's dispatch of 14,000 troops into its westernmost regions quickened their enthusiasm for the coming assault. But then, in early November, in a manner still not entirely explained, the Swedish envoy to Saxony learned of the allies' plans and passed the information on to Berlin. Frederick responded with his wonted promptitude. He sent orders to the Old Dessauer to ready the army gathered around Halle, and then he himself left to assume command of Prussian forces in Silesia. Worse swiftly followed. On 14 November word reached Dresden that the Russian government had unexpectedly reconsidered its decision of but a few weeks earlier: Elizabeth now limited Russian support to Saxon attacks on Silesia. In less than a week the two German allies had suffered both the loss of a secret and the distancing of a friend.

Irritated beyond measure, Frederick set 35,000 men of his Silesian army in motion toward Lusatia, determined to carry the war to Saxony. Since the Austrian army was entering Lusatia from Bohemia at almost the same moment, this placid eastern sector of Augustus's electorate suddenly became one of Europe's primary theaters. The Prussians first met a small Saxon contingent led by General Büchner. In an engagement fought near Grosshennersdorf on 23 November 1745, a Prussian force of 8,500 shattered a Saxon force of 5,500. When, on the next day, Prince Charles learned that Prussian troops had once again prevailed in battle, he led his Austrian soldiers in a disorderly withdrawal back into Bohemia. Frederick, meanwhile, unleashed his fury on the hapless electorate. He seized the town of Görlitz and its well-stocked magazine. He directed Prince Leopold to use the army at Halle to crush the western reaches of the electorate, and on 29 November the Old Dessauer led a surge of Prussians into Leipzig, Saxony's second city. There was a method to Frederick's rigor; he was less concerned with punishing than with intimidating Augustus. Thus, even as the blows fell east and west, Count Podewils extended the velvet glove to the Saxon government, offering formal peace if Saxony would withdraw from its Austrian tie and accede to the Convention of Hanover. Instead, the king-elector and his chief minister fled Dresden on 1 December, finding sanctuary in the Austrian dependency of Bohemia. In little more than one disastrous week, however, the Saxon state had been overrun.

Augustus's refusal to accede to the remorseless logic of military occupation was not as quixotic as it might at first seem. He and Brühl knew that the government at Vienna had finally decided to accept Saxon mediation aimed at ending Austrian belligerence with France. To that end Maria Theresa chose Count Frederick Harrach to journey to Dresden, with full powers to negotiate with a French envoy. The queen of Hungary armed him with negotiating ideas. In Italy she wanted an eastward shift for Charles Emmanuel's realm: Piedmont-Sardinia would give up Savoy to Don Philip and in return receive land in Lombardy from Austria. In the Low Countries she wanted a restoration of the status quo ante bellum, but Harrach was authorized to cede some small territories if France insisted. In Germany she wanted French recognition of Francis I's claim to the imperial dignity. The goal of these concessions was peace with France, not peace in Europe. If Vienna could free itself from its quarrel with Versailles, it could finally mobilize its full might against Prussia alone. The Saxon leaders shared this ambition, and therefore, though their realm was awash with Prussian troops, they looked beyond present troubles to an imminent renewal of Austrian fortunes in central Europe. It is true that the two allies were out of phase: Harrach left Vienna for Dresden on the night before Leipzig fell to the Prussians. But the allies agreed in placing more importance on the Austrian decision to come to terms with France than on the Prussian occupation of the electorate of Saxony.

KESSELSDORF

With Dresden chosen simultaneously as the site of the first truly significant peace talks since the Austro-Prussian negotiations of 1742 and as the target of a two-pronged Prussian offensive, the electorate of Saxony assumed center stage in Europe in December 1745. Count Rutowski was charged with protecting the city, and his Saxon army of 25,000 men, supplemented by General Grünne's nearby Austrian contingent of 10,000 men, constituted a formidable defense force for the capital. Meanwhile, three other large armies were bearing down on Dresden. From the south, out of Bohemia, came Prince Charles's Austrian army of 46,000. If it could link up with Rutowski's troops by Dresden, the Austro-Saxon army would number 81,000 troops—an aggregation that even Frederick's skill might have difficulty besting. From the west, out of Leipzig, came Prince Leopold's Prussian army of 33,000. From the east came Frederick's army, at 25,000 the smallest of the four but led by a commander now widely viewed as demonic. If combined, the

Prussian forces would number 58,000. The allies enjoyed several advantages in the campaign of maneuvering that ensued. They were operating among generally friendly people, and they could employ the Elbe valley as an avenue for their movements. Above all, both of their armies lay on the same side of the great river, and since they controlled Dresden they controlled the most important bridge that linked the two banks. The Prussians, conversely, were invaders—unwelcome soldiers amid resentful civilians. Since Frederick had now resolved to crush Saxon resistance by applying a policy of deliberate brutality, he could scarcely expect this Saxon animus to recede.

Contact between the hostile forces occurred on the morning of 15 December 1745 when Prince Leopold's army, approaching Dresden from the west, stumbled into the left flank of the Saxon army that Rutowski had lined up along the Zschoner Stream just east of Kesselsdorf. If an engagement was wanted, the opportunity now lay at hand. And fortune seemed to be favoring the Prussians, for by seizing their unexpected opportunity they might hope to launch a devastating flank attack on the Saxons, who, deployed against an anticipated attack from the north, were exposed and vulnerable. But Prince Leopold cast the advantages aside. A prisoner of conventional military thinking, he was blind to the possibility of rolling the enemy up from the left and insisted on positioning his troops in front of the enemy before signaling the attack. To manage this feat he marched his men across the front of the Saxons, thereby putting himself in the anomalous position of taking risks to be orthodox. But he got away with it, and by noon he was able to draw his Prussian army into line facing south and ready for combat. As soon as Rutowski realized that Prussians were nearby, he sent troops into Kesselsdorf to occupy it; as soon as Leopold had completed his deployment, he unleashed both infantry and cavalry against the town. With that strike the battle began.

Rutowski's plans were simple. He believed that the position he held at Kesselsdorf bore certain similarities to the position Maurice of Saxony had created at Fontenoy: his troops stood upon high ground, made still more defensible by the icy surface of the slope that fell away in front of them, while a gully on the left would play the funneling role of the Woods of Barry. Just as his brother had done in May, Rutowski proposed to hold his ground and cut down the hard-charging enemy with cannon fire. For a while the plan seemed to be working. In the center the allied artillery kept the numerically superior Prussian infantry at bay. Meanwhile, on the Saxon left the Prussian assault on Kesselsdorf was insufficient to dislodge the Saxon defenders. But at this point Rutowski miscalculated. Wanting to turn the tactical triumph on his left into a rout, he ordered his grenadiers to pursue the retreating

Prussians. These warriors charged forth, abandoning the protection afforded by the town and their hill crest, and were met by Leopold's formidable force of dragoons. A melee ensued, from which the Prussians emerged triumphant. This dramatic reversal of fortune left the town of Kesselsdorf indefensible, and so the Prussians swarmed in to capture a settlement that had been denied them scarcely an hour earlier. Possession of Kesselsdorf paid off almost immediately, for from its rubbled precincts the Prussians now moved against the flank of the Saxon center and converted a slow Saxon retreat before Prussian infantry pressure into a collapse. Before the sun was down on this short December day, the allied force had withdrawn, leaving the battlefield to Prince Leopold and the victorious Prussians.[25]

The engagement bore some resemblance to earlier battles in the war. Once again an army that fought against Prussia had forfeited an early success by breaking ranks. Once again the sheer toughness of the Prussian infantry had prevailed in the close-quarters fighting in the center. But there are aspects of the engagement that were perplexing. The allied right never got involved, essentially because Rutowski forbore summoning them. Moreover, Dresden itself was only seven miles away, and Prince Charles's large army—the vastest in Saxony—but a few hours distant. Yet it too was unsummoned. Why did Rutowski not call for aid? Why in fact did he actually direct Prince Charles to remain in the city? Speculation has focused on Rutowski's supposed greed for glory or on his suspicion that the engagement at Kesselsdorf was only a feint. Puzzlement over the battle does not end with Rutowski's actions, for it was inexcusable that Prince Charles, whatever his advice from Rutowski, did not march to join his ally. The Austro-Saxon aim was to defeat the Prussians; a yoking of Rutowski's and Charles's forces would have virtually assured that the battle now being joined would be a victory. Once again Prince Charles's unfitness for command—his want of ingenuity, energy, and confidence—had cost his sovereign dearly.

The battle at Kesselsdorf was one of the bloodiest of the war. The Prussian army numbered almost exactly 30,000; one-sixth of them were counted among the casualties. The allied army numbered 31,000; when figures for the dead, the wounded, the missing, and the captured were finally aggregated, somewhere between one-third and one-half of the initial army was gone.[26] The total casualty rate for the battle was therefore 25 percent at minimum and almost 33 percent for an upper limit—and either figure is distorted downward by the inclusion of the nonparticipating allied right. The hero of the day was Prince Leopold of Anhalt-Dessau, and on the morrow of the victory he led his delighted king around a battlefield still furzed with ice, showing Frederick where and how the invincible Prussian soldiers had again prevailed. The king took particular satisfaction in the reflection that his army had proved to be formidable even when led by a person other than himself. The Austrians, he believed, would be compelled to take note of that alarming truth.

THE TREATY OF DRESDEN

The battle at Kesselsdorf provided an inauspicious backdrop to Count Harrach's diplomatic mission to Dresden. Austria needed time and leverage to win France over, and the battle deprived Vienna of both. Nevertheless, arriving on the very day of the engagement, Harrach persevered. On the night of 15-16 December, even as the military commanders huddled nearby to prepare to withdraw to Pirna, Harrach met with a French diplomat and offered to cede the Flemish districts of Furnes, Ypres, and Beaumont to France and to grant the Italian districts of Parma, Piacenza, and Pavia to Don Philip. But with France demanding still more, the talks ended in disagreement. Besides, France was insisting that Prussia retain Silesia. Harrach concluded from this dismal exchange that an Austro-French agreement was not currently practicable. French rigidity did not, however, alter the fact that Austria's military situation was desperate. In every theater the tide of war had been running against Vienna. The defeat at Kesselsdorf had now driven Austria's closest ally, the electorate of Saxony, into hurried negotiations with the Prussians. If some step were not taken quickly to relieve the constricting pressure of the Spanish in Milan, the Scots in the Midlands, the French in Flanders, and the Prussians in Saxony, then Austria was in imminent danger of finding itself stripped of allies and naked before the joint might of France and Prussia. And so he turned to his secondary instructions, which allowed him, in the event of an emergency, to treat with Prussia.

Austria would quickly have found itself in a totally untenable position if Frederick II had wanted to use his control of Saxon territory to squeeze further concessions from Maria Theresa: Harrach's orders allowed him to hand over Silesia—nothing more. But Frederick was too shrewd to let a greedy impulse undo a long-term strategy. For months he had been seeking a way out of the war. All he wanted was an assurance that Silesia was his to keep. The king entered Dresden on 18 December 1745, displayed concern for the children of Augustus III still stranded in the city, and entertained—even cosseted—Harrach. Meanwhile, at nearby Bautzen, diplomats serving him met regularly with Saxon diplomats, their daily work a potent reminder to Harrach that unless he brought Austria promptly into the diplomatic arena, Saxony would unilaterally make peace with Prussia. Harrach was not a man to be intimidated by the king, but he was contending for high stakes with a mediocre hand. And so, of course, he finally folded. On Christmas Day, after two days of meetings with Count Podewils, Count Harrach accepted military reality and signed the document known as the Treaty of Dresden. This December decision is a foundational event in German history.

The abiding importance of the Treaty of Dresden is that it recognized the transfer of Silesia from Austria to Prussia. Austria retained, as it had in 1742, Cesky Tesin and Opava. In accepting the treaty, Maria Theresa was acknowledging that despite Frederick's illegal snatch-and-run foray of 1741 and despite his repudiation of a solemn peace concluded in 1742, Vienna still lacked the wit and weight to force him to disgorge his conquest. Obviously this acknowledgment was difficult for the empress-queen. She despised Frederick and his actions. By assenting to the Treaty of Dresden and ceding one-third of the lands of the Bohemian crown, the empress-queen was acquiescing in a truncation of her multinational realm that seemed to her radically unjust. As she sighed to Harrach in a letter dated 30 December 1745, she had never believed when the campaign had begun that she could endure so fatal a treaty, but now that it had been concluded she was "firmly resolved to uphold it sacredly."[27] And she was true to her word, for when war over Silesia was resumed yet again eleven years later, in another circumstance and under rapidly shifting diplomatic conditions, it was again Prussia and not Austria that unleashed the troops.

Everything else in the Treaty of Dresden must be read in light of the transfer of Silesia. Frederick granted his recognition to the new emperor and ended his opposition to Austrian use of the Bohemian vote in the electoral college. Frederick and Maria Theresa exchanged guarantees of each other's German holdings. Toward Saxony (which also concluded on Christmas Day in Dresden) Frederick was sterner. Prussia exacted an indemnity of 1 million thaler (£250,000) from the Saxons and refused to hand back those Saxons who had been conscripted into the Prussian army. Because they concluded together, Austria and Saxony could regard their alliance as remaining intact. But since each side blamed the other for the recent military disasters, the alliance was sorely weatherbeaten. Ratifications were promptly exchanged, and the Prussians thereupon pulled out of Saxony. Frederick meanwhile marched into Berlin a hero, Augustus returned to Dresden to gather up the pieces, and Maria Theresa, helplessly ensconced at Vienna, assembled her advisors to begin anew the search for territory.

Scarcely fourteen months earlier Austria's prospects had gleamed. The French were scrambling back from Madonna dell'Olmo; the Prussians were staggering out of Bohemia. Anchored in the south by the fastnesses of

Piedmont, in the east by the arms of Austria, and in the west by the wealth of Britain, the Worms allies had seemed redoubtably poised for decking triumphs with triumphs. What had happened? One explanation for later disappointments rests with changes in the French military leadership. By replacing Marshal Noailles with Maurice of Saxony, Louis XV had elevated genius to command. The distance between Noailles and Maurice was measured by the results at Dettingen and Fontenoy. A second explanation focuses on the flawed nature of the Treaty of Worms itself. By pointlessly provoking Genoa, the alliance drove the coastal republic into the enemy camp. The distance between Bourbons deprived of Genoese support and Bourbons fortified by it was measured by the difference between the Italian campaigns of 1744 and 1745. A third explanation draws attention to the opening of new theaters. Bringing the war to Scotland paralyzed Britain's capacity to aid its allies; bringing it to Saxony gave Frederick an opportunity to employ both of Prussia's armies rather than just one. But from Austria's perspective it is the fourth explanation that was conclusive. The year 1745 had been a military debacle for the Habsburg state. "We lost five battles during it," Bartenstein later wrote, "which had never before come to pass during the life of the house."[28] By December Vienna had been compelled to cut losses. Because Prussia had been freer than France to take swift advantage of Austria's plight, the Treaty of Dresden imposed an Austro-Prussian rather than an Austro-French peace. Prussian decisiveness continued to be a standing rebuke to French confusion.

Though the Treaty of Dresden left much uncertain—it resolved, after all, only the second Silesian War, not the sprawling pan-European struggle—it left one point indubitably clear: Prussia had prevailed. Under great pressure, isolated, and demographically outmanned, Frederick had defended his expanded realm in 1745 against every nibbling incursion and finally forced his exhausted foes to seek peace. It did not significantly dilute his success that Prussia had failed to keep Maria Theresa's husband from the imperial throne. It did not undermine his achievement that he had once again concluded a peace without France. Frederick had proved his garrison state to be formidable and imposed a settlement on his own terms. Now he was ready to preside over an oasis of peace amid a Europe that, from the cataracts of Lancashire to the bogs of Courland, was creaking beneath military cadences. To a French envoy he declared his intention in unnervingly bald terms: "I will see Prince Charles at the gateway of Paris without stirring."[29] The war was now France's to decipher.

The Austrians for their part assessed the treaty soberly. Postmortems on their army were clearly in order, and it did not escape the notice of the

Conference that the only commanders who enjoyed some combination of success and respect, aside from the creaky Traun, were such younger men as the perplexing Browne and the rising luminaries Daun and Lacy. Also in order was a reexamination of Austria's relationship with Britain. The Convention of Hanover had betrayed Austria's hopes for a German triumph; the Scottish revolution had reduced the island kingdom to a temporary nullity. And yet Britain had still strangely prevailed, since its German goal for at least a year had been to end the Silesian war so that the Bourbon war might be emphasized. An ally who is useless when called upon and deflective of one's own war aims is a poor ally at best. Consequently, there were those in the Conference who urged a reduced dependence on London. But amid all these demands for reexamination, none called for the war to cease. The Treaty of Dresden had redirected belligerence, redefined opportunities, and reawakened hopes. Maria Theresa and Count Bartenstein still presided over Austrian affairs, and their appetite for compensation, like some primal obsession, remained unsated.

P·A·R·T IV

The Reassertion of Tradition
December 1745 – October 1747

15

The Foundering of French Policy
(December 1745 — June 1746)

WAR WITHOUT PRUSSIA

Prussia's withdrawal stripped away the last element of structural ambiguity from the sprawling European war. What was unmistakably left was a recrudescence of the belligerence that had riven Europe between 1689 and 1713—a resumption of the Anglo-Austrian effort to confine Bourbon ambitions. The British took this threat very seriously, and therefore they applauded the Treaty of Dresden. By freeing the Austrians to aim their arms solely at the Bourbons, it realized the hopes envisioned in the Convention of Hanover. The treaty constituted, moreover, the second stroke of good news to cheer the British capital in the final week of 1745, for shortly before word of the settlement in Dresden arrived, the government learned that the army of Charles Edward Stuart, having reached Derby at the middle of the month, had begun withdrawing toward Scotland. The danger of a French assault along the south coast, though not eliminated, receded with each retreating step of the Jacobites.

Austria's view of war in the post-Dresden era, though not identical to Britain's, was complementary. Defined by Maria Theresa, it aimed at winning compensation for Austria in Italy, and its preliminary goal therefore was the recovery of Milan. The empress-queen had no sooner learned of the Treaty of Dresden than she sent instructions to Count Browne to lead his 10,000 troops out of Heidelberg and into Mantua. Two points may be made about Austria's designs. The first is that they did not treat the Austrian Netherlands as important. The empress-queen had never been very interested in this distant and indefensible province, and she calculated now that since French advances there actually threatened British and Dutch interests more than Austrian, the Maritime Powers would defend the region even without significant support from Vienna. The second point is that by 1746, with Bartenstein at her ear, Maria Theresa had lost all but a minimal regard for Austria's ties with Britain: too often had she witnessed a British defiance of Austrian interests. She would not break with George II; his money was welcome and his navy helpful. But neither would she count on him. Instead, insofar as possible, she would chart Vienna's course without consulting the winds from London.

In Madrid intransigent attitudes continued to hold sway. Spain alone among the major combatants had stood virtually aloof from the flurry of negotiations that marked the second half of 1745. The government was intent on imposing its will by force, not by words, and Don Philip's entrance into Milan at the end of 1745 had closed Gages's remarkable campaign with a glorious success that seemed to ratify the choice of means. Cheered by this triumph, the royal couple saw no reason to change their procedures. Indeed, they were remarkably insouciant about the future. They made no serious effort as 1745 ended to initiate talks with Austria about Lombardy. Yet neither did they send reinforcements to Gages, even though the commander was worried about the relative paucity of troops and his lack of artillery. No government entered the new year with a poorer sense of the changing structure and nature of the war.

France, as usual, was in a muddle. More so than at any time since d'Argenson assumed command, however, that need not have been the case. Late in 1744 the marquis's freedom of action had been confined by three inherited commitments. One of these—the promise to assist the Holy Roman Emperor—had dissolved with the death of Charles VII. A second—the obligation to work in tandem with Prussia—had now been superseded by Frederick II's withdrawal from the war. Only the pledge to assist Don Philip remained in force, and the military successes of 1745 offered ample opportunity for honoring that pledge. In principle, therefore, France was in a position to define a military and diplomatic policy that conformed to its own interests. The problem was that the Marquis d'Argenson could not identify those interests in any coherent way. His hope for Italy was to serve as midwife to the birth of an Italian federation, but that goal placed him in conflict with Spain, France's ally in the region. His hope for the Low Countries was peace, but that goal entailed exercising restraint in the only region that had witnessed unilateral French victories. D'Argenson's foreign policy was thus an inconsistent compound of dogma and sentimentality, contrived (it might seem) to disoblige friends, sacrifice successes, and create diplomatic gridlock. Such a policy was, by any reasonable standard, an awesome feat of incoherence.

This incoherence is most visible in d'Argenson's inability to grasp for peace. It is true that when the French learned early in January 1746 that the

Jacobites had begun to retreat from Derby, they concluded that Charles Edward's campaign had failed and that it would be useless to send French troops into England. But no one at Versailles sought to use the suspension of the invasion plans as a springboard for peace talks. In fact, when in February the Dutch States-General sent Count Wassenaer-Twickel back to France, the Marquis d'Argenson offered him little encouragement. Instead, d'Argenson pursued his peculiar Italian initiatives. On the day after Christmas 1745 — that is, one day after Harrach and Podewils came to terms in Dresden — Champeaux and Gorzegno concluded their secret talks by signing an agreement in the Piedmontese capital. For convenience we may call the document the Principles of Turin.[1] It envisioned the partition of Habsburg Italy by various claimants: Piedmont-Sardinia, Don Philip's putative realm, Modena, and Genoa. A supplement to the principles declared that France and Spain would pay subsidies to Piedmont-Sardinia equivalent to those that Turin was receiving from London. The implication of the principles was patent: Piedmont-Sardinia was abandoning its Austrian connection for a Bourbon tie. Although the document represented a victory for the Marquis d'Argenson, it was not an agreement likely to foster peace in Italy. Austria, after all, could not reasonably be expected to acquiesce in its own displacement from the peninsula. And the rage of Madrid at the prospect of losing some of its recent trophies, including Milan, was as predictable as the rising of the sun. It was not inconceivable — one need think only of the Treaty of Vienna of 1725 — that Spain and Austria might join forces in their anger to defend their common interests against France and Piedmont-Sardinia.

The most dramatic evidence that France was not hungry for peace at the opening of 1746 was afforded by Maurice of Saxony, who startled Europe by breaking out of winter quarters at the end of January to lay siege to Brussels, the city of 70,000 that served as capital of the Austrian Netherlands. This unexpected thrust bore many of Maurice's characteristic marks. It was the product of attentive preparations. It was superbly masked, first by accounts of Maurice's renewed infatuation with his sybaritic life of womanizing, concert-going, and cockfighting and then by rumors that the illustrious marshal had suffered a stroke and was lingering in Flanders only because he was too ill to return to Paris. Maurice was counting too on the tradition of allied torpor, for like any great commander, he fed his reading of the character of his enemy into his calculations. When a protracted winter thaw finally snapped under the onslaught of suddenly frigid weather, Maurice ordered 22,000 men into motion. Leaving Ghent and other staging areas on 28 January 1746, they vaulted four waterways with stunning ease. By 30 January they had surrounded Brussels. Fierce weather ravaged the besiegers, but Maurice drove them to new exertions. He also called upon Count Kaunitz to surrender. "It has never been my desire," he declared, "to turn Brussels into a battlefield; these great capitals, the adornments of their countries, should be declared to be open cities, as is Milan."[2] When the French made two breaches in the walls of Brussels, Kaunitz capitulated and then left for Antwerp, nursing still another grievance against the fecklessness of the Maritime Powers.[3] Maurice of Saxony, meanwhile, returned to France, a hero of mythic proportions, to lobby for his view that Versailles should now proceed to compel the United Provinces to leave the war by threatening to crush them if they refused.

THE CUNNING OF CHARLES EMMANUEL

The Treaty of Dresden rescued Piedmont-Sardinia from a grave predicament. The Sardinian monarchy could prosper only in the context of a Habsburg-Bourbon rivalry in Italy. If either Austria or Spain should withdraw from the peninsula, then Piedmont-Sardinia would be exposed to irresistible pressures from the other side to crop its ambitions and curtail its activities. Moreover, given the facts of geography, the threat was not symmetrical. Since Bourbon France bordered on Piedmont-Sardinia, the Bourbon factor in the equilibrium could never be eliminated. But the Austrian factor was potentially removable. Indeed, by late 1745 the removal appeared to have been effected, leaving the Piedmontese state enfolded in enmity. It is no wonder then that it sought protection in the Principles of Turin: though they implied a repudiation of the Worms alliance, they at least assured the continued existence of a Sardinian monarchy. The Treaty of Dresden then changed the calculations. As the king and his advisors understood the new situation, Maria Theresa would now shift the bulk of her German army to Italy. Since the Austro-Prussian peace afforded no compensatory relief to France or Spain, the Bourbon states could not be expected to match Vienna's Italian buildup. It was therefore plausible to believe that Austria would again be a formidable force in Italy, capable in conjunction with the Piedmontese of compelling the overextended Bourbons to abandon their conquests in Lombardy. Alliance with the Bourbons was no longer necessary. But since such a shift in the balance of forces could not occur instantaneously, it was incumbent on Piedmont-Sardinia to protract the negotiations designed to transform the principles into a treaty. Turin dared not act on its true view until the Austrians had established a significant base in the vicinity of the Po.[4]

Insofar as the Piedmontese were seeking to prolong their talks with France, they acquired two very unlikely allies in their broad strategy: the king and queen of Spain. Madrid found the Principles of Turin astonishing and execrable, for they proposed that Don Philip should relinquish Milan to Charles Emmanuel. When first notified of the contents of the Principles on 26 January 1746, Philip V exploded. "I dare not repeat his expressions," the stunned French ambassador wrote to Versailles.[5] Spain's formal response to France, drafted a few days later, labeled the principles "a dishonorable and profitless arrangement" portending "a shameful peace."[6] The Spanish, unable to imagine that Piedmont-Sardinia might find the principles unacceptable, announced that they would not enter into an agreement that gave more to a defeated Charles Emmanuel than to a victorious Don Philip. To underline their resolve, Philip V and Elizabeth Farnese dispatched one of Spain's leading grandees, the Duke of Huescar, to Versailles as ambassador extraordinary to direct the struggle against the principles. On his arrival in Paris, the young man bluntly declared that his instructions consisted of the injunction to "oppose the treaty by every means."[7]

With the cecity that characterized so much that he did, the Marquis d'Argenson walked directly into the Piedmontese trap. Indeed, by briefly introducing a scheme for an Italian confederation into the negotiations, he gave Turin adequate and plausible grounds for additional stalling. The Piedmontese, meanwhile, proceeded with great skill. After France relented in its campaign for remaking Italy, Gorzegno informed the French that Piedmont-Sardinia dared not sit forever between the two stools of Vienna and Versailles; if an agreement could not be reached by the end of February, Turin would regard itself as free of all commitments to Versailles. By setting this deadline, Gorzegno laid the basis for an honorable rather than a treacherous resumption of warfare at the opening of March and put pressure on France to show its own good faith by suspending military operations against the fortress at Alessandria.

A choicer proposal would have been hard to find. As one who had been arguing that the Dutch republic should be enticed rather than bludgeoned into cooperation, d'Argenson had already seen the possibility of a Piedmontese parallel. A full week before the principles were broached to Spain, he had written to Marshal Maillebois to inform him of the negotiations with Turin. He recommended that Maillebois should attack neither the Piedmontese army nor Liechtenstein's Austrian troops, lest he exacerbate Piedmontese suspicions. D'Argenson's conclusion—a statement that soon gained notoriety—advised the marshal that "thus today it is simply defensive and tranquility until the treaty is signed."[8] Charles Emmanuel soon learned of the letter, and his minister of war, Count Bogino, made use of the freedom of action it offered to gather a Piedmontese army. But because Maillebois did not interpret the letter to require him to raise the siege of Alessandria, Turin requested such an armistice in February. D'Argenson heard the request with sympathy and on 17 February 1746 authorized the end of the siege. It was an extraordinary decision: to show good faith, the marquis proposed to suspend the only form of direct pressure that France at that time was exerting on Piedmont-Sardinia.

D'Argenson never realized that catastrophe impended. Instead, he cheerfully lied to the Spanish, assuring them that the principles were only a response to the Treaty of Dresden and that the initiative had been Turin's. He prodded Louis XV into writing a letter to Philip V that defended the urgency of securing Charles Emmanuel: "Success is certain with him, and without him the contrary is almost certain. . . . Our enemies will be confounded by this stroke."[9] But nothing availed. Huescar stormed about Paris, tearing the cloak of secrecy from the talks. The royal couple invoked their Iberian version of common sense, inquiring why, when Bourbon arms were everywhere triumphant, Madrid should embrace a scheme that served only Piedmont-Sardinia. The Spanish even tried to bribe d'Argenson into compliance, offering him a Spanish title if he would repudiate his plan. To break the deadlock, the marquis finally concluded that a moderation of his attitude toward Spain was necessary. Since the armistice order had not yet left Paris, he adjusted its contents to make them more palatable to Madrid. Then to convey this message both to Charles Emmanuel at Turin and to Marshal Maillebois at Alessandria, d'Argenson summoned the marshal's son (and his own son-in-law), Count Maillebois. Meanwhile, however, with the advent of March the Piedmontese deadline expired, and Charles Emmanuel's troops began to move toward Asti and Alessandria. Because both towns were at several days' distance and Turin did want to tip its hand prematurely, the game with Count Maillebois was spun out a bit longer. But on 5 March 1746 the Piedmontese army caught the French garrison at Asti totally unawares and in a crushing assault reopened the war for Italy.

It was a devastating resumption for the Bourbons. Within a week they were in full retreat from their strongholds on the Tanaro. Their surprise and confusion testified with equal power to the fatuity of French intelligence-gathering and to the ability of the Piedmontese to disguise their intentions. When the attack on Asti began, the French commander of the garrison there protested in bewilderment that the warfare violated the peace just concluded between the two monarchs. On 8 March, after the Piedmontese had blasted two holes in the walls, Asti surrendered, and 5,000 French troops passed quickly into Piedmontese captivity. Marshal Maillebois collapsed when he learned of the capitulation: "I have death in my heart," he scribbled to d'Argenson.[10] Meanwhile, the Spanish commander at the siege of Alessandria, Count Lasci, received orders from Don Philip in Milan to raise the siege and withdraw toward Tortona.[11] Lasci complied, though Maillebois begged him not to. By 11 March the Tanaro River valley was again under Piedmontese control.

What had happened was a debacle for France, and it had occurred because d'Argenson had presumed himself wiser than his colleagues and the Spanish, and persuasive enough to convert the Piedmontese to right thinking. At least he had the grace to accept the blame. To those who indicted Maillbois *père et fils*, he declared that the marshal and the count were "innocent as the chaste Suzanne."[12] The marquis himself was inclined to fault his favorite whipping boys, the Spanish. They in turn denounced the marquis— for stupidity, treachery, shortsightedness, and an invincible bias against Iberians. Still, amid the muddle of Bourbon recriminations one point was clear: through controlled secrecy, steady diplomacy, and shrewd maneuverings, Charles Emmanuel had won a major victory against a more powerful enemy. With Piedmont-Sardinia revivified and with 30,000 Austrian troops relocated from Germany into Italy, the Bourbon position in the peninsula, so recently formidable, had become precarious and imperiled. The question was no longer how large Don Philip's realm might be but whether it would exist at all.

THE ROUT OF THE JACOBITES

When 5,000 Highlanders marched into Derby, a town less distant from London than Prague is from Linz, they nursed rather more substantial doubts about their enterprise than the frightened English realized. They looked at three hard facts. The English populace was not rising to support them; the government of George II had mobilized 30,000 troops against them; and their French allies had yet to appear. At meetings held on 16 December 1745, Lord George Murray advised Charles Edward that his army could not prevail if it lacked both popular and French support and faced an enemy that outnumbered it six to one. Since almost all the commanders concurred in Murray's views, Charles Edward submitted to the majority. "I must yield," he protested, "but I take God to witness that it is with the greatest reluctance, and that I wash my hands of the fatal consequences which I foresee, but cannot help."[13] The withdrawal—Charles Edward refused to style it a "retreat"—was less easy than the advance. The Jacobite troops yielded to demoralization and indiscipline. The English civilians, who had seemed largely indifferent when the momentum lay with the invaders, now turned hostile. And Edinburgh was meanwhile retaken by other forces loyal to George II. When the government at London realized what the Jacobite withdrawal implied, they replaced Cumberland with Lieutenant-General Henry Hawley, whose operative judgment about the Jacobites was that "I do and allwayes shall despise these Rascalls."[14] On 31 December—it was Charles Edward's twenty-fifth birthday—the Jacobite troops crossed the Esk and reentered Scotland.

Shortly thereafter the Jacobite camp enjoyed its final brief taste of success. By laying siege to Stirling Castle, still a loyalist stronghold, the Jacobites drew an overconfident Hawley forward from Edinburgh. The killing began on a blustery and wet 28 January 1746 when the loyalist cavalry rode out against the advancing Jacobite infantry near Falkirk and fell before a volley of fire. The Jacobites then charged the loyalist infantry. Only the loyalist right held against the charge, protecting the unruly retreat as best it could. Falkirk was a victory to be savored by the Jacobites: though it lasted only twenty minutes, it took 400 loyalist lives and cost the loyalists an even larger number of prisoners.[15] It also destroyed Hawley's reputation, and he was soon relieved of the command he had just assumed. Unfortunately for Charles Edward Stuart, the outcome at Falkirk did not alter the basic facts that defined the Scottish campaign. The government at London still controlled the sea and a far vaster panoply of resources. Though the 6,000 Dutch troops had been returned to the continent, they had been replaced by 5,000 Hessians. By choosing Cumberland to replace Hawley, the government signaled its commitment to implacable rigor in the war against the Jacobites. The duke entered Perth on 17 February, vengeful and determined, and a remorseless stalking began, as the loyalists tried to convert Scotland into an occupied province.

Before this pressure the Jacobites receded. Lord George Murray concluded that the prince's army would not be safe unless it found protection in the Highlands. Charles Edward resisted Murray's reasoning with the inevitable question: "Can we imagine, that where we go the enemy will not follow, and at last oblige us to a battle which we now decline?"[16] But postponing defeat seemed preferable to inviting it, and on 12 February the dispirited Jacobites began a disorderly retreat to the north, entering Inverness on 3 March. The loyalist garrison there withdrew by sea, taking all the available boats with them to prevent pursuit. Though poorly armed and abandoned by France, the Jacobites had no further haven to flee to and could only watch anxiously as the loyalist army drew near. Lord George Murray saw only one chance for success under these conditions—catching the loyalists unawares.

But a nocturnal march undertaken against the loyalists at Nairn on 26-27 April quickly degenerated into a nightmare. When Lord George learned that the loyalist camp had uncovered the surprise, he ordered a retreat to Culloden. All that his ill-chosen probe had done was to assure that a Jacobite army already suffering from want of food would now engage without sleep as well.

When Cumberland was informed of how the Jacobites had spent the night, he resolved on an immediate attack. The loyalists broke out of Nairn shortly after dawn, closed quickly on the Jacobites near Culloden, and by late on the morning of 27 April 1746 the two armies had fallen into line formation facing each other. Cumberland's army outwinged the Highlanders on both the right and the left. Because the ground was spongy and therefore unsuitable for a Highland Charge, Charles Edward elected to await a loyalist charge and deal with it as his troops had at Falkirk. This decision gave Cumberland the luxury of assailing an immobile foe with barrages of artillery, and for twenty minutes loyalist cannon fire lashed the Jacobite ranks. It was the first time the Highlanders had faced effective artillery fire; they were appalled at its destructiveness. When it became clear to Murray that Cumberland had no incentive to order a charge, the center and right of the Jacobite line lurched forward in a desperate effort to turn the tide. The ensuing fighting on the Jacobite right was vicious. The loyalists clubbed and bayoneted the wounded to death, leaving the battlefield, in the words of one observer, "bespattered with blood and brains."[17] At the other end of the line of battle the Highlanders, rather than advancing, broke and fled. But instead of saving their lives, this action led them directly into the grip of the cavalry on the loyalist right. Charles Edward watched the entire affair in disbelief. Earlier engagements had led him to think, against Murray's warning, that his men were invincible; a few hours at Culloden proved they were mortal. By 1:00 P.M. the Jacobite retreat was well under way. The battered right, disciplined to the end, withdrew to the sound of bagpipes. The left dissolved into the woods, hedgerows, ditches, and fields of Culloden.[18]

On the next day Charles Edward conferred for a final time with Lord George Murray—the two men would never meet again—and issued his last command: "Let every man seek his own safety the best way he can."[19] He then began the tortuous flight that ended, after months of disguises and deceptions, in his escape from the British Isles. Culloden had left him with no hope. While 9,000 loyalist troops had borne only 300 casualties, 5,400 Jacobite troops had suffered 1,560 casualties. And the end of the battle did not bring an end to the carnage. Wounded Highlanders were left to die unattended on the battlefield, and civilians between Culloden and Inverness were put to the sword. The activities that would earn for Cumberland his reputation as "the butcher" had begun. In its own slower way the British government also unleashed its punishments. Over 100 men were put to death for complicity in the rebellion. Over 1,000 were deported. Estates of the guilty were deemed forfeit. In an effort to destroy the power of the clans the heritable jurisdictions of the Scottish lords were abolished, and Parliament acted to disarm the Highlands and ban the use of Highland attire. The anglicization that the Lowlands had accepted peacefully was now to be imposed by force on the Highlands.

Four considerations explain the failure of the Scottish revolt. The first was the hostility of the English. Scotland's misfortune was to share an island with a more numerous people who distrusted Scottish particularism. The second factor, given the first, was the absence of any counterweight to the English. France acted for a while as if it would aid the Scots, but since the French government was waiting on the English Jacobites, who in turn were waiting on the French government, Versailles never mounted the grand offensive against England that Charles Edward counted on. The third factor was the unwillingness of a majority of Scots themselves to work for a Stuart restoration. No leading Scottish lord signed on. Scottish intellectuals were wary. Lowland Scots thought Charles Edward a disturber of the peace. The Presbyterian clergy thought him wicked. But the fourth factor is the critical one, for had it been different, so might the others. This factor is the character and capacity of Charles Edward himself. Though a hero to many and a demigod to a few, the Young Pretender was—the judgment is inevitable—unfit for the task he assumed. He lacked the intense resolve that marked Maria Theresa. He lacked the capacity for clear thinking that characterized Frederick II. He lacked the suppleness of strategy associated with Charles Emmanuel. He never understood that by attacking England he was compromising his claims on Scottish nationalism. He never understood that, as a Catholic, he frightened even those in England who disliked the Hanoverian dynasty. He lacked the wit either to engage the French or contact the Jacobites of England. He was lazy, selfish, petulant, and only haphazardly brave. He was—the most biting judgment of all—finally not interested in the Scots. The Young Pretender was truly his grandfather's grandson.

SORTING OUT THE PIECES

In the aftermath of the fall of Asti, the Marquis d'Argenson defined two goals for France: the fostering of warmer relations with Spain and the isolating of Austria. Cosseting Spain violated all his instincts. Nevertheless, what was needed, he now affirmed, was a dramatic sign of Versailles's commitment to

Madrid, and the two gestures decided on were almost theatrical. With the first, the French government directed Marshal Maillebois to subordinate himself and his troops in Italy to the commands of Don Philip. In effect, France accepted Spanish control of France's army in Italy. With the second gesture the French government sent Marshal Noailles to Madrid as a special representative from Louis XV. As a man untainted by the recent fiasco and a known critic of the Marquis d'Argenson, Noailles carried the credibility requisite to regaining Spanish confidence. While France was deliberating these gestures, the question naturally arose about how Italian territory might be extorted from the stubborn Austrians. D'Argenson proposed a solution he had once scorned: Flanders would be the price that France would pay to secure an Italian principality for Don Philip. Despite recent events, the marquis's penchant for spilling French blood on behalf of allies' goals burned unabated.

If cooperation with Spain was a policy imposed by d'Argenson's head on his reluctant heart, the corollary policy of weakening Austria had the marquis's unitary assent, and he set about trying to mobilize potential enemies of Vienna. One such foe was Turkey, but the Turks were not to be diverted from their commercially profitable peace with Vienna. With Saxony, however, another such foe, the marquis gained a modest triumph. There was, of course, no hope of roping Dresden back into a war it had so recently fled. But a lesser purpose—the weaning of Saxony from Austria—seemed realizable. On each side there were men who sought a Franco-Saxon rapprochement. Maurice wanted closer French ties with his half brother, the king of Poland. Count Brühl wanted closer Saxon ties with a state that he hoped to align, at some distant date, with Austria. Patently the motives on each side were in tension, but nevertheless on 21 April 1746 France and Saxony concluded a treaty of neutrality. Saxony won more from the agreement than France: Versailles pledged itself to pay an annual subsidy of 2 million livres (£80,000) for three years, even if Saxony, as part of the empire, should cooperate in imperial military activities. But Versailles was not without its winnings. Formerly lacking a major German ally, France now had one. In this season of French disasters, the treaty was savored as a solitary success.

It was the Low Countries that most intensely engaged d'Argenson's interest. But the two territories that lay within that region—the Austrian Netherlands and the Dutch republic—elicited dramatically dissimilar policies from the French. Toward the United Provinces Versailles remained conciliatory. After all, rapprochement with the republic would deprive Austria of an ally and place enormous pressure on Britain to end its belligerence; if Britain should leave the war, then Austria would be hopelessly outmatched. But toward the Austrian Netherlands the marquis urged the policy of the stick. The province, after all, was Austria's. Whenever negotiators should finally sit down to resolve the various disputes among the belligerents, it was likely that they would distribute territories among the combatants in accordance with the dictates of military success or failure. The more Austrian land that could be occupied, whether in Italy or the Low Countries, the more formidable the Bourbon position became. Only one consideration blunted this hope: France dared not to behave in a manner that might seem to threaten Dutch security, for then the collateral effort to lead the republic away from Austria would be splintered.

The extension of a velvet glove to the Dutch represented a modest shift in France's attitude. Only as the hope to engage Piedmont-Sardinia faded did d'Argenson begin to smile on Wassenaer-Twickel. Events then moved swiftly. Before February was out d'Argenson drafted a document titled *Ideas on the Peace*, which adumbrated a possible settlement. It proposed various Austrian cessions in the Low Countries, the dismantling of the fortifications at Luxembourg, and the restoration of Cape Breton to France. On Italy it was silent. The Dutch found the *Ideas* disappointing and dispatched Jacob Gilles, the second Greffier, to steady Wassenaer-Twickel's faltering grasp of Dutch interests. The British, to whom the Dutch forwarded the document, reacted with even greater asperity. But conversations continued, and the distance between the two camps finally narrowed to the point where it was measured only by four questions that in the context of 1746 apparently defied resolution. Should Britain be compensated for restoring Cape Breton to France? Should the Jacobites be granted any consideration whatsoever? Should France be allowed to strengthen its fortifications at Dunkirk? Should Austria be pressed to yield Tuscany? The Dutch, as was their wont, looked to Britain for guidance. Guided by the Duke of Newcastle, the ministry in London urged the suspension of meaningful talks with France. And so, by the end of May in 1746 the diplomatic dance was terminated, and each camp withdrew, to await the outcome of the incipient season of military campaigning. But both France and the Maritime Powers now had a more accurate understanding of the other side's views, and with the clearer vision of hindsight we can see that the long process of winding down the belligerence had finally begun.

Just how halting the process would be was demonstrated by France's actions in the Austrian Netherlands. While at Paris the diplomats were canvassing the possibilities of peace, at Antwerp Maurice resumed his resorption of Vienna's Atlantic province. The decision to focus military attention on the Austrian Netherlands was d'Argenson's. The Prince of Conti had asked to be given command of a large army in the Rhineland, but the marquis, anxious to avoid any action that might prompt a German rallying to Austria, prohibited French probes in the empire. Maurice of Saxony had advanced a detailed plan for invading the Dutch republic. Again d'Argenson imposed a veto, fearing in this instance that an attack on Dutch territory would strengthen rather than weaken London's commitment to Vienna. And so Maurice was required to return to his army in Flanders, swollen now to over 100,000 troops, and direct a dreary campaign of sieges. The bludgeoning of the city of Antwerp began on 20 March 1746, and, with Louis XV present to add luster to the day, on 3 June the outnumbered Austrians surrendered. As summer began, therefore, the French ruled Austrian Brabant and Austrian Flanders and menaced Austrian Hainault. They were making the Austrian Netherlands their own.

French fortunes in Italy, however, were a different story. The collapse of the Bourbon position at Asti triggered a failure in French morale that expressed itself in mounting desertions and debilitating illnesses. Within a month Maillebois lost 15,000 men from his army encamped around Novi. Farther east, at Piacenza, Gages's Spanish army sat immobilized. Both the commander and Don Philip, still ensconced at Milan, recognized the danger posed by the flood of Austrian troops into the region, but fearful of ignoring instructions from Madrid, neither was willing to initiate a retreat. Instead, they directed the French to abandon the ready avenue of escape through Genoa and to march eastward to join them. The Austrians, 45,000 strong, moved skillfully to entrap the isolated Bourbons. On 20 March, as Count Bernklau led the Austrians back into Milan, Don Philip fled his disease-ravaged capital for Pavia, as if, in the words of an observer, "after the loss of a pitched battle."[20] By April Guastalla and Reggio were in Austrian hands. At Parma the Austrian command then gathered to make plans for a decisive battle against the Bourbon troops scurrying into Piacenza from various directions. Throughout Europe interested observers wondered at the spectacle of Lombardy: what the Bourbons had effortlessly effected in 1745 the Austrians had undone with even greater dispatch in 1746.

Even as craggy Corsica was straining to liberate itself from Genoa, it became at the end of 1745 a small theater in the international war raging around it. On the island three men were struggling to impose three different orders on a traditionally restless people. Stefano di Mari was Genoa's agent. Abandoning the conciliatory posture of his predecessor Giustiniani, Mari turned to such tactics as the pillaging of churches to persuade Corsicans that they should not seek to dissolve their ties with the republic. Gian Pietro Gaffori dominated the revolutionary Consulate and commanded a force of 400 men. He dismissed the Genoese as lacking "the ability, the knowledge, and the will to govern well."[21] Amid civil disorder and political disarray, he offered the structure of justice and order. Not surprisingly, he won a healthy number of supporters. Domenico Rivarola, the third figure, swaggered about like a medieval princeling. Though posing as a liberator, he alienated almost all chiefs who might have joined him in the fight against Genoa and was dismissed by many as the "riff-raff of fortune" and a "blundering spirit."[22] But because he commanded 200 mercenaries, he could not be ignored. Between them these three leaders and others of lesser stature were carving the island up into little fiefdoms with shifting frontiers. National administration was nonexistent; the localities ruled essentially as they saw fit.

It was this jumble of ambitions that drew the outsiders in. Piedmont-Sardinia backed Rivarola. Charles Emmanuel publicly promised "our royal protection and assistance and the provision of all those aids that are in our power" and privately hoped that the condottiere's diversion in Corsica would force Genoa to withdraw troops from Finale.[23] Britain also intervened on behalf of the adventurer, placing its Mediterranean squadron at Rivarola's disposal. When Rivarola laid siege to Bastia in November 1745, British vessels came to his aid by subjecting the settlement to devastating naval fire. This success then induced the Austrians to add their own words of support, with Maria Theresa pledging "our protection and help."[24] In March 1746, with the hope of winning over Charles Emmanuel visibly disappointed, Louis XV finally projected France into the confusion by declaring that he supported the Genoese claim to Corsica and that he hoped to contribute "as promptly and as efficaciously as possible to the reestablishment of peace, order, and subordination in Corsica."[25] These four interventions, however, exercised little effect: France and Austria never sent troops to the island, and Britain and Piedmont-Sardinia soon suspended their dabbling in its affairs. Thus, by early July 1746, after six months of confusion, an equilibrium had emerged in Corsica, but no Corsican leader could be confident that foreign intervention would not rematerialize soon.

Meanwhile, by late in the spring of 1746, the competing belligerent alliances were recovering their vigor. In the Bourbon camp the chief healer of wounds was the Duke of Noailles. Though d'Argenson muttered about Spain being "a bad comrade in war, still worse in negotiations," and the Duke of Huescar (in effect) replied that the "good harmony that [the French] lauded as so useful to the two crowns was in substance only a blind acquiescence that they sought from us,"[26] Noailles ignored the former and overcame the latter, calming the sense of betrayal that each side felt toward the other. Meanwhile, to the north, a similar reconciliation was occurring in the Austro-British camp. London responded to the fall of Brussels by quickly increasing Maria Theresa's annual subsidy from £300,000 to £400,000 and by purchasing soldiers from Bavaria. The action was a timely gesture, designed to harden Dutch resolve and erode Austrian suspicions. Austria reciprocated with a return to a rhetoric of cooperation and professions of solidarity. Meanwhile, members of both alliances seemed to agree that further tests of arms were requisite to wringing peace from the gnarled war.

Only Piedmont-Sardinia stood somewhat apart from this structure of hostility. Charles Emmanuel had his winnings—the territory ceded him by the Treaty of Worms. What he wanted now was a way to recover Savoy from its Spanish occupiers. On the surface it would appear that that goal would make him a candidate for a closer tie with Maria Theresa and George II. But in fact the situation was more complicated. Even though the Spanish denounced Charles Emmanuel as a "faithless man with whom it is not possible to pursue a safe policy," the French continued to drop hints that they wanted to reach an accommodation with the king.[27] And even though Britain showered favors on Charles Emmanuel, increasing his subsidy by £100,000 to bring it to parity with Vienna's new grant, the Austrians were unforgiving that, by secretly dallying with French negotiators at Paris and Turin, he should even have contemplated a repudiation of the bonds with Vienna. So Charles Emmanuel entered the summer of 1746 as a nominal member of the refurbished Worms alliance, but sought after by one of his foes and contemned by one of his partners

THE TWO EMPRESSES

For a long time Alexis Bestuzhev had been using his access to the empress of Russia to spin a web of Prussophobia about her. He preached the dangers that Frederick's adventurism portended for Saxony and Poland, he extolled the virtues of cooperation with Austria, and he even suggested that since the army was potentially the most destabilizing of Russian institutions, it might be advisable to dispatch it for battle in foreign parts. Prussian action underlined these warnings. Frederick's swift devastation of Saxony sobered Elizabeth; his efforts to rouse the Turks enflamed her. Prussia was becoming the disturber of the peace, the despoiler of tranquility. On 21 January 1746 Bestuzhev proposed to Elizabeth that Russia conclude a defensive alliance with Austria. It was not the first time that the grand chancellor had broached the subject. But contrary to former practice, on this occasion the empress agreed. In her eyes Frederick had become the foremost threat to European stability. With that conclusion Maria Theresa won a victory she had sought since the outbreak of belligerence.

The negotiations to bring Austria and Russia together took place in St. Petersburg. Baron Pretlack represented the Austrian government; Alexis Bestuzhev himself negotiated for Elizabeth. Both sides guarded the secrecy of the talks so successfully that neither Hyndford nor Mardefeld could penetrate their purpose. The chief obstacle to a prompt treaty was the disagreement over the imminence of a war against Prussia. Russia wanted an immediate attack on Frederick's territories—we are left to imagine how that message, too late by a bare matter of months, was received in Vienna—while Austria, twice stung and now at peace with the rapacious Frederick, wanted only an assurance that when the inevitable third Silesian War arose, St. Petersburg would aid Vienna. By 25 April the treaty was in final form, and after a month of ineffectual haggling over minutiae, the Treaty of St. Petersburg was formally signed on 2 June 1746. Ironies abound in this juncture of Europe's two empresses—and the pact was quickly and popularly styled the "treaty of the two empresses"—but the greatest surely is that an agreement grounded in a common hatred of Prussia reached fruition almost six months after Prussia had stopped molesting its neighbors and had left the war.

The treaty was a defensive pact—that is, it specified that if either of the signatories became involved in a war with a third power, the other would assist it by supplying 30,000 troops. But there were important qualifications to that rule. Austria had no obligation if Russia's war was with Persia; reciprocally, Russia had no obligation if Austria's war was with Spain. The troop commitment reached only 15,000 if Austria's war was with France or Russia's with Sweden. Finally, the current war in Italy and the Low Countries was excepted from the treaty. But if the document muted its force in some directions, it featured incentives for belligerence in others. The anti-Prussian bias of its drafters was most visible in its stipulations that if Prussia attacked Austria, Russia, Poland, or an ally of Austria, not only would each signatory double its complement of troops but additionally Austria would regain Silesia. This clause put Vienna's opportunities under the Treaty of St. Petersburg into conflict with its obligations under the Treaty of Dresden. Much of the treaty remained a secret. But Europe knew enough about it to realize that the two giants of the east had finally made common cause. Hitherto Europe's most important neutral, Russia seemed on the brink of becoming Europe's vastest belligerent.

16

The Bourbons Fall Out
(June 1746 — December 1746)

PIACENZA

The walled town of Piacenza was a magnet for the various fighting forces in Italy in the spring of 1746. During March and April Spanish armies fell back on the town from both Milan and Parma, hounded by their swarming Austrian foes; the French drew near in May, harried by the cautious Piedmontese. The Austrians were surprised at these developments, for they had presumed that the numerical superiority of the Worms allies would induce their Bourbon foes to withdraw to the relative safety of Genoa. But Philip V and Elizabeth Farnese, having foreseen the possibility of faintheartedness in a son who beneath his "Spanish exterior" had a "French heart,"[1] had fortified Gages with the strictest orders: whatever else might happen, Piacenza was not to be relinquished. And since Louis XV, in his effort to reaffirm Bourbon solidarity, had ordered Maillebois to submit to Don Philip's commands "without regard to preserving his communications,"[2] the French marshal had no choice but to remain near his ally. Thus 100,000 soldiers, who only three months earlier had been scattered across the vast quadrilateral defined by Asti, Milan, Mantua, and Reggio, were now being compacted into the twenty-mile strand of the Po valley that extended from Stradella to Piacenza.

The commander of the Austrian army was the popular Prince Liechtenstein. He was supported by a staff of men who had been hardened by the rigors of German warfare: Nadasdy, Bernklau, and above all Browne. Complemented by the Piedmontese, his side enjoyed a potential margin of perhaps 15,000 men in troop strength. Objective factors thus pointed to an Austrian triumph in any coming confrontation. But Liechtenstein's health was poor, and while the Austrians devoted May to building their fortifications, moving their artillery into place south of the town, seizing outlying blockhouses, and requisitioning provisions from sullen civilians, Liechtenstein spent much of the spring living the life of an invalid. Gages, meanwhile, applied all of his considerable skill to making the Spanish position formidable. The Spanish army was encamped on the glacis of Piacenza, just south of the town. Gages had spurned the precincts of the walled city because its crumbling battlements were likelier to cramp than protect. Instead, he directed that ditches be dug, artillery emplaced, and the wider region scouted. He was determined, if a battle came, that the Austrians should pay heavily. He needed Maillebois's French troops if the Bourbons were to have any hope of success in the impending battle, but the French commander had dealt with Gages's entreaties for aid by temporizing, sending ten battalions forward to Piacenza but remaining himself at Novi. Only on 14 and 15 June 1746, in obedience to orders from Versailles, did the last and largest components of Maillebois's forces finally reach Piacenza.

Gages's Spanish army numbered at most about 25,000. Desertions had riddled its ranks as various elements staggered in from all points of the compass, and disease had weakened its morale. The Neapolitan and Genoese contingents had been especially susceptible to the ravages of "hunger, misery, and want and dearth, and fever and plague and sore throats and smallpox, with a hundred other calamities."[3] Maillebois's French army numbered about 15,000. It had once been far larger, but it too had suffered from desertion, and many of the men who had served at Alessandria now languished in Piedmontese captivity. Its arrival in mid-June, though increasing Bourbon strength considerably, also intensified the already severe demands that the Bourbon presence was making on the food supplies of the city. Liechtenstein's Austrian army numbered approximately 45,000. Though suffering from the same sort of material hardships that bedeviled the Bourbons, the Austrians at least expected to consummate their Italian campaign with a triumph in the vicinity of Piacenza. Trailing the French, and hence approaching but not yet on the scene on 15 June, was a part of Charles Emmanuel's Piedmontese army. This force numbered perhaps 10,000, and it drew near at a pace so slack as to suggest a preference for observing over fighting.

It was the fact that the forces of Piedmont-Sardinia were still a day's march away that impelled Maillebois to urge Gages to immediate action. The plan that the two commanders adopted on 15 June was Gages's, for he had studied the flat countryside that stretched off to the south from Piacenza and observed the Austrians methodically deploy their forces and guns for the coming engagement. He proposed that the Bourbons should encircle and enfold the Austrians. While a small force was keeping the Austrian center occupied with artillery fire, the Bourbon right (in the west) should sweep farther right before circling back against the left flank of the enemy. The Bourbon left (in the east), in a less elaborate move, should attack the Austrian right with the purpose of pushing it toward the center. Finally, a portion of the Bourbon right should detach itself and find a position behind the enemy. During the night of the fifteenth and sixteenth the Bourbons began to move out into battle formation. Unfortunately for the Bourbons, Count Browne foresaw what Gages would attempt. He therefore decided on 15 June to deploy his forces on the Austrian left along the eastern side of a canal, facing outward and ready to meet the encircling Bourbons head-on. The decisions facing the Marquis of Botta d'Adorno, commander of the Austrian right, were simpler on the evening of June 15, and he limited himself to placing his troops on alert; when the attack came, they would be ready. In general, the Austrian plan, like Traun's scheme when he bested the same Gages at Campo Santo, was to let the enemy waste itself in an attack against well-fortified positions and then to counterattack when the vigor of the assault was spent.

The battle began in earnest with the rising of the sun on 16 June 1746. While the Austrian artillery opened fire on the Bourbon camp, the French on the west and the Spanish on the east commenced their assault on the Austrian lines. Maillebois was so astonished at finding Browne's troops correctly lined up to meet his sweeping attack that he could only conclude that a spy had betrayed Gages's plan. And that was not his only problem. The French column that was supposed to sweep most broadly had misread the monotonous terrain during the night and, by cutting back to the east too soon, had jammed the French columns to its left into a smaller area than planned. Thus compacted, they were cannon fodder. Maillebois worked furiously to bring more men into action and thereby prevent the day from turning into a debacle. But Austrian fire was so fierce that the French never got close enough to engage in hand-to-hand combat. The final stroke was an Austrian infantry advance across the canal. The French attack collapsed, the fetid gullies became French graves, and not even the example of Maillebois himself, seizing a standard and calling for resistance, could restore coherence to the Bourbon right. By noon the struggle on the west wing was Austria's. On the eastern wing, however, the battle was far more even. The Spanish marched directly at their Austrian foes, and beneath the weight of their repeated assaults the Austrian infantry slowly yielded. Only when Bernklau was able to bring the Austrian cavalry into action was the Spanish advance finally checked. When, after midday, the Spanish line quivered and then broke, the Austrians were left with the ritualistic task of chasing their enemy back into Piacenza. By 2:00 P.M. the battle was over, and Don Philip, who had seen the Bourbon defeat developing, had already fled his observation post to hide amid the peddlers of the city.[4] Few would have suspected it that day, but in fact the question of domination in Lombardy had now been effectively answered for the next half century.

The extent of the Austrian victory is most visible in the casualty figures. Whereas Liechtenstein's forces lost only 3,400 men, 700 of whom were killed, Gages's Spanish troops suffered 9,000 casualties (including the missing and captured) and Maillebois's French troops endured 4,000 more. In all, the Bourbon armies buried about 4,500 of their men, saw another 4,800 led off into Austrian captivity, and bore a casualty rate of 33 percent—the highest for any major battle in the war thus far.[5] Piacenza was an abattoir. For Maria Theresa the day brought deliverance: her army had been valiant, her cavalry had been brilliant, and, as she told a diplomat in Vienna, "I want to hope that this event will dispel from my enemies any thought they may have of completely banishing me from Italy."[6] At Madrid, contrariwise, the recriminations flew, with chief blame being affixed to Gages, who, it was said, withheld essential cavalry elements from battle. "The operation," the Duke of Huescar wrote, "was lost for being badly conceived and badly managed."[7] In fact, the outcome should have surprised neither court. Gages had hoped to overcome his numerical disadvantage with a little cunning. Victory went, however, as it usually does, to the larger force. The task for the Bourbon armies was now to extricate themselves from Italy. A stroke of good luck befell them when, on 18 June 1746, Prince Liechtenstein tendered his resignation to Maria Theresa. Exhausted by his long illness, Liechtenstein believed that he could no longer bear responsibility for the empress-queen's army in Italy. Aware of the confusions in the Austrian camp, the Bourbons used the advantage to exit the city on 27 June, moving to the north bank of the Po. Conceived by Maillebois, this plan of escape was a bold one, for it put the outnumbered Bourbon armies on the wrong side of a mighty river and meant that they could reach safety only be recrossing it at a later time. But at least it allowed the 25,000 French and Spanish to escape from Piacenza.

THE IMPACT OF TWO DEATHS

In the early morning hours of 9 July 1746, barely three minutes after complaining of nausea and slumped in the arms of his wife, Philip V died. To say that an era in Spanish history ended with Philip's passing is not to overstate the implications of the event. Philip, who had held the throne (with one short interruption) for forty-six years, had presided over the fixing of Spain within

France's cultural and social orbit. His accession in 1700 had triggered a European war, and even after winning recognition for his claim, Philip had had problems. The nadir of Spanish fortunes was reached in 1719, when British gunship diplomacy forced Philip to swap Sicily for Sardinia. But then Spain began to recover. In the 1730s the Spanish royal couple succeeded in enthroning their own eldest son—though not Philip's eldest, for there had been an earlier marriage—as king of the Two Sicilies. At the same time the Spanish navy grew and the Spanish economy revived. The Bourbon Family Compact made Spain a partner, subordinate but powerful, with France. Throughout his life Philip V had yielded to the temptation to rely on others. But he had never been a nullity, and in the 1740s, with the futures of his own sons at stake, he had become virtually as fervent as his wife in seeking a realm for the coddled Don Philip. Royal deaths can overthrow international calculations in a moment: Charles VI's demise had triggered the current war, and Charles VII's had redirected it. The question buzzing through every European chancellory in the second half of July 1746 may be framed simply: with Philip V dead, how will Spanish policy change?

Much depended, of course, on the character and dreams of the new king. Not yet thirty-three years old, Ferdinand VI had already earned a reputation for being, in Elizabeth Farnese's words, "simple-minded."[8] Since his stepmother was far more solicitous for her own children, Ferdinand had not figured prominently in the shaping of Spanish policy during the war. Royal ministers, however, who must always keep actuarial probabilities in mind, had not entirely neglected him, and the Marquis of Ensenada had been especially successful at earning the respect of the prince while retaining the trust of the king. Nevertheless, Ferdinand acceded to the throne a self-confessed neophyte in matters of policy and diplomacy. His character traits thus assumed a special importance, and among the most prominent were a shy amiability, a love of music, a fear of being assassinated, a determination not to appear vacillating—and, most important of all, a uxoriousness that rivaled his father's. His spouse was the asthmatic Portuguese princess Maria Barbara, an intelligent consort who sang, composed, and performed at the harpsichord "with fine style and commendable skill."[9] She detested Elizabeth Farnese and contemned the French. Don Philip had already foreseen problems when he wrote to his mother about Maria Barbara: "we nourish a serpent in our bosom."[10] Of one thing everyone felt confident. Ferdinand VI —the first monarch of eighteenth-century Spain to be born on Spanish soil —would pursue a foreign policy more manifestly consistent with Spanish national interests than his predecessor had. "The king," Maria Barbara wrote, "is Spanish and deeply Spanish, and in no way French."[11]

As Ferdinand VI understood Spain's interests, the chief need was to end the war. Ensenada agreed. "Nothing," he declared, "is better than *Peace.*"[12] In the bedchamber Maria Barbara preached the same doctrine. This concerted advocacy won a prompt and important victory. Ferdinand had scarcely assumed power when he turned his limited attention to Italy. Summoning the Marquis de La Mina out of his forced retirement, he dispatched him to Lombardy to relieve Gages and fortified him with secret instructions to eschew fighting in favor of escape. With this—his swiftest and yet most important decision—Ferdinand set Spanish policy on a course that would lead finally to Madrid's extrication from the Italian war. The route, however, was tortuous. Ferdinand VI, after all, did not want Don Philip to wind up in Spain, where he would surely be an embarrassment and perhaps a threat. And Ensenada, alert to the international implications of national actions, explained that Ferdinand, by still insisting upon a principality for Don Philip, would enhance his own reputation. The effect of these considerations was to prompt the king to pursue the classic policy of the armed peace. Spain, one observer wrote, will "move toward peace by means of war."[13]

The constellation of individuals who exercised influence shifted early in the new reign. In Madrid itself, though Ensenada stayed in power, other ministers of the late king soon found themselves without influence. At Versailles, the most important of the foreign courts, Huescar replaced Campo-Florido. To Lisbon, now in light of the queen's Portuguese antecedents a vital capital, the Duke of Sotomayer was dispatched. These men, along with La Mina, constituted a team of lieutenants loyal to a new monarch rather than an old policy. Another figure of importance in the new reign was the celebrated castrato, Carlo Broschi (Farinelli), the greatest singer of his day. These changes in personnel portended, of course, a change in priorities for Spain. And no action symbolized the new order more publicly or strikingly than Ensenada's decision to strip Don Philip of the title and revenues of Grand Admiral. In the context of the ongoing war it was a declaration of rupture with the past.

Scarcely more than two weeks after Philip V died, a second death brought a second shock to Franco-Spanish relations. Ferdinand's half sister Maria Theresa, the wife of Louis XV's eldest son, succumbed in childbirth. Though neither she nor her husband exercised political influence, their marriage was one of the matrimonial links that helped bind Bourbon Spain to Bourbon France. Since the dead woman had a younger unwed sister, Maria Antonia, the Spanish court was quick to propose that this infanta replace the late one in the dauphin's marriage bed. But in a startling exercise of royal authority, His Most Christian Majesty unexpectedly demurred. He was encouraged in his adamance by the Marquis d'Argenson, who hoped to use the eligibility of the dauphin to rearrange France's diplomatic commitments. Alternative brides were promptly canvassed. D'Argenson suggested a daughter of Charles Emmanuel; Maurice of Saxony commended his own niece, the daughter of Augustus III; Marshal Belle-Isle urged consideration of Frederick II's sister. D'Argenson's gambit promptly failed, for the king of Sardinia rejected the scheme with the apposite remark that "the fiancee would need a safe-conduct to get to the wedding."[14] The other candidacies, however, remained alive throughout most of 1746. The significance of this peculiar episode lies less in its eventual outcome—the dauphin finally married Maria Josepha of Saxony—than in its opening phase. For reasons that baffled many and enraged some, Louis XV had chosen the occasion of the death of a Spanish princess to affront the crown of Spain at the very moment that France needed Spanish help in escaping from Italy.

THE CHARADE AT BREDA

The death of the king of Spain did not derail France's chief diplomatic initiative. Ever since the summer of 1742, French ministers had fixed their eyes on the United Provinces as the weakest link in the chain of foes that sought to fetter Louis XV. Technically, of course, the Dutch Republic was not even at war with France. But its nonbelligerent status had not prevented it from contributing troops to the Pragmatic Army in 1743, from participating against the French at Fontenoy, and from supplying the chief contingents that resisted the French seizures of fortresses in the Austrian Netherlands. In June 1746 d'Argenson sent the Marquis Puisieulx, a diplomat with experience in Naples, on a brief trip to the Dutch republic to try to nudge its leaders. Puisieulx adopted a stern position, proposing a peace settlement that included the return of Louisbourg to France, the establishing of Don Philip in Tuscany, and a guarantee for Silesia. He returned to France to report that peace was not at hand. But in fact he had sufficiently frightened the Dutch so that early in July Van der Heim sent word that Gilles had been given full powers to conclude a separate peace. The Dutch then asked the British to join them in the negotiations.

The Dutch action forced Britain's hand. The Duke of Newcastle had recently won the British government over to the view that, with France unbending, more was to be gained from military campaigns than from diplomatic parleys. But that calculation was credible only if the Dutch remained loyal to the Pragmatic Alliance. Therefore it was imperative that Britain appear to take Dutch concerns seriously. Newcastle had, however, another consideration to weigh—a consideration that made the situation rather more complicated. With Ferdinand VI's accession in Madrid, the British government concluded that the time was propitious for an effort to disengage Spain from France. The outcome at Piacenza lent plausibility to this hope. And the Portuguese background of the new queen of Spain suggested Lisbon as a fitting site for Anglo-Spanish talks. Newcastle asked Benjamin Keene, Britain's most skilled diplomat and an old hand at Iberian affairs, to travel to the Portuguese capital and contact the Spanish there. This roundabout diplomacy was unlikely to bear prompt fruit. Time, therefore, was what Britain needed. This is why the Dutch invitation was so embarrassing. At the very moment when Iberian affairs seemed to be offering attractive opportunities for Britain, Flemish affairs were driving the Dutch into a panicky quest for peace.

Newcastle decided that an immediate settlement with France must be avoided, lest a good peace be sacrificed to a swift one. So the technical issue at hand involved finding a satisfactory way of dealing with the Dutch allies. And since Britain dared not spurn the Dutch invitation entirely—an invitation endorsed, significantly, by the French—the issue reduced itself to improvising dilatory maneuvers. The first opportunity for delay arose with a dispute over the location of the negotiations. Britain insisted on a neutral site, and only after much talk did the choice fall on Breda, a Dutch town lying less than ten miles from the French frontier. Even after a site had been selected, Britain did nothing to quicken the pace of events. As Britain's representative Newcastle chose the Earl of Sandwich, a neophyte at diplomacy. Newcastle then equipped him for a deception by providing him with two sets of instructions, one public and the other secret. The public orders suggested that Britain, though seeking to broaden the talks to include Austria and Piedmont-Sardinia (and therefore Spain), was interested in hard-headed negotiations in cooperation with the Dutch. The insistence that Vienna and Turin be represented served Newcastle's purpose splendidly, for it was certain to induce delays. Meanwhile, the private written orders specified that Sandwich should refuse to accept: (1) neutrality for the Austrian Netherlands, (2) any transfer of Tuscany, or (3) the retrocession of Cape Breton. And to assure that priorities were understood, his private oral orders identified delay as his chief purpose at Breda.

For the task of dealing with the British at Breda, the Marquis d'Argenson turned again to Puisieulx, arming him with instructions appropriate to the representative of a dominant state. But the changing Italian situation obliged d'Argenson to add a new demand to Puisieulx's list: the restoration of Genoa and Modena to their prewar situations. D'Argenson warned Puisieulx that the talks might be long, and he urged patience on the envoy, enjoining him to maneuver the negotiations in such a fashion that, if they collapsed, the blame would be Britain's. D'Argenson was remarkably sanguine: since Spain would be loyal, since Piedmont-Sardinia would be tractable, since demands for peace were welling up in the Dutch republic, and since Sandwich was hungry for glory, Britain would come to understand the value of peace. However, only one thing was truly certain: since Sandwich was under instructions to drag the talks out and Puisieulx was under instructions not to break the talks off, the Breda conference would not come to any quick decisions.

Owing to a variety of factors, the conference did not open until 4 October 1746. Britain of course had made delay a matter of policy, and Sandwich was rich in stratagems, refusing, for example, to travel from The Hague to Breda until Puisieulx had done so. But Britain's purpose was served as well by two other elements—Van der Heim's death, which necessitated a governmental shuffling in the United Provinces and resulted in the elevation of Gilles to the position of Grand Pensionary and the appointment of Wassenaer-Twickel as the Dutch representative at Breda; and the ambiguity of military fortunes, which were prospering for the Bourbons in the Low Countries and for the Worms allies in Italy. At that first meeting Puisieulx stumbled into a British trap. To forestall British demands that Austria and Piedmont-Sardinia be represented, the French envoy declared that there was no need for Spain to send a diplomat to Breda, since France could speak for Spain. Sandwich seized on this incautious argument to insist that if Madrid was already represented, then Vienna and Turin could not be left out. The conference was thus deadlocked, and Puisieulx was forced to consult Versailles for instructions. When the negotiators regathered on 25 October, the French victory at Rocoux had intervened. But the Dutch still forbore concluding unilaterally with the French (despite the authorization given their negotiator to do so), because they feared the domestic consequences of breaking with Britain. And so Sandwich could hold his ground on the issue of participation and refuse to be stampeded into substantive discussions. Breda was becoming a conference of airbags.

When the conclave reassembled yet again on 18 November, its business was complicated by the presence in town of envoys from Austria and Piedmont-Sardinia. Their appearance shifted the question of representation from the realm of the theoretical to the realm of the concrete. Having been outmaneuvered by Sandwich in early October, Puisieulx was now wiser: he understood that Britain did not want the discussions to end, and he used this knowledge to advantage, refusing to allow either Austria's Count Ferdinand Harrach or Piedmont-Sardinia's Count Chavanne to be admitted to the conference, and threatening to walk out on the talks unless Britain backed away from supporting their participation. Sandwich gave way, and Gilles then came forward with the proposal that, after the pattern of the Gertruydenburg negotiations of 1710, the representatives from Vienna and Turin be allowed to sit in as spectators. Puisieulx opposed this compromise too, but d'Argenson, savoring the humiliation it implied for Austria, ordered the French diplomat to accept it. Further delay was then inevitable, for the approval of the governments at Vienna and Turin had to be secured. So even in defeat Britain carried the day, and the halting negotiations spun themselves out into December.

But other developments were also conspiring to clog any impulse toward peace at Breda. Harrach's orders, for example, revealed that Austria was not interested in peace. Bartenstein, after all, still directed foreign policy and was—in Robinson's words—"the most difficult man at this court to be brought to think of peace."[15] Britain was less overtly bellicose, banking on a diplomatic victory in Iberia rather than a military victory in Italy, but it was no more interested than Austria in coming to terms. And Piedmont-Sardinia, suddenly optimistic about military prospects in Liguria, also turned aside talk of a settlement. Puisieulx summarized the situation tersely: "the Dutch want peace and will not make it, the English don't want it but might make it. The Queen of Hungary flees from it and fears it and wins over her allies."[16] There was, in addition to all of these considerations, a further reason why the Breda conference lapsed into inconsequence. Diplomacy in wartime is contoured by military campaigning, and in the fall of 1746, as was so often the case in this equilibrated struggle, the two major theaters taught starkly dissimilar lessons.

ROCOUX

Campaigning in the Low Countries got off to a late start in 1746, for on each side command problems required cautious solutions. For France there was of course no dispute over who should command the main army: Maurice of Saxony stood as the heir of Turenne. But the Prince of Conti, whose pretensions might otherwise have been ignored, was related to the king, and in a strange compromise he was entrusted with an independent command over a smaller force. Maurice was frustrated by the political prohibition against attacking the United Provinces, and he lamented that he "could only lose from the continuation of the war, without hope of gaining anything."[17] For the Pragmatic Allies questions of command continued to be more divisive than solidifying. Maria Theresa chose her feckless and luckless brother-in-law,

Prince Charles of Lorraine, to lead the Austrian troops. Having dueled with Frederick II, he was now to test himself against Maurice. His presence meant that the Duke of Cumberland would not be generalissimo—and so Cumberland did not appear; instead, Sir John Ligonier assumed command of British troops. The Dutch commander was the inevitable Prince of Waldeck, selected because he had incumbency on his side and hence was the only choice available to a States General that did not wish to reopen the issue of the proper role of the Prince of Orange. By mid-1746 the French had amassed 200,000 troops in the Low Countries and the allies had gathered 90,000. But since the French were dispersed, holding fortresses and towns across foreign territory, that manpower gap would be considerably shortened if the two armies should ever join in battle.

Maurice moved into action in early July, convinced that, if glory could not be won, lives need not be lost. Like Traun in Bohemia in 1744, he determined to remove an enemy bloodlessly. By skillfully maneuvering his large army, he believed he could secure territory while avoiding engagements. The territory he coveted lay along the middle reaches of the Meuse River, and Maurice targeted three towns for conquest. The first was Mons, not essential to his Meuse strategy but a powerful fortress and an awkward enclave of Austrian authority lying within otherwise French-controlled Hainault. The second was Charleroi, which sat upon the chief tributary of the Meuse in this region, the Sambre. The third was Namur, the famous citadel commanding the confluence of the Sambre and Meuse. A fourth target, probably not attainable in the current year of campaigning, was the great fortress at Maastricht, sited fifty miles downstream from Namur and celebrated as the guardian of the eastern sector of the Dutch republic.

The task of taking Mons fell to Conti, and he proceeded with methodical thoroughness. On 11 July 1746 Mons surrendered, and Hainault passed unequivocally under French control. Conti then shifted his troops to Charleroi. Here too he enjoyed success, when on 2 August a squad of defenders fled from an outwork into the main fortress and neglected to bar the gate to their French pursuers. Meanwhile, however, even as Conti's military record acquired luster, his relations with Maurice turned positively hostile. Native-born French commanders often despised the German-born marshal who had restored France's military honor, and no one exceeded the proud Conti in feeling resentful about the Saxon's success. While the siege at Charleroi was proceeding, Maurice had approached Prince Charles's force at the Méhaigne river. He had requested aid of Conti and been denied what he sought. Maurice thereupon resolved upon a showdown with his rival. On 2 August, within hours of the surrender of Charleroi, Maurice and Conti met, and in a fiery conversation each made clear his unwillingness to serve under the other. An appeal to the king followed, and Louis XV promptly declared his preference for genius over consanguinity. On 12 August Conti wrote a terse note to Maurice to inform the marshal that he was leaving. Though only twenty-nine at the time and a general who had known much success, Conti never commanded again in the three decades of life left him.

Maurice now fixed his eye on Namur, a fortress famed for its sieges. He judged the investment of Namur itself to be a relatively straightforward enterprise and assigned it to the Count of Clermont. The more interesting task, in light of his determination to avoid battle, was keeping a relief army at bay. This role he gave to himself, and during the next two months Maurice gave lessons to all of Europe about the use of feints, ruses, and ripostes to disable the schemes of an enemy. In the process he even provided an opportunity for an army under Count Löwendahl to capture Huy. Three times in August and September Maurice declined combat: he wanted territory, not slaughter. Toward the end of the siege of Namur he even ordered the bombardments to cease, relying on shortages of food alone to induce the commandant to surrender. When on the first day of October 1746 the white flag rose over the citadel, the policy of bloodless conquest received its ultimate vindication. Since it was now too late in the year to tackle Maastricht and since the republic was still off limits, Maurice expected campaigning to wind down. "There was," he wrote to Frederick II, "nothing left for us to do."[18]

But he was wrong, for the allied army unexpectedly began to march southward along the western bank of the Meuse toward Liège. The decision was Prince Charles's, taken at Vienna's prompting. Maurice still had no taste for a pointless battle, but when the allies crossed the Jaar River, Maurice realized he was being offered an opportunity not merely to defeat the enemy force but to crush it. The allies encamped on a large triangle of land defined by the Jaar and the Meuse. They were strung out along a five-mile line, their backs to the Meuse. Their left (when they swung around to face the French) touched Liège but had neglected to occupy it. Their right was separated from the center by a ravine. They had no depth and were outnumbered. Maurice concluded that fools deserved a fool's fate. On 10 October he moved his army into position opposite the allies and, that evening, used an actress in a performing troupe to send a prearranged signal to his officers that the attack would commence the following day. The professional was determined to show the amateurs how the game was played.

Fog obscured the scene on the morning of 11 October 1746, but when the mists lifted around midday observers—for spectators actually flocked out from Liège to witness the impending battle—beheld two vast forces arrayed for combat. To the west were 120,000 French troops, strung in a four-mile-long arc that extended from close to the Jaar in the north to the outskirts of Liège in the south. Maurice commanded the French center, which faced the villages of Lier, Varoux, and Rocoux. Commanding on his right and menacing the town of Ance was Clermont, aided by Löwendahl and d'Estrées. The left was entrusted to the Marquis of Clermont-Gallerande. The allies deployed themselves as three national armies. On the left were 24,000 Dutch, anchored on Ance and regarded by all as the weakest element in the allied army. In the center were 24,000 British (including their German auxiliaries), formidably protected by the three central villages. On the right, on the far side of a ravine and hence isolated from the others, were 32,000 Austrians. Maurice's plan of battle presumed that the Austrians would not be able to link up with the British. He proposed to send his right, to whom his ablest commanders were assigned, to assail the feeble Dutch, driving a wedge between them and the stronger British. Once the Dutch had begun to give way, the infantry in the French center would surge forward against the British. If all went as planned, the Austrians would be isolated, the Dutch would collapse, and the British would be defeated.

In fact, however, two elements broke in the allies' favor. Maurice had counted on having much of the day to effect his devastation. But the weather prevented any action aside from artillery shelling until 2:00 in the afternoon. He therefore had only five hours in which to accomplish nine hours' worth of work. Then—absolutely unanticipated by anyone—the Dutch offered firm resistance, blunting Löwendahl's charge on Ance. When Maurice unleashed his infantry on the allied center, Rocoux fell quickly to the pressure and Varoux yielded soon thereafter. In this brutal struggle in the center, Maurice used his advantage in manpower, steadily feeding battalions into the maw to engage the British in a meat-grinder operation he knew he could not lose. But the afternoon was slipping away, and Maurice realized that the Austrians, thus far useless to their allies, might now become important as coverers of the imminent Dutch and British retreat. He therefore sent orders to Clermont-Gallerande to attack Prince Charles's army, an action that would distract it from any role as a protector of a retreat. But Clermont-Gallerande delayed two hours before beginning to harass the Austrians. In the interval the Dutch and British negotiated their retreat skillfully, crossing to the east of the Meuse behind the cover of dusk.[19]

The result was a major French victory but not the crushing blow that Maurice had hoped to inflict. The marshal acknowledged this truth, remarking that if he had been allowed two more hours of daylight he could have destroyed the Pragmatic force. The French suffered 3,750 casualties, one-third of them fatalities. The allies bore 7,000 casualties (including the missing and captured), of whom about 1,600 were killed. Since the battle had been vast—with 200,000 participants it was the largest of the century up to that point—the proportion of casualties to participants was rather low, especially when contrasted with engagements in the murderous Italian theater. But gross statistics disguise national differences: with 2,500 casualties the Dutch, from a force of 24,000, suffered two-thirds as many losses as the French from an army of 120,000.[20] Maurice himself took deepest satisfaction from the fact that under his training the French infantry, so unfit at Dettingen, had been transformed into a force capable of taking on the fearsome British. "I have as my sole weapon the buckle of truth," he soon wrote to Count Brühl. "I am feared, the king loves me, and the public places its hope in me."[21]

THE BOURBON COLLAPSE IN ITALY

While Bourbon fortunes were reaching new heights in the Low Countries, they plummeted in Italy. The battle of Piacenza shattered Gallispan hopes for the peninsula. The death of Philip V ended the era of strategic parallelism. Thereafter, the best that the embattled French and Spanish troops could hope for as they scrambled for protection in the summer of 1746 was that their leaders would recognize the utility of reciprocal support in retreat. That the withdrawal would not be easy was patent: not only were the Bourbons outnumbered, they were also blocked off from the safety of France by the Po River and the Apennine Mountains. Their chief asset was the persisting strain of reciprocal suspicion that wracked the Worms alliance, a suspicion that erupted again after the Bourbons fled Piacenza into Austrian Lombardy. The Austrian commander, Botta d'Adorno, wanted to protect his queen's territory, even if that meant driving the Bourbons west of the Ticino. The Piedmontese commander, Charles Emmanuel, resented the idea that his territory could be used as a refuse dump and insisted that his lands remain untransgressed. To obviate the clear danger of a disruption in the Worms alliance, Count Browne persuaded the commanders to adopt the ancient principle of the Golden Door. Rather than seeking a decisive engagement, the Worms allies would stay separated and try to funnel the outnumbered Bourbons southward back across the Po and then southwestward toward Genoa. By always allowing one route of egress to remain open, the allies would purge their territories of their enemy and still avoid battle.

By early August Maillebois had begun to suspect that his foes were adopting the strategy of Traun. On 9 August 1746, in the hope that he was right, he directed a passage across three bridges back to the south bank of the Po at the point where the Tidone flows into that river. The decision was a bold one, for it committed the Bourbons to the exposure of a river crossing while two hostile armies were in the vicinity. But Maillebois had judged Austro-Piedmontese thinking accurately—in fact, only at Rottofreno did Botta d'Adorno actually engage his enemy—and with the Austrians baying and gnawing at their heels, the Bourbons staggered into Tortona on 14 August. The Po was now forded, but the mountains still lay ahead. The task of vaulting them would not be Gages's. On 13 August La Mina arrived in the Spanish camp to replace the man who had earlier replaced him. "My whole care," La Mina later wrote, "was...to save the army without exposing a grenadier."[22] He assured Maillebois that he would continue to cooperate with his ally, but the French commander was skeptical. And the skepticism proved sound. Even when offered a chance to engage Browne's outnumbered army, La Mina refused to be diverted from retreat over the Apennines. On 23 August the Bourbons stumbled through the Bocchetta Pass and reached the temporary safety of the Genoese republic.

The Genoa they staggered into was panic-stricken. The great gamble of 1745—the decision to shed neutrality and to supply troops and provisions to the Bourbon camp—had manifestly failed. Although putative defenders were now filing down from the Bocchetta Pass, the citizenry and government of the republic could take little comfort from their arrival, for La Mina made clear his intention of merely marching through Genoa on his way to the French frontier, and Maillebois reluctantly declared that, without Spanish support, the French dared not stay either. That left Genoa surrounded by enemies. Botta d'Adorno and Browne were poised to challenge the feeble Bourbon garrisons left at the pass. Charles Emmanuel and the Piedmontese had moved farther west to approach the territory of the republic along the Bormida valley. And at sea British squadrons had begun to assist their Worms allies by bombarding the city. From this trio of foes Genoa could expect scant mercy. When Don Philip departed the city, he glibly exhorted a senatorial deputation: "Don't be afraid: it's a passing moment, it will be nothing."[23] The records do not reveal whether the senators laughed or wept.

Even as the French and Spanish withdrew toward Savona, the Austrians smashed their way into the republic. The invaders had expected a fierce challenge at the Bocchetta Pass, but none materialized. On 6 September 1746, relieved only that it was the Austrians rather than the Piedmontese to whom they surrendered, the Genoese authorities yielded the city to the conquerors. Botta d'Adorno, in disregard of pledges of lenity, quickly imposed an onerous indemnity of 3 million genovine (£800,000) upon the republic and began in addition to requisition supplies. His motives for such savagery were mixed. He wanted to punish Genoa for its insolence, and he needed money and supplies for his troops. But he also had a personal grudge to settle, for his family was Genoese in origin and his father had been exiled from the republic. Some observers thought the commander's faithlessness ill judged. But for the time being Austrian authority was irresistible in the city.

The fall of the city of Genoa left the extended arc of the republic virtually defenseless. The town of Savona (though not the citadel) surrendered to the Austrians on 9 September 1746, while Finale, the port long coveted by Piedmont-Sardinia, capitulated to Charles Emmanuel a week later. A major question now faced the Worms allies: what should their next objective be? Vienna and Turin had different answers. Having regained control of Lombardy, Maria Theresa wanted to send her army southward against Naples. Having expelled the Bourbons from Genoa, Charles Emmanuel wanted to dismember the republic and then dislodge the Spanish from Savoy. In fact, however, neither the queen of Hungary nor the king of Sardinia prevailed. Britain was footing much of the bill for this struggle, and in London the Duke of Newcastle, fretting at Maurice's success in the Netherlands, wanted to put pressure on Louis XV where he was most vulnerable— in the unprotected southeast corner of France. Exerting the power that flows from the purse, Britain's representatives imposed London's priorities on Vienna and Turin: the assembled land and sea commanders decided to strike through the western wing of the Genoese republic into Provence, carrying the war to France. "These operations," Newcastle soon wrote, "on the richest and most exposed part of the French dominions must be regarded as the principal object of the war."[24]

The only factor delaying the plunge into France was the immediate shortage of troops. Browne believed that a minimum of 30,000 was necessary, and so, after rushing toward the French frontier and capturing Nice on 17 October 1746, the Austrians halted their forward drive in order to allow time for reinforcements to catch up with the van. (On that same day the remnants of the French and Spanish armies, now numbering only 17,000, stumbled into France.) The Austrian advance was supported from the sea by fire from a British squadron. Except at Savona and Finale, the Piedmontese played a secondary role. Charles Emmanuel fully intended to lead the invasion of France itself, but he left command of the preliminary campaigning in Browne's hands. Thus, when Charles Emmanuel took to his bed with smallpox on 20 November, Browne was superbly prepared to assume full command of the 20,000 Austrian and 10,000 Piedmontese who had gathered at

Nice, and on the last day of November he began to send them across the 300 yards of the shallow but swift Var. The border that the Bourbons had transgressed in 1744 was now violated from the other direction.

The Bourbon armies had recoiled from their advancing foes like hounds from a flaming torch. Once safely across the Var, the Spanish army abandoned all pretext of Bourbon cooperation. Despite Maillebois's pleas for assistance, La Mina immediately led his troops into Savoy, where they joined their compatriots in the army of occupation and by their presence disabused Charles Emmanuel of any dreams of recovering his province by force. The Spanish departure left Maillebois with the daunting task of defending Provence alone. He quickly determined that resistance at the frontier would be suicidal, and so he proposed to withdraw the French troops from the coastal plains into the mountains behind the river Loup and from these lairs to prey upon the Austrian flanks. The Austrians and Piedmontese celebrated their invasion of France with numerous episodes of mayhem against civilians. Offshore the British squadron contributed to allied success with regular coastal bombardments. At Versailles the French government frantically tried to throw together a relief force. But in the opening weeks of December 1746 it was the Austrians who enjoyed the initiative in Provence. Browne was so confident of taking Antibes that, leaving Austrian artillery and British naval fire to reduce it to chars, he swept past it on the road to Toulon. There was little Provence could do for the time being except endure.

Bourbon unity, which had known its high point in March 1746, was now in tatters. But the reactions of the two courts to this disenchantment were sharply different. At Versailles the government concluded that slippage must be reversed. On 9 November, prodded by Marshal Noailles, the ministry decided to dismiss the tainted Maillebois from his command and replace him with a figure whom the Spanish respected, the indomitable Marshal Belle-Isle. The hero of Prague, as if resurrected, assumed command in early December. At Madrid, however, priorities were different. In his most important action since recalling Gages, Ferdinand VI raised Don José de Carvajal, forty-eight years of age and a man of wide administrative experience, to the rank of minister, entrusting him with direction of foreign policy. Within little more than a month the politically agile Carvajal had confined Ensenada to duties that did not bear directly on the war. "Spain," Carvajal declared, "must distance itself from France so as not to be subordinated to her."[25] He therefore wanted warmer ties with Britain. He would not reject France's friendship. But given the maritime nature of Spain's interests and given British possession of the former territories of Gibraltar and Minorca, Britain loomed as a more significant entity on the international scene, whether as friend or foe. With Spain angling for a British rapprochement, it was far from clear as winter set in whether French efforts to resuscitate the Bourbon alliance would succeed. And meanwhile France was faced with the imperative of purging Provence of invaders.

17

Further Revolutionary Intrusions
(December 1746 – May 1747)

THE GENOESE REVOLUTION

The republic of Genoa, mistress of the Ligurian Sea, was one of the small number of nonmonarchical sovereignties that existed in the interstices of the dynastic state system of Europe. Although only 50,000 people resided within the precincts of the city, Genoa the Proud was nevertheless a force to be reckoned with. Nature had given it a formidable northern wall, history had given it control over Corsica, and the ingenuity of its citizens had given it a financial paramountcy in the Mediterranean region. It had been, the famous phrase ran, a bank before it was a city. In 1744 the government had chosen to cast prudence to the winds and to aid the Bourbon monarchies in their war against the Worms allies. The decision divided the patriciate that guided Genoa's affairs. On one side stood the older noble families, who tended to think that abandonment of neutrality was reckless. They were supported by the merchants, who expressed fears of British reprisals. But on the winning side stood the nobility of more recent origin who mobilized a war party around the nationalistic conviction that the transfer of Finale to Piedmont-Sardinia would be a "terrible slaughter" and must be resisted.[1] In the triumphant Bourbon campaign of 1745, Genoa supplied men and artillery to the Gallispan army, lent money to the French and Spanish governments, and acquired military celebrity through the conduct of its troops at the siege of Tortona. But in 1746 this fragile world of success shattered. Instead, as Bourbons fled Italy, the Genoese war party vanished, and the government soon capitulated to the Austrians.

By surrendering, the Genoese turned themselves over to foreign troops who enjoyed brutalizing civilian populations and to a governor, the Marquis Botta d'Adorno, who savored his opportunity for revenge. With the army using whips to assure civilian order, the inhabitants suffered even more cruelly than the Bohemians in Prague during the French occupation of that city four years earlier. Nor were indignities at the hands of Germans the only misery the city endured. Peasants driven from the war-beset countryside brought inflation and starvation with them to the city. Above all, wearing everyone down, there was the enormous indemnity of 3 million genovine (£800,000) imposed by Botta d'Adorno. Where was such a vast sum of money to come from? The Austrians knew that Genoa was a banking center. They presumed that the financial institutions of the republic could be forced to disgorge funds. But the patricians, determined to shift the incidence of the imposition away from themselves and onto the broader though vastly poorer general population, guided the government to the decision that the indemnity should be met by tapping the great charitable foundation of Genoa, the Casa di San Giorgio. It is not surprising that those who bore this burden were not inclined to feel much compassion for a patriciate that, having blundered into a war, now sought to make others pay the chief price of the blunder.

On the evening of 5 December 1746 the combustible mixture caught fire. An Austrian work-gang lost control of a mortar it was dragging, and the piece got lodged in a ditch. When the commander tried to force some Genoese bystanders to assist in extricating it, he was greeted by a shower of cobblestones. The mob quickly swelled, and the Austrians, hoping for a more tranquil morrow, withdrew to their guardhouse. But neither night nor rain extinguished the blaze. On 6 December the protest spread to other precincts of the city. Barricades were flung up, cries of "liberty, liberty" and "weapons, weapons" bespoke a rising fervor, and with their armories pillaged the Austrians suddenly found themselves subject to sniping. The startled Botta d'Adorno tried to negotiate with the aroused citizenry. The equally startled Genoese patriciate splintered. Some squeezed their movable belongings into wagons and departed the scene of chaos. Others chose to support a movement they believed they could not defeat, hoping at least to channel it. The revolt quickly gained force. Churchmen enlisted, and people at the margins on society—prisoners, former soldiers, beggars—joined the fray. By 10 December it was clear that what had begun as a riot had become an insurrection. Faced with that tough truth, an incredulous Botta d'Adorno ordered an Austrian withdrawal from the city. In less than a week the Genoese had liberated themselves.

But now the pressing question obtruded: from what had they been liberated? In one sense the answer was clear. The Austrians had been the oppressors, and the Austrians must now be made to pay. Detained Austrian soldiers—those 2,500 whom ill luck had prevented from escaping—were abused by their captors, and Genoese citizens who had sympathized or collaborated with the occupiers were seized and incarcerated. Because Austrian troops still held many of the towns of the republic, a universal conscription was imposed on all males between the ages of seventeen and seventy, and reforms aimed at improving the efficiency of the militia were enforced. But for many in Genoa, the expulsion of the invader was insufficient. They sought to liberate Genoa from the patriciate too. Thus a rival government was quickly put in place, coexisting with the traditional one but based on broader principles of representation. Its central institution, created on 17 December 1746, was the Assembly, which contained delegates chosen by, among others, the stoneworkers, the fishmongers, the glassworkers, the jewelers, and the winemakers of the city. After 17 December the Senate and the Assembly—one representing the traditional order, the other presaging an alternative future—vied with each other to direct the city's affairs. Their competition would have been more intense still had they both not sensed that two constraints imposed an obligation for minimal cooperation upon them. The first was the continuing Austrian threat: Maria Theresa, enraged at Genoese disobedience, vowed to recover the city. The second was the need to secure French aid: the insurgents may have driven the occupiers out, but the monarchical government of Louis XV was exceedingly wary of aiding a republican revolution.

For a brief moment Genoa stood at the center of Europe's gawking attention. Foreign ministers and their advisors sought to find meaning, advantage, or hope in the bizarre events that thundered through the city. At Turin the revolution was seen as a "fatale catastrophe."[2] Though the Piedmontese army was able to crush the last resistance at Savona on 9 December 1746, the leaders at Turin sensed that with their king laid low and their enemy now aroused, future successes were likely to be scarce. The British too were dismayed, and Lord Hardwicke barked his wish that "Botta had been hanged when the Czarina would have had him hanged."[3] At Vienna, the third of the Worms capitals, the chief sentiment was rage. Maria Theresa sent orders to Botta d'Adorno to club the Genoese back into submission, and Francis I spoke for his wife when he said that "Botta must go to Genoa, whatever the cost."[4] Though ultimately decisive, the French reaction was in its first stage profoundly mixed. No more than Maria Theresa was the French government minded to tolerate republican insolence. But the French consul at Genoa wrote breathlessly that "nothing like this has ever been seen," and in noting that "the people attack the Germans in a fury," he underscored the strategic implications of the revolution.[5] Since Louis XV had already supported a revolutionary movement in Scotland, there seemed no compelling reason for him to abstain from offering similar support to a revolution in Genoa. By

February 1747, therefore, French funds were reaching the beleaguered city, and soon thereafter French and Spanish troops began evading British naval blockades to infiltrate and defend Genoa. During the same time the revolutionary zeal of the opening weeks slowly faded, and the Senate—the body with which the French dealt—gained the upper hand. The French intervention was thus doubly critical. It saved Genoa from an Austrian counterattack, and it saved the old regime from the new.

FRANCE CHANGES ITS HELMSMAN

"The d'Argenson's are tottering," Maurice of Saxony wrote to Count Brühl in December 1746; "the one for foreign affairs is so stupid that the king is ashamed of him."[6] For two disastrous years the Marquis d'Argenson had presided over the conduct of French foreign policy. It would be difficult to find a more egregious example of inept leadership in the entire span of the eighteenth century. He allowed himself to be gulled by Piedmont-Sardinia, in the process disarming his own forces and looking the fool when Charles Emmanuel attacked. He persisted in a foolish contempt for Spain, heedless of the strategic importance of the familial tie and preferring to ignore Spain when he could, scold it when he desired, and insult it as therapy. His fondness for Prussia was so unreflective that he construed Frederick II's slights as nothing but charades, deliberately chosen by the king to disguise his partiality toward Versailles. Finally there was Austria. Toward this state d'Argenson nourished a keen distrust. Since most political observers in France thought Britain a more dangerous foe than Austria, and since the Catholic hierarchy wanted easier relations with Catholic Vienna, d'Argenson's obsession with Austria seemed singularly peculiar.

And so an opposition coalesced at the court. To the core comprised of Maurepas, Tencin, and Noailles others attached themselves. Puisieulx concluded that d'Argenson was feeble as a policymaker, Vauréal deplored his tendency to disoblige friends, and his own brother—never on close terms with the marquis—found his military ideas appallingly naive. Maurice of Saxony stood somewhat apart from the political machinations of the ministers, but his views of d'Argenson's unfitness were widely known. "He is a firecracker," Maurice wrote; "if he is ignited, he will explode, for the whole kingdom—the king, the court, and the clergy—wishes it."[7] The case against the marquis was finally and decisively made by the Duke of Noailles. In a long December memorandum to Louis XV, the king's closest confidant marshaled an array of evidence to demonstrate a record of unparalleled fatuity. It was d'Argenson who had lost Italy, wasted time on the Dutch, and alienated

Spain. Above all, it was he who had squandered opportunities, such as the one afforded by the demise of Charles VII, to seek closer ties with Austria. He was, Noailles declared, an ideological dogmatist; he must, Noailles concluded, be dismissed.[8] It was the complacency of the sovereign that had hitherto protected d'Argenson from the consequences of his folly. Noailles's memorandum finally penetrated that complacency.

On 10 January 1747, having just finished dining at his brother's residence, the Marquis d'Argenson received a letter of dismissal from the king. He was not entirely surprised. The removal of Maillebois, d'Argenson's favorite general, had been a portent, especially since it had been the first stroke in the emerging French campaign to reverse the decay in Franco-Spanish relations. The king used the occasion of this dismissal to reassert his confidence in two other servants. The Count d'Argenson, who feared that his brother's fall would encompass his own, was confirmed in office. Maurice of Saxony was given yet another title: marshal-general. The dismissal of d'Argenson was almost universally applauded. The Duke of Luynes offered a balanced judgment: the marquis was high principled and well intentioned, "but unfortunately he lacks the talent necessary for success." Another journal-keeper preferred witticism: "it is generally said that the affairs with which the Marquis d'Argenson was charged were truly foreign to him." Maurice made his point with characteristic brevity: "Well, my dear count, the bomb has exploded."[9]

Louis XV chose to replace d'Argenson with the forty-five-year-old Marquis of Puisieulx. The king's wishes in matters of this sort were velleities. But all the obvious alternatives suffered from liabilities. The redoubtable Chauvelin was still too haughty for the king's taste. The acerbic Chavigny, one of d'Argenson's most incisive critics, lacked sufficient social standing. The Count of Saint-Séverin, though experienced and skilled, was Italian-born and hence unsuitable as foreign minister to a French monarch who already relied on a German-born general. Puisieulx had served in two important capacities, first as envoy to the king of the Two Sicilies and then as French representative at Breda. He thus understood both the northern and the Mediterranean aspects of the war. He had the support, moreover, of Joseph Pâris-Duverney, whom financial connections made ever more important as the expensive war continued. Finally, Marshal Noailles stood in his corner, convinced that Puisieulx would accept the Nestorian advice that d'Argenson had ignored. Peace is the object of war, Noailles counseled, "but to achieve it with security and advantage it is necessary to concert military operations with political measures."[10] The advice pointed up one of d'Argenson's greatest flaws—his failure to see fighting and negotiating as complementary activities in wartime. Puisieulx, less cocksure and more commonsensical, seemed likelier to grasp the relationship.

FRANCE REGAINS THE LIGURIAN INITIATIVE

France's first task at the opening of 1747, whoever might be guiding foreign affairs, was expelling the invaders from Provence. Marshal Belle-Isle had insisted, before accepting the command, that he be promised the requisite number of reinforcements. To aid him in the task he drafted the services of his younger brother, the Chevalier Belle-Isle, whose daring in Bohemia and at Rocoux had drawn favorable attention. He pulled troops whom Maillebois had stationed in lands north of the Loup back to more secure areas farther west. He won La Mina's and Spain's promise to help. Then he waited while reinforcements dribbled in from the Low Countries and Savoy, trading space for time. Meanwhile, Count Browne, though advancing against the thickening Bourbon alignment, was having second thoughts. The Genoese revolution was an unmitigated calamity—an abscess flaring deep behind his lines. And since payments to his Austrian troops were already in arrears, the Austrian portion of his army was low. Even his stock of effective artillery was spare. In these circumstances Browne calculated that the only way the Worms allies could sustain their occupation of Provence was to control a broader swath of French territory and live off of it. The proposal, of course, smacked of desperation, for Browne had only 30,000 troops on hand with scarcely a chance of seeing that total increase, while Belle-Isle had the resources of an affronted France and, closer at hand, La Mina's army to count on.

The French launched their expected counterattack on 21 January 1747. Fifty thousand strong (including 6,000 cavalry), they struck against the right flank of the overextended line of the Austrians and Piedmontese. Browne immediately signaled a retreat. Initially he hoped to hold at the Siagne River, but when he realized that Belle-Isle would again try to outflank him, he abandoned all ideas of retaining a corner of French territory and ordered his troops to end the siege of Antibes and withdraw back to the east of the Var. During the retreat the Piedmontese were hounded so closely that when they fired the bridge that had just led them to safety, the French were already beginning to cross it. By 3 February the Austrians and Piedmontese were clear of France. At the cost of only 100 men the French army—and vengeful French peasants—had imposed 4,000 casualties on the invaders. Primary blame for the debacle attaches to the British, who had imposed this plan of campaign upon their allies in the teeth of sound and warranted forebodings.

Browne's conduct of the Provence expedition won applause. Count Traun thought it extraordinary that, in addition to hanging on for two winter months in foreign territory without supplies, the army had been able successfully to extricate itself. But praise of that sort could not disguise the fact that the enterprise had failed.

Attention now shifted to the liberated city of Genoa. Unlike Milan, exposed on a plain, Genoa crouched behind a mountain range and honored a tradition of resistance. The ease of Botta d'Adorno's entry in September 1746 had been a fluke—the consequence of a swift demoralization and the desertion by allies. It could not, Maria Theresa was advised by her generals, be replicated by the Austrian army now nursing its injured pride at Novi. The empress-queen acceded to their arguments for strengthening her force in the region. She replaced Botta d'Adorno with Count Schulenburg in January 1747, conferred command of the entire Mediterranean theater on Browne in February, and authorized Browne to negotiate with Count Bogino about the details of Ligurian cooperation in March. The British had already pledged to enforce a naval blockade. As finally adumbrated, the plan for the siege called for applying pressure on all routes of access with the aim of starving the contumacious city into submission. At Maria Theresa's request, Browne entrusted command of the siege itself to Schulenburg. The British blockade took shape in February, the Austrian advance from Novi began in April, and on 3 May 1747 the formal planning came together when Austria and Piedmont-Sardinia concluded a treaty that confirmed earlier projections of placing 90,000 troops in the field in Italy—two-thirds of them Austrian and one-third Piedmontese.

Bourbon efforts to introduce reinforcements into the city were impeded by the fact that, with land routes held by the Austro-Sardinian army, only the sea afforded a route of access. And the sea was Britain's domain. So a risky cat-and-mouse game was begun, as Belle-Isle sent French and Spanish troop carriers out to coast along the Ligurian strand. Some were captured, some repulsed. But some slipped through, and by mid-April 1747 Belle-Isle had contrived to introduce 3,000 French and Spanish troops and 200,000 sorely needed livres (£8,000) into the city of Genoa. Initially French brigadier-general Mauriac commanded the Gallispans; at the Senate's invitation he accepted direction of the city's defenses. But on 30 April, in a dramatic gesture of Louis XV's solidarity with the Genoese, the Duke of Boufflers snuck into the city and superseded Mauriac. By infiltrating so grand a figure into the beleaguered city, France was telling the world that it did not intend to allow Genoa to fall back into Austrian control. Boufflers thrilled the Senate with a grand promise: "show me the danger, and I will seek my glory in protecting you from it."[11] At a remorseless price in casualties and prisoners, Belle-Isle contrived to provide Genoa with defenders.

Meanwhile, however, the question of where to open a second front vexed Bourbon counsels. La Mina proposed the most obvious course: a march along the Ligurian coast to Genoa. It would force the Austro-Sardinians to defend themselves front and back and put Spanish troops again on the most direct road to Piacenza, where Spain still hoped to install Don Philip. Belle-Isle, on the other hand, believed that Genoese and French purposes could best be jointly served by an attack on Piedmont-Sardinia. With d'Argenson gone from the foreign ministry, the policy of conciliation toward Turin was rejected. It was now time to try coercion. If Charles Emmanuel could be compelled to sue for peace, then Maria Theresa would be isolated in Italy and the long Bourbon struggle in the peninsula would be rewarded with victory. In the end the Gallispans decided to try both. Two separate but interrelated military movements in and around the northwest corner of Italy followed. The first involved preparations for the assault on the western reaches of Piedmont-Sardinia. The second was the struggle around the perimeter of Genoa. The major Austro-Sardinian attack on the city commenced on 21 May 1747, designed less to penetrate its walls than to confine it even further. But Genoa's defenses were strong, and the ensuing struggle, despite Boufflers's contracting of smallpox, was an exceedingly even one. As May passed into June, doubts about ultimate success in the struggle for Genoa were beginning to surface in both camps.

A TANGLE OF TONGUES

By the spring of 1747 the various combatants were showing visible signs of war-weariness. The United Provinces had, of course, never been avid for war: technically they had never even shed their nonbelligerent status. As early as 1742 France had begun to repent of its rash race into combat, and the Marquis d'Argenson had brought the search for peace to the forefront of French diplomacy. By early in 1744 Piedmont-Sardinia, now in possession of the lands ceded to it at Worms, joined those looking for peace. Though opinions in Britain varied, a peace party had coalesced by 1745 around Henry Pelham, the first lord of the treasury. The accession of Ferdinand VI in the middle of 1746 moved Spain into the camp of those belligerents who were eager to end the hostilities. Even Austria, though unregretfully bellicose in Italy, was receptive to peace overtures in the Netherlands. The fourth phase of the war was thus characterized by the simultaneous pursuit of preparations for combat and parleys for conciliation. The papal nuncio at Paris understood the dilemma confronting the statesmen of Europe. "All say that they sincerely want peace," he wrote in March 1747, "but each would like it with his advantage, which is the same as saying he does not want it."[12]

Within the anti-Bourbon camp the special preparations for the coming military campaign were diplomatic. The talks, held at The Hague at the opening of 1747 and attended by the various anti-Bourbon representatives sent to Breda, were designed essentially to identify obligations and allocate resources. For the first time in the war the Pragmatic and Worms alliances in effect met together to establish quotas for the struggle against the common French enemy. The documents that were signed on 12 January were surprisingly forceful. They specified that for the coming campaign in the Low Countries, Austria would supply 60,000 troops and Britain and the United Provinces would supply 40,000 each. Meanwhile, to the campaign in the Mediterranean theater, Austria would contribute another 60,000 troops, Piedmont-Sardinia would allocate 30,000 troops, and Britain would assign thirty warships. Britain also committed itself to granting subsidies of £400,000 to Maria Theresa and £300,000 to Charles Emmanuel. On paper, therefore, two formidable armies had been created. The Pragmatic Allies envisioned an army of 140,000 men; the Worms allies foresaw an army of 90,000, aided by an powerful naval presence. In each theater the predominance of power would thus rest with the anti-Bourbon camp. But the success of the Convention of The Hague depended on the fulfillment of these promises, and by 1747 the financial authorities in the belligerent states were without exception advising their foreign ministers that the money to meet such obligations was simply not available.

For that reason, and despite the planning for war-making, the states of Europe simultaneously explored possible paths to peace. In the various exchanges of views that ensued, no belligerent remained completely faithful to commitments to allies. In fact, in the winter and spring of 1747 virtually every conceivable bilateral conversation occurred. Nevertheless, we can make sense out of this intricately interrelated set of probings for peace if we keep in mind the precedence of two pairings over all others. The first involved efforts by French and Austrian negotiators to resolve the increasingly pointless belligerence that damaged both their nations. Saxony acted as intermediary in these conversations. The second involved efforts by British and Spanish representatives to settle the various quarrels that divided London from Madrid. In this instance, though not as centrally, it was Piedmont-Sardinia that played the role of intermediary. Though the two sets are not parallel, they nevertheless show some symmetries. In both cases each major protagonist knew, though perhaps sketchily, about its ally's dabbling with betrayal. In both cases each major protagonist hoped to steal a march on its nominal ally by coming to terms with one of its enemies and, in cooperation with that (former) enemy, imposing those terms or their corollaries on all other belligerents. No one wanted to be left in the cold; so everyone moved to secure the freezing out of others.

The cover for the Austro-French negotiations was the marriage of the dauphin to Maria Josepha, daughter of Augustus III of Saxony, on 9 February 1747. Late in 1746 the Duke of Richelieu traveled to Dresden, ostensibly to make arrangements for the imminent wedding but actually to discover if Saxony and Count Brühl were still interested in trying to broker an Austro-French rapprochement. The duke found the Saxons eager to help. Anxious above all else about unneighborly Prussia, they agreed with Noailles's advice to Louis XV that France should "give up the idea of annihilating the house of Austria."[13] The Loss brothers, Christian and Johann Adolf, already posted to Vienna and Versailles respectively, were the two players on Saxony's fraternal team of mediation. They had ascertained that there was interest in both their courts in an easing of tension between Louis XV and Maria Theresa. Acting on this understanding, Brühl cooperated with Richelieu in sketching out a set of peace proposals in Dresden, and on 27 December 1746 both men dispatched Count Saul to Vienna, where, in conjunction with Christian Count Loss, he was to invite Austrian reactions. The sticking point in the clandestine discussions that ensued was Italy. Saul proposed that Austria cede territory to Don Philip, either in Italy or the Low Countries; Bartenstein found such a proposal, in light of the rout of the Bourbon armies in Italy and the hollowness of Don Philip's claim, preposterous. Maria Theresa was meanwhile dreaming again of seizing Naples. And so Saxon offices failed to bring Vienna and Versailles together in the spring of 1747. But a network of diplomatic contacts was now in place.

The tale of Britain's and Spain's efforts to find mutually satisfactory terms in the winter and spring of 1747 is more convoluted. The range of issues dividing London from Madrid included the older matters of Gibraltar and Minorca; the more recent quarrels over the Asiento and the Annual Ship; and the question of Don Philip, whom Britain was at first inclined to exclude from Italy entirely. The talks at Lisbon, begun in the autumn of 1746, became deadlocked: Keene reported that the Spanish were dependent on France, Sotomayer reported that the British were too cocky of their power, and so Lisbon slowly resumed its status as a sleepy outpost of western Europe. That left the talks at Breda. One of Count Carvajal's first actions on assuming direction of Spanish foreign policy at the end of 1746 was to send to Breda one of the most extraordinary figures to surface during this protracted war—Don Melchior Rafael, Count Macanaz. A diplomat in the service of Spain early in Philip V's reign and a scholar of church-state relations, he had angered both crown and church and had consequently spent over thirty years in exile. The decades abroad had left their stamp: his language, a Dutch observer noted, was "one-third bad French, one-third trite Spanish, and the other third Basque."[14] Like many Spanish grandees before him, he dreamed of Hispanic grandeur and despised the French. The latter attitude made him a credible representative of Spanish independence, but the former rendered him hopeless as a negotiator. Still, that was the point, for, unbeknownst to Macanaz, Carvajal sent the seventy-seven-year-old count to Breda not to succeed but to fail. Carvajal was suspicious of congresses; he believed Spain could squeeze more out of bilateral horse-trading than out of multilateral squabbling.

There was thus a peculiar symmetry to what ensued. Sandwich had been sent to Breda with instructions to prevent the negotiations from reaching any conclusions. Macanaz now thundered into town, and if his instructions did not require him to block progress in the talks, that nevertheless was the purpose for which he had been sent. As unwitting confederates, these two men succeeded in their task: France refused to permit a Spanish representative to be seated, the final Breda meeting broke up over the issue on 16 March 1747, and by May everyone was acknowledging that the negotiations hatched by d'Argenson and used by Puisieulx had run their fruitless course. But even while succeeding in their primary function, the two men—a youth not yet thirty and a graybeard nearing eighty—began to explore the alternative of an Anglo-Spanish peace treaty. Macanaz promptly made some astonishing proposals. Asserting Ferdinand VI's right to impose settlements on Europe, he assigned Tuscany to Don Philip, restored Silesia to Maria Theresa, and encouraged Austria to seek territories west of the Rhine. The man sent to spoil Breda was preaching the spoliation of France as well.

Anyone who considers this grab bag of proposals closely will quickly suspect, as his auditors did, that Macanaz was bereft of his senses. He builds, Harrach wrote, "Spanish castles in the air."[15] Nevertheless, because the other diplomats could never be totally certain that Macanaz spoke without authority, they dealt with him cautiously. For a while it appeared that Sandwich and Macanaz might actually contrive to concoct an Anglo-Spanish document.[16] But both men were out of their depth, rushing ahead where their governments dared not tread. Moreover, by May, with the season of campaigning well under way, military events were again assuming priority over diplomacy. From Carvajal's perspective the controlling fact was the presence of an outnumbered Spanish army maneuvering amid and in conjunction with two French armies in Italy. Spain was hostage to its ally, and much as Carvajal resented the Iberian kingdom's dependence, he dared not disoblige his powerful friend. On 13 May 1747 a letter of recall was dispatched to Macanaz. Understandably, William Bentinck was later to dismiss the entire Breda interlude as "a complication of foolishness and rascality."[17]

THE DUTCH REVOLUTION

If Genoa was a bank before it was a city, the United Provinces were a mart before they were a state. Northern Europe's only important republic, the United Provinces were also the wealthiest nation per capita in all of Europe. Largely (but far from exclusively) Protestant, industrious in both trade and agriculture, proud of their liberties, and more widely educated and generally tolerant than any other Europeans, the Dutch were a people who for over three centuries had played a major role in European affairs. But by the fifth decade of the eighteenth century they were experiencing difficulties. The once boisterous economy had lost its momentum and may actually have begun a secular contraction. The constitution, which in earlier days had been one of the glories of Dutch civilization, seemed increasingly dysfunctional, except to the ruling patrician elite. Though proud of a splendid past, the republic in the middle of the eighteenth century was cautious, not bold, reactive, not enterprising. Its politics, its attitudes, and increasingly its self-identity took the protection of trade as their touchstone. Yet only by the most generous of standards can the collection of entities that comprised the United Provinces be called a nation. Each of the constituent provinces retained virtually total control over its domestic affairs.[18] Only for foreign affairs was it deemed necessary to assemble a supraprovincial body. Styled the States General, this institution consisted of delegates from the provinces. A Secret Committee screened topics that came before the States General, and no proposal could be put into practice until it had been passed by the Secret Committee, the States General, and the provinces. Any province could thus veto a measure. No single office served, even nominally, as the chief executive office of the republic. Instead, each province elected its own Stadholder. In principle, therefore, there might be seven different Stadholders at any one time. In practice the chief member of the House of Orange—the closest approximation to a royal house in the United Provinces—usually held several stadholderships simultaneously, and the rest sat vacant. In principle too all the provinces were equal, but in practice Holland, by far the largest and richest of them, and Amsterdam, the dominant city in Holland, tended to assume direction of Dutch affairs. Holland preferred to leave its stadholership vacant, and its dominance was reflected in the fact that yet another provincial officer, the Grand Pensionary of Holland, was the closest thing to a foreign minister that the Dutch republic possessed.

Control over this monument to decentralization rested with the regent class—families of extensive commercial wealth who lived in large urban homes and whose sense of class solidarity was intensifying under the pressure of economic stagnation. Though the character and degree of their power varied from province to province, the pattern of regent dominance was everywhere the same. This system left the large majority of the people without a vote. The middling classes had one institution they could call their own: the civic guard, traditionally staffed from their ranks. The poor, whether urban or rural, had none, and while, in the comparative prosperity of the republic Dutch peasants were vastly more comfortable than their Neapolitan or Bohemian counterparts, they were not satisfied with their exclusion. One poor citizen called himself "a miserable hired horse. . . , which is driven ahead with bloody whiplashes" from the regents.[19] And even though the teachings of the clergy, the need for favor if one hoped to advance, and the general expectation that society be hierarchical all conduced to render the poor acquiescent, the volume of grumbling about the oligarchic system was mounting.

Broadly speaking, the regents fell into two political camps. The dominant group in the early 1740s may be called the Oligarchic party, though, rather unhelpfully, they in fact styled themselves the "true patriots."[20] The French faction that was demanding a looser Anglo-Dutch affiliation was a subset of this party. So too were the moderate republicans, led by Anthonie Van der Heim. The regional strength of the Oligarchic party lay in Holland and especially in Amsterdam, but it had adherents in all the provinces. The rivals of the Oligarchs were the Orangists—"patriots" by self-designation. As the party of the Prince of Orange, they recalled the triumph of William III in 1672. Just as Jan de Witt's stadholderless regime had then seemed impotent before the Louis XIV, so now did Van der Heim's and Gilles's regime seem to quail before Louis XV. The current prince of Orange was Willem Karel Hendrik Friso, and he was already stadholder of the rural provinces of Friesland, Groningen, and Gelderland. He was an unlikely national hero—crook-backed, legalistic, cautious. But the Prince of Orange possessed three advantages in any struggle for power: he was George II's son-in-law; he attracted the support of the growing number of people who were becoming disenchanted with the rule of the Oligarchic party; and in William Bentinck, he had the services of the republic's most dynamic politician. The Orangists had one demand: make the Prince of Orange stadholder of all the provinces and entrust him with sufficient authority to turn back the French. Bentick's words to the Prince of Orange defined the Orangist position:

> Whether or not there is money, whether or not it can be found, whether or not cattle die, whether the spirits are well- or evilly-disposed, whether the majority is for or against, Your Serene Highness must always expressly and openly take sides against France and declare that if in 1572, in 1672, in 1688, and in 1702 we had yielded as we now do, we would still sit under France, in popery and slavery.[21]

In the spring of 1747 French patience with Dutch efforts to enjoy the best of two worlds ran out. Maurice of Saxony had fully 136,000 troops under his command. His foes, despite the paper promises made at The Hague, could scarcely field 100,000. Maurice therefore enjoyed the luxury of both numerical superiority and strategic freedom, and he proposed to replicate the success of the previous year by denying his enemies provisions, by forcing them to yield territory or to face battle, and finally by crushing them. Meanwhile, he also took aim at the republic. On 17 April the French envoy at The Hague announced that France would no longer respect the neutrality of a state that so blatantly aided its enemies, and Maurice sent Löwendahl and two columns of troops crashing into the western reaches of the Generality. Noailles's final directive to Maurice, a model of transcendent silliness, may have tempered the attack somewhat: invasion, the marshal cautioned, "is an extreme remedy which they want to administer gently, without however prejudicing the firmness and vigour of the execution."[22] But any French reservations were lost on the Dutch. For the first time since the outbreak of European hostilities, Dutch soil had been violated.

The Oligarchic party had hitherto had one irrefutable justification for its policy: the republic had been spared the misery of war. With French troops shredding that defense, the Oligarchs stood exposed to the recriminations of all. The province of Zeeland, next in line if the French attack in the west continued, abandoned all hope of receiving aid from The Hague. It turned to the British, requesting the presence of a naval squadron to defend its twisting coastline. On 19 April 1747 four British vessels arrived; by 23 April a squadron was offshore. Then on the night of 24-25 April the civic guard took to the streets in behalf of the Prince of Orange, and on 28 April the States of Zeeland voted unanimously to make him the Stadholder, the Captain-General, and the Admiral of the province. Meanwhile, the uprisings spilled over from Zeeland into Rotterdam, Doordrecht, The Hague, and even Amsterdam, as Holland's middling classes, able at last to vent their anger at the Oligarchs, poured into the streets and flashed Orange ribbons from thousands of rooftops. In a tumultuous session of 29 April, made more infuriate still by the crowd that swarmed about the building and attacked delegates who showed their faces, the States General agreed that the Prince of Orange's demands could not be refused. Several days were required to assure the observance of legalities—and in the meantime it was found necessary to hide the hysterical Gilles in the home of William Bentinck—but finally on 3 May the province of Holland, without a dissenting vote, raised Willem to the stadholdership. On the same day Utrecht unanimously chose the prince, and Overijssel followed in a similar manner on 10 May. In less than two weeks a revolution had blown through the United Provinces, making the thirty-five-year-old Prince of Orange the first person in the history of the republic to hold the stadholdership of every Dutch province simultaneously. And there was more. On 4 May the States General named the prince Captain-General (he thus replaced Waldeck) and Admiral of the Republic, and on 15 May the legislature voted to increase the size of the army he commanded by 30,000 men. In this moment of crisis all Dutch politicians were prepared to defer to the prince.

And yet William IV was an oddly ambivalent leader. While the republic writhed on his behalf, he remained at distant Leeuwarden. Not until 12 May 1747 did he arrive in The Hague, whereupon he spoke of war and glory, hoping "under God's blessing to be able to be a savior" and to restore "the splendor and respect of old."[23] But then not until 17 May, by which time the French controlled all Dutch lands lying west of the Scheldt, did he set out for beleaguered Zeeland. And he meanwhile resisted appeals from Bentinck and Sandwich to assail the Oligarchs and sound the tocsin of broader participation. As a consequence of these actions, the realization slowly dawned that William IV was a deeply flawed ruler. The republic had undergone, in William's own words, an "astonishing and sudden revolution."[24] But it was as if William believed that the gaps in men, supplies, and spirit would now dissolve before a mere wave of his Orange hand. In the last analysis William IV was unfit for the office he had seized. His political experience was confined to two rural northern provinces, his military knowledge was drawn from books, and his vision for the future was clouded by romantic notions of Orange destiny. History, in short, was not repeating itself: William IV was not William III.

The obvious international beneficiary of these events was Britain. If the United Provinces should make peace with France or prove unable to prevent a French occupation, the Pragmatic alliance would be at an end. The question thus suggests itself: did the British government give aid to the cause of the Prince of Orange? The evidence is ambiguous. The case for active British participation rests on such points as the remarkable promptitude with which the naval squadron appeared off Zeeland in April 1747, the guarded references to "support to the well-meaning" found in some of Sandwich's letters, and the British readiness to supply funds to the Bentincks for bribing Dutch officials.[25] The case against active British participation is similarly oblique. Aside from the silence of the instructions—surely, on balance, evidence against rather than for intervention—there is the fact that in 1744 William Bentinck sought British support for an Orangist uprising and was spurned by Carteret. It may be true that 1747 was not 1744 and Newcastle not Carteret. But the precedent indicates that Britain appreciated the difficulties—not to mention the embarrassment and harm if the scheme failed—of meddling with the constitutional order of another country. If, however, we cannot be confident of Britain's role in these events, we can at least be clear about its response. "Nothing," Newcastle wrote on 2 May 1747, "can exceed the joy and satisfaction that I have from the great event that has happened in Holland."[26]

Finally, it is worth noting that though the revolution in the United Provinces seemed to threaten to reverse military momentum in the Low Countries in precisely the manner that the revolution in Genoa had reversed it along the Mediterranean, in fact the Dutch revolution did not undo French military advantages, and William IV, by speaking of complementing the "sword in one hand" with the "olive branch in the other," revealed that he understood this truth.[27] He assumed command of a nation exhausted by war. There is no doubt that the revolution triggered a new wave of anti-French feeling in the republic. Some citizens even credited absurd stories linking the Oligarchs to the French invasion. But anti-French feeling did not, in the prostration of 1747, translate into a pro-war sentiment. Sandwich and Newcastle misread the Dutch mind: they anticipated a rush of belligerence. Chesterfield knew better. As Gilles—still, significantly, the Grand Pensionary—advised William within a month, the republic lacked the funds needed for warring. Revolution or not, peace was as desirable as ever.

18

Athens and Sparta
[May 1747 – October 1747]

CAPE ORTEGAL

The advent of a new admiralty board late in 1744 opened that vital office of British defense operations to new ideas. In September 1745 Admiral Edward Vernon, drawing on a term then forty years old, called for the creation of a Western Squadron. Vernon felt that Britain lacked a coherent maritime strategy. He wanted to see the British navy freed from transatlantic convoy duty so that it might seek to destroy any aggregation of enemy ships that risked coming out of its anchorage. To that end he proposed the formation of a large squadron, standing about fifty miles out to sea off the French coast, comprised of a sufficient number of ships of the line, frigates, and sloops to allow its commander to observe Brest, Lorient, and Rochefort and to attack a squadron issuing from any of them. "A western squadron," Vernon wrote, ". . . might face [the Bourbons'] united force, cover both Great Britain and Ireland and be in condition to pursue them wherever they went, and be at hand to secure the safe return of our homeward bound trade from the East and West Indies."[1] The new board heard Vernon's proposal sympathetically, for it had already experimented with an embryonic version of the squadron. Admiral George Anson, whose circumnavigation of the globe in the early years of the decade had borne significant scientific and medical fruit, found the proposal particularly exciting. Having won pledges to expand the size of the squadron, Anson assumed personal command of it in August 1746. He was a disciplinarian, persuaded by experience that success attended the side with the better-trained seamen. With this appointment the full-blown Western Squadron emerged—seventeen ships of the line, six fifty-gunners, four frigates, and two sloops.

The France against which they were aimed was increasingly respectful of Britain's naval might. In the West Indies, for example, Britain was squeezing

France's sugar empire, less interested in conquering territory (a victory that would only increase the competition for existing British planters) than in laying waste production in the more efficient French islands. In the northern climes of America the advantage was again Britain's, as France's effort in 1746 to recover Louisbourg failed. In the still more distant swells of the Indian Ocean, France had enjoyed a greater measure of success in the imperial struggle, for the fate of France's Asian empire lay with two very capable men — Mahe de la Bourdonnais, the Governor of the Islands (effectively, of Martinique), and Joseph-François Dupleix, the Commandant-General of India (operating from Pondichery and serving the French East India Company). Bourdonnais had weathered gales, disease, and food shortages to appear with a small squadron off Nagappattinam, south of Pondichery, to harry a British squadron into port in Ceylon. Then Bourdonnais and Dupleix combined to attack Madras, which capitulated after a short siege in September 1746. But with ultimate success in India almost at hand, Bourdonnais and Dupleix fell into a sharp quarrel and lost the opportunity to capture Fort St. David (Cuddalore), Britain's sole settlement on the Coromandel Coast. Thus even halfway around the world French efforts were stalled.

With nothing less than the French empire at stake, Maurepas began early in 1747 to plan another attempt at recovering Cape Breton while simultaneously gathering forces to be used in protecting Pondichery. His problem was that he needed to get the reinforcements past Britain's Western Squadron and through to the distant American and Indian theaters. On 14 May Anson's squadron sighted a French squadron to its south. Bearing northwest, the enemy consisted of a small number of ships of the line escorting a convoy of more than thirty French transports out into the Atlantic. Commanded by Admiral Jonquière, this force was actually comprised of two distinct elements. One was intended for America, the other for India. The French hoped, by combining the two sections during their running of the gauntlet of European waters, to form a force large enough to deter a British attack. Anson did not know what France intended this force to do, but from its size he realized that it constituted a major effort, not a feint, and he resolved to smash it. He possessed a considerable advantage in numbers — fourteen ships with fifty or more guns compared to Jonquière's six — and with the wind out of the north-northeast, he closed quickly. Lacking the stomach for a hopeless engagement, Jonquière sent the convoys away to the west-southwest. He then signaled a flight, hoping that at least a few of his ships would escape. Anson responded immediately and appropriately, changing the flag signal from line of battle ahead to general chase. The British then bore down on the disordered French squadron.

The battle that ensued helped define the technique of chase for the rest of the century. Since the British ships were swifter, the British van caught up with the French rear. But rather than have the lead British ship drop out of the chase and confine its attention to the French ship it had come abreast of, Anson directed the ships in his squadron to catch up with an enemy vessel, damage it with gunfire, and then sail on ahead to overtake the next available French ship, leaving the disabled one for the British ships that followed. In this fashion the outnumbered and outgunned French were passed down the British line, savaged and ravaged by the fire of each succeeding British vessel. The French fought bravely: the battle, in fact, became a byword for French fortitude. And many transports in the convoys successfully reached American or Indian waters. But despite these achievements, the engagement was a decisive victory for Britain.[2] Every French ship that fought was captured by the British. Others fell too, so that the final total of captured vessels was eighteen. Not a single ship of the line reached its extra-European destination. About 800 French seamen died. The value of the prizes approximated £300,000. In little more than three hours, the Western Squadron had demolished the work of months.

Custom has attached no single title to this maritime engagement. The "battle of Cape Ortegal"—using the name of the Spanish spit that probably was the closest landfall—will serve our purposes adequately. Its outcome meant that Britain was finally asserting the kind of supremacy at sea that its allies had hoped for and its enemies feared. Anson was—for the second time—a hero, and on this occasion he was rewarded with a peerage, becoming Baron Anson. It is true that he had enjoyed a superiority of power so great that defeat was almost inconceivable. But in large part that superiority was of his own manufacturing: he was the one who had insisted that the concept of the Western Squadron made sense only if the squadron was ample enough to outweigh any plausible enemy. Moreover, though defeat may have been implausible, a crushing victory was not inevitable. By drilling his men, Anson had transformed mediocre seamen into skilled sailors and motley crews into coordinated teams. "I could plainly see that my ships made a much hotter fire," he wrote afterward, "and much more regular than theirs."[3] In France, by contrast, the mood was despondent. The Dutch revolution had already alarmed the kingdom's leaders. Now came this naval debacle, and stocks responded by falling 10 percent in value. If Maurice of Saxony was making France the Sparta of Europe, Vernon and Anson were transforming Britain into Athens.

DEADLOCK IN ITALY

On 3 June 1747 the pause in the war for Genoa came to an abrupt end, as Marshal Belle-Isle pushed forty battalions eastward across the Var and into Nice. After long and often acrimonious discussions with La Mina, he had persuaded the Spanish commander that the reentry into Italy should be two-pronged. The southern column, by advancing along the coastal route and regaining seriatim the various Mediterranean towns held by the Piedmontese, would be the first prong; its task was eventually to draw near to the city of Genoa and attack the rear of its Austro-Sardinian besiegers. The northern column, assembling in Dauphiné as the Ligurian assault was launched, would soon be ready to strike into the heart of Piedmont. This second prong, by threatening Turin itself, was designed to force Charles Emmanuel to break off his cooperation with the Austrians and to call his troops home. The coastal advance quickly became a triumphal procession. Only Vintimiglia offered a resistance that the attackers could regard as irksome, and even its garrison capitulated before the end of June. July thus opened with the promise that Belle-Isle and La Mina would soon shatter the alliance between Vienna and Turin that for almost four years had foiled Bourbon hopes in Italy.

Then, precisely as fortune seemed to be breaking the Bourbons' way, there arrived jolting instructions from northern France. Displaying that sovereign disregard for sound advice and common sense that marked him as a royal fool, Louis XV once again interposed his judgment in the strategic delibera-tions of the Gallispan army. On the hauntingly familiar grounds that it was essential to subordinate strategy to kinship, Louis XV endorsed La Mina's plan. Belle-Isle was thunderstruck. The king even acknowledged that Belle-Isle's plan was wiser in the short run and likelier to secure France's long-run goals. He therefore acquitted Belle-Isle of responsibility for any failures that might result from following royal orders. The French marshal, in receipt of the royal letter on 9 July 1747, could do little more than supplicate La Mina not to abandon the northern prong entirely. In some measure he succeeded: after three days he wrung from the Spanish commander permission to launch a trimmed-down attack on Piedmont from Dauphiné. The invaders would not be as numerous as Bourcet had envisioned, nor would they have the reinforcements that he had planned for. But at least they would march.

The Piedmontese had watched the growing aggregation of French troops in Dauphiné with understandable concern. The war for Piedmont was enter-ing its fourth year, and while the wall of mountains had demonstrated its capacity to blunt French attacks in 1744 and 1745, it had proved more porous than expected. Therefore, even though he already had a scattered army of 55,000 men, Charles Emmanuel sought and received reinforcements for the various garrisons that dotted the slopes and valleys of his Alpine curtain. The French army against which these preparations were being taken totaled 25,000 men by early July. Though in principle outnumbered by the Piedmontese, the French enjoyed the advantage of concentration of forces: Charles Emmanuel was obliged to defend all the passes into his realm, but the French would assail only one of them. The commander of the invading army was to be the Chevalier Belle-Isle, younger brother and alter ego of the marshal. It was widely believed that the marshal entrusted his brother with this daunting but potentially illustrious assignment so that the family might claim a second baton. It is certain that the marshal thought his brother the fittest candidate for flinging audacity into the faces of the Piedmontese. Though fretful about his brother's impetuosity, he was also counting on it.

On 14 July 1747 the French advance began. Following Bourcet's advice, the Chevalier Belle-Isle chose the Dora Riparia River as the route of access into Piedmont because charts suggested that Exilles (the chief fortress on the Dora Riparia) was marginally less formidable than Cuneo, and because Bourcet had been raised in the region of the Dora Riparia and knew it intimately. The initial target was Exilles, a fortification that Charles Emmanuel was defending with 15,000 men. The king believed that the best place for meeting the French was on the slope that led uphill to a ridge called Assietta. From this slope and ridge the Piedmontese could hope to control access to nearby Exilles. Charles Emmanuel directed his troops to plant obstacles across the slope—sod redoubts, piles of rock, and above all an array of eighteen-foot wooden palisades bristling with sharpened crests. If his plan worked, the French would exhaust and maim themselves in struggling to surmount the obstacles and the rise, all the while exposing themselves to fire from hidden Piedmontese musketeers.

On 19 July elements of the French army approached the slope. The Chevalier Belle-Isle had divided his forces into three columns and had sent them by three parallel routes toward Exilles. The central column, commanded by the Marquis d'Arnault, was given the chilling task of attacking into the face of the various obstacles with which the Piedmontese had littered the slope. What ensued in the late afternoon became celebrated as the most one-sided bloodbath of the war. Neither of the flanking columns moved decisively enough to influence the events in the center. There, lashed on by determined officers, the French struggled up the slope, disassembling the various man-made impediments as they proceeded, while withering musket fire from concealed and protected hideouts exacted a severe toll. Four times the French fell back before the onslaught; each time they returned to the struggle. Toward the end, as soldiers strained toward the crest of the ridge, the battle produced tableaux that were soon to transfix a disbelieving Europe. The living climbed over piles of the dead as they tried to surmount the palisades. Defenders rained bullets and rocks down on the relentless blood-drenched attackers. It was late in the battle, after d'Arnault had been killed, before the Chevalier Belle-Isle left his hillock of observation to rush into the carnage. He was a desperate man, seeking by his example to stir his staggered troops to renewed efforts. Promptly wounded by enemy fire, he nevertheless managed to approach the top of the ridge and plant a French flag. But then a second shot ripped through his body and he fell lifeless. Their head and heart struck down, the dispirited French troops could endure no more punishment. A retreat, more orderly than the butchery might have portended, began at once, and the French staggered back to Barcelonette. Meanwhile, well before nightfall on this high summer day, the Piedmontese could celebrate a victory of historic proportions.[4]

When they learned of the battle of Assietta, the politically lettered in France were stunned. French casualties totaled 5,300, and for the first and only time in the war a clear majority of these—perhaps 3,700—were fatalities. Casualties represented 25 percent of those engaged, and for d'Arnault's column, which marched into the most hellish sector of the battle, the proportion was far higher. When this total was contrasted with the figure of 229 Piedmontese and Austrian casualties, most of them wounded rather than killed, the one-sided character of the slaughter became apparent.[5] Charles Emmanuel had picked his site well. But the obverse of that judgment was that Marshal Belle-Isle, by badgering La Mina into approving the invasion, had sacrificed several thousand French soldiers in a hopeless endeavor. Maurice of Saxony, whose renown the marshal had hoped to surpass with his Italian exploits, pronounced a severe but essentially accurate judgment on both the marshal and the king: "Ambition has always been the ruin of any scheme in which the Belle-Isle brothers have had a hand. . . . What is surprising is that the court of France makes the same mistakes with the same people over and over again."[6]

In earlier years the Austro-Piedmontese victory at Assietta would have opened up a vista of possibilities in the west to the Worms allies. But by 1747 ambitions were banked. Maria Theresa instructed Browne to turn back to the Ligurian coast and "to take all pains to secure the prompt conquest of Genoa."[7] The empress-queen could hope for no more because, for the first time since the war had reached Italy, Austria's will and capacity to sustain belligerence were visibly deteriorating. The total size of the Austrian army had been declining since peaking at 204,000 troops in 1745. Despite the promises made at The Hague in January 1746, Austria had fallen far short of its target of 60,000 troops for Italy in 1747. In the instructions that Maria Theresa sent to Browne after the battle of Assietta, there was a portentous injunction for the commander to "conserve" his troops. Meanwhile, some of the Warasdiners brought from Hungary left camp and unilaterally headed for home. This was nothing less than a mutiny. Under the pressure of a long, tedious, and increasingly pointless belligerence, discipline was cracking.

Since the French no longer wanted to make war along the painful Piedmontese front, and since the Austrians were increasingly unable to make war in the region, the series of small cross-border raids that occurred in September 1747 and the skirmishes that surrounded Ventimiglia virtually brought hostilities in northwest Italy to a close. Even without the benefit of a peace treaty, hostilities—except in Corsica—were winding down. What was left was a standoff. The Bourbons had failed to penetrate Piedmont; the Worms allies had failed to regain Genoa. The reasons for the decrescendo are not obscure. The war had devastated northwestern Italy. A journalist who visited Genoa, the most ravaged state, wrote that "everything has been swept away—the doors, the shutters, the gates, the panes. And on seeing the countryside one would believe that it is one of those uncultivated lands that human ingenuity has never cared to clear."[8] Moreover, talk of a European settlement was in the air. No one in authority believed that a major campaign on the eve of peace talks was likely to pay dividends equivalent to its costs. And so belligerence in Italy subsided into sniping, observing, and launching occasional raids.

LAFFELD

As summer approached in the Low Countries, Maurice of Saxony was basking in the conviction that the campaign of 1747 would be successful and perhaps bloodless. He knew that the Pragmatic Army had suffered a shortfall of 40,000 troops and that his own forces thus outnumbered the enemy's by 136,000 to 100,000. He knew that despite the revolution, the Dutch republic had not intensified its military effort. From frequent conversations with Puisieulx and Louis XV, he knew that France was pursuing peace in several capitals. Maurice had no taste for wasting lives. So he chose the course of watchful waiting, hopeful that want of supplies would force the outnumbered enemy to flee. If, contrary to wisdom, the allies chose to engage, Maurice would enjoy two advantages—the larger army and the choice of the site. With these advantages he could anticipate a French victory. And with the victory would come the freedom to attack either Bergen-op-Zoom in the west or Maastricht in the east. Maurice was thus sanguine.

The details of the campaign depended on the enemy's actions. But the outcome did not. Whatever the Pragmatic Allies chose to do, Maurice believed that France had strength adequate for prevailing.

There ensued a brief game of cat-and-mouse. The Duke of Cumberland, again in command of the allied army, was determined to shadow the French. For his part, Maurice was determined to outwait the undersupplied Pragmatic Allies, feigning a dash in one direction and bluffing a march in another until they withdrew and left him in command of the region. Only the Demer River separated the two forces, and on most days in June the armies could observe each other. Finally, however, Louis XV, who was traveling with his troops, wearied of the war of nerves that Maurice was conducting. He determined that Maastricht could and should be taken, and so, even as the feints continued, Maurice began to turn his mind to the problem of seizing the most redoubtable fortress in the Low Countries. A successful battle was the prerequisite to a successful siege, and so the immediate task confronting Maurice was to maneuver his own army (and the enemy's) so that when the inevitable battle ensued, the advantages of topography and formation were France's. He effected this goal with two superbly executed deceptions. The first tricked Cumberland into dogging smaller forces led by d'Estrées and Clermont while Maurice covertly moved the main French army by forced marches into position just west of Maastricht. The second—in a sense the reversal of the first—cozened a startled Cumberland into believing that a major portion of the French force was occupying the important Heights of Herderen when in fact this strategic ground was seized by only 12,000 troops. By the evening of 1 July 1747 Maurice of Saxony had realized his scheme of deployment, and the allies, again caught off guard, were scrambling to recover.

Almost a quarter of a million fighting men were crowded into a region no larger than twenty-five square miles and thick with obscure hamlets. The French totaled almost 125,000 while the Pragmatic Allies exceeded 100,000 in number. Even the dense armies of Rocoux could not match these figures. The French faced north, their line extending five miles from Elderen through Herderen and Montenaken to the outskirts of Wilre. The allies faced south. Their right, composed of the Austrians, lay west of Great Spauwen. A small ravine separated the right from the bulk of the allied army. Their center, formed by the Dutch, stretched from Great Spauwen to the ground in front of Vlitingen. The allied left—the British, Hanoverians, and Hessians—ran eastward from Laffeld and extended toward, but did not reach the outworks of, the fortress at Maastricht. The gap between the allied army and the fortress gave Maurice his tactical vision. He proposed to send his infantry crashing down upon the allied left-center around Laffeld, drawing attention to this embattled sector, and then to unleash both cavalry and infantry on a flanking attack from his right down the western bank of the Jaar River to cut the allies off from Maastricht.

Mindful of the inconveniences a late start had imposed on him at Rocoux, Maurice quickly pulled his army into readiness in the early morning of 2 July 1747, and despite sodden ground and a steady rain at 10:00 A.M. he signaled the attack. Artillery fire had already prepared the way. But almost immediately things began to go wrong for the French. While still lining his forces up, Maurice had seen Laffeld aflame. He had assumed from this firing of the town that the allies had abandoned it and formed their lines behind it. And such indeed had been Cumberland's plan. But Sir John Ligonier, embarking on the most extraordinary day of his life, persuaded the duke that just as the devastated town of Fontenoy had anchored the French in 1745, so too could the ruined hamlet of Laffeld protect the allies in 1747. Thus, when the French grenadiers assaulted the village, they found not a deserted, charred settlement but a fortified defense post, bristling with artillery. Maurice then sent a second attack forward, but it too found the resistance too formidable and broke off. In a sense Maurice was achieving his purpose: he had drawn Cumberland's attention to Laffeld. But the price was turning out to be far higher than the Saxon had reckoned. When Maurice sent a third wave against Laffeld, some of the most sanguinary fighting of the battle occurred. The French shot and bayoneted their way into the village only to be expelled. Two additional French assaults were required before the attackers finally gained the ground they had been contending for.

And so, though with far higher losses than he had expected, Maurice appeared by 2:00 P.M. to be ready to cap the triumph at the hamlet of Laffeld by releasing his attack on the right. But again Ligonier intervened. Stationed with massed cavalry at the rear of the allied line, Sir John had thus far not seen much action in this battle of infantries. But when Maurice ordered Count d'Estrées and the French right to isolate the Pragmatic Allies from Maastricht and to turn their flank, Sir John on his own initiative led the allied cavalry out against the French. The wide plain above the Jaar afforded a splendid theater for mounted exploits, and there immediately ensued the most spectacular cavalry engagement of the war. With unexpected ferocity and speed, the allies' first charge beat back the French and crippled the French effort to drive a wedge between Maastricht and the allied army. Elsewhere along the extended line of battle, however, the French were prevailing, and when Cumberland launched Ligonier's cavalry on its second charge, its purpose was not so much to block a French attack as to cover the general allied retreat. Once again the allied cavalry was successful, but on this occasion their success led them into trouble. Cutting clean through the French cavalry, they found themselves surrounded by well-armed French infantrymen. Ligonier hoped to escape capture by posing as a Frenchman— born in France, he spoke the language well—but the star of the Order of Bath betrayed his nationality, and he was taken prisoner. The allied situation had meanwhile become desperate, and they organized a withdrawal under the cover of the Austrian cavalry. By nightfall the vastest battle of the war was at an end.[9]

Laffeld was a French victory. But rather than a crushing triumph it was a compromised one, falling considerably short of Maurice's and Louis XV's hopes. French casualties totaled 10,000, twice the number of allied casualties.[10] The sum of 15,000 makes Laffeld the costliest battle of the war in the Low Countries.[11] "Would it not be better," a sobered Louis XV declared as he viewed the bodies amid the mud, "to think seriously of peace than to have so many brave people killed?"[12] And France's embarrassment did not end with its disproportionate number of casualties. Maurice had engaged so that he might clear the way to Maastricht. Instead, his enemy, though beaten, had escaped in good order, and the mistress of the Meuse remained for the time being inviolable. For the first time in several years it became acceptable to criticize the great general, with some observers wondering if he might actually be seeking to protract the war. Maurice indicted himself: "the mistakes which we committed that day have deprived us of the advantage which we should have drawn from it."[13] This debate, however, tended to obscure the Saxon's very real accomplishments. He had moved a vast army in a coherent and swift fashion, demonstrating that it was possible to infuse organic unity and surprising speed into a fighting force of more than 100,000 men. The lesson would not be lost on Bonaparte. He had superbly coordinated the use of musket fire and artillery, using each to complement the other in a fashion that suggests affinities to the nineteenth century. He had cleared the region from Antwerp to Maastricht of the enemy. And he had displayed all these accomplishments even while once again protecting the king from the dangers that his majesty so foolishly courted. With good reason Maurice was disappointed but not dejected.

The Pragmatic Allies were ambivalent about the battle. Cumberland dashed off a letter to Newcastle in which he called it a "brisk but not very successful affair."[14] The Dutch, however, were more pleased with the outcome, since it suggested that France could not yet invest Maastricht. In assessing the role of participants, major attention focused on Cumberland and Ligonier. The former, whose reputation had blossomed at Fontenoy and Culloden, now became the target of criticisms. He had, to be sure, been brave, so openly exposing himself to the enemy that at one point only his well-handled sword spared him from spectacular capture. But he had also reversed himself (under Ligonier's prodding) on how best to use the hamlet of Laffeld and can most charitably be described as having stumbled onto a reasonably effective scheme. Sir John Ligonier, though languishing in captivity, was roundly praised. His cavalry had performed with the steely sureness that only the Austrian and Prussian cavalry had evinced previously in the war, and his decision to charge the French right as it moved on Wilre was seen as the stroke that prevented a crushing French victory. When Maurice introduced his distinguished prisoner to Louis XV, his words bespoke his respect: "Sire, I present to your Majesty a man who has defeated all my plans by a single glorious action."[15]

The belief that peace was essential propelled Maurice into a remarkable initiative. Using Ligonier as an intermediary, he proposed to Cumberland that the two commanders meet to work out peace terms for Europe. "We two princes," he soon wrote, "will settle more things in an hour than ministers will in a month."[16] The presumption of the proposal is so extraordinary that it defies belief to think that Louis XV—who was, after all, in the French camp after Laffeld—was unconsulted and unapproving. Weary of slaughter and diplomatic nit-picking, Maurice was suggesting that the generals impose a peace. Cumberland approved of the idea of a meeting, but for three reasons the British government, and especially the Duke of Newcastle, was hostile. First, the new Dutch government, still flushed with hope, counseled rejection. Second, neither Austria nor Piedmont-Sardinia would take kindly to British bullying. Third, Cumberland was untried as a negotiator and Maurice was contemptuous of diplomatic niceties. Newcastle thus directed Cumberland to proceed with deliberate slowness and dispatched the Earl of Sandwich, who had returned to Britain to electioneer, back across the Channel. Sandwich at least could be trusted, and he was skillful at dragging talks out. Meanwhile, Louis XV himself began to have second thoughts, for he did not want Maurice to convey the impression that France was a pushover. On 5 August 1747, at Louis's direction, Maurice informed the British that Versailles would not desert its allies. This assertion destroyed the hope of an immediate end to the war. Nevertheless, even though the fanciful notion of a generals' peace had been derailed, negotiations were again on the European agenda.

OVERTURES AND OUTRAGES

Those charged with guiding the war policies of the European states responded to Laffeld in a variety of ways. One course of action, still alive despite Britain's coolness and France's cooling, sought surcease from war through diplomacy. Even the Duke of Newcastle dared not try to thwart the general view in the British government that profferings of peace must be attended to seriously, and so the French were informed that if they submitted specific proposals, the British would treat with them. Versailles took Britain's cautiously affirmative response to their approach as an opportunity to be seized. This judgment altered the diplomatic environment of the war. Ever since 1742 the French had regularly probed Austrian intentions. Now in July and August of 1747 the French finally decided that a combination of Austrian diplomatic stubbornness, French maritime vulnerability, and British financial strength elevated Britain past Austria to the role of the adversary with whom peace prospect s must be explored. But Laffeld invited another response, and Maurice of Saxony was prompt to embrace it. Stung by criticism of his conduct at the battle, he determined to refute all those who were suddenly voicing doubts about his military wisdom. His plan rested on the simple proposition that an outnumbered enemy could not adequately defend two separate fortifications at once. He ordered Count Löwendahl, who was encamped with 30,000 troops halfway on the road to Brussels, to march immediately on Bergen-op-Zoom and lay siege to the Dutch fortress at the mouth of the Scheldt. Maurice believed that the Pragmatic Allies had only two possible responses to this challenge. Either they could rush defenders from Cumberland's army across Brabant to reinforce Bergen-op-Zoom, in which case they would fatally weaken their hold on Maastricht. Or they could keep Cumberland's army intact to defend Maastricht, in which case Löwendahl would discover a way to make Bergen submit. Whichever response the allies chose, France seemed certain to win one of the two gateways to the Dutch republic.

The diplomats took the stage before the soldiers. On 11 September 1747, after weeks of preparations, Count Puisieulx and Lord Sandwich met at Liége. Unlike the discussions at Breda, which the Dutch had brokered and attended, the talks this day were strictly bilateral. The presumption that underlay the bilaterality was made explicit when the two men agreed that they could not bind their allies, but that since they represented—in Sandwich's words—"the two principal Powers engaged in this war," they could promote peace by working to harmonize their views on the central issues.[17] The conversation between Puisieulx and Sandwich revealed four points of major contention between France and Great Britain. The first involved Louisbourg, with Puisieulx threatening that if Britain did not return the fortress, France would retain its conquests in the Low Countries. The second point of contention involved maritime Flanders. Sandwich insisted that France demolish its seaside fortifications at Dunkirk and nevertheless hand over Furnes. Puisieulx declared that France would accept demolition or yield Furnes, but not both. On Don Philip—the third point of contention—the two men were sharply at odds: Britain would not force its allies to provide the feckless prince with a realm, while France would not abandon Spain or Spanish demands. The fourth point touched close to the hearts of the two monarchs involved. Sandwich wanted France to repudiate all support for the house of Stuart. Puisieulx replied that a declaration of the sort Britain sought would humiliate Louis XV. One day of discussions sufficed to convince both men that the two kingdoms were still too far apart for diplomacy to work its emulsifying effect. But they agreed before departing that a peace congress would be in order.

As the diplomats left Liège, the soldiers seized the spotlight. Löwendahl had responded promptly to Maurice's order by marching to Bergen-op-Zoom. The difficulties confronting him were legion. The perimeter of marshland rendered the traditional technique of investment almost useless, the outworks were notoriously formidable, the adjacent river and sea assured the fortress of maritime support, and if—despite all these obstacles—an invader managed to approach the fortress, there remained the explosive countermines to be contended with. It is easy to understand why the allies were confident that *la Pucelle*, designed by the celebrated Menno van Coehoorn, would remain impregnable. Löwendahl established his siege with 12,000 men, holding back the remaining 18,000 as an army of observation. The defense of Bergen was in the hands of General Cronstrom and his international garrison of 4,000. Cronstrom, eighty-six years old, urged the townsfolk to screw up their courage and proceed with their lives as if all were normal. "Bergen-op-Zoom is a virgin," he proclaimed, "and she shall die like the daughter of the brave old Roman Virginius before she shall be polluted and ravished from us by the faithless Gaul."[18] Most observers concluded that Maurice had underestimated the vulnerability of Bergen. But the marshal resisted the importunities of his excited correspondents, confident that what had been true in July remained true in September: if Cumberland bolted, Maastricht would fall, while if the Pragmatic commander held his ground, Löwendahl would contrive to find a way to take Bergen-op-Zoom.

The confidence was well placed. Despite the impediments presented by man and nature, the French slowly drew closer to the great fortress. Löwendahl measured his progress in yards, but he calculated that the daily artillery shelling was taking a toll of lives in the town, and he suspected that the town was vulnerable to a surprise attack. And so at 4:30 on the morning of 16 September 1747, the French launched an assault, storming the outworks and chasing away the groggy and frightened defenders without a fight. A detachment of French soldiers then mounted the walls and, once inside, opened the gates. The mass of the French army swept through. The opposition they expected at this point barely materialized. Cronstrom himself was at first disbelieving, and then—to quote a French report—"awakened from his pyrrhonism, he did not await the outcome of this affair; he retreated from the town."[19] In startlingly swift order, and with casualties numbering only 500, the French found themselves masters of a famous Dutch town, its celebrated fortress, and 2,000 of its former defenders.[20]

It was at this point that something indefinable snapped in the French army. The siege of Bergen-op-Zoom had been protracted, and the French were angry that their foes had not surrendered earlier. With a conquered town lying before them and resistance at an end, the invaders unexpectedly abandoned the restraint and discipline that had made them a coherent fighting force and began a rampage through the streets and squares of Bergen-op-Zoom, ripping down dwellings, stealing whatever caught their fancy, and putting the civilian populace to the sword. Captured casks transformed their angry frenzy into a besotted madness. By 10:00 A.M. 2,000 civilians had perished under the butt, the blade, and the boot of the crazed French; another 1,000 lay wounded. Only then, sated with victims and alcohol, did the French army sink into a posttraumatic torpor, allowing the cries of keening children to replace the tumult of rushing troops and the crackle of misused muskets. Though Count Löwendahl promptly declared his regret at the dissolution of discipline, informed European opinion was staggered. When Maurice of Saxony learned of the events at Bergen-op-Zoom, he acted promptly to protect his lieutenant's reputation by suggesting a baton for him: "there is no middle course," Maurice told Louis XV; "either you must hang him or make him Marshal of France."[21] Since the former was unthinkable, the latter became necessary.

From a strategic perspective the fall of Bergen-op-Zoom marked a signal defeat for the Dutch. The government of the new stadholder could no longer indulge in emotionalism, and its reflections on the implications of Löwendahl's success gave new force to the arguments for peace. But the mass killing of civilians confused the republic's capacity to respond effectively. As reports of the massacre gained currency, an anti-French rage swept through the people, making peace talks less rather than more acceptable. The British government, less directly involved, was also less touched by a sense of indignation at French atrocities. Instead, increasingly aware of Dutch ineffectiveness and in receipt of Dutch requests for expanded financial aid, London was finally giving serious consideration to the possibility of peace. "Can anything be more absurd," Newcastle fumed, "than that the Republic should be pressing us every day to continue the war, and decline at the same time declaring war themselves."[22] In the aftermath of the taking of Bergen-op-Zoom, the various armies in the Low Countries moved into winter quarters. That action allowed the governments of Europe five months to try to sort domestic matters out and to extricate themselves from the increasingly hated war. And if anyone still needed to be taught why war should be hated, the example of Bergen-op-Zoom could now be cited.

OUESSANT

Disappointing by land, the campaigning season of 1747 brought Britain triumphs unparalleled by sea. The presence of the Western Squadron kept most French ships in their home ports lest they meet the fate of Jonquière's fleet. The most signal midyear success of the Western Squadron began on the last day of June 1747, when a detachment of ships sighted a French convoy returning from the West Indies, protected by three men-of-war. During the course of four days the British squadron chased the defending ships away and then collected forty-eight prizes. Meanwhile, to redress the balance in India, where the loss of Madras rankled, the British gathered an expeditionary force of six large ships and 2,000 men to be sent to the Coromandel Coast. The experience at Cartagena in 1741 had underlined the importance of a unitary command, and so the Indian expedition was entrusted solely to Rear Admiral Edward Boscawen. Though the expedition did not finally sail for Asia until the autumn, the fact that Britain, while establishing maritime paramountcy in wartime Europe, could still afford to assemble the largest force ever sent to aid the East India Company indicates just how dominant the Royal Navy had become.

And yet Count Maurepas dared not abandon the seas entirely to Britain, for such an abdication would hand over French trade and the French empire as invaluable hostages to the enemy. Thus he labored to put together a still larger force than Jonquière had had at his disposal when Anson had bested him, and he assigned command of the force, with orders to escort a vast convoy to safety, to the sixty-five-year-old Marquis de l'Étandère, a veteran of twenty-two naval campaigns. Neither the reliable commander nor his apprehensive crews could muster much confidence for the job that lay ahead. Indeed, Admiral Conflans, the grand old man of the French naval establishment, warned against the plan. The British learned quickly of activity at Brest, Rochefort, Ferrol, and even Carthagena, and they suspected that France (perhaps with Spanish support) was refitting its battered fleet for another challenge. Ordinarily the task of facing this challenge would have fallen to Sir Peter Warren, Anson's successor. But when ill health forced Warren to step down, command then passed, temporarily it was believed, to Edward Hawke, barely forty years old. Hawke had distinguished himself at Toulon, commanding the *Berwick* in the only action of that lugubrious battle that merited being called heroic.

The Western Squadron spent the summer and early fall of 1747 restlessly on the move. Hawke was like Anson (and Maurice and Frederick): he insisted that his men keep their skills honed through constant practice, and he strove to infuse in them a sense of pride in themselves and their country. Since his squadron numbered twelve ships of the line and two fifty-gunners, he was confident that he would outnumber his foe if any action occurred. At 7:00 A.M. on the morning of 25 October 1747, with drinking water running short and winter beckoning, the grand French flotilla was finally sighted off to the southwest of the British. Sprawled across the ocean 140 miles west of Ouessant Island and sailing from Brest to the West Indies, it consisted of 252 merchantmen guarded by seven ships of the line and one fifty-gunner. Signaling general chase, Hawke closed quickly on the enemy. The Western Squadron boasted as fine a complement of captains as any naval unit ever possessed—Hawke himself, George Romney, and Philip Saumarez among others. It is understandable that their excitement ran high: it was now within the power of the Royal Navy to extinguish the French maritime challenge entirely.

The action began about noon. In an effort to save the convoy, l'Étanduère had authorized it to escape to the northwest while the French line bore to the southwest. He knew that the British would chase his line rather than the merchantmen. Besides, though outnumbered fourteen to eight, his ships were well built and large, with five of them actually exceeding in size any of the British vessels. His own ship, the *Tonnant*, boasted eighty guns, fourteen more than Hawke's flagship, the *Devonshire*. And he held the windward gage. Initially, the British line adopted tactics similar to those chosen by Anson off Cape Ortegal. But fairly quickly the battle became disordered. Hawke gave considerable discretionary latitude to his commanders; they rewarded him with sound tactical decisions. By 2:00 P.M. the French rear was conquered, two ships having been taken as prizes and the rest sent reeling. In every respect, except perhaps in the display of coarse courage, the British crews were acquitting themselves more efficiently than the French. The one-on-one, fight-to-the-kill method proved devastating to the French; Hawke adopted it with such éclat that the *Devonshire* collected three prizes during the fateful day. Moreover, Britain's advantage in ammunition—the Western

Squadron fired 4,000 shots to the French squadron's 1,800—took a remorseless toll. By 6:00 P.M. the dismasted French squadron was reduced to a set of defenseless corks bobbing on the unsteady sea. As night fell there could be no doubt that what Anson had begun Hawke had finished. France no longer had a navy.[23]

In the aftermath of this second large engagement of 1747—which I style the battle of Ouessant[24]—Hawke spoke with laconic assuredness. "They took," he reported of the French, "a great deal of drubbing."[25] Of the six French ships seized as prizes, four were totally devoid of masts while the other two retained only their foremasts. Whereas British casualties had numbered 750, the French had lost the services of 4,000 men. Since a seaman is both rarer and more highly skilled than a soldier, these losses weighed far more heavily on France's war-making capacity than losses of a similar magnitude incurred in land actions. Meanwhile, the convoy that the French ships of the line had been guarding was not forgotten amid the blasts of battle and toasts of triumph. Hawke sent a sloop to the Leeward Islands to notify the British commander in the region that a French convoy was on the way. Thus forewarned, the British were able to pounce on the French merchantmen when they sailed into range, seizing forty vessels as prizes and capturing 900 seamen. With this episode of early December, the sad tale of the ill-fated convoy from Brest wound down to a close. Thomas Arne was not alone in these years in noting that Britannia ruled the waves.

By the end of 1747 France was almost literally defenseless by sea. Warren told Newcastle that George II "had more French ships in his ports than remained now in the ports of France. . . We could beat them with their own ships."[26] Half of all French crewmen sat in British captivity. Therefore, although France exercised military dominance on land, smothering the Austrian Netherlands and squeezing the Dutch Republic, Britain nevertheless controlled the seas, denying France access to its empire and use of its commerce. If Maurice of Saxony symbolized one kind of invincibility, then Lord Anson and Sir Edward Hawke—for his service Hawke was invested into the Order of Bath—represented an alternative variety. At the opening of December 1746 an equilibrium had been struck between French successes in the Low Countries and Austrian successes in Italy. The Genoese revolution had allowed France to undo that equilibrium to its own advantage in the first half of 1747. But meanwhile a more universal equilibrium had emerged, pitting the lord of the land against the the mistress of the sea. It was a classic contest of the sort that Thucydides had already dissected.

P·A·R·T V

A Peace of Exhaustion
(October 1747 – October 1748)

19
The Collapse of the Case for War
(October 1747 – April 1748)

THE IMPERATIVE OF PEACE

Wherever one listened as 1747 drew its final breaths, the talk in the chancellories of Europe was of the need for peace. In the case of Piedmont-Sardinia the urgency was felt because, with Italian warfare stalemated, only a negotiated cessation of hostilities seemed capable of dislodging the Spanish from Savoy. Spain sought peace because Ferdinand VI was reluctant to send his army out on yet another campaign of bloody Italian fighting. "I regard peace," Carvajal wrote at the end of October 1747, "as most necessary for the kingdom."[1] Austria was unprecedentedly receptive to peace because though its heartland basked in the tranquility that the Treaty of Dresden had brought to Germany, its more distant possessions were suffering. Maurice of Saxony sucked at the wealth of the Austrian Netherlands with vampiric intensity, Lombardy was so saddled with debt that fully half of its tax revenues were required to service the obligation, and Milan bent before a cyclonic inflation. None of these conditions—whether in Turin, Madrid, or Vienna—was precisely new. But in aggregate they created a force of novel intensity. "May the Almighty bring about the end soon," the empress-queen prayed; "the situation will not be better in two months, and not even so good."[2]

Even in Britain the pressures for peace were rising. Stock prices, which had peaked in 1743, were now slipping ominously, sinking in 1747 to levels not seen since 1724. To some observers a crisis of confidence seemed near at hand, and as 1747 came to an end, it was far from clear that the government loan that would be launched early in the new year would find a market.[3] Even the commercial situation, generally exciting as a consequence of Britain's maritime mastery, had its murky elements. The long-term growth in the profitable trade with Portugal had been reversed by the war, and the value of imports from the West Indies had fallen to levels not seen in a quarter of a century. Strategic considerations, as summarized by Lord Anson, were even more alarming. Britain, he asserted, could never hope to match the size of France's army. Therefore, Britain could not humble France. Even control of the seas was not enough to extort Louis XV's submission. Since Britain had already contrived to protect the Viennese succession in the empire while preserving most of the Habsburg realm intact, it had secured its primary continental goals. If continued fighting offered, at best, the prospect of a war of attrition, it was far the wiser choice for Britain to seek a prompt peace. The Sardinian envoy in London felt the mood of the government when he reported that the British "want to speed up a peace, whatever the cost. That is the only thing that is sure and certain here."[4]

Across the Channel, the situation smacked of paradox. No current belligerent could boast of military successes like France's: under the direction and tutelage of Maurice of Saxony, French armies had won triumphs that had defied Turenne, Condé, and Luxembourg. And yet no belligerent gasped under the burden of war like France: by almost every economic measure, and in almost every realm of economic activity, France was suffering. Military mobilization provided its predictable disruptions, as men were plucked from workshops and farms and dropped into a vast armed machine. Financial exigency distorted and then drained France's capital markets, involving the kingdom in a borrowing competition with Britain that it could not hope to win. Ill success at sea desiccated foreign trade, leaving merchants without products, consumers without goods, and the kingdom without its regular commercial income. Even the fatal caprice of an untoward climate took its toll on the grain harvests, obliging even many of those whom war and its attendant social disruptions spared to submit to the cruelty of famine, disease, and exposure. By late in 1747 France was a land immured in widespread misery.

To the ministers of France the concatenation of economic and demographic disasters left the kingdom with scant room for maneuver. Maurice of Saxony might be lobbying for a peace worthy of Fontenoy—a peace that expanded France's territory, humbled Piedmont-Sardinia, and reminded the Dutch of their vulnerability—but the ministers were far less demanding. They believed that a continuation of the war could only multiply France's afflictions. Britain, after all, was effectively invulnerable; the naval disasters of 1747 had reduced France to the expedient of manning its outnumbered ships with men who had never been to sea. France on the other hand was frighteningly exposed: its trade stood ransom, its empire lay defenseless, and with rumbles of mobilization from the east even its continental military advantage might soon be overborne by the arrival of Russian troops. Some urged that France use its paramountcy in the Low Countries to launch an offensive against the hapless Dutch, thereby bringing pressure to bear on Britain to seek a negotiated settlement. But the majority of the ministers thought that a French conquest of the United Provinces—though militarily feasible—would be likely to bring the Holy Roman Empire and Prussia back into the war as defenders of the republic and send Spain scurrying into the enemy camp in order to protect its trade with the Dutch. Odd as it might seem for a kingdom that had seized a portion of the commercial and agricultural heartland of Europe, France needed peace more sorely than any other combatant.

Because every belligerent was looking for a way to extricate itself from the war, it was easy to agree that talks among the combatants would be useful. Thus, even as a conference at Breda broke apart in the spring of 1747, the negotiators took pains to promise that a new conference would be convoked in the coming months. The campaign of 1747 had underlined the need for that conference, for the total effect of the engagements at Cape Ortegal, Assietta, Laffeld, Bergen-op-Zoom, and Ouessant had been the solidification of stalemate. Therefore, even before the armies had moved into winter quarters, the promise of the spring (as reaffirmed at Liège) was activated, and Aix-la-Chapelle, celebrated for its baths and for the tomb of Charlemagne, was chosen as the site for negotiations. On 20 November the town received the formal application to accommodate the aspiring peacemakers. Aix-la-Chapelle thus became the focal point of European hopes and prayers.

THE MATRIX OF NEGOTIATIONS

It is time to recall the issues that divided the combatants. They display a bedeviling multifariousness, and one reason that the War of the Austrian Succession is usually regarded as so complex is that the issues at stake were so diverse. Yet they need not be seen as peculiarly arcane. It is only to be expected that a struggle that blended several analytically distinct conflicts into one sprawling war would generate a set of issues that did not allow of consistent and mutually satisfactory solutions.

Four categories of problems divided Europe as 1747 ended.

Territorial disputes were the first category. The conflict had begun as a territorial struggle when Prussia seized Silesia. That particular territorial dispute had been settled by the Treaty of Dresden, but three other major ones remained, all of them very much alive as Europe ended its seventh year of warring.

1. The territorial dispute with the widest strategic significance revolved upon the future of the Austrian Netherlands, now bearing the burden of French occupation. What was to become of them? One theoretical possibility was that France might keep them. This option, however, would destroy the peace talks, for the Austrians, the British, and the Dutch were not willing to countenance Versailles's acquisition of the province. In practical terms, therefore, the issue was more confined: should Versailles hand them back to Vienna in their entirety, or should Louis XV keep a portion as a token of the success of his army? The allies were predictably of the former view. The French were uncertain. Louis found himself, almost against his will, hankering after a trophy of some sort to justify all his efforts. But Pâris-Duverney advised him that if he wanted to promote the trust "so necessary for the reestablishment of public tranquillity," he needed to honor his promise not to grab land.[5] Still, possession of the Austrian Netherlands gave France its chief element of leverage in any peace talks: if the enemies of Versailles were not forthcoming, France could balk at ending its occupation.

2. The territorial dispute with the broadest economic significance was the quarrel over America. The continent was a diverse place; its economic landscape offered a variety of prospects. But there was one constant element throughout the variety: at point after point, British interests were challenging Bourbon interests—France's in the north, Spain's in the south. Moreover, it was in America that Britain had won its only territorial conquest of the war—the great fortress at Louisbourg and the consequent command of access to the Canadian interior. Predictably, London was reluctant to hand back this prize—a reluctance that moved the pacific Henry Pelham to call Louisbourg "a stumbling-block to all negotiations."[6] Just as France was determined not to relinquish the Austrian Netherlands unless properly rewarded, so too was Britain committed to retaining its authority over Cape Breton until France proved munificently forthcoming.

3. Italy offered Europe's diplomats their most gnarled territorial dilemma. The very intricacy of the Italian issues gave some observers their grounds for optimism. "It is principally through Italy," the Duke of Richelieu advised the Marquis of Puisieulx, "that you will make peace."[7] At the heart of the problem sat Don Philip, already known as the "carrier pigeon."[8] Spain had entered the continental war in order to secure him a principality; the change of monarchs in Madrid had crippled but not eliminated this purpose. France supported Spain in this goal, in large measure because Louis XV felt familial obligations to his son-in-law, but also because, having given his pledge, the king felt that he could not retreat from his word while retaining his honor. The Bourbons' chief diplomatic ally in this effort to find a domain for Don

Philip was Britain, for London reasoned that if it wanted a compliant Spain when West Indian issues came up for discussion, it needed a contented Spain when Italian issues were resolved. There were only two possible suppliers for this putative principality—Austria and Piedmont-Sardinia. Neither therefore was sympathetic to Don Philip's pretensions. But each hoped the other might provide some territory. The prince was thus a peculiarly fortunate man. Though he was insignificant himself, his cause had transcended his status and emerged as the key to unlocking a peace.

Disputes about overseas trade were the second category of issues. In America the protagonists were chiefly Britain and Spain. Madrid detested British merchants who, under the cloak of the Asiento and the Annual Ship, intruded into its empire; they concluded that New Spain needed protection against the sedition, heresy, and espionage associated with these interlopers. Consequently, Spain had suspended a trade that was at once sanctioned by international agreement, profitable to Britain, and emblematic of London's confidence that prosperity lay along the Atlantic. The disagreement was the classic one between an energetic outsider and a suspicious traditionalist, and Britain had chosen to make war over the matter. In India the chief protagonists were Britain and France. Each had its own trading settlements, each its local allies. The region was vast, but equally vast was the promise of wealth. The War of the Austrian Succession was not primarily concerned with trade. But neglecting the commercial component in its complex constitution would be an error. Britain never made war in the eighteenth century without a visible commercial motive.

Questions of dynastic recognition constituted the third category of issue. International acknowledgment of one's right to rule enhanced security, conferred prestige, and dampened disaffection. Three rulers were hungry for such recognition.

1. The first was Francis I. France had withheld recognition of his imperial dignity in 1745. By 1747 French officials had no basis for disputing the title, but they still were not inclined to surrender gratis a blessing that might command a concession.

2. The second monarch seeking recognition was George II. The Jacobite revolution of 1745 had reawakened the long-smoldering British fears that the Hanoverians might be displaced. France, moreover, had abetted the pretender's forces. Britain was reluctant to settle with France unless, as part of the settlement, Versailles explicitly repudiated the Stuart cause.

3. The third monarch, not even a belligerent, was Frederick II. The Treaty of Dresden had recognized his right to Silesia, but Frederick had little reason to believe that Maria Theresa would honor that recognition if circumstances

ever offered the opportunity to reclaim the province. So the king wanted international guarantees, and the imminent peace treaty was a good place to begin collecting them.

A fourth category of issues involved *two disputes over the full exercise of sovereignty*. The first arose in the Austrian Netherlands, where the Barrier Treaty conferred on the Dutch the right to station troops in Austrian fortresses and on the Maritime Powers the right to block Austrian plans to change the tariffs for the province. Austria hoped to use the imminent negotiations to eliminate the infringements of its sovereignty; the Maritime Powers intended to defend them. The second dispute arose over the harbor at Dunkirk, which by the terms of the Treaty of Utrecht could not be fortified. France had used the outbreak of war to ignore the limitations stipulated by the treaty. Britain, fearful that the port might again become a nest of privateers, wanted to restore the prewar situation; France naturally enough demurred.

As European diplomats surveyed the situation on the eve of the peace talks, they worried about two other possible intrusions: the emergence of unexpected linkages among issues and the further dissolution of the already weakened alliances. Linkages, for example, could subvert expectations. Charles Emmanuel warned Osorio that "God would not wish to have Holland saved at the expense of Italy."[9] A French diplomat suspected that "the affairs of Italy are the ones that the English have closest to their heart, because they are the rub for those in America."[10] Whether such linkages could actually be embedded in a peace settlement was uncertain; whether they would be proposed allowed of no doubt. And so all the courts nursed apprehensions about being asked or forced to make sacrifices for some broader good. Unfriendly diplomacy might yet succeed where unfriendly arms had failed. Another kind of fear arose from the patently frayed nature of the wartime alliances. The Bourbon allies were deeply suspicious of each other; the Worms allies were, if anything, even more estranged. French leaders thought Spain's ministers to be parochial and stupid; Spanish ministers held their French counterparts to be faithless liars. Britain charged Austria with willful blindness, Piedmont-Sardinia suspected Britain of deliberate maritime negligence, and Austria accused Piedmont-Sardinia of unprincipled greed. A major question thus arose in all belligerent capitals: should we work to placate our allies, or should we preempt them by concluding a treaty with the enemy? The bias was toward strengthening ties that were already in place, and so—again, other things being reasonably equal—the diplomats of Europe devoted more energy to revitalizing existing alliances than to probing for new ones. But this allocation of energy did not dissolve fears of being betrayed.

These considerations allow us to summarize the hopes and priorities of each of the major belligerents as peace drew near.

Austria wanted the abrogation of the Treaty of Worms and some measure of territorial indemnification for the loss of Silesia. Though her armies had failed against Prussia and been chased from Genoa, Maria Theresa held to her belief that Austria deserved a favorable settlement. Her chief asset as diplomats began to gather was her general aloofness from the rush for peace: it was entirely plausible that the empress-queen would choose to continue the war if she could not receive suitable terms. *Britain* wanted France to vacate the Netherlands, Spain to open up its American empire to British traders, and both to disavow the Stuarts. Britain's leverage in the coming talks consisted of its control of the seas and its consequent capacity to throttle French trade. If the Bourbons were not forthcoming, moreover, the blockade might be extended to Spain. The possession of Louisbourg was another British advantage. Britain's weakness lay in the failure of its army. If France could not be extruded from the Netherlands, the very foundations of British security were in peril. *France* held the oddest of positions. Its goals seemed altruistic to the point of self-abasement. Rather than seeking territory for itself (aside from the return of Louisbourg), Versailles sought it for Spain's Don Philip. Rather than demanding indemnities for itself, it demanded considerations for the feeble Electoral Palatine, the dislodged Duke of Modena, and the embattled republic of Genoa. Since French armies occupied the Austrian Netherlands and parts of the Dutch republic, the government at Versailles held what must, from a military perspective, be regarded as an extraordinarily powerful hand. And yet the French position was deeply flawed, for military success had been accompanied by economic debilitation. *Piedmont-Sardinia,* as became the smallest of the major combatants, had the most confined goals. For Italy as a whole Turin sought only the maintenance of an effective equilibrium between Habsburg and Bourbon influence. In its own theater of concern Turin wanted basically the evacuation of Savoy and the upholding of the Treaty of Worms. If it secured these several aims, then it would emerge from the war with its security enhanced, its old realm intact, and with several new acquisitions appended in the east. Charles Emmanuel would thereby be a clear winner. *Spain,* finally, seemed a paradox. Its government had changed in almost every respect since the outbreak of the war—in monarchs, in ministers, in military leaders—and yet its goal of placing Don Philip in an Italian domain remained oddly unaltered. Of all the great powers, Spain was the most relentlessly focused in its demands.

QUI DESIDERAT PACEM . . .

While Europe talked of peace, it prepared for war. This conduct did not betray a want of sincerity. It reflected instead the lesson of recent years that peace talks often aborted. Its most dramatic exemplification in the waning year was the British and Dutch purchase of Russian soldiery. Sobered by the outcome at Laffeld, the British government directed Lord Hyndford at the opening of August 1747 to solicit Russian military help for the campaign in the west. The ensuing negotiations were difficult. Britain's continuing inability to defeat the French army gave Alexis Bestuzhev grounds for believing that Russia should be amply rewarded for its assistance. So too did the fact that the Dutch republic, invigorated by its revolution, was willing to join the British in hiring Russian troops. Hyndford plied the Russian ministers with extravagant gifts, and on the last day of November 1747 a convention was concluded. In return for £300,000 per year, the empress Elizabeth would supply 30,000 troops to the Pragmatic Allies. As soon as the ratifications of the convention were exchanged on 8 February 1748, the Russian army began its westward advance. Elizabeth entrusted command to Prince Vasilii Anikitich Repnin, a cavalry officer with artillery experience, and to show her determination to be of real assistance to her allies, Elizabeth sent not just the stipulated 30,000 men but instead a fuller force of 37,000. Proudly accoutered, fiercely loyal, and impressively disciplined, the army set out across Poland. Its advance traversed the winter and penetrated the spring, bringing with each passing day Europe's only fresh army nearer to the theaters of warfare.

Publicly, the ministers at Versailles professed to be unconcerned. The Russian troops were proceeding with such deliberateness that, even though the French expressed respect for the empress's legions, they declared that they saw no need to flinch before an enemy that still lay beyond the Vistula and rested every third day. The French also professed to believe that the attractions and opportunities of the west would precipitate mass desertions from the Russian army. Truth, however, belied appearance at Versailles. With negotiations approaching, the French ministers preferred not to appear alarmed. But they were. Austria and Britain had secured the permission of various German states to allow unobstructed passage to the Russians; Frederick himself declined to object. The transit, Puisieulx wrote, "is sad and shameful for Germany—sad because she will be the victim, shameful because in all her annals an equally contemptible example cannot be found."[11] But the transit also menaced France. In fact, unless some diplomatic or military stroke interceded, within half a year 37,000 Russians—"a fine body of troops" in the words of an admiring British observer[12]—would be banging on the doors of Alsace.

The Anglo-Dutch cooperation that allowed Russian troops to be hired manifested itself in other ways as well. During the summer of 1747 the Dutch had assumed the uncharacteristic role of cheerleader of belligerence, and in August William Bentinck traveled to Britain to steel the pro-war faction and to negotiate troop commitments for the campaign of 1748. There was, however, an element of the ludicrous in this Dutch effort to infuse resolve into the Pragmatic Alliance. The United Provinces had, after all, never declared war on France. This awkward truth deeply compromised the Dutch position: how could the republic criticize British sloth when it was itself unwilling to formalize its belligerence? William IV recognized the moral absurdity of his stance. He therefore looked for an opportunity to bring Dutch practice and Dutch professions into closer congruence. When rage swept through the United Provinces after the fall of Bergen-op-Zoom in October 1747, he seized the opportunity to issue a promise (unconstitutional but potent) that if the talks at Aix-la-Chapelle were unproductive of peace when spring came, the republic would declare war on France. These maneuvers removed the chief obstacle to an Anglo-Dutch troop agreement, and on 26 January 1748 a convention was accepted. Its terms provided that Britain and the United Provinces would each supply 66,000 troops for the Low Countries in 1748 and that Austria (represented in these talks by Count Batthyany) would supply a further 60.000. The figures were somewhat misleading, for although each Maritime Power was pledging 26,000 more troops than it had supplied in 1747, each fudged its total by factoring in 15,000 Russian troops. Nevertheless, the convention posited an allied army of 192,000 in the Low Countries for the coming campaign.

Plans for allied actions in the Italian theater also took shape as 1747 ended. The wretched results of 1747 had intensified the mutual rancors of the three governments. But as long as Italian issues remained unresolved and Don Philip's putative realm undefined, the allies had sufficient reasons for hanging together. In November a colloquy of troubled military leaders gathered at Milan. Browne knew that he commanded a demoralized army, Colonel Wentworth recalled that both the Austrian and the Piedmontese commanders had lied to him about the sizes of their armies, and General de la Roque (of Piedmont-Sardinia) pushed for allied endorsement of a plan that would have made Charles Emmanuel the commander-in-chief of the allied army even when he was not present. After considerable haggling the conferees concluded an agreement not unlike the one of the previous May. Austria and Piedmont-Sardinia pledged to put 90,000 men into the field, two-thirds supplied by Vienna and one-third by Turin. Britain promised to support these operations with cash and a maritime blockade. A happy Newcastle exulted:

"Two hundred thousand in Flanders, ninety thousand in Italy, and a fleet to sweep all before it; I begin now to talk a little big."[13]

In the Bourbon camp by the winter of 1747-48 a striking divergence had appeared. Spain's once formidable enthusiasm for war was spent. Ferdinand VI had no stomach for dispatching still more Spanish troops to die in foreign lands, and Count Carvajal reckoned peace to be the prerequisite to any Anglo-Spanish accord. Besides, since Spanish troops already occupied Savoy, Spain had adequate means for wringing a settlement for Don Philip out of the imminent negotiations. But in France the advocates of action still exercised influence. Count Saint-Séverin, soon to be traveling to Aix-la-Chapelle, linked the battlefield to the negotiating table when he suggested the directive that he believed Puisieulx should issue to Maurice of Saxony, Count d'Argenson, and Pâris-Duverney: "Gentlemen, it is your business to put me in condition to act usefully in my office."[14] It goes without saying that Maurice was already aware of the linkage. And so, while Spain curled up to await events, Maurice devoted the winter to consulting with Belle-Isle and Noailles about a scheme to render the United Provinces absolutely defenseless. He proposed, in short, to cap his career by seizing Maastricht.

Jointly administered by the Dutch republic and the bishop of Liège, this great gateway sat athwart the Meuse. It posed the trickiest problem for a would-be besieger of any site in the Low Countries. Because it occupied both banks of the river, it could be encircled only by an army that divided itself. And effecting such a division was not easy. Although within the precincts of the city there were bridges to keep the east and west banks in communication, outside of the city there were few bridges—none at all to the north—and if the Pragmatic Allies foresaw a French crossing, they could mobilize to resist it, with all the advantages that a large army holding a bridgehead invariably enjoys. The city itself was formidable. Its fortifications were sturdy, its earthworks dotted with reinforcing trees and decked with stabilizing grasses. A garrison of 10,000 manned the defense works. For reasons such as these, Maastricht was regarded as Europe's most impregnable fortified city. But Maurice relished challenges, and Maastricht, which had eluded him after Laffeld, represented both a set of technical problems to be overcome and a blemish to be purged from his record. He knew that with peace near at hand, he was unlikely to have another opportunity to command armies in a major war. And he was not unhappy that peace was approaching. "I desire," he wrote (coincidentally on the day of the massacre at Bergen-op-Zoom), "only rest."[15] But Maurice was a soldier, and in the last analysis he had a soldier's idea about how to realize his goal. Diplomats, he believed, obeyed the outcomes of battles: "the peace," he stated, "will be made in Maastricht."[16]

PROBING AND PRODDING

The tale of diplomatic maneuvering that is about to unfold is marked by false starts, hesitations, misunderstandings, and deceptions. Six points should be kept in mind, for they will be useful guideposts amid the confusions, disappointments, and lies that littered Europe's path to peace. First, because no belligerent has actually been defeated, the settlement, as it emerges, will be a compromise. Second, the already frayed alliances will tend to become more tattered still as fighting yields to parleying and to a situation in which each negotiator can nurse hopes of luring an enemy away from its allies. Third, much business will be conducted bilaterally rather than multilaterally; secrecy, after all, is the prerequisite to poaching. Fourth, among the various bilateral possibilities, only two will offer a reasonable prospect of ending a general war: a Franco-British settlement and a Franco-Austrian settlement. Fifth, France will therefore be in an enviable structural position: it alone has two roads to peace—one through London and the other through Vienna. Sixth, France will hold still another advantage, inasmuch as it is the only combatant that has renounced all ambition for acquiring territory. When Louis XV proudly declared that he wanted to negotiate "as a king and not as a merchant,"[17] it was this freedom from avarice that he was trumpeting.

The exclusion of Anglo-Spanish talks from this list may seem puzzling. That exclusion reflects Spain's dependent status within the Bourbon alliance, as Britain determined that it could neither use Spain to extract a peace from France nor seduce Spain into severing its ties with France. Several months were required, however, before these truths became evident. The on-and-off Anglo-Spanish colloquies, suspended when the Breda conference dissolved, resumed in August 1747 when Benjamin Keene shifted his residence from Lisbon to Madrid. They gained momentum the next month when Carvajal dispatched General Ricardo Wall, an Irish Jacobite, to London to represent Ferdinand VI. Each side was initially optimistic, and on one issue the two countries even made headway, with Britain finally abandoning all reservations about planting Don Philip in an Italian principality. The linking of Parma (which belonged to Vienna) and Piacenza (which, as a result of Worms, was Turin's) was quickly fixed upon as constituting a suitably acceptable realm. But on the other matters dividing London from Madrid—the Asiento, the Annual Ship, even Gibraltar—no meeting of the minds was possible. In November the talks broke off. Carvajal still wanted an Anglo-Spanish rapprochement; he remained, however, without resources to effect it.

During the same autumn Austria and France resumed their own protracted discussions. Unlike the Anglo-Spanish talks, which quickly lost all cloak of secrecy, the Austro-French exchanges were confidential. The two states managed this remarkable feat by avoiding direct contact, either in Paris or in Vienna, and by resorting instead to Saxon intermediaries. Count Brühl had labored since 1745 to reconcile Maria Theresa's realm to Louis XV's, and he was delighted when both powers showed themselves ready to use Saxon diplomats to transmit proposals back and forth. The Loss brothers were still at their posts, and so fraternal solidarity supplemented Saxon resolve in providing security for the delicate discussions. The obstacles to a Franco-Austrian settlement lay chiefly in Vienna, where Maria Theresa, emotionally exhausted by a war that was coterminous with her reign, had lapsed into a prickly irresolution. She was drawn to peace, for only under its conditions could she hope to complete the administrative reforms she was asking Count Haugwitz to oversee. She was also tempted to break with Britain, for Bartenstein had persuaded her that London's interests were fundamentally at variance with Austria's. And yet her hunger for compensation for Silesia was unappeased, and had Britain not vetoed an attack on Naples, she would gladly have seen the Kingdom of the Two Sicilies sacked by Austrian troops. Only as winter approached did the empress-queen finally begin to resolve her confusions. France seemed sympathetic to her insistence that, having yielded territory to Charles Emmanuel at Worms, she should not now be expected to cede territory to Don Philip at Aix-la-Chapelle. By suggesting that the Bourbon prince be given Savoy as his reward, France seemed to commit itself to the view that Piedmont-Sardinia should be required to help pay for the peace. These signs of French understanding won her over: in December her government authorized Count Kaunitz to negotiate a separate peace with France.

Meanwhile, delegates to the projected congress at Aix-la-Chapelle were being named. Two diminutive combatant states were to be on hand. Genoa nominated Maria Francesco D'Oria; Modena selected Count Monzone. Even one noncombatant made an appearance, as the United Provinces, playing their juridically ambiguous role to the end, designated a five-man team headed by Count William Bentinck to protect Dutch interests at the talks. Piedmont-Sardinia chose the calm and quiet Count Chavanne, who by long experience in Madrid and attentive listening at Breda had been armed with a full knowledge of his friends' and adversaries' views. Spain selected Jaime Masones de Lima, the younger brother of the Marquis of Sotomayer, a friend of Carvajal's and a veteran of the Italian campaigns. Masones had succeeded Macanaz at the very end of the Breda colloquies and, though a novice at diplomacy, was already evincing the shrewdness of mind that would bring him into the Council of State many years later.

The central representatives were those from Vienna, London, and Versailles. Austria nominated Count Kaunitz. His experience at Turin and Brussels was a recommendation, but Maria Theresa nominated him chiefly because she found his memoranda compact and cogent, his antipathy to Britain congenial, and his plans for closer ties with France well founded. Britain nominated the Earl of Sandwich. Breda had scarcely been a triumph for the young peer, but Newcastle felt confident that with Sandwich at Aix-la-Chapelle, Britain would be spared the embarrassment of irregular initiatives. France chose Count Saint-Séverin. This nomination offended French chauvinists, who, already piqued that France's war effort was led by a Saxon, now had to stomach a peace effort led by a Neapolitan. But in choosing the count, the foreign minister thwarted Belle-Isle's hope that the man who had begun the conflict might be permitted to end it. And the choice also allowed Puisieulx to place a figure with wider diplomatic experience than either Kaunitz or Sandwich possessed at the heart of peace negotiations.

The first surprise of the new year came in February 1748, when Count Charles Bentinck, the younger brother of William, arrived in London with the astonishing request that Britain should lend £1 million to the United Provinces; otherwise, Charles declared, the republic would not be able to contribute to the Pragmatic war effort. Newcastle immediately realized that if Charles Bentinck told the truth, the Pragmatic Allies had no option but to seek peace. Needing more information, the duke dispatched the Duke of Cumberland to the republic to provide a British analysis of the Dutch situation. Cumberland's report, submitted after a tour of the republic in March, confirmed all that Count Charles Bentinck had said. Instead of a standing army of 130,000 men, the Dutch fighting force numbered scarcely more than one-third of that total. Since many of these troops were former prisoners of war and since the republic was out of money, it was doubtful that the Dutch could assemble even 10,000 men at Breda, much less the promised 51,000. Moreover, the Prince of Orange was himself a convert to peace. Cumberland declared that war could not be sustained, and Newcastle, though despondent, assented: "we seem," he wrote almost wistfully, "to have all been in a dream."[18]

The collapse of the Maritime Powers' military strength lent new urgency to another British initiative. For two years ministers in London had been alarmed by Britain's continuing inability to secure closer ties with Prussia. Though Carteret was gone, his strategic hopes for Germany retained force: Britain and Prussia were natural Protestant allies against Catholic France. The decision to pay Russian troops to march across central Europe intensified that concern. Frederick's fear of Russia was legendary. If he responded to the Anglo-Dutch initiative by rejoining France, then the purchase of troops would serve only to widen the war rather than to shorten it. Newcastle chose Henry Legge, a young man fortified with good connections, for a mission to Berlin. Legge consulted with British diplomats at The Hague, Aix-la-Chapelle, and Hanover on his way to Berlin. In the uncertain conditions of the spring of 1748, Britain and Prussia needed access to each other's ears, and the Legge mission was designed to reopen Anglo-Prussian conversations.

Had the government in London known of the secret Austro-French talks that Saxony was brokering, Britain's concern would have been deeper still. In mid-February, after much tugging and hauling, the two courts tentatively agreed to two documents—a preliminary article and a secret one. The preliminary article defined a territorial settlement for Europe. Its general rule was that each belligerent power should retain or recover the possessions it held when the war began. The only important exception allowed Parma and Piacenza to become the principality of Don Philip, with the understanding that if he inherited the Neapolitan crown or died without heirs, the two states would revert to Austria. The similarity between this agreement and the tentative Anglo-Spanish compromise on Italy was not a coincidence; Spain passed information on to France. The secret article addressed the issue of Silesia. In it Austria stated that it had no intention of breaking the Treaty of Dresden, and France agreed to exclude any mention of Silesia from the final treaty. As for the rest of the world—the Low Countries, North America, India, the high seas—Austria declared that it did not take sides in the dispute between France and Britain. Kaunitz, when he read the two articles, called the work "a masterpiece."[19]

Well he might. A settlement crafted in accordance with the terms set forth in the two articles would have been an Austrian triumph—almost a resurrection of the Pragmatic Sanction. By proposing to hand back Genoese and Mantuan territory that her troops had won, Maria Theresa was making that purpose absolutely clear. It is true that as a nod of appreciation toward Britain, the Austrians expressed a willingness to cede Furnes to France if London refused to relent from its demand that the fortifications at Dunkirk be demolished. But otherwise the Austrians paid no heed to London's needs. And toward Piedmont-Sardinia they were almost vindictive. Guided by Bartenstein, Maria Theresa had consistently proclaimed that the Treaty of Worms was conditional upon success for *both* of the contracting parties. Since Turin's winnings in the northern part of Italy had not been matched by any Viennese conquests in the south, Piedmont-Sardinia had no right to retain its trophies. The preliminary article ratified Austria's interpretation of the treaty. Not only did it reclaim the western section of Lombardy for

Vienna, it also stipulated that if Don Philip left his new holding along the Po for a finer realm in the south, it would revert in its entirety to Austria. Piedmont-Sardinia, in sum, would gain nothing from the war.

What the Austrians failed to realize was that France had a strategy of its own. If they had thought seriously about the articles, they would have concluded that the commitments were too good to be credible. But the antipathy toward Turin and the resentment toward London bit deep. The Austrians were therefore off their guard in dealing with the suddenly accommodating French. Convinced of the justice of their own views, they believed that Versailles had done nothing more than submit to the promptings of equity in coming around to a pro-Austrian position. And so, even when France suddenly confounded Austrian expectations at the end of March by insisting that the articles required several adjustments, Vienna was not alarmed. The adjustments were not minor: once again reversing itself, Versailles proposed that Don Philip receive Savoy rather than Parma and Piacenza; reawakening dormant issues, Versailles called for compensation for Louis XV's loyal German ally, the Elector Palatine. The Austrians, however, remained blithely confident. "It is a good sign," Kaunitz was advised, "that the French Court proposes to conclude with you [at Aix-la-Chapelle] in two or three discussions."[20] There is no escaping the inference that the Austrians walked into the French lair because their eyes were obstinately closed.

By the middle of March 1748 the diplomatic representatives of the belligerent powers were beginning to arrive in Aix-la-Chapelle.[21] In accordance with custom every road into the old imperial city was posted with signs that, in both French and German, proclaimed its neutrality. A dispute over ceremonials—virtually predictable in such a setting—quickly broke out, and the ensuing delay worked to the advantage of the participant with the strongest hand, the court of Versailles. France, after all, had two negotiating partners to choose between. Unwilling to foreclose either possibility prematurely, Puisieulx authorized Saint-Séverin to establish contact with both Kaunitz and Sandwich, and to use the delay to maintain separate bilateral conversations with each. Thus the French representative could provoke a bidding war between London and Vienna and settle in the end with the capital that was more forthcoming. Meanwhile, lest the Pragmatic Allies think that they might have the luxury of time, Maurice of Saxony set about effecting the grand military deceit wherewith he planned to capture Maastricht. The French economy may have been decrepit, but all the short-term advantages seemed to lie with Versailles, and with Maurice menacing and the Russians distant, the allies could not be confident that a longer term was worth waiting for.

THE PRELIMINARY TREATY

The man who had declared that peace would be made in Maastricht began a final flex of his muscle at the opening of April 1748. From a modern viewpoint the plan that Maurice devised sounds like simplicity itself. But in an age that knew neither instantaneous communications nor the swift transport of troops, it was a scheme that was bold in vision and daring in implementation. The deceit involved gathering the machinery for a siege at the northwestern end of the French line. The purpose of this activity was to induce the Pragmatic commanders to believe that the attack would fall on Breda or 's Hertogenbosch. Meanwhile, to place troops on the eastern side of the Meuse, Maurice sent Löwendahl and his army back into France, where, marching swiftly, they crossed to the right bank in Luxembourg and then began a northward advance through Verviers on Maastricht. To divert eyes from Löwendahl's march, Maurice exploited the fact that he himself was regarded as Europe's foremost man of war. First he stayed in Paris, freezing his apprehensive enemies. Then, when he moved, it was only to confirm what French preparations portended, for by arriving at Bergen-op-Zoom on 2 April 1748 he seemed to suggest that the campaign would commence in the west. In fact, he had arrived only to pick up the army destined for a different appointment. With the swiftness that Maurice alone was able to extract from large forces in this war, the French army then reversed itself and sped eastward, gathering troops from various encampments as it went. Maurice's troops and Löwendahl's then converged on Maastricht, one army on each bank. Siege equipment arrived from higher up the river. By 9 April the investment of the city had begun. By 15 April Maastricht and its garrison of 10,000—half Dutch, half Austrian—was cut off and isolated.

Less than twenty miles of flat countryside separated Aix-la-Chapelle from Maastricht. "You are going to hear the roar of the cannon," Maurice wrote puckishly to Saint-Séverin; "I do not know if the sound of this agreeable music will lift spirits to thoughts of peace or to a war-like ardor."[22] From both London and Vienna came unequivocal signs that France's enemies heard the martial strains and were redoubling their efforts to find a way out of the war before France had destroyed the Dutch republic. The Austrian proposal demonstrated that Vienna would not allow its contempt for Piedmont-Sardinia to block a settlement. Accepting the French suggestion that Don Philip's principality be Savoy, Maria Theresa proposed that until the Spanish prince succeeded his elder brother in Naples (at which time he would return Savoy to Piedmont-Sardinia), Charles Emmanuel should enjoy the control and revenues of Parma and Piacenza. The aim was simple: the king of

Sardinia would thereby be protected against a calamitous loss of revenue and prestige. Britain's reactions to the events on the Meuse were, however, even more startling. Newcastle first directed Sandwich to accept the cession of Parma and Piacenza to Don Philip. He then authorized him to yield on Finale. Finally, reversing the policy he had adhered to since rising to power, Newcastle authorized Sandwich to sign a peace treaty even if London's allies refused to join in. Newcastle still wanted to protect the Treaty of Worms, and so—ignorant of the substance of Austro-French talks—he added the injunction, certain to enflame the Austrians, that when the prince succeeded to the throne in Naples, Parma and Piacenza should revert to "their present possessors." That phrase implied that while Austria would recover Parma, Piedmont-Sardinia would be awarded most of Piacenza. Clearly, by 20 April 1748 Saint-Séverin was in the enviable position of having both of France's enemies virtually supplicating him for peace.

But the structure of the situation also meant that Saint-Séverin could no longer defer answering the question that from the beginning of the peace talks had been the central issue for France: should Versailles conclude with London or with Vienna? Thus far, Vienna had been the negotiating partner, and the two countries had apparently moved very close to an accord. Kaunitz's latest offer may indeed be seen as ending all Austro-French disagreement. And yet a major difficulty lingered. Though a settlement with Austria would allow France to discharge its Italian and Spanish obligations honorably and efficiently, it would leave Cape Breton in British hands. And since a settlement with Austria would involve a French withdrawal from the Austrian Netherlands (for otherwise Austria would not conclude), it would require France to give up its key point of leverage against Britain and thus deprive France of any means of forcing Britain to hand the North American treasure back. The difficulty went further: though a peace treaty with Austria would probably sever the diplomatic tie between London and Vienna, France could not be sure that it would force London to make peace. In light of Britain's overwhelming dominance on the seas, the prospect of a maritime war with Britain was chilling to the French. If an unequivocal end to the war, involving a restitution of Cape Breton, was Versailles's goal, only a treaty with Britain could effect it.

Saint-Séverin and the French officials advising him came to this conclusion by pondering several different considerations. The first was Britain's influence with its close allies. The Dutch and the Piedmontese were so dependent on London that the French felt confident that Britain could impose a settlement on them. A second consideration was Britain's influence with Russia. Only Britain, as paymaster, could suspend the advance of the

Russian troops whenever it chose. A third consideration was Britain's desire to please Prussia. This desire made Britain willing—as Austria was not—to accept France's view that a guarantee of Silesia should be included in the treaty. A final consideration was Britain's role as subsidizer of Austrian troops. It was difficult to imagine how a straitened Austrian government could contrive to deal with the loss of British aid without reducing the military effectiveness of the empress-queen's arms. The sum of these considerations was the patent truth that a treaty with Britain offered France the prospect of a general peace while a treaty with any other power left loose ends. Puisieulx's advice to Saint-Séverin summarized the situation: "the articles offered you [by the Austrians] are more alluring than England's, but if we can conclude with London, there will be less trouble, more safety, and more speed."[23]

By the fourth week in April 1748 Saint-Séverin and Sandwich were engaged in substantive and semisecret negotiations. Because Sandwich and Kaunitz had discovered that they did not like each other, they had little occasion to get together. Because each thought the other was France's dupe, they had little reason to consult. Kaunitz continued to expect a swift agreement, despite minor problems, and an Austrian observer, faintly puzzled at French delays, could declare only that he "would not wish to be in Puisieulx's place and have the deaths at Maastricht and in Italy on [his] conscience, when he could make peace with the stroke of a pen."[24] Sandwich, meanwhile, deeply involved in the intrigue, kept in almost daily contact with Bentinck. The Dutch envoy's mood was sober: "if peace is to be made, it must be made, and if not as we would, then as we may."[25] On 28 April Saint-Séverin played his final hand, informing Sandwich that Austria and Spain were on the verge of concluding a peace treaty that would punish Piedmont-Sardinia. The report was a lie, but it wrought its desired effect. Though doubting the story, Sandwich dared not risk ignoring it, and so, on 30 April 1748 Sandwich placed his signature on the document that he and Saint-Séverin had cobbled together only the day before. Count Bentinck and his Dutch colleagues also affixed their signatures. The preliminary treaty of peace thereby came into existence.

The haste with which it had been thought out and drafted left the preliminary treaty a flawed document. But the whole purpose of a preliminary treaty is to suggest the outlines of a settlement, not to specify every final detail. Its terms provided a useful agenda for discussion. We shall consider them under five headings.

The dominant theme of restoration

Under the preliminary treaty, the Austrian Netherlands were to be restored to Vienna; Cape Breton was to be restored to France; the various territories seized, held, or assailed in the East and West Indies were to be recovered by their prewar possessors; even Genoa and Modena were to recover whichever lands had been taken from them. One restoration was, however, qualified. Although Britain was to regain the Asiento and the right of the Annual Ship, it was to enjoy these opportunities only "for the years of non-use"—a turn of phrase that was open to a variety of interpretations. Another restoration—Dunkirk's—was thoroughly ambiguous. By referring to "standing treaties" when defining the types of seaside fortifications that would be permitted, the document simply reopened Britain's and France's long disagreement over how references to Dunkirk in earlier treaties were to be interpreted.

One exception

The preliminary treaty identified one exception to the dominant theme: the creation of an Italian state for Don Philip. This new principality would consist of Parma, Piacenza, and tiny Guastalla. Since Parma belonged to Austria, the proposal entailed yet another truncation of Maria Theresa's inheritance. Since Piacenza was part of Piedmont-Sardinia's winnings at Worms, the proposal also promised to anger Charles Emmanuel. Without incurring the wrath of Vienna and Turin in this way, however, Sandwich could not have won Saint-Séverin's consent to the preliminary treaty. Foreseeing the possibility that Don Philip might succeed his elder brother in Naples or die without a male heir, Sandwich and Saint-Séverin added the provision that in either instance the territories that comprised the principality being created for him would revert to their "present possessors." This stipulation was Britain's effort to limit Charles Emmanuel's anger, but since it implicitly made the Treaty of Worms its point of reference, it offered effective recognition to an accord that Maria Theresa hoped to invalidate.

The promise of widened legitimacy

To four ruling houses that were seeking international recognition for some range of their territorial claims the preliminary treaty offered the promise of widened legitimacy. Versailles made two inevitable but important concessions: it agreed that Francis I was indeed the Holy Roman Emperor and, by abandoning the house of Stuart, it recognized the right of George II to reign in Britain. Then, in a convenient exercise of reciprocal back-scratching, France supported Hanover's unexpected claim for compensation from Spain for seventeenth-century debts, while Britain agreed that the final treaty should settle the Elector Palatine's claim (against Vienna) to the fief of Pleistein, a sliver of land embedded in Bavaria's dominion of the Upper Palatinate. The latter two claims were reminders that when giants shake up the dust of the earth, enterprising midgets can sometimes contrive to collect valuable fallout.

Three guarantees

The preliminary treaty also offered three important guarantees. First, it reaffirmed the international guarantee of the Pragmatic Sanction, suitably adjusted to take into account Vienna's territorial losses during the war. Second, it offered Charles Emmanuel an unequivocal guarantee for all of his dominions, singling out the remaining trophies of Worms for explicit mention. These first two guarantees balanced each other: they established international defenses for the new Italian equilibrium established by the war; and they delimited the realms of Vienna and Turin in the Po valley, further legitimizing the Treaty of Worms but also pledging Europe through an international instrument to uphold the sizable residue of Maria Theresa's inheritance. Third, the preliminary treaty offered a guarantee of Prussia's possession of Silesia and Klodzko. This inclusion was a patent affront to Vienna, for Berlin, having left the war in 1745, was not even a party to the peace talks.

Ending the war

Finally, the preliminary treaty established a schedule for winding down the war. First it addressed the issue of bringing fighting to a conclusion. It specified that an armistice on land should take effect six weeks after the signing of the preliminary treaty—that is, on 15 June—and that an armistice at sea should follow three months after the signing. The maritime armistice represented a recognition of geographical reality: the East and West Indies were distant realms, and there seemed no sound reason to impose a striking of arms prior to the period in which combatants could be expected to learn of it. The continental armistice, however, had a political flavor. Only a day, after all, was needed to deliver word of the treaty to Maastricht. But France did not want Maastricht and the advantages it promised to slip away under the cover of a premature peace, and so Saint-Séverin insisted that Maurice be allowed a space of time sufficient for completing his task there. After setting terms for the two armistices, the preliminary treaty fixed the conditions for restoring a true peace to Europe. Here again France controlled the decisions. Although the public document stated that none of the cessions, restitutions, guarantees, and recognitions would take effect until all the interested parties had acceded to its terms, a secret and separate article pledged the three signatories—Britain, France, and the United Provinces—to push ahead to a final accord even in the face of opposition from nonsignatories. A government that persisted in its opposition would be in danger of forfeiting whatever winnings the treaty promised it. The secret article defined the political situation at Aix-la-Chapelle: Athens and Sparta were powerful enough to give the law to Europe.[26]

20

The Triumph of the Diplomats
(April 1748 — October 1748)

COPING WITH A SOW'S EAR

If no one wins the war, no one wins the peace. Though compelling, the logic of that statement was resisted by at least some in every belligerent state (except Britain) as the terms of the preliminary treaty became known. In Italy the disappointments were exclusively territorial. The representative of Modena declared that his battered duchy would regard mere restitution as insufficient and insist instead on territorial compensation for its contributions. The envoy from Genoa advanced the same argument, and since the Treaty of Aranjuez had promised territorial gains to the republic, he was not shy about proclaiming his sense of betrayal by the Bourbons. Piedmont-Sardinia nursed two grievances. Despite the Treaty of Worms, neither the promised territory of Finale nor the portion of Piacenza already ceded to Turin were to be Charles Emmanuel's. The loss of Finale surprised few. It had, after all, not been Austria's to cede in the first place. With Piacenza, however, the situation was different. Austria's claim to the territory had been indisputable and so the cession to Turin had been thoroughly legitimate; and at the very moment when Sandwich and Saint-Severin consigned the territory to Don Philip, it was controlled by Piedmontese troops. To oblige Charles Emmanuel to hand over Piacenza was to require him to give up what was his property both de jure and de facto. And so not until 30 May 1748, a month after the signing at Aix-la-Chapelle, did the three Italian states finally declare their accession to the preliminary treaty. They were not thereby abandoning all plans of lobbying for changes in the final settlement, but they were at least acknowledging, howsoever reluctantly, that the basic structure of the preliminary treaty should provide the terms of reference for drawing up a definitive treaty.

The plaints emitted by Turin were as nothing compared to the howls that emanated from a stunned Madrid. "It is not possible," Ferdinand VI raged, "that the King of France has done this. He treats us like the Duke of Modena!"[1] This reaction might well seem excessive. After all, strictly speaking (Turin having won at Worms and Prussia at Dresden), Madrid was the most unambiguous victor in the document drafted at Aix-la-Chapelle: Don Philip was to receive his coveted principality, and Britain was denied any gains at Spain's expense in the New World. But the Spanish ministers did not compute success by reference to the situations of the other states of Europe. Rather, they invoked the Treaty of Fontainebleau, which stood for them, as the Treaty of Worms did for Piedmont-Sardinia, as the baseline against which to measure the success of the belligerence. By this canon the terms proposed by Sandwich and Saint-Séverin were patently disappointing. Milan would remain with Vienna; Minorca and Gibraltar would remain with Britain; the Asiento and the Annual Ship would run their terms.

It was a sign of the new realism in Spanish foreign policy, however, that fury quickly yielded to calculation. Carvajal realized that the vague terminology employed by Sandwich and Saint-Séverin in defining the American settlement was susceptible to a variety of readings, and he therefore directed his efforts to assuring that that reading would be Spanish. Everything turned on how one chose to interpret the key phrase "for the years of non-use." Since the treaty that gave the rights of the Asiento and the Annual Ship to Britain had expired in 1743, London could not lay claim to any rights in Spanish America after that date. Since the treaty had been ratified in 1713, London could claim no rights prior to that date. The issue therefore revolved upon determining the number of years between 1713 and 1743 that Britain had been denied its rights. From Carvajal's perspective, the deprivation had begun only in 1739, with the outbreak of the War of Jenkins' Ear, and so the phrase in question defined a span of but four years—from 1739 to 1742 inclusive. Britain, however, viewed matters differently. The South Sea Company reminded the government of the many years—eleven in all—when the hostile policies of Alberoni and Ripperda had made the exercise of British rights impossible and won Newcastle's endorsement of the judgment that Britain had been denied the use of its legal rights for a total of fully fifteen years.

Spanish diplomats in the field were skeptical of France's willingness to represent Madrid's views on the matter forcefully. "The government," Huescar wrote from Paris, "plots our abasement with perseverance and steadiness."[2] France, however, was casting about for ways to regain credit with Spain and was prepared to be a far more vigorous advocate of Spanish interests than Huescar expected. It was Carvajal who most clearly sensed this French disposition and who saw the great advantage that lay in it. The swift change in his mind can be measured by the remarkable words he penned as early as 14 May: "the preliminaries are not bad, except for the clause which allows the prolongation of the Asiento and the years of the Annual Ship; if this is removed we shall rest satisfied."[3] Masones resented this decision to leave Spanish matters in French hands. But on 28 June 1748 Spain acceded to the preliminary treaty.

Over the course of seven harsh years Maria Theresa had learned to temper her rigor with flexibility, and so, to the surprise of many, Vienna was the first of the nonnegotiating capitals to accede to the provisional treaty, doing so on 25 May. Nevertheless, disappointment bit deep. Kaunitz had made Austria's three objections public: the treaty obliged Maria Theresa to cede yet another territory, it offered guarantees to Berlin's and Turin's booty, and it was a violation of Britain's promise not to negotiate secretly with the enemy. But Kaunitz had gone to Aix-la-Chapelle persuaded that in the long term France would be a more valuable ally than Britain, and although the conclusion of the preliminary treaty had shown him that a diplomatic revolution would be difficult to effect, it did nothing to alter his conviction that it would be advantageous. Prompt accession, allowing a resumption of his talks with Saint-Séverin, was therefore appropriate. Nevertheless, the government at Vienna advised Kaunitz to be vigilant and cautious. "It is better," his instructions stated, "to rely on one's own strength in the future than to beg for foreign money and thereby remain in eternal subordination."[4]

Once Austrian accession had readmitted Kaunitz to the negotiating game at Aix-la-Chapelle, he directed his energies to effecting two changes in the preliminary arrangements. Neither would be minor. The first involved the postwar status of the Austrian Netherlands, which Kaunitz now proposed to clear of all Dutch troops. To the Maritime Powers the sudden appearance of the issue was a total surprise: they had assumed that the matter had been settled a generation earlier by the Barrier Treaty. Kaunitz's second proposed change was procedural in form but substantive in implication. He urged that instead of using one general treaty to end the war, the negotiators resort to the practice of Utrecht by employing a set of bilateral conventions, each designed to resolve a particular problem between two interested states. The government at Vienna noted that "no single example is to be found where the affairs of so many belligerent powers have been pulled together into a single treaty."[5] But Kaunitz's real goal in advancing this proposal was to create a situation in which the guarantees of the Treaties of Dresden and Worms, because they were irrelevant to bilateral issues, would be dropped from consideration.

The preliminary treaty provoked vigorous discussion among the British. Horace Walpole was amazed at what he construed as French carelessness: "wonderful it is what can make the French give us such terms, or why they have lost so much blood and treasure to so little purpose!" The Duke of Cumberland, however, believed that he saw the stamp of French shrewdness on the agreement: "it is too plain that our situation and pacific disposition was thoroughly known to the enemy, and they took advantage of it."[6] Most commentators expressed surprise that the treaty was not more severe. Moreover, while protecting British interests in a difficult hour, it had not neglected the interests of Britain's allies. The Dutch were to recover Zeeland, the Piedmontese were to receive international recognition to their residual winnings, and Austria was to regain the Austrian Netherlands. Newcastle was therefore annoyed that these allies did not seem more appreciative of Sandwich's labors. Vienna's objections were, to be sure, predictable; that, after all, was Bartenstein's manner. But Turin's denunciations struck Newcastle as ill judged, ill considered, and ill tempered—though, in a paradoxical way they were also serviceable, for in the eyes of Vienna one of the few points in the treaty's favor was its capacity to irritate Turin.

It was in France that the treaty aroused the highest passions. Whereas Britons could at least agree in their evaluation of the utility of its terms, the French lacked consensus even on this point. If the purpose of the struggle had been to win territory, then one could only agree with the bluff old soldier, Maurice of Saxony, that the treaty was absurd. Maurice's words bespoke his sense of bewildered betrayal: "I . . . promise you to fight to the death for truths that I do not understand."[7] But not everyone agreed that the war had been one of conquest. For those who saw it as a campaign to weaken Austria it could be adjudged a qualified success. "Here is France," Saint-Séverin wrote, "almost at the point of accomplishing its great design of humbling the House of Austria. We must now work to do the same to England, so that we will have no further powers to fear."[8] But there was yet another way of assessing the treaty. To those who were impressed chiefly by France's darkening economic prospects, the treaty was less a triumph than a salvation. "Necessity in our internal affairs requires it," Count d'Argenson declared; "our military successes have been fortunate, but this state needs repose."[9] That the public was so divided portended major long-term problems for France. Within a year many in France adopted as a favorite designation of contempt the pithy phrase "idiotic as the peace."

SPIKING THE GUNS

Just as the investment of Maastricht had hastened the signing of the provisional treaty, so now did the signing of the treaty hasten the surrender of the city. The Pragmatic Allies lacked all means of reinforcing their garrison or driving off the besieger. Although the garrison had scored heavily in several well-placed sorties against the French, the long-term outcome could not be in doubt. And so in the second week of May, after Maurice allowed the allied troops to march out of Maastricht with the honors of war, the French army occupied the city and began to clean up its dung-filled streets and fetid quarters. Löwendahl was installed as governor. All sought to forget the casualty figures, which amounted to 10,500 among the defenders and 7,000 among the besiegers. The conquest of Maastricht was a fitting climax to the career of Maurice of Saxony, the man who had emerged from the War of the Austrian Succession with the reputation as Europe's greatest soldier.

By the third week of May in 1748, northern Italy was the only continental area still framing hostile armies. When in February an Austrian attack on the defenders of Genoa failed at Voltri, Count Browne concluded that he lacked the forces requisite to penetrating the republic's defense perimeter in that sector. Obliged by order of Maria Theresa to maintain pressure on Genoa, he shifted his attention to the eastern end of the republic, where the port town of Spezia invited attack. But after the signing of the preliminary treaty made any reliance on British cooperation unwise, he adjusted again and targeted a string of small Apennine settlements situated to the north of Spezia. The fighting that ensued was fierce. But then word arrived that Maria Theresa had acceded to the preliminary treaty. An end to this pointless bloodletting seemed therefore in order, and Richelieu promptly proposed that both sides lay down their arms. Browne, as sick of the killing as the Frenchman, agreed; and on 15 June 1748, at the village of San Pietro Vara, the Austrians and French published their Italian armistice. Though the Spanish and Genoese did not immediately accept it, neither did they violate it. Thus, on that date peace returned to Europe.[10]

The conclusion of the preliminary treaty raised a question about the purpose of the approaching army of 37,000 Russians. The threat of their intrusion into western Europe had been a powerful prod for France to seek a settlement, but they had now served their purpose. Financial exigency argued for their prompt return to their homeland. But to send the troops back to Russia courted two dangers. It would lift the allies' only guns from Louis XV's head, and it might enrage the prickly Elizabeth Petrovna, whose acquiescence in the expedition had been based on her expectations of triumphs. Newcastle and Sandwich therefore urged that Britain continue to pay for the troops' westward march and meanwhile try to negotiate a swap with France, offering to send the 37,000 Russians back home if Versailles would recall a similar number of its own men from the Low Countries. On 2 August 1748 Sandwich and Saint-Séverin concluded a convention that traded the 37,000 Russians for 38,700 French soldiers. And even prior to that agreement, instructions had gone out to the Russians, first, to halt their advance, and then, one week later, to withdraw. Though the Rhine had been their goal, they never came farther west than Franconia. The Austrians were startled at the decision, the French delighted, the British relieved.

Oddly for a conflict that had begun as a Carribean quarrel between London and Madrid, Britain's Jamaica squadron and Spain's Havana squadron had never engaged each other. When the British commander, Rear Admiral Sir Charles Knowles, learned in mid-July 1748 that the Anglo-French conflict was suspended, he turned his attention to the nonacceding Spanish. He wanted to seize their treasure fleet before a peace was imposed. The commander of the Havana squadron, Admiral Andres Reggio, understood his British counterpart well, and so he moved to protect Spain's transatlantic sinew of bullion. Knowles missed the annual treasure fleet, but on 1 October 1748, while cruising in Cuban waters, his spread-out squadron drew down on Reggio's. A straggling engagement ensued, in which two squadrons of equal size—six ships of the line in each—tried to punish one another. By capturing one Spanish ship and damaging Reggio's flagship, the British won the day. Knowles continued prowling until, on 16 October, he learned of Spain's belated accession to the preliminary treaty. With his consequent breaking off of the chase, the war in the West Indies concluded. On the other side of the globe, where the final stages of belligerence pitted Britain against France, the fighting ended at almost exactly the same time. Edward Boscawen's relief squadron arrived on the Coromandel Coast in August 1748. But his siege of Pondichery ran afoul of Dupleix's cunning defense measures and the autumnal monsoon. With a ubiquitous dampness making entrenchment impossible, powder unpredictable, vision beclouded, and disease rife, Boscawen raised the siege on 17 October 1748. At this decision every belligerent gun in the War of the Austrian Succession had been stilled. A week later—such was the state of eighteenth-century communications—Boscawen and Dupleix learned of the preliminary agreement.

THE DIPLOMATIC REVOLUTION PREFIGURED

It may well be wondered why so much time elapsed between the signing of the preliminary treaty and the signing of the definitive treaty. After all, with France and Britain having determined to act bilaterally and with the major issues virtually resolved, it might seem that there was little to be done beyond refining the hasty prose of Saint-Séverin and Sandwich. Sadly for those who lost their lives in the final five months of the war, matters were not that simple. Both the contents of the preliminary treaty and the speed with which it had been drafted aroused anxiety in France and Britain. Austria was not averse to delay, if only because the terms proposed in April were so distasteful. Spain and Piedmont-Sardinia had their own axes to grind. Finally, the demobilization of fighting forces, begun in the spring of 1748, had the perverse effect of protracting the formal belligerence. With the British navy dismissing seamen as swiftly as it could process their releases and with the French army selling off its supplies at Maastricht, it was apparent that no combatant was empowering itself to coerce the negotiators. Diplomacy would therefore be free, amid sumptuous parties and balls, to wend its own tortuous path toward a settlement.

To understand these byways we must cast our view ahead eight years. Europe was again at war. But the contours of the conflict begun in 1756 were radically different from the shape of belligerence ending in 1748. Whereas in the earlier struggle France, Spain, and Prussia had opposed Britain, Austria, Piedmont-Sardinia, and the United Provinces, in the latter one France found itself for much of the time allied with Austria alone, struggling against Britain and Prussia. Only toward the end of the war did Spain lend support to its Bourbon neighbor. As for the Piedmontese and the Dutch, they remained on the sidelines throughout the entire conflict. The core of this international transformation lay in the creation of a Vienna-Versailles axis: enemies for centuries, Austria and France finally determined in the interwar years to make common cause against Prussian untrustworthiness. So tectonic was the shift in alliances that in English-language texts the event is conventionally called the Diplomatic Revolution. The term conveys the sense of astonishment and unease that the forging of an alliance between Versailles and Vienna provoked. It implies that a past has been repudiated. What is important from our perspective is that during the long hiatus in 1748 between the drafting of the preliminary treaty and the acceptance of the final treaty, virtually every element of the Diplomatic Revolution was anticipated.

One aspect of that future was a closer cooperation between Britain and Prussia. Frederick II had rejoiced quietly when Britain sent Henry Legge on his mission to Berlin in the spring of 1748, for this newest approach from London meant that Prussia's two years of isolation and exposure were over. Frederick lavished time upon Legge and, as a blandishment, dropped the calculated confidence that "to be the ally of France was to be her slave."[11] To his envoy in St. Petersburg he explained that "as long as I am on good terms with England and in agreement with her, I have nothing to fear from Russia."[12] Eager to supersede Sandwich at Aix-la-Chapelle, Henry Legge became caught up in this heated atmosphere of amity and decided to risk exceeding his orders. Though instructed to do nothing that might jeopardize Anglo-Austrian friendship, he labored to create an Anglo-Prussian alliance explicitly predicated on procedures that were inimical to Austrian interests. Frederick II offered no resistance to Legge's initiative, and so as July opened British and Prussian diplomats in Berlin were trying to find words that would knit Britain and Prussia closer together.

If the Anglo-Prussian parleys in Berlin were unsettling in their implications, the Austro-French talks that quickly resumed at Aix-la-Chapelle were potentially earth-shaking. Once again it was Saxony that tried to broker an agreement. Baron Kauderbach, posted by Count Brühl to observe the activities at Aix-la-Chapelle, brought Saint-Séverin and Kaunitz back into contact in the aftermath of the preliminary treaty. The former spoke as if the treaty were "soft wax, from which I will make a dog, a cat, a cook, a monkey, finally whatever I like."[13] The latter pretended to forget the recent betrayal. Then, using Kauderbach as a medium, the two men sent proposals back and forth that, seasoned by Kauderbach's personal contributions, encompassed nothing less than the remapping of Europe. Mounting in extravagance as the summer proceeded, the terms under discussion finally envisioned Austria's recovery of Silesia and France's acquisition of Flanders. At one tense moment an excited Kaunitz wrote that "I live between hope and fear."[14] Only in September did everyone involved learn that the bizarre exchange of proposals was chiefly a concoction of Kauderbach's, and the talks, already faltering, collapsed. But as long as Saint-Séverin saw himself as a disciple of Fleury, rebuilding the prewar cooperation between Vienna and Versailles, while Kaunitz saw himself as a secular missionary, leading Austria out of bondage to Britain, there remained a dispositional basis for Austro-French parleys.

The complement to these anticipations of federal revolutions were the anticipations of experiments with neutrality. Spain's probe was tepid. The Duke of Huescar might "foresee that it will be necessary to live with equal distrust of France and England,"[15] but until French support had helped Spain wring a satisfactory settlement from the negotiations, Madrid dared not break with Versailles. Piedmont-Sardinia enjoyed wider latitude, and so during the summer of 1748 Charles Emmanuel authorized his agents to explore a variety of startling options—a dynastic marriage between his own son and one of Louis XV's daughters, a joint Prussian-Piedmontese assault on Austria, the carving of a corridor to the sea across Genoese territory. The most dramatic harbinger of the future, however, was seen in the United Provinces. As long as the French had threatened to engulf the republic, the Dutch dared not let their revolutionary politics get out of hand. But once the preliminary treaty was signed, they lost all inhibitions about leaving the republic exposed and gave themselves over to thrashing out the implications of the revolution. By the summer of 1748 a national self-absorption, marked by riots and tax revolts, had rendered the republic virtually deaf to promptings from abroad. By the time that William IV maneuvered quarreling Amsterdam factions into a compromise resolution of their differences in September 1748, he had learned that the citizens of the republic did not relish being a tail to Britain's dog. It was a lesson that he and the advisors of his successor would not soon forget.

The flaw in these various national experiments with a new international order was that they failed to promote the translation of the preliminary treaty into a definitive document. The first power to grasp the implications of experimentation was Britain. So important was the securing of peace that Newcastle, though famously fearful of travel by sea, decided to leave Britain for the first time in his life and accompany George II during the monarch's visit to his beloved electorate. He had already set forth his own priorities: "my politics with regard to the King of Prussia are that he should be gained by way of additional strength (if possible) to the old alliance, but not be substituted in the place of the House of Austria to form a new chimerical system."[16] In light of this reasoning, it is not surprising that the duke was enraged when he learned that Legge had overleapt his instructions. The priority that the duke placed upon maintaining Anglo-Austrian solidarity led him to invite Britain's envoy to Vienna, Sir Thomas Robinson, to serve as Sandwich's coadjutor at Aix-la-Chapelle. Then Newcastle cajoled his brother Henry Pelham into approving a payment of £100,000 to Austria in compensation for the 4,000 cavalry troops that Austria had supplied to the allied armies in the Low Countries as part of the abortive campaign of 1748.[17] Newcastle saw his task vis-a-vis Vienna as one of calming troubled waters. Neither diplomatic gaffes nor misplaced parsimony was to be allowed to stir up the sea.

This precept, however, proved difficult to honor. With Kaunitz continuing to negotiate with Saint-Séverin and missives from Vienna continuing to insist that the general treaty be broken up into its various bilateral constituent parts, Newcastle found himself unable to hew to a consistent policy toward Britain's putative ally. At the opening of August he directed Sandwich to demonstrate Britain's good faith by revealing to Kaunitz all the secrets about Anglo-French conversations. (William Bentinck gasped that "Bartenstein himself will laugh up his sleeve at having frightened us."[18]) But at the end of the month he was discussing a combined Anglo-French-Dutch military action to impose an Italian settlement on Austria. Not even the dispatching of Sir Thomas Robinson to Aix-la-Chapelle softened the Austrians. To Maria

Theresa and her ministers it mattered little that he knew Austria well; he had, after all, consistently deployed that information to undermine Austrian interests.

For a month the British alone seemed fully to understand the necessity of ending the war before testing new international configurations. But in August the French began to join them. As early as 17 June 1748 the government at Versailles had instructed Saint-Séverin to conclude a treaty swiftly and "without the showy and useless formality of a congress."[19] Puisieulx later summoned Saint-Séverin home, ostensibly to award him the *cordon bleu*, but in fact to tell him that unless Kaunitz could immediately offer substantive concessions that would justify prolonging the Anglo-French war, Saint-Séverin was to abandon the Austrian gambit and conclude a treaty with Sandwich. To enforce this directive Puisieulx sent Du Theil, the veteran of Breda and the chief clerk of the foreign ministry, back to Aix-la-Chapelle with Saint-Séverin and confined each man with the instruction that he must secure the approval of his colleague before committing France to any terms. The meaning of the French action was not lost on Sandwich: France, he declared, was at last ready to bring the war to a swift close. Had Sandwich known Madame Pompadour's parting words to Saint-Séverin he would have been even more pleased. "Do not return without peace," the king's mistress commanded, "the king no longer wants war."[20]

THE TREATY OF AIX-LA-CHAPELLE

And so Athens and Sparta submitted again to the logic of April. If peace was the goal of negotiations, then there was no point in wasting time with countries that could not impose peace on their allies. Count Kaunitz, by asserting that "there is no power in Europe less dangerous to France than the House of Austria," had set forth a principle upon which future Austro-French cooperation could be founded.[21] But France's immediate need was not an ally whose interests did not conflict with its own. Instead, its immediate need was peace. And only Britain could deliver that desideratum. By acceding to the preliminary treaty, the government in London had acknowledged that it had not won the war and could not hope to impose a victor's peace. By restoring Sandwich's authority to conclude a treaty without Austrian concurrence, the government signaled its unwillingness to let Austria veto a peace that served London's needs. France therefore chose finally to deal with London rather than Vienna. When the Venetian ambassador at Paris spoke of "the predominance and superiority of France and England in the affairs of Europe" at the opening of July 1748, he was referring to their monopoly of the power to make peace.[22] Maurice of Saxony's army and Lord Anson's navy had brought Europe to this pass.

Between the last week in August and the middle of October everything finally fell into place at Aix-la-Chapelle. The culminating sequence of events required the crafting of four interlocking and critical compromises, the first treating the claims of Piedmont-Sardinia, the second dealing with the claims of Spain, the third imposing a chronological asymmetry on the process of restitution, and the fourth involving the status of the Barrier. Although it is impossible to date these compromises precisely, it is easy to discern their structures. The first brought Austria and Britain back into a muted cooperation with each other, and thus, despite the visibility of portents of future problems, the arrangement showed that the Anglo-Austrian alliance had not yet decayed beyond repair. The second critical compromise was struck between the two great belligerent camps. It removed the last major wartime issue between hostile (in distinction to nominally allied) powers and thus cleared the path to a final treaty. The third critical compromise afforded France the assurance it needed that, in evacuating its troops from the Low Countries, it would not abandon its leverage with Britain, whose compliance with the American terms could be neither signaled nor confirmed for months. And the fourth critical compromise removed the last obstacle to French troop withdrawals from the occupied Austrian Netherlands. Of such designs are treaties wrought when none has swept the field.

The climactic period began when, toward the end of August, Piedmont-Sardinia suddenly raised three new demands at Aix-la-Chapelle. Britain, hoping to salvage some of the honor it had lost at Charles Emmanuel's court through its complicity in the preliminary treaty, allowed itself to be associated with Piedmont-Sardinia's aspirations. Matters remained at this pass into the second week in September. But then on 13 September Kaunitz received two instructions from home, unexpectedly authorizing him to accept a single unified treaty and to concede to Turin's first (and least important) demand, which strengthened Charles Emmanuel's grasp on his remaining Worms winnings. Two motives account for Vienna's volte-face. In immediate terms Austria was responding to Britain's renewed threat that it might be obliged to sign a treaty that Austria declared unacceptable. More broadly, Maria Theresa was now unspeakably sick of what she would soon style "a so bloody and tenacious war."[23] The letter of September signaled her recognition that what had been done at Dresden in December 1745 and at Aix-la-Chapelle in April 1748 could not be undone. With this concession from Kaunitz it became possible for Sandwich to abandon his support of other Piedmontese demands. A stunned Chavanne accused Austria and the

Maritime Powers of plotting "to hold Your Majesty [Charles Emmanuel] in dependence."[24] But Piedmont-Sardinia was isolated in its disappointment. For with these two concessions the first critical compromise was effected: Vienna resigned its claims to the western Parmesan in favor of Turin, and Britain resigned all advocacy of any additional Piedmontese pretensions.

France was pleased at the outcome of the Anglo-Austrian compromise. It meant that neither Genoa nor Spain was to be unexpectedly affronted by a resurgent Worms alliance. Attention could now be turned to a second unre-solved issue—the peculiar matter of determining the duration of Britain's nonuse of its commercial rights in Spanish America—and even though France was not a protagonist in this particular dispute, Saint-Séverin had evinced no inclination to allow a medial number between four and fifteen to be bandied about. When the resolution of Piedmont-Sardinia's claims left the issue of nonuse standing alone, Britain was suddenly under enormous pres-sure to concede the point. Its arguments for a longer term of years were juridically suspect. Moreover, if Britain chose to insist that the duration of nonuse was a matter of fundamental importance, then it risked forfeiting its hopes for weaning Spain from France. Happily for London, there was a way to save a margin of face. Britain and the United Provinces wanted to enhance in some small degree the chance that Austria and Piedmont-Sardinia might some day recover the lands they were ceding to Don Philip. For that reason, among others, they had endorsed delimiting the prince's inheritance-worthy offspring to male children alone. Don Philip already had a son. There was no reason to suspect he would not have more. The matter thus seemed close to moot. And so, reluctantly but deliberately, France and Spain agreed to the addition of the adjective "male" to the clause that treated eventualities for the new principality. Britain in turn accepted defining the term of nonuse at four years' duration.

To understand the third critical compromise, we need to recall that Cape Breton Island lay far across the sea. Since France was evacuating the Low Countries in return for Britain's departure from Louisbourg, and since everyone—France included—wanted to clear the Netherlands of foreign troops as quickly as possible, it was necessary to devise a mechanism whereby France could be confident that, having complied with its own oblig-ation, it would receive Cape Breton in due course. Without such assurance, France ran the risk of giving up its chief trophy and learning months later that Britain had reneged. The solution was simplicity itself. France could acquire the requisite assurance by holding British hostages as tokens of Britain's good faith. Once Britain had complied with the terms of the treaty, the hostages could return home. (Such was the spirit of the age—or the fatigue of the war—that no one would conceive that Britain might prefer to sacrifice hostages rather than surrender a fortress.) Two young volunteer peers, handsomely provided for by the British government, soon arrived in France. Like Belle-Isle in Britain, they then discovered that the life of the high-born hostage can be thoroughly diverting.

The last issue requiring resolution was the identity of the army—the Dutch or the Austrians—to whom the French should hand over the fortresses in the Low Countries that they had occupied. From France's point of view the matter was immaterial. But the Pragmatic Allies were in disarray on the matter. Count Kaunitz wanted the limitations imposed on Austrian sovereignty by the Barrier treaty definitively removed. The Bentincks on the other hand lobbied on behalf of the maintenance of the Barrier Treaty. Caught in the middle, the British tried to extract benefit from embarrassment by striking the stance of mediator. During the first two weeks of October, they succeeded in transacting a compromise, from which both the Austrians and the Dutch could draw modest satisfaction. Insofar as all parties agreed that the treaty should recognize the empress-queen's sovereignty in the Netherlands while referring specifically to neither the Barrier Treaty nor the question of duties, the compromise suited Austrian interests. Insofar as all parties concurred in identifying the Dutch as the people to whom the French would in fact relinquish the fortresses, the compromise suited Dutch interests. With this compromise the final impediment to peace had been swept away, and after two summarizing meetings at Bentinck's residence—"the Court of Holland," as it was styled—on 9 and 10 October 1748 the French and British came to terms.

A week later, on 18 October 1748, only two days short of the eighth anniversary of Charles VI's death, the accredited plenipotentiaries of Louis XV, George II, and the States General affixed their signatures to the document of peace. The text they signed is known as the Treaty of Aix-la-Chapelle. Two days later Spain's envoy acceded to the treaty. Masones's brief delay signaled Spain's annoyance that Don Philip had been, in Spain's eyes, short-changed. But Carvajal revealed Madrid's truer opinion when he congratulated Huescar that Spain was "at peace and free of troubles and ambushes. It is most excellent, considering the circumstances."[25] On 23 October Austria's representative gave his concurrence. Kaunitz was not pleased with the treaty, and so he approved of his recent orders to delay accession and thereby to demonstrate "that except out of necessity we do not take an interest in so wicked, deficient, and (like its preliminaries) monstrous and in many parts even more vexing work."[26] Piedmont-Sardinia was even slower to accept the unpleasant fact. Charles Emmanuel was profoundly irritated that the treaty involved a partial repudiation of Worms. Only after representatives of the first four signatories concluded a convention on 25 October that committed them to enforcing the treaty even if Turin held out did the king yield to reason. On 7 November Chavanne gave a formal accession. Even as the oak leaf finally falls, so too had peace finally come.

The definitive treaty decreed a settlement very similar to the one outlined in the preliminary treaty. The general principle was still one of restitution. The chief exception was still the creation of a principality for Don Philip in northern Italy, comprised of Parma, Piacenza, and Guastalla and inheritable by male heirs. The term of Britain's nonuse of its trading rights was set at four years. Recognition for the Pragmatic Sanction (as that patent was modified by the treaty itself) and for Prussian claims to Silesia and Klodzko remained in the document. There were two interesting omissions. First, all references to the order of the Golden Fleece were expunged: it had proved impossible to reconcile Austrian and Spanish claims to the grandmastership of the order. Second, the acknowledgment that Francis I was Holy Roman Emperor also disappeared, for Maria Theresa had decided that French recognition of her husband's title was irrelevant and her pursuit of it demeaning. Counterbalancing the omissions were five substantive additions. The first added the Treaty of Vienna of 1738 to the list of pacts reaffirmed by the current treaty. The effect of this addition was to provide further recognition for the Bourbons' claim to Naples. The other four additions all dealt with the technical problems of implementing the restitutions. They fixed a timetable (six weeks after the exchange of ratifications), specified what the occupying armies were allowed to do until required to surrender the territories they held, imposed on Britain the obligation of supplying hostages to assure compliance, and called for commissioners from the contracting states to deal with the various disputes that a wholesale swapping of territories seemed likely to precipitate.

The formal exchange of ratifications occurred between 19 November and 6 December 1748, triggering the implementation of the various withdrawals, relinquishings, releases, and swaps that comprised the restitutions. Spain immediately opened its ports to British ships, and Austria promptly received French goods. Commissioners gathered at Brussels to oversee the details of the settlement in the Low Countries. Not everything went smoothly, however. France, as loyal to its allies in the nascent era of peace as it had been in the defunct era of war, refused to hand over the capital of the Austrian Netherlands until Austria had restored the Modenese enclaves in Hungary to their rightful sovereign and had reimbursed the Genoese gentlemen whose wealth it had confiscated. Only on 28 January 1749 did the French finally depart from Brussels. Italian exchanges occurred even later. Browne, Belle-Isle, and La Mina began meeting in Nice on 29 November 1748 to thrash through the problems. The general terms of an exchange of prisoners and a distribution of captured artillery were readily accepted, a conference held on 21 January 1749 settled the details, Don Philip assumed command in Parma on 18 March, and by the end of the same month every bit of western European territory—both in Italy and the Low Countries—was in the hands of its rightful owner. The sense of relief was universal. "God spare us from ever seeing them again," a Savoyard abbé sighed as the Spanish departed, and he spoke for the victims of occupation everywhere.[27]

"There has been no Congress," the abbé Mably later wrote, "where affairs have been treated with less patience and maturity. . . . To speed the peace people were content with sketching out the topics."[28] Consequently, Mably concluded, the peace created by the Treaty of Aix-la-Chapelle was brief. In fact, strictly speaking, there was no congress at all, for the negotiators never gathered together, save at concerts and balls. Instead, responsibility for devising a treaty fell essentially to the French and the British. And they proceeded in an unusual fashion. Rather than dividing the peacemaking into topical components, the central negotiators treated the various issues as a bundle, sometimes emphasizing one element, sometimes another, but never totally segregating them. The indictment is that the negotiators became prisoners of their own little world—their own concerns and hopes, their own sense of momentum and urgency, their own readings of their colleagues. The criticism is unfair. Some quarrels lay beyond the hope of human remediation in 1748. There is no way, for example, that the negotiators at Aix-la-Chapelle could have extinguished Austria's belief that it had been plundered of Silesia. There is no way they could have resolved the nascent Anglo-French contention for empire. Moreover, at the core of the policy of each of the major protagonists there lay a fundamental ambivalence. The British wavered between threatening and conciliating Austria, uncertain about which tack was likelier to make an ally tractable. The French vacillated between an Austrian and a British peace, unclear about which option dealt with a fuller range of French needs. And the Austrians alternated between a French and a British future, unsure of the implications that each alternative carried for their security. As long as these fundamental strategic matters were unresolved in the capitals of Europe, the peacemakers at Aix were forced to confine themselves to the concrete and immediate issue of ending the belligerence. To have expected more of them is to ask for what the world has never known: the war to end all wars.

21

The Balance Sheet

AN OVERVIEW OF THE WAR

The war that lasted 2,865 days began when the young king of Prussia, barely half a year on the throne and incautiously eager for fame, launched a snatch-and-run operation to deprive the young and even less experienced archduchess of Austria of the province of Silesia. It expanded from a regional clash into a global conflict because Frederick II managed to align his own ambitions with the aspirations of a variety of national leaders and because he contrived to exploit the tensions along two of the fundamental political fault lines of Europe. The yoking of ambitions was largely adventitious. Frederick did not know, for example, that Marshal Belle-Isle hungered for glory or that Lord Carteret and the Marquis d'Argenson would come to power as friends of Prussia, and he knew only in a general sense that the royal couple of Spain nursed broad designs for their children. But the broader cleavages of Europe were commonplaces to the king and essential to his project. The first pitted Britain against Spain in a contention for imperial advantage. The second pitted France against the Habsburg realm in a contention for dominance in Europe. Frederick knew that although he had the power to grab Silesia from the far larger Austrian state, he might not have the power to retain it single-handedly once the young ruler in Vienna was finally able to mobilize her far-flung army. He calculated that he could succeed only within the arena of a vaster war. It did not matter to him whether Britain or Spain wound up as his ally, whether he would find himself helping Austria defend itself against France or helping France humble Austria. All that was important was that an attack on Austria should trigger a broader conflict. And because there were other, smaller states intruding on the scene, each with its own territorial ambitions, Frederick was confident that his own rupture of the peace would prompt someone else to break it too. This confidence was not misplaced; before 1741 ended almost all of Europe was at war.

From one perspective the war of the 1740s was really four separate con-
flicts. The first took place in Germany, where Prussia decisively defeated
Austria. In German history this conflict is treated under the rubric of the first
two Silesian wars. The second occurred in Italy, where after much loss of life
Piedmont-Sardinia and Spain made minor territorial gains. This conflict is
sometimes styled the War of the Alps. The third was waged in the Low
Countries, where France, after a slow start, occupied most of the Austrian
Netherlands and made inroads against the Dutch republic. The final conflict
occurred on the high seas, where Britain, also after a slow start, asserted its
dominance over the combined naval might of France and Spain. To view the
belligerence of the decade as something other than a single entity is, however,
to miss the point. The four conflicts were bound not merely by synchrony
but also by military, financial, and diplomatic links. When Austria was compelled to recall its army from Alsace in 1744 to protect Bohemia, the military
connection between the German and the Atlantic wars was underlined.
When Austria poured troops across the Alps in the months after the Treaty
of Dresden, the link between Italy and Germany was highlighted. The financial linkages are similarly clear, especially in the case of Britain. As paymaster
of the anti-Bourbon alliances, Britain used its resources to impose its own set
of theater priorities on Austria. Since London's money was more readily
available for campaigns against France than for campaigns against Prussia,
Austria was compelled to adjust its own strategic thinking to Britain's.
Diplomatic linkages emerged whenever negotiators tried to extricate Europe
from the war, for the balanced reassignment of real estate that was the prerequisite of any ratification of peace presupposed territorial equivalencies
across theaters. The most famous example of this presupposition was
Britain's insistence that Louisbourg would not be returned to Versailles
unless France left the Low Countries. But it should not be forgotten that
Spain had its own plan for the Low Countries—using them as a lever to pry
loose a broader principality for Don Philip—and that Austria proposed
swapping the Austrian Netherlands for Bavaria. The hoary assumption that
sovereigns could exchange peoples and places to suit their own interests
reigned with undiminished force in the 1740s.

The interested observer can learn many things from a close study of the
War of the Austrian Succession. For example, the two states that profited
most from the war—Prussia and Piedmont-Sardinia—were led by soldier-
kings. It is also notable that the most important battle of the war was neither
the largest (Laffeld) nor the most celebrated (Fontenoy) but the first. Had
Mollwitz resulted in a defeat for Prussia, the war would probably have been
confined to Germany, and the subsequent course of German history would

probably have been significantly different. Thus Mollwitz was like the even smaller battle that occurred thirty-seven years later at Saratoga. It is again notable that a war undertaken by France to eviscerate Austria—Belle-Isle sought Vienna's "annihilation"—should have had so few major engagements between French and Austrian armies.[1] In fact, although Austrian units added to the ranks of allied armies at Dettingen, Fontenoy, Rocoux, and Laffeld while French troops constituted an important constituent of the Bourbon forces at Piacenza, only in the dueling in Upper Austria, Bavaria, and Bohemia did armies predominantly Austrian fight armies predominantly French. Finally, it is notable that for the second time in as many decades a war in western and central Europe was hastened to its close by the approach of troops from Russia. Having established its superiority to Sweden, the giant of the east was beginning to make its might felt in Versailles and London.

As an object lesson in the old military truth that overextension will be punished the War of the Austrian Succession can hardly be surpassed. France reached too far into Bohemia in 1742 and could not retrieve an exposed army. By advancing beyond the Rhine and the Tiber in 1744, Austria left itself vulnerable to an attack in the rear. Prussia plunged into Bohemia in 1744 and promptly found its army engulfed in a sea of civilian hostility. Although the Bourbons seized much of northern Italy in 1745, they were forced to relinquish it the following year when their attenuated lines of communication proved too brittle. Austria committed the symmetrical error late in 1746, pushing into Provence and then discovering that it could not guard its rear and flanks. The only campaigns that succeeded were those directed by the Prussians against Silesia and by the French against the Low Countries. The common elements in these campaigns are basic: both confined themselves to adjacent targets, and neither left vulnerabilities in its wake. For a conflict that has struck many observers as indecipherable, the War of the Austrian Succession displays an awesome capacity to abide by the rules.

It was not for want of advocates that peace was kept so long at bay. Friends it had in great number—Walpole and Fleury, Van der Heim and Gilles, Ormea and Ensenada, even Frederick and Maurice. But each advocate qualified his advocacy with stipulations. And behind all the hopes and conditions there lurked the unsettling truth that peace could not be achieved until every single combatant was willing to support it. The war might have ended in 1741 had France not chosen to expand a local conflict into a continental one. It might have ended in 1742 had Austria not been bent upon securing compensation. In 1743 the stumbling block was Britain, eagerly forging a broad alliance and unwilling to forgo testing its efficacy. In 1744 the chief problem was Prussia, determined to reenter the war and steal more

ᐟfrom Austria. In 1745 the Treaty of Dresden offered the combatants a splendid opportunity to withdraw, but neither Spain nor Austria was prepared to accept the status quo in Italy, and Britain, though under assault, was unwilling to consider surrendering Louisbourg. The obstacle in 1746 was Austria again, moving to the offensive and seemingly on the verge of success. In 1747 Britain reemerged as the chief hindrance, fearful that the Pragmatic Alliance could not survive a controversial peace and preferring war to isolation. In wartime it lies within the competence of any major power to veto peace.

Against this shifting background of an enduring resistance to peace, the men deputed by their respective governments to wring a settlement from the turmoil labored at their task. Almost from the beginning of the war there were official representatives of combatant states seeking a negotiated peace. From 1743 on I doubt that a month passed without some proposal for peace being tendered in some belligerent capital. More significantly, I calculate that during about 60 percent of the duration of the war active negotiations for peace—whether at Paris or Vienna, Berlin or Breslau, Worms or The Hague, Breda or Aix-la-Chapelle—were in progress. This was not a war that lingered because no one tried to stop it. It was a belligerence, as most are, that acquired a life of its own.

Not surprisingly, therefore, the war was a great demolisher of dreams. Even Frederick II, the figure who most clearly approximates a victor, reaped a fair portion of pain, for his hopes of 1744 were blighted in the ill-considered Bohemian campaign. Yet the king's story is success itself when compared to the frustrations of others. Marshal Belle-Isle hoped to make France the dominator of Europe. Before the war was over he spent time in British captivity and lost his beloved brother in peripheral Alpine skirmishing. Maria Theresa embodied adamance amid asthenia. But her vision of an Austria vindicated and recompensed crumbled beneath the blows of Prussian arms, Piedmontese diplomacy, and British indifference. Lord Carteret hoped to enlist all of non-Bourbon Europe into a coalition that could begin the selective dismemberment of France. Before the war was over he saw his coalition evaporate, his appointment disappear, and his career as a celebrated British tippler commence. The Marquis d'Argenson plotted a reorganization of Italy, a diminution of Spanish influence at Versailles, and the establishment of a beneficent French hegemony over Europe. He broke under the weight of botched Italian negotiations, mounting Spanish hostility, and a general rejection of the idea that beneficence can be a principle of foreign policy. Elizabeth Farnese dreamed of crushing the house of Savoy in her campaign to make Don Philip a major Italian prince. When the war ended she sat separated from power, a bitter spectator of an Italy that, though home to her princeling son, was more than ever subject to the influence of still expanding Piedmont-Sardinia. The point is clear. Those who presumed to try to bend the power of war to their own purposes in the 1740s absorbed one of history's enduring lessons: war is the great chastener of pride.

THE INTERNATIONAL MATRIX

The abiding significance of the War of the Austrian Succession lies in a negative fact: it frustrated France's hope of establishing a hegemony over major portions of non-Bourbon Europe. This hope assumed two forms over the course of the belligerence. In its earlier guise it focused on Germany. When Marshal Belle-Isle schemed to bring France into the war, his intention was precisely to install someone beholden to France on the throne of the Holy Roman Empire. Then, when the French discovered that German soil was peculiarly barren, they shifted their attention northwestward. In this later guise, and with Count Maurepas as chief planner, France envisioned replacing the Protestant house of Hanover with the Catholic house of Stuart on the throne of Britain. But Britain was no more receptive to armies bearing French dreams than Germany had been, and by mid-1746 France's goals had finally shrunk to the more modest proportion of serving as Europe's disinterested arbiter that the Marquis d'Argenson had oddly placed at the heart of his foreign policy. Historians have long appreciated the implications of the thwarting of French ambitions in the days of Louis XIV and Napoleon Bonaparte. That Europe repulsed the challenge to its equilibrium in the reign of Louis XV should pass neither unremarked nor uncelebrated.

The truth about France's ambitions leads to a corollary truth: Lord Carteret had a sounder understanding of what was at stake in the 1740s than Charles Emmanuel III, Count Bartenstein, or Jacob Gilles. Carteret's great shortcoming lay not in his powers of diagnosis but in his choice of prescriptions. To contend with France on the battlefield of France's own choosing — that is, to oppose Bourbon military might with anti-Bourbon military might — was folly. To suppose that all of the non-Bourbon states would gladly suppress their mutual distrusts in order to collaborate in an anti-Bourbon coalition was naive. It thus fell to Carteret's successors to discover the better remedy, by stumbling into a naval and economic policy that compensated for France's armed power and by understanding that the best they could hope for from Prussia was disengagement. But Carteret bequeathed to his successors a sound understanding of the danger threatening equilibrated Europe. It was this view which in turn decreed that not until France should subside into more traditional and limited goals — goals that were susceptible to compromise through diplomacy—would it be possible to work seriously for peace.

By concluding in what amounted to a standoff, with France triumphant on land and Britain triumphant at sea, the War of the Austrian Succession demonstrated that a Britain bent upon belligerence with France had at last found its métier. The span from 1689 to 1815 is often regarded as the Second Hundred Years' War. Throughout this period France possessed Europe's mightiest army. British leaders understood from the beginning that their kingdom's insular status afforded it valuable protection against Gallic legions, and they learned in the opening chapters of the protracted duel that the financial resilience of the kingdom allowed it to mobilize continental hirelings to do much of the actual fighting. But only slowly did the British discover that besting France need not entail sending great numbers of British-sponsored troops against French armies. Rather, France could be paralyzed if Britain could deny to the French effective use of the seas and access to their empire. The great vindication for this strategy still lay ahead, in the crushing defeat that Britain would administer to the muscle-bound Bourbon kingdom in the Seven Years' War. But Louisbourg, Cape Ortegal, and Ouessant hinted at what the next war held in store. Almost without Europe's cognizance, London was becoming a global military power.

Although the war left little doubt that Britain and France stood apart from the other powers of Europe as nations with global interests, it also unsettled the traditional alliances in which these two powers figured so prominently. Indeed, this development was precisely a consequence of the mounting disparities between the expansive visions of Britain and France and the more regional focuses of their allies. But it became visible only when discontented satellites began to explore the possibility that by changing sides they might secure more sympathetic partners. There was even a measure of symmetry in the development. In one camp sat a bitter Austria, reckoning strength almost solely in terms of territorial possessions, and riveting its gaze on the Hohenzollern kingdom to the north. Since its traditional ally, Great Britain, showed little enthusiasm for confining Prussia, Austria became receptive to French overtures, and in 1756, when war next broke out in Europe, Austria and France were united as allies against Prussia and Britain. Meanwhile, in the other camp sat a discontented Spain, unable to share France's excitement for German and Flemish matters, having little stake in South Asian concerns, and coveting allies with whom its trade interests were complementary rather than competitive. While the War of the Austrian Succession was still being fought, Anglophile ministers whom Ferdinand VI had appointed undertook approaches to Britain, and in 1750 Madrid and London resolved outstanding commercial disputes. As a consequence of this rapprochement, when hostilities resumed in 1756 Spain chose the path of neutrality, disavowing obligations to France. The War of the Austrian Succession was a powerful solvent of alliances.

In addition to rearranging Austria's alliance structure in the west, the war also refurbished Vienna's alliance structure in the east. In this region, where Europe slowly dissolved into Asia, Russia stood as Austria's large but quarrelsome ally. Despite the treaty of 1726, St. Petersburg spent most of the War of the Austrian Succession disappointing Vienna's hopes. The conclusion of the Treaty of St. Petersburg in 1746, however, ended this era of rancor and launched the two states into a long period of cooperation. Although Russia was a rising power while Austria had begun its long recessional, both states were traditional in outlook and had many interests potentially in common. Russia needed insurance against a possible Prussian attack; Austria needed a powerful ally to counter the weakening of its positions in Germany (against Prussia) and Italy (against Piedmont-Sardinia). Brought together as a consequence of Alexis Bestuzhev's lobbying and Bartenstein's forbearance, the two states soon discovered that their mutual interests extended far beyond anti-Prussianism. An Austrian rescript of 1748 states that "similar perils confront both lands—namely, that both have unjust, arrogant, and faithless enemies and false and . . . confused friends."[2] In 1756 Austria and Russia joined to make war on Prussia and Britain, and during the next hundred years they cooperated in the dismemberment of Poland, the resistance to revolutionary France, and the suppression of central European nationalisms. Not until the Great War did the two imperial states completely repudiate cooperation and make war against each other. The outcome of that cataclysm underlined precisely how vital the Vienna-St. Petersburg axis had been to each: by 1919 Russia was revolutionized and the Austrian realm splintered.

In Germany the war upset a precarious but long-standing equilibrium. The central element in that balance was a ranking of states that placed Austria in a status of indefeasible preeminence while positioning a clutch of smaller states—Bavaria, Prussia, and Saxony—as rivals jockeying for the second slot. But what made sense in 1648 was far less incontrovertible by 1740. Despite the breadth of its holdings, Austria was a state awash with trouble. Meanwhile, Prussia had broken free from the pack of contenders, and by virtue of a series of able rulers, a commitment to bureaucratic efficiency, and the cultivation of a superb army, the Prussian state had become the first plausible German challenger to Austria's dominance in central Europe. In the War of the Austrian Succession the kingdom of Prussia, with bold (and unprincipled) leadership and a measure of luck, used its accumulating advantages to make good its challenge. But in doing so it of necessity shattered the received understanding of how Germany operated. Where once there had been no question about which state was supreme in the Teutonic world, the new order took the conflict for supremacy between Vienna and Berlin as its axiom.

If the war brought disequilibrium to Germany, it brought a profound balance to Italy. The territorial shifts that came as a consequence of the war were important, but the deeper meaning of the conflict lay not in transfers of sovereignty but in lessons of allegiance and interest. The War of the Spanish Succession had seen Austria try to make Italy a Habsburg dependency. The War of the Polish Succession had seen France try to drive the Habsburgs out of the peninsula. The joint result of the two struggles was the establishment of an equilibrium. The effect of the War of the Austrian Succession was to confirm and harden this result. It is true that by assuring Don Philip his claims to Parma and Piacenza, the war extended the Bourbon family empire by a small degree. Far more important, however, were the return of Piedmont-Sardinia to the anti-Bourbon camp and the election of the duke of Tuscany to the dignity of Holy Roman Emperor. Both developments served to define limits to Bourbon ambitions in Italy by intimating that any further Bourbon assault upon the status quo would be met by an Austro-Piedmontese riposte. Not until revolution engulfed France in the final decade of the eighteenth century would external forces again intrude upon the tranquility of Italy.

THE REVOLUTIONS

It is not surprising that war, inherently a destructive force, should ravage even the subtle bondings of society. The ordinary activities of the vast majority of people are rooted in custom. We have expectations about how others will behave, assumptions about how public decisions are arrived at, habits of obedience or initiative. War disorders these customs. It disrupts patterns of life, imposes fiscal burdens, calls people from their allotted tasks, and inflicts pain. Human beings can endure a significant measure of dislocation: we are adaptable and tough. But at some point, for societies as for individuals, a limit is reached. In its commoner form this upwelling of wrath focuses on an intruding foreign foe. In Savoy the wrath fell on the Spanish, in Moravia on the Prussians, in Piedmont on the French, in Liguria on the Austrians. But in its rarer form the surge of rage can turn inward, seeking nothing less than an overhaul of institutions of governance that have been indicted for irrelevance or oppression. Such surges we are accustomed to style revolutions, and the War of the Austrian Succession was the stage for four: the protracted and convoluted struggle for the command of Corsica, the quixotic effort to free Scotland from English rule, the bloody uprising of the Genoese against oligarchs held to be traitorous, and the anachronistic appeal by the commercial Dutch to models from the past. No symptom of the disintegrative force of war is more striking than its capacity to overturn political orders.

It is instructive, therefore, to analyze the revolutions that attended Europe's years of belligerence, and a fruitful point of departure is a study of the Scottish and Corsican situations. In the large view the revolutions in the two countries arose from the same set of circumstances. In each the power of the clans and clan leaders was extensive and directed toward the maintenance of older and deeply seated traditions governing social organization, the administration of justice, and the appropriateness of violence. Each was ruled by a more powerful neighboring state, and in each there was a sense that the imperial power misgoverned in the dependency. Moreover, there were similarities between the two imperial relationships. In each case a vigorously commercial and visibly wealthy nation (England and Genoa) exercised authority over an overwhelmingly rural and desperately poor nation (Scotland and Corsica). This is a powerful parallel: in both Corsica and Scotland the tradition and purpose of clan rule was being challenged by absentee governors whose methods were viewed as illegitimate and whose aims were seen as predatory.

Clearly there are important points at which similarity breaks down. Scotland was more socially diversified than Corsica, and hence support for the revolt was less widespread in Scotland. Corsica shared a religious confession with Genoa, whereas many in Scotland scorned the Church of England as fiercely as they contemned government from England. Scotland was not geographically isolated in the manner that Corsica was; thus it was far easier for England to send troops into Scotland than for Genoa to send them into Corsica. And reciprocally, the Corsicans were quicker than the Scots to use guerrilla techniques against their foes. Scotland sat on the edge of the European world, its fate of little concern to the powers of the center, while Corsica sat athwart Mediterranean trade lines and found its affairs scrutinized in Madrid, Versailles, Turin, and London. Above all, the Scots—or at least those who supported the revolt—had a clear leader in the scion of the dispossessed house of Stuart; the Corsicans were asked to choose among competing claimants for leadership, each of them operating with some important disabilities. The many differences give distinctive textures to the two revolts, explaining their separate courses, but they should not disguise the underlying similarities in origin. In both cases the leaders of a traditional rural society used the opportunity afforded by a general war to try to drive out their commercially energetic overlords.

The revolts in Genoa and the United Provinces were of a different stripe. Both states were republics, both were wealthy, and both depended upon trade for the winning and the maintaining of their wealth. Political power in both states rested with a patrician oligarchy. Because war was deemed to be inimical to trade, both initially turned to neutrality when their neighbors took up arms in the 1740s; both nevertheless became caught up in the belligerence. In both, the ensuing revolution was an urban phenomenon, triggered when the oligarchic rulers, already distrusted by the poor and weak, proved themselves unable to perform even the elementary governing task of protecting the homeland against foreign invasion. The revolutionaries in both cases began their protests by asserting that the defense of the homeland required a change in government. Quickly, however, their attention turned to domestic matters as well, and they began calling for a return to the putatively purer politics of the past. Further evolution occurred when, under the pressure of unfolding events, they found themselves forced to temper these historical arguments with bolder ideas that anticipated in peculiar and inexact ways the platforms of the great Atlantic revolutions that lay a generation or two ahead.

There were of course differences between the two republican uprisings. The Dutch tried to hide the fact that a change of government was being extorted by power, and in truth, from a technical point of view, they successfully conformed (although barely) to correct constitutional practice in installing the new regime; the Genoese on the other hand made no effort to disguise their resort to *force majeure* not only to oust the invaders but then to establish a new and parallel government. Moreover, the Dutch revolt was virtually bloodless while the Genoese revolution became celebrated for its sanguinary character. But even when these differences are tallied, it is the similarities that dominate the scene. In both republics a patrician class, already suspected of practicing the politics of personal pelf, compounded its failings by allowing a foreign foe to invade; in both cases the middling and poorer orders then seized command of the state, albeit temporarily, and tentatively explored the kinds of solutions that in the final two decades of the century the Americans and the French would be able to craft with greater confidence. If the troubles in Corsica and Scotland took their origin in the communal solidarity of a precommercial society, the troubles in Genoa and the United Provinces took their origin from the tendency of commerce to foster aspirations of liberty. In short, the revolutions in Corsica and Scotland were hostile to the social and economic forces that were changing the

European world; the revolutions in Genoa and the United Provinces were expressions of those selfsame forces.

CALCULATING THE CARNAGE

War kills. Much else can be said about this human enterprise, but in the final reckoning the abiding truth about war is that it is lethal. In the War of the Austrian Succession, belligerence killed in a wide variety of ways. Soldiers died in battle—abruptly if decapitated by an artillery missile, slowly if felled by a bayonet thrust and left helpless while blood ebbed away. They died in the weeks and months after a battle, as sepsis exacted its toll from a world that did not understand infection. They died in camps far from the front, where the spread of contagious diseases was checked only by acquired immunities. They died on marches, where exhaustion, foul weather, and penurious rations were their frequent companions. They even died while trying to escape from the armies that had compelled their service, for neither a suspicious civilian populace nor a wrathful commander was inclined to be kindly toward a trooper who had left his assignment. And the fatal effects of war were felt far beyond the boundaries of the standing armies of the age. Civilians died when armies fought in their neighborhoods. They died when armies encamped in their vicinity and began the ruthless requisitioning that they needed in order to keep themselves in fighting trim. They died when they were unfortunate enough to live in a town that a commander chose to defend. They died when they were unfortunate enough to live in a town that another commander chose to occupy. They died when the trampling of boots interrupted a growing season at a crucial moment, leaving the region without food for the next year. They even died when armies en route to distant theaters left the infectious diseases they carried with them as memorials of their visits. Though scarcely exhaustive, this list should manage to suggest the range of ways in which war could be lethal. As Frederick II wryly noted, "we somewhat forget what brotherly love is whenever we make war."[3]

Perspective in these matters remains important. Most studies suggest that when measured against the standards of bloodiness that other major wars in the seventeenth and eighteenth centuries set, the War of the Austrian Succession was not notably sanguinary. "My sentiments," Lord Stair wrote to Marshal Noailles after Dettingen, "are and always will be, to make war with all the generosity and all the humanity possible."[4] No battle in the war was as destructive of life as either Malplaquet, the most savage confrontation in the earlier War of the Spanish Succession, or Zorndorf, the bloodiest engagement of the later Seven Years' War. And these two eighteenth-century wars were, in their turn, less slaughterous than the fabled belligerences of the preceding century, when religious ideology and military entrepreneurialism combined to make warfare a scourge almost beyond belief. But even allowing for perspective, one must finally come away from a study of the war of the 1740s with a profound sense of humankind's capacity for evil. A Russian historian, Boris Z. Urlanis, has made a study of battle fatalities in modern wars. I calculate that he applied an inappropriate multiplier to his gross figures and hence exaggerated the number of deaths from combat in the War of the Austrian Succession. But even by my more conservative reckoning fully 100,000 soldiers lost their lives as a consequence of military engagements in the war.[5] That figure is grim as it stands; and yet it is only a starting point for any calculation of carnage.

For the havoc wrought by war can never be confined to members of the fighting forces. The Spanish treated occupied Savoy as if it were a satrapy, despoiling its lands with requisition gangs, impoverishing its people with ever-mounting tax assessments, and intimidating the restless with a policy of burning houses. When a "delegation general" was formed, the people took to styling it a "desolation general."[6] The British army in the Rhineland sometimes pillaged churches, looted villages, and stole cattle; rather more regularly British naval detachments brought seaside villages into submission by landing demolition parties; and when it came to dealing with Jacobite Scots, the British armed forces resorted to methods that sometimes approached savagery. The Prussians were famous for the dispatch with which they could administer exemplary brutalities in an occupied territory; a French observer expressed the general sense of dismay at Prussian severity when he remarked that "not since the Goths"—he chose his parallel with Gallic appositeness—"has war been waged in this fashion."[7] But the grimmest example of war's capacity to make the defenseless its victims arose along the Ligurian coast, where in 1747 a vindictive Austrian army laid siege to Genoa. Irregular troops conducted a campaign worthy of eastern Europe: they burned villages, carved up luckless citizens, and castrated priests. Before the six-month campaign was broken off, 24,000 people—the vast majority of them noncombatants—had perished of hunger, disease, or murder. It would be misleading to suggest that brutal behavior by soldiers was either typical or widely condoned. But it was not infrequent, especially among units of irregulars, and if it was rarely authorized, it was even more rarely punished. Military commanders understood that they had important tasks to accomplish; if civilians could help them achieve their goals, then it seemed perfectly appropriate to enlist such aid, even if it was involuntary and secured at the price of lives.

In light of the uncertainty surrounding casualty figures for a group of individuals as readily defined and counted as combatants are, it may seem folly to guess—no other word will do—at the casualty figures for a group as amorphous as the noncombatants. And yet no calculation of the cost of the war that ignores the fates of civilians can be deemed adequate. What makes this task particularly intricate for the historian of the 1740s is the fact that war was not the only scourge sweeping Europe during the decade. There is also the impact of climatic aberrancies to be reckoned with. Bad weather begot famine, which in turn begot disease. Those whom hunger weakened illness later dispatched. The problem for the historian is to find a way to separate those deaths attributable essentially to war from those deaths attributable chiefly to the climate. It is no easy task of analysis. Yet an American historian, Myron P. Gutmann, has proposed an apposite method, and although his results apply only to a portion of one theater, they are suggestive. He concludes that dislocation associated with war was a major rather than a peripheral contributor to the periodic crises of subsistence that wracked the continent in the eighteenth century. If Gutmann's line of analysis is valid for all of Europe, then it is clear that many of the deaths that might at first be attributable to the vagaries of the weather should in fact be attributed to belligerence.[8] Though I can do no more than advance impressions, they coincide with Gutmann's conclusions. I think it likely that during the course of the war perhaps four times as many noncombatants as combatants died as a direct consequence of military activities. Or, to put the matter quantitatively, to the 100,000 men in arms who perished as a consequence of the war must be added an additional 400,000 civilians if we are to have a sound sense of the scope of lives lost. We are thus led to the stark conclusion that the War of the Austrian Succession killed half a million people.

To the vast majority of people in eighteenth-century Europe, war was a calamity, for it added a new and weighty burden to lives already struggling against immiseration. An observer from Geneva caught this truth by noting in 1747 that "when one sees the purposes of a war as bloody and expensive as this one, one cannot avoid saying that princes are cruel and deceitful."[9] For most people this sense of senselessness was complemented by a sense of helplessness. The most prolific political writer of the generation lamented that "we have only the liberty of secretly contemplating the evils before our eyes, somewhat as physicians contemplate the diseases of humankind, without being able either to cure them or to prevent people from dying."[10] It has been said that nothing serves the cause of peace more effectively than a taste of war, and the conflict of the 1740s bears witness to the aptness of the dictum; by 1744 almost everyone was a proponent of peace. Some of course had resisted the call for bellicosity from the beginning. But vindication of their judgment brought them scant solace. Sir Robert Walpole was, according to his son, "quite shocked at living to see how terribly his own conduct is justified."[11] And the very course of events—as if to prove that the gods of history savored irony—reserved places with such hopeful names as Holy Grounds (Campo Santo), Pale Red Church (Falkirk), and the High Mountain of Peace (Hohenfriedberg) for some of the most bloody engagements of the war. The final truth must be the first truth: War kills. For that reason if for no other I choose to end this study with the epigram that stood on the title page of the 1743 edition of Van Hoey's letters. It is the prayer that is ever apposite.

Da pacem, Domine, in diebus nostris.

■ NOTES ■

NOTES TO CHAPTER 1

1. Marquis de Vogüé, and Auguste Le Sourd, eds., *Campagnes de Jacques de Mercoyrol de Beaulieu, Capitaine au Régiment de Picardie (1743-1763)* (Paris: Librairie Renouard, 1915), p. 8.

2. The foregoing discussion is based on several works. The most prominent are: John Childs, *Armies and Warfare in Europe 1648-1789* (New York: Holmes and Meier, 1982); Spenser Wilkinson, *The Defence of Piedmont, 1742-1748* (Oxford: Oxford University Press, 1927); Christopher Duffy, *The Army of Frederick the Great* (London: David and Charles, 1974); Christopher Duffy, *The Army of Maria Theresa* (New York: Hippocrene, 1979); Jean Lambert Alphonse Colin, *Les campagnes de Maréchal de Saxe*, 3 vols. (Paris: Librairie Militaire R. Chapelot & Cie, 1901-1906); Olaf Groehler, *Die Kriege Friedrichs II.* (East Berlin: Deutscher Militärverlag, 1968); E. H. Skrine, *Fontenoy and Great Britain's Share in the War of the Austrian Succession* (Edinburgh: W. Blackwood and Sons, 1906); David Chandler, *The Art of Warfare in the Age of Marlborough* (London: B. T. Batsford, 1976); Andre Corvisier, *Armies and Societies in Europe, 1494-1789*, trans. Abigail T. Siddall (Bloomington, Ind.: Indiana University Press, 1979).

3. Charles Pierre Victor, Count Pajol, *Les guerres sous Louis XV*, vols. 2-3 (Paris: Formin-Diderot, 1883-84), III, 471.

4. Duffy, *Army of Frederick II*, pp. 139-40; Evan Charteris, *William Augustus, Duke of Cumberland: His Early life and Times (1721-1748)* (London: Edward Arnold, 1913), p. 196.

5. John L. Sutton, *The King's Honor and the King's Cardinal: The War of the Polish Succession* (Lexington, KY; University of Kentucky Press, 1980), p. 138.

6. Martin Van Creveld, *Supplying War: Logistics from Wallenstein to Patton* (Cambridge: Cambridge University Press, 1978).

7. John Creswell, *British Admirals of the Eighteenth Century: Tactics in Battle* (Hamden, Conn.: Archon Books, 1972), pp. 35-39 makes several of the points that follow.

8. Sir Herbert William Richmond, *The Navy in the War of 1739-48*, 3 vols. (Cambridge: Cambridge University Press, 1920), 3:86.

NOTES TO CHAPTER 2

1. *The Theatre of the Present War in the Netherlands and upon the Rhine* (London: J. Bindley, 1745), p. 11.

2. British Library, Additional Manuscripts 32814, fol. 204.

3. Victor-L. Tapié, "Contribution a l'étude des relations entre la France et l'Autriche avant la guerre de succession d'Autriche," in *Österreich und Europa: Festgabe für Hugo Hantsch zum 70. Geburtstag*, n.e. (Vienna: Verlag Styria, 1965), p. 148; Adolf Beer, "Holland und der österreichische Erbfolgekrieg," *Archiv für österreichische Geschichte* 46 (1871): 302; P.G.M. Dickson, "English Commercial Negotiations with Austria, 1737-1752," in *Statesmen, Scholars and Merchants*, ed. Anne Whitman et al. (Oxford: Oxford University Press, 1973), p. 96; Tapié, "Contribution," p. 142.

4. Albert, Duke of Broglie, *Frédéric II et Marie Thérèse, 1740-1742*, 2 vols. (Paris: Calman Levy, 1883), I: 241.

5. Carlo Baudi di Vesme, "Le pace di Aquisgrana (1748): una pagina di storia delle relazioni internazionali," *Bolletino storico-bibliografico subalpino* 66 (1968): 104.

6. Broglie, *Frédéric II et Marie Thérèse*, I: 231.

7. Jeremy Black, "Foreign Policy in the Age of Walpole," in *Britain in the Age of Walpole*, ed. Jeremy Black (New York: St. Martin's, 1984), p. 155.

8. John B. Owen, *The Rise of the Pelhams* (London: Methuen, 1957), p. 183.

9. Jeremy Black, "The Development of Anglo-Sardinia Relations in the First Half of the Eighteenth Century," *Studi piemontesi* 12 (1983): 59.

10. C. R. Andolenko, *Histoire de l'armée russe* (Paris: Flammarion, 1967), p. 59.

11. Broglie, *Frédéric II et Marie Thérèse*, I:82.

12. Arthur McCandless Wilson, *French Foreign Policy During the Administration of Cardinal Fleury, 1726-1743* (Cambridge, Mass.: Harvard University Press, 1936), p. 323.

13. Gustav Berthold Volz, "Die Politik Friedrichs des Grossen vor und nach seiner Thronbesteigung," *Historische Zeitschrift* 151 (1935): 500; Broglie, *Frédéric II et Marie Thérèse*, I: 62.

14. Gerhard Ritter, *Frederick the Great*, trans. by Peter Paret (Berkeley: University of California Press, 1974), p. 7.

NOTES TO CHAPTER 3

1. Josef Kallbrunner and Clemens Biener, eds., *Kaiserin Maria Theresias Politischen Testament* (Vienna: Verlag für Geschichte und Politik, 1952), p. 29.

2. Karl Theodore von Heigel, ed., "Die Correspondenz Karls VII. mit Josef Franz Graf von Seinsheim, 1738-1743," *Königlich Bayerischen Akademie der Wissenschaften. Abhandlungen der Historischen Klasse* vol. 14, part 1 (1879): 113. The French is as peculiar as the English.

3. Maurice Sautai, *Les préliminaires de la guerre de la succession d'Autriche* (Paris: Librairie Militaire R. Chapelot, 1907), p. 114.

4. Alfred, Cardinal Baudrillart, *Philippe V et la cour de France*, 5 vols. (Paris: Librairie de Paris, 1890-1900), 5: 2.

5. Volz, "Politik," p. 516.

6. *Recueil des instructions données aux ambassadeurs et ministres de France depuis les traités de Westphalie jusqu'à la révolution française*, 28 vols. (Paris: F. Alcan, 1884-), vol.7: *Bavière, Palatinat, Deux-Ponts*, ed. A. Lebon, xxi-xxii.

7. Sautai, *Préliminaires*, p. 152.

8. *Politische Correspondenz Friedrich's des Grossen*, vols. 1-4, edited by J. G. Droysen *et al.* (Berlin: Alexander Duncker, 1879-80), 1:97.

9. Ritter, *Frederick*, p. 82.

10. Alfred, Ritter von Arneth, *Maria Theresia*, 10 vols. (Vienna: W. Braumüller, 1863-79), 3:438.

11. *Politische Correspondenz*, 1: 147, 148.

12. The tiny county of Klodzko (Glatz), projecting south from Silesia into a fold opened up by Moravia and Bohemia, was not technically part of Silesia.

13. Edward Vehse, *Memoirs of the Court of Prussia*, trans. Franz C. F. Demmler (London: T. Nelson, 1854), p. 160.

14. Reinhold Koser, *König Friedrich der Grosse*, 2 vols. (Stuttgart: Cotta'sche Buchhandlung, 1901), 1:77.

15. Eugen Guglia, *Maria Theresia: Ihr Leben und ihre Regierung*, 2 vols. (Munich: R. Oldenbourg, 1917), 1:65.

16. Arneth, *Maria Theresia*, 1:382.

17. Colmar Grünhagen, *Geschichte des ersten schlesischen Krieges*, 2 vols. (Gotha: Perthes, 1881), 1:225.

18. Wilson, *Fleury*, p. 333.

19. Baudrillart, *Philippe V*, V, 6.

20. Baudrillart, *Philippe*, V, 22.

21. Grünhagen, *Geschichte*, I, 275-76.

22. Hans Portzek, *Friedrich der Grosse und Hannover in ihrem gegenseitigen Urteil* (Hildesheim: August Lax, 1958), p. 12.

23. *Politische Correspondenz*, I, 179.

24. Koser, *König Friedrich*, I, 93.

25. *Politische Correspondenz*, I, 223.

26. Duffy, *Army of Maria Theresa*, p. 100.

27. Koser, *König Friedrich*, I, 98.

28. Gustav Adolph-Auffenberg Kowarow, "Das Zeitalter Maria Theresias," in *Unser Heer: 300 Jahre österreichisches Soldatentum im Krieg und Frieden* (Vienna: Fürlinger, 1963), p. 122.

29. The words are those of an Austrian soldier. Christopher Duffy, *The Military Life of Frederick the Great* (New York: Atheneum, 1986), p. 31.

30. For accounts of the battle see: *Die Kriege Friedrichs des Grossen, Vols. 1-5* (Berlin: Ernst Siegfried Mittler, 1890-95), Part 1, Vol. 1, 388-425; *Kriege unter der Regierung Maria Theresia. Österreichischer Erbfolge-Krieg 1740-1748*, 9 vols. (Vienna: L. W. Seidel & Sohn, 1896-1914), II, 225-50.

31. Figures of this sort are famously imprecise and uncertain. Casualties include the dead, the wounded, the captured, and the missing (for battle was a splendid cover for desertion). Two fine modern sources—Groehler, *Kriege*, p. 32, and Chandler, *Art*, p. 306—are in substantial agreement on these figures.

32. [J. Cognazzo,] *Freymüthiger Beytrag zur Geschichte des österreichischen Militairdienstes* (Frankfurt: n.p., 1789), p. 15; Chandler, *Art*, p. 130.

33. Cognazzo, *Freymüthiger Beytrag*, p. 14.

NOTES TO CHAPTER 4

1. *Politische Correspondenz*, I, 224.

2. Karl Theodor von Heigel, *Die oesterreichische Erbfolgestreit und die Kaiserwahl Karl VII.* (Nördlingen: Beck, 1877), p. 157. Although within a few months reports were circulating of a second Treaty of Nymphenburg, formally binding France and Bavaria and ostensibly concluded on 22 May, the spuriousness of this claim and the fraudulence of the purported text now seem beyond dispute.

3. Though dated 5 June 1741, the treaty was signed the previous day. It is more conventionally called the Franco-Prussian Treaty of 1741, perhaps to distinguish it from the so-called Treaty of Breslau of 1742, which, to add to the confusion, was actually signed in Berlin and which will, in this study, be styled the Treaty of Berlin.

4. Broglie, *Frédéric II et Marie Thérèse*, I, 351.

5. James Leitch Wright, Jr., *Anglo-Spanish Rivalry in North America* (Athens, Georgia: University of Georgia Press, 1971), p. 94.

6. Rohan Butler, *Choiseul*, vol. I: *Father and Son, 1719-1754* (Oxford: Clarendon Press, 1980), 270.

7. B. McL. Ranft, ed., *The Vernon Papers* (London: Navy Record Office, 1958), p. 211.

8. For these figures I have followed W. Adolphe Roberts, *The Caribbean: The Story of Our Sea of Destiny* (Indianapolis: Bobbs-Merrill, 1940), p. 216, and W. N. Hargreaves-Mawdsley, *Spain under the Bourbons, 1700-1833: A Collection of Documents* (Columbia, S.C.: University of South Carolina Press, 1973), p. 104. Some sources report smaller figures on both sides.

9. Douglas Edward Leach, *Roots of Conflict: British Armed Forces and Colonial America 1677-1763* (Chapel Hill, N.C.: University of North Carolina Press, 1986), p. 57.

10. Hargreaves-Mawdsley, *Spain under the Bourbons*, p. 106.

11. Some have calculated that Britain lost 20,000 lives in the Caribbean adventure of 1741. William Coxe, *Memoirs of the Kings of Spain of the House of Bourbon* (London: Longman, 1815), III, 24. That figure, though probably high, is not implausible.

12. On the battle for Cartagena, see Richmond, *Navy in the War*, I, 111-24; Robert Beatson, *Naval and Military Memoirs of Great Britain, from the year 1727 to the present time* (London: Strachan, 1790-1804), I, 86-115.

13. With this coronation Maria Theresa became Queen of Hungary, the title she will conventionally be known by until 1745. In fact, owing to the peculiarity of Hungarian tradition—which recognized no queenship—Maria Theresa was crowned *king* of Hungary.

14. Beer, "Holland," p. 307.

15. Broglie, *Frédéric II et Marie Thérèse*, II, 18-19.

16. *Politische Correspondenz*, I, 265.

17. On 23 June 1741 a Franco-Bavarian convention on finances was finally concluded in Paris. France promised to pay Bavaria an annual subsidy of two million livres (£80,000).

18. British Museum, Additional MSS 32697, fo. 426.

19. Sautai, *Préliminaires*, p. 399.

20. Sautai, *Préliminaires*, p. 401.

21. Manfred Schlenke, *England und das friderizianische Preussen 1740-1763* (Munich: Verlag Karl Albert, 1963), pp. 108-109.

22. Walther Mediger, *Moskaus Weg nach Europa: Der Aufstieg Russlands zum europäischen Machtstaat im Zeitalter Friedrichs des Grossen* (Braunschweig: Georg Westermann Verlag, 1952), p. 386.

23. François-Marie Arouet Voltaire, *Histoire de la guerre de 1741*, edited by Jacques Maurens (Paris: Garnier Frères, 1971), p. 17.

24. Arneth, *Maria Theresia*, I, 268.

25. The town is now located in Slovakia, hence the name. In German it is Pressburg; in Hungarian it is Pozsony.

26. Joseph was the longed-for male heir. Though the queen made good use of the presence of her son at Bratislava, he had not come to impress the Hungarians. Rather the approach of the French and Bavarians toward Vienna from the west had prompted his guardians to dispatch him further east for safety.

27. Johann Christoph Allmayer-Beck, "Das Heer der Kaiserin," in *Maria Theresia und ihre Zeit*, ed. Walter Koschatzky (Vienna: Residenz Verlag, 1980), p. 84.

28. William Coxe, *History of the House of Austria*, 3d ed., 4 vols. (London: George Bell, 1877), III, 259; Adolf Unzer, *Die Convention von Klein-Schnellendorf (9. October 1741)* (Frankfurt-am-Main: Reitz & Koehler, 1889), p. 9.

29. Arneth, *Maria Theresia*, I, 245.

30. Peter Claus Hartmann, *Karl Albrecht—Karl VII. Glücklicher Kurfürst, Unglücklicher Kaiser* (Regensburg: Friedrich Pustet, 1985), p. 183.

31. Carl Friedrich, Count Vitzthum von Eckstaedt, ed., *Maurice Comte de Saxe et Marie-Josephe de Saxe, Dauphine de France: lettres et documents inédits* (Leipzig: Ludwig Denicke, 1867), p. 406.

32. Sautai, *Préliminaires*, p. 372.

33. Uriel Dann, *Hannover und England: Diplomatie und Selbsterhaltung* (Hildesheim: August Lax, 1986), p. 44.

34. Gert Brauer, *Die hannoversch-englischen Subsidienverträge 1702-1748* (Aalen: Scietia Verlag, 1962), p. 118.

35. Almost simultaneously France readied itself at home. On 29 August 1741 the new higher levels for the dixième were established and orders issued to collect it strictly.

36. Maurice Sautai, *Les débuts de la guerre de la succession d'Autriche* (Paris: Librairie Militaire R. Chapelot, 1910), p. 279.

NOTES TO CHAPTER 5

1. *Politische Correspondenz*, I, 323.

2. Adolf Unzer, *Die Convention von Klein-Schnellendorf (9. Oktober 1741)* (Frankfurt-am-Main: Reitz & Koehler, 1889), p. 49.

3. Grünhagen, *Geschichte*, II, 18.

4.   Charles Albert received his first hints of the agreement on 19 October, two days before he decided to change directions.

5.   Butler, *Choiseul,* p. 287.

6.   Duffy, *Army of Maria Theresa,* p. 151. The date of the letter is uncertain, and it may even have been written after the fall of Prague.

7.   Butler, *Choiseul,* p. 272.

8.   Jon Machlip White, *Marshal of France: The Life and Times of Maurice, Comte de Saxe (1696-1750)* (Chicago: Rand McNally, 1962), p. 110.

9.   Accounts of the fall may be found in Butler, *Choiseul,* pp. 296-301, and Broglie, *Frédéric II et Marie Thérèse,* II, 130-33.

10.   Baudrillart, V, 73.

11.   Sautai, *Préliminaires,* p. 400.

12.   Broglie, *Frédéric II et Marie Thérèse,* II, 141.

13.   Since father and son were both christened Leopold, it was conventional to distinguish them as the Old Dessauer and the Young Dessauer.

14.   Butler, *Choiseul,* p. 307.

15.   R. N. Bain, *The Daughter of Peter the Great* (Westminster: A. Constable, 1889), p. 87.

16.   Sir Richard Lodge, "The Treaty of Worms," *English Historical Review* 44 (1929): 229.

17.   P.G.M. Dickson, *Finance and Government Under Maria Theresa 1740-1780* (Oxford: Clarendon Press, 1987), II, 161.

18.   Austria, Bavaria, Bohemia, Cologne, the Electoral Palatine, Hanover, Mainz, Prussia, and Trier.

19.   Wilson, *French Foreign Policy,* p. 342.

20.   Fritz Wagner, *Kaiser Karl VII. und die grossen Mächte 1740-1745* (Stuttgart: W. Kohlhammer, 1938), p. 212.

21.   B. Auerbach, *La France et le Saint Empire Romain Germanique depuis la paix de Westphalie jusqu'à la révolution française* (Paris: Librairie Ancienne Honore Champion, 1912), p. 313.

NOTES TO CHAPTER 6

1.   Hartmann, *Karl Albrecht,* p. 209.

2.   Karl Roider, ed., *Maria Theresa* (Englewood Cliffs, N.J.: Prentice-Hall, 1973), p. 23.

3.   Erich Hillbrand, *Die Einschliessung von Linz 1741/42,* vol. 15 of *Militärhistorische Schriftenreihe* (Vienna: Oeterreichische Bundesverlag für Unterricht, Wissenschaft und Kunst, 1970) is the fullest study of the blockade of Linz.

4.   The story has several versions. I have followed Horace Mann's. Wilmarth S. Lewis et al., eds, *The Yale Edition of Horace Walpole's Correspondence* (New Haven: Yale University Press, 1981), XVII, 380.

5. Arneth, *Maria Theresia,* II, 24.

6. *Politische Correspondenz,* II, 24.

7. Vitzthum, *Saxe,* p. 447.

8. *Politische Correspondenz,* II, 77.

9. *Politische Correspondenz,* II, 208. For an analysis and account of this campaign, see Erich Bleich, *Der mährische Feldzug Friedrich II. 1741/42* (Berlin: R. Sieble, 1901).

10. Angelo Tamborra. "La pace di Aquisgrana del 1748 e la politica della Santa Sede," in *Archivio storico italiano* 117 (1959): 523.

11. Maximilien Henri, Marquis de St.-Simon, *Histoire de la guerre des Alpes ou campagne de MDCCXLIV par les armées combinées d'Espagne et de France* (Amsterdam: Rey, 1770), p. iii.

12. Don Joseph de Campo-Raso, *Continuacion à los Commentarios del Marques de S. Felipe desde el año de MDCCXXXIII* (Madrid: Imprenta Real, 1793), IV, 188.

13. The prince would never return to Spain, though he had twenty-three years of life ahead. In fact, he would not see his wife again until 1749.

14. The term *Napolispani* is used in L. A. Muratori, *Annali d'Italia dal principio dell'era volgare sino all'anno 1750* (Naples: Giovanni Gravier, 1773), XII, 245, and elsewhere.

15. Schlenke, *England,* p. 183.

16. British Library Add. MSS 32701, fol. 190.

17. Lewis, ed., *Walpole's Correspondence,* XVII, 410.

18. *Politische Correspondenz,* II, 145.

19. *Politische Correspondenz,* II, 158.

20. Chandler, *Art of Warfare,* p. 306; Groehler, *Kriege,* p. 41.

21. The words are those of a Prussian participant, Christophe Ludwig von Stille. *Les campagnes du roi avec des réflexions sur les causes des évènements* (Berlin, 1762), I, 102.

22. Groehler, *Kriege,* p. 41.

23. On the battle of Chotusitz, accounts of which differ in salient details, see Arneth, *Maria Theresa,* II, 50-55; Koser, *König Friedrich,* I, 168-71; Grünhagen, *Geschichte,* II, 242-48; *Kriege Friedrichs des Grossen,* part I, vol. I, 227-72; *Kriege unter Maria Theresia,* II, 591-682.

24. Grünhagen, *Geschichte,* II, 273.

25. Arneth, *Maria Theresia,* II, 466.

26. Alfred, Ritter von Arneth, "Johann Christoph Bartenstein und seine Zeit," in *Archiv für österreichische Geschichte* 46 (1871): 40.

27. Butler, *Choiseul,* p. 322.

28. Hyndford revealed his Austrian instructions to Podewils. The Prussian minister thus knew exactly how far his foe was prepared to go, always useful information in a negotiation.

29. Arneth, "Bartenstein," p. 41.

30. *Politische Correspondenz*, II, 210.

31. *Politische Correspondenz*, II, 207-209, 7.

32. Émile G. Leonard, *L'armée et ses problemes au XVIIIe siècle* (Paris: Plon, 1958), p. 131.

33. Sir Richard Lodge, "The So-Called Treaty of Hanau," *English Historical Review* 38 (1923): 387.

NOTES TO CHAPTER 7

1. Wagner, *Kaiser*, p. 332.

2. Arneth, *Maria Theresia*, II, 79.

3. Guglia, *Maria Theresia*, I, 181.

4. Lodge, "Treaty of Worms," p. 239.

5. Carlo Baudi di Vesme, *Studi sul XVIII secolo: le prime manifestazioni della rivoluzione d'occidente in Francia e nelle repubbliche oligarche (1748-1775)* (Turin: Palazzo Carignano, 1972), p. 30.

6. Butler, *Choiseul*, p. 331.

7. Duke of Broglie, *Frédéric II et Louis XV, 1742-44*, 2 vols. (Paris: Calmann Levy, 1885), I, 23-24.

8. Arneth, *Maria Theresa*, II, 184.

9. René Bouvier and André Laffargue, *La vie napolitaine au XVIII siècle: prélude au voyage à Naples* (Paris: Hatchette, 1956), p. 140.

10. Domenico Carutti, *Storia del regno di Carlo Emmanuele III* (Turin: Ered. Botta, 1859), II, 42.

11. Baudrillart, *Philippe V*, V, 117.

12. Edouard Revel, "Les Espagnols en Savoie, 1742-1749," in *Mémoires et documents publiés par la Société Savoisienne d'Histoire et d'Archaeologie* 62 (1925): 220.

13. Voltaire, *Histoire*, p. 33.

14. Capitaine Bernard, "Le siège de Prague (1742)," in *Revue retrospective; recueil des pièces intéressantes et de citations curieuses* 11 (1890):271. See also Ottokar Weber, "Die Occupation Prags durch die Franzosen und Baiern 1741-1742," in *Mittheilungen des Vereines für Geschichte der Deutschen in Böhmen* 34 (1896): 1-92.

15. Butler, *Choiseul*, p. 341.

16. Wagner, *Kaiser*, p. 342.

17. Charles Philippe Albert, Duke of Luynes, *Mémoires*, 17 vols. (Paris: Firmion Didot Fréres, 1860-65), IV, 362.

18. Butler, *Choiseul*, p. 327.

19. Broglie, *Frédéric II et Louis XV*, I, 105.

20. Butler, *Choiseul*, p. 359.

21. Butler, *Choiseul,* p. 360.

22. Broglie, *Frédéric II et Louis XV,* I, 144.

23. Broglie, *Frédéric II et Louis XV,* I, 149.

24. Chevert was virtually the first Frenchman to get into Prague in November 1741 and the last to leave in January 1743.

25. Robert Joseph Kerner, *Bohemia in the Eighteenth Century: A Study of Political, Economic, and Social History, with special reference to the reign of Leopold II, 1790-1792* (New York: Macmillan, 1932), p. 32.

NOTES TO CHAPTER 8

1. The words are President des Brosses'. G. Baguenault de Puchesse, "Le pape Benoît XIV et la France. Missions à Rome de Tencin et de Choiseul (1740-1757)," in *Revue d'histoire diplomatique* 17 (1903): 481.

2. Camille Rousset, ed., *Correspondance de Louis XV et du Maréchal de Noailles,* 2 vols. (Paris: Paul Dupont, 1865), I, 181.

3. Arneth, *Maria Theresia,* II, 276.

4. On the battle of Campo Santo, see Chandler, *Art,* p. 306; Arneth, *Maria Theresia,* II, 187; Wilkinson, *Defence,* pp. 73-80; Chevalier de Powerer, *Tableau de la guerre de la pragmatique sanction en Allemagne et en Italie* (Bern: Nouvelle Société Typographique, 1784), I, 239-48; Muratori, *Annali,* XII, 267-68; and George Louis Le Rouge, *Recueil des sièges et batailles pour servir à l'histoire des guerres de 1741* (Paris: 1754), n.p.

5. The comparable figure for Mollwitz was 23 percent. For Chotusitz it was 20 percent.

6. A. van Hoey, *Lettres et négociations 1743-4, pour servir à l'histoire de la vie de Cardinal de Fleury* (London: John Nourse, 1743), p. 79.

7. Broglie, *Frédéric II et Louis XV,* I, 279.

8. Historical Manuscripts Commission, *Report on the Manuscripts of Mrs. Stopford-Sackville, of Drayton House, Northamptonshire,* 2 vols. (London: Mackie, 1904), I, 290.

9. Wagner, *Kaiser,* p. 415.

10. Max Spindler, ed., *Handbuch der bayerischen Geschichte,* vol 2: *Das alte Bayern: Der Territorialstaat vom Ausgang des 12. Jahrhunderts bis zum Ausgang des 18. Jahrhunderts* (Munich: C. H. Beck'sche, 1966), II, 470.

11. Hartmann, *Karl Albrecht,* p. 281.

12. Frederick II, *Mémoires de Frédéric II,* ed. by B. Boutaric and E. Campardon, Vol. I of *Histoire de mon temps* (Paris: Henri Plon, 1866), p. 189.

13. Michael Orr, *Dettingen 1743* (London: Charles Knight, 1972), p. 59.

14. *The Operations of the British and the Allied Arms, during the Campaigns of 1743 and 1744, Historically Deducted* (London: M. Cooper, 1744), p. 16.

15. Again I follow Chandler, *Art,* p. 306. His figures are lower than those mentioned in many sources. Estimates range as high as 6,000 for the French and 2,350 for the allies. For a description of the battle, see *Kriege unter der Regierung der Kaiserin-Königin Maria Theresia. Oesterreichischer Erbfloge-Krieg 1740-1748,* 9 vols. (Vienna: L. W. Seidel & Sohn, 1896-1914), IV, 298-316; Orr, *Dettingen.*

16.   Leonard, *L'armée*, p. 131.

17.   *Campagne de Monsieur le Maréchal, duc de Noailles, en Allemagne, l'an 1743, contenant les lettres de ce maréchal et celles de plusieurs officiers généraux au roi et à M. d'Argenson*, 3 vols. (Amsterdam: Rey, 1760-61), I, 25.

18.   Historical Manuscripts Commission, *Report on the Manuscripts of Mrs. Franklin-Russell-Astley of Chequers Court, Bucks*. (London: Mackie, 1900), pp. 260-61.

19.   Bain, *Daughter*, p. 107.

20.   *Politische Correspondenz*, II, 409-10.

21.   Basil Williams, "Carteret and the So-Called Treaty of Hanau," *English Historical Review* 49 (1934): 686.

22.   Baudrillart, *Philippe V*, V, 151.

23.   The two documents were titled "Project and Ideas" and "Project of Secret Assurance." Together they have been called the Treaty of Hanau, though they were assuredly not a treaty.

24.   Sir Richard Lodge, *Studies in Eighteenth-Century Diplomacy, 1740-1748* (London: J. Murray, 1930), p. 17n. The words are those of a Hessian observer.

25.   Carutti, *Storia del regno*, I, 214.

26.   Domenico Carutti, *Storia della diplomazia della Corte di Savoia*, 4 vols (Turin: Fratelli Bocca, 1880), IV, 208.

27.   Carlo Baudi di Vesme, *La politica mediterranea inglese nelle relazioni degli inviati italiani a Londra durante la cosidetta "guerra di successione d'Austria" 1741-1748* (Turin: Gheroni, 1952), p. 64.

28.   Carutti, *Storia del regno*, I, 239.

29.   Archibald Ballantyne, *Lord Carteret: A Political Biography, 1690-1763* (London: Richard Bentley, 1887), p. 293.

NOTES TO CHAPTER 9

1.   Baudrillart, *Philippe V*, V, 161-3.

2.   Wilkinson, *Defence*, p. 98.

3.   P. Coquelle, *L'alliance franco-hollandaise contre l'Angleterre 1735-1788* (Paris: Librairie Plon, 1902), p. 15.

4.   Broglie, *Frédéric II et Louis XV*, II, 18.

5.   Richmond, *Navy*, I, 236.

6.   An extended account of the battle may be found in Richmond, *Navy*, II, 8-49. Briefer accounts are in Cesareo Fernandez Duro, *Armada española desde la unión de los reinos de Castilla y de Aragon* (Madrid: Sucesores de Rivadeneyra, 1900), VI, 299-314; G. Lacour-Gayet, *La marine militaire de la France sous le règne de Louis XV*, pp. 150-55.

7.   Baudrillart, *Philippe V*, V, 189; Lacour-Gayet, *Marine*, p. 156.

8.   Wilkinson, *Defence*, p. 100.

9. Charteris, *Cumberland*, p. 151.

10. Butler, *Choiseul*, p. 491.

11. Arneth, *Maria Theresia*, II, 265.

12. Guglia, *Maria Theresia*, I, 209.

13. Jean Lambert Alphonse Colin, *Louis XV et les Jacobites: le projet de débarquement en Angleterre de 1743-44* (Paris: Librairie Militaire R. Chapelot et Cie, 1901), p. 186.

14. *Politische Correspondenz*, III, 42.

15. *Politische Correspondenz*, III, 67.

NOTES TO CHAPTER 10

1. Enrique de Tapia Ozcariz, *Carlos III y su epoca: biografia del siglo XVIII* (Madrid: Aguilar, 1962), p. 147.

2. Arneth, *Maria Theresia*, II, 358.

3. For fuller accounts of the second battle of Velletri, see Christopher Duffy, *The Wild Goose and the Eagle: A Life of Marshal von Browne, 1705-1757* (London: Chatto, 1964), pp. 96-105; Pietro Giuseppe Maria Buonamici, *Denkwürdigkeiten des italienischen Krieges vom Jahre 1744 bis 1748. Aus dem Lateinischen Übersetzt* (Breslau: Korn, 1756), pp. 95-110; Giuseppe Pasquali, *Le due battaglie di Velletri 1744-1849* (Velletri: Cesare Bertini, 1891); Manuel Danvila y Collado, *Reinado de Carlos III*, vol, 1: *Educación política de D. Carlos de Borbon. Infante de España* (Madrid: El Progreso Editorial, 1893), pp. 245-48.

4. Casualty figures for both sides come from Chandler, *Art*, p. 306. I am not aware of a breakdown between Spanish and Neapolitan casualties.

5. Wilkinson, *Defence*, p. 123.

6. Wilkinson, *Defence*, p. 131.

7. Wilkinson, *Defence*, p. 129.

8. Bourcet drew on Luxembourg, Catinat, and Berwick. But he was more systematic. Napoleon Bonaparte drew on Bourcet. See P. J. de Bourcet, *Principes de la guerre de montagnes* (Paris: Imprimerie Nationale, 1775).

9. Wilkinson, *Defence*, p.140.

10. Wilkinson, *Defence*, pp. 153-56. Chandler, *Art*, p. 306, gives higher figures: 3,000 Bourbon casualties, 1,500 Piedmontese casualties.

11. Voltaire, *Histoire*, p. 105.

12. Carlo Buffa di Perrero, *Carlo Emmanuele III di Savoia a difesa delle Alpi nella campagna del 1744* Turin: Fratelli Bocca, 1887), p. 164.

13. Hermann Weber, *Die Politik des Kurfürsten Karl Theodor von der Pfalz während der österreichischen Erbfolgekrieges (1742-1748)* (Bonn: Ludwig Röhrscheid, 1956), p. 79.

14. *Politische Correspondenz*, II, 239.

15.   Approximately 161,000 French were in the entire region, facing approximately 145,000 allied troops.

16.   Dutch neutrality explained Noailles's orders to Maurice: if he met foreign troops, he was to ask of what country; if they said they were Dutch, he was to ask if they were simply Dutch or also auxiliaries of Austria; only in the final instance was he to fight.

17.   Arneth, *Maria Theresia*, II, 546.

18.   Colin, *Campagnes*, II, 267.

19.   Ballantyne, *Carteret*, p. 297.

20.   The similarity of this name to Wasner's is unfortunate. They are in fact two separate individuals, Wassenaer-Twickel serving the Dutch and Wasner serving the Austrians.

21.   Arneth, *Maria Theresia*, II, 547.

22.   Oskar Teichman, *Pandour Trenck: An Account of the Life of Baron Franciscus von der Trenck, 1710-1749* (London: John Murray, 1927), p. 122; Vogüé and Le Sourd, eds, *Campagnes de Mercoyrol*, p. 28.

23.   Broglie, *Frédéric II et Louis XV*, II, 326.

24.   Bain, *Daughter*, p. 113.

25.   Sir Richard Lodge, "Russia, Prussia, and Great Britain, 1742-4," *English Historical Review*, XLV (1930), 604.

26.   *Politische Correspondenz*, III, 245,

27.   Arneth, "Bartenstein," p. 41.

NOTES TO CHAPTER 11

1.   Arneth, *Maria Theresia*, II, 557.

2.   Albert, Duke of Broglie, *Marie Thérèse impératrice* (Paris: Calman Levy, 1888), I, 18.

3.   Arneth, *Maria Theresia*, II, 429.

4.   *Politische Correspondenz*, III, 314.

5.   Broglie, *Marie Thérèse Impératrice*, I, 82.

6.   Jakob Anton Friedrich Logan-Logejus, *Meine Erlebnisse als Reiteroffizier unter dem Grossen König in den Jahren 1741-1759* (Breslau: Wilh. Gottl. Korn, 1934), p. 66.

7.   On the battle, see: Buffa di Perrero, *Carlo Emmanuele III*, pp. 214-38; *Kriege unter der Regierung*, VIII, 506-25; Butler, *Choiseul*, I, 536-40; Henri Moris, *Operations militaires dans les Alpes et les Apennins pendant la guerre de la succession d'Autriche (1742-1748)* (Paris: I. Baudoin, 1886), pp. 53-69.

8.   Butler, *Choiseul*, p. 540; [Jaime Miguel Guzman,] Marques de La Mina, *Memorias militares*, ed. Antonio Canovas del Castillo (Madrid: Fortanet, 1898), II, 11.

9.   Buffa di Pererro, *Carlo Emmanuele III*, p. 237.

10.   The figure for the Bourbons is taken from Butler (*Choiseul*, p. 540), who distinguishes (as I do) between casualties in the battle and casualties in the other actions of that busy day. It is by conflating these two separate categories that other sources increase the total of Bourbon casualties to 4,000 or more.

11. Butler, *Choiseul,* p. 547.

12. René-Louis de Voyer de Paulmy, Marquis D'Argenson, *Journal et mémoires,* ed. E.J.B. Rathery (Paris: V. Jules Renouard, 1862), III, 432.

13. Edgar Zévort, *Le Marquis d'Argenson et le ministère des affaires étrangères du 18 Novembre 1744 au 10 Janvier 1747* (Paris: Germer Ballière, 1879), p. 42.

14. The characterization was delivered by Count Haslang, an imperial diplomat. Elisabeth Charlotte Broicher, *Der Aufstieg der preussischen Macht von 1713 bis 1756* (Cologne, 1955), p. 122.

15. Owen, *Rise,* p. 238.

16. Treaties with Mainz (April 1744) and Cologne (July 1744) supplemented the Treaty of Worms (September 1743) and the many treaties defining Britain's relationship with Austria—the most recent of which was the Treaty of London (August 1744).

17. British Library, Add. MSS 35407, fol. 280.

18. Geoffrey Jules Marcus, *A Naval History of England,* Vol. I: *The Formative Centuries* (London: Longmans, 1961), p. 254.

19. Olivier Bernier, *Louis the Beloved: The Life of Louis XV* (Garden City, N.Y.: Doubleday, 1984), p. 115.

20. Franz Ehgartner, *Der Regierungsanfang des Kurfürsten Maximilian III. Joseph von Bayern: Ein Beitrag zur Geschichte des Friedens von Füssen (1745)* (Würzburg: H. Stürtz, 1910), p. 76.

21. Heigel, *Erbfolgestreit,* p. 294.

22. Georg Preuss, *Der Friede von Füssen* (Munich: H. Luneburg, 1894), p. 19.

23. *Politische Correspondenz,* IV, 24.

24. Alois Schmid, *Max III. Joseph und die europäischen Mächte: die Aussenpolitik des Kurfürstentums Bayern von 1745-1765* (Munich: R. Oldenbourg, 1987), p. 52.

NOTES TO CHAPTER 12

1. *Politische Correspondenz,* IV, 59.

2. *Politische Correspondenz,* IV, 123.

3. Broglie, *Marie Thérèse Impératrice,* I, 251-52.

4. D'Argenson, *Journal,* IV, 279.

5. Butler, *Choiseul,* I, 574. The quotation was not reported until the following November.

6. The document is printed in Gaetan de Raxis de Flassan, *Histoire générale et raisonée de la diplomatie française* (Paris: Treuttel et Wurtz, 1811), V, 243-44. Zévort ignored it, unable to find it in the archives. But Butler argues—and the balance of probability seems to me to support this view—that it was incinerated in the fire at the library of the Louvre in 1871. *Choiseul,* p. 578.

7. Colin, *Campagnes,* III, 10.

8. Albert, Duke de Broglie, *Maurice de Saxe et le Marquis d'Argenson, 1746-1747,* 2 vols. (Paris: Calmann Levy, 1891), I, 102.

9.   Arneth, *Maria Theresia*, III, 399.

10.   Schmid, *Max III. Joseph*, p. 76.

11.   Ehgartner, *Maximilian III. Joseph*, p. 65.

12.   Guglia, *Maria Theresia*, I, 246.

13.   Butler, *Choiseul*, I, 577.

14.   Franco Venturi, "Genova a metà del settecento," *Rivista storica italiana* LXIII (1967), 738.

15.   Baudrillart, *Philippe V*, V, 275.

16.   Skrine, *Fontenoy*, p. 137. 26,000 were militiamen. Though the Bourbon army coalescing in Italy was marginally larger than the French army in the Low Countries, it was gathered from five countries—France, Spain, Naples, Modena, and Genoa.

17.   Rex Whitworth, *Field-Marshal Lord Ligonier: A Story of the British Army, 1702-1770* (Oxford: Clarendon Press, 1958), p. 92.

18.   Colin, *Campagnes*, III, 107.

19.   Much has been written about the square. Yet we still do not know whether Cumberland ordered it—the eminent military writer Folard had speculated about such a device—or whether it formed under the exiguities of the situation.

20.   Colin, *Campagnes*, III, 118.

21.   For fuller accounts of the battle of Fontenoy, see Jean Baptiste Joseph Sahuguet d'Amarzit, Baron d'Espagnac, *Histoire de Maurice, Comte de Saxe*, 2 vols., new edition (Paris: Philippe-Denys Pierres, 1775), II, 58-85; Colin, *Campagnes*, III, 85-144; Charteris, *Cumberland*, pp. 170-89; *Kriege unter der Regierung*, IX, 59-135; Skrine, *Fontenoy*, passim.

22.   Charteris, *Cumberland*, p. 189; White, *Marshal*, p. 164.

23.   A comment on these figures is called for, because the differences among the sources is greater than usual for Fontenoy. Estimates for the size of the French army range from 49,000 to 60,000. Estimates for the size of the Pragmatic Army range from 47,000 to 53,000. Both Colin (51,000 to 49,000) and Chandler (53,000 to 52,000) say that the allies had the larger force. Approximately 15% of combatants were casualties, a figure higher than Dettingen's but lower than the proportion of casualties at Mollwitz, Chotusitz, or Campo Santo. See Skrine, *Fontenoy*, pp. 188-90; Vienna, Kriegsarchiv, Manuskripte/ Allgemeine Reihe/162 (Gaston Bodart, "Les troupes belges au service de l'Autriche 1714-1801").

24.   White, *Marshal*, p. 164.

25.   *Politische Correspondenz*, IV, 134-35.

26 .   Rudolf Keibel, *Die Schlacht von Hohenfriedberg* (Berlin: A. Bath, 1899), p. 34.

27.   Broglie, *Marie Thérèse Impératrice*, II, 58.

28.   Johann Gustav Droysen, *Geschichte der preussischen Politik*. Part V: *Friedrich der Grosse*, 2 vols. (Leipzig: Veit & Comp., 1876), II, 487.

29.   Reinhold Koser, *Geschichte Friedrichs des Grossen*, 2 vols. (Berlin: J. G. Cotta'sche Buchhandlung, 1921), I, 493.

30. Logan-Logejus, *Erlebnisse,* pp. 91-93.

31. For fuller descriptions of the battle of Hohenfriedberg, see Keibel, *Schlacht; Kriege unter der Regierung,* VII, 451-96; *Kriege Friedrichs des Grossen,* Part II, Vol. II, 219-44.

32. I am following Groehler, *Kriege,* pp. 59-60, and Chandler, *Art,* p. 306, which are in substantial agreement.

33. Stille, *Campagnes,* II, 223.

NOTES TO CHAPTER 13

1. D'Argenson, *Journal,* IV, 331.

2. Lewis, ed., *Walpole Correspondence,* XIX, 78.

3. Marcus, *Naval History,* p. 261.

4. Fairfax Downey, *Louisbourg: Key to a Continent* (Englewood Cliffs, N.J.: Prentice-Hall, 1965), p. 215.

5. Downey, *Louisbourg,* p. 102.

6. Warren was made a rear admiral; Pepperell became America's first (and last) baronet.

7. William Coxe, *Memoirs of the Administration of the Right Honourable Henry Pelham,* 2 vol. (London: Orme, 1829), I, 284.

8. *Politische Correspondenz,* IV, 190.

9. *Politische Correspondenz,* IV, 247.

10. Joseph Posch, *Die Kaiserwahl Franz' I. 1745,* Vienna dissertation (Vienna, 1949), p. 37.

11. Zévort, *D'Argenson,* p. 104. The reader should keep this incautious phrase in mind.

12. Mack Walker, *Johann Jakob Moser and the Holy Roman Empire of the German Nation* (Chapel Hill, N.C.: University of North Carolina Press, 1981), pp. 154-58.

13. Several African contingents were included in Spain's army. The appearance of black troops aroused much comment in Italy.

14. For the battle of Bassignana, see Buonamici, *Denkwürdigkeiten,* pp. 195-211; Carutti, *Storia,* I, 291-93; Wilkinson, *Defence,* pp. 217-19.

15. Chandler, *Art,* p. 306.

NOTES TO CHAPTER 14

1. Though conventionally called the battle of Soor, the fighting actually occurred closer to Burkersdorf. The Austrians marched through Soor to reach the hills around Burkersdorf.

2. Edith Simon, *The Making of Frederick the Great* (Boston: Little, Brown, 1963), p. 254.

3. For accounts of the battle, see Arneth, *Maria Theresia,* III, 115-18; Koser, *König Friedrich,* I, 273-74. A full account is in Hans Stabenow, *Die Schlacht bei Soor* (Frankfurt-am-Main: Voigt und Gleiber, 1901).

4.   At Campo Santo the victorious Austrians had been outnumbered, but only by 2,000 men.

5.   I follow Groehler here, *Kriege*, pp. 63, 64 (who silently corrects Koser's misprints) and Chandler, *Art*, p. 306.

6.   Friedrich Freiherr von Trenck, *Merckwürdige Lebensgeschichte*, 4 vols. (Berlin: Friedrich Vieweg, 1787), I, 47.

7.   Johannes Kunisch, *Der Kleine Krieg: Studien zum Heerwesen des Absolutismus* (Wiebaden: Steiner, 1973), p. 27.

8.   Guglia, *Maria Theresia*, I, 272

9.   *Politische Correspondenz*, IV, 299.

10. Zévort, *D'Argenson*, p. 33.

11. Arneth, *Maria Theresia*, III, 447.

12. Voltaire, *Histoire*, p. 228.

13. Katherine Tomasson and Francis Buist, *Battles of the '45* (New York: Macmillan, 1962), p. 49.

14. These are the words of an observer. Tomasson and Buist, *Battles*. p. 71.

15. On the battle, see Tomasson and Buist, *Battles*, pp. 51-71.

16. A treaty of 1719 obliged the Dutch to supply troops, when asked. France was angered by the Dutch action, for the States General sent men who had surrendered at Tournai and Dendermond and who were therefore, in accordance with the terms of their release, not to engage. The Marquis d'Argenson protested sharply and renounced the commercial treaty of 1739.

17. Tomasson and Buist, *Battles*, p. 79.

18. Skrine, *Fontenoy*, p. 283.

19. Jean Sareil, *Les Tencins: Histoire d'une famille au dix-huitième siècle d'après de nombreux documents inédits* (Geneva: Droz, 1969), p. 383.

20. Broglie, *Marie Thérèse Impératrice*, II, 338.

21. D'Argenson, *Journal*, IV, 333.

22. Bavid Baynes Horn, "Saxony in the War of the Austrian Succession," *English Historical Review* XLIV (1929), 35.

23. Reinhold Becker, *Der Dresdener Friede und die Politik Brühls* (Leipzig: S. Hirzel, 1902), p. 11.

24. Paul Karge, *Die russisch-österreichische Allianz von 1746 und ihre Vorgeschichte* (Göttingen: Robert Peppmüller, 1887), p. 124.

25. On the battle see Walter von Bremen, *Die Schlacht bei Kesselsdorf am 15. Dezember 1745* (Berlin: Ernst Siegfried Mittler und Sohn, 1888).

26. Chandler, *Art*, p. 307 puts allied casualties at 10,500; Groehler, *Kriege*, pp. 68-69 puts them at 14,500.

27. Arneth, *Maria Theresa*, III, 445.

28. Arneth, "Bartenstein," p. 185. Bartenstein had Fontenoy, Hohenfriedberg, Bassignana, Soor, and Kesselsdorf in mind.

29. Broglie, *Marie Thérèse Impératrice*, II, 375.

NOTES TO CHAPTER 15

1. D'Argenson called it the "Treaty of Turin," and Broglie and Lodge accepted the usage, though the latter noted the inappropriateness of the term. We need not honor that misleading custom. Albert, Duke of Broglie, *Maurice de Saxe et le Marquis d'Argenson, 1746-1747*, 2 vols. (Paris: Calman Levy, 1891), I, 138; Lodge, *Studies*, 104-106.

2. White, *Marshal*, p. 172.

3. On the siege of Brussels, see Broglie, *Maurice de Saxe*, I, 37-43; Espagnac, *Saxe*, II, 130-49.

4. This argument is controversial. Many historians, for a variety of reasons, believe that Charles Emmanuel was sincere in his negotiations with France. The view I have presented seems to me more consistent with the full range of facts.

5. Edward Armstrong, *Elizabeth Farnese: "The Termagant of Spain"* (London: Longmans, Green & Co., 1892), p. 382.

6. Zévort, *D'Argenson*, p. 38.

7. D'Argenson, *Journal*, IV, 296. Huescar's task was in fact to persuade Louis XV to dismiss d'Argenson.

8. The awkwardness of the translation reflects the awkwardness of the original. Broglie publishes the full text of the letter. *Maurice de Saxe*, I, 147-48.

9. Zévort, *D'Argenson*, p. 36.

10. Broglie, *Maurice de Saxe*, I, 201.

11. Baudrillart has established that Don Philip issued these orders *before* he knew of the fall of Asti and as a consequence of Don Philip's fear that France and Piedmont-Sardinia were on the verge of becoming allies! V, 383-84.

12. Broglie, *Maurice de Saxe*, I, 210.

13. Eveline Cruickshanks, *Political Untouchables: The Tories and the '45* (New York: Holmes & Meier, 1979), p. 101.

14. Tomasson and Buist, *Battles*, p. 105.

15. On the battle of Falkirk, see Tomasson and Buist, *Battles*, pp. 108-24.

16. James Michael Hill, *Celtic Warfare 1595-1763* (Edinburgh: John Donald, 1986), p. 111.

17. Hill, *Celtic Warfare*, p. 146.

18. On the battle see Jeremy Black, *Culloden and the '45* (New York: St. Martin's, 1990); Tomasson and Buist, *Battles*, pp. 163-95; Frank McLynn, *Charles Edward Stuart: A Tragedy in Many Acts* (New York: Routledge, 1988); pp 248-64; David Daiches, *The Last Stuart: The Life and Times of Bonnie Prince Charlie* (New York: G. P. Putnam's Sons, 1973), pp. 210-16.

19. Tomasson and Buist, *Battles*, p. 204.

20.   *Storia di Milano*, XII: *L'età delle riforme (1706-1796)* (Milan: Treccani degli Alfieri, 1959), p. 229.

21.   Silvio Pellegrini, "La Corsica e i Savoia nel secolo XVIII," *Nuova rivista storica* VIII (1924): 107. The quotation dates from 1748, but it accurately reflects Gaffori's views in 1745.

22.   Christian Ambrosi, *La Corse insurgée et la seconde intervention française au XVIIIe siècle (1743-1753)* (Grenoble: Imprimerie Allier, 1950), p. 70.

23.   Giuseppe Roberti, "Carlo Emmanuele III e la Corsica al tempo della guerra de successione austriaca," *Rivista storica italiana* IV (1889): 680.

24.   Roberti, "Carlo Emmanuele," p. 685.

25.   Ambrosi, *La Corse*, p. 73.

26.   Zévort, *D'Argenson*, p. 322; Pio Zabala y Lera, *El Marqués de Argenson y el pacto de familia de 1743* (Madrid: Editorial Voluntad, 1928), p. 216.

27.   Zabala y Lera, *Marqués*, p. 212.

NOTES TO CHAPTER 16

1.   The terms are Don Philip's own, uttered to a confidant. Victor Meduna, *Der Krieg in Italien gegen Spanien, Neapel und Frankreich 1746* (Vienna: Institut für österreichische Geschichtsforschung, p. 80).

2.   Wilkinson, *Defense*, p. 251.

3.   Though the translation misses the rhythm, the words are from a poem about the suffering in Piacenza in the spring of 1746. Emilio Nasalli-Rocca di Corneliano, *Piacenza sotto la dominazione sabauda (1744-1749)* (Piacenza: A. Del-Maino, 1929), p. 86.

4.   On the battle of Piacenza, see: Buonamici, *Denkwürdigkeiten*, pp. 252-55; Duffy, *Wild Goose*, pp. 120-25; Moris, *Opérations*, pp. 167-72; Meduna, *Krieg*, pp. 54-67.

5.   Meduna, *Krieg*, 67; Browne MSS 38.

6.   Arneth, *Maria Theresia*, III, 449.

7.   Didier Ozanam, ed., *La diplomacia de Fernando VI: corerespondencia reservada entre D. Jose de Carvajal y el Duque de Huescar, 1746-1749* (Madrid: C.S.I.C., 1975), p. 96.

8.   Broglie, *Maurice de Saxe*, I, 358.

9.   Angela Garcia Rives, *Fernando VI y Doña Barbara de Braganza (1748-1759): Apuntes sobre su reinado* (Madrid: Julio Cosano, 1917), p. 17.

10.   Harold Acton, *The Bourbons of Naples (1734-1825* (London: Methuen, 1957), p. 65.

11.   Joao Albino Pinto Ferreiro, ed., *Correspondência de D. João V e D. Bàrbara de Bragança Rainha de Espanha (1746-1747)* (Coimbra: Livraria Gonçalves, 1945), p. 49.

12.   Antonio Rodriguez-Villa, *Don Cenon de Somodevilla, Marqués de la Ensenada* (Madrid: M. Murillo, 1878), p. 31.

13.   Baudrillart, *Philippe V*, V, 467.

14.   Baudrillart, *Philippe V*, V, 473.

15. Lodge, *Studies*, p. 180.

16. Broglie, *Maurice de Saxe*, II, 35.

17. Butler, *Choiseul*, p. 639.

18. Butler, *Choiseul*, p. 658.

19. For accounts of Rocoux, see Broglie, *Maurice de Saxe*, I, 424-25; Whitworth, *Ligonier*, pp. 137-40; Jean Baptiste Joseph Sahuguet d'Amerzit, Baron d'Espagnac, *Journal historique de la dernière campagne de l'armée du roi en 1746* (The Hague: Henry Scheurleer, 1747), pp. 165-84; *Kriege unter der Regierung*, IX, 386-452.

20. Vienna, Kriegsarchiv, Bodart, *Troupes*, p. 217; d'Espagnac, *Journal*, p. 185; Butler, *Choiseul*, p. 661.

21. Carl Friedrich, Count Vitzthum von Eckstaedt, *Die Geheimnisse des sächsischen Cabinets. Ende 1745 bis Ende 1756*, 2 vols. (Stuttgart: J. G. Cotta'schen Buchhandlung, 1866), I, 135-36.

22. Ozanam, *Diplomacia*, pp. 12-13.

23. Broglie, *Maurice de Saxe*, I, 379.

24. Lodge, *Studies*, p. 216.

25. Carlo Baudi di Vesme, "La Spagna all'epoca de Ferdinando VI e il matrimonio spagnuolo de Vittorio Amadeo III (1749)," *Bolletino storico-bibliografico subalpino* LI (1953), 135.

NOTES TO CHAPTER 17

1. Venturi, "Genoa," p. 736.

2. Venturi, "Genoa," p. 749. The words are Arthur Villette's, paraphrasing the view of Piedmontese officials.

3. Lodge, *Studies*, p. 203.

4. Annibale Bozzola, "La controversia austro-sarda sulla capitulazione del 6 settembre 1746," *Bolletino storico-bibliografico subalpino* 36 (1934), 70.

5. Gaston-E. Broche, *La république de Gênes et la France pendant la guerre de la succession d'Autriche (1740-1748)*, 3 vols. (Paris: Société Française d'Imprimerie et de Librairie), III, 13.

6. Butler, *Choiseul*, p. 671. [Translation slightly modified.]

7. L. Rankin, *The Marquis d'Argenson and Richard II* (London: Longmans, Green, and Co., 1901), p. 80.

8. Rousset, ed., *Correspondance*, II, 252-76.

9. Luynes, *Mémoires*, VIII, 79; Edmond-Jean-François Barbier, *Chronique de la régence et du règne de Louis XV (1718-1763) ou Journal de Barbier*, 7 vols. (Paris: G. Charpentiers, 1885), IV, 214; Vitzthum, ed., *Geheimnisse*, I, 146.

10. Flassan, *Histoire générale*, IV, 354.

11. Arneth, *Maria Theresia*, III, 291.

12.   Tamborra, "Pace," p. 525.

13.   Rousset, ed., *Correspondance*, II, 255.

14.   Pieter Geyl, *Willem IV en Engeland tot 1748 (Vrede van Aken)* (The Hague: Martinus Nijhoff, 1924), p. 335.

15.   Arneth, *Maria Theresia*, III, 469.

16.   A copy of the project worked out by Macanaz and Sandwich is printed in Maria Dolores Gómez Molleda, "El 'caso Macanaz' en el Congreso de Breda," *Hispania* XVIII (1958): 121-28.

17.   C. Gerretson and P. Geyl, eds., *Briefwisseling en Aanteekeningen van Willem Bentinck, Heer van Rhoon*, Vol. I: *Tot aan de Praeliminarien van Aken (30 April 1748)* (Utrecht: Kemink en Zoon, 1934), p. 265.

18.   The provinces were: Friesland, Gelderland, Groningen, Holland, Overijsel, Utrecht, and Zeeland. Additionally the United Provinces held the strip of land that bordered the Austrian Netherlands. Jointly controlled by all seven provinces, it was appropriately called the land of the Generality.

19.   J. A. Van Houtte, et al., eds., *Algemene Geschiedenis der Nederlanden* (Utrecht: W. de Haan, 1955), VIII, 1.

20.   I take the terminology from Margaret C. Jacob, *The Radical Enlightenment: Pantheists, Freemasons and Republicans* (New York: Barnes and Noble, 1972), p. 734. There is no single generally accepted English-language term for this group. The "Republican party" is sometimes used; even "the regents" (despite its patent ambiguity) is sometimes employed.

21.   Pieter Geyl, *Geschiedenis van de Nederlandse Stam* (Amsterdam: Wereldbibliothek, 1962), IV, 1091.

22.   Butler, *Choiseul*, p. 687.

23.   Geyl, *Willem IV*, p. 338.

24.   Michel Richard, *Les Orange-Nassau* (Lausanne: Editions Rencontre, 1968), p. 217.

25.   British Library, Add. MSS 32806, fol. 124.

26.   British Library, Add. MSS 32808, fol. 101.

27.   Th. Bussemaker, ed., *Archives ou correspondance inédite de la maison d'Orange-Nassau*, 4th ser., I (Leiden: A. W. Sijthoff, 1908), p. 31.

NOTES TO CHAPTER 18

1.   Richard C. Saxby, "The Western Squadron and the Blockade of Brest," *History Today* 23 (1973): 20.

2.   Accounts of the battle of Cape Ortegal may be found in Richmond, *Navy in the War*, III, 86-95; Lacour-Gayet, *Marine militaire*, 181-84; and Beatson, *Naval and Military Memoirs*, I, 357-62.

3.   N.A.M. Rodger, *The Wooden World: An Anatomy of the Georgian Navy* (Annapolis, MD: Naval Institute Press, 1986), p. 58.

4.   For extended accounts of the battle of Assietta, see Andrea Vignetta, *Battaglia dell'Assietta* (Pinerola: P. P. Giuseppini, 1960), and Vittorio Dabormida, *la bataille de l'Assiette 1747: étude historique*, trans. L.-Ch. Laporte (Paris: Spectateur Militaire, 1884), *passim*. Contemporary accounts vary enormously. The engagement is sometimes called the battle of Exilles.

5. These figures are taken from Dabormida, p. 141; Vignetta, *Battaglia*, p. 8; and Wilkinson, *Defence*, p. 309 (despite an error in addition). But Broglie, following Marshal Belle-Isle's bowdlerized account of the battle, puts French casualties at 1,500. *Maurice de Saxe*, II, 317-18.

6. White, *Marshal*, p. 222.

7. Guglia, *Maria Theresia*, I, 299.

8. Venturi, "Genova," p. 784.

9. Good accounts of the battle of Laffeld may be found in White, *Marshal*, pp. 212-19; Whitworth, *Ligonier*, pp. 151-54; Broglie, *Maurice de Saxe*, II, 270-75; Butler, *Choiseul*, pp. 689-96; Jean Baptiste Joseph Sahuguet d'Amarzit, Baron d'Espagnac, *Campagne de l'armée du roi en 1747* (The Hague: Henry Scheuleer, 1747), pp. 175-230.

10. There is the usual range of estimates. I follow Whitworth, *Ligonier*, p. 155. Bodart, *Troupes*, p. 218, in a breakdown of allied casualties, gives a total of 5,782, with the Hanoverians and the British bearing the brunt of the toll. D'Espagnac, *1747*, 238, however, puts French casualties at only 5,000 (half of them fatalities) and Vogüé and Le Sourd, eds., *Campagnes*, p. 96, goes even lower, to 4,200 (contrasted to 9,500 allied casualties). Pajol, *Guerres*, III, 542, cites figures of 8,700 French casualties and 10,000 allied. Clearly the reader must treat all figures, including mine, cautiously.

11. Expressed as a *percentage* of participants, the casualty figure of 7 percent is, of course, far lower than the corresponding figure for most other battles. The lowness is a consequence of the fact that the western ends of the two lines, including almost the entire Austrian force, did not engage.

12. Broglie, *Maurice de Saxe*, II, 276.

13. Butler, *Choiseul*, p. 694.

14. British Library, Add. MSS 32711, 473.

15. Skrine, *Fontenoy*, p. 333.

16. Broglie, *Maurice de Saxe*, II, 340. Ligonier traveled to the British camp on parole and, in accordance with its terms, later returned to French captivity.

17. Lodge, *Studies*, p. 286.

18. Duffy, *Siege Warfare*, II, 107.

19. Vienna, Kriegsarchiv, Brown's MSS, 39.

20. I take these figures from White, *Marshal*, pp. 225-28. If the whole siege is considered, French casualties are higher — 1,000 dead and 4,000 wounded. André Louis Woldemar Alphée, Marquis de Sinéty, *Vie du maréchal de Lowendahl* (Paris: Librairie Bachelin-Deflorenne, 1867), II, 124.

21. Skrine, *Fontenoy*, p. 337.

22. British Library, Add. MSS 32810, 72.

23. A full account of the battle may be found in Ruddock F. Mackay, *Admiral Hawke* (Oxford: Clarendon Press, 1965), pp. 69-88. See also Richmond, *Navy in the War*, III, 104-10; Beatson, *Naval and Military Memoirs*, I, 365-70; Raoul Victor Patrice Castex, *Les idées militaires de la marine au XVIIIe siècle: de Ruyter à Suffren* (Paris: L. Fournier, 1911), pp. 223-28.

24. On the principle that the nearest landfall supplies the name. The more conventional titles are the second battle of Cape Finisterre and the battle of Belle-Isle.

25. Alfred Thayer Mahan, *Types of Naval Officers Drawn from the History of the British Navy* (Boston: Little, Brown, 1901), p. 92.

26. Mackay, *Admiral Hawke*, p. 87.

NOTES TO CHAPTER 19

1. Maria Dolores Gómez Molleda, "El Pensamiento de Carvajal y la política internacional española del siglo XVIII," *Hispania* 15 (1955): 128.

2. Robert Pick, *Empress Maria Theresa: The Earlier Years, 1717-1757* (New York: Harper and Row, 1966), p. 185.

3. It is worth noting, however, that the percentage of Britain's wartime expenses borne by borrowing was lower during the war of 1739-48 than for any eighteenth-century war until the very end of the century.

4. Carutti, *Storia della diplomazia*, IV, 305.

5. Butler, *Choiseul*, p. 723.

6. Coxe, *Memoirs of Pelham*, I, 284.

7. Albert Duke of Broglie, *La paix d'Aix-la-Chapelle, 1748* (Paris: Calman Levy, 1891), p. 16.

8. Baudi di Vesme, "Pace," 66:105. It reflected the transitory nature of his stays in realms he claimed.

9. Carutti, *Storia della diplomazia*, IV, 305.

10. Baudi di Vesme, "Pace," 66:103.

11. Auerbach, *France*, p. 333.

12. M. S. Anderson, *Britain's Discovery of Russia 1553-1815* (London: Macmillan, 1958), p. 114.

13. British Library, Add. MSS 32811, f. 102.

14. Butler, *Choiseul*, p. 679.

15. Vitzthum, ed., *Saxe*, p. 510.

16. Broglie, *Paix*, p. 104.

17. Broglie, *Paix*, p. 73.

18. Lodge, *Studies*, p. 316.

19. Arneth, *Maria Theresia*, III, 480.

20. Adolf Beer, "Zur Geschichte des Friedens von Aachen im Jahre 1748," *Archiv für österreichischen Geschichte* 47 (1871): 73.

21. Sandwich and Chavanne arrived on 17 March, Kaunitz on 18 March, William Bentinck on 25 March, Saint Severin on 26 March, Masones on 17 April, d'Oria on 19 April, and Manzone on 16 May.

22.   Broglie, *Paix,* pp. 107-108.

23.   Arneth, *Maria Theresia,* III, 484.

24.   Arneth, *Maria Theresia,* III, 483. Bernhard Poll, "Zur Geschichte des Aachener Friedens 1748," *Zeitschrift des Aachener Geschichtsvereins* 81 (1971): 27-90, prints abridgements of many of Kaunitz's reports between February and June 1748.

25.   Paul-Emile Schatzman, *The Bentincks: The History of a European Family,* trans. Steve Cox (London: Weidenfeld and Nicolson, 1976), p. 145.

26.   Three works are central to our understanding of what happened at Aix-la-Chapelle: Lodge, *Studies*; Beer, "Zur Geschichte,"; and Baudi di Vesme, "Pace."

NOTES TO CHAPTER 20

1.   Baudi di Vesme, "Pace," 65:298.

2.   Ozanam, ed., *Diplomacia,* p. 47.

3.   Jean Olivia McLachlan, *Trade and Peace with Old Spain* (Cambridge: Cambridge University Press, 1940), p. 208. Punctuation altered.

4.   Guglia, *Maria Theresia,* I, 306.

5.   Beer, "Zur Geschichte," p. 54.

6.   Lewis, ed., *Walpole Correspondence,* XIX, 482; Lodge, *Studies,* pp. 340.

7.   Broglie, *Paix,* pp. 170-73.

8.   Arneth, *Maria Theresia,* III, 485.

9.   Broglie, *Paix,* p. 160.

10.   Almost. Corsica continued to smolder, where shards of the Bourbon and Worms armies were on the alert, their conduct circumscribed (after mid-September 1748) only by an imperfect armistice.

11.   Sir Richard Lodge, *Great Britain and Prussia in the Eighteenth Century* (Oxford: Clarendon Press, 1923), p. 66.

12.   *Politische Correspondenz,* VI, 123.

13.   Beer, "Zur Geschichte," p. 41.

14.   Beer, "Zur Geschichte," p. 49.

15.   Ozanam, ed., *Diplomacia,* p. 48.

16.   British Library, Add. MSS 32715, f. 166.

17.   This sum should not be confused with the identical sum promised by Britain as a subsidy for Austrian *infantry* in the Low Countries. It too was eventually paid—in 1749—but as a matter of policy not justice, since no one could pretend that Vienna had complied with this particular commitment.

18.   Lodge, *Studies,* p. 394.

19. *Recueil*, 23, *Holland*, III, 165.

20. Broglie, *Paix*, p. 263.

21. William J. McGill, "Wenzel Anton von Kaunitz and the Congress of Aix-la-Chapelle, 1748," *Duquesne Review* 14 (1969), 160.

22. Baudi di Vesme, "Pace," 65: 283.

23. Kalbrunner and Biener, eds., *Politisches Testament*, p. 82.

24. Baudi di Vesme, "Pace," 66: 376.

25. Ozanam, ed., *Diplomacia*, pp. 44-45.

26. Arneth, *Maria Theresia*, III, 488.

27. Maurice Daniel, "Don Philippe: Généralissime de l'armée espagnole de Savoie (1742-1748)," *Mémoires de l'Académie des Sciences, Belles-Lettres et Arts de Savoie*, 6th ser., 4 (1960): 155.

28. Baudi di Vesme, "Pace," 65: 265.

NOTES TO CHAPTER 21

1. *Recueil des instructions . . . Autriche*, p. 20.

2. Beer, "Zur Geschichte," p. 39.

3. Arnold Berney, *Friedrich der Grosse: Entwicklungsgeschichte eines Staatmannes* (Tübingen: J.C.B. Mohr, 1934), p. 164.

4. Orr, *Dettingen*, p. 4.

5. Boris Zesarewitsch Urlanis, *Bilanz der Kriege: die Menschenverluste Europas vom 17. Jahrhundert bis zur Gegenwart*, trans. Gerhard Hartmann (Berlin: Deutscher Verlag fur Wissenschaften, 1965), pp 60-64. Urlanis calculates that approximately 400,000 casualties resulted from engagements during the war. I agree. On the grounds that the average ratio of wounded to dead in the eighteenth century was 2.4:1, he estimates the number of fatalities at about 120,000. My counts suggest that the ratio during the War of the Austrian Succession was about 3:1, and so the total of deaths is reduced to about 100,000. As an indication of how conservative my judgment is and of how uncertain the procedures of historians are, it is worth noting that Jack Levy, *War in the Modern Great Power System, 1495-1975* (Lexington, KY: University Press of Kentucky, 1983), p. 90, says that 359,000 military personnel died as a result of battle during the war.

6. Jean Nicolas, *La Savoie au XVIIIe siècle. Noblesse et bourgeoisie* (Paris: Maloine, 1978), II: 556-58.

7. Broglie, *Frédéric II et Marie Thérèse*, II, 210.

8. See Myron P. Gutmann, *War and Rural Life in the Early Modern Low Countries* (Princeton: Princeton University Press, 1980), especially p. 173.

9. Baudi di Vesme, "Pace," 66: 423.

10. Jean Rousset de Missy, *Histoire mémorable des guerres entre les maisons de France e3 d'Autriche*, 4 vols. (Amsterdam: Ryckhoff, 1743), IV, 325-26.

11. Lewis, ed., *Walpole Correspondence*, XVIII, 458.

■ BIBLIOGRAPHY ■

BOOKS

Acerra, Martine; Merino, José; and Meyer, Jean, eds. *Les marines de guerre européennes: XVII-XVIIIe siècles*. Paris: Presses de l'Université de Paris-Sorbonne, 1985.

Acton, Harold. *The Bourbons of Naples (1734-1825)*. London: Methuen, 1957.

Ailly, Antoine Jean d', Jr. *Willem Bentinck van Rhoon en die Diplomatieke Betrekkingen tusschen Engeland en de Nederlansche Republiek gedurende de Laatste Jaren vóór den Vrede van Aken in 1748*. Amsterdam: J. H. de Wit, 1898.

Albertini, P.-L., and Rivollet, G. *La Corse militaire: ses généraux: monarchie, révolution, 1er empire*. Paris: Peyronnet, 1958.

Alger, John I. *The Quest for Victory: The History of the Principles of War*. Westport, CT: Greenwood Press, 1982.

Allmayer-Beck, Johann Christoph. "Das Heer der Kaiserin." In Walter Koschatzky, ed., *Maria Theresia und ihre Zeit*, pp. 83-90. Vienna: Residenz Verlag, 1980.

Alonso, José Ramón. *Historia política del ejército español, 1700-1931*. Madrid: J. Benita, 1974.

Altamira y Crevea, R. *Historia de España y de la civilizacion española*. 5 vols. Barcelona: Heredros de J. Gill, 1928-30.

Ambrosi, Christian. *La Corse insurgée et la seconde intervention française au XVIIIe siècle (1743-1753)*. Grenoble: Imprimerie Allier, 1950.

Anderson, M. S. *Britain's Discovery of Russia 1553-1815*. London: Macmillan, 1958.

— — —. *Europe in the Eighteenth Century, 1713-1783*. London: Holt, Rinehart and Winston, 1961.

Andolenko, C. R. *Histoire de l'armée Russe*. Paris: Flammarion, 1967.

Anes, Gonzalo. *El antiguo régimen: los Borbones*. Madrid: Ediciones Alfaguara, 1975.

Anson, Walter Vernon. *The Life of Admiral Lord Anson: The Father of the British Navy 1697-1762*. London: John Murray, 1912.

Antoine, Michel. *Le conseil du roi sous le regne de Louis XV*. Geneva: Librairie Droz, 1970.

Antonetti, Pierre. *Histoire de la Corse*. Paris: Robert Laffont, 1973.

Aranda, Joaquin M. *El Marqués de la Ensenada: Estudios sobre su administración*. Madrid: Los Hijos de M. G. Hernàndez, 1898.

Argenson, Rene-Louis de Voyer de Paulmy, Marquis d'. *Journal et mémoires*. Vols. 4-5. Edited by E.J.B. Rathery. Paris: V. Jules Renouard, 1862-63.

Armstrong, Edward. *Elizabeth Farnese: "The Termagant of Spain."* London: Longmans, Green & Co., 1892.

Arneth, Alfred Ritter von, ed. *Briefe der Kaiserin Maria Theresia an ihre Kinder und Freunde*. 4 vols. Vienna: Wilhelm Braumüller, 1881.

— — —. *Maria Theresia*. 10 vols. Vienna: W. Braumüller, 1863-79.

Arvers, P., ed. *Les guerres des Alpes: guerre de la succession d'Autriche (1742-1748)*. 2 vols. Paris: Librairie Militaire Berger-Levrault, 1892.

Auerbach, B. *La France et le Saint Empire Romain Germanique depuis la paix de Westphalie jusqu'à la révolution française*. Paris: Librairie Ancienne Honore Champion, 1912.

Bain, R. N. *The Daughter of Peter the Great*. Westminster: A. Constable, 1899.

Balázs, Eva H. "Die Königin von Ungarn." In Walter Koschatzky, ed., *Maria Theresia und ihre Zeit*, pp. 97-104. Vienna: Residenz Verlag, 1980.

Ballantyne, Archibald. *Lord Carteret: A Political Biography 1690-1763*. London: Richard Bentley, 1887.

Bamford, Paul Walden. *Forests and French Sea Power, 1660-1789*. Toronto: University of Toronto Press, 1956.

Barbier, Edmond-Jean-François. *Chronique de la régence et du règne de Louis XV (1718-1763) ou Journal de Barbier*. 7 vols. Paris: G. Charpentiers, 1885.

Barker, Thomas M. *Army, Aristocracy, and Monarchy: Essays on War, Society, and Government in Austria, 1618-1780*. New York: Columbia University Press, 1982.

Baudi di Vesme, Carlo. *La politica mediterranea inglese nelle relazioni degli inviati italiani a Londra durante la cosidetta "guerra di successione d'Austria" 1741-1748*. Turin: Gheroni, 1952.

— — —. *Studi sul XVIII secolo: le prime manifestazioni della rivoluzione d'occidente in Francia e nelle repubbliche oligarchie (1748-1775)*. Turin: Palazzo Carignano, 1972.

Baudrillart, Alfred, Cardinal. *Philippe V et la cour de France*. 5 vols. Paris: Librairie de Paris, 1890-1900.

Baugh, Daniel A. *British Naval Administration in the Age of Walpole*. Princeton, NJ: Princeton University Press, 1965.

Baumgart, Peter. "Die Annexion und Eingliederung Schlesiens in den friderizianischen Staat." In Peter Baumgart, ed. *Expansion und Integration: Zur Eingliederung neugewonnener Gebiete in den preussischen Staat*. Cologne: Böhlau Verlag, 1984.

Beatson, Robert. *Naval and Military Memoirs of Great Britain, from the year 1727 to the present time*. 6 vols. London: J. Strachan, 1790-1804.

Becke, A. F. *An Introduction to the History of Tactics 1740-1905*. London: Hugh Rees, 1909.

Becker, Reinhold. *Der Dresdener Friede und die Politik Brühls*. Leipzig: S. Hirzel, 1902.

Becker y Gonzalez, Jeronimo. *España y Inglaterra: sus relaciones políticas desde las paces de Utrecht*. Madrid: Ambrosio Perez, 1907.

Bedarida, Henri. *Les premiers Bourbons de Parme et l'Espagne (1731-1802)*. Paris: Librairie Ancienne Honore Champion, 1928; reprint ed., Paris: Librairie Marcel Didier, 1969.

Benedikt, Heinrich. *Als Belgien österreichisch war*. Vienna: Verlag Herold, 1965.

— — —. *Kaiseradler über den Apennin. Die Österreicher in Italien 1700-1866*. Vienna: Verlag Herold, 1964.

Bercé, Yves-Marie. *Révoltes et révolutions dans l'Europe moderne (XVIe-XVIIIe siècles)*. Paris: Presses Universitaires de France, 1980.

Bergamini, John D. *The Spanish Bourbons: The History of a Tenacious Dynasty*. New York: G. P. Putnam's Sons, 1974.

Berney, Arnold. *Friedrich der Grosse: Entwicklungsgeschichte eines Staatsmannes*. Tübingen: J.C.B. Mohr, 1934.

Bernier, Olivier. *Louis the Beloved: The Life of Louis XV*. Garden City, NY: Doubleday, 1984.

Bernis, François-Joachim de Pierre, Cardinal. *Mémoires et lettres*. 2 vols. Edited by F. Masson. Paris: E. Plon, 1878.

Bertling, M. *Die Kroaten und Panduren in der Mitte des XVIII. Jahrhunderts und ihre Verwendung in den Friderizianischen Kriegen*. Berlin: Herman Blanke, 1912.

Beskrovnyi, Liubomir Grigorevich. *Russkaia armiia i flot v XVIII v.* Moscow: Academy of Science of the USSR, 1958.

Biggs, William. *The Military History of Europe, &c from the Commencement of the War with Spain in 1739 to the Treaty of Aix-la-Chapelle in 1748.* London: R. Baldwin, 1755.

Binder, Sidonia. *Carl Graf Batthyany, Nachmals Fürst, Feldmarschall, Minister der Niederlande und Erzieher Joseph II.* Vienna, 1976.

Bindoff, S. T. *The Scheldt Question to 1839.* London, 1945.

Birke, Adolf M., and Kluxen, Kurt, eds. *England und Hannover/England and Hanover.* Munich: K. G. Saur, 1986.

Black, Jeremy. *British Foreign Policy in the Age of Walpole.* Edinburgh: John Donald, 1985.

———. *Culloden and the '45.* New York: St. Martin's, 1990.

———. "Foreign Policy in the Age of Walpole." In Jeremy Black, ed., *Britain in the Age of Walpole,* pp. 145-69. New York: St. Martin's, 1984.

Black, Jeremy, ed. *The Origins of War in Early Modern Europe.* Edinburgh: John Donald, 1987.

Black, Jeremy, and Woodfine, Philip, eds. *The British Navy and the Use of Naval Power in the Eighteenth Century.* Leicester: Leicester University Press, 1988.

Blainey, Geoffrey. *The Causes of War.* New York: Free Press, 1973.

Blanning, T.C.W. *Reform and Revolution in Mainz, 1743-1803.* London: Cambridge University Press, 1974.

Blaschke, Karlheinz. *Zur Bevölkerungsgeschichte Sachsens vor der industriellen Revolution.* Weimar: Hermann Bohlaus, 1967.

Bleich, Erich. *Die mährische Feldzug Friedrichs II. 1741/42.* Berlin: R. Sieble, 1901.

Blet, H. *Histoire de la colonisation française.* Vol. 1. Grenoble: B. Artaud, 1946.

Bodart, Gaston. *Losses of Life in Modern Wars: Austria-Hungary; France.* Oxford: Clarendon Press, 1916.

Boom, Ghislaine de. *Les ministres plénipotentiares dans les Pays-Bas autrichiens, principalement Cobenzl.* Brussels: Lamertin, 1932.

Borkowsky, Ernst Otto. *Die englische Friedensvermittlung in Jahre 1745. Ein Beitrag zur Geschichte der geheimen Diplomatie König Georges II.* Berlin: F. Berggold, 1884.

Boroviczény, Aladar von. *Graf von Brühl: Der Medici, Richelieu und Rothschild seiner Zeit.* Zurich: Amalthen, 1930.

Boudard, René. *Gênes et la France dans la deuxième moitié de XVIIIe siècle.* Paris: Mouton, 1962.

Bourcet, P. J. de. *Principes de la guerre de montagnes.* Paris: Imprimerie Nationale, 1775.

Boutry, Maurice. *Intrigues et Missions du Cardinal de Tencin.* Paris: Émile-Paul, 1902.

Bouvier, René, and Laffargue, André. *La vie napolitaine au XVIIIe siècle: Prélude au voyage à Naples.* Paris: Hatchette, 1956.

Bouvier, René, and Soldevila, C. *Ensenada et son temps: le redressement de l'Espagne au XVIIIe siècle.* Paris: Fernand Sorlot, 1941.

Brancaccio, Nicola. *L'esercito del vecchio Piemonte (1560-1859).* Rome: Amministrazione della Guerra, 1922.

Braubach, Max. *Diplomatie und geistiges Leben im 17. und 18. Jahrhundert.* Bonn: Röhrscheid, 1969.

———. *Versailles und Wien von Ludwig XIV. bis Kaunitz. Die Vorstadien der diplomatischen Revolution im 18. Jahrhundert.* Bonn: Ludwig Röhrscheid, 1952.

Braudel, Ferdinand, and Labrousse, E., eds. *Histoire économique et sociale de la France.* Vol. 2: *Des derniers temps de l'âge seigneurial aux préludes de l'âge industriel (1660-1789).* Paris: Presses Universitaires de France, 1970.

Brauer, Gert. *Die hannoversch-englischen Subsidienverträge 1702-1748*. Aalen: Scientia Verlag, 1962.

Bremen, Walter von. *Die Schlacht bei Kesselsdorf am 15 Dezember 1745*. Berlin: Ernst Siegfried Mittler und Sohn, 1888.

Brennan, James F. *Enlightened Despotism in Russia: The Reign of Elizabeth, 1741-1762*. New York: Peter Lang, 1987.

Brewer, John. *The Sinews of Power: War, Money, and the English State 1688-1783*. New York: Alfred A. Knopf, 1989.

Broche, Gaston-E. *La république de Gênes et la France pendant la guerre de la succession d'Autriche (1740-1748)*. 3 vols. Paris: Société Française d'Imprimerie et de Librairie, 1935.

Broglie, Albert, Duke of. *Frédéric II et Louis XV, 1742-44*. 2 vols. Paris: Calmann Levy, 1885.

———. *Frédéric II et Marie Thérèse, 1740-1742*. 2 vols. Paris: Calmann Levy, 1883.

———. *Marie Thérèse impératrice, 1744-1746*. 2 vols. Paris: Calmann Levy, 1888.

———. *Maurice de Saxe et le Marquis d'Argenson, 1746-1747*. 2 vols. Paris: Calmann Levy, 1891.

———. *La paix d'Aix-la-Chapelle, 1748*. Paris: Calmann Levy, 1891.

Broicher, Elisabeth Charlotte. *Der Aufstieg der preussischen Macht von 1713 bis 1756*. Cologne: University of Cologne dissertation, 1955.

Browning, Reed. *The Duke of Newcastle*. New Haven, Conn.: Yale University Press, 1975.

Bruijn, J. R. *De Admiraliteit van Amsterdam in Rustige Jaren 1713-1751: Regenten en Financiën, Schepen en Zeevarenden*. Amsterdam: Scheltma & Holkema, 1970.

Brun, Vincent Félix. *Guerres maritimes de la France: Port de Toulon*. 2 vols. Paris: Henri Plon, 1861.

Buffa di Perrero, Carlo. *Carlo Emmanuele III di Savoia a difesa delle Alpi nella campagna del 1744*. Turin: Fratelli Bocca, 1887.

Buonanmici, Pietro Giuseppe Maria [later Count Castruccio]. *Denkwürdigkeiten des italienischen Krieges vom Jahre 1744 bis 1748. Aus dem Lateinischen übersetzt*. Breslau: Korn, 1756.

Büsch, Otto. *Militärsystem und Sozialleben im alten Preussen 1713-1807: Die Anfänge der sozialen Militarisierung der preussisch-deutschen Gesellschaft*. Berlin: Walter de Gruyter, 1962.

Bussemaker, Th., ed. *Archives ou correspondance inédite de la maison d'Orange-Nassau*. 4th ser. Vol. 1. Leiden: A. W. Sijthoff, 1908.

Butler, Rohan. *Choiseul*. Vol. 1, *Father and Son 1719-1754*. Oxford: Clarendon Press, 1980.

Campagnes de Monsieur le Maréchal de Maillebois, en Westphalie. L'an 1741, & 1742. Amsterdam: Rey, 1772.

Campagnes de Monsieur le Maréchal, duc de Coigny, en Allemagne, l'an 1743 et 1744, contenant plusieurs lettres de ce maréchal et celles de plusieurs autres officiers généraux au roi et à M. d'Argenson. 8 vols. Amsterdam: Rey, 1761.

Campagne de Monsieur le Maréchal, duc de Noailles, en Allemagne, l'an 1743, contenant les lettres de ce maréchal et celles de plusieurs officiers generaux au roi et à M. d'Argenson. 3 vols. Amsterdam: Rey, 1760-61.

Campo-Raso, Don Joseph de. *Continuacion à los Commentarios del Marques de S. Felipe desde el a:o de MDCCXXXIII*. Madrid: Imprenta Real, 1793.

Capra, Carlo, and Sella, Domenico. *Il Ducato di Milano dal 1535 al 1796*. Turin: UTET, 1984.

Carrias, E. *La pensée militaire française*. Paris: Presses Universitaires de France, 1960.

Carsten, F. *Princes and Parliaments in Germany from the Fifteenth to the Eighteenth Century*. Oxford: Clarendon Press, 1959.

Carter, Alice Clare. *The Dutch Republic in Europe in the Seven Years War*. London: Macmillan, 1971.

———. *Neutrality or Commitment: The Evolution of Dutch Foreign Policy, 1667-1795*. London: Edward Arnold, 1975.

Carutti, Domenico. *Storia della diplomazia della Corte di Savoia*. 4 vols. Turin: Fratelli Bocca, 1880.

———. *Storia del regno di Carlo Emmanuele III*. Turin: Ered. Botta, 1859.

Castex, Raoul Victor Patrice. *Les idées militaires de la marine du XVIIIe siècle: De Ruyter à Suffren*. Paris: L. Fournier, 1911.

Cesari-Rocca, Colonna de, and Villat, Louis. *Histoire de Corse*. Paris: Ancienne Librairie Furne, 1916.

Chandler, David. *The Art of Warfare in the Age of Marlborough*. London: B. T. Batsford, 1976.

———. *Atlas of Military Strategy*. New York: Free Press, 1980.

Charliat, P. *Trois siècles d'économie maritime française*. Paris: Marcel Rivière, 1931.

Charteris, Evan. *William Augustus, Duke of Cumberland: His Early Life and Times (1721-1748)*. London: Edward Arnold, 1913.

Childs, John. *Armies and Warfare in Europe 1648-1789*. New York: Holmes and Meier, 1982.

[Cognazzo, J.] *Freymüthiger Beytrag zur Geschichte des österreichischen Militairdienstes*. Frankfurt: n.p., 1789.

Colin, Jean Lambert Alphonse. *Les campagnes de Maréchal de Saxe*. 3 vols. Paris: Librairie Militaire R. Chapelot & Cie, 1901-1906.

———. *Louis XV et les Jacobites: le projet de débarquement en Angleterre de 1743-44*. Paris: Librairie Militaire R. Chapelot et Cie, 1901.

Conn, Stetson. *Gibraltar in British Diplomacy in the Eighteenth Century*. New Haven: Yale University Press, 1942.

Coquelle, P. *L'alliance franco-hollandaise contre l'Angleterre 1735-1788*. Paris: Librairie Plon, 1902.

Cornet, Henri, ed. *Siège de Prague (1742). Journal authentique d'un Lieutenant-Ingénieur dans l'Armée Autrichienne devant Prague*. Vienna: Tendler, 1867.

Corvisier, Andre. *L'armée française de la fin du XVIIe siècle au ministere de Choiseul: Le soldat*. 2 vols. Paris: Pressses Universitaires de France, 1964.

———. *Armies and Societies in Europe, 1494-1789*. Translated by Abigail T. Siddall. Bloomington: Indiana University Press, 1979.

Costa de Beauregard, Joseph Henri, Marquis de. *Mémoires historiques sur la maison royale de Savoie*. Vol. 3. Turin: Pierre Joseph Pic, 1816.

Coxe, William. *History of the House of Austria*, 3rd ed. 4 vols. London: George Bell and Sons, 1877.

———. *Memoirs of the Administration of the Right Honourable Henry Pelham*. 2 vols. London: Orme, 1829.

———. *Memoirs of the Kings of Spain of the House of Bourbon*. 3 vols. London: Longman, 1813-15.

Craig, Gordon A. *The Politics of the Prussian Army 1640-1945*. Oxford: Clarendon Press, 1955.

Cregreen, Eric. "The Changing Role of the House of Argyll in the Scottish Highlands." In N. T. Phillipson and Rosalind Mitchison, eds., *Scotland in the Age of Improvement: Essays in Scottish History in the Eighteenth Century*. Edinburgh: Edinburgh University Press, 1970.

Creswell, John. *British Admirals of the Eighteenth Century: Tactics in Battle*. Hamden, CT: Archon Books, 1972.

Creveld, Martin Van. *Supplying War: Logistics from Wallenstein to Patton*. Cambridge: Cambridge University Press, 1978.

Crousse, Franz. *Les guerres de la succession d'Autriche dans les provinces belgiques, campagnes de 1740 à 1748*. Paris: L. Baudoin, 1885.

Crowhurst, Patrick. *The Defence of British Trade, 1689-1815.* London: W. & J. Mackay, 1977.

Cruickshanks, Eveline, ed. *Ideology and Conspiracy: Aspects of Jacobitism, 1689-1759.* Edinburgh: John Donald, 1982.

— — —. *Political Untouchables: The Tories and the '45.* New York: Holmes & Meier, 1979.

Cruickshanks, Eveline, and Black, Jeremy, eds. *The Jacobite Challenge.* Edinburgh: John Donald, 1988.

Dabormida, Vittorio. *La bataille de l'Assiette 1747: étude historique.* Translated by L.-Ch. Laporte. Paris: Spectateur Militaire, 1884.

Daiches, David. *The Last Stuart: The Life and Times of Bonnie Prince Charlie.* New York: G. P. Putnam's Sons, 1973.

Dann, Uriel. *Hanover and Great Britain 1740-1760: Diplomacy and Survival.* London: Leicester University Press, 1991.

Danvila y Collado, Manuel. *Reinado de Carlos III.* Vol. 1, *Educación política de D. Carlos de Borbón, Infante de España.* Madrid: El Progreso Editorial, 1893.

Dardel, Pierre. *Navires et marchandises dans les ports de Rouen et du Havre au XVIIIe siècle.* Paris: S.E.V.P.E.N., 1963.

De Forest, Louis Effingham, ed. *Louisbourg Journals 1745.* New York: Society of Colonial Wars in the State of New York, 1932.

Dette, Erwin. *Friedrich der Grosse und sein Heer.* Göttingen: Vandenhoek & Ruprecht, 1914.

De Vries, Jan. *Economy of Europe in an Age of Crisis, 1600-1750.* Cambridge: Cambridge University Press, 1976.

Diarium Pragense: Das ist ausführliche Beschreibung Aller dessen, was sich von Anfang des letzten Böhmischen Kriegs an sowohl bey der Belagerung und Eroberung der königlichen Haupt-Stadt Prag. N.p., 1744.

Dickson, P.G.M. "English Commercial Negotiations with Austria, 1737-1752." In Anne Whitman et al., eds., *Statesmen, Scholars, and Merchants,* pp. 81-112. Oxford: Oxford University Press, 1973.

— — —. *Finance and Government under Maria Theresa 1740-1780.* 2 vols. Oxford: Clarendon Press, 1987.

— — —. *The Financial Revolution in England: A Study in the Development of Public Credit 1688-1756.* London: St. Martin's, 1967.

Discailles, Ernest. *Les Pays-Bas sous le regne de Marie-Thérèse (1740-1780).* Brussels: C. Muquart, 1873.

Dolleczek, Anton. *Geschichte der österreichischen Artillerie von den frühesten Zeiten bis zur Gegenwart.* Vienna: Kreisel & Gröger, 1887.

Doria, Francesco Maria. *Della storia di Genova negli anni 1745. 1746. 1747.* [Modena:] n.p., 1748.

Downey, Fairfax. *Louisbourg: Key to a Continent.* Englewood Cliffs, NJ: Prentice-Hall, 1965.

Droysen, Johann Gustav. *Geschichte der preussischen Politik.* Part 5, *Friedrich der Grosse.* Vol. 2. Leipzig: Veit & Comp., 1876.

Duffy, Christopher. *The Army of Frederick the Great.* London: David and Charles, 1974.

— — —. *The Army of Maria Theresa: The Armed Forces of Imperial Austria 1740-1780.* New York: Hippocrene, 1977.

— — —. *Fire and Stone: The Science of Fortress Warfare 1660-1860.* New York: Hippocrene, 1975.

— — —. *The Military Life of Frederick the Great.* New York: Atheneum, 1986.

— — —. *Russia's Military Way to the West: Origins and Nature of Russian Military Power 1700-1800.* Boston: Routledge and Kegan Paul, 1981.

— — —. *Siege Warfare.* Vol. 2, *The Fortress in the Age of Vauban and Frederick the Great 1660-1789.* Boston: Routledge and Kegan Paul, 1985.

— — —. *The Wild Goose and the Eagle: A Life of Marshal von Browne, 1705-1757.* London: Chatto, 1964.

Duffy, Michael, ed. *The Military Revolution and the State 1500-1800.* Exeter: University of Exeter, 1980.

Dukes, Paul. *The Making of Russian Absolutism 1613-1801.* New York: Longman, 1982.

Dumortous, Pierre. *Histoire des conquêtes de Louis XV. tant en Flandres que sur le Rhin, en Allemagne & en Italie, depuis 1744, jusques à la paix conclue en 1748.* Paris: Chez de Lormel, 1759.

Dunthorne, Hugh. *The Maritime Powers 1721-1740: A Study of Anglo-Dutch Relations in the Age of Walpole.* New York: Garland, 1986.

Earle, E. M., ed. *Makers of Modern Strategy.* Princeton, NJ: Princeton University Press, 1944.

Egido Lopez, Teofanes. *Opinion publica y oposicion al poder en la Espa:a del siglo XVIII (1713-1759).* Valladolid: Sever-Cuesta, 1971.

Egret, Jean. *Louis XV et l'opposition parlementaire, 1715-1774.* Paris: Librairie Armand Colin, 1970.

Ehgartner, Franz. *Der Regierungsanfang des Kurfürsten Maximilian III. Joseph von Bayern: Ein Beitrag zur Geschichte des Friedens von Füssen (1745).* Wurzburg: H. Sturtz, 1910.

Erskine, David, ed. *Augustus Hervey's Journal.* London: William Kimber, 1953.

Espagnac, Jean Baptiste Joseph Sahuguet d'Amarzit, Baron d'. *Campagne de l'armée du roi en 1747.* The Hague: Henry Scheuleer, 1747.

— — —. *Cartes et plans pour l'intelligence des deux éditions in-12 de l'histoire du Maréchal de Saxe.* Paris: n.p., n.d.

— — —. *Histoire de Maurice, Comte de Saxe.* 2 vols. New edition. Paris: Philippe-Denys Pierres, 1775.

— — —. *Journal historique de la dernière campagne de l'armée du roi en 1746.* The Hague: Henry Scheurleer, 1747.

Eszlry, Kroly. *La pragmatique sanction hongroise et celle des pays et provinces héréditaires des Habsbourg.* Paris: Librairie gen. de droit et de jurisprudence, 1952.

Faesch, Georg-Rudolph. *Geschichte der oesterreichischen Erbfolgekrieges von 1740-8.* 2 vols. Dresden: Walther, 1787.

Fernandez Duro, Cesareo. *Armada española desde la unión de los reinos de Castlla y de Aragon.* Vol. 6. Madrid: Sucesores de Rivadeneyra, 1900.

Filion, Maurice. *Maurepas: Ministre de Louis XV (1715-1749).* Montreal: Leméac, 1967.

— — —. *La pensée et l'action coloniale de Maurepas vis-à-vis du Canada 1723-1749: l'âge d'or de la colonie.* Ottawa: Leméac, 1972.

Fisher, H.E.S. *The Portugal Trade: A Study of Anglo-Portuguese Commerce 1700-1770.* London: Methuen, 1971.

Flassan, Gaetan de Raxis de. *Histoire générale et raisonée de la diplomatie française.* 7 vols. Paris: Treuttel et Wurtz, 1811.

Fleury, Jacques, Vicomte. *La cour aux armées pendant la guerre de succession d'Autriche.* Paris: Librairie Plon, 1926.

— — —. *Le secret de maréchal de Belle-Isle.* Paris: Firmin-Didot, 1934.

Foord, Archibald S. *His Majesty's Opposition 1714-1830.* Oxford: Clarendon Press, 1964.

Ford, Douglas. *Admiral Vernon and the Navy.* London: T. Fisher Unwin, 1907.

Forster, Robert. *The Nobility of Toulouse in the Eighteenth Century: A Social and Economic Study.* Baltimore, MD: The Johns Hopkins Press, 1960.

Forster, Robert, and Greene, Jack, eds. *Preconditions of Revolution in Early Modern Europe*. Baltimore, MD: The Johns Hopkins Press, 1970.

France. Archives diplomatique, Commission des. *Recueil des instructions données aux ambassadeurs et ministres de France depuis les traités de Westphalie jusqu'à la révolution française*. 28 vols. Paris: F. Alcan, 1884- .

Fred, W. *Briefe der Kaiserin Maria Theresia*. Translated by Hedwig Kubin. Munich: Georg Müller, 1914.

Frederick II. *Mémoires de Frédéric II*. Edited by B. Boutaric and E. Campardon. Vol. 1, *Histoire de mon temps*. Paris: Henri Plon, 1866.

Fritz, Paul Samuel. *The English Ministers and Jacobitism between the Rebellions of 1715 and 1745*. Toronto: University of Toronto Press, 1975.

Fromm, Elias. *Der Kaiserwahl Franz I.: Ein Beitrag zur deutschen Reichsgeschichte des achtzehnten Jahrhunderts*. Gnesen: Lange, 1883.

Fuller, J.F.C. *British Light Infantry in the Eighteenth Century*. London: Hutchinson & Co., 1925 (?).

Furlani, Silvio, and Wandruszka, Adam, eds. *Österreich und Italien: Ein bilaterales Geschichtsbuch*. Vienna: Jugend und Volk, 1973.

Gagliardo, John C. *Reich and Nation: The Holy Roman Empire as Idea and Reality, 1763-1806*. Bloomington: Indiana University Press, 1980.

Garcia Rives, Angela. *Fernando VI y Doña Barbara de Braganza (1748-1759): Apuntes sobre su reinado*. Madrid: Julio Cosano, 1917.

A General View of the Present Politics and Interests of the Principal Powers of Europe; Particularly of Those at War. London: W. Webb, [1747?].

Gerhard, Dietrich. *England und der Aufstieg Russlands*. Munich: R. Oldenbourg, 1933.

Gerretson, C., and Geyl, Pieter, eds. *Briefwisseling en Aanteekeningen van Willem Bentinck, Heer van Rhoon*. Volume 1, *Tot aan de Praeliminarien van Aken (30 April 1748)*. Utrecht: Kemink en Zoon, 1934.

Geyl, Pieter. *Geschiedenis van de Nederlandse Stam*. Vol. 4. Amsterdam: Wereldbibliothek, 1962.

― ― ―. "Historical Appreciations of the Holland Regent Regime." In A. O. Sarkissian, ed., *Studies in Diplomatic History and Historiography in Honour of G. P. Gooch*, pp. 287-303. New York: Barnes and Noble, 1961.

― ― ―. *Williem IV en Engeland tot 1748 (Vrede van Aken)*. The Hague: Martinus Nijhoff, 1924.

Giarelli, F. *Storia di Piacenza*. 2 vols. Piacenza: Vicenzo Porta, 1889.

Gibbon, Edward. *Autobiography*. Edited by Dero A. Saunders. New York: Meridien, 1961.

Girdlestone, Cuthbert. *Jean-Philippe Rameau: His Life and Work*. London: Cassell and Company, 1957.

Gooch, G. P. *Louis XV: The Monarchy in Decline*. London: Longmans, Green, 1956.

Gorani, Giuseppe, Count. *Memorie de giovanezza a di guerra*. Milan: A. Mondadari, 1936.

Gradish, Stephen F. *The Manning of the British Navy during the Seven Years' War*. London: Royal Historical Society, 1980.

Graham, Gerald S. *Empire of the North Atlantic: The Maritime Struggle for North America*, 2d ed. Toronto: University of Toronto Press, 1958.

Groehler, Olaf. *Die Kriege Friedrichs II*. East Berlin: Deutscher Militarverlag, 1968.

[Grosley, Pierre Jean.] *Mémoires sur les campagnes d'Italie de MDCCXLV et MDCCXLVI*. Amsterdam: Marc-Michel Rey, 1747.

Grünhagen, Colmar. *Geschichte des ersten schlesischen Krieges*. 2 vols. Gotha: Perthes, 1881.

Guglia, Eugen. *Maria Theresa: Ihr Leben und ihre Regierung*. 2 vols. Munich: R. Oldenbourg, 1917.

Guibal, Cornelis Jan. *Democratie en Oligarchie en Friesland tijdens de Republiek.* Assen: Van Gorcum, 1935.

Guichonnet, Paul, ed. *Histoire de la Savoie.* Toulouse: Edouard Privat, 1973.

Gutmann, Myron P. *War and Rural Life in the Early Modern Low Countries.* Princeton, NJ: Princeton University Press, 1980.

Guy, Alan J. *Oeconomy and Discipline: Officership and Administration in the British Army 1714-63.* Manchester: Manchester University Press, 1985.

Gwyn, Julian. *The Enterprising Admiral: The Personal Fortune of Admiral Sir Peter Warren.* Montreal: McGill-Queen's University Press, 1974.

Hall, Thad E. *France and the Eighteenth-Century Corsican Question.* New York: New York University Press, 1971.

Hamilton, Earl J. *War and Prices in Spain, 1651-1800.* In *Harvard Economic Studies* 81. Cambridge, MA.: Harvard University Press, 1947.

Hargreaves-Mawdsley, W. N. *Eighteenth-Century Spain, 1700-1788: A Political, Diplomatic and International History.* London: Macmillan, 1979.

— — —. *Spain under the Bourbons, 1700-1833: A Collection of Documents.* Columbia, SC: University of South Carolina Press, 1973.

Hart, Sir Basil Henry Liddell. *The Ghost of Napoleon.* London: Faber and Faber, 1933; reprint ed., Westport, CT: Greenwood Press, 1980.

Hartmann, Peter Claus. *Karl Albrecht-Karl VII.: Glücklicher Kurfürst Unglücklicher Kaiser.* Regensburg: Friedrich Pustet, 1985.

Hassell, W. v. *Die schlesischen Kriege und das Kurfürstentum Hannover.* Hanover: Hahn, 1879.

Hatton, Ragnhild. *The Anglo-Hanoverian Connection 1714-1760; The Creighton Trust Lecture.* London: University of London, 1982.

— — —. *George I: Elector and King.* Cambridge, MA: Harvard University Press, 1978.

Hatton, Ragnhild, and Anderson, M. S., eds. *Studies in Diplomatic History: Essays in Memory of David Bayne Horn* (New York: Archon, 1970).

Heeckeren, Emile de, ed. *Correspondance de Benoît XIV.* Paris: Plon, 1912.

Heigel, Karl Theodor von. *Die oesterreichische Erbfolgestreit und die Kaiserwahl Karls VII.* Nördlingen: Beck, 1877.

Heigel, Karl Theodor von, ed. *Das Tagebuch Kaiser Karl's VII aus der Zeit des österreichischen Erbfolgekrieges.* Munich: M. Rieger, 1883.

Heinermann, Erich. *England und Maria Theresia bis zum Berliner Frieden.* Vienna: University of Vienna dissertation, 1965.

Helm, Ernest Eugene. *Music at the Court of Frederick the Great.* Norman: University of Oklahoma Press, 1960.

Hennings, Fred. *Und Sitzet zur linken Hand. Franz Stephan von Lothringen, Gemahl der selbstregierenden Königin Maria Theresa und Römischer Kaiser.* Vienna: Paul Neff, 1961.

Hill, James Michael. *Celtic Warfare 1595-1763.* Edinburgh: John Donald, 1986.

Hillbrand, Erich. *Die Einschliessung von Linz 1741/42. Vol. 15 of Militärhistorische Schriftenreihe.* Vienna: Österreichische Bundesverlag für Unterricht, Wissenschaft und Kunst, 1970.

Hinrichs, Carl, ed. *Friedrich der Grosse und Maria Theresia: Diplomatische Berichte von Otto Christoph Graf v. Podewils.* Berlin: R. v. Decker, 1937.

Historical Manuscripts Commission. *Report on the Manuscripts of Lady Du Cane.* London: Ben Johnson & Co., 1905.

― ― ―. *Report on the Manuscripts of Mrs. Franklin-Russell-Astley of Chequers Court, Bucks.* London: Mackie & Co., 1900.

― ― ―. *Report on the Manuscripts of Mrs. Stopford-Sackville, of Drayton House, Northamptonshire.* 2 vols. London: Mackie & Co., 1904.

― ― ―. *Report on the Manuscripts of the Duke of Buccleuch and Queensbury, K.G., K.T., preserved at Montagu House, Whitehall.* 3 vols. London: Eyre and Spottiswoode, 1899.

Hoey, A. van. *Lettres et négociations 1743-4, pour servir à l'histoire de la vie du Cardinal de Fleury.* London: John Nourse, 1743.

Hohäusel, Annamaria. *Der österreichische Verbündete zwischen 1740 und 1745 im Spiegel der englischen Historiographie.* Vienna, 1971.

Horn, D. B. *The British Diplomatic Service 1689-1789.* Oxford: Clarendon Press, 1961.

― ― ―. *Great Britain and Europe in the Eighteenth Century.* Oxford: Oxford University Press, 1967.

― ― ―. *Sir Charles Hanbury Williams & European Diplomacy (1747-58).* London: George G. Harrap, 1930.

Houlding, J. A. *Fit for Service: The Training of the British Army, 1715-1795.* Oxford: Clarendon Press, 1981.

Howe, Martin A. S. *Spain: Its Greatness and Decay (1479-1788),* 3d ed. Cambridge: University Press, 1925.

Hubert, Eugène. *Les garnisons de la barrière dans les Pays-Bas Autrichiens (1715-1782).* Vol. 59 of *Mémoires couronnés et mémoires des savants étrangers.* Brussels: Royal Academy, 1901-3.

Hübner, Carl. *Zur Geschichte der kursächsischen Politik beim Ausbruch des österreichischen Erbfolgestreites.* Leipzig: Oswald Schmidt, 1892.

Huffel, Wilhelmina C. van. *Willem Bentinck van Rhoon: Zijn Persoonlijkheid en Leven 1725-1747.* The Hague: Martinus Nijhoff, 1923.

Hughes, B. P. *Firepower: Weapons Effectiveness on the Battlefield, 1630-1850.* New York: Charles Scribner's Sons, 1974.

Immich, Max. *Geschichte des europäischen Staatensystems von 1660 bis 1789.* Berlin: R. Oldenbourg, 1905.

Jacob, Margaret C. *The Radical Enlightenment: Pantheists, Freemasons and Republicans.* London: George Allen & Unwin, 1981.

Jacquet, Jean-Louis. *Les Bourbons d'Espagne.* Lausanne: Éditions Rencontre, 1968.

Jarvis, Rupert C. *Collected Papers on the Jacobite Risings.* 2 vols. New York: Barnes and Noble, 1972.

Jonge, Johan Karel Jakob de. *Geschiedenis van de Diplomatie gedurende den Oostenrijkschen Successie-Oorlog en het Congress van Aken (1740-1748).* Leiden: Jacobus Hazenberg Cs. Zoon, 1852.

Jorissen, Theod. *Historische Bladen.* 2 vols. Haarlem: H. D. Tjeenk Willink, 1889.

Jouan, René. *Histoire de la marine française des origines jusqu'à la révolution.* Paris: Payot, 1932.

Jowanowitsch, Jowan B. *Warum hat Friedrich der Grosse an der Schlacht bei Kesselsdorf nicht teilgenommen?* Berlin: E. Ebering, 1901.

Kaiser, David. *Politics and War: European Conflict from Philip II to Hitler.* Cambridge, MA: Harvard University Press, 1990.

Kallbrunner, Josef, and Biener, Clemens, eds. *Kaiserin Maria Theresias Politisches Testament.* Vienna: Verlag für Geschichte und Politik, 1952.

Kalshoven, A. *De Diplomatieke Verhouding tusschen Engeland en de Republiek der Vereen. Nederlanden 1747-1756.* The Hague: Martinus Nijhoff, 1915.

Kania, Hans. *Das Verhalten des Fürsten Leopold von Anhalt-Dessau vor der Schlacht von Kesselsdorf.* Potsdam: Kramer'sche Buchfruckerei, 1901.

Karge, Paul. *Die russisch-österreichische Allianz von 1746 und ihre Vorgeschichte.* Göttingen: Robert Peppmüller, 1887.

Keep, John L. H. *Soldiers of the Tsar: Army and Society in Russia 1462-1874.* Oxford: Clarendon Press, 1985.

Keibel, Rudolf. *Die Schlacht von Hohenfriedberg.* Berlin: A. Bath, 1899.

Kennett, Lee. *The French Armies in the Seven Years' War: A Study in Military Organization and Administration.* Durham, NC: Duke University Press, 1967.

Kerner, Robert Joseph. *Bohemia in the Eighteenth Century: A Study in Political, Economic, and Social History, with special reference to the reign of Leopold II, 1790-1792.* New York: Macmillan, 1932.

Khevenhüller-Metsch, Johann Josef. *Aus der Zeit Maria Theresias. Tagebuch des Fürsten Johann Josef Khevenhüller-Metsch, Kaiserlichen Oberhofmeisters 1742-1776.* 7 vols. Edited by R. von Khevenhüller-Metsch and H. Schlitter. Vienna: A. Holzhausen, 1907-25.

Kiraly, Béla, and Rothenberg, Gunther E., eds. *War and Society in East Central Europe.* Vol. 1: *Special Topics and Generalizations in the 18th and 19th Centuries.* New York: Brooklyn College Press, 1979.

Kirsten, E., Buchholz, E. W., and Kollman, W., eds. *Raum und Bevölkerung in der Weltgeschichte.* 2 vols. WHrzburg: A. G. Ploetz, 1956.

Kitchen, Martin. *A Military History of Germany: From the Eighteenth Century to the Present Day.* Bloomington: Indiana University Press, 1975.

Klingenstein, Grete. *Der Aufstieg des Hauses Kaunitz: Studien zur Herkunft und Bildung des Staatskanzlers Wenzel Anton.* Göttingen: Vandehoek und Ruprecht, 1975.

— — —. "Institutionelle Aspekte der österreichischen Aussenpolitik im 18. Jahrhundert." In Erich Zöllner, ed., *Diplomatie und Aussenpolitik Österreichs,* pp. 74-93. Vienna: Österreichischer Bundesverlag, 1977.

Komarów, Gustav Adolph-Auffenberg. "Das Zeitalter Maria Theresias." In no editor, *Unser Heer: 300 Jahre österreichisches Soldatentum im Krieg und Frieden,* pp. 109-68. Vienna: Furlinger, 1963.

Koschatzky, Walter, ed. *Maria Theresia und ihre Zeit: Eine Darstellung der Epoche von 1740-1780 aus Anlass der 200. Wiederkehr des Todestages der Kaiserin.* Vienna: Residenz Verlag, 1980.

Koser, Reinhold. *Geschichte Friedrichs des Grossen.* 2 vols. Berlin: J.G. Cotta'sche Buchhandlung, 1921.

— — —. *König Friedrich der Grosse.* 2 vols. Stuttgart: Cotta'sche Buchhandlung, 1901.

Kretschmayr, Heinrich. *Maria Theresia.* Leipzig: L. Staackmann, 1938.

Die Kriege Friedrichs des Grossen. Vols. 1-5. Berlin: Ernst Siegfried Mittler, 1890-95.

Kriege unter der Regierung der Kaiserin-Königin Maria Theresia. Österreischer Erbfolge-Krieg 1740-1748. 9 vols. Vienna: L. W. Seidel & Sohn, 1896-1914.

Kühling, Theodor. *Der Assoziationsplan 1743/44 mit besondere Berücksichtigung den Stellungnahme Friedrichs d. Gr.* Bonn: P. Hauptmann, 1914.

Kunisch, Johannes. *Feldmarschall Loudon: Jugend und erste Kriegsdienste. Archiv für österreichische Geschichte* 128/3. Vienna: Hermann Böhlaus, 1972.

— — —. *Der kleine Krieg: Studien zum Heerwesen des Absolutismus. Frankfurter Historische Abhandlungen* 4. Wiesbaden: Steiner, 1973.

— — —. *Staatsverfassung und Mächtepolitik: Zur Genese von Staatenkonflikten im Zeitalter des Absolutismus.* Berlin: Duncker & Humblot, 1979.

Küntzel, Georg. *Fürst Kaunitz-Rittberg als Staatsmann.* Frankfurt am Main: Moritz Diesterweg, 1923.

Lacombe, Hilaire de. *La politique française en allemagne et en Italie de 1740 à 1748.* Paris: Charles Douniol, 1872.

Lacour-Gayet, G. *La marine militaire de la France sous le règne de Louis XV*, 2d ed. Paris: Honoré Champion, 1910.

Lafuente, Don Modesto, and Valera, Don Juan. *Historia general de España desde los tiempos primitivos hasta la muerte de Fernando VII*. Vol. 13. Barcelona: Montanes y Simon, 1889.

Lameire, Irenée. *Les déplacements de souveraineté en Italie pendant les guerres du XVIIIe siècle*. Paris: Arthur Rousseau, 1911.

La Mina, [Jaime Miguel Guzman,] Marques de. *Memorias militares*. 2 vols. Edited by Antonio Cànovas del Castillo. Madrid: Fortanet, 1898.

Lamontagne, Roland. *Ministere de la Marine, Amérique et Canada; d'après les documents Maurepas*. Montreal: Leméac, 1966.

Leach, Douglas Edward. *Roots of Conflict: British Armed Forces and Colonial Americans 1677-1763*. Chapel Hill: University of North Carolina Press, 1986.

LeDonne, John P. *Absolutism and Ruling Class: The Formation of the Russian Political Order 1700-1825*. New York: Oxford University Press, 1991.

Leeb, I. Leonard. *The Ideological Origins of the Batavian Revolution: History and Politics in the Dutch Republic, 1747-1800*. The Hague: Martinus Nijhoff, 1973.

Le Glay, Andre. *Histoire de la conquête de la Corse par les Français: La Corse pendant la Guerre de la Succession d'Autriche*. Paris: Librairie A. Picard & Fils, 1912.

Lenman, Bruce. *The Jacobite Risings in Britain 1689-1746*. London: Eyre Methuen, 1980.

Leonard, Emile G. *L'armée et ses problemes au XVIIIe siècle*. Paris: Librairie Plon, 1958.

Le Rouge, [George Louis]. *Recueil des sièges et batailles pour servir à l'histoire des guerres de 1741*. Paris: n.p., 1754.

Levy, Jack S. *War in the Modern Great Power System, 1495-1975*. Lexington: University Press of Kentucky, 1983.

Lewis, Wilmarth S., et al., eds. *The Yale Edition of Horace Walpole's Correspondence*. Vols. 17-19. New Haven, CT: Yale University Press, 1981-82.

Liss, Peggy. *Atlantic Empires: The Network of Trade and Revolution, 1713-1826*. Baltimore: Johns Hopkins University Press, 1983.

Lodge, Sir Richard. *Great Britain and Prussia in the Eighteenth Century*. Oxford: Clarendon Press, 1923.

— — —. *Studies in Eighteenth-Century Diplomacy, 1740-1748*. London: J. Murray, 1930

Lodge, Sir Richard, ed. *Private Correspondence of Chesterfield and Newcastle. The Transactions of the Royal Historical Society* 44, 3rd ser. London: Royal Historical Society, 1930.

— — —. *The Private Correspondence of Sir Benjamin Keene, K.B.* Cambridge: University Press, 1933.

Logan-Logejus, Jakob Anton Friedrich. *Meine Erlebnisse als Reiteroffizier unter dem Grossen König in den Jahren 1741-1759*. Breslau: Wilh. Gottl. Korn, 1934.

Longworth, Philip. *The Three Empresses: Catherine I, Anne and Elizabeth of Russia*. London: Constable, 1973.

Louisbourg in 1745: The Anonymous Lettre d'un Habitat de Louisbourg. Translated by George M. Wrong. Toronto: Warwick Bro's & Rutter, 1897.

Luynes, Charles Philippe Albert, Duke of. *Mémoires*. 17 vols. Paris: Firmion Didot Frères, 1860-65.

Macartney, C. A., ed. *The Habsburg and Hohenzollern Dynasties in the Seventeenth and Eighteenth Centuries*. New York: Harper & Row, 1970.

— — —. *Maria Theresa and the House of Austria*. Mystic, CT: Lawrence Verry, 1969.

Mackay, Ruddock F. *Admiral Hawke*. Oxford: Clarendon Press, 1965.

Mahan, Alfred Thayer. *Types of Naval Officers Drawn from the History of the British Navy*. Boston: Little, Brown, 1901.

Mahrer, Eva. *Die englisch-russischen Beziehungen während des österreichischen Erbfolgekrieges*. Vienna: University of Vienna dissertation, 1972.

Malo, Henri. *Les derniers corsaires: Dunkerque (1715-1915)*. Paris: Émile-Paul Frères, 1925.

Marcus, Geoffrey Jules. *Heart of Oak: A Survey of British Sea-Power in the Georgian Era*. London: Oxford University Press, 1975.

―――. *A Naval History of England*. Vol. 1, *The Formative Centuries*. London: Longmans, 1961.

Marczali, Henry. *Hungary in the Eighteenth Century*. Cambridge: Cambridge University Press, 1910.

Marion, Marcel. *Histoire financière de la France depuis 1715*. Vol. 1, *1715-1789*. Paris: A. Rousseau, 1914; reprint ed., New York: Burt Franklin, n.d.

Martinez de Campos y Serrano, Carlos. *España bélica: el siglo XVIII*. Madrid: Aguilar, 1965.

Masnovo, Omero. *La condotta della Repubblica di Genova durante la guerra di successione austriaca*. Asti: V. Mobrico succ. Brignolo, 1920. [Also in *Bolletino storico-bibliografico subalpino* 22 (1920): 270-307.]

Mauvillon, Eléazar. *Histoire de la dernière guerre de Bohême*. 4 vols. Amsterdam: n.p., 1750.

McCusker, John J. *Money and Exchange in Europe and America, 1600-1775*. Chapel Hill: University of North Carolina Press, 1978.

McKay, Derek. *Prince Eugene of Savoy*. New York: Thames and Hudson, 1978.

McKay, Derek, and Scott, Hamish Marshall. *The Rise of the Great Powers 1648-1815*. New York: Longman's, 1983.

McLachlan, Jean Olivia. *Trade and Peace with Old Spain, 1667-1750*. Cambridge: Cambridge University Press, 1940.

McLennan, John Stewart. *Louisbourg from Its Foundation to Its Fall, 1713-58*. London: Macmillan, 1918.

McLynn, Francis J. *France and the Jacobite Rising of 1745*. Edinburgh: Edinburgh University Press, 1981.

―――. *The Jacobite Army in England. 1745: The Final Campaign*. Edinburgh: John Donald, 1983.

McLynn, Frank. *Charles Edward Stuart: A Tragedy in Many Acts*. New York: Routledge, 1988.

―――. *The Jacobites*. London: Routledge & Kegan Paul, 1985.

McNeill, William H. *The Pursuit of Power: Technology, Armed Force, and Society since A.D. 1000*. Chicago: University of Chicago Press, 1982.

Mecatti, Giuseppe Maria. *Diario della guerra d'Italia tra i borbon-liguri, e i sard-austriaci*. 2 vols. Naples: Giovanni di Simone, 1748.

Mediger, Walther. *Moskaus Weg nach Europa: Der Aufstieg Russlands zum europäischen Machtstaat im Zeitalter Friedrichs des Grossen*. Braunschweig: Georg Westermnann Verlag, 1952.

Meduna, Victor. *Der Krieg in Italien gegen Spanien, Neapel und Frankreich 1746*. Vienna: Institut fur österreichische Geschichtsforschung, 1923.

Meisenburg, Friedrich. *Der deutsche Reichstag während des österreichischen Erbfolgekrieges (1740-1748)*. Dillingen: Schwäbische Verlagsdruckerei, 1931.

Mémoires de l'élection de l'empereur Charles VII. The Hague: Libraires Associés, 1742.

Meyer, Christian, ed. *Briefe aus der Zeit des ersten Schlesischen Krieges*. Leipzig: Hermann Dege, 1902.

Mikoletzky, Hanns Leo. *Österreich: das Grosse 18. Jahrhundert*. Vienna: Österreichischer Bundesverlag für Unterricht, Wissenschaft und Kunst, 1967.

Mols, Roger. *Introduction a la démographie historique des villes d'Europe du XIVe au XVIIIe siècle*. 3 vols. Louvain: J. Duculot, 1954.

Moris, Henri. *Opérations militaires dans les Alpes et les Apennins pendant la guerre de la succession d'Autriche* (1742-1748). Paris: I. Baudoin, 1886.

Moscati, Ruggero, ed. *Direttive della politica estera Sabauda da Vittorio Amadeo II a Carlo Emmanuele III*. Milan: Istituto per gli studi di politica internazionale, 1941.

Müller, Michael G. *Polen zwischen Preussen und Russland: Souveranitätskrise und Reformpolitik*. Berlin: Colloquium Verlag, 1983.

Müller, Paul. *Zur Schlacht beit Chotusitz*. Berlin: E. Ebering, 1905.

Muratori, L. A. *Annali d'Italia dal principio dell'era volgare sino all'anno 1750*. Vol. 12. Naples: Giovanni Gravier, 1773.

Murdoch, Alexander. *"The People Above": Politics and Administration in Mid-Eighteenth Century Scotland*. Edinburgh: John Donald, 1980.

Murphy, Orville T. *Charles Gravier, Comte de Vergennes: French Diplomacy in the Age of Revolution 1719-1787*. Albany, NY: SUNY Press, 1982.

Murris, R. *La Hollande et les Hollandais au XVIIe et XVIIIe siècles vus par les Français*. Paris: Librairie Ancienne Honore Champion, 1925.

Nasalli-Rocca di Corneliano, Emilio. *Piacenza sotto la dominazione sabauda (1744-1749)*. Piacenza: A. Del-Maino, 1929.

Nicolas, Jean. *La Savoie au XVIIIe siècle. Noblesse et bourgeoisie*. 2 vols. Paris: Maloine, 1978.

Nicolle, Jean. *Madame de Pompadour et la société de son temps*. Paris: Albatross, 1980.

Niedhart, Gottfried. *Handel und Krieg in der britischen Weltpolitik 1738-1763*. Munich: Wilhelm Fink, 1979.

Nitsche, Georg. *Österreichische Soldatentum im Rahmen deutscher Geschichte*. Berlin: Freytag, 1937.

Noël, Jean-François. "L'opinion publique en Bohême et le 'règne' de Charles-Albert de Bavière (1741-1742)." In *Études européennes: mélanges offerts "Victor-Lucien Tapié*, pp. 280-92. Paris: Sorbonne, 1973.

Nolhac, Pierre de, ed. *Correspondance du Comte d'Argenson, Ministre de la Guerre*. Paris: Albert Messein, 1922.

Novotny, Alexander. *Staatskanzler Kaunitz als geistige Persönlichkeit*. Vienna: Brüder Hollinek, 1947.

Oettinger, Bruno. *Untersuchungen zur Schlacht bei Kesselsdorf*. Berlin: Th. F. Schemmel, 1902.

Ogle, Arthur. *The Marquis d'Argenson: A Study in Criticism, being the Stanhope Essay: Oxford, 1893*. London: T. Fisher Unwin, 1893.

The Operations of the British and the Allied Arms, during the Campaigns of 1743 and 1744, Historically Deducted. London: M. Cooper, 1744.

Orr, Michael. *Dettingen 1743*. London: Charles Knight, 1972.

Ostoja, Andrea. *Genova nel 1746: una mediazione milanese nelle trattative austro genovesi*. Bologna: Libreria Antiquaria Palmaverde, 1954.

Owen, John B. *The Rise of the Pelhams*. London: Methuen & Co., 1957.

Ozanam, Didier, ed. *La diplomacia de Fernando VI: correspondencia reservada entre D. Jose de Carvajal y el Duque de Huescar, 1746-1749*. Madrid: C.S.I.C., 1975.

Pajol, Charles Pierre Victor, Count. *Les guerres sous Louis XV*. Vols. 2-3. Paris: Formin-Diderot, 1883-84.

Palmer, Colin A. *Human Cargoes: The British Slave Trade to Spanish America, 1700-1739.* Urbana: University of Illinois Press, 1981.

Palmer, R. R. "Frederick the Great, Guibert, Bulow: From Dynastic to National War." In Edward Mead Earle, ed., *Makers of Modern Strategy: Military Thought from Machiavelli to Hitler,* pp. 49-74. Princeton, NJ: Princeton University Press, 1944.

Pamlenyi, Ervin, ed. *A History of Hungary.* London: Collet's, 1975.

Pares, Richard. *Colonial Blockade and Neutral Rights, 1739-1763.* Oxford: Clarendon Press, 1938.

———. *War and Trade in the West Indies.* Oxford: Clarendon Press, 1936.

Parker, Geoffrey. *The Military Revolution: Military Innovation and the Rise of the West, 1500-1800.* Cambridge: Cambridge University Press, 1988.

Parry, J. H. *Trade and Dominion: The European Overseas Empires in the Eighteenth Century.* London: Weidenfeld and Nicolson, 1971.

Parry, J. H., and Sherlock, P. M. *A Short History of the West Indies,* 3d ed. London: St. Martin's, 1971.

Pasquali, Giuseppe. *Le due battaglie di Velletri 1744-1849.* Velletri: Cesare Bertini, 1891.

Peckham, Howard H. *The Colonial Wars, 1689-1762.* Chicago: University of Chicago Press, 1964.

Pemberton, W. Baring. Carteret: *The Brilliant Failure of the Eighteenth Century.* London: Longmans, Green, 1936.

Phillipson, N. T., and Mitchison, Rosalind, eds. *Scotland in the Age of Improvement.* Edinburgh: University of Edinburgh Press, 1970.

Pichler, Henriette. *Johann Leopold Freiherr van Bärnklau 1700-1746.* Vienna, 1940.

Pick, Robert. *Empress Maria Theresa: The Earlier Years, 1717-1757.* New York: Harper and Row, 1966.

Pinto Ferreira, Joao Albino, ed. *Correspondência de D. João V e D. Bárbara de Bragança Rainha de Espanha (1746-1747).* Coimbra: Livraria Gonçalves, 1945.

Piot, Guillaume Joseph Charles. *La règne de Marie-Thérèse dans les Pays-Bas Autrichiens.* Louvain: Fonteyn, 1874.

Pirie, Valorie. *His Majesty of Corsica: The True Story of the Adventurous Life of Theodore 1st.* New York: Appleton-Century, 1939.

Pitman, Frank Wesley. *The Development of the British West Indies, 1700-1763.* New Haven, CT: Yale University Press, 1917.

Politische Correspondenz Friedrich's des Grossen. Vols. 1-4. Edited by J. G. Droysen et al. Berlin: Alexander Duncker, 1879-80.

Pomponi, Francis. *Histoire de la Corse.* Paris: Hatchette, 1979.

Portzek, Hans. *Friedrich der Grosse und Hannover in ihrem gegenseitigen Urteil.* Hildesheim: August Lax, 1958.

Posch, Joseph. *Die Kaiserwahl Franz' I. 1745.* Vienna, 1949.

Post, John D. *Food Shortage, Climatic Variability, and Epidemic Disease in Preindustrial Europe: The Mortality Peak in the Early 1740s.* Ithaca, NY: Cornell University Press, 1985.

Pounds, N.J.G. *An Historical Geography of Europe 1500-1840.* Cambridge: Cambridge University Press, 1979.

[Powerer, Chevalier de.] *Tableau de la guerre de la pragmatique sanction en Allemagne et en Italie.* 2 vols. Bern: Nouvelle Société Typographique, 1784.

Prebble, John. *Culloden.* London: Secker and Warburg, 1961.

Preuss, Georg. *Der Friede von Füssen.* Munich: H. Luneburg, 1894.

Pribram, Alfred Francis, ed. *Österreichische Staatsverträge. England.* 2 vols. Innsbruck: Wagner, 1907-13.

Priestly, Herbert Ingram. *France Overseas through the Old Regime.* New York: Appleton-Century, 1939.

Prims, Floris. *Antwerpen onder Lodewijk XV (1746-1748).* Antwerp: Vlijt, 1945.

Prinzing, Friedrich. *Epidemics Resulting from Wars.* Oxford: Clarendon Press, 1916.

Pritchard, James. *Louis XV's Navy 1748-1762: A Study of Organization and Administration.* Kingston, Ont.: McGill-Queen's University Press, 1987.

Quazza, Guido. *Il problema italiano e l'equilibrio europaeo. 1720-1738.* Turin: Palazzo Carignana, 1965.

―――. *Le riforme in Piemonte nella prima metà del Settecento.* 2 vols. Modena: Societa tipografica editrice modenese, 1957.

Quimbey, Robert S. *The Background of Napoleonic Warfare: The Theory of Military Tactics in Eighteenth-Century France.* New York: AMS Press, 1979.

Ranft, B. McL., ed. *The Vernon Papers.* London: Navy Records Society, 1958.

Ranke, Leopold von. *Memoirs of the House of Brandenburg, and History of Prussia, during the Seventeenth and Eighteenth Centuries.* Vol. 3. Translated by Sir Alexander and Lady Duff Gordon. London: John Murray, 1849.

Rankin, L. *The Marquis d'Argenson and Richard II.* London: Longmans, Green, and Co., 1901.

Reddaway, W. F. *Frederick the Great and the Rise of Prussia.* New York: G. P. Putnam's Sons, 1904.

Rediker, Marcus. *Between the Devil and the Deep Blue Sea: Merchant Seamen, Pirates, and the Anglo-American Maritime World 1700-1750.* Cambridge: Cambridge University Press, 1987.

Redlich, F. *De Praeda Militari: Looting and Booty 1500-1815.* Wiesbaden: Franz Steiner, 1956.

Regele, Oskar. *Generalstabschefs aus vier Jahrhunderten: Das Amt des Chefs des Generalstabes in der Donaumonarchie: Seine Träger und Organe von 1529 bis 1918.* Vienna: Herold, 1966.

Rendu, Eugène. *L'Italie et l'empire allemagne.* 2d ed. Paris: E. Dentu, 1859.

Richard, Michel. *Les Orange-Nassau.* Lausanne: Editions Rencontre, 1968.

Richelieu, Louis Francois Armand de Plessis, Duc de. *Mémoires authentiques du maréchal de Richelieu.* Edited by A. de Boislisle. Paris: Société de l'Histoire de France, 1918.

Richmond, Sir Herbert William. *The Navy in the War of 1739-48.* 3 vols. Cambridge: Cambridge University Press, 1920.

―――. *Statesmen and Sea Power.* Oxford: Clarendon Press, 1946.

Riley, James C. *International Government Finance and the Amsterdam Money Market, 1740-1815.* Cambridge: Cambridge University Press, 1979.

―――. *The Seven Years War and the Old Regime in France: The Economic and Financial Toll.* Princeton, NJ: Princeton University Press, 1986.

Ritter, Gerhard. *Frederick the Great.* Translated by Peter Paret. Berkeley: University of California Press, 1974.

Roberts, W. Adolphe. *The Caribbean: The Story of Our Sea of Destiny.* Indianapolis, IN: Bobbs-Merrill, 1940.

Rodger, N.A.M. *The Wooden World: An Anatomy of the Georgian Navy.* Annapolis, MD: Naval Institute Press, 1986.

Rodrigues Villa, Antonio. *Don Cenon de Somodevilla, Marqués de la Ensenada.* Madrid: M. Murillo, 1878.

Rogers, H.C.B. *The British Army of the Eighteenth Century.* New York: Allen & Unwin, 1977.

Roider, Karl A., Jr. *Austria's Eastern Question 1700-1790*. Princeton, NJ: Princeton University Press, 1982.

Roider, Karl, ed. *Maria Theresa*. Englewood Cliffs, NJ: Prentice-Hall, 1973.

Rolt, Richard. *An Impartial Representation of the Conduct of the Several Powers of Europe engaged in the Late General War*. 4 vols. 2d ed. London: S. Birt, 1754.

Ross, Steven. *From Flintlock to Rifle: Infantry Tactics 1740-1866*. Rutherford, NJ: Fairleigh Dickinson University Press, 1979.

Rostaing, M. de. *Leben und Thaten sowohl des Grafens von Löwendahl, als der beyden Herzoge von Noailles und Richelieu*. Leipzig: Johann Samuel Heinsius, 1749.

Rothert, Wilhelm. *Hannover unter dem Kurhut 1648-1815*. Hanover: Adolf Sponholtz, 1916.

Rousset, Camille, ed. *Correspondance de Louis XV et du Maréchal de Noailles*. 2 vols. Paris: Paul Dupont, 1865.

Rousset de Missy, Jean. *État politique de l'Europe*. 11 vols. The Hague: A. Moetjens, 1742-49.

———. *Histoire mémorable des guerres entre les maisons de France et d'Autriche*. 4 vols. Amsterdam: Ryckhoff, 1743.

Rowen, Herbert H. *The Princes of Orange: The Stadholders in the Dutch Republic*. Cambridge: Cambridge University Press, 1988.

St-Simon, Maximilien Henri, Marquis de. *Histoire de la guerre des Alpes ou campagne de MDCCXLIV par les armées combinées d'Espagne et de France*. Amsterdam: Rey, 1770.

Sareil, Jean. *Les Tencins: Histoire d'une famille au dix-huitieme siècle d'après de nombreux documents inédits*. Geneva: Droz, 1969.

Sars, R. de. *Le recrutement de l'armée permanente sous l'ancien régime*. Paris: Rouseeaue, 1920.

Satow, Sir Ernest. *The Silesian Loan and Frederick the Great*. Oxford: Clarendon Press, 1915.

Sautai, Maurice. *Les débuts de la guerre de la succession d'Autriche*. Paris: Librairie Militaire R. Chapelot, 1910.

———. *Les préliminaires de la guerre de la succession d'Autriche*. Paris: Librairie Militaire R. Chapelot, 1907.

Savio, Pietro. *Asti occupata e liberate (1745-1746)*. Asti: Michele Varesio, 1927.

Schazman, Paul-Emile. *The Bentincks: The History of a European Family*. Translated by Steve Cox. London: Weidenfels and Nicolson, 1976.

Schieder, Theodor. *Friedrich der Grosse: Ein Königtum der Widersprüche*. Frankfurt: Propyläen, 1983.

Schipa, Michelangelo. *Il regno di Napoli al tempo di Carlo di Borbone*. Naples: Luigi Pierro, 1904.

Schlenke, Manfred. *England und das friderizianische Preussen 1740-1763*. Munich: Verlag Karl Albert, 1963.

Schlösser, Susanne. *Der Mainzer Erzkanzler im Streit der Häuser Habsburg und Wittelsbach um das Kaisertum 1740-1745*. Wiesbaden: Franz Steiner Verlag, 1986.

Schmid, Alois. "Bayern und die Kaiserwahl des Jahres 1745." In Pankraz Fried and Walter Ziegler, eds., *Festschrift für Andreas Kraus*, pp. 257-76. Kallmünz: Michael Lassleben, 1982.

———. *Max III. Joseph und die europäischen Mächte: Die Aussenpolitik des Kurfürstentums Bayern von 1745-1765*. Munich: R. Oldenbourg, 1987.

Schmid, Julius. *Der öster. Erbfolgekrieg. Feldzug 1745, Italien*. Vienna: Institut für österreichische Geschichtsforschung, 1923.

Schmidt, Otto Eduard, ed. *Minister Graf Brühl und Karl Heinrich von Heinecken, Briefe und Akten*. Berlin: B. G. Teubner, 1921.

Schop Soler, Ann Maria. *Die spanisch-russischen Beziehungen im 18. Jahrhundert.* Wiesbaden: Otto Harrassowitz, 1970.

Schröter, Gustav Adolph. *Die Nymphenburger Vertrag vom 22. Mai 1741.* Berlin: R. Trenkel, 1911.

Scott, Hamish M. "Verteidigung und Bewahrung: Österreich und die europäischen Mächte 1740-1780." In Walter Koschatzky, ed., *Maria Theresia und ihre Zeit*, pp. 47-54. Vienna: Residenz Verlag, 1980.

1682-1982. K. (u.) K. Infanterie-Regiment Nr. 27 "König der Belgier." Graz: Stadtmuseum Graz, 1982.

Senftner, Georg. *Sachsen und Preussen im Jahre 1741, zugleich ein Beitrag für Klein-Schnellendorf.* Berlin: E. Ebering, 1905.

Shaw, John Stuart. *The Management of Scottish Society, 1707-1764: Power, Nobles. Laweyers, Edinburgh Agents and English Influences.* Edinburgh: John Donald, 1983.

Shellabarger, Samuel. *Lord Chesterfield and His World.* New York: Biblio and Tannen, 1971.

Sheridan, Richard B. *Sugar and Slavery: An Economic History of the British West Indies, 1623-1775.* Baltimore: The Johns Hopkins University Press, 1974.

Simeoni, Luigi. *L'assorbimento austriaco del ducato estense e la politica dei Duchi Rinaldo e Francesco III.* Modena: Blondi e Parmeggiani, 1919.

Simon, Edith. *The Making of Frederick the Great.* Boston: Little, Brown and Co., 1963.

Sinéty, André Louis Woldemar Alphée, Marquis de. *Vie du maréchal de Lowendahl.* 2 vols. Paris: Librairie Bachelin-Deflorenne, 1867.

Skalweit, Stephan. *Frankreich und Friedrich der Grosse: Der Aufstieg Preussens in der öffentlichen Meinung des "ancien regime."* Bonn: Ludwig Röhrscheid, 1952.

Skrine, Francis Henry Bennett. *Fontenoy and Great Britain's Share in the War of the Austrian Succession.* Edinburgh: W. Blackwood and Sons, 1906.

Smith, Annette M. *Jacobite Estates of the Forty-Five.* Edinburgh: John Donald, 1982.

Spannagel-Heitmar, Auguste. *Beiträge zur Geschichte des österreichischen Erbfolgekrieges.* Vienna: University of Vienna dissertation, 1949.

Speck, W. A. *The Butcher: The Duke of Cumberland and the Suppression of the 45.* Oxford: Blackwell, 1982.

Spindler, Max, ed. *Handbuch der bayerischen Geschichte. Vol. 2, Das alte Bayern; Der Territorialstaat vom Ausgang des 12. Jahrhunderts bis zum Ausgang des 18. Jahrhunderts.* Munich: C. H. Beck'sche, 1966.

Spon, Jean François, Baron de. *Mémoires pour servir à l'histoire de l'Europe, depuis 1740. jusqu'à la Paix-Generale, signées à Aix-la-Chapelle le 18. October 1748.* 2 vols. Amsterdam: La Compagnie, 1749.

Stabenow, Hans. *Die Schlacht bei Soor.* Frankfurt-am-Main: Voigt und Gleiber, 1901.

Stadelmann, Gustav. *Bibliographie der Schlacht Dettingen nebst Verzeichnis der vorhandenen Abbildungen und Plane.* Aschaffenburg: J. Kirsch, 1929.

Stanley, George F. G. *New France: The Last Phase 1744-1760.* Toronto: McClelland and Stewart, 1968.

Steele, I. K. *Guerillas and Grenadiers: The Struggle for Canada, 1689-1760.* Toronto: Ryerson Press, 1969.

[Stille, Christoph Ludwig von.] *Les campagnes du roi avec des réflexions sur les causes des évènements.* 2 vols. Berlin: 1762.

Storia di Milano. Vol. 12, *L'età delle riforme (1706-1796).* Milan: Treccani degli Alfieri, 1959.

Strachan, Hew. *European Armies and the Conduct of War.* London: Allen & Unwin, 1983.

Strieder, Jacob. *Kritische Forschungen zur österreichischen Politik vom Aachener Frieden bis zum Beginne des siebenjährigen Krieges.* Leipzig: Quelle & Meyer, 1906.

Stryienski, Casimir. *The Daughters of Louis XV (Mesdames de France)*. Translated by Cranstoun Metcalfe. London: Chapman & Hall, 1912.

Sutton, John L. *The King's Honor and the King's Cardinal: The War of the Polish Succession*. Lexington: University of Kentucky Press, 1980.

Sylva-Tarouca, Egbert. *Der Mentor der Kaiserin: der weltliche Seelenführer Maria Theresias*. Zurich: Amalthea, 1960.

Symcox, Geoffrey, ed. *War, Diplomacy, and Imperialism 1618-1763*. New York: Harper, 1973.

Tapia Ozcariz, Enrique de. *Carlos III y su epoca: biografia del siglo XVIII*. Madrid: Aguilar, 1962.

Tapié, Victor-L. "Contribution à l'étude des relations entre la France et l'Autriche avant la guerre de succession d'Autriche." In *Österreich und Europa: Festgabe für Hugo Hantsch zum 70. Geburtstag*, pp. 133-48. Vienna: Verlag Styria, 1965.

— — —. *L'Europe de Marie-Thérèse: Du baroque aux lumières*. Paris: Fayard, 1973.

— — —. *The Rise and Fall of the Habsburg Monarchy*. Translated by Stephen Hardman. New York: Praeger, 1971.

Teichman, Oskar. *Pandour Trenck: An Account of the Life of Baron Franciscus von der Trenck, 1710-1749*. London: John Murray, 1927.

Thadden, Franz-Lorenz von. *Feldmarschall Daun: Maria Theresias grösster Feldherr*. Vienna: Herold, 1967.

The Theatre of the Present War in the Netherlands and upon the Rhine. London: J. Bindley, 1745.

Tomasson, Katherine, and Buist, Francis. *Battles of the '45*. New York: Macmillan, 1962.

Trenck, Friedrich Freyherr von. *Merkwürdige Lebensgeschichte*. 4 vols. Berlin: Friedrich Vieweg, 1787.

Tschuppik, Karl. *Maria Theresia*. Amsterdam: Allert de Lange, 1934.

Unser Heer. 300 Jahre osterreicher Soldatentum in Krieg und Frieden. Vienna: Fürlanger, 1963.

Unzer, Adolf. *Die Convention von Klein-Schnellendorf (9 Oktober 1741)*. Frankfurt-am-Main: Reitz & Koehler, 1889.

Urbanski, Hans. "Unveröffentlichte Aufzeichnungen Karls von Lothringen." In Walter Koschatzky, ed., *Maria Theresia und ihre Zeit*, pp. 91-96. Vienna: Residenz Verlag, 1980.

Urlanis, Boris Zesarewitsch. *Bilanz der Kriege: die Menschenverluste Europas vom 17. Jahrhundert bis zur Gegenwart*. Translated by Gerhard Hartman. Berlin: Deutscher Verlag der Wissenschaften, 1965.

Vagts, Alfred. *History of Militarism*. Rev. ed. New York: Free Press, 1959.

Valsecchi, Franco. *L'Italia nel settecento, dal 1714 al 1788*. Milan: Arnoldo Mondadori, 1959.

Vandal, A. *Une ambassade française en Orient sous Louis XV. La mission de Marquis de Villeneuve 1728-1741*. 2d ed. Paris: Plon, 1887.

— — —. *Louis XV et Élisabeth de Russie*. Paris: Plon, 1882.

Van Houtte, Hubert. *Les occupations étrangères en Belgique sous l'Ancien Régime*. 2 vols. Ghent: Van Rysselberghe & Rombaut, 1930.

Van Houtte, J. A., et al., eds. *Algemene Geschiedenis der Nederlanden*. Vols. 7-8. Utrecht: W. de Haan, 1953-55.

Vartanian, Aram. *La Mettrie's l'Homme Machine: A Study in the Origins of an Idea*. Princeton, NJ: Princeton University Press. 1960.

Vattel, Emmerich de. *The Law of Nations; or, Principles of the Law of Nature*. Translated from the French. Philadelphia: P. H. Nicklin & T. Johnson, 1829.

Vaucher, P. *Robert Walpole et la politique de Fleury (1731-1742)*. Paris: Plon, 1924.

Vehse, Edward. *Memoirs of the Court of Prussia*. Translated by Franz C. F. Demmler. London: T. Nelson, 1854.

Venturi, Franco. *Ricerche sull'Italia durante la guerra de successione austriaca*. Turin: Tirrenia, 1967.

Vignetta, Andrea. *Battaglia dell'Assietta*. Pinerola: P. P. Giuseppini, 1960.

Vitzthum von Eckstaedt, Carl Friedrich, Count. *Die Geheimnisse des sächsischen Cabinets. Ende 1745 bis Ende 1756*. 2 vols. Stuttgart: J. G. Cotta'schen Buchhandlung, 1866.

Vitzthum von Eckstaedt, Carl Friedrich, Count, ed. *Maurice Comte de Saxe et Marie-Josephe de Saxe, Dauphine de France: lettres et documents inédits*. Leipzig: Ludwig Denicke, 1867.

Vogüé, Marquis de, and Le Sourd, Auguste, eds. *Campagnes de Jacques de Mercoyrol de Beaulieu, Capitaine au Regiment de Picardie (1743-1763)*. Paris: Librairie Renouard, 1915.

Voltaire, François-Marie Arouet. *Histoire de la guerre de 1741*. Edited by Jacques Maurens. Paris: Garnier Frères, 1971.

Voogd, Nico Johannes Jacque de. *De Doelistenbeweging te Amsterdam in 1748*. Utrecht: H. de Vroede, 1914.

Vries, Joh. de. *De Economische Achteruitgang der Republiek in de achttiende eeuw*. Leiden: H. E. Stenfert Kroese, 1968.

Wagner, Fritz. *Kaiser Karl VII. und die grossen Mächte 1740-1745*. Stuttgart: W. Kohlhammer, 1938.

Waliszewski, K. *La dernière des Romanov, Elisabeth Ire; Impératrice de Russe 1741-1762*. 2d ed. Paris: Plon, 1902.

Walker, Mack. *Johann Jakob Moser and the Holy Roman Empire of the German Nation*. Chapel Hill: University of North Carolina Press, 1981.

Walter, Friedrich. *Männer um Maria Theresia*. Vienna: Adolf Holzausen, 1951.

Wandruszka, Adam. *Österreich und Italien im 18. Jahrhundert*. Vienna: Verlag für Geschichte und Politik, 1963.

Wangermann, Ernst. *The Austrian Achievement, 1700-1800*. London: Thames & Hudson, 1973.

Ward, Adolphus William. *Great Britain & Hanover: Some Aspects of the Personal Union*. Reprint ed. New York: Haskell House, 1971.

Weber, Hermann. *Die Politik des Kurfürsten Karl Theodor von der Pfalz während des österreichischen Erbfolgekrieges (1742-1748)*. Bonn: Ludwig Röhrscheid, 1956.

Weber, Ottocar. *Die Occupation Prags durch die Franzosen und Baiern 1741-1743*. Prague: J. G. Calve'schek, 1896.

Weigand, Emanuela. *Die englisch-österreichische Beziehungen im österreichischen Erbfolgekrieg*. Vienna: University of Vienna dissertation. 1953.

Weigley, Russell F. *The Age of Battles: The Quest for Decisive Warfare from Breitenfeld to Waterloo*. Bloomington: Indiana University Press, 1991.

White, Jon Machlip. *Marshal of France: The Life and Times of Maurice, Comte de Saxe (1696-1750)*. Chicago: Rand McNally, 1962.

Whitworth, Rex. *Field-Marshal Lord Ligonier: A Story of the British Army, 1702-1770.* Oxford: Clarendon Press, 1958.

Wilkinson, Spenser. *The Defence of Piedmont, 1742-1748*. Oxford: Oxford University Press, 1927.

Williams, Glyndwr. *The Expansion of Europe in the Eighteenth Century: Overseas Rivalry, Discovery, and Exploitation*. New York: Walker and Company, 1967.

Wilson, Arthur McCandless. *French Foreign Policy during the Administration of Cardinal Fleury, 1726-1743.* Cambridge, MA: Harvard University Press, 1936.

Woolf, Stuart. *A History of Italy 1700-1860: The Social Constraints of Political Change.* London: Methuen, 1979.

Wright, Charles, and Fayle, C. Ernest. *A History of Lloyds.* London: Macmillan, 1928.

Wright, James Leitch, Jr. *Anglo-Spanish Rivalry in North America.* Athens: University of Georgia Press, 1971.

Wright, William E. *Serf, Seigneur and Sovereign: Agrarian Reform in Eighteenth-Century Bohemia.* Minneapolis: University of Minnesota Press, 1966.

Yorke, Philip C. *The Life and Correspondence of Philip Yorke, Earl of Hardwicke, Lord High Chancellor of Great Britain.* 3 vols. Cambridge: Cambridge University Press, 1913.

Youngson, A. J. *After the Forty-Five: The Economic Impact on the Scottish Highlands.* Edinburgh: Edinburgh University Press, 1973

Z°°°°, Major. *La guerre de la succession d'Autriche (1740-1748). Campagne de 1744 . . . 1745.* Paris: Chapelot, 1913.

Zabala y Lera, Pio. *El Marqués de Argenson y el pacto de familia de 1743.* Madrid: Editorial Voluntad, 1928.

Zeller, Gaston. *Aspects de la politique française sous l'ancien régime.* Paris: Presses Universitaires de France, 1964.

———. *Histoire des relations internationales.* Vol. 3, *Les temps modernes.* II. *De Louis XIV à 1789.* Paris: Hachette, 1955.

Zévort, Edgar. *Le Marquis d'Argenson et le ministère des affaires étrangères du 18 Novembre 1744 au 10 Janvier 1747.* Paris: Germer Balliere, 1879.

JOURNAL ARTICLES

Abrate, Mario. "Ricerche per la storia economica dell'artigliera nella prima metà del XVIII secolo." *Nuova Rivista Storica* 53 (1969): 146-66.

Anderson, Olive. "The Establishment of British Naval Supremacy at Sea and the Exchange of Naval Prisoners of War." *English Historical Review* 75 (1960): 77-89.

Arese, Franco. "Le supreme cariche della Lombardia austriaca, 1706-1796." *Archivio storico lombardo* 10th ser., 5 (1979-80): 535-98.

Arneth, Alfred, Ritter von. "Johann Christoph Bartenstein und seine Zeit." *Archiv für österreichische Geschichte* 46 (1871): 1-214.

Atkinson, C. T. "Jenkins' Ear, the Austrian Succession War and the 'Forty-Five: Gleanings from Sources in the Public Records Office." *Journal of the Society for Army Historical Research* 22 (1943): 280-98.

Aubert, Hippolyte. "La cour d'Espagne et la situation de la Savoie en 1746, d'aprs une correspondance contemporaine." *Revue d'histoire diplomatique* 5 (1891): 253-74.

Baguenault de Puchesse, G. "La pape Benoît XIV et la France. Missions à Rome de Tencin et de Choiseul (1740-1757)." *Revue d'histoire diplomatique* 17 (1903): 481-88.

Bamford, Paul. "French Shipping in Northern European Trade, 1660-1789." *Journal of Modern History* 26 (1954): 207-19.

Baudi di Vesme, Carlo. "La crisi europea del 1745-46 e l'Italia." *Bolletino storico-bibliografico subalpino* 48 (1950): 84-117.

———. "La guerra di successione d'Austria e la politica di Casa Savoia. Rassegna critica degli studi vecchi e nuovi." *Rivista storica italiana* 58 (1941): 215-34.

————. "L'influenza del potere marittimo nella guerra di successione d'Austria." *Nuova rivista storica* 37 (1953): 19-43.

————. "La pace di Aquisgrana (1748): une pagina di storia delle relazioni internazionali." *Bolletino storico-bibliografico subalpino* 65 (1967): 249-314; 66 (1968): 103-74, 365-428; 67 (1969): 483-593.

————. "La Spagna all'epoca de Ferdinando VI e il matrimonio spagnuolo di Vittorio Amadeo III (1749)." *Bolletino storico-bibliografico subalpino* 51 (1953): 123-55.

Beattie, J. M. "The Pattern of Crime in England, 1600-1800." *Past and Present*, no. 62 (1974): 47-95.

Beer, Adolf. "Holland und der österreichische Erbfolgekrieg." *Archiv für österreichische Geschichte* 46 (1871): 297-418.

————. "Zur Geschichte des Frieden von Aachen im Jahre 1748." *Archiv für österreichische Geschichte* 47 (1871): 3-195.

Benedikt, Heinrich. "Corsica und die Türkei." *Mitteilungen des Instituts für österreichische Geschichtsforschung* 63 (1955): 412-29.

————. "Die europäische Politik der Pforte vor Beginn und während des Österreichisches Erbfolgerieges." *Mitteilungen des österreichischen Staatsarchiv* 1 (1948): 137-92.

Berger, Peter. "Dir Pragmatische Sanktion und ihre Zeit." *Der Donauraum* 9 (1964): 1-2.

Bernard, Capitaine. "Le siège de Prague (1742)." *Revue retrospective; recueil des pièces intéressantes et de citations curieuses* 11 (1890): 268-84.

Bien, David D. "The Army in the French Enlightenment: Reform, Reaction, and Revolution." *Past and Present* no. 85 (1979): 68-98.

Black, Jeremy. "British Foreign Policy and the War of the Austrian Succession, 1740-48: A Research Priority." *Canadian Journal of History* 21 (1986): 313-31.

————. "The Development of Anglo-Sardinian Relations in the First Half of the Eighteenth Century." *Studi piemontesi* 12 (1983): 48-59.

————. "French Foreign Policy in the Age of Fleury Reassessed." *English Historical Review* 103 (1988): 359-84.

————. "The Problems of the Small State: Bavaria and Britain in the Second Quarter of the Eighteenth Century." *European History Quarterly* 19 (1989): 5-36.

Bleckwenn, H. "Zur Handhabung der Geschütze bei der friderizianischen Feldartillerie." *Zeitschrift für Heereskunde* 29 (1965): 96-105.

Bozzola, Annibale. "La controversia austro-sarda sulla capitulazione del 6 settenbre 1746." *Bolletino storico-bibliografico subalpino* 36 (1934): 29-73.

Braubach, Max. "Johann Christoph Bartensteins Herkunft und Anfänge." *Mitteilungen des Instituts fur Österreichische Geschichtsforschung* 61 (1953): 99-149.

————. "Die österreichische Diplomatie am Hofe des Kurfürsten Clemens August von Köln 1740-1756." *Annalen des Historischen Vereins für den Niederrhein* 111 (1927): 1-80; 112 (1928): 1-70; 114 (1929): 87-136.

Brilling, Bernhard. "Die Intervention des Kurfürsten und Erzbischofs von Köln zugunsten der Prager und böhmischen Juden im Jahre 1745." *Annalen des Historischen Vereins für den Niederrhein* 174 (1972): 122-37.

————. "Ein Interventionsbrief der Hamburger Gemeinde für die Prager Juden vom Jahre 1745." *Zeitschrift für die Geschichte der Juden* 1 (1964): 37-42.

Broglie, J.V.A., Duke of. "Le Cardinal de Fleury et la pragmatique sanction." *Revue historique* 20 (1882): 257-81.

— — —. "Études Diplomatiques: Fin du ministere du Marquis d'Argenson." *Revue des deux mondes* 96 (1889): 313-49, 721-50; 97 (1890): 54-85, 770-809; 98 (1890): 313-46, 522-46; 99 (1890): 48-93.

— — —. "Un manifeste diplomatique de Voltaire." *Revue d'histoire diplomatique* 1 (1887): 13-26.

Brown, Raymond Lamont. "General George Wade: Roadmaker in the Highlands." *History Today* 29 (1979): 147-54.

Browning, Reed. "The British Orientation of Austrian Foreign Policy, 1749-1754." *Central European History* 1 (1968): 299-323.

Büchsel, Hans Wilhelm. "Oberschlesien im Brennpunkt der grossen Politik 1740-1742." *Forschungen zur brandenburgisch-preussischen Geschichte* 51 (1939): 83-102.

Buffinton, Arthur H. "The Canada Expedition of 1746: Its Relation to British Politics." *American Historical Review* 45 (1940): 552-80.

Butel, P. "L'économie maritime française au XVIIIe siècle." *Vierteljahrschrift für Sozial- und Wirtschaftsgeschichte* 62 (1975): 289-308.

Carignani, G. "Il partito austriaco nel regno di Napoli al 1744." *Archivio storico per le province Napoletane* 6 (1881): 37-73.

Castillo, Alvaro. "Coyuntura y crecimento de la economía española en el siglo XVIII." *Hispania: revista española de historia* 31 (1974): 31-54.

Castro, Giovanni de. "Carlo Emmanuele III e il Milanese." *Archivio storico lombardo* 10 (1883): 474-513.

Cegielski, Tadeusz. "Preussische 'Deutschland- und Polenpolitik' in dem Zeitraum 1740-1792." *Jahrbuch für die Geschichte Mittel- und Ostdeutschlands* 30 (1981): 21-27.

Chagniot, Jean. "Une panique: les Gardes Françaises à Dettingen (27 Juin 1743)." *Revue d'histoire moderne et contemporaine* 24 (1977): 78-95.

Chandler, David G. "War and the Past: The Logistics of Military History." *History Today* 31 (1981): 47-48.

Cormier, Paul. "Albert de Broglie (1821-1901), historien diplomatique." *Revue d'histoire diplomatique* 86 (1972): 5-20.

Costet, Corvette. "La stratégie britannique de 1739 à 1748." *Revue Maritime*, n.s., no. 178 (1934): 434-64.

Czikann-Zichy, Moricz. "Die Pragmatische Sanktion in der ungarischen Geschichte." *Donauraum* 9 (1964): 18-25.

Daniel, Maurice. "Don Philippe: Généralissime de l'armée espagnole de Savoie (1742-1748)." *Mémoires de l'Académie des Sciences, Belles-Lettres et Arts de Savoie* 6th ser., 4 (1960): 141-55.

Davis, R. "English Foreign Trade, 1700-1774." *Economic History Review*, 2d ser., 15 (1962): 285-303.

De Boom, Ghislaine. "L'archiduchesse Marie-Elisabeth et les grandes maîtres de la cour." *Revue belge de philologie et d'histoire* 5 (1926): 493-506.

Delsante, Ubaldo. "Don Filipo di Borbone e la guerra di successione austriaca." *Archivio storico per le province parmensi*, 4th ser., 26 (1974): 371-412.

Diaz, Furio. "Aspetti e problemi di storia della Toscana nella settecento." *Rivista storica italiana* 91 (1979): 286-312.

Di Vittorio, Antonio. "Un caso di correlazione tra guerre, spese militari e cambiamenti economici: le guerre asburgiche della prima età del XVIII secolo e loro ripercussioni sulla finanza, e economia dell'impero." *Nuova rivista storica* 66 (1982): 59-81.

Doerflinger, Thomas M. "The Antilles Trade of the Old Regime: A Statistical Overview." *Journal of Interdisciplinary History* 6 (1976): 397-415.

Dossetti, Manuela. "Aspetti demografici del Piemonte occidentale nei secoli XVII e XVIII." *Bolletino storico-bibliografico subalpino* 75 (1977): 127-238.

Fann, Willard R. "Peacetime Attrition in the Army of Frederick William I, 1713-1740." *Central European History* 11 (1978): 323-34.

Ferrandis Torres, Manuel. "El equilibrio europeo de Don Jose de Carvajal y Lancester." *Revista historica* [Valladolid], 2d ser., 1 (1924): 157-63.

Fisher, H.E.S. "Anglo-Portuguese Trade, 1700-1770." *Economic History Review*, 2d ser., 16 (1963-64): 219-33.

Florovsky, A. V. "Russo-Austrian Conflicts in the Early 18th Century." *Slavonic and East European Review* 47 (1969): 94-114.

Freudenberger, Herman. "The Woolen-Goods Industry of the Habsburg Monarchy in the Eighteenth Century." *Journal of Economic History* 20 (1960): 383-406.

Furlani, Silvio. "I preliminari di Aquisgrana nella critica di un opusculo contemporaneo." *Nuova rivista storica* 31 (1947): 110-24.

Galand, Michele. "Le journal secret de Charles de Lorraine, gouverneur-général des Pays-Bas autrichiens." *Revue belge de philologie et d'histoire* 62 (1984): 289-301.

Geyl, Pieter. "Holland and England during the War of the Austrian Succession." *History*, n.s., 10 (1925-26): 47-51.

———. "Willem IV en Engeland." *De Gids* 88, part 2 (1924): 79-117, 328-66

Glover, Richard. "War and Civilian Historians." *Journal of the History of Ideas* 18 (1957): 84-100.

Gómez Molleda, Maria Dolores. "El 'caso Macanaz' en el Congreso de Breda." *Hispania* 18 (1958): 62-128.

———. "El pensamiento de Carvajal y la política internacional española del siglo XVIII." *Hispania* 15 (1955): 117-37.

Graham, G. S. "The Naval Defence of British North America, 1739-1763." *Transactions of the Royal Historical Society*, 4th ser., 30 (1948): 95-110.

Gras, Yves. "Les guerres 'limitées' du XVIIIe siècle." *Revue historique de l'armée* 26 (1970): 22-36.

Grillon, Pierre. "Un incident diplomatique franco-anglais au XVIIIe siècle: l'arrestation et la détention du Maréchal de Belle-Isle (1744-1745)." *Revue d'histoire diplomatique* (April-June 1962): 97-116.

Groehler, Olaf. "Probleme der preussischen Kriegskunst im Zeitlater der Schlesischen Kriege (1740-1763)." *Zeitschrift für Militärgeschichte* 5 (1966): 286-301.

Guéry, Alain. "Les finances de la monarchie française sous l'ancien regime." *Annales; Économies, Sociétés, Civilizations* 33 (1978): 216-39.

Harding, R. H. "Sir Robert Walpole's Ministry and the Conduct of the War with Spain, 1739-41." *Bulletin of the Institute for Historical Research* 60 (1987): 299-320.

Hay, Douglas. "War, Dearth and Theft in the Eighteenth Century: The Records of the English Courts." *Past and Present*, no. 95 (1982): 117-60.

Hayes, James. "The Royal House of Hanover and the British Army, 1714-60." *Bulletin of the John Rylands Library* 40 (1957-58): 328-57.

Heigel, Karl Theodore von, ed. "Die Correspondenz Karls VII. mit Josef Franz Graf von Seinsheim, 1738-1743." *Königlich Bayerischen Akademie der Wissenschaften. Abhandlungen der Historischen Klasse* 14, part 1 (1879): 71-133.

Hermann, Otto. "Von Mollwitz bis Chotisitz: ein Beitrag zur Taktik Friedrichs des Grossen." *Forschungen zur Brandenburgischen und Preussischen Geschichte* 7 (1894): 313-61.

Horn, David Baynes. "Saxony in the War of the Austrian Succession." *English Historical Review* 44 (1929): 33-47.

Hrazky, Josef. "Johann Christoph von Bartenstein, der Staatsmann und Erzieher." *Mitteilungen des österreichischen Staatsarchivs* 11 (1958): 221-51.

Hufton, Olwen. "Social Conflict and Grain Supply in Eighteenth-Century France." *Journal of Interdisciplinary History* 14 (1983): 303-31.

Huyon, Alain. "L'obligation militaire en France sous l'ancien régime." *Revue historique des armées*, no. 147 (1982): 5-17.

Ibanez de Ibero, Carlos. "El Marqués de la Ensenada y su politica exterior." *Revista de Historia Militar* 9 (1965): 143-56.

Ingrao, Charles. "The Pragmatic Sanction and the Theresian Succession." *Topic: A Journal of the Liberal Arts*, no. 34 (1980): 3-18.

Jankovic, Branimir. "The Characteristics of Balkan Diplomacy in the Eighteenth Century." *East European Quarterly* 9 (1975): 389-404.

Japikse, N. "De Aard der Volksbewegingen van 1747 en 1748." *De Gids* 4th ser., 28 (1910), 4th part: 315-31.

John, A. H. "War and the English Economy, 1700-1763." *Economic History Review*, 2d ser., 7 (1954-55): 329-44.

Kamen, H. "Melchior de Macanaz and the Foundation of Bourbon Power in Spain." *English Historical Review* 80 (1965): 699-716.

Kann, Robert A. "Aristocracy in the Eighteenth Century Habsburg Empire." *East European Quarterly* 7 (1973): 1-13.

Kannegieter, J. Z. "Het valsche Nymphenburger Tractaat en zijn vermoedlijke auteur." *Tijdschrift voor Geschiedenis* 55 (1940): 121-69.

Kaplan, Steven Laurence. "Lean Years, Fat Years: the 'Community' Granary System and the Search for Abundance in Eighteenth-Century Paris." *French Historical Studies* 10 (1977): 197-230.

Kematmüller, Rittmeister. "Die österreichische Administration in Bayern 1743-45." *Mittheilungen des K. und K. Kriegs-archiv* neue Folge, 9 (1895): 317-58.

Kittel, Ed. "Correspondenz der von der Stadt Eger (1742) an der Hoflager Karl VII. nach Frankfurt Abgeordneten." *Archiv für österreichische Geschichte* 56 (1877): 181-228.

Klima, Arnost. "Industrial Development in Bohemia 1648-1781." *Past and Present* 11 (1957): 87-99.

Koehl, Robert L. "Heinrich Brühl: A Saxon Politician of the Eighteenth Century." *Journal of Central European Affairs* 14 (1954): 311-28.

Koser, Reinhold. "Friedrich der Grosse und die Familie Broglie." *Historische Zeitschrift* 51 (1883): 54-76.

———. "Der preussische Staatsschutz von 1740-1756." *Forschungen zur Brandenburgischen und Preussischen Geschichte* 4 (1891): 529-51.

———. "Zur Schlacht bei Mollwitz." *Forschungen zur Brandenburgischen und Preussischen Geschichte* 3 (1890): 479-91.

———. "Der Zerfall der Koalition von 1741 gegen Maria-Theresia." *Forschungen zur Brandenburgischen und Preussischen Geschichte* 27 (1914): 169-88.

Lebrun, François. "Les crises démographiques en France aux XVIIe et XVIIIe siècles." *Annales; économies, sociétés, civilizations* 35 (1980): 205-34.

Lefevre, J. "Les nominations faites dans la magistrature pendant l'occupation française 1746-1747." *Revue belge de philologie et d'histoire* 13 (1934): 697-711.

Le Glay, André. "Une mission délicate. Le cas d'un ambassadeur génois " Florence (1743)." *Revue d'histoire diplomatique* 11 (1897): 541-64.

Lenman, Bruce. "The Jacobite Diaspora 1688-1746: From Despair to Integration." *History Today* 30 (1980): 7-10.

Lentze, Hans. "Die Pragmatische Sanktion und das Werden des österreichischen Staates." *Der Domauraum* 9 (1964): 3-12.

Léonard, Émile-G. "La question sociale dans l'armée française au XVIIIe siecle." *Annales; économies, sociétés, civilisations* 3 (1948): 135-49.

Lodge, Sir Richard. "The Continental Policy of Great Britain 1740-60." *History* n.s., 16 (1930-31): 246-51.

―――. "An Episode in Anglo-Russian Relations during the War of the Austrian Succession." *Transactions of the Royal Historical Society* 4th ser., 9 (1926): 63-83.

―――. "The First Anglo-Russian Treaty, 1739-42." *English Historical Review* 43 (1928): 354-75.

―――. "The Hanau Controversy in 1744 and the Fall of Carteret." *English Historical Review* 38 (1923): 509-31.

―――. "Lord Hyndford's Embassy to Russia, 1744-9." *English Historical Review* 46 (1931): 48-76, 389-422.

―――. "The Maritime Powers in the Eighteenth Century." *History* n.s., 15 (1930-31): 246-51.

―――. "The Mission of Henry Legge to Berlin, 1748." *Transactions of the Royal Historical Society* 4th ser., 14 (1931): 1-38.

―――. "Russia, Prussia, and Great Britain, 1742-4." *English Historical Review* 45 (1930): 579-611.

―――. "Sir Benjamin Keene: A Study in Anglo-Spanish Relations." *Transactions of the Royal Historical Society* 4th ser., 15 (1932): 1-43.

―――. "The So-Called Treaty of Hanau." *English Historical Review* 38 (1923): 384-407.

―――. "The Treaty of Abo and the Swedish Succession." *English Historical Review* 43 (1928): 540-71.

―――. "The Treaty of Worms." *English Historical Review* 44 (1929): 220-55.

Malone, Joseph J. "England and the Baltic Naval Stores Trade in the Seventeenth and Eighteenth Centuries." *Mariner's Mirror*, no. 4 (1972): 375-95.

Manno, A. "L'esercito piemontese. Lo stato attuale degli studi." *Bolletino storico-bibliografico subalpino* 65 (1967): 404-33.

Marczali, Heinrich. "Vitam et sanguinem!" *Historische Zeitschrift* 117 (1917): 413-31.

Martel, André. "Le renouveau de l'histoire militaire en France." *Revue historique*, no. 497 (1971): 107-26.

McGill, William J. "The Roots of Policy: Kaunitz in Italy and the Netherlands, 1742-1746." *Central European History* 1 (1968): 131-49.

―――. "The Roots of Policy: Kaunitz in Vienna and Versailles, 1749-1753." *Journal of Modern History* 43 (1971): 228-44.

―――. "Wenzel Anton von Kaunitz and the Congress of Aix-la-Chapelle, 1748." *Duquesne Review* 14 (1969): 154-67.

McLynn, F. J. "Issues and Motives in the Jacobite Rising of 1745." *The Eighteenth Century: Theory and Interpretation* 23 (1982): 97-133.

Mevorah, Barouh. "The Imperial Court-Jew Wolf Wertheimer as Diplomatic Mediator (during the War of the Austrian Succession)." *Scripta Hierosolymitana* 23 (1972): 184-213.

Michael, Wolfgang. "Die englische Koalitionsentwurfe des Jahres 1748." *Forschungen zur Brandenburgischen und Preussischen Geschichte* 1 (1888): 527-72.

Mikoletzky, H. L. "Franz Stephan von Lothringen als Wirtschaftspolitiker." *Mitteilungen des Österreichischen Staatsarchivs* 13 (1960): 231-57.

Mirowski, Philip. "The Rise (and Retreat) of a Market: English Joint Stock Shares in the Eighteenth Century." *Journal of Economic History* 41 (1981): 559-77.

Morineau, Michel. "Budgets de l'état et gestion des finances royales en France au dix-huitieme siècle." *Revue historique* 264 (1980): 289-336.

Narotchnitsky, A. "Deux tendances des relations franco-russes." *Revue historique* 91 (1967): 99-124.

Noël, Jean-François. "Traditions universalistes et aspects nationaux dans la notion de saint-empire romain germanique au XVIIIe siècle." *Revue d'histoire diplomatique* 82 (1968): 193-212.

Oglesby, J.C.M. "Spain's Havana Squadron and the Preservation of the Balance of Power in the Carribean, 1740-1748." *Hispanic Historical Review* 49 (1969): 473-88.

Otruba, Gustav. "Die Bedeutung englischer Subsidien und Antizipationen für die Finanzen Österreichs 1701-1748." *Vierteljahrschrift für Sozial- und Wirtschaftsgeschichte* 51 (1964): 192-234.

Ozanam, Didier. "Un project de mariage entre l'infante Maria Antonia, soeur de Ferdinand VI, et le dauphin fils de Louis XV (1746)." *Estudios de historia moderna* 1 (1951): 129-77.

Paillé, Marc. "The French Privateer Du Teillay Which Carried Prince Charles Edward to the Highlands (1745)." *Mariner's Mirror* 63 (1977): 309-10.

Pandiani, Emilio. "La cacciata degli austriaci de Genova nell'anno 1746." *Miscellanea di storia italiana* 3d ser, 20 (1924): 275-516.

Pares, Richard. "American versus Continental Warfare, 1739-1763." *English Historical Review* 51 (1936): 429-65.

Paret, Peter. "The History of War." *Daedalus* (spring 1971): 376-96.

Parker, Geoffrey. "The 'Military Revolution,' 1560-1660 — a Myth?" *Journal of Modern History* 48 (1976): 195-214.

Pellegrini, Silvio. "La Corsica e i Savoia nel secolo XVIII." *Nuova rivista storica* 8 (1924): 597-613.

Petrie, Sir Charles A. "Estudio de las relaciones anglo-españolas: Fernando VI y Sir Benjamin Keene." *Estudios americanos* 16 (1958): 107-26.

Phillips, Carla Rahn. "The Spanish Wool Trade, 1500-1780." *Journal of Economic History* 42 (1982): 775-95.

Poggi, Guido. "Guerre sulle Alpi Marittime (anno 1745)." *Rivista militare italiana* 7 (1933): 1428-64, 1623-49.

Poll, Bernhard. "Zur Geschichte des Aachener Friedens 1748." *Zeitschrift des Aachener Geschichtsvereins* 81 (1971): 6-142.

Price, Jacob M. "New Time Series for Scotland's and Britain's Trade with the Thirteen Colonies and States, 1740 to 1791." *William and Mary Quarterly*, 3d ser., 32 (1975): 307-25.

———. "The Rise of Glasgow in the Chesapeake Tobacco Trade, 1707-1775." *William and Mary Quarterly*, 3d ser., 10 (1954): 179-99.

Quazza, Guido. "La politica dell'equilibrio nel secolo XVIII." *Nuove questioni di storia moderna* 2 (1964): 1181-1216.

Regele, Oskar. "Die Schuld des Grafen Reinhard Wilhelm von Neipperg am Belgrader Frieden, 1739, und an der Niederlage bei Mollwitz." *Mitteilungen des Österreichischen Staatsarchivs* 7 (1954): 373-98.

Revel, Edouard. "Les Espagnols en Savoie, 1742-1749." *Mémoires et documents publiés par la Société Savoisienne d'Histoire et d'Archéologie* 62 (1925): 99-245.

Roberti, Giuseppe. "Carlo Emmanuele III e la Corsica al tempo della guerra de successione austriaca." *Rivista storica italiana* 4 (1889): 665-98.

Roberts, J. M. "L'aristocrazia lombarda nel XVIII secolo." *Occidente* 8 (1952): 305-25.

Roider, Karl A., Jr. "The Perils of Eighteenth-Century Peacemaking: Austria and the Treaty of Belgrade, 1739." *Central European History* 5 (1972): 195-207.

— — —. "The Pragmatic Sanction." *Austrian History Yearbook* 8 (1972): 153-58.

Roloff, G. "Friedrich und das Reich während des Ersten und Zweiten Schlesischen Krieges." *Forschungen zur Brandenburgischen und Preussischen Geschichte* 25 (1913): 445-59.

Rule, John C. "The Maurepas Papers: Portrait of a Minister." *French Historical Studies* 4 (1965): 103-8.

Russell, Peter E. "Redcoats in the Wilderness: British Officers and Irregular Warfare in Europe and America, 1740 to 1760." *William and Mary Quarterly* 3d ser., 35 (1978): 629-52.

Sànchez Diana, José María. "España y la politica exterior de Federico II de Prusia (1740-1786)." *Hispania* 15 (1955): 191-230.

Saxby, Richard C. "The Western Squadron and the Blockade of Brest." *History Today* 23 (1973): 20-29.

Schieder, Theodor. "Friedrich der Grosse und Machiavelli — das Dilemma von Machtpolitik und Aufklärung." *Historische Zeitschrift* 234 (1982): 265-94.

Schmidhofer, Ernst. "Das irische Element im kaiserlichen Heer." *Österreich in Geschichte und Literatur* 19 (1975): 81-90.

Schmidt, Hans. "Der Einfluss der Winterquartiere auf Strategie und Kriegsfuhrung des Ancien Régime." *Historisches Jahrbuch* 92 (1972): 77-91.

Schnitter, Helmut. "Die Schlacht von Fontenoy—ein Beispiel für das Durchbruchsproblem in der Kriegskunst des 18. Jahrhunderts." *Militärgeschichte* 19 (1980): 446-53.

Schrijver, Elka. "Bergen op Zoom: Stronghold on the Scheldt." *History Today* 26 (1976): 749-52.

Schwann, Mathieu. "Der Tod Kaiser Karls VII. und seine Folgen." *Forschungen zur Brandenburgischen und Preussischen Geschichte* 13 (1900): 77-104.

— — —. "Der Wendepunkt im Zweiten Schlesischen Kriege." *Forschungen zur Brandenburgischen und Preussischen Geschichte* 12 (1899): 483-507.

Sosin, Jack. "Louisbourg and the Peace of Aix-la-Chapelle, 1748." *William and Mary Quarterly* 3d ser., 14 (1957): 516-35.

Staszewski, Jacek. "Die polnisch-sächsische Union und die Hohenzollernmonarchie (1697-1763)." *Jahrbuch für die Geschichte Mittel- und Ostdeutschlands* 30 (1980): 28-34.

Stein, Robert. "The French Sugar Business in the Eighteenth century: A Quantitative Study." *Business History* 22 (1980): 1-17.

Stephenson, David. "The Highland Charge." *History Today* 32 (1982): 3-8.

Swanson, Carl E. "American Privateering and Imperial Warfare, 1739-1748." *William and Mary Quarterly*, 3d ser., 42 (1985): 357-82.

— — —. "The Profitability of Privateering: Reflections on British Colonial Privateers during the War of 1739-1748." *American Neptune* 42 (1982): 36-56.

Sweet, Paul R. "Prince Eugene of Savoy and Central Europe." *American Historical Review* 57 (1951): 47-62.

Tamborra, Angelo. "La pace di Aquisgrana del 1748 e la politica della Santa Sede." *Archivio storico italiano* 117 (1959): 522-40.

Tapié, Victor-L. "Le legs de Marie-Thérèse." *Revue d'histoire diplomatique* 88 (1974): 5-20.

Temperley, Harold W. V. "The Causes of the War of Jenkins' Ear, 1739." *Transactions of the Royal Historical Society*, 3d. ser., 3 (1909): 197-236.

Theissen, J. S. "Het Subsidie-Verdrag van 1747 met Hessen-Kassel." *Bijdragen voor Vaderlandsche Geschiedenis en Oudheidkunde*, 6th ser., 7 (1928): 49-94.

Valsecchi, F. "Il problema italiano nella politica europea: Aquisgrana." *Acme* 5 (1952): 255-73.

Van Dijk, H., and Roorda, D. J. "Sociale Mobiliteit onder Regenten van de Republiek." *Tijdschrift voor Geschiedenis* 84 (1971): 306-28.

Venturi, Franco. "Genova a metà del settecento." *Rivista storica italiana* 63 (1967): 732-95.

Volz, Gustav Berthold. "Friedrich Wilhelm I. und die preussische Erbansprüche auf Schlesien." *Forschungen zur Brandenburgischen und Preussischen Geschichte* 30 (1917): 55-67.

———. "Die Politik Friedrichs des Grossen vor und nach seiner Thronbesteigung." *Historische Zeitschrift* 151 (1935): 486-527.

———. "Das Rheinsberger Protokoll von 29. Oktober 1740." *Forschungen zur Brandenburgischen und Preussischen Geschichte* 29 (1916): 67-93.

Wandruszka, Adam. "Milano e Vienna nel settecento e nell'ottocento: considerazioni storiografiche." *Archivio storico lombardo* 101 (1976): 16-25.

Waquet, Jean-Claude. "La Toscane après la paix de Vienne (1737-1765): prépondérance autrichienne ou absolutisme lorrain?" *Revue d'histoire diplomatique* 93 (1979): 202-22.

Weber, Ottokar. "'Diarium' über die Belagerung und Occupation Prags durch die Preussen im J. 1744." *Mittheilungen des Vereines für Geschichte der Deutschen in Böhmen* 34 (1896): 321-70.

———. "Die Occupation Prags durch die franzosen und Baiern 1741-1742." *Mittheilungen des Vereines für Geschichte der Deutschen in Böhmen* 34 (1896): 1-92.

Wessely, Kurt. "The Development of the Hungarian Military Frontier until the Middle of the Eighteenth Century." *Austria History Yearbook* 9-10 (1973-74): 55-110.

Williams, Basil. "Carteret and the So-Called Treaty of Hanau." *English Historical Review* 49 (1934): 684-87.

Woolf, S. J. "Economic Problems of the Nobility in the Early Modern Period: the Example of Piedmont." *Economic History Review*, 2d ser., 17 (1964): 267-83.

Zeller, Gaston. "Le principe d'équilibre dans la politique internationale avant 1789." *Revue historique* 80 (1956): 25-37.

Zernack, Klaus. "Das preussische Königtum und die polnische Republik im europäischen Mächtesystem des 18. Jahrhunderts (1701-1763). *Jahrbuch für die Geschichte Mittel- und Ostdeutschlands* 30 (1981): 4-20.

MANUSCRIPT COLLECTIONS

London. British Library. Newcastle Papers. Add. MSS 32685-33083.

Vienna. Haus-, Hof- und Staatsarchiv. Friedensakten 62 ("Histoire de la paix d'Aix-la-Chapelle du 18. Oct. 1748").

Vienna. Kriegsarchiv. Brown's MSS 38-39.

Vienna. Kriegsarchiv. Manuskripte/Allgemeine Reihe/162 (Gaston Bodart, "Les troupes belges au service de l'Autriche 1714-1801").

■ INDEX ■